LAURA LEMAY'S
WEB WORKSHOP

MICROSOFT®
FRONTPAGE™ 98

Denise Tyler

Series Editor: Laura Lemay

201 West 103rd Street
Indianapolis, Indiana 46290

President:	Richard K. Swadley
Publisher and Director of Acquisitions:	Jordan Gold
Director of Product Development:	Dean Miller
Executive Editor:	Christopher Denny
Indexing Manager:	Johnna L. VanHoose
Director of Marketing:	Kelli S. Spencer
Product Marketing Manager:	Kim Margolius
Marketing Coordinator:	Linda Beckwith

Acquisitions Editor
Christopher Denny

Development Editor
Fran Hatton

Software Development Specialist
Patricia J. Brooks

Production Editor
Nancy Albright

Indexer
John Sleeva

Technical Reviewer
Jeff Perkins

Editorial Coordinators
Mandie Rowell
Katie Wise

Technical Edit Coordinator
Lynette Quinn

Resource Coordinators
Deborah Frisby
Charlotte Clapp

Editorial Assistants
Carol Ackerman
Andi Richter
Rhonda Tinch-Mize
Karen Williams

Cover Designer
Alyssa Yesh

Book Designer
Alyssa Yesh

Copy Writer
David Reichwein

Production Team Supervisors
Brad Chinn
Andrew Stone

Production
Cyndi Davis-Hubler
Jennifer Dierdorff
Ayanna Lacey
Chris Livengood

What's New in FrontPage 98

What's new in FrontPage 98? Goodness gracious, there are so many new enhancements and improvements that it makes the head spin. For example, the following list shows the new features that are available in FrontPage:

Auto Thumbnail	Generate a thumbnail version of any image on your page and automatically link to the larger original.
Banner Ad Manager	Create rotating banners and advertisements, complete with transition effects, for your Web site with easy-to-use dialog boxes.
Cascading Style Sheets	Use the Style button from many dialog boxes to set cascading style sheet properties, enabling you to customize colors, backgrounds, fonts, margins, and more. Create pages that use a consistent appearance and that can easily be changed on a global basis.
CDF Channel Wizard	Take advantage of push technology with the CDF wizard. This enables visitors to subscribe to content and automatically receive it on any desktop that runs Internet Explorer 4.0.
Database Region Wizard	The Active Server Pages (ASP) Database Region Wizard walks you through the process of creating pages that incorporate dynamic Web queries.
Design Time ActiveX	Receive support for Design Time ActiveX Controls.
Dynamic HTML	Create animated text, extend your form fields, create expandable nested lists, and create page transitions automatically, using dynamic HTML code—*without programming!*
Hit counter	Want to track how many times a page has been visited? Use the new hit counter on your FrontPage-enabled pages.
Hover buttons	Use buttons that highlight or change appearance when the mouse cursor is moved over them.
MCIS membership integration	Integrate with servers provided under the Microsoft Commercial Internet Services membership.
Shared borders	Designate regions on your pages in which to place content that repeats from page to page. Edit the original file and each page automatically updates for you.
Themes	Change the look of your entire Web site with the click of a button. Choose from dozens of professionally designed Web themes that use the latest Web technologies—*without programming!*
Web navigation	Design a navigation system for your Web. Automatically generate navigation bars. Create a printout of your navigation system.

If that list isn't long enough for you, there are many enhancements as well. You have improved support for Active Server Pages, better browser support, a very cool WYSIWYG Frameset Editor, enhanced form creation, multiple views in the FrontPage Editor and Explorer, text overlays on images, enhanced toolbars for image editing and table creation, and a host of other great enhancements. FrontPage 98 has really come of age in this release!

Letter from the Series Editor

Writing about technology is hard work. Writing about anything is hard work; all writers deal with the isolation, the tight deadlines, the constant fear that every word you write is the worst word that has ever been put to paper. But the worst part about writing about technology isn't any of these things; the worst part is simply dealing with change. Just when you think the book is done, that the last corrections are made, that the beastly thing is finally off to the printers and you can sit back and have a margarita and actually talk to the friends you've neglected for the last few months…someone goes and changes all the technology, and you've got to start all over again.

Nowhere is this tendency more pronounced these days than on the Web. The browser wars set the pace of a new product with new features every few months, and the tool makers scramble to catch up. Lose ground, and your competitor will pound you.

The first version of this book was widely acclaimed as one of the best books out there on FrontPage. I have scads of e-mail to prove it. Why was it so popular? Because it did more than just tell you what the buttons and the menus do. The first FrontPage book explained how to use FrontPage well, how to use it to accomplish the sorts of things real people are using it for in the real world. Like all the *Laura Lemay's Web Workshop* books, this book helps get you up and running and useful as fast as possible, without bogging you down in a lot of theory or details.

In this book, Denise Tyler not only brings the content of the book up to date with the new version of the software, but also improves on the concept itself. This book goes further and deeper into the sorts of things you can do with FrontPage, incorporating the comments and suggestions from readers to make reading this book more interesting and the tasks more useful. Just as FrontPage 98 offers more features for the Web designer or author over what previous versions did, this book offers an equal amount of improvement over its predecessor.

Good luck and enjoy!

Laura Lemay

LAURA LEMAY'S
WEB WORKSHOP

MICROSOFT®

FRONTPAGE™ 98

Dedication

To Mom, Dad, Bob, Paul, Celeste, and Jessie—the best family anyone could have.

Overview

Contents

Part II Starting with the Basics 113

Acknowledgments

A sizable team of talented individuals stands behind a book. As I work more and more with the folks at Sams.net, I grow increasingly impressed and appreciative of the knowledge, dedication, and friendship that they continue to share. Thanks to Chris Denny, as always, for the marvelous opportunity he gave me years ago and for being a good friend. Many thanks to Fran Hatton for her endless supply of suggestions, cheer and atta-girls—I owe you some (even though we never did get to Cancun); to Nancy Albright for her skillful editing, sharp eyes, and extreme patience; and to Jeff Perkins for his outstanding technical editing and comments. I again thank Laura Lemay for being the driving force and inspiration behind this book and its predecessors.

A special thank you to Crystal Erickson, my stepdaughter and partner in crime in this book. Her unique sense of humor and creative artistic ability added a special flair to the projects and generated a lot of laughs along the way.

About the Author

Denise Tyler is a computer graphics artist and animator, and former engineer with 15 years of technical writing experience. She has been creating graphics and animation for games, multimedia, and Web pages for four years. Her previous books include *Fractal Design Painter 3.1 Unleashed, Laura Lemay's Web Workshop: Advanced FrontPage 97,* and best-sellers *Laura Lemay's Web Workshop: Microsoft FrontPage* and *Laura Lemay's Web Workshop: FrontPage 97.* She is also co-author of the best-seller *Tricks of the Game Programming Gurus.*

Tell Us What You Think!

As a reader, you are the most important critic and commentator of our books. We value your opinion and want to know what we're doing right, what we could do better, what areas you'd like to see us publish in, and any other words of wisdom you're willing to pass our way. You can help us make strong books that meet your needs and give you the computer guidance you require.

Do you have access to the World Wide Web? Then check out our site at http://www.mcp.com.

NOTE: If you have a technical question about this book, call the technical support line at 317-581-3833 or send e-mail to support@mcp.com.

As the team leader of the group that created this book, I welcome your comments. You can fax, e-mail, or write me directly to let me know what you did or didn't like about this book—as well as what we can do to make our books stronger. Here's the information:

Fax: 317-581-4669

E-mail: programming_mgr@sams.mcp.com

Mail: Christopher Denny
         Comments Department
         Sams.net Publishing
         201 W. 103rd Street
         Indianapolis, IN 46290

Introduction

FrontPage 98 is the third-generation release of one of the hottest Web development programs available. The popularity of this program is well-deserved. Not only does FrontPage 98 provide you with a WYSIWYG page editor, but it also provides site management tools that enable you to maintain your Web sites with ease.

How to Use This Book

Because of the plethora of new features in FrontPage 98, I decided to focus the first part of the book on getting everyone familiar with the interfaces and general commands. In Part I, "Learning Your Way Around," you get an overview of the FrontPage 98 features. Read this part if you are new to FrontPage or if you want to familiarize yourself with some of the exciting new features in this new, and *totally awesome*, version of FrontPage:

❏ Chapter 1, "Installing FrontPage 98," shows you how to install or upgrade a previous version of FrontPage to FrontPage 98.

❏ Chapter 2, "About the FrontPage Server Extensions," explains why you need the FrontPage Server Extensions in some cases. You learn, by analogy, what the Server Extensions do and how to find an Internet Service Provider that has the FrontPage Server Extensions installed.

❏ Chapter 3, "FrontPage Explorer Basics," gives you an overview of the new FrontPage 98 interface in the FrontPage Editor. You learn the functions of each of the FrontPage Explorer views and how to do basic tasks in the FrontPage Explorer.

❏ Chapter 4, "FrontPage Editor Basics," shows you the new FrontPage 98 interface in the FrontPage Editor. You learn about the toolbars and each of the tabs you can use to change how you create and edit your Web pages. Basic tasks are covered in this chapter.

❏ Chapter 5, "Lightning-Speed Web Design," gives you an overview of the many Web and page templates and wizards that you can use to create Web pages. If you want to examine some of the great features found in FrontPage 98, this is a great place to start. The pages are chock-full of examples that show you how to create, lay out, and configure your pages.

❏ Chapter 6, "What To Do?" shows how you can use Tasks view to create and manage a to do list in your Web. You no longer need sticky notes to keep track of the changes you need to make to your pages.

- ❏ Chapter 7, "Real-Life Examples I: Using What You've Got," steps you through creating a Web with the Corporate Presence Wizard. Although the Web is small, the pages utilize many of the exciting new features that you'll learn more about in the remainder of the book. Here is where the real hands-on experience begins!

For those who prefer to jump in the water without testing the temperature, the chapters found in Part II, "Starting with the Basics," teach you how to add basic content to your Web pages. Here, you learn how to build your pages from the ground up. The chapters in Part II are as follows:

- ❏ In Chapter 8, "Designing Your Web Navigation," you learn how to use Navigation view in the FrontPage Explorer to automatically generate navigation bars that link to important pages in your Web. Not only does Navigation view automatically link your pages for you, but it's a great planning tool and the best place to start with your Webs!

- ❏ In Chapter 9, "Getting from Here to There," you learn how to add hyperlinks to your pages. Without hyperlinks, your page will stand on its own—and you learn how to get from "here" to "there" within and outside your Web site.

- ❏ In Chapter 10, "Composing and Editing Pages," you learn how to add basic content to your Web pages. Add features such as headings, paragraph styles, text, and fonts, and learn the typical uses for each type of character style.

- ❏ In Chapter 11, "Organizing Information into Lists," you create and compose the basic types of lists: numbered lists, bulleted lists, definition lists, directory lists, and menu lists.

- ❏ In Chapter 12, "Your Tables Are Ready," you learn how to use tables to enhance the layout of your pages.

- ❏ In Chapter 13, "Real-Life Examples II: Keeping it Plain and Simple," you begin to design a site of your own and focus on many of the tasks you learned about in this section. Your Web uses a built-in navigation system, and you set the groundwork for your entire Web site.

In Part III, "Advanced Techniques," you learn how to really dress up your pages. Using advanced features such as themes, images, animation, active content, framesets, and the basic Web components, your Web site begins to come alive with color, animation, and navigation. The following are the chapters in this part:

- ❏ In Chapter 14, "Using FrontPage Style Sheets and Themes," you learn how to assign a theme to your Web site. At the touch of your button, you can change the total appearance of your Web site—navigation buttons, bullets, banners, horizontal rules, fonts, text colors, and more! You also learn how to create your own themes.

❏ In Chapter 15, "Working with Images and Sound," you learn how to insert and modify images on your pages and how to add background sounds to your pages. You also learn when it's best to use each of the Web image formats.

❏ In Chapter 16, "Working with Animation and Active Content," you add animation, sound, and active graphics and features to your Web. Use hover buttons, banner ads, Search components, and more!

❏ In Chapter 17, "Integrating with Other Editors," you learn how to use FrontPage 98 in concert with other types of software. By configuring other editors, you can open and edit other types of content from within the FrontPage Explorer.

❏ In Chapter 18, "Frames: Pages with Split Personalities," you learn how to use the new and improved FrontPage 98 frames view. Now you can view and edit each feature of your frameset from within FrontPage 98. Learn how to build a frameset and how to place your Web pages into each frame.

❏ In Chapter 19, "Using FrontPage Components," you learn how to use the FrontPage Web components to automate and simplify Web changes. Learn how to add timestamps, tables of contents, and comments to your pages. Include pages and images on your pages on specific dates. These handy utilities help you organize and manage your time as well as your site!

❏ In Chapter 20, "Real-Life Examples III: Dressing Up Your Webs," you combine all the tasks you learned in this section of the book into your Web project. You add more pages and build a frameset. You automate your content with some of the FrontPage components. You customize your Web theme and add images and animation. Now your Web site is getting exciting!

In Part IV, "Working with Forms," you learn how to add interactivity to your Web site. Using forms, you can receive data from those who visit your site. You learn how to develop forms quickly and easily with the FrontPage 98 Forms Wizard, how to add and configure form fields, how to integrate your forms with IDC database connector files and Active Server Pages, and how to configure the FrontPage 98 form handlers:

❏ Chapter 21, "Quick and Easy Forms," steps you through the process of creating several forms with the Forms Wizard.

❏ Chapter 22, "Adding and Editing Form Fields," shows you how to add form fields to your pages and how to configure the properties of each type of form field.

❏ Chapter 23, "Configuring Form Handlers," shows you how to assign and configure the FrontPage 98 form handling components and how to assign your own custom scripts to process forms.

❏ Chapter 24, "Real-Life Examples IV: Adding Interactivity," adds some forms to your Web site project. You learn how to create and configure a variety of forms, including a discussion group.

In Part V, "Still More Advanced Techniques," you really get into the nitty-gritty of what makes all the advanced features of FrontPage tick. Some of these features are browser-specific and may not be compatible with older browsers—but you still learn how to reach the largest audience possible. You learn how to add Java applets and Netscape plug-ins to your pages and how to use your own HTML code to customize your pages even further. You peek behind the scenes of the FrontPage themes to learn how to create your own cascading style sheets and themes. You learn how to insert ActiveX controls and scripts into your pages. Here are the chapters:

❏ Chapter 25, "Using Java Applets and Netscape Plug-Ins," shows you how to insert and configure Java applets and Netscape plug-ins.

❏ Chapter 26, "Using Your Own HTML," shows you how use HTML view in the FrontPage Editor to add your own HTML code. You also learn when it is best to use the HTML Markup Bot to add enhanced features in your Web page.

❏ Chapter 27, "Using Styles," peeks behind the scenes of your themes. You learn how to add cascading style sheet styles to your pages and how to create your own customized themes.

❏ Chapter 28, "Working with ActiveX and Scripts," shows you how to add ActiveX and scripts to your pages.

❏ Chapter 29, "Real-Life Examples V: Using Browser-Specific Features," teaches you how to use all the features mentioned in this section so that your Web pages reach the largest audience possible.

In Part VI, "Publishing and Maintaining Your Webs," you learn about the personal Web servers that are provided with FrontPage 98 and how to administer your Web site with each of them. You also learn how to install, uninstall, and upgrade the FrontPage Server Extensions. Before your pages go out on the Web, you give your site a final check, using features that help you verify your hyperlinks, your spelling, your grammar, and more. You also learn how to create private Webs that are open to registered users only. The following are the chapters in this part:

❏ Chapter 30, "Using the FrontPage Personal Web Server," shows you how to install and configure the FrontPage Personal Web Server, and the administration tasks that are specific to this server.

❏ Chapter 31, "Using the Microsoft Personal Web Server," shows you how to install and configure the Microsoft Personal Web Server, the additional features you can use with it, and the administration tasks that are specific to this server.

- ❏ In Chapter 32, "Administering Your Webs," you learn how to manage the FrontPage Server Extensions and how to do general administration tasks.
- ❏ Chapter 33, "Designing Private Webs," shows you how to create a registration form for a private Web and how to configure a private Web site. You also learn how to use subscriptions.
- ❏ Chapter 34, "Testing and Publishing Your Webs," places your Web pages in their final destination—out on the Web! You learn how to use the Publish FrontPage Web command to post your pages to your Internet Service Provider's server or to your intranet. You also learn where you can go to publicize your Web.

Get ready to create Web sites the new and improved FrontPage 98 way! If you have any questions, stop by the support site for this book at the following URL:

`http://www.fpworkshop.com`

And thanks for choosing this book!

PART

I

Learning Your Way Around

ONE
Installing FrontPage 98

Have you ever wished you could create your own Web pages, but hesitated because you didn't want to learn what HTML tags did? When you use a text editor to create your Web pages, do you get a lot of surprises when you view your pages in a browser? Are you tired of fixing and maintaining links on your site? Have you always wished you could create navigation bars, complete with graphics, in an instant?

Good news is in store. The latest release of FrontPage not only helps you create Web pages with a WYSIWYG page editor, but you can create and maintain a complete navigation system for your Web site. Not only does FrontPage 98 take care of the navigation, but with the click of a button you can assign an entirely new theme to all the Web pages on a site. There are some very exciting new features in FrontPage 98 that I can't wait to show you!

If you're upgrading from a previous version of FrontPage, there are a couple of things you should know before you run the setup program. Many of the new features found in FrontPage 98 will not work with previous versions of the FrontPage Server Extensions. These include themes, Navigation view, and shared borders, which you will learn more about later in this book. If you take advantage of these new features and publish or save them to a server that has older FrontPage Server Extensions installed, the features will not work.

You learn more about the FrontPage Server Extensions in Chapter 2, "About the FrontPage Server Extensions." See Chapter 8, "Designing Your Web Navigation," to learn more about how to use Navigation view in the FrontPage Explorer and what shared borders are. See Chapter 14, "Using FrontPage Style Sheets and Themes," to learn how quickly you can change the look of your entire Web site.

You can install FrontPage 98 to a different directory on your hard disk and use it in conjunction with a previous version of FrontPage. The FrontPage 98 Server Extensions are backward-compatible with older versions of the FrontPage Explorer and FrontPage Editor. The server you used with the previous version remains on TCP/IP port 80, and the new FrontPage 98 server is installed to TCP/IP port 8080. The new FrontPage 98 Server Extensions are installed on both ports.

You can install FrontPage 98 to a different directory than your previous versions if you want to keep more than one version of FrontPage on your system. Previous versions of FrontPage will work with the new Server Extensions. Use the following steps:

1. From the Windows 95 Start Menu, choose Settings | Control Panel. The Control Panel dialog box appears.

2. Double-click Add/Remove Programs. The Add/Remove Program Properties dialog box appears, opened to the Install/Uninstall tab.

3. Click the Install button. The Install Program from Floppy Disk or CD-ROM dialog box appears.

4. Insert the FrontPage 98 CD-ROM into your CD-ROM drive and click Next to continue. The Run Installation Program dialog box appears, and the path to the FrontPage 98 Setup program appears in the Command line for installation program field.

5. Click Finish. Setup prepares files for installation, and the Microsoft FrontPage 98 Setup screen appears.

If you are running Windows 95 and you have access control set to Share Level, you may receive the following message:

```
Setup has detected that your computer is set to 'share level' access control.
If you want to set access permissions for your FrontPage Webs, please select
Cancel to exit setup and change the Access Control setting in the Network
dialog of the Control Panel to 'user level.'
```

User Level access control applies when you log on to a Windows NT Domain or Windows NT Server:

❏ If you are installing FrontPage 98 on a standalone Windows 95 system, choose OK to continue with the installation.

❏ If you want to reconfigure your system to use User Level Access Control to a Windows NT Domain or Windows NT Server, choose Cancel. Exit Setup and change your access control through the Network applet in the Windows 95 control panel. Enable File and Print Sharing in the Configuration tab of the Network dialog box, then select User-level access control in the Access Control tab of the Network dialog box. Finally, run the FrontPage 98 Setup program again.

To install or upgrade to Microsoft FrontPage 98, complete the following steps:

1. The Welcome screen shown in Figure 1.1 appears. Click **N**ext to continue.

Figure 1.1.
The Welcome screen begins the setup process of FrontPage 98.

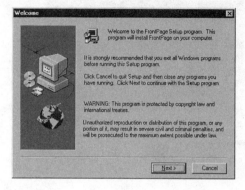

2. The FrontPage Registration screen shown in Figure 1.2 appears. Enter your name in the **Na**me field and your company name (if applicable) in the **C**ompany field. Click **N**ext to continue.

Figure 1.2.
Enter your name and company name in the FrontPage Registration screen.

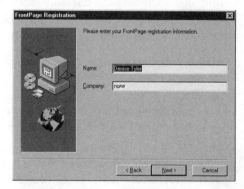

3. The Confirm FrontPage Registration screen shown in Figure 1.3 appears. If your registration information is correct, click **Y**es. Click **N**o to repeat step 2.

Figure 1.3.
Confirm your registration information in the Confirm FrontPage Registration screen.

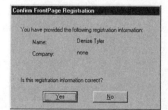

4. The License screen shown in Figure 1.4 appears. Click **Y**es if you agree to the license terms or **N**o to cancel installation.

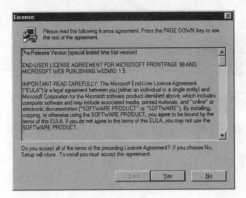

5. If Setup detects a previous version of FrontPage on your system, the Destination Path screen shown in Figure 1.5 appears:

   ❏ To upgrade your previous version of FrontPage to FrontPage 98, install FrontPage 98 in the same directory as the previous version. Setup detects the directory of the previous installation and enters the path in the Destination Directory section of the Destination Path screen. Choose **N**ext to continue the installation.

   ❏ To use your previous version of FrontPage in conjunction with FrontPage 98, click the **B**rowse button to choose a new installation folder for FrontPage 98. The Choose Directory dialog box shown in Figure 1.6 appears. Enter a new installation path in the **P**ath field or use the Drives and Directories lists to install FrontPage 98 to an existing folder on your system. Choose OK to return to the Destination Path panel. Setup asks whether you want the new folder to be created. Choose **Y**es. Then choose **N**ext from the Destination Path panel to continue installation.

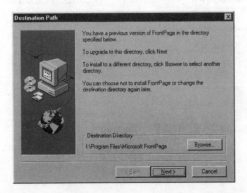

Figure 1.6.
Choose your installation directory in the Choose Directory dialog box.

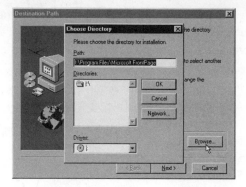

6. The Setup Type screen shown in Figure 1.7 appears:

   ❏ Choose **T**ypical to install the FrontPage client, the Microsoft Personal Web Server, and the FrontPage Server Extensions. Proceed to step 7 for a new installation or click **N**ext and continue with step 8 for an upgrade installation.

   ❏ Choose **C**ustom to select the FrontPage 98 components to install on your system.

Figure 1.7.
Choose Typical or Custom installation from the Setup Type screen.

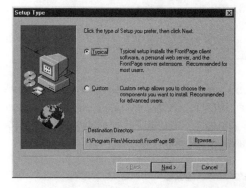

7. The default installation directory is `c:\Program Files\Microsoft FrontPage`:

   ❏ To install FrontPage 98 to the default installation directory, click **N**ext to continue.

   ❏ To change the installation folder, click the **B**rowse button. The Choose Directory dialog box appears. Enter the new path in the **P**ath field or use the Dri**v**es and **D**irectories lists to locate an existing drive and directory. Click the N**e**twork button to map a network drive, if necessary. After you choose your directory, click OK to return to the Setup Type screen. Setup asks whether you want to create the directory. Click **Y**es to continue or **N**o to cancel. Then click **N**ext on the Setup Type screen to continue.

8. If you selected the Custom installation option, the Select Components screen shown in Figure 1.8 appears. Check or uncheck any or all of the following FrontPage 98 components to install on your system:

> FrontPage 98
> Proofing Tools and Converters
> Additional FrontPage Themes
> Additional Clipart
> FrontPage Personal Web Server
> Server Extensions Resource Kit
> Server Extensions Administration Forms

Click **N**ext to continue.

Figure 1.8.

Choose the components you want to install from the Select Components screen.

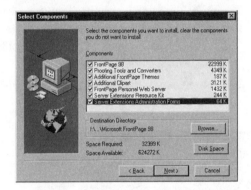

9. If you selected to install the FrontPage Personal Web Server, the Choose Microsoft FrontPage Personal Web Server Directory screen shown in Figure 1.9 appears. The default installation directory for the Personal Web Server is `c:\FrontPage Webs`.

Figure 1.9.

Select the directory to which you want to install the FrontPage Personal Web Server from the Choose Microsoft FrontPage Personal Web Server Directory screen.

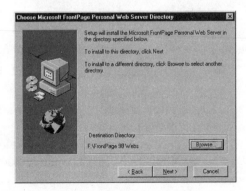

You learn more about the FrontPage Personal Web Server in Chapter 30, "Using the FrontPage Personal Web Server."

❏ To install the FrontPage Personal Web Server to the default installation directory, click **N**ext to continue.

❏ To change the installation folder, click the **B**rowse button. The Choose Directory dialog box appears. Enter the new path in the **P**ath field or use the Dri**v**es and **D**irectories lists to locate an existing drive and directory. Click the N**e**twork button to map a network drive, if necessary. After you choose your directory, click OK to return to the Setup Type screen. Setup asks whether you want to create the directory. Click **Y**es to continue or **N**o to cancel. Then click **N**ext from the Choose Microsoft FrontPage Personal Web Server Directory screen to continue. Setup copies files to your hard drive.

10. If Setup detects an existing Web server on your computer, the FrontPage Personal Web Server screen shown in Figure 1.10 appears. It informs you that Setup configures the FrontPage 98 server to run on TCP/IP port 8080. To connect with the FrontPage 98 server through the FrontPage Explorer or through your browser, you need to append the 8080 port to your server's URL. For example, if your server name is *myserver*, specify a URL as follows:

❏ **http://myserver** creates, opens, or browses Webs on your previous server, which is more than likely installed on TCP/IP port 80.

❏ **http://myserver:8080** creates, opens, or browses Webs on the new FrontPage 98 server, which will be installed on TCP/IP port 8080.

Figure 1.10.

The FrontPage Personal Web Server screen appears if you are installing the FrontPage Personal Web Server on a computer that already has a Web server installed.

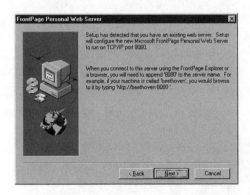

11. If you are performing a Typical installation, the Restart Windows screen appears. Choose Yes, I want to restart my computer now to restart your system or No, I will restart my computer later to return to Windows 95 after setup is complete. Then choose OK to complete the installation.

If you are performing a new or upgrade Custom installation and elected to install the FrontPage Personal Web Server, the Administrator Setup for FrontPage Personal Web Server dialog box shown in Figure 1.11 appears.

Enter your administrator name (no spaces, tabs, or colons are allowed) in the Name field and your administrator password in the Password field. Retype the password in the Confirm password field. Then choose OK to continue with step 11.

Figure 1.11.

Enter your administrator name and password in the Administrator Setup for FrontPage Personal Web Server dialog box.

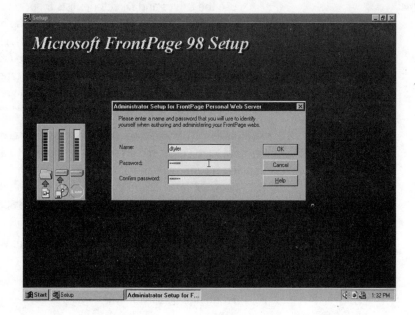

12. Setup installs the Server Extensions, and the Setup Complete dialog box shown in Figure 1.12 appears:

    ❑ To exit Setup without starting the FrontPage Explorer, uncheck the Start the FrontPage Explorer now checkbox and click Finish.

    ❑ To exit Setup and start the FrontPage Explorer, check the Start the FrontPage Explorer now checkbox and click Finish.

Figure 1.12.

The Setup Complete screen appears after Setup copies the files to your computer.

The first time you start the FrontPage Explorer, FrontPage determines your machine's hostname and TCP/IP address. Choose OK to complete this procedure. If FrontPage determines this information successfully, a dialog box reports your hostname and you can start using FrontPage. Choose OK to open the FrontPage Explorer, after which you see the Getting Started dialog box. This dialog box is explained in Chapter 3, "FrontPage Explorer Basics."

Workshop Wrap-Up

The FrontPage 98 installation program is a typical Windows installation setup program. If you are performing a new installation, setup should be very straightforward. If you are performing an upgrade, first decide whether you want to install over your previous version or to a new directory on your hard drive. Remember that if you make the latter choice, your old version of FrontPage and your existing Web content and server use port 80, and your new FrontPage 98 Webs will reside on port 8080.

Next Steps

In the next chapter, "About the FrontPage Server Extensions," you learn when you need to use the FrontPage Server Extensions and which FrontPage 98 features require them. You can also see the following chapters, which relate to the setup and administration of the Personal Web Servers that you can use with FrontPage 98:

❑ See Chapter 30, "Using the FrontPage Personal Web Server," for information on how to administer your Webs using the FrontPage Personal Web Server.

❑ See Chapter 31, "Using the Microsoft Personal Web Server," to learn what advantages you receive with this Personal Web Server and how to administer your FrontPage Webs.

❑ See Chapter 32, "Administering Your Webs," for Web administration tasks that are used with either of the previously mentioned Personal Web Servers.

Q&A

Q: I performed an upgrade installation. When Setup installed the Server Extensions on my existing Web server, my computer seemed to hang. Is something wrong?

A: When Setup performs an upgrade installation and installs the FrontPage 98 Server Extensions on your existing server, it replaces all the Server Extensions files and indexes (the files in the directories that begin with _vti) in each of your existing Webs. If you have a lot of content on your old server, this could take several minutes. The only indicator that Setup is performing this operation is periodic access to your hard drive. When the process is complete, you receive a notification that your Server Extensions have been upgraded. If your existing Web server contains many Webs, expect this process to take some time.

Q: I elected to use the Microsoft Personal Web Server with FrontPage 98, but the setup program installs this server to drive C. I don't have a lot of room left on that hard drive, and I'd rather move it to another. How do I change it?

A: See Chapter 31 for instructions on how to move your Webshare folder to another hard drive and how to change the settings to point to the new directory.

Q: Should I back up my existing Web content before I upgrade my installation?

A: You don't have to, but it might be a good idea. If you run into problems during installation, you have a copy to fall back on.

TWO

About the FrontPage Server Extensions

In the "old days" of Web page development, if you wanted to add forms and other advanced features to your Web pages, you had to learn how to write programs and scripts in other scripting languages, such as CGI, Perl, Java, JavaScript, or VBScript. Though you can still take the plunge and learn about these languages, you have the FrontPage components at your disposal. This is one of the things that make FrontPage unique—the FrontPage components enable you to incorporate advanced features in your Web pages without having to write programs and scripts yourself. The FrontPage components are custom CGI scripts and programs that take the place of these scripts so you don't have to do all that dirty work.

Some of the FrontPage components, such as the form handlers discussed in Chapter 23, "Configuring Form Handlers," need the FrontPage Server Extensions to work properly. You have these extensions installed on your local computer, which is why the forms work on your own computer. If your pages use these FrontPage components, you also need to make sure that your Internet Service Provider has the FrontPage Server Extensions installed on its server as well. The Server Extensions are installed on your machine when you install Microsoft FrontPage.

What Is a Server?

In its most basic definition, a server is a computer that provides services on a network. The World Wide Web, which is that part of the Internet on which Web pages are published, is basically a *huge* network of servers that are connected through phone lines. WWW servers respond to a special type of protocol called the Hypertext Transfer Protocol (HTTP).

When you install FrontPage on your computer, you can choose between one of two Personal Web Servers that run on the Windows 95 operating system. These servers are discussed in Chapter 30, "Using the FrontPage Personal Web Server," and Chapter 31, "Using the Microsoft Personal Web Server." Though the capabilities of these two servers differ slightly, they basically serve the same function. They enable you to create and test your Web pages on your local computer, without having to connect to the Internet.

What the FrontPage Server Extensions Do

For someone who is new to the Internet and Web page development, the FrontPage Server Extensions can be a bit confusing. Therefore, I'll try to explain what the FrontPage Server Extensions do. Please indulge me while I use an analogy…

As you look at Figure 2.1, imagine that you have taken a trip to France. You decide that you want to go to the Louvre to view the vast collection of art there. When you arrive, you join people from all over the world who are converging on this museum to view the same incredible masterpieces that you want to see. Some of the tourists speak English, some speak Spanish, some speak German, some speak Italian, and so forth—but none speaks French.

You, and many others, would like to learn about the history of one of these masterpieces even though you don't speak French. The people at the museum realize this, so they employ a host of tour guides who are familiar with several different languages. The four individuals that stand between the groups of people and the masterpiece in Figure 2.1 are the tour guides. Those who speak English follow a tour guide that speaks English; those who speak Italian follow a tour guide that speaks Italian, and so on. All are happy, because they are able to understand and learn about the masterpieces in their own language.

So how does this relate to the Internet and your FrontPage Web site? As you compare your Web site to Figure 2.2, think of your Web site as the "masterpiece" that you want the whole world to see. As you design your pages, you decide to incorporate some of the advanced features, such as forms and form handlers, on one of your masterpieces. You decide to use the FrontPage components as form handlers, because you don't know how to speak other form handling languages, such as CGI, Perl, Java, and so on.

Figure 2.1.

International tourists listen to tour guides speak about works of art in a museum.

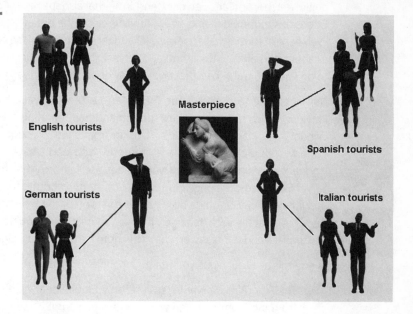

Figure 2.2.

In a similar manner, the FrontPage Server Extensions translate the features on your page into a language the server understands.

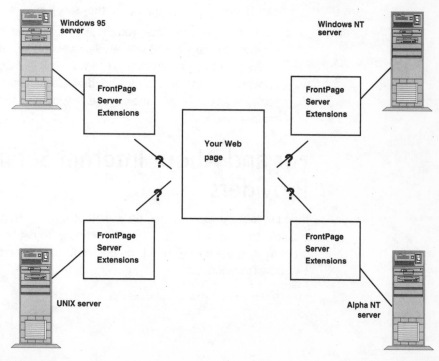

The FrontPage Personal Web Server or Microsoft Personal Web Server that you installed on your computer equates to one of the visitors at the museum, and it speaks "Windows 95." At the same time you installed FrontPage, you also installed a "tour guide"—the FrontPage Server Extensions—that also speaks Windows 95. Your Server Extensions tour guide looks at your masterpiece (the data that a user enters on your Web page in form fields, for example) and tells your server (the visitor at the museum) all about it. Thanks to the FrontPage Server Extensions, your server knows what it has to do with the data that it receives from the form—and that's why it works.

Now it is time to publish your Web site to a server hosted by an Internet Service Provider, which more than likely runs on another operating system, such as UNIX or Windows NT. Your ISP's server is "a visitor from another country" and doesn't speak Windows 95. For all intents and purposes, you don't have to worry about what language this visitor speaks. If your pages use features that require the FrontPage Server Extensions, the only thing you need to worry about is that your ISP has teamed up with its own tour guide by installing a version of the FrontPage Server Extensions that is compatible with its server. If it has, your ISP's tour guide can also look at your masterpiece and tell its server what it needs to know in a language that it understands.

I hope this analogy helps you realize a couple of things:

❏ The FrontPage Server Extensions on your personal Web server differ slightly from the FrontPage Server Extensions on your ISP's server. They basically perform the same functions, but they speak in different languages.

❏ Because of this difference, you shouldn't copy your Windows 95 Server Extensions onto your ISP's server. Basically, this includes any files that reside in directories that begin with _vti. When you use the FrontPage Explorer's Publish FrontPage Web command, discussed in Chapter 34, "Testing and Publishing Your Webs," the server extension files are not copied to the remote server.

For and About Internet Service Providers

If you're looking for a service provider that has the FrontPage Server Extensions installed, there are more than enough to choose from. Microsoft keeps an extensive list of them at the following URL, on the FrontPage Web Presence Providers Referral List shown in Figure 2.3:

```
http://microsoft.saltmine.com/frontpage/wpp/list/
```

Figure 2.3.

Microsoft keeps an extensive list of providers on the FrontPage Web Presence Providers Referral List on their site.

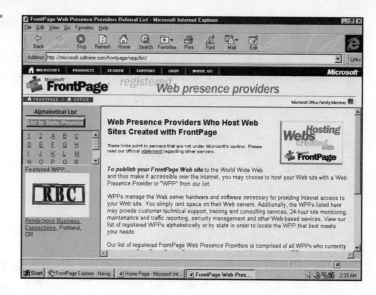

If your service provider doesn't have the Server Extensions installed, good news is in store. The FrontPage Server Extensions are available for several other platforms and operating systems. Point your ISP in the direction of the Microsoft FrontPage Web Presence Providers page, shown in Figure 2.4. There, it can review the requirements for obtaining and installing the Server Extensions, as well as the operating systems and Web servers for which FrontPage Server Extensions are available. The URL is

```
http://www.microsoft.com/frontpage/wpp.htm
```

Figure 2.4.

Information for Web Presence Providers also appears on the Microsoft FrontPage Web Presence Providers page on Microsoft's Web site.

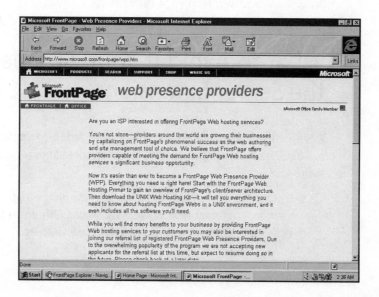

At press time, FrontPage Server Extensions were available for the following Web servers running on the UNIX platform: Apache 1.0.5, 1.1.1 and 1.1.3; CERN 3.0; NSCA 1.5.2; Netscape Commerce Server 1.12; Netscape Communications Server 1.12; Netscape Enterprise 2.0; and Netscape FastTrack 2.0. The following UNIX operating systems and platforms are supported:

AIX 3.2.5, 4.x
BSD/OS 2.1 (Intel Architecture)
Digital UNIX 3.2c, 4.0 (Alpha)
HP/UX 9.03, 10.01 (PA-RISC)
IRIX 5.3 (Silicon Graphics)
Linux 3.0.3 (Intel, from Red Hat Software)
Solaris 2.4, 2.5 (SPARC)
SunOS 4.1.3, 4.1.4 (SPARC)

For servers running on the Microsoft Windows NT operating system on Intel *x*86 Win32 architecture, the following Web servers are supported: Internet Information Server 2.0 or higher; O'Reilley and Associates Web Site; Netscape Commerce Server 1.12; Netscape Communications Server 1.12; Netscape Enterprise 2.0; Netscape FastTrack 2.0; and FrontPage Personal Web Server.

The following Web servers are supported on the Alpha NT Server 4.0 (or higher) and Alpha NT Workstation 4.0 (or higher) operating systems: Microsoft Internet Information Server 2.0 or higher and Microsoft Peer Web Services.

The following Web servers running under Windows 95 are supported: Microsoft Personal Web Server; FrontPage Personal Web Server; O'Reilly and Associates Web Site; and Netscape FastTrack 2.0.

What to Avoid if Your ISP Doesn't Have the Server Extensions

If you already have a Web site but your ISP does not have the FrontPage Server Extensions installed, there are some features included in FrontPage 98 that you should avoid using on your pages unless you know how to program or use alternatives for them:

❏ *FrontPage Image Maps*. If you want to use image maps, be sure to change them to a different type, such as NCSA or CERN. Instructions for this are included in Chapter 9, "Getting from Here to There."

❏ *Hit Counter.* The Hit Counter provided with FrontPage 98 runs only on a server that has the FrontPage Server Extensions installed.

❏ *Forms and Form Fields.* Avoid the use of forms and form fields unless you know how to program and use alternatives for the following three form handlers:

Save Results Form Handler. This FrontPage form handler is typically used to process general forms. For alternatives, use custom CGI, ASP, ISAPI, or NSAPI scripts, as discussed in Chapter 23.

Discussion Form Handler. This FrontPage form handler is used to create discussion groups and is discussed in Chapter 24, "Real-Life Examples IV: Adding Interactivity."

Registration Form Handler. This FrontPage form handler is used to register users for a private, or protected, Web site. It is designed for use with the FrontPage Server Extensions only. For more information, see Chapter 33, "Designing Private Webs."

Workshop Wrap-Up

You now know some of the basics about the FrontPage Server Extensions. For additional information, visit Microsoft's site, where the most recent information about the Server Extensions is kept.

Next Steps

To learn more about the Personal Web Servers and the FrontPage Server Extensions, refer to the following chapters:

❏ See Chapter 30, "Using the FrontPage Personal Web Server," to learn how to administer your FrontPage Webs using the FrontPage Personal Web Server.

❏ See Chapter 31, "Using the Microsoft Personal Web Server," to learn how to administer your FrontPage Webs using the Microsoft Personal Web Server.

❏ See Chapter 32, "Administering Your Webs," to learn general Web administration tasks, such as making general changes to your Web sites.

❏ See Appendix B, "FrontPage Reference," for a list of online resources that are available for the FrontPage Server Extensions and additional information for Web Presence providers.

Q&A

Q: Do I have to use a provider that has the FrontPage Server Extensions?

A: Not necessarily, but if you're new to Web development and want to use advanced features on your site (such as forms), you can implement them without a lick of programming by using any of the FrontPage components and selecting a service provider that has the FrontPage Server Extensions. Of course, you can always be adventurous and learn how to write your own scripts using CGI, Perl, or other scripting languages.

Q: If my service provider doesn't have the FrontPage Server Extensions, do I have to keep all the server extension files and directories on my computer?

A: You probably should, especially if you use any of the FrontPage components in your Web. Even when you use the FrontPage components that do not require the Server Extensions (such as the Include, Table of Contents, or Timestamp components), there is certain configuration information stored on your computer in relation to them. This configuration information is stored in your FrontPage Web. If you delete the FrontPage Web on your computer and later import your pages from your ISP's server into a new FrontPage Web on your computer, your pages are imported as straight HTML without the configuration information. You'll need to reinsert and reconfigure the FrontPage components that you used in your original Web. If you do decide to delete one of your FrontPage Webs, make a backup copy of all files and directories, including all the _vti directories, in case you need to revise your pages later.

Q: If my service provider uses the FrontPage Server Extensions, do I need any files from its server on my local computer?

A: No, you don't. The server extension files on the ISP's server perform the same functions as those you already have on your computer. You have everything you need on your system to make them work properly.

Q: When I transfer my Web to my service provider's site, will my Server Extensions overwrite my ISP's?

A: No. When you publish a Web to a remote site, the only files that are transferred are your Web pages, images, and other files that you included on your Web site. Any files located in directories that begin with _vti do not, and should not, get transferred to your ISP's server.

THREE

FrontPage Explorer Basics

The FrontPage Explorer provides many features that enable you to manage your Web sites with ease. If you are new to FrontPage, you will delight in the way the FrontPage Explorer helps you maintain the integrity of the links in your site. When you rename or move files, FrontPage asks whether you want to update any links on other pages to reflect the changes. You can tell at a glance what pages link to and from any page in your site. Imagine verifying dozens or hundreds of internal and external hyperlinks in a matter of minutes! These are some of the tried and true features that have made FrontPage a leading program for Web page developers.

The new features in the FrontPage Explorer are even more exciting! With FrontPage 98, you can design a complete navigation system that generates navigation bars for you. As you make changes to your Web site, the navigation bars automatically update to reflect the changes. Tired of your background and colors? Change the look of your entire site with the click of a button, choosing from dozens of professionally designed Web themes.

This chapter gives you a quick overview of the new FrontPage Explorer and what each of the different views are used for. You'll also learn about some of the basic commands that enable you to make changes to the structure of your Web sites.

In this chapter, you

- ❏ Become familiar with the FrontPage Explorer interface
- ❏ Learn what the different views in the FrontPage Explorer are used for and which chapters in this book provide additional information on them
- ❏ Learn how to use the FrontPage Explorer to create new pages and folders in your Web
- ❏ Select, move, and rename pages in your Web
- ❏ Learn how to open pages in the FrontPage Editor from the FrontPage Explorer
- ❏ Learn how to view and edit the properties of the files in your Web and how to add comments to them

Tasks in this chapter:

- ❏ Choosing a View
- ❏ Displaying the Status Bar and Toolbar
- ❏ Creating New Folders
- ❏ Changing Pages
- ❏ Opening Pages
- ❏ Viewing and Editing File Properties
- ❏ Exiting the FrontPage Explorer

Getting Started with FrontPage

You start FrontPage from the Windows 95 Start menu. Choose Start | Programs | Microsoft FrontPage. The Getting Started dialog box shown in Figure 3.1 appears. From this dialog box, you can open an existing FrontPage Web or create a new FrontPage Web. The steps to create or open Webs are discussed in more detail in Chapter 5, "Lightning-Speed Web Design."

For now, choose Cancel from the Getting Started dialog box to familiarize yourself with the new FrontPage 98 interface.

Figure 3.1.
The Getting Started dialog box appears the first time you open the FrontPage Explorer. Choose Cancel to examine the new FrontPage 98 interface.

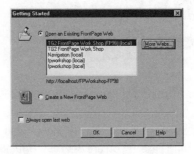

The FrontPage Explorer Interface

The FrontPage Explorer interface is divided into two main panes. The Views pane, which appears along the left side, enables you to choose one of many ways to view your Web sites. The right side of the FrontPage Explorer workspace changes, depending on the view you select.

Choosing a View

You can choose a FrontPage Explorer view in one of two ways. The quickest way is to use the Views pane at the left side of the FrontPage Explorer interface. You can also select a view by choosing one of the commands from the View menu. Each of the views is described in the following sections.

Folders View

Folders view, shown in Figure 3.2, displays the pages in your Web in folders. The folders that exist in your Web are listed in the left portion of Folders view. When you click on a folder name, its contents are displayed in the Contents portion of Folders view.

When you view your Web in Folders view, you can sort the files in each folder by clicking the column heading that appears at the top of the Contents portion on the right side of Folders view. Your Web content can be sorted by Name (filename), Title (the title of the Web page or file), Size, Type (folder or file extension), Modified Date, Modified By (the last author to work on the file), or Comments.

To view your Web in Folders view, use one of the following:

❏ Choose the Folders icon from the FrontPage Explorer Views pane.

❏ Choose **V**iew | **F**olders.

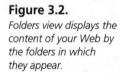

Figure 3.2.
Folders view displays the content of your Web by the folders in which they appear.

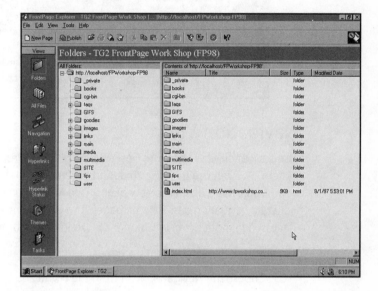

All Files View

When you want to view all the pages and files in your Web, choose All Files view, which is shown in Figure 3.3. When you view your Webs in All Files view, each page or file in your Web is displayed. You can sort the list by Name (filename), Title (title of the Web page or document), In Folder (folder in which the page appears), Orphan (whether the page is reachable from other pages or not), Size (size of the page in KB), Type (file extension), Modified Date (date that the page was last edited), Modified By (name of the author who last modified the page or file), and Comments.

To view your Web in All Files view, use one of the following:

❏ Choose the All Files icon from the FrontPage Explorer Views pane.

❏ Choose **V**iew | **A**ll Files.

Figure 3.3.
Use All Files view to view all the pages and files in your Web in one list.

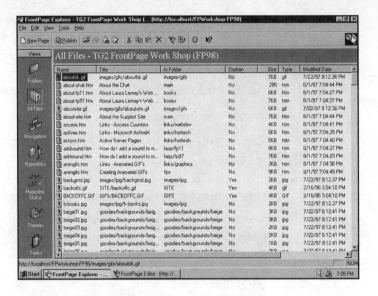

Navigation View

Use Navigation view, shown in Figure 3.4, to plan and design your Web site navigation system. You can use this view to design a hierarchical navigation system throughout your Web. After you create new pages from Navigation view, you can automatically generate navigation bars for your pages. This exciting new feature of FrontPage 98 is discussed in more detail in Chapter 8, "Designing Your Web Navigation."

To view your Web in Navigation view, use one of the following:

❑ Choose the Navigation icon from the FrontPage Explorer Views pane.

❑ Choose **V**iew | **N**avigation.

Hyperlinks View

Hyperlinks view, shown in Figure 3.5, is another way that you can display your Web site in a hierarchical manner. This view is divided into two panes. All Pages view displays the pages in an expandable hierarchical list. You can expand and contract the tree to view all pages that are linked to one of the pages in your Web.

To view your Web in Hyperlinks view, use one of the following:

❑ Choose the Hyperlinks icon from the FrontPage Explorer Views pane.

❑ Choose **V**iew | **H**yperlinks.

Figure 3.4.

Use Navigation view to design and view the navigation system in your Web.

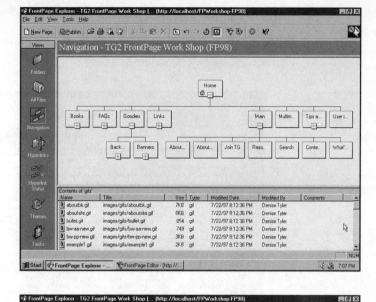

Figure 3.5.

Use Hyperlinks view to display the links to and from a Web page in a hierarchical tree.

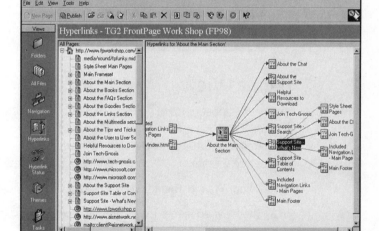

Hyperlink Status View

Use Hyperlink Status view, shown in Figure 3.6, to view the status of the hyperlinks in your Web. You can verify and repair both internal and external hyperlinks with rapidity and ease. For more information on how to use Hyperlink Status view, see Chapter 34, "Testing and Publishing Your Webs."

To view your Web in Hyperlink Status view, use one of the following:

❏ Choose the Hyperlink Status icon from the FrontPage Explorer Views pane.

❏ Choose **V**iew I Hyperlink **S**tatus.

Figure 3.6.
Use Hyperlink Status view to review, verify, and repair your hyperlinks—both internal and external to your Web site.

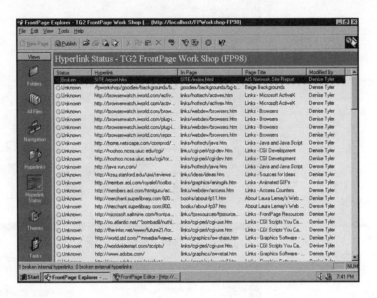

Themes View

Change the appearance of your entire Web site in a flash with Themes view, shown in Figure 3.7. Choose from one of dozens of themes for your Web site, each with its own banners, buttons, bullets, and horizontal rules. For a complete discussion of themes, see Chapter 14, "Using FrontPage Style Sheets and Themes."

To view your Web in Themes view, use one of the following:

❏ Choose the Themes icon from the FrontPage Explorer Views pane.

❏ Choose **V**iew I **T**hemes.

Tasks View

As your Web site grows, you can quickly forget exactly what pages you need to work on. You can use Tasks view, shown in Figure 3.8, to help in that regard. You can maintain a To Do List for every FrontPage Web you create; Chapter 6, "What To Do?" shows you how.

Figure 3.7.

Change the appearance of your entire Web site in a flash by choosing a theme in Themes view.

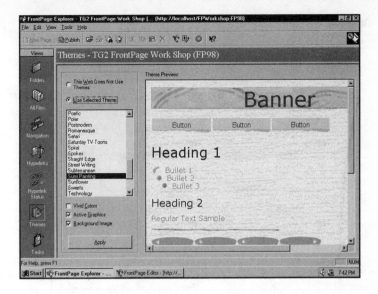

To view your Web in Tasks view, use one of the following:

❏ Choose the Tasks icon from the FrontPage Explorer Views pane.

❏ Choose **V**iew | Tas**k**s.

Figure 3.8.

Use Tasks view to organize, view, and complete tasks in your To Do List.

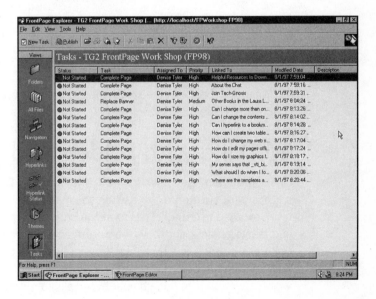

Displaying the Status Bar and Toolbar

The FrontPage Explorer has a status bar and toolbar that can be displayed or hidden. The status bar is located at the bottom of the FrontPage Explorer workspace and provides brief descriptions of what each menu command or toolbar button accomplishes. To display the status bar in the FrontPage Explorer, choose **V**iew | **S**tatus Bar. Repeat the command to hide the status bar.

The FrontPage Explorer toolbar, shown in Figure 3.9, is located beneath the Menu List. The buttons on the toolbar provide quick access to the commands you most commonly use in the FrontPage Explorer. From left to right, the commands are: Create New Page, Publish FrontPage Web, Open FrontPage Web, Print Navigation View, Cross File Find, Cross File Spelling, Cut, Copy, Paste, Delete, Up One Level, Show FrontPage Editor, Show Image Editor, Stop, and Help.

Figure 3.9.

The FrontPage Explorer's toolbar provides quick access to the most commonly used commands.

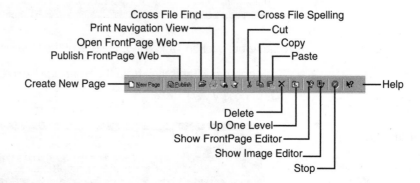

To display the toolbar in the FrontPage Explorer, choose **V**iew | **T**oolbar. Repeat the command to hide the toolbar.

Working with Folders and Pages

One of the advantages of working with the FrontPage Explorer is the ease with which it keeps track of your Web site when you make changes to it. Web sites constantly grow, evolve, and change. The FrontPage Explorer keeps track of your changes as you add, delete, rename, and move them. You can easily organize your pages into sections that focus on specific topics. Pages are easily moved from one folder to another by dragging and dropping, and the FrontPage Explorer is even smart enough to ask whether you want to update your hyperlinks to reflect the changes. The following sections discuss some of the more common ways that you can use FrontPage to make changes to the structure of your Web site.

Creating New Folders

As your Web grows, it becomes more and more difficult to keep track of pages if they are all contained in one directory. You can easily organize pages with similar content into their own directories. It is very easy to create new subfolders within your Web and move pages into them.

To create a new folder in your current Web, follow these steps:

1. From the FrontPage Explorer, choose **V**iew I **F**olders or click the Folders icon in the Views pane.

2. In the All Folders pane, click the folder beneath which you want to create the new subfolder. The folder becomes highlighted, and the pages contained in the folder appear in the Contents pane.

3. Choose **F**ile I **N**ew I **F**older. FrontPage creates a new folder in the Contents window, as shown in Figure 3.10. The folder is initially named New_Folder and is surrounded by a bounding box and highlighted, waiting for you to enter a new folder name.

4. Enter a name for the folder. The folder must be named according to the conventions used by your server, and the name cannot contain spaces.

5. Press Enter or click outside the bounding box to apply the name to the folder.

Figure 3.10.
Creating a new folder in the FrontPage Explorer.

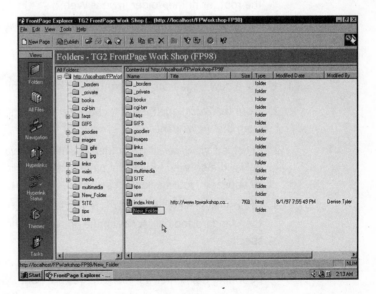

Changing Pages

You can use the FrontPage Explorer to create new pages in your Web, to rename or move pages into different folders, to copy pages from one folder into another, and to delete pages from your Web.

Creating New Pages

When you create a new page from any view in the FrontPage Explorer, you create a blank page. The background color of the page is white, and the text and hyperlink colors are set at their default values (black for text color, blue for hyperlink color, purple for visited hyperlink color, and red for active hyperlink color). It is the same type of page that you create when you choose the Normal Page template from the FrontPage Explorer.

You can create a new page from Folders, All Files, or Navigation view in the FrontPage Explorer. Depending on the view you select, the page is created in a different location.

❏ When you create a new page in Folders view, your new page is created in the current folder. If, for example, you want to create a new page in the _private folder of your Web, select the folder from Folders view and then choose the New Page command or button.

❏ When you create a new page in All Files view, your new page is created in the root, or home, folder in your Web.

❏ When you create a new page in Navigation view, you create a new page in a specific location in your navigation system. The page itself is saved in your Web's root, or home, folder.

To create a new page from the FrontPage Explorer, follow these steps:

1. From the FrontPage Explorer, choose the Folders, All Files, or Navigation icon from the Views pane.

2. In Folders view, select the folder in which you want to create the new page. In Navigation view, select the page beneath which you want your new page to appear in your navigation system.

3. Choose **F**ile | **N**ew | **P**age (Ctrl+N) or click the Create New Page button on the Standard toolbar. A new page appears in the directory or location you specify.

4. With the default name of the page highlighted and surrounded by a bounding box, enter the filename for the page you want to create and press Enter. Your page is created in the location you selected.

Renaming Pages

In FrontPage 98, it is extremely easy to rename files in your Web. When you rename pages from Folders view, All Files view, or the files pane in Navigation view of the FrontPage Explorer, FrontPage checks to see whether any pages include a link to the page that you are renaming. If so, FrontPage asks whether you want to update the hyperlinks on those pages. Your links keep right on working!

When you rename a page from the navigation pane in Navigation view, you are not renaming the page itself. Instead, you are editing the label that appears in the navigation bar. For more information about Navigation view, see Chapter 8.

To rename a page or file:

1. From the FrontPage Explorer, choose **V**iew I **F**olders, **V**iew I **A**ll Files, or **V**iew I **N**avigation. Alternatively, click the Folders, All Files, or Navigation icon from the Views pane in the FrontPage Explorer.

2. Click on the filename you want to rename from one of the following locations:

   Folders view   Select the filename you want to change from the
                       Contents pane in the folder in which your page
                       appears.

   All Files view   Select the filename you want to change from the
                       Name column.

   Navigation view   Select the filename you want to change from the
                       files pane in the lower portion of Navigation view.

3. Click on the filename again, or choose **E**dit I **R**ename, or press F2. The filename becomes surrounded by a bounding box, as shown in Figure 3.11.

4. Enter the new page name in the bounding box.

5. Press Enter or click outside the bounding box to apply the new name to the page. If any pages in your Web contain links to this page, FrontPage asks whether you want to update the links. Choose **Y**es to rename the page and update the links, **N**o to rename the page without updating the links (this causes broken links in your Web), or **C**ancel to keep the page name you currently have.

Selecting Pages

You can move or delete one or more pages at a time in your FrontPage Webs. To select multiple pages, use one of the following steps:

❑ To select a contiguous range of pages, folders, or a combination of pages and folders, click on the first item in the list and then Shift-click the last item. All pages between the two pages you click are also added to the selection.

Figure 3.11.

Renaming a page in the FrontPage Explorer.

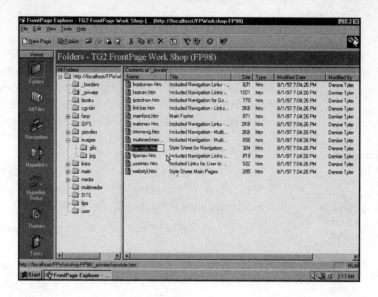

❏ To select two or more pages that are not in a contiguous set, click to select the first page or folder. Press the Ctrl key and click each additional page or folder you want to select.

❏ To select all folders and files in your Web site, choose **E**dit I Select **A**ll (Ctrl+A) from the home folder in your Web.

❏ To select all files in a single folder in your Web, first select the folder from the All Folders pane in Folders view. Then choose **E**dit I Select **A**ll (Ctrl+A).

Deleting Pages

To delete a selection of pages or folders from the FrontPage Explorer, use one of the following procedures:

❏ Choose **E**dit I **D**elete.

❏ Press the Delete button on the Standard toolbar.

❏ Press the Delete key on your keyboard.

❏ Right-click the selected pages or folders and choose **D**elete from the pop-up menu.

After you choose one of these procedures, the Confirm Delete dialog box appears, asking whether you are sure you want to delete the files or folders you selected. Choose **Y**es to delete one page or folder at a time, Yes to **A**ll to delete the entire selection, **N**o to cancel the deletion of one page or folder at a time, or Cancel to abort the procedure.

CAUTION: When you delete a folder from your Web, you delete all the pages contained in that folder. If the folder also contains subfolders that have their own pages, those are deleted also. Use caution when you delete folders! If you accidentally delete a page or folder, you cannot undo this action. You'll have to re-create the page or folder.

Copying and Moving Pages

You can easily move files or copy files from one folder to another. This task is most easily accomplished in Folders view. To move a page into a new folder, all you need to do is drag and drop, as shown in Figure 3.12.

Figure 3.12.
You can drag and drop one or more files from one folder into another to copy or move them.

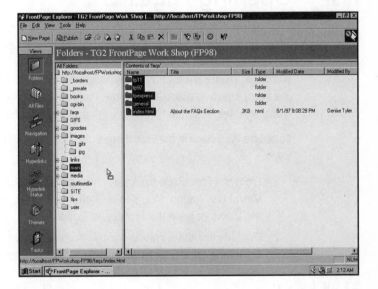

To copy or move a file:

1. From the Contents section of Folders view, highlight the file or files you want to relocate or copy, as discussed in the earlier section "Selecting Pages."

2. *To move the files into a new folder,* left-click and drag the file or files into the All Folders pane. When the folder to which you want to move the files is highlighted, release the mouse button.

3. *To create copies of pages in the same folder,* left-click and drag the mouse and release the mouse button in the Contents view of the current folder.

4. *To create copies of pages in another folder*, left-click and drag the file or files into the All Folders pane, until the folder to which you want to copy the files is highlighted. Press the Ctrl key before and while you release the mouse to make copies of the files in the new folder.

NOTE: By default, FrontPage uses the same filenames when you copy files into a different folder. When you copy files into the same folder, FrontPage names copies of files for you. If you copy a file named `index.htm`, for example, the copy is named `index_copy(1).htm`. Rename the files appropriately.

 ## Opening Pages

You can use the FrontPage Explorer to open pages in the FrontPage Editor. You can also double-click on a file of any type and open it in an associated editor. For example, if you want to open a Word document, an Excel spreadsheet, or an Access database, you can associate an editor with each file type. When you double-click on the filename, the file opens in its associated editor. For information on how to configure editors in FrontPage, see Chapter 17, "Integrating with Other Editors."

To open a Web page in the FrontPage Editor from the FrontPage Explorer, follow these steps:

1. From the FrontPage Explorer, choose **V**iew | **F**olders, **V**iew | **A**ll Files, or **V**iew | **N**avigation. You can also choose Folders, All Files, or Navigation from the Views pane in the FrontPage Explorer.

2. Double-click the filename for the Web page that you want to open. The FrontPage Editor opens and displays the page for editing.

Viewing and Editing File Properties

You can view the properties of any file in your Web from the FrontPage Explorer. Use the **E**dit | Properties command from Folders, All Files, or Navigation view to accomplish this. When you view file properties from the FrontPage Explorer, you can add comments to your page. These comments appear in the Contents pane of Folder view, in All Files view, and in the navigation pane of Navigation view.

To view and edit file properties from the FrontPage Explorer, follow these steps:

1. From the FrontPage Explorer, choose **V**iew | **F**olders, **V**iew | **A**ll Files, or **V**iew | **N**avigation. You can also choose Folders, All Files, or Navigation from the Views pane in the FrontPage Explorer.

2. Highlight the Web page or file whose properties you want to view. Choose **E**dit I Proper**t**ies, or press Alt+Enter, or right-click and choose Proper**t**ies from the pop-up menu. The Properties dialog box appears, opened to the General tab shown in Figure 3.13.

Figure 3.13.

Use the General tab in the Properties dialog box to view properties for a file in your Web.

3. The General tab displays the filename, its title, file type (extension), file size, and location. If the file has an extension other than `.htm` or `.html`, you can edit the title of the page. For example, the title for an image defaults to the folder and filename, and a title such as `images/aboutsite.gif` is very nondescriptive. To edit the title to something more appropriate, such as `About the Site Banner Graphic`, change the text in the Title field.

4. Use the Summary tab, shown in Figure 3.14, to add comments to any file in your Web. For example, if you want to make a note of the colors or fonts you used in a graphic, you can add them to the comments. Then, if you need to create similar graphics, you can remember color settings or font faces and sizes that you selected for your images.

Figure 3.14.

Use the Summary tab in the Properties dialog box to add comments to any file in your Web.

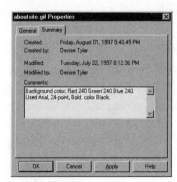

Select **F**ile I Proper**t**ies in the FrontPage Editor to edit the titles of your Web pages. Use the Title field in the General tab of the Page Properties dialog box to edit the titles of your Web pages.

Exiting the FrontPage Explorer

As you make changes to your Web in the FrontPage Explorer, all changes are immediately updated on your hard disk. You do not have to save any changes to your Web before you exit.

To exit the FrontPage Explorer, choose **File** I **Ex**it or click the X button in the upper-right corner of the FrontPage Explorer window. The FrontPage Editor remains open, and any pages from the Web you were working on remain opened in the FrontPage Editor.

Workshop Wrap-Up

This chapter gave you a quick tour of some of the main features in the FrontPage Explorer. You'll learn more about how to use many of these features in the chapters to come. You learned what each view in the FrontPage Explorer is used for and how to perform some of the basic tasks available to you from the FrontPage Explorer.

Next Steps

In the next chapter, "FrontPage Editor Basics," you'll get a quick tour of the FrontPage Editor. You'll learn about the various commands and toolbars available in this program and about some of the new features available in FrontPage 98.

For additional information about the features available in the FrontPage Explorer, refer to the following chapters:

- ❑ See Chapter 5, "Lightning-Speed Web Design," to learn about some of the Web templates and wizards available in the FrontPage Explorer.
- ❑ See Chapter 6, "What To Do?" to learn how to use the FrontPage Tasks view and how to maintain To Do lists in your Webs.
- ❑ See Chapter 7, "Real-Life Examples I: Using What You've Got," to learn how to combine some of the many FrontPage Web and page templates and wizards to create a Web site quickly and easily.
- ❑ See Chapter 8, "Designing Your Web Navigation," to learn how to use the commands and features available in the FrontPage Explorer's Navigation view.
- ❑ See Chapter 14, "Using FrontPage Style Sheets and Themes," to learn more about how to choose and create themes for your Web pages.
- ❑ See Chapter 17, "Integrating with Other Editors," to learn how to configure FrontPage to work with specific editors for several different types of files.

❑ See Chapter 34, "Testing and Publishing Your Webs," to learn how the FrontPage Explorer helps you quickly verify and repair links inside your Web and links to the World Wide Web.

Q&A

Q: Do I have to use the FrontPage Explorer while I develop my Web site?

A: You don't have to, but once you learn the many ways that the FrontPage Explorer helps you maintain your Web sites there may be no turning back. Having the ability to track the status of your links, move and rename pages without creating broken hyperlinks, change the entire look of your Web site, use common content from page to page—and more—make the FrontPage Explorer one Web developing companion you won't want to do without!

Q: Do I always have to create new Webs, or can I use content that I already have on the Internet?

A: You can import existing content into a FrontPage Web. Use the FrontPage Explorer to manage the pages in your site and use the FrontPage Editor to further enhance your pages. You learn how to import existing content into a FrontPage Web in Chapter 5.

Q: Why are some of the folder names in my Web preceded by an underscore character?

A: Folder names that are preceded by an underscore serve special functions in a FrontPage Web. These folders are hidden from the view of search bots, because they typically hold pages that contain partial content (such as a header or footer that appears on more than one page in your Web). Discussion group articles are also stored in folder names that are preceded by underscores. Typically, all but the _private folder are hidden from view in the FrontPage Explorer. You can display all hidden folders in your Web by choosing the **T**ools | **W**eb Settings command and checking the Show documents in **h**idden directories option in the Advanced tab of the FrontPage Web Settings dialog box.

FOUR

FrontPage Editor Basics

Now that you've had a quick overview of the FrontPage Explorer interface, it's time to take a tour of the other major component in FrontPage—the FrontPage Editor. Here is where you create, code, and preview your Web pages. Forget all those HTML tags and syntax. When you work in the FrontPage Editor, you don't touch any of those tags unless you really want to tweak and customize your pages.

If you've been working with previous versions of FrontPage, you'll see many nice enhancements to the FrontPage 98 Editor. As in previous versions, you develop your pages in true WYSIWYG mode. You can also view and edit the HTML code of your Web page. Major enhancements in FrontPage 98 include the ability to view and edit framesets and to preview sounds, animation, and other active content on your pages.

About the FrontPage Editor

The FrontPage Editor is used to create your Web pages. It is a WYSIWYG editor, meaning that what you see on your page is a good representation of how the page looks on the Web, using the most popular browsers. The FrontPage Editor does a great job of conforming to standards and generating "legal" HTML code. FrontPage 98 supports HTML 3.2 and then some, because it also supports Internet

Explorer 4.0 features, such as Dynamic HTML, Cascading Style Sheets, Channel Definition Files, and more. It makes your job a lot easier as a result: You can create forms and framesets in a flash, add color and emphasis to text, add images, create image maps and transparent GIFs, and use a host of other great features—all without touching a bit of HTML code.

 # Opening the FrontPage Editor from the FrontPage Explorer

As a general rule, you want to keep the FrontPage Explorer open while you create and edit pages for your Web sites. The FrontPage Explorer is used in conjunction with the FrontPage Editor to manage the hyperlinks in your Web and to make sure they remain working as you make changes to your pages.

To open the FrontPage Editor from the FrontPage Explorer, use one of two methods:

❏ Choose **T**ools I Show FrontPage **E**ditor.
❏ Click the Show FrontPage Editor button on the FrontPage Explorer toolbar.

You can return to the FrontPage Explorer at any time during your editing session.

To return to the FrontPage Explorer, use one of two methods:

❏ From the FrontPage Editor, choose **T**ools I Show FrontPage **E**xplorer.
❏ Click the Show FrontPage Explorer button on the Standard toolbar in the FrontPage Editor.

The FrontPage Editor Workspace Tabs

The FrontPage Editor workspace is displayed in several different tabs. The tab strip is located at the bottom of the workspace. Normally, there are at least three tabs:

❏ Use the Normal tab when you want to edit your Web page in WYSIWYG mode. This is the tab you will most likely use the most. Figure 4.1 shows a Web page displayed in the WYSIWYG editor.
❏ Use the HTML tab when you want to manually edit the HTML code in your Web page. An example is shown in Figure 4.2.

❏ Use the Preview tab when you want to preview what your Web page will look like on the Internet. When you use the Preview tab, you'll hear background sounds, see animation and active content, and preview other features that may not display in the FrontPage Editor's normal workspace.

Figure 4.1.

You create and edit pages in the Normal tab in the FrontPage Editor.

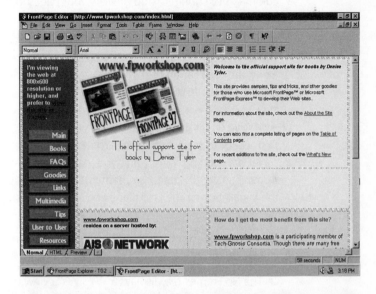

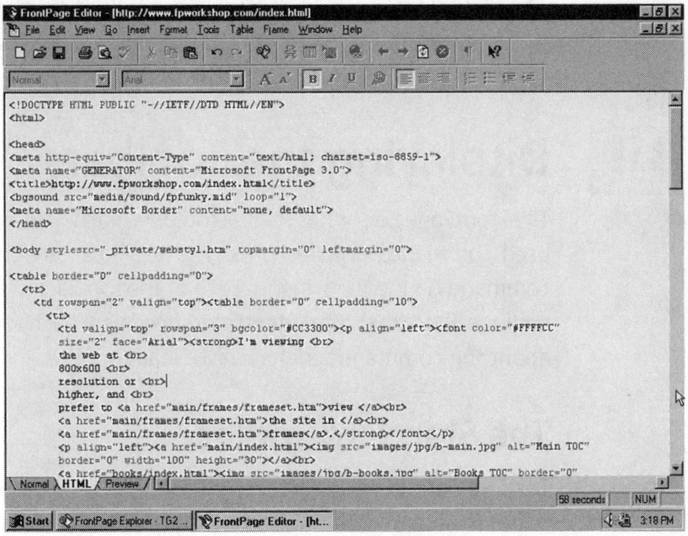

Figure 4.2.

You can view the code of your pages using the HTML tab in the FrontPage Editor.

See Chapter 26, "Using Your Own HTML," for further information on how you can add your own HTML code to your pages.

NOTE: Individual browsers handle certain features differently (tables are a good example), so it's wise to keep a variety of browsers on hand to fully test your pages before you publish them. You can use the **F**ile I Preview in **B**rowser command to configure and preview your pages in the browsers that you prefer.

If you are not running your server with the FrontPage Server Extensions while you browse your Web in the Preview tab, you receive the following message along the top margin of the workspace when a page contains features that require the FrontPage Server Extensions:

```
This page may not preview correctly because it contains one or more
➥components that require a Web server."
```

First, check to see whether the FrontPage Explorer and your personal Web server are running. If they are, you may need use the FrontPage Server Administrator, discussed in Chapter 32, "Administering Your Webs," to check the installation of the FrontPage Server Extensions.

When you're working on a frameset page, two additional tabs become available in the FrontPage Editor:

❏ The No Frames tab displays a WYSIWYG view of the page that the user sees when he or she does not have a frame-compatible browser.

❏ The Frames Page HTML tab enables you to view and edit the HTML code for the frameset.

Displaying the Toolbars

The FrontPage Editor has several toolbars, each of which provides access to frequently used commands and features. The toolbars can be displayed or hidden through commands in the View menu. Each of the toolbars is described briefly in the following sections. Refer to the chapters referenced near each toolbar for additional information about the commands that each toolbar contains.

The Standard Toolbar

The Standard toolbar, shown in Figure 4.3, provides a quick way to access common page creation and editing commands. Table 4.1 shows the commands in the toolbar as they appear from left to right and the menu commands that are associated with them.

Table 4.1. Commands in the Standard toolbar.

Toolbar Button	Associated Menu Command
New	**F**ile I **N**ew (select Normal Page)
Open	**F**ile I **O**pen
Save	**F**ile I **S**ave
Print	**F**ile I **P**rint
Preview in Browser	**F**ile I Preview in **B**rowser
Check Spelling	**T**ools I **S**pelling
Cut	**E**dit I **C**ut
Copy	**E**dit I **C**opy
Paste	**E**dit I **P**aste
Undo	**E**dit I **U**ndo
Redo	**E**dit I **R**edo
Show FrontPage Explorer	**T**ools I Show Fro**nt**Page Explorer
Insert FrontPage Component	**I**nsert I Front**P**age Component
Insert Table	T**a**ble I **I**nsert Table
Insert Image	**I**nsert I **I**mage
Create or Edit Hyperlink	**E**dit I Hyperlin**k**
Back	**G**o I **B**ack
Forward	**G**o I **F**orward
Refresh	**V**iew I **R**efresh
Stop	No command equivalent
Show/Hide Paragraph Marks	**V**iew I Format **M**arks
Help	**H**elp I Microsoft FrontPage **H**elp

To toggle the display of the Standard toolbar, choose **V**iew I **S**tandard Toolbar.

Figure 4.3.
The Standard toolbar.

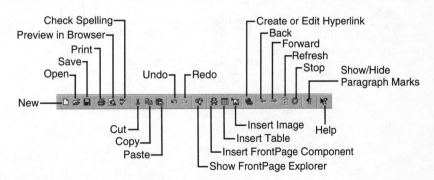

The Format Toolbar

The Format toolbar, shown in Figure 4.4, contains buttons that access text and paragraph style formatting commands. The toolbar buttons and associated menu commands are shown in Table 4.2.

Table 4.2. Commands in the Format toolbar.

Toolbar Button	Associated Menu Command
Change Style	**F**ormat I **P**aragraph
Change Font	**F**ormat I **F**ont
Increase Text Size	**F**ormat I **F**ont
Decrease Text Size	**F**ormat I **F**ont
Bold	**F**ormat I **F**ont
Italic	**F**ormat I **F**ont
Underline	**F**ormat I **F**ont
Text Color	**F**ormat I **F**ont
Align Left	**F**ormat I **P**aragraph
Center	**F**ormat I **P**aragraph
Align Right	**F**ormat I **P**aragraph
Numbered List	**F**ormat I Bullets and **N**umbering
Bulleted List	**F**ormat I Bullets and **N**umbering
Decrease Indent	No menu equivalent
Increase Indent	No menu equivalent

To display or hide the Format toolbar, choose **V**iew I **F**ormat Toolbar.

Figure 4.4.
The Format toolbar.

Learn how to format paragraphs and text in Chapter 10, "Composing and Editing Pages."

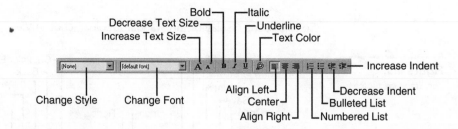

The Image Toolbar

The Image toolbar, shown in Figure 4.5, provides commands that enable you to create image maps and transparent GIFs and to make modifications to the images on your pages. There are no menu equivalents for the commands in the Image toolbar. For further information on these features, see Chapter 15, "Working with Images and Sound."

From left to right, the commands are Select, Rectangle, Circle, Polygon, Highlight Hotspots, Text, Make Transparent, Crop, Washout, Black and White, Restore, Rotate Left, Rotate Right, Reverse, Flip, More Contrast, Less Contrast, More Brightness, Less Brightness, Bevel, and Resample.

To display or hide the Image toolbar, choose **V**iew I **I**mage Toolbar.

Figure 4.5.
The Image toolbar.

Learn how to create image maps in Chapter 9, "Getting from Here to There." You create transparent GIFs in Chapter 15.

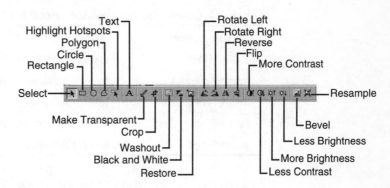

The Forms Toolbar

The Forms toolbar, shown in Figure 4.6, provides commands that enable you to place form fields on your page. Table 4.3 shows the buttons that appear in the Forms toolbar and the associated menu commands.

Table 4.3. Commands in the Forms toolbar.

Toolbar Button	Associated Menu Command
One-Line Text Box	**I**nsert I For**m** Field I One-Line **T**ext Box
Scrolling Text Box	**I**nsert I For**m** Field I **S**crolling Text Box
Check Box	**I**nsert I For**m** Field I **C**heck Box
Radio Button	**I**nsert I For**m** Field I **R**adio Button
Drop-Down Menu	**I**nsert I For**m** Field I **D**rop-Down Menu
Pushbutton	**I**nsert I For**m** Field I **P**ush Button

To display or hide the Forms toolbar, choose **V**iew I **Fo**rms Toolbar.

Figure 4.6.
The Forms toolbar.

Learn how to create
forms and form fields in
Chapter 21, "Quick and
Easy Forms," and
Chapter 22, "Adding
and Editing Form
Fields." Learn how to
assign form handlers in
Chapter 23, "Configur-
ing Form Handlers."

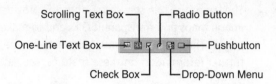

The Advanced Toolbar

The Advanced toolbar (see Figure 4.7) provides commands that enable you to place advanced features in your Web pages. Table 4.4 shows the buttons in the Advanced toolbar and the menu commands that are associated with them.

Table 4.4. Commands in the Advanced toolbar.

Toolbar Button	Associated Menu Command
Insert HTML	**I**nsert I **F**ront**P**age Component (choose Insert HTML)
Insert ActiveX Control	**I**nsert I **A**dvanced I **A**ctiveX Control
Insert Java Applet	**I**nsert I **A**dvanced I **J**ava Applet
Insert Plug-In	**I**nsert I **A**dvanced I **P**lug-In
Insert Script	**I**nsert I **A**dvanced I Scri**p**t

To display or hide the Advanced toolbar, choose **V**iew I **A**dvanced Toolbar.

Figure 4.7.
The Advanced toolbar.

Learn how to add
advanced features to
your pages in Chapter
25, "Using Java Applets
and Netscape Plug-Ins,"
Chapter 26, "Using
Your Own HTML," and
Chapter 28, "Working
with ActiveX and
Scripts."

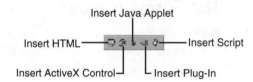

The Table Toolbar

The Table toolbar, shown in Figure 4.8, is used to create and edit tables and cells. Table 4.5 shows the buttons that are available in the Table toolbar and the menu commands that are associated with them.

Table 4.5. Commands in the Table toolbar.

Toolbar Button	Associated Menu Command
Draw Table	Ta**b**le I Draw Ta**b**le
Eraser	No menu equivalent

Toolbar Button	Associated Menu Command
Insert Rows	Table | Insert Rows or Columns
Insert Columns	Table | Insert Rows or Columns
Delete Cells	Table | Delete Cells
Merge Cells	Table | Merge Cells
Split Cells	Table | Split Cells
Align Top	No menu equivalent
Center Vertically	No menu equivalent
Align Bottom	No menu equivalent
Distribute Rows Evenly	Table | Distribute Rows Evenly
Distribute Columns Evenly	Table | Distribute Columns Evenly
Background Color	Table | Table Properties (assigned with Background Color drop-down menu)

To display or hide the Forms toolbar, choose View | Table Toolbar.

Figure 4.8.
The Table toolbar.

Learn how to create tables and add content to their cells in Chapter 12, "Your Tables Are Ready."

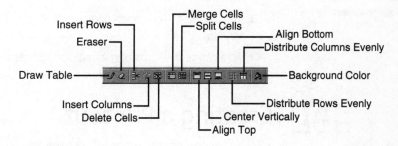

The Status Bar

Like the FrontPage Explorer, the FrontPage Editor has a status bar that can be displayed or hidden. The status bar provides descriptions of the menu commands and toolbar buttons as you drag your mouse over a command.

To display the status bar in the FrontPage Editor, choose View | Status Bar. Choose the command again to hide the status bar.

Viewing Format Marks

When you first open or create a page in the FrontPage Editor, you see paragraph and format marks displayed on the page. If you find this distracting, you can toggle display of the format marks on or off.

To toggle display of the format marks on your pages, choose **V**iew | Format **M**arks or click the Show/Hide button on the Standard toolbar.

Working with Pages

Throughout this book, you'll use the FrontPage Editor to generate pages that can be saved to your Web. You'll learn how to create pages from templates and wizards, and how to create pages on your own. The pages range from simple, text-only pages to those with advanced features—such as forms, frames, and tables—that enhance your page layout. You begin each page with the **F**ile | **N**ew command in the FrontPage Editor. The rest can be as straightforward or as creative as you choose.

Working with Multiple Pages

See Chapter 5, "Lightning-Speed Web Design," for further information on FrontPage's Web and page templates.

When you have several pages open at once in the FrontPage Editor, you can arrange the windows to overlap each other or to tile in the FrontPage Editor workspace:

❑ To display all your open pages in overlapping windows, choose **W**indow | **C**ascade.

❑ To arrange all your open pages so that they do not overlap, choose **W**indow | **T**ile.

❑ To arrange the icons of minimized pages at the bottom of the FrontPage Editor's window, choose **W**indow | **A**rrange Icons.

Creating a Printout

You can create a printout of any Web page, using commands in the File menu. The Page Setup command enables you to specify the page margins, header, and footer. The Print Preview command enables you to preview your page before you print it. Then, select your printer and the number of copies you want to print by using the Print command.

Previewing the Printout

Use the **F**ile | Print Pre**v**iew command in the FrontPage Editor to preview what your printed page will look like. To preview your printed page, follow these steps:

1. Open the page that you want to print in the FrontPage Editor.

2. Choose **F**ile | Print Pre**v**iew. A preview of your page appears, as shown in Figure 4.9.

Figure 4.9.

To preview your page before you print a hard copy, choose File | Print Preview.

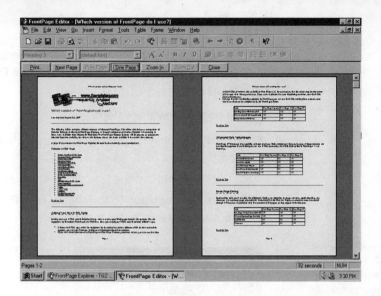

3. To preview the pages in your printout, choose one of the following buttons on the Print Preview toolbar, located at the top of the screen:

   ❏ To preview the next page in your printout, click the **N**ext Page button.

   ❏ To return to the previous page in the printout, click the Pre**v** Page button.

   ❏ To preview two pages at the same time, click the **T**wo Page button, after which the button is renamed to **O**ne Page. To return to a single page display, click the **O**ne Page button.

   ❏ To increase the magnification of the page in the preview screen, click the Zoom **I**n button.

   ❏ To decrease the magnification of the page in the preview screen, click the Zoom **O**ut button.

4. After you preview your printout, you have two options:

   ❏ To print out the pages and return to the FrontPage Explorer, click **P**rint. The Print dialog box appears, and you can configure the number of copies you want to print.

   ❏ To return to the FrontPage Explorer without printing your pages, click **C**lose.

Printing Your Page

You can print your page from the Print Preview screen, as mentioned in the earlier section "Previewing the Printout," or by choosing the **F**ile | **P**rint (Ctrl+P) command or toolbar button.

To print your page, follow these steps:

1. Open the Print dialog box, shown in Figure 4.10, using one of the following methods:

    ❑ Choose **P**rint from the Print Preview screen.

    ❑ From the FrontPage Editor, choose **F**ile | **P**rint (Ctrl+P) or click the Print button on the Standard toolbar.

Figure 4.10.
Use the Print dialog box to select your printer and specify the pages and number of copies you want to print.

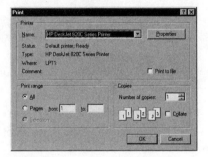

2. Enter or choose the following settings in the Print dialog box:

Printer: **N**ame:	Select your printer from the drop-down menu. Click the **P**roperties button to select settings that are unique to the printer you selected.
Printer: Print to fi**l**e:	Choose this option if you want to print your Navigation view to a file on your hard drive rather than to your printer. The file is saved with a `.prn` extension by default.
Print range: **A**ll	Choose this option to print all the pages in Navigation view.
Print range: Pa**g**es	Choose this option to print one or more of a range of pages in Navigation view. Enter the starting and ending page numbers in the **f**rom and **t**o fields.

| Copies: Number of **c**opies: | Enter the number of copies that you want to print in this field. |
| Copies: **C**ollate | Check this option if you want to collate multiple copies. Your printer must support collating. |

3. Choose OK to print your pages. You return to the FrontPage Editor, and the files are printed.

Browsing Your Web with the FrontPage Editor

As you design your pages, you can use the Normal tab in the FrontPage Editor to browse through the pages in your Web. To navigate through hyperlinks in your pages, follow these steps:

1. From the Normal tab in the FrontPage Editor, select the text, image, or hotspot that navigates to another page.

2. Choose **G**o | Follow Hyperlin**k**, or press Ctrl+Click, or right-click and choose Follow Hyperlink from the pop-up menu. The FrontPage Editor opens the destination page in your browser.

3. To return to the originating page, choose **G**o | **B**ack or press the Back button on the Standard toolbar.

4. To navigate forward to a hyperlink that you already followed, choose **G**o | **F**orward or press the Forward button on the Standard toolbar.

5. To refresh the display of the page in your browser, choose **V**iew | **R**efresh (F5) or press the Refresh button on the Standard toolbar.

See Chapter 19, "Using FrontPage Components," to learn how to follow hyperlinks in Include components. See Chapter 8 to learn how to follow hyperlinks in navigation bars.

Exiting the FrontPage Editor

When the changes and additions to your pages are complete, you can exit the FrontPage Editor. If you have one or more pages opened in the FrontPage Editor, you are prompted to save any unsaved changes before you exit.

Closing Your Pages

To close a page that is opened in the FrontPage Editor, choose **F**ile | **C**lose or click the X button in the upper-right corner of the page window. If there are any unsaved changes on your page, you will be prompted to save them before the page closes. You are also prompted to save any images, sounds, and other page enhancements that have not yet been saved to your FrontPage Web.

See Chapter 5 to learn how to save pages into your FrontPage Web or to your hard disk. See Chapter 15 to learn how to save images to your FrontPage Web.

Exiting the FrontPage Editor

To exit the FrontPage Editor, use one of the following procedures.

❑ Choose **F**ile | **C**lose (Ctrl+F4).

❑ Press the X button at the upper-right corner of the FrontPage Editor window.

Workshop Wrap-Up

Now you have a general idea of how to find your way around the FrontPage Editor. You've learned about several different tabs and views in which you can create and edit your pages. You also learned which toolbars provide access to the most commonly used commands and how to exit the FrontPage Editor when you're finished.

Next Steps

In the next chapter, you'll learn about the Web and page templates and wizards that are provided with FrontPage and how you can combine them to create Web sites that contain multiple pages that are already linked together for you. The following chapters show you how to add basic features in your pages with the FrontPage Editor:

❑ See Chapter 9, "Getting from Here to There," to learn how to create and edit hyperlinks.

❑ See Chapter 10, "Composing and Editing Pages," to learn how to add basic content such as headings, paragraphs, and text and font formatting to your pages.

❑ See Chapter 11, "Organizing Information into Lists," to learn how to insert and format your information in a variety of list types.

❑ See Chapter 12, "Your Tables Are Ready," to learn how to use tables to achieve advanced layout in your pages.

Q&A

Q: Can I open other types of documents in the FrontPage Editor besides Web pages?

A: You can open a variety of word processing formats, including Rich Text Format and text documents. The FrontPage Editor also enables you to open and edit processed `.html` pages that use extensions such as `.asp` (Active Server Pages), `.htx` (for Internet Information Server Internet database connection), and others. For more information on importing and using these various file formats, see Chapter 17, "Integrating with Other Editors."

Q: Can I use the FrontPage Editor to edit Web pages that reside on my hard drive instead of those that exist in a FrontPage Web?

A: Yes, you can. You learn more about this in Chapter 5.

FIVE

Lightning-Speed Web Design

Are you someone who likes to get things done quickly and efficiently? I am. Sometimes my creativity is blocked, and other times I just want to get the groundwork done in a hurry so that I can get to the fun part of dressing up the pages. That is what I enjoy the most.

If you are pressed for time or short on ideas for pages, FrontPage has a bountiful supply of Web and page templates and wizards that will quickly help you set the groundwork for your Web site. Many of the pages are designed for business purposes. You can modify the content in any way you choose.

In this chapter, you get an overview of the many Web and page templates and wizards provided with FrontPage. You also learn how to do basic tasks, such as creating, opening, and saving Webs and pages.

Getting Started with Webs

The Getting Started with Microsoft FrontPage dialog box, shown in Figure 5.1, provides a means of creating and opening Webs quickly.

Figure 5.1.

The Getting Started dialog box offers quick access to commonly used Web commands.

Choose one of the following commands from the dialog box to open or create a FrontPage Web:

❑ *Open an Existing FrontPage Web*. For additional information, see the section "Opening an Existing FrontPage Web," later in this chapter.

TIP: To remove a Web name from the Getting Started dialog box, right-click on the name you want to remove and choose **R**emove from List from the pop-up menu.

❑ *Create a New FrontPage Web*. For additional information, see the task "Creating a New FrontPage Web."

❑ *Always open last Web*. Check this box if you want to resume with the last Web that you were editing when you last used the FrontPage Explorer.

 # Enabling or Disabling the Getting Started Dialog Box

You can disable the Getting Started dialog box from the FrontPage Explorer. To return to the FrontPage Explorer from the FrontPage Editor, choose **T**ools I Show Fro**n**tPage Explorer or click the Show FrontPage Explorer button on the Standard toolbar. Then, disable the Getting Started dialog box as follows:

1. From the FrontPage Explorer, choose **T**ools I **O**ptions. The Options dialog box appears, opened to the General tab shown in Figure 5.2.

2. In the General FrontPage Explorer Options section, check the Show **G**etting Started dialog checkbox to enable the dialog box. To disable it, uncheck this option.

3. Click OK to exit the Options dialog box. The change takes effect the next time you start the FrontPage Explorer.

Figure 5.2.

Use the General tab in the Options dialog box to disable the Getting Started dialog box.

The Web Templates and Wizards

When you create a new Web in FrontPage, you can select from a number of different Web templates and wizards. You choose one of the templates and wizards from the New FrontPage Web dialog box, which is described later in this chapter in the task "Creating a New FrontPage Web."

The Web templates and wizards save you a great deal of time. When you use the Web templates and wizards, FrontPage automatically creates several different pages that are already linked together for you. Shared borders display content that is similar from page to page. What remains is for you to customize the content on the pages.

Businesses and corporations may find several of the Web templates and wizards provided with FrontPage to be of interest. The Corporate Presence Wizard is an ideal way to create a business Web site where your products and services are highlighted. The Customer Support Web and the Discussion Web Wizard feature discussion groups that contain threaded messages. The Customer Support Web features pages that provide communications for customer relations, whereas the Project Web features pages for project coordination.

To start a personal Web site quickly, choose the Personal Web template. This creates a Web that contains a personal home page along with a favorites page, an interests page, a photo album, and a list of favorite links.

The following sections briefly describe the Web templates and wizards that are available with FrontPage.

The Corporate Presence Wizard

The first screen of the Corporate Presence Wizard is shown in Figure 5.3. This wizard, discussed in greater detail in Chapter 7, "Real-Life Examples I: Using What You've Got," creates several pages that get a corporate Web site up and running quickly. The site includes several pages:

- ❑ The home page provides a general introduction to your company. It can include an introduction, a mission statement, a company profile, and contact information.

- ❑ The What's New page announces recent changes to your site and links to pages that tell recent news about your company.

- ❑ Products and Services pages describe the products and services that your company has to offer. Each product sheet can contain a product image, pricing information, and an information request form. Each service page can include a list of capabilities, reference accounts, and an information request form.

- ❑ The Table of Contents page contains a list of all the pages on your site. It is generated automatically through the use of a Table of Contents component.

- ❑ The Feedback Form enables users to tell you what they think about your company, your Web site, or your products and services. You can store users' results to an HTML or text file on your Web site.

- ❑ The Search Form enables users to search through all the pages in your site for words or a combination of words.

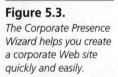

Figure 5.3.
The Corporate Presence Wizard helps you create a corporate Web site quickly and easily.

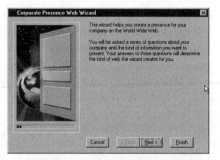

The Discussion Web Wizard

The Discussion Web Wizard helps you create your own customized discussion group. The first screen of the Discussion Web Wizard is shown in Figure 5.4. You can create a discussion group in a Web site of its own or add a discussion group to an existing

Web site. The discussion group can be included in a public or private Web and can be placed within framesets or regular pages. An article submission form is automatically created for you. You can also add a Table of Contents, search form, threaded replies, and a confirmation page.

You will find additional information on how to use the Discussion Web Wizard in Chapter 24, "Real-Life Examples IV: Adding Interactivity."

Figure 5.4.
The Discussion Web Wizard helps you design discussion groups for public and private Web sites.

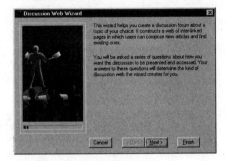

The Customer Support Web

The Customer Support Web template creates a Web that contains a number of different pages, some of which are shown in the list in Figure 5.5. This Web provides interactive support with your customers. Though it is primarily designed around providing support for software products, it can easily be modified to suit any purpose. Included in the collection are the following pages:

- ❏ A Customer Support section, complete with Bug Report Form, Discussion Group, Download page, Customer Feedback page, Frequently Asked Questions page, Search page, Suggestions from Customers page, Technical Notes, and What's New page
- ❏ A Customer Support discussion group, complete with its own Search page, article submission form, a Welcome page, and page headers and footers

The Project Web

The Project Web template creates pages that include two discussion groups. One section of the Project Web provides an area where files, pages, and a discussion group relating to a project are stored. The other section of the Project Web creates a section where Knowledge Base articles and a discussion group are located. Figure 5.6 shows a partial list of the pages created in the Project Web.

Figure 5.5.

The Customer Support Web creates several pages that provide a customer support site on the Internet.

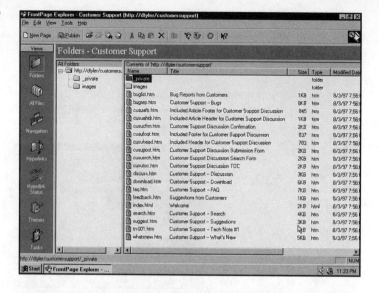

Figure 5.6.

The Project Web template creates two discussion groups and additional pages that help you coordinate projects on an intranet or the Internet.

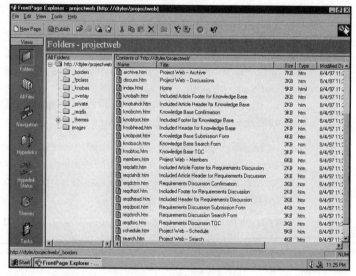

The Personal Web Template

The Personal Web template creates a personal Web site with five Web pages contained in it. Besides a home page, the site includes a Favorite Sites page, an Interests page, a Favorites page, and a Photo Album page. Figure 5.7 shows this site in Navigation view in the FrontPage Explorer. Navigation systems are created for you automatically any time you create Webs with this template or any of the others mentioned in the previous sections.

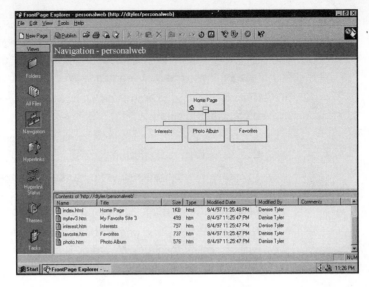

Figure 5.7.
The Personal Web Template creates a home page and four additional pages that list personal favorites and interests.

The Empty Web and the One-Page Web

The Empty Web template creates a Web site that contains no pages. Typically, you use this Web when you want to start a Web site from scratch or when you want to import existing content into a Web. The one-page Web can be used for the same situations. It creates a blank home page in the Web.

Creating a New FrontPage Web

You use the New FrontPage Web dialog box, shown in Figure 5.8, to create new Webs. This dialog box enables you to choose from the Web templates and wizards that have already been discussed.

Figure 5.8.
Use the New FrontPage Web dialog box to create a Web from one of several different Web templates and wizards.

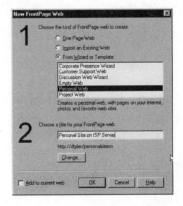

To create a new Web, follow these steps:

1. From the Getting Started dialog box, choose **C**reate a New FrontPage Web and click OK or choose **F**ile | **N**ew | FrontPage **W**eb (Ctrl+N) from the FrontPage Explorer. The New FrontPage Web dialog box appears.

2. In the Choose the kind of FrontPage Web to create section, select the type of Web you want to create:

   ❏ To create a Web that contains a single blank home page, select the **O**ne Page Web radio button.

   ❏ To create a Web that enables you to import content from a folder on your local or network hard drive or from a site on the World Wide Web, select the **Im**port an Existing Web radio button.

   ❏ To create a Web using one of the FrontPage Web templates and wizards, check the From **W**izard or Template button and select the template or wizard that you want to use.

3. In the Choose a **t**itle for your FrontPage web field, enter a descriptive title for your Web site, such as `Personal Site on`, followed by your server name.

4. To edit the URL for your Web site, click the **C**hange button. The Change Location dialog box shown in Figure 5.9 appears. Use this dialog box to identify the server and the folder name for your Web.

Figure 5.9.
Use the Change Location dialog box to edit the server address and folder in which your Web will appear.

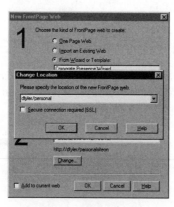

5. Use the drop-down menu in the Change Location dialog box to select a server on which to create your Web site, or enter a server name and folder name in the Please specify the location of the new FrontPage **w**eb field. The following examples show some typical entries:

`myserver/myweb`	Creates a Web named `myweb` on the server installed at port 80 on your local computer, but may prompt you to connect to the Internet before connecting to your server. If your FrontPage server was installed to port 8080, use `myserver:8080/myweb`.
`localhost/myweb`	Creates a Web named `myweb` on the server on your local computer. You will not be prompted to connect to the Internet. If your FrontPage 98 server was installed to port 8080, use `localhost:8080/myweb`.
`127.0.0.1/myweb`	Creates a Web named `myweb` on the server on your local computer. You will not be prompted to connect to the Internet. If your FrontPage 98 server was installed on port 8080, use `127.0.0.1:8080/myweb`.
`www.webserver.com`	Creates a Web in the root directory on a server or domain name on the World Wide Web. You will be prompted to connect to the Internet and will probably be required to enter a user name and password to gain access to the site.
`www.webserver.com/myweb`	Creates a Web named `myweb` in a folder beneath the root directory on a server on the World Wide Web. This is the most common format for those who have personal sites with an Internet service provider.

6. If the server on which you want to create your Web supports Secure Socket Layer communications, check the **S**ecure connection required (SSL) checkbox.

7. Choose OK to return to the New FrontPage Web dialog box.

8. If the URL you enter in the Choose a title for your FrontPage web field already exists, the Add to current web checkbox enables it.

9. Choose OK again to create your Web site. If you created a Web from a template, your pages appear in the FrontPage Explorer. If you created a Web from a wizard, your pages appear in the FrontPage Explorer after you complete the steps in the Wizard.

Importing an Existing Web from Folders on Your Hard Drive

The Import Web Wizard enables you to import content from an existing Web site into a FrontPage Web. You can use the Import Web Wizard to import content from your local or network hard drive or from a site on the World Wide Web. The Wizard enables you to set limits to the amount you download as well. Follow these steps:

1. From the New FrontPage Web dialog box, choose **Im**port an Existing Web.

2. In the Choose a **t**itle for your FrontPage Web field, enter a descriptive title for your Web site.

3. To edit the **U**RL for the Web site on the server you want to publish to, click the **C**hange button. The Change Location dialog box appears. Edit the URL as mentioned earlier in the task "Creating a New FrontPage Web" and choose OK to return to the New FrontPage Web dialog box.

4. Choose OK to create the Web. The first screen in the Import Web Wizard appears.

5. To import your content from a folder on your local or network hard drive, select the From a source **d**irectory of files on a local computer or network radio button, as shown in Figure 5.10.

Figure 5.10.

You can import content from a folder on your local or network hard drive.

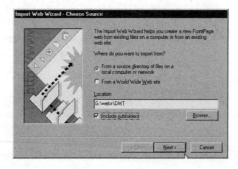

6. Enter the path to the files in the **L**ocation field or click the **B**rowse button to locate the folder in the Browse for Folder dialog box shown in Figure 5.11. After you select the folder, click OK to return to the Import Web Wizard.

7. Check the Include **s**ubfolders checkbox to include all files and folders beneath the folder you want to import.

8. Choose **N**ext to continue. The Edit File List screen shown in Figure 5.12 appears. To exclude files from the list, highlight the file or files that you want to exclude and click the **E**xclude button. Click **R**efresh to deselect all the files.

Figure 5.11.

Select the folder from which you want to import your content in the Browse for Folder dialog box.

Figure 5.12.

Use the Edit File List screen to exclude files from the list of files to be imported.

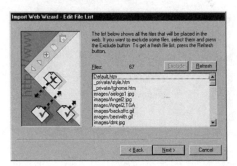

9. Choose **N**ext to continue. The Import Web Wizard notifies you that it has all the answers it needs. Click Finish to import your pages. FrontPage imports all the files and folders into your Web.

Importing an Existing Web from the World Wide Web

The Import Web Wizard also enables you to import content from a site on the World Wide Web. When you import a site from the Internet, you can set limits to the amount that you download.

To import content from the World Wide Web, follow these steps:

1. From the New FrontPage Web dialog box, choose **Im**port an Existing Web.

2. In the Choose a **t**itle for your FrontPage web field, enter a descriptive title for your Web site, such as **Personal Site on**, followed by your server name.

3. To edit the **U**RL for the Web site on the server you want to publish to, click the **C**hange button. The Change Location dialog box appears. Edit the URL as mentioned earlier in the task "Creating a New FrontPage Web" and choose OK to return to the New FrontPage Web dialog box.

4. Choose OK to create the Web. The first screen in the Import Web Wizard appears.

5. To import a Web site from the World Wide Web, check the From a World Wide Web site radio button and enter the URL in the Location field, as shown in Figure 5.13. You can also enter a specific folder from which to start, such as the following:

www.yourserver.com/webname/folder/

Figure 5.13.
You can also use the Import Web Wizard to import content from an existing site on the World Wide Web.

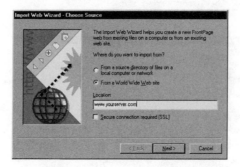

6. Choose **N**ext to continue. The Choose Download Amount screen shown in Figure 5.14 appears. If you want to limit the amount of downloading you do, you can set limits in this screen:

Figure 5.14.
The Choose Download Amount screen enables you to reduce download times by setting limits on what you import.

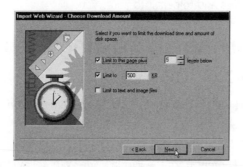

❏ To limit the number of levels you want to download, check the Limit to this page plus checkbox. Enter the number of levels below the folder in the levels below field. Uncheck this option to download the entire site.

❏ To limit the total number of kilobytes you want to download, check the **L**imit to checkbox and enter the number of KB you want to limit the download to. Uncheck this option to download the entire site.

❏ To limit the download to text and image files only, check the Limit to text and image **f**iles checkbox.

7. Choose **N**ext to continue. The Import Web Wizard notifies you that it has all the answers it needs. Click Finish to import your pages. FrontPage imports all the files and folders into your Web.

Opening Existing Webs

The Getting Started with Microsoft FrontPage dialog box provides commands to open your most recent Web and to open any other FrontPage Web that exists on your server or hard drive. You can also open Webs from the FrontPage Explorer.

Opening an Existing FrontPage Web

You can open an existing Web from the Getting Started dialog box as follows:

1. From the Getting Started dialog box, choose the **O**pen an Existing FrontPage Web radio button.

2. Double-click the Web that you want to open from the list of Webs on your server or highlight the Web name and choose OK. The Web opens in the FrontPage Explorer.

If the Web that you want to open does not appear on the list, you may need to log on to another server. Click the **M**ore Webs button. The Open FrontPage Web dialog box shown in Figure 5.15 appears. You can open this dialog box in one of two ways:

❏ From the Getting Started with Microsoft FrontPage dialog box, choose the **M**ore Webs button.

❏ From the FrontPage Explorer, choose **F**ile | **O**pen FrontPage Web. The Open FrontPage Web dialog box shown in Figure 5.15 appears.

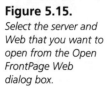

Figure 5.15.
Select the server and Web that you want to open from the Open FrontPage Web dialog box.

To open the Web, follow these steps:

1. In the Select a **W**eb server or disk location field, choose the server on which you created your Web from the drop-down menu.

FrontPage 98 can open Webs existing on servers that support the Secure Socket Layer (SSL). Web pages on a secure Web start with `https://` instead of `http://`. This indicates a secure link. When you open a secure Web for the first time, you must select the **S**ecure connection required (SSL) option in the Open FrontPage Web dialog box. If you don't check this option, you will receive a message that access has been denied.

NOTE:
If you use the Open FrontPage Web command to open a Web on a server that does not have the FrontPage Server Extensions installed, you receive a message that the server could not complete your request and that the requested URL `/_vti_bin/shtml.exe/_vti_rpc` was not found on the server. You can use the Import Web Wizard, discussed in the earlier task "Importing an Existing Web from the World Wide Web" to import the pages from the server into a FrontPage Web on your local computer.

2. Check the **S**ecure connection required (SSL) checkbox if you want to connect to a server that supports Secure Socket Layer (SSL) communications.

3. Click the **L**ist Webs button. The names of the existing Webs on the server appear in the **F**rontPage Webs found at location list. (This step might not be necessary if you choose the server from the Web **S**erver or File Location drop-down menu.)

4. From the FrontPage W**e**bs list, double-click the Web you want to open or highlight the name of the Web you want to open and choose OK. Enter your name and password if the Name and Password Required dialog box appears. The Web opens in the FrontPage Explorer.

NOTE:
The Name and Password Required dialog box appears the first time you open or create a Web after starting the FrontPage Explorer. Enter the name and password you configured in the FrontPage Server Administrator while installing FrontPage to your local computer.

Opening Your Most Recent Web

You can open the most recent Web you worked on in one of two ways:

❑ From the Getting Started with Microsoft FrontPage dialog box, check the **A**lways open last web checkbox to automatically open the last Web you worked on each time you start FrontPage.

❑ From the FrontPage Explorer, choose **F**ile | **1** *webname*, where *webname* is the name of the last Web you worked on.

Working with Pages

When you work with pages in FrontPage, you do most of your work in the FrontPage Editor. You should also have the FrontPage Explorer running concurrently. By doing so, you maintain your links and organize all your Web pages and images into folders.

By far, the quickest way to create pages is to use the templates and wizards provided with FrontPage. In addition to the seven Web templates and wizards, there are several page templates and wizards; by studying their construction, you learn many of FrontPage's features. As you become more familiar with the FrontPage features, you can customize the templates to better suit your needs.

Creating a Page from a Template

After you open or create a FrontPage Web, you can easily add pages to it. To create a page from a template, do the following:

1. From the FrontPage Explorer, choose **T**ools | Show FrontPage **E**ditor or use the Show FrontPage Editor button on the toolbar. The FrontPage Editor opens and initially displays a blank page.

2. From the FrontPage Editor, choose **F**ile | **N**ew (Ctrl+N). The New dialog box shown in Figure 5.16 appears.

Figure 5.16.
Use the New Page dialog box to select the template or wizard from which you want to create your page.

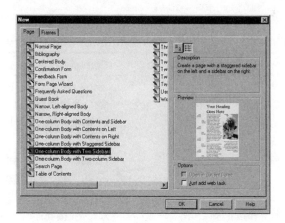

3. From the Template or Wizard list, highlight the template from which you want to create your page. All available templates are listed in Tables 5.1 and 5.2.

4. Click OK or press Enter. Your page appears in the FrontPage Editor.

Old Style Templates and Wizards

The most popular page templates from previous versions of FrontPage are also included in FrontPage 98. These pages include features that you will most commonly use in personal Web sites. Figure 5.17 shows thumbnails of each page, and Table 5.1 lists the old style page templates.

Figure 5.17.
Old style page templates.

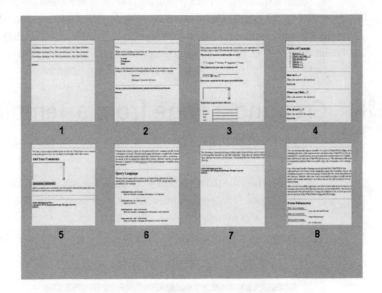

Table 5.1. Old style page templates and wizards.

Page Template or Wizard	Comments
Normal Page	Blank page; used to start your pages from scratch. You can create a normal page quickly by using the New button on the Standard toolbar.
Bibliography	Presents a list of reference material, including author and publication name and publisher information. (See thumbnail #1 in Figure 5.17.)
Confirmation Form	A form that is returned to a user after he or she submits data into another form on your page. (See thumbnail #2 in Figure 5.17.)
Feedback Form	A general-purpose feedback form that can be modified for any purpose. (See thumbnail #3 in Figure 5.17.)

Page Template or Wizard	Comments
Form Page Wizard	A wizard that helps you create forms by entering the questions you want to ask. Discussed in Chapter 21, "Quick and Easy Forms."
Frequently Asked Questions	Presents a list of questions and links to their answers. (See thumbnail #4 in Figure 5.17.)
Guest Book	Enables users to place comments on your site. (See thumbnail #5 in Figure 5.17.)
Search Page	Enables users to search through your site for a word or phrase. (See thumbnail #6 in Figure 5.17.)
Table of Contents	Generates a table of contents of all pages on your site, beginning with a specified page. (See thumbnail #7 in Figure 5.17.)
User Registration	A form to enter a username and password to gain entry into a protected Web. (See thumbnail #8 in Figure 5.17.)

New Style Page Templates

The new page templates furnished with FrontPage 98 are fully compatible with the new features in FrontPage 98. Most of them use tables to achieve advanced layout in your Web pages. The pages present information in one, two, or three columns. Some pages feature sidebars where you can place your navigation. Figure 5.18 shows thumbnails of each page, and Table 5.2 lists the new style page templates.

Table 5.2. New style page templates and wizards.

Thumbnail #	Page Template or Wizard
Thumbnail 1	Centered Body
Thumbnail 2	Narrow, Left-aligned Body
Thumbnail 3	Narrow, Right-aligned Body
Thumbnail 4	One-column Body with Contents and Sidebar
Thumbnail 5	One-column Body with Contents on Left
Thumbnail 6	One-column Body with Contents on Right
Thumbnail 7	One-column Body with Staggered Sidebar

continues

Table 5.2. continued

Thumbnail #	Page Template or Wizard
Thumbnail 8	One-column Body with Two Sidebars
Thumbnail 9	One-column Body with Two-Column Sidebar
Thumbnail 10	Three-column Body
Thumbnail 11	Two-column Body
Thumbnail 12	Two-column Body with Contents on Left
Thumbnail 13	Two-column Body with Two Sidebars
Thumbnail 14	Two-column Staggered Body
Thumbnail 15	Two-column Staggered Body with Contents and Sidebar
Thumbnail 16	Wide Body with Headings

Figure 5.18.
*New style page
templates.*

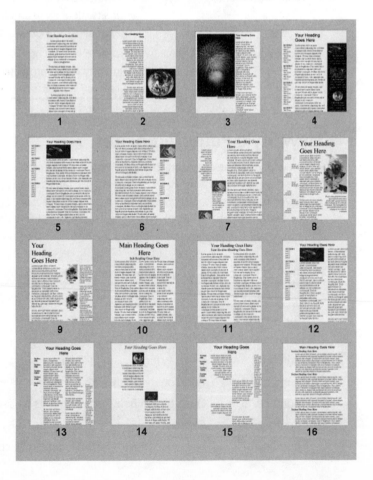

Opening Existing Pages

To open a page from your current Web, follow these steps:

1. From the FrontPage Editor, choose **F**ile | **O**pen (Ctrl+O) or click the Open button on the Standard toolbar. The Open dialog box shown in Figure 5.19 appears.

Figure 5.19.
Use the Open dialog box to open a page in your current Web, from the World Wide Web, or from your local or network hard drive.

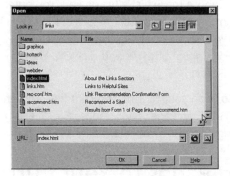

2. From the list of files in your current Web, double-click the filename you want to open or highlight the filename and choose OK. To open a page in a subfolder in your Web, double-click the folder, then double-click the filename. The page opens in the FrontPage Editor.

To open a page from the World Wide Web, follow these steps:

1. From the FrontPage Editor, choose **F**ile | **O**pen (Ctrl+O) or click the Open button on the Standard toolbar. The Open dialog box appears.

2. Use one of the following methods to open the page:

   ❏ Enter the URL of the page you want to open in the **U**RL field and choose OK.

   ❏ Select the Use your Web Browser to select a page or file button located to the right of the **U**RL field. Your browser opens and you can navigate to the page you want to open in the FrontPage Editor. After you navigate to the page, return to the Open dialog box in the FrontPage Editor, where the URL of the page will appear in the **U**RL field. Click OK to open the page in the FrontPage Editor.

NOTE: Labels for the buttons in the Open and Save As dialog boxes appear when you hover your mouse over the button.

To open a page from your local or network hard drive, follow these steps:

1. From the FrontPage Editor, choose **F**ile I **O**pen (Ctrl+O) or click the Open button on the Standard toolbar. The Open dialog box appears.

2. Use one of the following methods to open the page:

   ❏ Enter the path to the page you want to open in the **U**RL field and choose OK.

   ❏ Choose the Select a file on your computer button located to the right of the **U**RL field. Use the Select File dialog box to locate the page on your local or network hard drive. Double-click the folder and filenames or highlight the file and click OK. The page opens in the FrontPage Editor.

You can also open your four most recent files from the File menu in the FrontPage Editor. From the FrontPage Editor, choose **F**ile I **1**, **F**ile I **2**, **F**ile I **3**, or **F**ile I **4**. The lowest number designates the most recent file.

Saving Pages to Your Current Web

After you create or edit your pages, you save them to your FrontPage Web. The Web can be located on your server or on your local or network hard drive. If there is no Web open when you save the page, you will be prompted to open a Web and save the page again.

To save your page to the current Web, follow these steps:

1. From the FrontPage Editor, choose **F**ile I **S**ave (Ctrl+S) or click the Save button on the Standard toolbar. The Save As dialog box shown in Figure 5.20 appears.

Figure 5.20.
The Save As dialog box.

2. By default, the page is saved to the root folder in your current Web. If you created a new page at the same time you created a hyperlink from an existing page, the page is saved to the same folder in which the originating page appears. To select a different folder, double-click the folders in the Save As dialog box to select another one.

3. In the **U**RL field, enter a filename for the new page.

4. In the **T**itle field, enter a title for your new page.

5. Click OK or press Enter to save the file to the current Web.

Saving Pages as Files

You can also use the Save As dialog box to save your page to another location on your local or network hard disk.

1. From the FrontPage Editor, choose **F**ile | Save (Ctrl+S) or click the Save button on the Standard toolbar. The Save As dialog box appears.

2. In the **U**RL field, enter the path to which you want to save the file in the URL field or proceed with step 3 to locate a folder on your local or network hard drive.

3. To locate a folder on your local or network hard drive, click the Select a file on your computer button to the right of the **U**RL field. The Save As File dialog box appears.

4. Use the Save **i**n box to locate the folder on your hard drive that you want to save the file in.

5. In the Save as **t**ype field, select the type of file that you want to save:

HTML Files	`(*.htm; *.html)`
Preprocessed HTML	`(*.htx; *.asp)`
Hypertext Templates	`(*.htt)`

6. Click **S**ave. Your page is saved to the directory and you return to the FrontPage Editor. If your page includes images, sound, or other elements, you are asked whether you want to save them to the same folder.

Saving All Pages

If you have a number of pages opened in the FrontPage Editor, you can save or update pages in your Web by using the Save All command. This command saves only the pages that have not yet been saved to your Web.

To save any pages that contain changes, choose **F**ile I Save All. Any pages that you have previously saved to your Web but which include revisions will be updated to the folders to which they were saved. To save any pages that have not yet been saved to your current Web or to a folder on your local or network hard drive, use the procedures discussed in the sections "Saving Pages to Your Current Web" and "Saving Pages as Files."

Creating Templates of Your Own

Sure, the templates and wizards provided with FrontPage do save you time—but you think they need more spice. You'd like to develop your own page templates from which you can choose. You'll find that using templates is the best way to save time while maintaining a consistent look and feel in your Web site. FrontPage enables you to create your own templates on which to base the pages in your Web.

Building the Template

When you build your page template, complete as much of the typical page content as you can. Add your color schemes; choose your background, text, and link colors; and add background images. Enter as much general content as you can and use the **I**nsert I FrontPage Component command to add comments to your page where you think your memory might need refreshing later. The more common ground you create on your template, the less you have to remember when you edit the content. This makes everything consistent.

Saving a Page as a Template

Choose the **F**ile I **S**ave command to save a page as a template. The Save As dialog box includes an option button that lets you save a page as a template. Use the following steps:

1. After your page is complete, choose **F**ile I **S**ave (Ctrl+S) or click the Save button on the Standard toolbar. The Save As dialog box appears.

2. Enter a URL for the template in the URL field. Limit the number of letters in the URL to 8 characters or less. For example, if you want to create a template for a guest book, enter a URL of `gstbook.htm`.

3. Enter a title for the page in the **T**itle field. This title will also appear in the New Page dialog box after you save your page as a template. Therefore, the title should be descriptive enough so that you know what Web or page your template will be used for. For example, enter the following:

   `My Custom Guest Book`

4. Click the As Template button. The Save As Template dialog box shown in Figure 5.21 appears.

5. The URL and title you entered in steps 2 and 3 appear by default in the **T**itle and **N**ame fields of the Save As Template dialog box. Leave these settings as they are.

6. Enter a description for the template. When you create a new page based on the template, this description appears at the bottom of the New Page dialog box. Enter the following description:

   Template for Guest Book on Personal Web Site

7. Click OK to save the page as a template.

If you installed FrontPage using the default settings, a new directory named `gstbook.tem` is created in the `Program Files/Microsoft FrontPage/Pages` subdirectory. Now, whenever you create a new page, this template is listed in the New Page dialog box.

Figure 5.21.

The Save As Template dialog box enables you to save your Web page as a template. Later, you can select your template from the New Page dialog box when you create a new Web page.

Workshop Wrap-Up

This chapter discussed many of the built-in templates and wizards provided with FrontPage. Much work and thought has gone into these pages. The Webs and pages generated with FrontPage can save you a great deal of time.

In this chapter, you learned how to create, open, and save Webs and pages from the FrontPage Explorer and the FrontPage Editor. You got a general overview of the templates and wizards provided with FrontPage and how to use them to create your own Web sites.

Next Steps

In the next chapter, you'll learn how you can add and manage a To Do list for each of your Web sites. Your Web will certainly change and grow in size over time, and the FrontPage To Do list helps you keep track of the pages that need changing.

To learn how to edit the pages covered in this chapter, check out the following chapters:

❑ To add or edit bookmarks and links, see Chapter 9, "Getting from Here to There."

❑ To create and edit the various types of lists, see Chapter 11, "Organizing Information into Lists."

❑ To work with images and other enhancements, see Chapter 15, "Working with Images and Sound."

❑ To add or edit the basic FrontPage components included on your pages, see Chapter 19, "Using FrontPage Components."

❑ To edit the form fields included in these pages, see Chapter 22, "Adding and Editing Form Fields." Chapter 23, "Configuring Form Handlers," shows you how to edit the properties of the form handling components on your pages.

Q&A

Q: Can I use FrontPage to save pages to a Web that does not have the FrontPage Server Extensions installed?

A: You can use the Publish FrontPage Web command to publish your Web pages to servers that do not have the FrontPage Server Extensions installed. See Chapter 34, "Testing and Publishing Your Web," for instructions on how to accomplish this.

Q: Can I create my own Web templates and wizards?

A: The CD-ROM that comes with the retail version of FrontPage 98 includes a FrontPage 98 Developer's Kit. This kit provides files and utilities that enable you to create your own Web templates and wizards. Full instructions on how to accomplish this are also included in the developer's kit.

SIX

What To Do?

"I've got sticky notes all over my monitor! Aaagh!"

Sound familiar? As the number of pages in your Web grows, you will discover that it is hard to keep track of which pages you need to add or revise—especially if your Web has many pages or if multiple people work on them at once. It also adds to the confusion if you lose track of who is doing what and what needs to be done.

Don't get me wrong. Sticky notes are one of the greatest inventions to come around in a long time, and I use them a lot. I use them less now, however, because I use FrontPage to design my Web site. I use the To Do list to keep track of things for me. I can see through to my monitor screen again.

What To Do Lists Do

Think of your To Do list as the personal information manager of Web development. You use the To Do list to track what needs to be done on a Web site or on a particular page. If you are developing a site in which multiple authors work on the same Web, you can learn quickly what tasks you are responsible for. You can use the To Do list to remind yourself of whom you need to consult about your pages, attach notes to other authors about what they need to do on the page, and so on. Essentially, anything you put on a sticky note can go on your To Do list. You can get those sticky notes off your monitor and into the computer where they belong!

In this chapter, you

- ❏ Manually add items to the To Do list from the FrontPage Explorer and the FrontPage Editor
- ❏ Learn the best way to add items to the To Do list
- ❏ Add tasks to the To Do list when you create a link to a new page
- ❏ Add tasks to the To Do list when you verify internal and external links
- ❏ Sort tasks by category
- ❏ Complete and delete tasks from the To Do list

Tasks in this chapter:

- ❏ Creating Tasks for Any Type of File
- ❏ Assigning a Task to Your Current Page
- ❏ Adding General Tasks
- ❏ Assigning Tasks to New Pages
- ❏ Adding Tasks to Broken Links
- ❏ Creating Tasks for Spelling Errors
- ❏ Showing the To Do List
- ❏ Adding Task Details or Modifying Tasks
- ❏ Completing Tasks
- ❏ Closing the To Do List
- ❏ Printing the To Do List

Suppose, for example, that three people work on a Web site. The administrator develops the overall content. Another author adds the artwork. The third author adds special HTML code or enhanced features to the pages. The To Do list helps you coordinate what these folks have to do.

What Are To Do Tasks?

Tasks are items that need to be completed on a page. Each task has a name, a responsible person, and a description. You can make the task as simple or as detailed as you like. For example, if you work on your own, you can enter a task, such as `Complete survey page`. Because you are responsible for the entire job, you know what you have to do.

When you coordinate with others on a page, you might have an idea that falls outside your normal area of expertise. It is better to assign that task to someone else who can handle it better. You can attach the task to the page—along with a description of your idea—and assign it to another author.

Don't Let the List Manage You

When you add tasks to your To Do list, keep the list as compact as possible. For example, if five items on a page need to be completed and you are responsible for three of them, bundle those three tasks into one description. You can always edit the description after you complete one of the tasks. Otherwise, you can imagine how big a To Do list gets if you enter five tasks for each of 100 pages. In that case, the To Do list is managing you. Remember: The To Do list is there to save you time—not to create more work.

As a general rule, if an item depends on the actions of another individual—even, perhaps, a customer—it is a good idea to add a task for it.

Working with To Do Lists

There are several ways to add tasks to a To Do list. Some wizards, such as the Corporate Presence Wizard, add them automatically. In other cases, you add tasks manually after you examine the pages to see what needs to be done.

You can add a task to a To Do list in several ways:

- ❏ You can add a task manually from the FrontPage Explorer or from the FrontPage Editor.
- ❏ You can add a task automatically when you create a link to a new page.

❏ You can add a task automatically when you verify broken links in your Web.

❏ You can add tasks when you do across-the-web spell-checking.

 ## Creating Tasks for Any Type of File

You can use the FrontPage Explorer to add a task to any page, graphics image, or other type of file in the current Web. Follow these steps:

1. Open the Web in the FrontPage Explorer by using **F**ile I **O**pen FrontPage Web or by choosing the Open FrontPage Web button on the toolbar.

2. Select Folders, All Files, Navigation, or Hyperlinks view from the Views area of the FrontPage Explorer.

3. Right-click on the name of the page, image, or file to which you want to attach a task. For example, in Figure 6.1, a task is being added to an image in the Web. A pop-up menu appears.

Figure 6.1.
Highlight the Web page, image, or other file to which you want to attach a task.

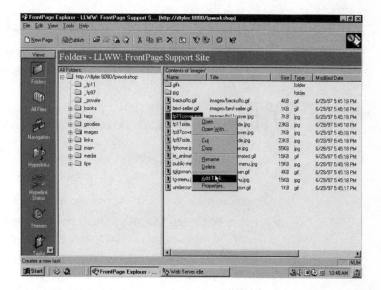

4. From the pop-up menu, choose **A**dd Task. The New Task dialog box shown in Figure 6.2 appears.

5. Assign a name for the task in the **T**ask Name field.

6. Type the name of the author to which the task is assigned in the **A**ssign To field.

7. Enter a description for the task in the **D**escription field. The description can contain as much information as you see fit.

8. Assign a priority to the task. Anything that relates to completing the text content of the page is a **H**igh priority. **M**edium priority might involve fixing broken URLs, revising content, or running a spell check. Adding extra elements that merely enhance the appearance of the page are **L**ow priority.

9. Choose OK. The task is added to the To Do list.

Figure 6.2.
Use the New Task dialog box to add items to your To Do list.

Assigning a Task to Your Current Page

If you're working on a page and don't have time to complete it, you can use the FrontPage Editor to add a task to the currently opened page.

NOTE: When you add tasks from the FrontPage Editor, the task is added to the opened Web page. You cannot add a task for an image or other type of file from the FrontPage Editor.

1. Open the page to which you want to attach the task in the FrontPage Editor.

2. Choose **E**dit I **A**dd Task. If you have not yet saved your page to the Web, FrontPage asks whether you would like to save it. Choose **Y**es and use the Save As dialog box to save the page to a folder in your current Web. After you save your page to the Web, the New Task dialog box appears, as shown in Figure 6.3.

3. Assign a name for the task in the **T**ask Name field.

4. Type the name of the author to which the task is assigned in the **A**ssign To field.

5. Enter a description for the task in the **D**escription field. The description can contain as much information as you see fit.

6. Assign a **H**igh, **M**edium, or **L**ow priority to the task.

7. Choose OK. The task is added to the To Do list.

Figure 6.3.

You can assign a task to the currently opened page in the FrontPage Editor.

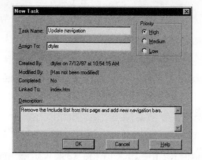

NOTE: When you add a task from the FrontPage Editor, the page to which you add a To Do task must exist in the currently opened Web. Sometimes you might open a page from one Web and not save or close it before you open another Web. When you return to that page in the FrontPage Editor and try to add a task to it, you get an `Unable to Open To Do List` message. To resolve this problem, open the Web from which you opened the page and add the task again.

 ## Adding General Tasks

Sometimes you might have tasks of a general nature that apply to more than one page or to your entire Web. You can add a task from the To Do list itself. Tasks added this way do not attach to a particular page, but they can serve as a reminder of something else in your Web that needs to be completed.

To add tasks of a general nature, as shown in Figure 6.4, display your Web in Tasks view. If you right-click anywhere within Tasks view, a pop-up menu appears, and you can choose to add a task to your Web.

Figure 6.4.

You can enter tasks that are not linked to any page or file in your Web.

To add a general task, follow these steps:

1. From the FrontPage Explorer, choose the Tasks icon from the Views list.
2. Right-click anywhere within the Tasks view in the right portion of your screen. A pop-up menu appears, displaying three commands: New **T**ask, Task Histor**y**, and Web **S**ettings.
3. Choose New **T**ask. The New Task dialog box appears. The Linked To field shows that the task is not linked to any page.
4. Assign a name for the task in the **T**ask Name field.
5. Type the name of the author to which the task is assigned in the **A**ssign To field.
6. Enter a description for the task in the **D**escription field.
7. Assign a **H**igh, **M**edium, or **L**ow priority to the task.
8. Choose OK. The task is added to the To Do list.

 # Assigning Tasks to New Pages

You can create a link to a new page from the Create Hyperlink dialog box shown in Figure 6.5. Instead of opening the new page in the FrontPage Editor, you can add a task to your Web that reminds you to create the content on the page. When you add a task to a new page, FrontPage creates the Web page based on the template you select, but the page will not open in the FrontPage Editor.

To create a new page and add a task to your To Do List, follow these steps:

1. Open the originating page in the FrontPage Editor. Select the text, image, or hyperlink which the user clicks to navigate to the new page.
2. Choose the Create or Edit Hyperlink button on the Standard toolbar. The Create Hyperlink dialog box appears.
3. Click the Create a page and link to the new page button (the last button shown at the right of the **U**RL field). The New dialog box appears.
4. From the Options section, check the Just **a**dd web task checkbox, as shown in Figure 6.5.
5. Click OK. The Save As dialog box appears.
6. Choose a folder in your current Web in which to save the page. Enter a **U**RL for the page in the URL field and a page title in the **T**itle field.
7. Choose OK. The page is added to your Web, and a task is added to the To Do List.

Figure 6.5.
You can add a task automatically to the To Do list when you create a link to a new page.

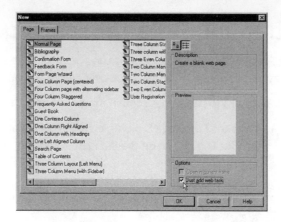

TASK Adding Tasks to Broken Links

In Chapter 34, "Testing and Publishing Your Webs," you will learn how to verify internal and external links before you publish your Web. When you have broken links in your Web that you don't have the time to repair, you can add a task to your To Do List.

To add a task to a broken hyperlink, follow these steps:

1. After you do the Verify Links procedure (discussed in Chapter 34) right-click on the broken link in the Task list you want to add the task to. A pop-up menu appears, displaying four commands: **V**erify, Edit **H**yperlink, Edit **P**age, and **A**dd Task.

2. Choose **A**dd Task. The New Task dialog box appears, as shown in Figure 6.6.

3. Enter the name of the person to which you want to assign the task in the **A**ssign To field.

4. The **T**ask Name field automatically displays a task named `Fix broken hyperlink`. You cannot change this. In addition, the **D**escription field lists the URL that was verified as broken. You can edit the description to provide additional information, if necessary.

5. Choose OK. The new task is added to your To Do List.

Figure 6.6.
You can add a task automatically when you verify the links in your Web.

Creating Tasks for Spelling Errors

In Chapter 34, you will learn how to do across-the-web spell-checking. This is a handy way to give your Web a final once-over before you publish it.

To add tasks to pages that contain misspelled items, follow these steps:

1. From the FrontPage Explorer, choose **T**ools I **Sp**elling (F7) or click the Cross File Spelling button on the Standard toolbar. The Spelling dialog box appears.
2. Before you begin your spell-check, check the Add a task for each page with misspellings checkbox at the bottom of the dialog box, as shown in Figure 6.7.
3. Select how you want to do the spell check (All pages or Selected pages).
4. Click **S**tart to begin the spell-check. After your spell check is complete, the pages that contain misspelled words will be added to your To Do List.

For additional information about across-the-web spell checking, see Chapter 34.

Figure 6.7.
You can add To Do tasks when you do across-the-web spell-checking.

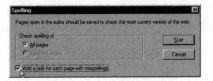

Showing the To Do List

Once you add tasks to the To Do list, you can use it to keep track of what has been done or who is assigned to a particular task. The To Do List appears in the FrontPage Explorer when you choose Tasks from the Views section. Figure 6.8 shows a Web displayed in Tasks view.

Figure 6.8.
View your Web in Tasks view to see all the tasks attached to your Web.

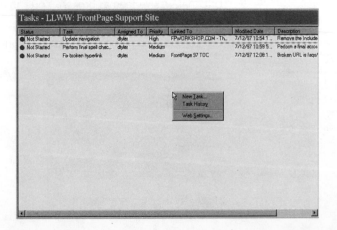

The To Do list arranges tasks in columns. You can sort the tasks by category by clicking the appropriate column heading. The categories are

See Chapter 30, "Using the FrontPage Personal Web Server," and Chapter 31, "Using the Microsoft Personal Web Server," for instructions on how to add additional authors to your Web site.

❑ *Status.* This column displays the status of the task.

❑ *Task.* This is the name of the task. By default, tasks are listed in the order in which they were entered.

❑ *Assigned To.* This column shows the author who is responsible for completing the task. Of course, if you are working alone, there is only one author—you.

❑ *Priority.* This column sorts tasks by priority. High-priority tasks appear at the top of the list, followed by medium-priority and low-priority tasks.

❑ *Linked To.* If multiple tasks are assigned to a page, you can sort the To Do list to display them conjointly. This column shows the title of a page, the URL of a page, or a graphics file.

❑ *Modified Date.* This column displays the date and time that the task was added or last modified.

❑ *Description.* You can also sort tasks by their descriptions. You enter a description when you add tasks manually. Some descriptions are entered by wizards, such as the Corporate Presence Wizard. Task descriptions are also entered when you verify links. You can edit the descriptions at any time.

When you right-click anywhere within Tasks view, a pop-up menu appears. This menu is also displayed in Figure 6.8, and it provides quick access to several frequently used commands:

New **T**ask | When you click this button, the New Task dialog box appears and you can add a task to the page or file that you currently have selected.

Task Histor**y** | Click this button to show or hide the display of completed tasks in your Web.

Web **S**ettings | Click this button to open the FrontPage Web Settings dialog box. If you want to add tasks to pages that are contained in hidden directories (folders that are preceded by an underscore), you use the Advanced tab to display documents in hidden directories. For more information, see Chapter 32, "Administering Your Webs."

 # Adding Task Details or Modifying Tasks

Task details are the elements that make up a task: its name, the person assigned to it, and its description. Sometimes, you need to modify a task, especially if it was added automatically by a wizard or through the Create Link or Verify Links dialog boxes. You

modify tasks by using the Task Details dialog box. This dialog box is similar to the New Task dialog box shown in Figures 6.2 through 6.4, except that you are allowed only to modify who the task is assigned to and the description of the task.

To modify a task:

1. From the FrontPage Explorer, display your Web in Tasks view.
2. From Tasks view, double-click the task you want to modify. The Task Details dialog box appears.
3. Assign the task to a new author or edit the description of the task, as necessary.
4. Click OK to revise the task. Click Cancel to close the dialog box without revising the task.

Completing Tasks

To complete a task, it is best to open the page from the To Do list itself. It is much easier to keep track of the tasks this way. This is a good habit to get into if many authors work on the same Web. The To Do list tracks who is assigned to a page or a task.

To complete a task from the To Do list:

1. From the FrontPage Explorer, display your Web in Tasks view.
2. From Tasks view, open the Task Details dialog box, using one of the following methods:
   - ❏ Highlight the task you want to complete and choose **E**dit I Do Ta**s**k.
   - ❏ Right-click on the task you want to complete and choose Do Ta**s**k from the pop-up menu.
   - ❏ Double-click the task you want to modify. The Task Details dialog box appears. Click the Do **T**ask button.
3. After the page or file opens in the FrontPage Editor or the editor that is associated with the file type you have configured, revise the page as indicated by the task.
4. Choose **F**ile I **S**ave (Ctrl+S) or click the Save button on the Standard toolbar (in the FrontPage Editor) to save the page or file to the Web. You are asked whether you want to mark the task as complete. Choose **Y**es to complete the task or **N**o to keep the task in the To Do list.

Deleting or Marking Tasks Complete

What if you forgot to open the page from the To Do list and completed what you were supposed to do? What if you mistakenly added a task to the wrong page? There are commands that remedy those situations as well. To delete a task from your To Do list or to mark a task complete, follow these steps:

1. From the FrontPage Explorer, display your Web in Tasks view.
2. Right-click the task that you want to mark as complete or to delete. A pop-up menu appears.

   ❏ To remove a task from the task list but keep it in your task history, choose **M**ark Complete. The Status column in the Task List displays the task as completed.

   ❏ To remove a task from the task list and the task history, choose **D**elete. The Confirm Delete dialog box appears and asks whether you are sure that you want to delete the task. Choose **Y**es to delete the task, **N**o to cancel.

Printing the To Do List

The Print command is disabled when you display your Web in Tasks view. To print your list, you need to use a roundabout method. The items in your To Do list exist in a Web file in the `_vti_pvt` directory on your server. Suppose that you installed your FrontPage Web content to a directory called `D:\FrontPage Webs\Content`. The Web is named `PersonalWeb`. The To Do list HTM file, then, appears in the `D:\FrontPage Webs\Content\PersonalWeb\_vti_pvt\_x_todo.htm` directory.

If you want to print the To Do list from the FrontPage Editor, you can open the file from the currently opened Web by following these steps:

1. From the FrontPage Editor, choose **F**ile I **O**pen (Ctrl+O) or use the Open button on the Standard toolbar. The Open File dialog box appears.
2. Choose the Use your web browser to select a page button, which appears at the right of the URL field. Your browser window opens.
3. In the Address field, enter the path to the To Do list page. The file is found in the following path if you installed FrontPage with the default settings. You will need to replace the webname in the path with the name of the Web in which you created the To Do list. If you are using Internet Explorer 4.0 with Shell Integration, you can browse to the correct folder:

   `c:\FrontPage Webs\Content\webname\_vti_pvt\_x_todo.htm`

4. The page appears in your browser. Choose **F**ile I **P**rint (Ctrl+P) to print the To Do list.

Workshop Wrap-Up

To Do lists help make Web development much easier. Your desk will be clear of notepaper, and you will be able to see your monitor. Keep in mind that you are in charge of your To Do list—not the other way around. Keep items as basic as you can while still getting your intent across. You are sure to discover that To Do lists are an excellent management tool.

In this chapter, you learned how and when to add tasks to a To Do list in several ways. Whether you add tasks manually or automatically, you can keep track of your Web projects much better with a To Do list.

Next Steps

In Chapter 7, "Real-Life Examples I: Using What You've Got," you will combine some of the many templates available with FrontPage to create a corporate Web site. These templates help you get a Web site up quickly. You can also study the pages that are created by the templates to learn more about how FrontPage components are used. In the section that follows, you will progress from basic concepts, such as entering text on your pages, to organizing information in lists and creating tables:

❏ In Chapter 9, "Getting from Here to There," you learn how to create and edit links and bookmarks.

❏ Chapter 10, "Composing and Editing Pages," outlines the basics of entering paragraphs, text styles, headings, and other types of text effects in your pages.

❏ In Chapter 11, "Organizing Information into Lists," you discover the different kinds of lists that you can use for organizing information. You also learn how to add enhanced features to lists.

❏ In Chapter 12, "Your Tables Are Ready," you use tables to enhance the layout of your pages.

Q&A

Q: If I mark a task as completed or delete it by mistake, is there any way to get it back in the To Do list?

A: No. You must enter the task again if you want it to reappear as an unfinished task.

Q: When an author logs in to a Web, is there an easy way to tell how many tasks he has to complete in that Web?

A: Yes. There can be many tasks in the To Do list. The easiest way to find the tasks assigned to a particular author is to sort the list by the Assigned To field. This groups all the tasks assigned to an author.

Q: In the examples in this chapter, three authors are assigned to the Web. What if one author quits? Can the other authors complete his tasks?

A: Yes. An author can modify, complete, or delete a task assigned to another author. The procedures are the same as discussed in this chapter.

Q: I want to assign a task to another author, but I do not know who the other authors are. How can I get this information?

A: The Web administrator assigns the authors for the Web. Unfortunately, the only way to view the authors assigned to the Web is by using the Tools I Permissions command, which only an administrator can use. To remedy this, the administrator can add a general task to the To Do list by using the Add Task button in the To Do List dialog box. He might create a task such as this:

Task Name:	Authors assigned to this Web.
Assign To:	The administrator's name.
Priority:	**H**igh (keeps it at the top of the list).
Linked T**o**:	(It won't be linked to any page.)
Description:	The authors assigned to this Web are Becky, Sam, and Tom.

SEVEN

Real-Life Examples I: Using What You've Got

In this chapter, you

- ❏ Create a small corporate presence Web using the Corporate Presence Web Wizard
- ❏ Get a peek at all of the exciting new features that help you create dynamic Web sites, complete with graphics and navigation system
- ❏ Examine some of the enhanced features in FrontPage 98 and learn where you can read in this book for additional help on a particular page

Tasks in this chapter:

- ❏ Building the Presence
- ❏ Displaying Hidden Directories
- ❏ Examining Your Pages
- ❏ Adding Content to the Home Page
- ❏ Completing the Product Pages

In the previous chapters, you learned about the FrontPage Explorer and FrontPage Editor interfaces and how to create Webs and pages using the FrontPage templates and wizards. Now you'll get a chance to see one of the Web templates in action. By using the built-in templates and wizards of FrontPage, you not only develop Web pages in the blink of an eye, but you also get a chance to learn about the FrontPage 98 features that pack the most punch—the FrontPage components, built-in navigation generation, themes and cascading style sheet support, and active content.

The small Web you create in this chapter uses the Corporate Presence Web Wizard to generate a small number of pages. However, when you peek under the hood of what goes behind these pages, you see a lot of features that save you a great deal of time. Here is where the fun begins!

TASK

Building the Presence

In Chapter 5, "Lightning-Speed Web Design," you were introduced to the Web templates and wizards that are provided with FrontPage 98. Now, you'll get some hands-on experience in using the Corporate Presence Web Wizard. This wizard provides a way for you to get several pages out on the Web quickly. The pages are focused on getting the word out about your company and the products and services you have to offer. You can find examples of the small Web you create in this chapter on the CD-ROM that is furnished with this book. The Web files are located in the `Book\Chap07\Examples` directory on the CD-ROM.

To begin your corporate presence Web, follow these steps:

1. Choose **F**ile | **N**ew | FrontPage **W**eb (Ctrl+N) or choose the New FrontPage Web button on the FrontPage Explorer toolbar. The New FrontPage Web dialog box appears.

2. In Section 1, choose the From **W**izard or Template radio button and high-light Corporate Presence Web Wizard from the list of available Web templates and wizards.

3. In Section 2, enter `ACME Corporation Web Site` as the title for your FrontPage Web.

4. Notice that, beneath the field where you entered the title, the URL defaults to `http://servername/acmecorporatio`, where *servername* is the name of the server that resides on your local computer. To change the name of the Web folder, click the **C**hange button. The Change Location dialog box appears.

5. In the Please specify the location of the new FrontPage web field, edit the portion of the URL that reads `acmecorporatio` to read `acmecorp`. Choose OK to return to the New FrontPage Web dialog box.

6. Choose OK. The FrontPage Explorer creates temporary files, and the Corporate Presence Web Wizard dialog box shown in Figure 7.1 appears.

7. Click **N**ext to choose the pages that you want to include in the Web.

Figure 7.1.

The Introductory Screen of the Corporate Presence Web Wizard.

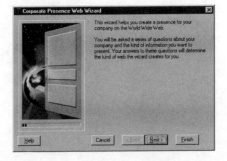

Selecting Your Pages

The second screen in the wizard, shown in Figure 7.2, asks what types of pages you want to include in your Web site. The home page is required, and you do not have the option of unchecking the page. In this screen, complete the following steps:

Figure 7.2.

Select the pages you want to include in your Web from this screen.

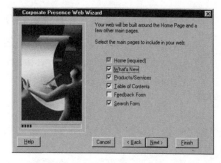

1. Select the following additional pages for your Web site:

   What's New
   Products/Services
   Table of Contents
   Search Form

2. Click **N**ext to continue.

Choosing Your Home Page Content

The third screen of the Corporate Presence Web Wizard prompts you to choose the sections you want to appear on your home page. To complete the screen shown in Figure 7.3, follow these steps:

Figure 7.3.

Select the sections you want to appear on your home page from this screen.

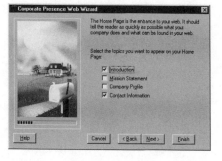

1. Select the following options:

   Introduction
   Contact Information

2. Click Next to continue.

Telling What's New on the Site

In the fourth screen, select the type of information you want to appear on your What's New page. Keep this simple and select only one option. To complete the screen shown in Figure 7.4, do the following:

1. Select Web Changes.

2. Click Next to continue.

Figure 7.4.
Select the content for your What's New page in this screen.

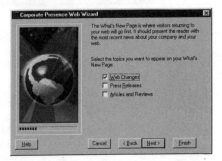

Selecting Your Products and Services

In the fifth screen, you select how many products and services pages you want to add to your Web site. ACME Corporation is a manufacturer and primarily offers products. This company does not need services description pages. To complete the screen shown in Figure 7.5, follow these steps:

1. In the Products field, enter 1.

2. In the Services field, enter 0.

3. Click Next to continue.

Figure 7.5.

From this screen, select how many products and services pages you want to create.

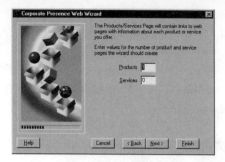

Selecting Your Products Page Options

In the sixth screen, shown in Figure 7.6, you choose the options for your products pages. The services pages options are disabled because you elected not to include them in the previous screen. You won't select the Information Request Form option in this example. To complete this screen, follow these steps:

1. Select the following options:

   Product **I**mage
   Pricing Information

2. Click **N**ext to continue.

Figure 7.6.

Select the options for your products pages in this screen.

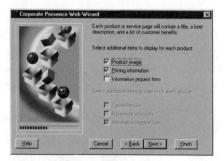

Choosing Your Table of Contents Page Options

In the seventh screen, you select the options for your table of contents page. To complete the screen shown in Figure 7.7, follow these steps:

1. Leave the **K**eep page list up-to-date automatically option unchecked. Because the corporate presence Web could end up containing a lot of pages, this saves a lot of time. By leaving the option unchecked, the table of contents page does not regenerate the page list each time you add or move pages.

You can regenerate the table of contents list manually at any time by opening the table of contents and resaving it to your Web.

2. The **S**how pages not linked into web option will not be included either. By leaving this unchecked, only the pages that are hierarchically linked to your home page appear in the table of contents. Any pages that are unreachable by navigation through the home page do not appear.

3. Select the **U**se bullets for top-level pages option.

4. Click **N**ext to continue.

Figure 7.7.
Select your table of contents page options in this screen.

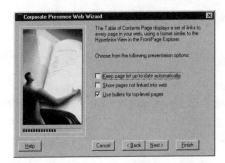

Selecting Options for Your Header and Footer

In the eighth screen of the Corporate Presence Web Wizard, shown in Figure 7.8, you are asked what you want to appear at the top of each page (the page header) and at the bottom of each page (the page footer). You can include links to your main Web pages in the top section, bottom section, or both. Some prefer to place links at the top of the page so that users can navigate to other pages as soon as the page opens. Others like to place links at the bottom of the page, which makes navigation more convenient when the user reads the entire page and reaches the bottom. Still others like to place the navigation bars in both places. Choose both so you have all bases covered.

Figure 7.8.
Select what you want to appear at the top and bottom of each page from this screen.

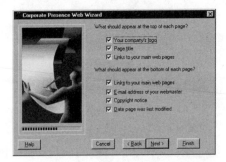

To complete this screen, follow these steps:

1. You are asked what should appear at the top of each page. Select all three options (Your company's **l**ogo, Page **t**itle, and **L**inks to your main web pages).

2. You are asked what should appear at the bottom of each page. Select all four options (Link**s** to your main web pages, **E**-mail address of your webmaster, **C**opyright Notice, and **D**ate page was last modified).

3. Click **N**ext to continue.

Adding an Under Construction Icon

In the ninth screen, shown in Figure 7.9, you are asked whether you want to include an under construction icon on your pages. Most people realize sites are always under construction, and many feel these icons are a bit redundant. I elected not to include them by choosing N**o**. If you would rather include the under construction icons, choose **Y**es. Remember to remove them when your pages are done! Then, click **N**ext to continue.

Figure 7.9.

If you want to include an under construction icon on unfinished pages, choose Yes from this screen.

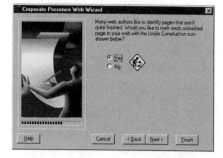

Entering Your Company Location

In the tenth screen, shown in Figure 7.10, you enter your company name and location. I used a rather overused fictitious company name in my examples; if you'd rather use your own company name, go ahead. The one-word version of the name is an abbreviation that appears in all the page titles. You can edit them later. To complete this screen, you can respond with the values I entered or enter your own responses as follows:

1. What is the full n**a**me of your company?

   `ACME Corporation` (or your company name)

2. What is the **o**ne-word version of this name?

   `ACMECORP` (or a one-word version of your company name)

3. What is your company's **s**treet address?

123 Busy Street, Anycity, NY 00001 (or your company's street address)

4. Click **N**ext to continue.

Figure 7.10.
Enter your company name and location in this screen.

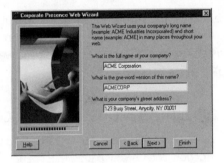

Enter Your Company Contact Information

In the eleventh screen, shown in Figure 7.11, you enter company contact information. To complete this screen, respond to the questions as follows:

1. What is your company's **t**elephone number?

313-555-1212 (or your company telephone number)

2. What is your company's FA**X** number?

313-555-1213 (or your company fax number)

3. What is the e-mail address of your **w**ebmaster?

webmaster@acmecorp.com (or your e-mail address because you're the webmaster)

4. What is the e-mail address for general **i**nfo?

marketing@acmecorp.com (or your company's marketing or sales department e-mail address)

5. Click **N**ext to continue.

Figure 7.11.
Enter your company contact information in this screen.

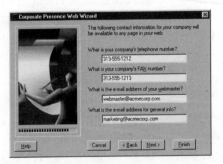

Choosing Your Web Theme

On the twelfth screen, shown in Figure 7.12, you choose a graphical theme for your Web. You can continue with the Corporate Presence Web Wizard without selecting a theme by choosing the Next button. The Expedition web theme will be used by default.

Figure 7.12.

The twelfth screen gives you the option to select a graphical theme for your corporate presence Web.

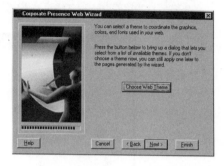

See Chapter 14, "Using FrontPage Style Sheets and Themes," for more information about how to choose and create Web themes.

To select a theme for your sample site, follow these steps:

1. Click the Choose Web Theme button. The Choose Theme dialog box shown in Figure 7.13 appears.

2. From the left portion of the screen, choose the **U**se Selected Theme radio button. Scroll down the list of themes and select the Technology theme.

3. Select the following options:

   Vivid **C**olors
   Active **G**raphics
   Background Image

4. Choose OK to return to the Corporate Presence Web Wizard.

5. Click **N**ext to continue to the next screen.

Figure 7.13.

Choose a graphical theme for your Web site from this screen.

Creating the Web

The final screen in the wizard asks whether you want to view Tasks view after your Web is created. You do not want to view it at this time because you have more pages to add, so uncheck the **S**how Tasks view after web is uploaded option.

To create the Web site, click the **F**inish button. Your Web site appears in the Explorer window. Figure 7.14 shows the Web in the Navigation view of the FrontPage Explorer.

Figure 7.14.
Your Web appears in the FrontPage Explorer. Here, it is shown in Navigation view.

See Chapter 6, "What To Do?" for an in-depth look into the FrontPage Tasks view commands.

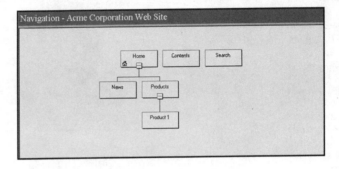

Reviewing the Web

Based on the options that you selected in the Corporate Presence Web Wizard, your Web site has six pages in the root folder. There are others that you aren't able to see yet, and I'll show you how to access them in the following task. The pages that appear in the Web's home folder are shown in Table 7.1. The images that appear in the Web's images folder are shown in Table 7.2.

Table 7.1. Pages in the ACMECorp Web's home folder.

Page Name	Page Title
index.htm	Home
news.htm	ACMECORP News Page
prod01.htm	ACMECORP Product 1
products.htm	ACMECORP Products Page
search.htm	ACMECORP Search Page
toc.htm	ACMECORP Table of Contents Page

Table 7.2. Images in the ACMECorp Web's `images` folder.

Page Name	Page Title
`logo.gif`	A placeholder image for the company logo graphic. You replace this image with your own company logo.
`prodimg.gif`	A placeholder image that appears on the ACMECORP Product 1 page. You replace this image with a photo of the product discussed on the Web page.
`smallnew.gif`	A small graphic that you can place near the new items on your What's New page.

 # Displaying Hidden Directories

You're probably wondering where all those images in the Web theme are coming from. One of the reasons you can't see them is that they exist in hidden directories. This is discussed in more detail in Chapter 14. For now, all you need to know is how to display those directories so that you can learn where to find additional pages and images in your Web. To display the documents in hidden directories, follow these steps:

1. From the FrontPage Explorer, choose **T**ools | **W**eb Settings. The FrontPage Web Settings dialog box appears.

2. Click the Advanced tab, shown in Figure 7.15.

3. In the Options section, check the Show documents in **h**idden directories checkbox.

4. Click OK. FrontPage asks whether you want to refresh the Web. Answer Yes.

 **Figure 7.15.**
Use the FrontPage Web Settings dialog box to display hidden folders in your Web.

Now, you notice some additional folders in your Web. These additional folders (`borders`, `fpclass`, `overlay`, and `themes` and its subfolders) hold all files and images that are associated with your Web themes and navigation borders. Table 7.3 contains a brief explanation of the contents of each of these hidden folders and where you can find more information about them.

Table 7.3. General contents of the hidden folders.

Folder Name	Contents Description
_borders	Stores the Web pages that are used for your Web's *shared borders*. You will learn more about shared borders in Chapter 8, "Designing Your Web Navigation."
_fpclass	Stores the FrontPage Java applets that are associated with the active content on your Web. In the case of the corporate presence Web you created in this chapter, there are two files that are associated with hover buttons. To learn more about hover buttons, see Chapter 16, "Working with Animation and Active Content." To learn more about using Java applets, see Chapter 25, "Using Java Applets and Netscape Plug-Ins."
_overlay	Stores the navigation buttons and banner images used in your Web theme.
_themes	Used to store additional files and images associated with your Web themes. Files include images, cascading style sheets, and information files used with FrontPage. For more information about these files, see Chapter 27, "Using Styles."

 ## Examining Your Pages

Now, take a look at each page you created in your Web. Decide what you need to do to pull them all together. The following sections contain a list of general pointers for you and the chapters where you can learn how to complete the pages.

The Border Pages

The Top Border page is located in the `_borders` folder in your Web and uses a filename of `top.htm`. This page includes a generic graphic that reads Company Logo. Replace this with your own company logo, as shown in Figure 7.16.

To learn how to insert images into your pages, see Chapter 15, "Working with Images and Sound."

The left border contains a navigation bar. To learn how to make changes to this page, see Chapter 8.

The bottom border contains the page footer information. Besides using a navigation bar, this page also includes a Substitution component, which you can learn more about in Chapter 19, "Using FrontPage Components."

Figure 7.16.

Replace the logo image in the Top Border page with your own company logo.

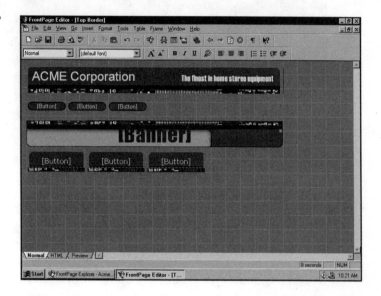

TASK Adding Content to the Home Page

Take a look at your home page. In Figure 7.17, you see the portion of the page that appears directly beneath the banner images and navigation buttons. This page is located in your Web's main folder and is named index.htm, default.htm, or whatever you choose to name your default home page.

To complete your home page, do the following:

1. Complete an introductory paragraph or section at the top of the page, where indicated by the comment (the purple text on the page).

Learn more about inserting and editing comments in Chapter 10, "Composing and Editing Pages."

2. Complete an introduction to the Contact Information section, where indicated by the comment.

3. Most of the contact information has been entered for you by the Corporate Presence Web Wizard. There is also a blank space in which you can add sales contact information.

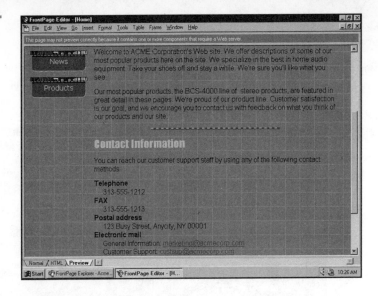

Figure 7.17.
Complete the home page with an introductory paragraph about your company.

The News Page

The ACMECORP News Page is basically the What's New page in your Web. You can give the page a new title by choosing **F**ile l Page Propert**i**es from the FrontPage Editor. As you add new items to the site, place text, descriptions, and links to the new pages on this page, as shown in Figure 7.18. Dress it up by adding a New icon here and there (a New icon is included in your Web's images folder) and add some graphics to draw interest. Don't forget to remove the under construction icon if it's there.

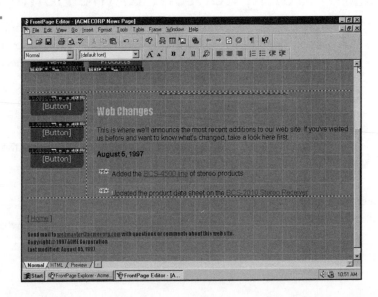

Figure 7.18.
As you add new items to the site, provide links to them on the What's New page.

TASK

Completing the Products Pages

When you create one products or one services page, you have the opportunity to add any other global elements to the page before you create additional pages from it. You can then save the page as a template.

See Chapter 5 to learn how to make templates from your Web pages. You'll also learn how to make templates in Chapter 13, "Real-Life Examples II: Keeping It Plain and Simple."

After you create your custom products pages from your template, you need to title each page appropriately to describe the product you are highlighting on the page. Change the title that appears on the page and use the **F**ile I Page Properties command to change the title that appears at the top of your browser window and in the site's table of contents. Use Navigation view to change the title that appears on the navigation buttons, if desired.

To complete additional items on the page, follow these steps:

1. Obtain a photo of the product and insert it on your page in place of the placeholder graphic. Add a caption beside or beneath the photo.

2. Enter a description of the product where noted on the page. This portion of the page should look similar to Figure 7.19.

Figure 7.19.

Complete the product information section of the page.

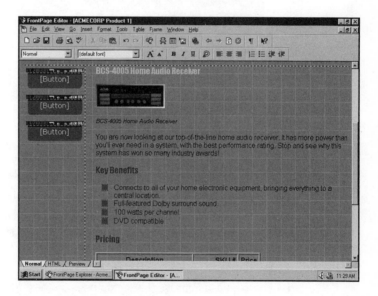

3. Add the key benefits of the product in the Key Benefits area. If you need to create more bullets for your Key Benefits list, copy one of the existing bullets into your clipboard using Ctrl+C and paste it into another location on the page using Ctrl+V—a quick and easy way to insert multiple images on a page.

4. Complete the pricing information in the table that appears in the Pricing section of the page, which should look similar to Figure 7.20.

5. Remove the under construction icon, if necessary.

Figure 7.20.

Complete the key benefits and pricing information sections for each product.

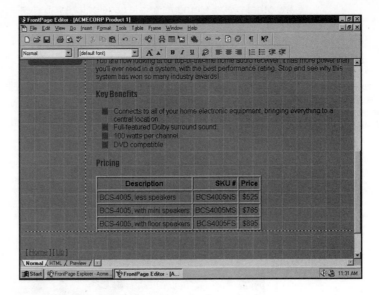

The Products Page

The ACMECORP Products Page, shown in Figure 7.21, links to all the products pages on your company's site. You start the page with a brief overview of the products you provide. Then, you create a list of products on the page, providing links to each of your products pages (described in the previous section).

The Search Page

The ACMECORP Search Page, shown partially in Figure 7.22, uses a Search component that enables a user to search through your site for a word or phrase. You'll learn how to configure this Search component in Chapter 16.

TIP: You can improve the search page by the addition of a query language section, as shown in Figure 7.22. You can create a new page by using the Search Page template (selected from the New Page dialog box) and copying the query language section from it into your corporate presence Web search page.

Figure 7.21.

The products page provides links to all the product sheets on your site.

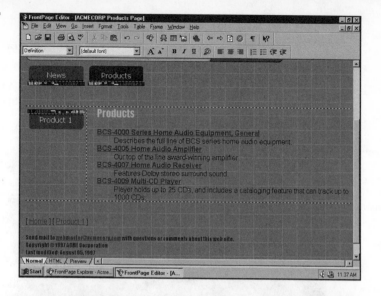

Figure 7.22.

You can improve the search page by adding a query language section so users know how to enter search terms.

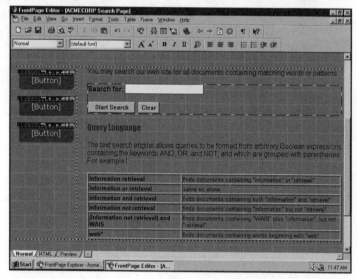

The Search WebBot on this page is configured to search through your entire Web. When the Search WebBot finds documents that match the user's search terms, it returns a list of pages that includes the date of the page and its file size (in kilobytes).

The Table of Contents Page

For the ACMECORP Table of Contents Page, you need to add an introductory paragraph that highlights the contents of your Web site, as shown in Figure 7.23. The Table of Contents WebBot included on the page does the rest for you automatically. By default, the table of contents lists all pages in your Web that begin with your home page (index.htm).

Figure 7.23.
Complete the table of contents with an introductory paragraph.

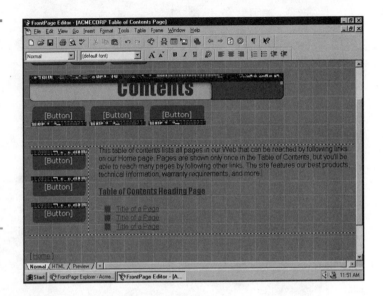

You learn how to configure and use a Table of Contents WebBot in Chapter 19.

Workshop Wrap-Up

Creating large Web sites is no longer tedious. Combining Webs and pages with FrontPage makes the job a snap. You can add pages to your Webs to your heart's content. As your page library grows, the job gets even easier.

In this chapter, you learned how to create a small Web from the Corporate Presence Web Wizard. You examined many of the exciting new features included within the pages and learned where you can receive additional help in this book. You can easily add additional pages to this Web by selecting additional templates or wizards from the FrontPage Editor.

Next Steps

In the next chapter, you learn how to create a navigation system for your Web. Using Navigation view in the FrontPage Explorer, you can create new pages or drag and drop pages from within your current Web to link all your pages together automatically and create navigation bars that automatically appear on all your pages.

To complete the pages in your corporate presence Web, see the following chapters for help:

❏ See Chapter 9, "Getting from Here to There," to learn how to add links to your pages.

❏ See Chapter 10, "Composing and Editing Pages," to learn how to edit or add more content to your pages.

❏ See Chapter 12, "Your Tables Are Ready," to learn how to use tables to enhance your page layout.

❏ See Chapter 15, "Working with Images and Sound," to learn how to add images, background sounds, and animation to your pages.

❏ See Chapter 19, "Using FrontPage Components," to learn more about the basic WebBots used in the corporate presence Web pages.

Q&A

Q: Those graphics in the navigation system are really big. Is there any way to make them smaller?

A: You need to reduce the size of the images by using an image editing program. Keep in mind, though, that the images have to be large enough to contain the text that appears on the buttons. Chapter 14 shows you how you can use your own images in themes.

Q: What are those files in the `_fpclass` folder that end with a `.class` extension?

A: Those files are Java applets—nifty little routines that add extended features to your Web pages. In this case, they are the routines that make hover buttons change their appearance when you move the mouse over them. Hover buttons are discussed in more detail in Chapter 16. Java applets are discussed in Chapter 25. Appendix B, "FrontPage Reference," includes a list of Java-related books written by Laura Lemay.

Q: OK, how about those files that end with `.css`, `.utf8`, and `.inf` in the `_themes` folders?

A: Themes work in conjunction with cascading style sheets, which are always saved with a `.css` extension. This is an up-and-coming Web technology that enables you to customize the look and feel of your Web pages with customized text colors, font faces, and more. The `.inf` and `.utf8` extension files are information files used by FrontPage. You can learn more about these files in Chapter 27.

Q: What happens if my company changes its name in the future? Do I have to go back through all those pages and edit the information?

A: No, you don't, and there are a couple of reasons why. First, all your company information is stored in the corporate presence Web as configuration variables. The configuration variables are placed on your pages through the use of the FrontPage Substitution component. Configuration variables and Substitution components are discussed in Chapter 19. In addition, the Web you created in this chapter employs a feature called *shared borders*. Basically, shared borders enable you to create a bit of content on one page and use it repeatedly and in the same location from page to page. For example, the footers on the page are all the same, and they all use the _borders/bottom.htm page in your Web. For more information about shared borders, see Chapter 8.

PART

II

Starting with the Basics

EIGHT

Designing Your Web Navigation

In the previous section, you learned your way around the new FrontPage interface. You also learned how the FrontPage 98 Tasks view helps you keep track of items that you need to add to your site. Tasks view enables you to say goodbye to sticky notes—but Navigation view helps you say goodbye to the proverbial notebook, paper placemat, or dinner napkin.

How many times have you had an idea for a Web site? Several, I bet. Now think back to how many times the idea has changed along the way. Eventually, you have a stack of papers piled up, with pages crossed out, edges torn, and eraser marks all over the place. Your notes are written in five different colors of ink or pencil, and soon they are illegible.

With FrontPage 98, you don't have to plan your Web pages on placemats any more. Using Navigation view in the FrontPage Explorer, you can plan your site while you create a complete navigation system for your Web. Plan, create, and link your Web pages in a few simple steps. As you make changes to your Web, the navigation bars change along with it—automatically! The hardest part of the whole job is figuring out what you're going to put on your site.

Navigation Terminology

Before you get into designing the navigation system for your Web site, review some of the terminology used in the FrontPage 98 Explorer. You will find the following terms used frequently in Navigation view and navigation bar procedures:

❏ You can easily design a navigation system for your Web site using *Navigation view* in the FrontPage Explorer. By doing so, FrontPage 98 automatically generates *navigation bars* that provide hyperlinks to other pages in your Web. When you change or move pages, the navigation bars are updated for you automatically.

❏ The *active page* is the page that you are currently editing in the FrontPage Editor.

❏ A *parent page* is a page that provides navigation links to one or more *child pages* that discuss a similar topic or area of interest.

❏ Each *child page* is accessed from the navigation bar on its parent page. These pages usually provide more detailed information than that included on the parent page.

❏ All the child pages that share a common parent page are *peer pages*. They usually share a common focus.

❏ When you design a navigation system in FrontPage Explorer, you can designate areas of your pages in which to include your navigation bars. These areas are known as *shared borders* and are automatically generated on all pages or selected pages in your Web.

NOTE: Navigation bars and shared borders are an alternative to framesets, which are discussed in Chapter 18, "Frames: Pages with Split Personalities." They provide a consistent navigation system throughout your Web and enable visitors to browse through related pages easily. If your Web site uses frames, you should not use shared borders and navigation bars, because they may make your Web site confusing to navigate.

Using Navigation View

Although you can design your navigation system at any time, you may find it easiest to plan your Web site in Navigation view. In this chapter, you'll begin a navigation system for a personal site. You envision a main section that holds general pages and other sections that focus on topics that you are interested in. Assume, for example, that you want to create a Web site that contains the following areas:

❏ The Main area, for general pages such as a guest book, a table of contents, and a search page

❏ The Links area, for pages that link to your favorite sites on the World Wide Web

❏ The Interests area, for pages that describe one or more topics in which you are interested

❏ The Discussion area, for pages that provide a discussion group that focuses on a topic of your choice

❏ The Cool Stuff area, for pages that show off all the flashy Web page talents you have

You learned how to create new Webs in Chapter 5, "Lightning-Speed Web Design." You'll also step through the entire process of creating a new Web and designing a complete navigation system in Chapter 13, "Real-Life Examples II: Keeping It Plain and Simple."

The first part of the process, of course, is to create a Web site that stores your pages. You can begin the process with either the One Page Web or the Empty Web template if you are building your Web site from the ground up. The only difference between the two Web templates is that the One Page Web template creates a blank home page for you, whereas the Empty Web template does not.

Viewing Your Web in Navigation View

After you create your FrontPage Web, you can use Navigation view to plan and create new pages for it. The nice thing about planning your site in Navigation view is that FrontPage automatically generates navigation bars for you. This new feature of FrontPage 98 takes a *lot* of repetitive tasks out of your Web site design—while being incredibly easy to use! You have the option of creating text-only navigation bars or navigation bars that use a combination of graphics and text.

After you create or open a Web, use one of the following procedures to view your Web in Navigation view:

❏ From the FrontPage Explorer, choose **V**iew | **N**avigation.

❏ Click the Navigation icon in the FrontPage Explorer Views pane, as shown in Figure 8.1.

Navigation view is divided into two panes. The upper portion of the screen contains the *navigation pane*. It displays the structure of your Web in a graphical manner. At this point, only the home page appears in the navigation pane, because you have not yet begun to develop your navigation system.

At the bottom of Navigation view is the *files pane*. This pane lists the files and folders in your current Web, similar to the files and folders lists in Windows Explorer or to the FrontPage Explorer's Folders view.

Figure 8.1.

The Navigation icon in the FrontPage Explorer Views pane enables you to view your Web in Navigation view.

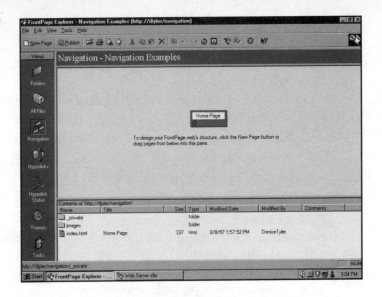

Creating a New Page in Navigation View

In the section "Using Navigation View," I discussed some sections that might exist in a typical personal Web site. Now you'll see how easy it is to plan and create the structure of the Web site. You begin by creating new pages for your Web while in Navigation view.

To create new pages for the Main, Links, Interests, Discussion, and Cool Stuff sections in the Web, follow these steps:

1. Click on the Home Page icon in the navigation pane to select it.

2. Click the **N**ew Page button in the FrontPage Explorer toolbar to create a new page. FrontPage asks whether you want to create navigation bars that link your pages together and whether they will be placed in the borders of each page. Choose **Y**es to continue. A page titled New Page 1 appears in the navigation pane.

3. Click the New Page button four more times. Four new pages appear beneath the Home Page icon in the navigation pane. They are labeled New Page 2 through New Page 5.

4. To assign the labels that appear in the navigation bars for each page, right-click the New Page 1 icon and choose **R**ename from the pop-up menu. You can also click the New Page 1 label once to select it and then again to edit

the name. The name becomes surrounded by a bounding box and becomes highlighted so you can rename the page. Enter `Main` and press Enter to rename the page.

5. Repeat step 3 to rename the remaining pages in your Web, as shown in the following list. When you're finished, your navigation pane should look like the following, as shown in Figure 8.2:

New Page 2	Links
New Page 3	Interests
New Page 4	Discussion
New Page 5	Cool Stuff

You now have five new pages in the navigation pane, but they haven't been saved in your Web yet. If you click the Folders icon in the Views pane, you should see your pages appear in the main folder of your Web. The next time you return to Navigation view, your pages appear in the files pane, as shown in Figure 8.2.

Figure 8.2.

After you select Folders view and return again to Navigation view, the new pages are displayed in the files pane.

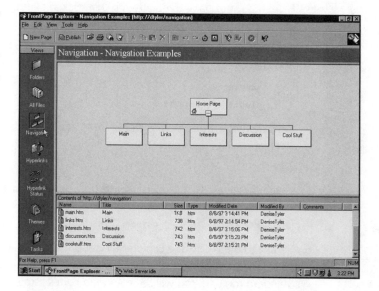

NOTE: When you create new pages in Navigation view, the FrontPage Explorer does not enable you to select a template. The normal page template is used. In addition, The text that you entered for the page name also appears as the filename. For example, the Table of Contents page uses a filename of `tableofcontents.htm`, the Search Page uses a filename of `searchpage.htm`, and so on.

Adding Pages from Your Current Web

You've probably noticed that when you create new pages in the FrontPage Explorer's Navigation view, you are not given the opportunity to select a template on which to base your new page. You can create new pages in the FrontPage Editor and then drag them into the navigation pane from the files pane. In the following task, you create four new pages for the main section and add them to your navigation bars.

To add four more pages to your navigation bar, follow these steps:

1. From the FrontPage Explorer, choose **T**ools I Show FrontPage **E**ditor or select the Show FrontPage Editor button on the Standard toolbar. The FrontPage Editor opens with a blank page and displays placeholders for your navigation bars.

2. From the FrontPage Editor, choose File I **N**ew (Ctrl+N). The New Page dialog box appears.

3. From the list of page templates, double-click Table of Contents. A new Table of Contents page appears in the FrontPage Editor.

4. Choose File I **S**ave (Ctrl+S). Enter the following in the URL and Title fields and choose OK to save your page to the home folder in your Web:

   URL: `contents.htm`
   Title: `Table of Contents`

5. Repeat steps 2 through 4 to create three additional pages, using these templates, URLs, and page titles:

Template	URL	Title
Search Page	`search.htm`	`Search Page`
Two-column Body	`whatsnew.htm`	`What's New`
Guest Book	`gstbook.htm`	`Guest Book`

6. Return to the FrontPage Explorer by using the FrontPage Explorer icon in your taskbar or by choosing the Show FrontPage Explorer button on the Standard toolbar. You will see your new pages listed in the files pane, as shown in Figure 8.3.

7. Click the `contents.htm` page in the files pane. Keep the left mouse button pressed and drag it into the navigation pane. As you drag the page, a ghosted representation of the page follows your mouse cursor. Release the mouse button when the ghosted image of the contents page attaches itself to the Main page in the navigation pane, as shown in Figure 8.4.

Figure 8.3.

Return to FrontPage Explorer's Navigation view after you create four new pages in the FrontPage Editor. Your new pages appear in the files pane.

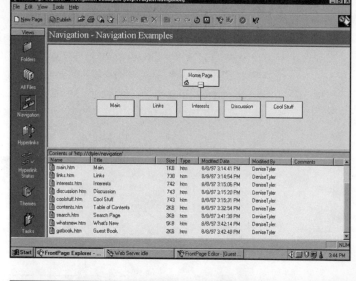

Figure 8.4.

Release the mouse button when the page you are dragging from the file page attaches itself to the page you want to link it to in the navigation pane.

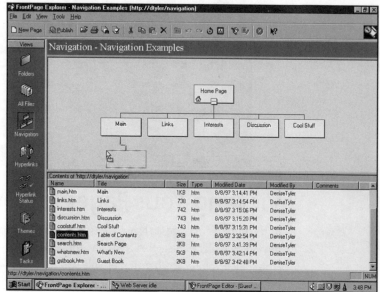

8. Repeat step 7 to attach the remaining three new pages to the Main page in Navigation view. Attach them in this order: `search.htm`, `whatsnew.htm`, and `gstbook.htm`. Your Navigation view should now look like the one in Figure 8.5.

TIP: You can also drag and drop pages within the same level to rearrange the order in which the pages will appear in your navigation bar. Release the mouse button when the ghosted image of the page appears before, after, or between any of the pages in your Navigation view.

You can move the border between the navigation pane and the files pane to improve your view of one of the panes.

Figure 8.5.
Four pages have been added from the current Web into Navigation view.

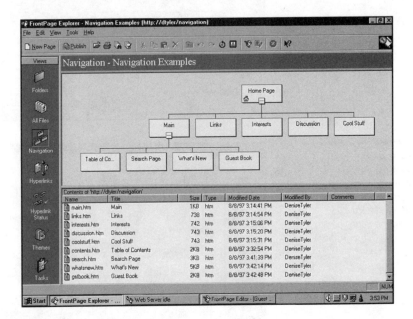

Viewing Your Pages in Navigation View

As the number of pages in Navigation view increases, you'll find that you need to scroll through the hierarchical tree to review the pages. There are a couple of buttons in the FrontPage Explorer toolbar that enable you to change the way pages are displayed in the navigation panel. You can rotate the tree or zoom out to display all the pages in your navigation system.

Rotating the Navigation View

By default, the navigation pane displays the top level in your navigation hierarchy at the top of the page, the next level beneath it, and so on. You can rotate the pages in Navigation view so that the tree is displayed horizontally—the top level appears at the left, the second level to its right, the third level to the right of the second level, and so on. An example is shown in Figure 8.6.

Figure 8.6.

You can rotate the pages in Navigation view to display the hierarchical tree horizontally.

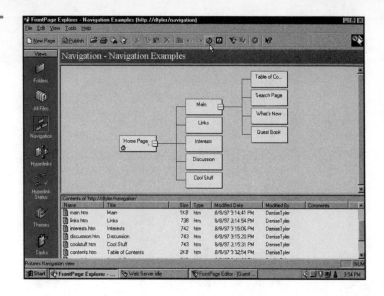

To toggle between vertical (top to bottom) and horizontal (left to right) display of your pages in Navigation view, use one of the following methods:

❏ From the FrontPage Explorer, choose **V**iew | R**o**tate.

❏ From the Standard toolbar, choose the Rotate button (shown in Figure 8.6).

 # Sizing Navigation View to Fit the Screen

You can also display your entire Web structure in the navigation pane so that you can view all the pages without scrolling. This is accomplished with the Size to Fit command or toolbar button.

To toggle between normal viewing and Size to Fit mode in Navigation view, use one of the following methods:

❏ From the FrontPage Explorer, choose **V**iew | Si**z**e To Fit.

❏ From the Standard toolbar, choose the Size to Fit button (shown in Figure 8.7).

NOTE: When you view your pages in Size to Fit mode, the Size to Fit button on the toolbar is depressed, and a checkbox appears to the right of the **V**iew | Si**z**e To Fit command.

Figure 8.7.

You can display your entire Web structure in the navigation pane with the Size to Fit command or toolbar button.

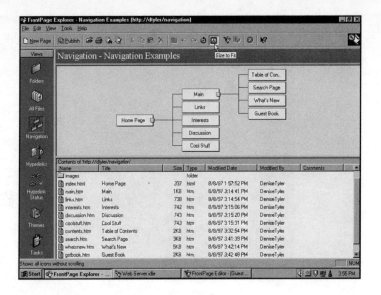

TASK

Expanding and Collapsing the Tree

If you have many pages in your Web, even the Size to Fit command or toolbar button will not display all the pages in your Web so that you can read them. You can reduce the number of pages that display in the navigation pane and expand or contract the tree to view certain levels. The top portion of Figure 8.8 shows your Web in Size to Fit mode before the pages in the Main Section are contracted. The lower portion of Figure 8.8 shows the navigation pane after the pages in the Main Section are contracted. They enable you to do the following:

❑ To contract a level in the hierarchical tree displayed in Navigation view, click the minus sign (-) on the page icon at the level you want to contract. The minus sign appears at the bottom or right side, depending on whether you are viewing your tree vertically or horizontally.

❑ To expand a level in the hierarchical tree, click the plus sign (+) on the bottom or right side of the page icon you want to expand.

Figure 8.8.
Click the minus sign (-) to contract a level and the plus sign (+) to expand a level in your hierarchical tree.

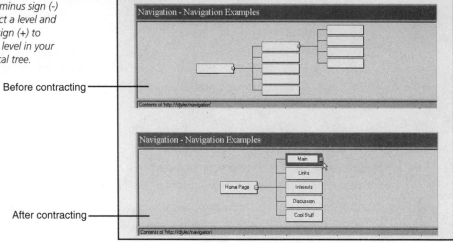

Before contracting

After contracting

 ## Undoing and Redoing Navigation Changes

If you want to undo the most recent change you made to your navigation system, you can use the **E**dit | **U**ndo command in the FrontPage Explorer. The **E**dit | **R**edo command undoes the Undo and reverts back to your change. To summarize:

❑ To undo a change to your navigation system, choose **E**dit | **U**ndo (Ctrl+Z) or press the Undo button on the FrontPage Explorer Standard toolbar.

❑ To revert back to your change, choose **E**dit | **R**edo (Ctrl+Y) or press the Redo button on the Standard toolbar.

 ## Creating a Printout

You can create a printout of your Web as it appears in Navigation view. This is a handy feature that enables you to keep a hard copy of the navigation structure of your Web site.

NOTE: Before you print your Navigation view, be sure to expand or contract the hierarchical tree to view the pages you want to include in the printout. Choose the **V**iew I **R**efresh (F5) command while in Navigation view to reset Navigation view so that it displays all pages in your navigation system. Pages that exist in your Web but which have not yet been added to the navigation system will not appear in the printout.

Previewing the Printout

You can use the **F**ile I Print Pre**v**iew command while in Navigation view to preview what your printout will look like. To preview your printed pages, follow these steps:

1. From Navigation view in the FrontPage Explorer, choose **F**ile I Print Pre**v**iew. A preview of your navigation structure appears, as shown in Figure 8.9.

Figure 8.9.

To preview your Navigation view before you print a hard copy, choose File I Print Preview.

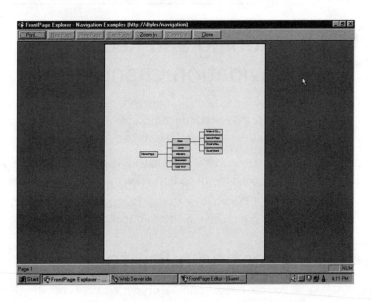

2. To preview the pages in your printout, choose one of the following buttons on the Print Preview toolbar, located at the top of the screen:

   ❑ To preview the next page in your printout, click the **N**ext Page button.

   ❑ To return to the previous page in the printout, click the Pre**v** Page button.

   ❑ To preview two pages at the same time, click the **T**wo Page button, after which the button is renamed **O**ne Page. To return to a single page display, click the **O**ne Page button.

❏ To increase the magnification of the page in the preview screen, click the Zoom **I**n button.

❏ To decrease the magnification of the page in the preview screen, click the Zoom **O**ut button.

3. After you preview your printout, you have one of two options:

❏ To print the pages and return to the FrontPage Explorer, click **P**rint. The Print dialog box appears, and you can configure the number of copies you want to print.

❏ To return to the FrontPage Explorer without printing your pages, click **C**lose.

Printing Navigation View

You can print Navigation view from the Print Preview screen, as mentioned in the previous section "Previewing the Printout," or by choosing the **F**ile | **P**rint Navigation View (Ctrl+P) command or toolbar button.

To print your Navigation view, follow these steps:

1. Open the Print dialog box, shown in Figure 8.10, using one of the following methods:

❏ Choose **P**rint from the Print Preview screen.

❏ From Navigation view in the FrontPage Explorer, choose **F**ile | **P**rint Navigation View (Ctrl+P) or click the Print Navigation View button on the Standard toolbar.

Figure 8.10.

Use the Print dialog box to select your printer and specify the pages and number of copies you want to print.

2. Enter or choose the following settings in the Print dialog box, shown in Figure 8.10:

Printer: **N**ame: Select your printer from the drop-down menu. Click the **P**roperties button to select settings that are unique to the printer you selected.

Printer: Print to file:	Choose this option if you want to print your Navigation view to a file on your hard drive rather than to your printer. The file is saved with a `.prn` extension.
Print range: **A**ll	Choose this option to print all the pages in Navigation view.
Print range: Pa**g**es	Choose this option to print one or more of a range of pages in your Navigation view. Enter the starting and ending page numbers in the **f**rom and **t**o fields.
Copies: Number of **c**opies:	Enter the number of copies that you want to print in this field.
Copies: C**o**llate	Check this option if you want to collate multiple copies. Your printer must support collating.

3. Choose OK to print your pages. You return to the FrontPage Explorer, and the files are printed.

Deleting Pages

You can use either the navigation pane or the files pane in Navigation view to delete pages. When you delete pages from the navigation pane, you can choose to delete the page from your navigation bars or to delete the page from both the navigation bar and your Web. When you delete a page from the files pane, it deletes the page from both the navigation bar and the Web.

To delete a page from the navigation pane, follow these steps:

1. From the navigation pane, click the page you want to delete.

2. Press the Del key. The Delete Page dialog box appears (see Figure 8.11).

3. To delete the page from Navigation view (and therefore from your navigation bars), select the **R**emove this page from all Navigation bars radio button. To delete the page from Navigation view and your FrontPage Web, select the **D**elete this page from the FrontPage web radio button.

4. Choose OK. The page is deleted.

Figure 8.11.
Use the Delete Page dialog box to delete a page from your navigation bars or from your FrontPage Web.

To delete a page from the files pane, follow these steps:

1. From the list of files in the files pane, click the page you want to delete.

2. Press the Delete key. The Confirm Delete dialog box shown in Figure 8.12 appears. If the current page links to other pages beneath it, a list of pages appears in the Items to delete field.

3. Choose **Y**es to delete the current page or Yes to All to delete the current page and all pages in the Items to delete field. Choose **N**o to cancel and return to the FrontPage Explorer.

CAUTION:
If you delete a page from your current Web, you cannot undo the action. You need to re-create the pages to get it back. Use caution!

Figure 8.12.
The Confirm Delete dialog box asks whether you are sure that you want to delete pages from your navigation bars.

TASK # Opening a Page from Navigation View

Now that you've learned your way around the FrontPage Navigation view, it's time to see what you've created as a result of your planning. First, you need to open one of the pages in the FrontPage Editor. In the following task, you'll open the home page (`Default.htm`, `index.htm`, or whatever your default home page filename is).

To open a page from Navigation view, double-click the page you want to open. You can select the file from either the navigation pane or the files pane. The page opens in the FrontPage Editor.

Using Navigation Bars

The navigation bars that you automatically create in Navigation view do not appear on your Web pages until you place them there. FrontPage 98 provides a couple of ways that you can apply your navigation bars to your pages. The first method, discussed in the next section, applies navigation bars and other repetitive page elements on your pages for you automatically. The second method, discussed in the later section "Adding a Navigation Bar to a Single Page," enables you to place navigation bars on a page that you choose.

Using Shared Borders

Fortunately, you don't have to add your navigation bars to each of the pages in your Web. FrontPage 98 has a solution for that task as well, and it involves a feature called *shared borders*. You can use shared borders to display any elements that repeat from page to page—navigation bars, page footers, banner graphics, or other items that are used repeatedly from page to page.

When you design your Web in Navigation view (as you've already begun in this chapter), you can use the shared borders in the FrontPage Explorer to automatically add a navigation bar to each page displayed in Navigation view.

Shared borders are automatically created and enabled for you when you create a Web from one of the FrontPage Web templates or wizards, with the exception of the Discussion Web Wizard. You can use the Shared Borders dialog box, discussed in the next section, to modify or disable the shared borders, if desired.

Using the Same Shared Borders on All Pages in Your Web

If you did not create your Web structure in Navigation view or by using one of the FrontPage Web templates and wizards, you can use the Shared Borders command on the FrontPage Explorer toolbar to enable shared borders in your Web site.

As you work your way through the Real-Life Examples chapters that appear at the end of each section in this book, I'll present more examples of how you can apply shared borders in your pages.

In the following task, you'll specify a top shared border for all the pages in your small Web. This shared border will appear on all the pages in your Web that have child pages.

To add a shared border to the top of every page in your Web, follow these steps:

1. With your Web opened in the FrontPage Explorer, choose **T**ools I Shared **B**orders. The Shared Borders dialog box appears (see Figure 8.13).

Figure 8.13.
You can apply shared borders to the top, left, right, or bottom of each page in your Web.

2. In the Borders to include section, check one or more of the following choices to display a shared border in a designated region of the page, or uncheck the option to remove the shared border in that region. As you check one or more options, a horizontal or vertical line appears in the page preview at the left side of the dialog box to indicate the regions on your page that will contain shared borders:

Top	Displays a shared border at the top of each page. Select this option for the Web you have created for this chapter.
Left	Displays a shared border at the left side of each page.
Right	Displays a shared border at the right side of each page.
Bottom	Displays a shared border at the bottom of each page.

3. Choose OK. The shared border settings are applied to all the pages in your Web.

4. From any view in the FrontPage Explorer, double-click the Home Page to open it in the FrontPage Editor. The home page opens, and your page displays the navigation bar that takes you to each of the sections in your Web, as shown in Figure 8.14.

Figure 8.14.

The navigation bar on the home page takes you to the main sections in the Web.

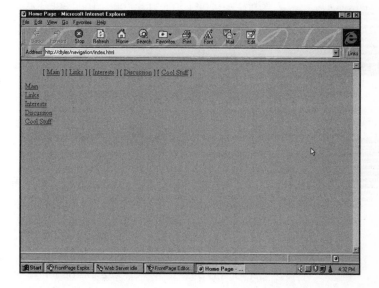

5. Choose **F**ile | Preview in **B**rowser to preview your home page in the browser and resolution of your choice. The home page opens in your browser.

6. Click the navigation button that links to the Main Section page. The page opens in your browser and displays the navigation bar that lists the main pages in the Web.

7. Return to the home page, using the Home Page navigation button or the Back button in your browser. Now, click the Links section button. Notice that there is no navigation bar on this page. The reason for this is that there are no pages beneath the Links page in the Web's Navigation view. The Links Section page is "the end of the road" until you add pages beneath it in Navigation view in the FrontPage Explorer.

Using Borders on Specific Pages in Your Web

You can also apply borders from the FrontPage Editor. When you do so, you can use either the Web default shared borders that you configured in the earlier section "Using the Same Shared Borders on All Pages in Your Web," or you can use a setting that applies to your current page only.

To add borders from the FrontPage Editor, follow these steps:

1. Open the page that you want to apply the shared border to in the FrontPage Editor.

2. Choose **T**ools | Shared **B**orders. The Page Borders dialog box shown in Figure 8.15 appears.

Figure 8.15.
Use the Page Borders dialog box to apply borders to a specific page in your Web.

3. In the Borders to include section, check one of the following options:

   Use **w**eb default   Choose this option to use the shared border settings that you have set for all the pages in the Web. When you select this option, the settings listed in step 3 are disabled.

   Set for this **p**age only Choose this option to set borders for your active page only. The Web default settings will be overridden, and you can choose the borders you want to include in the following step.

4. If you selected Set for this page only in step 2, check one or more of the following choices to display a shared border in a designated region of the page, or uncheck the option to remove the shared border in that region. As you check one or more options, a horizontal or vertical line appears in the page preview at the left side of the dialog box to indicate the regions on your page that will contain shared borders:

   Top   Displays a shared border at the top of each page. Select this option for the Web you have created for this chapter.

   Left   Displays a shared border at the left side of each page.

| **R**ight | Displays a shared border at the right side of each page. |
| **B**ottom | Displays a shared border at the bottom of each page. |

5. Choose OK. The border settings are applied to your current page.

Adding a Navigation Bar to a Single Page

You can also add a navigation bar to one page at a time. This enables you to control which of your pages you want the navigation bars to appear on and enables you to choose a different type of navigation bar or to specify a different level of pages than is used in the default settings.

To add the navigation bar to a specific page, follow these steps:

1. With your page opened in the FrontPage Editor, position the insertion point where you want to place the navigation bar.

2. Choose **I**nsert | **N**avigation Bar. The Navigation Bar Properties dialog box shown in Figure 8.16 appears.

Additional examples of navigation bars and shared borders are furnished on the CD-ROM that accompanies this book. You can find them in the `Book\Chap29\Examples` folder on the CD-ROM. These examples will show you how to tackle a variety of situations.

Figure 8.16.

Use the Navigation Bar Properties dialog box to configure options for your navigation bar.

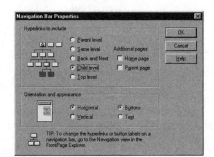

NOTE: A small graphic representation of the pages that the navigation bar will link to appears at the left side of the Navigation Bar Properties dialog box. As you select your options in steps 2 and 3, the preview graphic will change to display the pages that the navigation bar links to. The yellow and red rectangle in the graphic represents the *active page* (the page on which you are inserting the navigation bar). The red rectangles represent the pages that the navigation bar on the current page will link to.

3. From the Hyperlinks to include section, select the level of hyperlinks that you want to appear in the navigation bar. For your home page, select the **C**hild level option. The options you can select from are as follows:

Parent level   Choose this option to create a navigation bar that links to all the pages in the same level as the parent page.

Same level   Choose this option to create a navigation bar that links to all the *peer pages* of the current page.

Back and Next   Choose this option to create a navigation bar that links to the peer pages that appear before and after your current page.

Child level   Choose this option to create a navigation bar that links to the pages on the level beneath your current page.

Top level   Choose this option to create a navigation bar that links to all the pages in the top level of your Web.

4. In the Additional pages section, check one or both of the following options to include additional pages in the navigation bar (leave both these options unchecked for your home page):

Ho**m**e Page   Check this box to include a link to the home page in your Web, in addition to the pages you selected in Step 3.

P**a**rent Page   Check this box to include a link to the parent page, in addition to the pages you selected in Step 3.

5. In the Orientation and appearance section, select how you want your navigation bar to appear. You can select horizontal or vertical orientation and create text-only or graphic navigation buttons. For your home page, select Hori**z**ontal | Te**x**t.

The options are as follows:

Hori**z**ontal   Choose this option to position the links in the navigation bar in a horizontal (left to right) line on your page. This choice is good for navigation bars that appear on the top or bottom of your page.

Vertical   Choose this option to position the links in the navigation bar in a vertical (top to bottom) arrangement on your page. This choice is good for navigation bars that will appear at the left or right side of your page.

B**u**ttons   Check this box to create navigation buttons that are compatible with the graphic theme you select for your Web. For more information on themes, see Chapter 14, "Using FrontPage Style Sheets and Themes."

Te**x**t   Check this option to create text-only links in your navigation bar.

6. Choose OK. The navigation bar appears on your page.

Modifying a Navigation Bar

After you create your navigation bars and place them on your pages, you can use the commands previously discussed in this chapter to modify your navigation bars in several different ways:

❏ To change the text labels that appear in the navigation bars, use Navigation view in the FrontPage Explorer. Edit the page titles that appear in the navigation pane, similar to the way you assigned page titles in the section "Creating a New Page in Navigation View," earlier in this chapter.

❏ To change the pages that appear in the navigation bars, use the navigation pane in the FrontPage Explorer. Add, delete, or move pages in your navigation structure as outlined in the earlier section "Changing Pages in Navigation View." As you make changes to your navigation system, all your navigation bars update to reflect the changes.

❏ You can use the Navigation Bar Properties dialog box, discussed in the earlier section "Adding a Navigation Bar to a Page," to change the pages that a navigation bar points to. You can also use this dialog box to change from graphic navigation bars to text navigation bars or to change the layout of the navigation bar from horizontal to vertical. To reopen the Navigation Bar Properties dialog box, open the page on which you want to change the navigation bar. Double-click the navigation bar to open the Navigation Bar Properties dialog box. Modify the settings in the dialog box and choose OK to update the changes.

❏ Remember that when you change a navigation bar that appears in a shared border region on a page, the changes will also apply to any other pages that share the same border settings. If you move a navigation bar from a top shared border to a bottom shared border, for example, the change applies to each page that uses that shared border setting.

❏ To change the fonts, colors, and graphics that appear on all the pages in your Web, select a new theme from Themes view in the FrontPage Explorer. To apply changes of this nature to only one page in your Web, select a new theme from the FrontPage Editor. To learn more about themes, see Chapter 14.

Deleting Navigation Bars

It's easy enough to delete a navigation bar, but depending on where you delete it from, you achieve different results.

Here are the steps to delete a navigation bar:

1. Open the page that you want to modify in the FrontPage Editor.
2. Select the navigation bar that you want to delete:

   ❏ If the navigation bar appears in a page that does not use shared borders, the navigation bar is deleted from the active page only.

   ❏ If the navigation bar appears on a page that does use shared borders, but appears in the body of the page instead of a shared border region, the navigation bar is removed from the active page only.

   ❏ If the navigation bar appears within a shared border region on a page, the navigation bar is removed from the current page and all other pages that share the same border region.

3. Delete the navigation bar, using one of the following methods:

   ❏ Choose **E**dit | Cle**a**r or press the Delete key to remove the navigation bar from your page.

   ❏ Choose **E**dit | Cu**t** (Ctrl+X) to remove the navigation bar from your page and place it into your Windows clipboard. You can paste it into another page using **E**dit | **P**aste (Ctrl+V).

 # Changing Shared Borders

You can change the contents of a shared border at any time. When you edit a shared border, the changes you make are automatically updated in any page that shares the same border.

To modify the placement of shared borders, use one of the following procedures:

❏ Choose **T**ools | Shared **B**orders from the FrontPage Explorer to modify the placement of shared borders on all pages in your Web, as discussed in the earlier section "Using the Same Shared Borders on All Pages in Your Web." The changes you make in the Shared Borders dialog box apply to all the pages in the current Web that use the Web's default shared borders.

❏ Choose **T**ools | Shared **B**orders from the FrontPage Editor to modify the placement of shared borders on your current page, as discussed in the earlier section "Using Shared Borders on Specific Pages in Your Web."

To modify the contents of a shared border:

1. Open any page that contains a shared border in the FrontPage Editor.
2. Click inside the shared border region. The shared border becomes surrounded by a bounding box.

3. Modify the contents of the shared border as necessary.

4. Choose **F**ile | **S**ave (Ctrl+S) to save the changes to your Web. Any pages that use the same shared border will automatically update with the changes.

Workshop Wrap-Up

When you use Navigation view in the FrontPage Explorer, you not only provide links to the key sections and pages in your Web, but you make it easier for your site visitors to find their way around. You learned in this chapter how to create automatic navigation bars that update themselves when you make changes to your Web. You also learned how to use shared borders to place repeated content on all or selected pages in your Web. You'll learn more about these features in Chapter 13.

Next Steps

In the next chapter, you learn how to add basic content to your pages by placing headings, paragraphs, and fonts on your pages. You also learn how and when to use different types of paragraphs and characters.

For other information that relates to the topics discussed in this chapter, refer to the following chapters:

❑ See Chapter 14, "Using FrontPage Style Sheets and Themes," to learn more about the themes that are used in your navigation bars.

❑ See Chapter 15, "Working with Images and Sound," to learn how to modify the images used in your navigation bars from within the FrontPage Editor.

❑ See Chapter 16, "Working with Animation and Active Content," to learn more about the hover buttons used in your navigation bars.

❑ See Chapter 19, "Using FrontPage Components," to learn about other ways you can economize your time while making changes to your Web site.

❑ See Chapter 25, "Using Java Applets and Netscape Plug-Ins," to learn more about Java applets, such as those used for the hover buttons.

❑ See Chapter 27, "Using Styles," to learn what goes on behind the scenes of your navigation bars and your Web page themes.

Q&A

Q: Is there any way to select a page template other than the Normal page template when I create new pages in Navigation view?

A: Not from within the FrontPage Explorer. If you want to base pages on existing templates, you need to create the pages in the FrontPage Editor, save them to your Web, and then drag the pages into your Navigation view. These steps are covered in the "Adding Pages from Your Current Web" section.

Q: Does my Internet Service Provider have to have the FrontPage Server Extensions installed in order for me to use navigation bars and shared borders?

A: To track the links to your pages, you do need to design your shared borders with the FrontPage Server Extensions running. However, when you publish your pages, the navigation bars are saved in standard HTML format. You can publish pages that use this feature to an ISP that does not have the FrontPage Server Extensions installed!

Q: Are the navigation bars created by FrontPage 98 compatible with every browser, or do I have to recommend a specific browser with which to view them?

A: If your navigation bars use active graphics, they incorporate hover buttons. These types of buttons are discussed further in Chapter 16. Hover buttons are actually small Java applets, so you need to recommend a browser that is capable of displaying Java applets. The most current versions of Netscape Navigator/Communicator and Internet Explorer are sure to support the latest and greatest features, but it's always best to test your pages in several different browsers to be sure.

Q: Can I change the font that is used in my text navigation bars?

A: The fonts used with your navigation bars are determined by the theme you use. Cascading style sheet tags are used to determine the fonts and colors of the fonts. For more information about cascading style sheets, see Chapter 27.

Q: The navigation buttons that are used for my theme are way too big. How can I make them smaller?

A: All the images used in your navigation bars are stored in your `_themes` subfolders. Chapter 14 tells a bit more about what goes on behind the scenes with themes and how you can modify existing ones or create your own.

Q: How do I follow a hyperlink in a navigation bar from the FrontPage Editor? When I select the navigation bar, the Go | Follow Hyperlink command is disabled.

A: Place the mouse over the navigation button or text in the navigation bar and use the Ctrl+Click shortcut to follow the hyperlink.

NINE

Getting from Here to There

The first time I went on the Internet, what I thought would be only a one-hour browsing session lasted four hours. I began by looking for information on graphic development. I did a Web search for related pages. The search returned thousands of pages, so I picked one that sounded promising. Once I got to the site, I went deeper into areas that were more relevant to the topics in which I was interested. Each site led me to another. It was like having a huge library in my living room.

Hyperlinks and bookmarks are what give Web pages this level of interactivity. Without them, you cannot easily enable people to see what is on your site or to find other sites with similar information. With hyperlinks and bookmarks, a user can simply click a mouse on text or a graphic to navigate to all types of pages, download files, find newsgroups, and send e-mail.

In this chapter, you

- ❏ Create bookmarks on your pages and navigate to specific places on them
- ❏ Create hyperlinks to Web pages, files, and other Web protocols
- ❏ Use images as hyperlinks and designate specific areas in an image for navigating to other pages
- ❏ Use the FrontPage Editor to follow hyperlinks

Tasks in this chapter:

- ❏ Creating a Web for This Chapter
- ❏ Creating and Hyperlinking to Bookmarks
- ❏ Creating Text Hyperlinks
- ❏ Linking to a New Page Based on a Template
- ❏ Creating Hyperlinks from the FrontPage Explorer
- ❏ Inserting Images and Adding Alternative Representations
- ❏ Using Clickable Images
- ❏ Creating Hotspots
- ❏ Hyperlinking to Pages and Files
- ❏ Sending Mail Through a Hyperlink

Creating a Web for This Chapter

For the tasks in this chapter, create a new Empty Web from the FrontPage Explorer. Name the Web **hyperlinks**. To create the Web, follow these steps:

1. From the FrontPage Explorer, choose **F**ile | **N**ew | FrontPage **W**eb (Ctrl+N). The New FrontPage Web dialog box appears.

2. Check the From **W**izard or Template radio button and highlight Empty Web.

3. In the Choose a **t**itle for your FrontPage web field, enter **Hyperlinks Examples**. The URL beneath the Web title changes to http://*server*/hyperlin (or http://*server*:8080 if the FrontPage 98 Server was installed to port 8080), where *server* is the name of the server that exists on your computer.

4. Click the **C**hange button to change the URL for the Web. The Change Location dialog box appears. Edit the hyperlin portion of the URL to read hyperlinks. Then choose OK to return to the New FrontPage Web dialog box.

5. Choose OK again to create your Web. The empty Web appears in the FrontPage Explorer workspace.

6. From the FrontPage Explorer views list, choose the Themes icon. The Web is displayed in Themes view.

7. Select the **T**his Web Does Not Use Themes radio button, then click **A**pply.

8. Choose **V**iew | **F**olders or click the Folder icon in the FrontPage Explorer Views list to switch to Folder view.

9. Choose **F**ile | **I**mport. The Import File to FrontPage Web dialog box appears.

10. Click the **A**dd File button. The Add File to Import List dialog box appears.

 11. Locate the directory on the CD-ROM that accompanies this book that contains the project files for this chapter. There are 13 files located in the Book\Chap09\Project Files. Highlight all the files and click **O**pen. You return to the Import File to FrontPage Web dialog box, and all files are highlighted.

12. Click OK. The pages import into the home directory of your Web.

13. Select all the images in the home folder in your Web and move them to the images folder in your Web. The images are renamed and moved.

 ## Creating Bookmarks

Just as bookmarks serve as placeholders when you read a book, they perform basically the same function on a Web page. Bookmarks mark a specific spot on a page. A page that contains bookmarks typically has a small table of contents at the top that hyperlinks the user to bookmarked headings on the page. At the end of the bookmark's section, another hyperlink takes the user back to a bookmark located at the top of the page or at the table of contents.

The Windsurfing Links page (`windsurf.htm`) that you imported into your Web from the CD-ROM is the page used in the following task. Open the page to complete the following task.

To create a bookmark on your page, follow these steps:

1. From the FrontPage Explorer, double-click `windsurf.htm`, located in your Web's home directory. The page opens in the FrontPage Editor.

2. Position the cursor to the left of the heading that reads Windsurfing Links. Click to select the heading.

3. Choose **E**dit | **B**ookmark. The Bookmark dialog box appears (see Figure 9.1).

Figure 9.1.
You create a new bookmark with the Bookmark dialog box.

4. By default, the text that you select for the bookmark appears in the **B**ookmark Name field. Although FrontPage enables you to create bookmark names that contain spaces, some browsers do not recognize them and the bookmarks might not work properly. It is a good idea to keep bookmarks fairly short because it saves typing when linking to them from another page in the Web. In the **B**ookmark Name field, enter `top`.

5. Choose OK or press Enter. The heading on your page becomes underlined with a dotted line, indicating that it is a bookmark.

6. Position the cursor to the left of the heading in the second section that reads Other Sites About Windsurfing. Click to select the heading.

7. Choose **E**dit | **B**ookmark. The Bookmark dialog box appears. Assign a bookmark name of `sites` and choose OK or press Enter. Another bookmark is created.

8. Scroll down the page to the third section and position the cursor to the left of the heading that reads Windsurfing Newsgroups. Click to select it.

9. Choose **E**dit | **B**ookmark. The Bookmark dialog box appears. Assign a bookmark name of `news` and choose OK or press Enter. You create a third bookmark.

10. Choose **F**ile | Save (Ctrl+S) or click the Save button on the Standard toolbar. The page is saved to your Web.

Hyperlinking to Bookmarks

Now that you have created some bookmarks on the sample page, you want to create hyperlinks from the contents section of the page to the bookmarks. To create the links, follow these steps:

1. Scroll to the top of the page until you see the Contents section of the page. Position your cursor to the left of the bulleted list item that reads Other Sites about Windsurfing. Click to select the item.

2. Choose **E**dit I Hyperlin**k** (Ctrl+K), **I**nsert I Hyperlin**k** (Ctrl+K), or the Create or Edit Hyperlink button on the Standard toolbar. The Create Hyperlink dialog box appears.

3. From the list of pages in your Web, highlight `windsurf.htm`, which should appear at the top of the list.

4. In the Optional section at the bottom of the Create Hyperlink dialog box, choose the `sites` bookmark from the **B**ookmark drop-down list, as shown in Figure 9.2. Then choose OK or press Enter. A link to the bookmark is created.

Figure 9.2.
From the Create Hyperlink dialog box, choose the sites bookmark on the `windsurf.htm` *page.*

5. Position your cursor to the left of the bulleted list item that reads Windsurfing Newsgroups. Click to select the item.

6. Click the Create or Edit Hyperlink button on the Standard toolbar. The Create Hyperlink dialog box appears.

7. From the list of pages in your Web, highlight `windsurf.htm`, which should appear at the top of the list.

8. In the Optional section at the bottom of the Create Hyperlink dialog box, choose the `news` bookmark from the **B**ookmark drop-down list. Then choose OK or press Enter. A link to the bookmark is created.

9. Select the text at the bottom of the second section that reads Back to Top. Choose the Create or Edit Hyperlink button on the Standard toolbar. This time, repeat steps 6 and 7 to create a hyperlink to the top bookmark.

10. Repeat step 8 for the Back to Top link at the bottom of the third section on the page.

TIP: You can also copy the first Back to Top hyperlink to your clipboard using Ctrl+C and paste it into other locations on your page by using Ctrl+V.

11. Choose **F**ile | **S**ave (Ctrl+S) or click the Save button on the Standard toolbar. The page is updated in your Web.

 # Visiting Bookmarks

You can visit a bookmark on your page without creating a hyperlink to it. Use the following steps:

1. With the page that contains the bookmarks opened in the FrontPage Editor, choose **E**dit | **B**ookmark. The Bookmark dialog box appears.

2. In the **O**ther Bookmarks on this Page field, select the bookmark that you want to visit.

3. Click **G**oto. The FrontPage Editor scrolls to the bookmark.

4. Click OK or Cancel to close the Bookmark dialog box.

You also can visit a bookmark on another page. Suppose you have the page oriental.htm, which is named "Cooking Great Chinese Food." On it is a section called "Picking Fresh Vegetables," with the bookmark freshveggies. When you create a hyperlink to this bookmark, the URL looks like this:

oriental.htm#freshveggies

To visit a bookmark on another page, do the following:

1. Place the pointer anywhere within the text on the originating page that the user clicks to go to the bookmark on another page.

2. Choose **T**ools | Follow **H**yperlink. The FrontPage Editor opens the other page and scrolls to the bookmark that you want to visit on the page.

Removing Bookmarks

Removing a bookmark is easy:

1. Place the mouse pointer anywhere within the text of the bookmark (indicated by a dotted underline).
2. Choose **E**dit l **B**ookmark and then click the **C**lear button in the Bookmark dialog box. The bookmark is removed, but the text associated with it remains on your page.

TIP: To delete the bookmark and its associated text, select the text and use the Delete key.

Hyperlinks: Reaching Outward

It is convenient to jump to different locations on a page, but that is not what the Web is all about. *The Web is about reaching outward.* To accomplish this, you provide hyperlinks on your pages. Hyperlinks can take users to other pages in your Web, to pages in other people's Webs, to newsgroups, and to other types of Internet protocols. You can even put a hyperlink on your page to get e-mail delivered to your mailbox. FrontPage enables you to create text hyperlinks, image hyperlinks, and clickable image hyperlinks (or image maps) very easily.

Creating Text Hyperlinks

As you learned in Chapter 8, "Designing Your Web Navigation," FrontPage generates navigation bars for you automatically. They provide a way for the user to navigate to key pages in your Web site. You can easily create a text navigation bar that links to the main pages or sections in your Web. Then you can use an Include Page component to place the same navigation bar on multiple Web pages.

Refer to Chapter 8 for information on how FrontPage can generate navigation bars automatically for you. See Chapter 19, "Using FrontPage Components," for more information about Include Page components.

Now you'll work on the text navigation page that you imported into your FrontPage Web for this chapter:

1. From the FrontPage Editor, choose **F**ile l **O**pen (Ctrl+O) or click the Open button on the Standard toolbar. The Open File dialog box appears.
2. Double-click `textnav.htm`. The page opens in the FrontPage Editor.
3. Select the text that reads Kandy's Home Page, as shown in Figure 9.3. This is the text which the user clicks to navigate to the home page.
4. Select **E**dit l **Hyperlin**k (Ctrl+K) or click the Create or Edit Hyperlink button on the toolbar. The Create Hyperlink dialog box appears. For the link to Kandy's

Home Page, continue with the following task, "Linking to a New Page Based on a Template."

Figure 9.3.

Select the text you want the user to click on to navigate to the page.

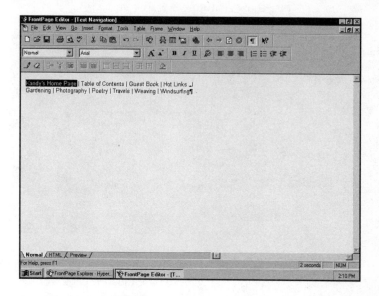

 # Linking to a New Page Based on a Template

Right now, you don't have any pages in your Web to which to link. In FrontPage, it's easy to create a new page and link to it at the same time. When you create a new page in this manner, you can base the new page on one of the many page templates provided with FrontPage 98.

You should have the Create Hyperlink dialog box opened at this time from the preceding task. From here, choose the Create a page and link to the new page button shown in Figure 9.4. Use the following steps:

Figure 9.4.

Choose the Create a page and link to the new page button to create a hyperlink to a new page.

1. From the Create Hyperlink dialog box, select the Create a page and link to the new page button. The New dialog box appears, opened to the Page tab shown in Figure 9.5.

Figure 9.5.
Use the New dialog box to select a template on which you want to base the new Web page.

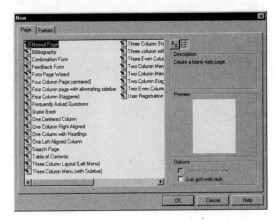

2. From the list of page templates in the Page tab, select the template on which you want to base the new page. For this example, choose the Normal Page template.

3. Choose OK or press Enter. A new page appears in the FrontPage Editor.

4. Choose **F**ile | **S**ave (Ctrl+S) or click the Save button on the Standard toolbar. The Save As dialog box appears.

5. Enter the filename `index.htm` (or your default home page filename) in the **U**RL field. In the **T**itle field, enter `Kandy's Home Page`.

6. A list of all the folders in your Web appears in the Save As dialog box. By default, the home folder is displayed here. Choose OK to save Kandy's Home Page to this folder.

NOTE: To save a page in a different folder in your current Web, double-click the folder name in which you want to save the page and then choose OK to save your page. You can also use the Create New Folder button that appears to the right of the Look **in** drop-down menu in the Save As dialog box to create a new folder in your Web.

7. Click the Back button on the FrontPage Editor Standard toolbar to return to the `textnav.htm` page.

8. Complete steps 1-7 for the remaining links in the navigation bar. Table 9.1 lists the page template you should select when you create each page and the page URL you should use when you save your pages to the Web. Save all the pages to the home directory in your Web. Figure 9.6 shows the navigation bar with all links completed.

TIP: If you drag your mouse over the hyperlinks in the navigation bar after you create them, the destination URL appears in the status bar at the bottom of your screen. Use this for quick verification that your hyperlinks go where you want them to go!

Figure 9.6.
The navigation bar now contains links to all the main pages in the Web.

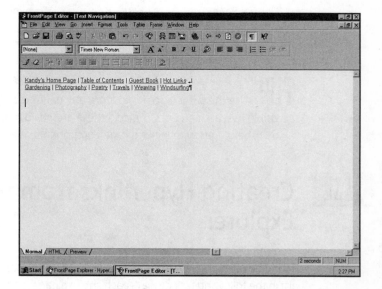

9. After you complete all the links shown in Table 9.1, return to the textnav.htm page one last time. Save the text navigation bar to your Web by using the **F**ile I **S**ave command (Ctrl+S) or by clicking the Save button on the Standard toolbar. Close the page by using the **F**ile I **C**lose command or by clicking the X button located in the right corner of the menu command line.

10. Return to the FrontPage Explorer. Click and drag the textnav.htm page to move it from your Web's home directory into the _private directory. FrontPage renames the page _private/textnav.htm.

Table 9.1. New pages in Kandy's place.

Page Template	Page URL	Page Title
Normal Page	`index.htm`	Kandy's Home Page
Table of Contents	`toc.htm`	Table of Contents
Guest Book	`guestbk.htm`	Guest Book
Normal Page	`hotlinks.htm`	Hot Links
Normal Page	`garden.htm`	Gardening
Normal Page	`photos.htm`	Photography
Normal Page	`poetry.htm`	Poetry
Normal Page	`travels.htm`	Travels
Normal Page	`weaving.htm`	Weaving
Normal Page	`surfing.htm`	Windsurfing

TIP: Use the `private` folder to store any pages that you don't want to be visible in search engines. Among these are navigation bars that you will place on other pages with Include Page components.

 # Creating Hyperlinks from the FrontPage Explorer

You can also create text hyperlinks to pages in your Web by dragging pages from the FrontPage Explorer into a page that is opened in the FrontPage Editor. The navigation list in the following task displays each link to a page in the Web on a different line and is suitable to use in the contents section of a frame set. You'll find it easier to create links in this manner if you have both the FrontPage Explorer and the FrontPage Editor open and visible onscreen at the same time, as shown in Figure 9.7.

The navigation list shown in Figure 9.8 was created by dragging pages from the FrontPage Explorer to an open page in the FrontPage Editor. Afterwards, it was arranged into a bulleted list.

Figure 9.7.

Drag pages from the FrontPage Explorer into an opened page in the FrontPage Editor to create text links easily.

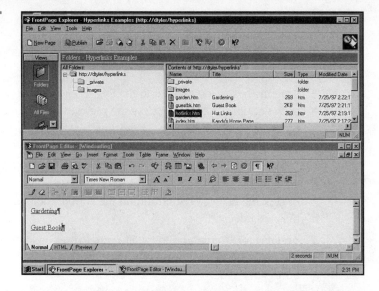

Figure 9.8.

Links to the main pages were created by dragging pages from the FrontPage Explorer into the FrontPage Editor.

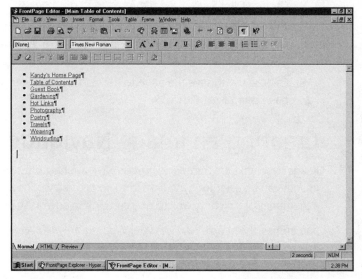

To create text links from the FrontPage Explorer, use the following steps:

1. Position the FrontPage Explorer and the FrontPage Editor so that you can access both screens easily.

2. From the FrontPage Explorer, choose Folders view.

3. From the FrontPage Editor, use the New button on the Standard toolbar to create a new page based on the Normal Page template. A blank page appears in the FrontPage Editor.

4. From Folders view in the FrontPage Explorer, click and drag the `index.htm` page from the FrontPage Explorer into your opened page in the FrontPage Editor. Release the mouse button on the first line. A link to the page appears after you release the mouse.

5. Drag the remaining pages into the FrontPage Editor, one at a time, placing each new link on the line below the previous one. Create the links in this order: `toc.htm`, `guestbk.htm`, `garden.htm`, `hotlinks.htm`, `photos.htm`, `poetry.htm`, `travels.htm`, `weaving.htm`, and `surfing.htm`.

6. Select all the text links on the page using **E**dit | Select All (Ctrl+A). Choose Bulleted List from the Change Style drop-down menu in the Format toolbar or click the Bulleted List button on the Format toolbar. The links appear in a bulleted list.

7. Add any text formatting to the links that you like. In my example, I changed the font to Arial and reduced the size by clicking the Decrease Font Size button one time.

8. Choose **F**ile | **S**ave. The Save As dialog box appears. In the **U**RL field, enter `maintoc.htm`. In the **T**itle field, enter `Main Table of Contents`.

9. From the list of files and folders in your current Web, double-click the `_private` folder.

10. Choose OK to save the page to the `_private` folder in your Web. Close the page using **F**ile | **C**lose.

Creating an Image Navigation Bar

Themes, a new feature provided with FrontPage 98, uses Cascading Style Sheet tags in conjunction with Navigation view to automatically create text and image navigation bars for you. For more information on designing Web navigation, refer to Chapter 8. See Chapter 14, "Using FrontPage Style Sheets and Themes," for more information about using FrontPage 98 themes.

Image hyperlinks are commonly used as navigational buttons and navigation bars, but images can be used for hyperlinks in all sorts of ways. For example, you can provide a thumbnail of a picture, which users can click to download or display in a larger view.

Sometimes, the people who visit your Web site are not using browsers that can display images. These browsers are becoming increasingly rare, but other browsers provide the option of turning off image display. Many people choose not to download images because of the time involved. This is not a problem when images are placed on a page just to be seen. When they serve a function, however, you must provide an alternative for people who do not want to download all that artwork. You can provide a text version elsewhere on the page, or you can specify an alternative text representation. You'll use the latter approach in the following task.

Inserting Images

This navigation bar consists of two rows with five buttons each. Each navigation graphic is 100 pixels wide, making each row a total of 500 pixels wide. The images should already be present in your current Web because you imported them at the beginning of this chapter.

Here are the steps:

1. From the FrontPage Editor, use the New button on the Standard toolbar to create a normal page. A blank page opens in the FrontPage Editor.

2. With the insertion point on the first line, use the Insert | Image command or the Insert Image button on the Standard toolbar command five times in succession. Each time, the Image dialog box appears. Double-click the images folder in the Image dialog box and insert the images in the first row in the following order: home.jpg, contents.jpg, guestbk.jpg, garden.jpg, and hotlinks.jpg.

3. At the end of the first row, press Shift+Enter or choose Insert | Break and select Normal Line Break from the Break Properties dialog box. The insertion point moves to the next line.

4. Using the same procedure outlined in step 3, insert the following images into the second row: photos.jpg, poetry.jpg, travels.jpg, weaving.jpg, and windsurf.jpg. When you're done, your page should look like the one in Figure 9.9.

Figure 9.9.

Insert 10 images from your current Web into the new page, placing five images on each line.

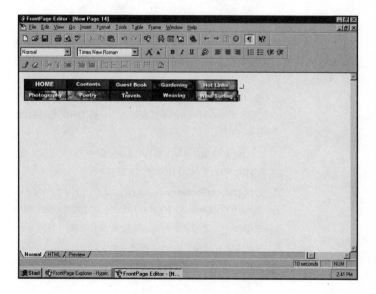

Adding Alternative Text Representations and Links

Creating image hyperlinks is just as simple as creating text hyperlinks. To create an image hyperlink, you need only click an image and then choose Edit | Hyperlink

(Ctrl+K) or use the Create or Edit Hyperlink button on the Standard toolbar.

What happens when users have graphics turned off in their browsers and then they can't read where your image hyperlinks are supposed to take them? One solution is to provide an alternative text representation for the image that you are using as a hyperlink. The text that you enter in the alternative text representation field appears before an image is loaded onto the page and displays whether or not users have graphics turned on in their browsers. The following steps show one way to create an image hyperlink while you add an alternative representation at the same time:

1. Click the Home graphic and press Alt+Enter, or right-click the Home graphic and choose Image Properties from the pop-up menu. The Image Properties dialog box shown in Figure 9.10 appears.

Figure 9.10.
You can create links and add alternative text representations from the Image Properties dialog box.

2. By default, the filename and file size of the current image appears in the Alternative Representations: Te**x**t field. Replace this entry with the word Home.

3. In the Default Hyperlink: **L**ocation field, click the B**r**owse button. The Edit Hyperlink dialog box appears.

4. Double-click the index.htm page that appears in the home directory in your Web. You return to the Image Properties dialog box. Click OK to create the hyperlink and alternative text representation.

5. Repeat steps 1 through 4 for each additional image on the page, creating links to the appropriate page for each navigation button. Add alternative text representations, as shown in Table 9.2.

6. Choose **F**ile I **S**ave (Ctrl+S) or click the Save button on the Standard toolbar to save the page to the Web. The Save As dialog box appears.

7. In the **U**RL field, enter buttons.htm. In the **T**itle field, enter Graphic Navigation Buttons.

8. Double-click the _private folder in the Save As dialog box and choose OK to save the page to the _private folder.

Table 9.2. Links and alternative text for Navigation bar.

Button Label	Alternative Text	Links To
Contents	Contents	toc.htm
Guest Book	Guest Book	guestbk.htm
Gardening	Gardening	garden.htm
Hot Links	Hot Links	hotlinks.htm
Photography	Photography	photos.htm
Poetry	Poetry	poetry.htm
Travels	Travels	travels.htm
Weaving	Weaving	weaving.htm
Windsurfing	Windsurfing	surfing.htm

See Chapter 15, "Working with Images and Sound," for more information about inserting images into your pages.

Setting Clickable Image Style

Before you get into creating clickable images, you should know what type of clickable image style you need to create. If your Web resides on a server that has the FrontPage Server Extensions installed, you will probably want to use FrontPage image map style, which is the default setting. However, if your Internet Service Provider (ISP) does not have the Server Extensions installed, you'll need to select another image map style. If you are not certain what kind you will need, verify this information with your ISP.

To change the image map style, follow these steps:

1. From the FrontPage Explorer, choose **T**ools I **W**eb Settings. The FrontPage Web Settings dialog box appears.

2. Choose the Advanced tab, shown in Figure 9.11.

Figure 9.11.
Use the Advanced tab in the FrontPage Web Settings dialog box to change the clickable image style.

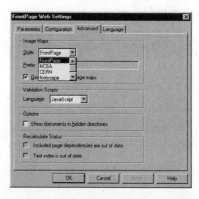

3. In the Image Maps section, choose the image map type you want to create from the **S**tyle selection box. Available choices are the following:

❑ FrontPage (default) generates image map data for FrontPage-enabled servers.

❑ NCSA generates image map data for NCSA servers. The default path to the image map handler is `/cgi-bin/imagemap`.

❑ CERN generates image map data for CERN servers. The default path to the image map handler is `/cgi-bin/htimage`.

❑ Netscape generates image map data for Netscape servers. There is no default path for an image map handler.

❑ <None>. FrontPage does not generate HTML to support image maps.

4. If you choose an image map type other than FrontPage or <None>, enter the URL of the server-side image map handler in the **P**refix field. If you are uncertain of the URL, verify this information with your ISP. The default paths are listed in step 3.

5. Check the **G**enerate client-side image maps checkbox to generate client-side HTML for image maps. If you uncheck this option, FrontPage does not generate HTML that supports client-side image maps.

NOTE: When you generate client-side image maps, the destination URL of each hotspot on the page is encoded directly in your Web page and the hyperlink is processed by your browser. They are more efficient than server-side image maps because the server does not have to process them. Client-side image maps are not supported by all browsers. If you select a style other than <None> in step 4 and check the Generate client-side image maps button, FrontPage generates both client-side and server-side HTML.

6. Choose OK to exit the FrontPage Web Settings dialog box. FrontPage asks whether you want to refresh the Web so the changes take effect. Answer **Y**es to refresh the Web.

Creating a Home Page with a Clickable Image

Clickable images, also known as *image maps,* are graphics that contain hotspots. An image can contain more than one hotspot to navigate to different pages in your Web. They are useful and enable you to add creativity to the hyperlinks on your pages.

To create the home page, follow these steps:

1. From the FrontPage Editor, choose **F**ile | **O**pen (Ctrl+O), or click the Open button on the Standard toolbar. The Open dialog box appears. Double-click `index.htm` to open the page.

2. Choose **I**nsert | **I**mage or click the Insert Image button on the Standard toolbar. The Image dialog box appears.

3. Double-click the `images` folder; then double-click `imagemap.jpg`. The image appears on your page.

4. Center the image using the Center button on the Format toolbar.

Creating Hotspots

You can turn any graphic on your page into a clickable image. Simply select the image, create a hotspot or hotspots on it, and assign a hyperlink to the hotspot. The Image toolbar includes buttons that let you add hotspots to an image. By default, the toolbar displays at the bottom of the FrontPage Editor workspace, as shown in Figure 9.12. There are three types of hotspots: rectangular, circular, and polygonal.

Figure 9.12.
Hotspots are created using the buttons on the Image toolbar.

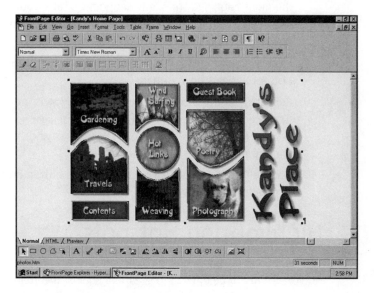

Figure 9.12 shows hotspots added to the image on Kandy's Home Page. You create them as follows:

1. Click the image to select it. The Image toolbar is enabled. If the Image toolbar is not displayed, choose **V**iew | **I**mage Toolbar.

2. To add a rectangular hotspot, click the Rectangle button on the Image toolbar. Position the mouse at the upper-left corner of the Guest Book

rectangle on the image and click and drag to the lower-right corner. Then release the mouse button. The Create Hyperlink dialog box appears.

3. From the home directory in your Web, double-click `guestbk.htm`. The hotspot appears on your page and the hyperlink is created.

4. Repeat steps 2 and 3 for the Contents rectangle in the image, creating a link to `toc.htm` in your current Web.

5. To create a circular hotspot for the Hot Links portion of the graphic, select the Circle button on the Image toolbar. Click to begin the circle in the center of the Hot Links circle and drag outward until the entire circle is enclosed. Release the mouse button to open the Create Hyperlink dialog box.

6. From the home folder in your Web, double-click `hotlinks.htm`. The circular hotspot appears on your page. If you didn't get the hotspot centered correctly, click and drag from the center of the hotspot to move it.

7. To create a polygonal hotspot for the Gardening section of the graphic, click the Polygon button on the Image toolbar. Start the polygon by clicking at any starting point around the border of the hotspot area. As you move the mouse, the outline follows your cursor. Click to set a second point and move the mouse again. Continue to set points until an outline is drawn around the area. End the hotspot by clicking at your starting point. The Create Hyperlink dialog box appears.

8. From the home folder in your Web, double-click `garden.htm`. The polygonal hotspot appears on your page.

9. Repeat steps 7 and 8 for the remaining polygonal hotspots in the image. Create links to `surfing.htm` (for Windsurfing), `poetry.htm` (for Poetry), `travels.htm` (for Travels), `weaving.htm` (for Weaving), and `photos.htm` (for Photography).

10. Choose **F**ile I **S**ave (Ctrl+S) or click the Save button on the Standard toolbar to save the page to your Web.

Highlighting Hotspots

You sometimes need to adjust the hotspots on your page so that they do not overlap. However, it might be difficult to see them against the image on which they appear. You can use the Highlight Hotspots command to find hotspots easier:

1. Click the image to activate the Image toolbar.

2. Click the Highlight Hotspots button, which is the next-to-last button on the Image toolbar. The image disappears and you can see the hotspot areas, as in Figure 9.13. To return to normal view, click outside the image or press the Highlight Hotspots button again.

Figure 9.13.

*Use the Highlight
Hotspots button to view
hotspots easily.*

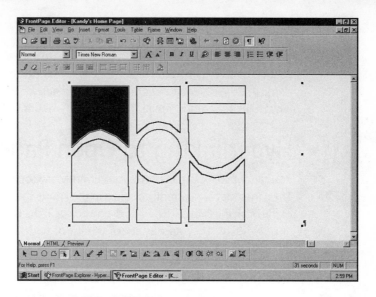

TASK ## Changing Hotspots

You need to select a hotspot to move, resize, or delete it. To select a hotspot, do the
following:

1. Click the image where the hotspot appears.
2. Select the hotspot by clicking it. It becomes surrounded by a bounding box
   with sizing handles at each corner.

To move a hotspot, use the following steps:

1. Select the hotspot.
2. Left-click and drag the hotspot to a new location; use the Escape key before
   you release the mouse to return the hotspot to its original position. Alternatively, use the Up, Down, Left, and Right arrow keys to nudge the hotspot
   one pixel at a time to a new location.

To resize a hotspot, follow these steps:

1. Select the hotspot.
2. Click and drag any of the resizing handles or resizing points in the hotspot.
   They are designated by small squares.

To delete a hotspot, follow these steps:

1. Select the hotspot.
2. Use the **E**dit | Cle**a**r command or press the Delete key.

Where You Can Hyperlink

In the previous tasks, you learned how to create links to new pages and to pages in your current Web. You can also create links to open pages, to pages or files on the World Wide Web, and to files on your local or network hard drive. You can also create a hyperlink that sends e-mail. These procedures are shown in the following tasks.

Hyperlinking to Open Pages

You can hyperlink to pages that you currently have opened in the FrontPage Explorer. The pages that are currently opened in the FrontPage Editor are displayed at the top of the list in the Create Hyperlink dialog box or in the Edit Hyperlink dialog box shown in Figure 9.14. They appear above the list of folders in your current Web and are represented by an icon that shows a red quill pen on the page. To hyperlink to open pages:

Figure 9.14.

Pages that are currently opened in the FrontPage Editor are represented by icons that show a red quill pen on the page. They appear above the list of folders in your Web.

1. Select the text, image, or hotspot on which you want the user to click to navigate to the page.
2. Select **E**dit I Hyperlin**k** (Ctrl+K) or click the Create or Edit Hyperlink button on the toolbar. The Create Hyperlink dialog box appears.
3. Double-click the filename of the open page that you want to link to. You create a hyperlink to the open page.

Hyperlinking to the World Wide Web

You can create hyperlinks to pages on the World Wide Web, including pages that exist in other Webs on your own personal Web server. You also can create hyperlinks to other Web protocols. Table 9.3 describes the protocols to which you can hyperlink.

Table 9.3. Web protocols.

Protocol	Description and Sample URL
file	Specifies a file on your local or network computer. Sample URL is `file://localhost/directory/filename.ext`.
ftp	File transfer protocol. Used for a file that is accessible across the Internet. Sample URL is `ftp://www.anyserver.com/downloads/program.zip`.
gopher	Gopher protocol. Creates a link to a directory-based protocol. Sample URL is `gopher://anygopher.tc.university.edu/2`.
http	Hypertext transfer protocol. Enables Web clients to retrieve information from Web hosts. Sample URL is `http://www.anyserver.com/mylink.htm`.
https	Hypertext transfer protocol with Secure Systems Layer (SSL) support. Enables Web clients to retrieve information from Web hosts using secure connections. Sample URL is `https://www.secureweb.com/mylink.htm`.
mailto	Creates a link to an e-mail address. Sample URL is `mailto:myemail@www.myprovider.com`.
news	Retrieves files from a Usenet newsgroup. Sample URL is `news.alt.example.nosuchgroup`.
telnet	Used for a remote telnet login session. Sample URL is `telnet://yourname:password@yourhost:port`.
wais	Provides hyperlinks to database information on Wide Area Information Servers. Sample URL is `wais://yourhost:port/database`.

NOTE: Your files might end up on a system that is case sensitive. This is typical of servers that run on UNIX systems. As a general rule, most Web developers use all lowercase letters when they enter URLs to avoid conflicts with case sensitivity.

When you create a hyperlink to a page, file, or protocol on the World Wide Web, you can enter its URL in the **U**RL field of the Create Hyperlink or Edit Hyperlink dialog box. You can also select the Use your Web Browser to select a page button, shown in Figure 9.15, to locate the page with your browser. The following steps describe the latter method.

Figure 9.15.

Select the Use your Web Browser to select a page button to locate a page to link to.

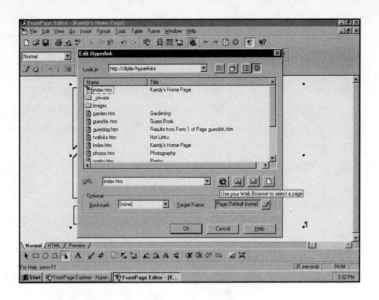

To link to a page that you locate with your browser, follow these steps:

1. Select the text, image, or hotspot on which you want the user to click to navigate to the page.

2. Select **E**dit I Hyperlin**k** (Ctrl+K) or click the Create or Edit Hyperlink button on the toolbar. The Create Hyperlink dialog box appears.

3. Enter the absolute URL (the full path) to the page or file that you want to link to in the **U**RL field, or choose the Use your Web Browser to select a page button that appears at the right of the **U**RL field. Your browser opens.

4. Use your browser to navigate to the page or file that you want to link to. When you reach the page, return to the FrontPage Editor. The full path to the page or file appears in the URL field of the Create Hyperlink dialog box.

5. To hyperlink to a bookmark on the page, select one of the existing book-marks from the **B**ookmark field. If there are no bookmarks on the page, the list will be empty.

6. Click OK to create the hyperlink.

Hyperlinking to Files on Your Local or Network Computer

If you are designing a Web site for a corporate intranet, you can easily create links to pages or files on a local or network computer. If your Web site resides on a server that is hosted by an Internet Service Provider, links to files on your local or network hard drive will result in a File Not Found message when a user tries to navigate to the page.

When you create a hyperlink to a page, file, or protocol on your local or network hard drive, you can enter its path in the **U**RL field or select the Make a hyperlink to a file on your computer button shown in Figure 9.16 to locate the page with your browser. The following steps describe the latter method.

Figure 9.16.

Select the Make a hyperlink to a file on your computer button to hyperlink to a page or file on your local or network hard drive.

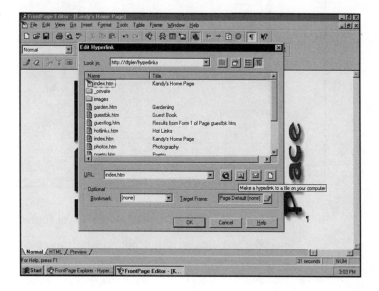

To link to a page or file on your local or network hard drive, follow these steps:

1. Select the text, image, or hotspot on which you want the user to click to navigate to the page.

2. Select **E**dit I Hyperlin**k** (Ctrl+K) or click the Create or Edit Hyperlink button on the toolbar. The Create Hyperlink dialog box appears.

3. Enter the full path to the page or file that you want to link to in the **U**RL field or choose the Make a hyperlink to a file on your computer button that appears at the right of the **U**RL field. The Select File dialog box appears.

4. Use the Look **i**n drop-down menu to locate the folder in which the page or file that you want to link to appears. Double-click the page or file to create the hyperlink. You return to the FrontPage Editor.

 # Sending Mail Through a Hyperlink

You can also use the Create Hyperlink dialog box to create a hyperlink to an e-mail address. When the user follows this link, he or she can compose an e-mail message and send it to the e-mail address designated by the hyperlink. You create a hyperlink to an e-mail address by choosing the Make a hyperlink that sends E-mail button shown in Figure 9.17.

Figure 9.17.

Select the Make a hyperlink that sends E-mail button to create a hyperlink to an e-mail address.

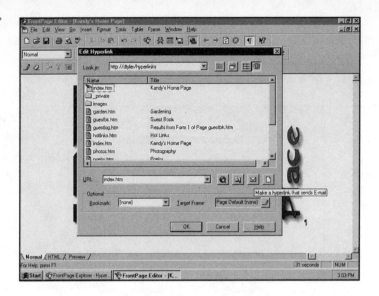

To create a hyperlink that sends e-mail to an e-mail address, follow these steps:

1. Select the text, image, or hotspot on which you want the user to click to navigate to the page.

2. Select **E**dit | Hyperlin**k** (Ctrl+K) or click the Create or Edit Hyperlink button on the toolbar. The Create Hyperlink dialog box appears.

3. Enter the full path to the E-mail address in the **U**RL field (for example, `mailto:bsmith@www.server.com`) or choose the Make a hyperlink that sends E-mail button that appears at the right of the **U**RL field. The Create E-mail Hyperlink dialog box appears.

4. In the Type an E-mail address field, enter the e-mail address that you want to link to, such as `bsmith@www.server.com`. Choose OK or press Enter to return to the Create Hyperlink dialog box.

5. Click OK to create the hyperlink and return to the FrontPage Editor.

Changing and Fixing Hyperlinks

You can use the FrontPage Editor to navigate to and from links on your pages. In addition, links can be changed, unlinked, and deleted very easily through the Edit Hyperlink dialog box. You'll also learn how to recalculate links when you make changes to them and how to add extended attributes to links.

Following Hyperlinks

The FrontPage Editor has built-in browsing capabilities that enable you to follow the hyperlinks in your Webs and the World Wide Web. Although not a high-powered browser, it enables you to test your hyperlinks as you design them.

To follow a bookmark, a text hyperlink, or an image hyperlink forward, use these steps:

1. From the FrontPage Editor, place the mouse pointer anywhere within the text or image hotspot that contains the hyperlink, or select any part of the hyperlink.

2. Select **G**o I Follow **H**yperlink or press Ctrl and click the left mouse button. If you follow a hyperlink to a bookmark, the FrontPage Editor scrolls to the bookmark. If you follow a hyperlink to another page, it opens in a new window in the FrontPage Editor.

3. After you follow a bookmark hyperlink, a text hyperlink, or an image hyperlink forward, choose Go I **B**ack or use the Back button in the FrontPage Editor Standard toolbar to return to the page from which you navigated. The originating page reopens at the location of the hyperlink that you followed.

Sometimes the server to which you are following a hyperlink is unresponsive. You can stop the process by clicking the Stop button on the FrontPage Editor Standard toolbar.

Changing, Unlinking, and Deleting Hyperlinks

It is a fact of life on the Web that sites have a tendency to evolve and change. Ten pages quickly become dozens. They are renamed, relocated, deleted, or divided into other pages.

To change the URL of a text hyperlink or an image hyperlink, do the following:

1. Select the hyperlink that you want to change. For a text hyperlink, place the mouse pointer anywhere within the text that contains the hyperlink or select any part of it. For an image hyperlink, select the image or the hotspot within the image that contains the hyperlink.

2. Use the **E**dit I Hyperlin**k** command or click the Create or Edit Hyperlink button in the FrontPage Editor toolbar. The Edit Hyperlink dialog box appears.

3. Edit the **U**RL in the URL field or choose the appropriate button (Use your Web Browser to select a page, Make a hyperlink to a file on your computer,

Make a hyperlink that sends E-mail, or Create a Page and link to the new page). Complete the hyperlink as outlined in the tasks in this chapter; then choose OK to exit the Edit Hyperlink dialog box.

To unlink a hyperlink, follow these steps:

1. Select the characters that you want to delete within the text hyperlink.
2. Choose **E**dit | **Un**link. The hyperlink is deleted from the text—or the part of the text—that you selected. The text associated with the hyperlink remains.

To delete a text hyperlink or an image hyperlink, use the following steps:

1. Select the hyperlink that you want to delete. For a text hyperlink, place the mouse pointer within the text associated with the hyperlink. For an image hyperlink, select the image or hotspot in the image that contains the hyperlink.
2. Select **E**dit | Hyperlin**k** or click the Create or Edit Hyperlink button on the toolbar. Then click Clear. Alternatively, you can press the Delete key.

Recalculating Hyperlinks

When multiple authors work on the same Web at the same time, you can easily lose track of who has done what. Likewise, when you create Webs with wizards or import pages into your Web, you sometimes see a red triangle beside the page when you are in the FrontPage Explorer's Outline view. This usually occurs when a page that contains a hyperlink is imported to a Web before the destination page is imported. Use the Recalculate Hyperlinks command to update the Web display in the FrontPage Explorer. In many cases, this command gets rid of those red triangles.

To update the Web display or to create the text index for the Search component, use the **T**ools | **R**ecalculate Hyperlinks command. The FrontPage Explorer refreshes the display of the Web.

Workshop Wrap-Up

You've learned quite a lot about creating and using hyperlinks with FrontPage. You are now set to tackle building your Web site from the ground up. Plan the areas that you want to include on your site, and the rest will happen over time. Rome was not built in a day; neither will your custom pages be. Sites constantly evolve and change as new standards are developed for the Internet. The more you become familiar with what is out there and what you can do, the more you can incorporate into your site.

In this chapter, you learned how to navigate through your pages and out to other areas of the Internet by using bookmarks and hyperlinks. You learned how to hyperlink pages with text, images, and image maps.

Next Steps

In the next chapter, you learn about the basic elements that make up a page—paragraphs, headings, and text styles. You learn when to use them and how to arrange content for the best appearance.

For additional information that relates to the topics discussed in this chapter, check out the following chapters:

❑ Chapter 15 shows you how to import images into your Web and onto your pages.

❑ Learn how to configure target frames with Chapter 18, "Frames: Pages with Split Personalities."

❑ See Chapter 34, "Testing and Publishing Your Webs," to learn how to verify hyperlinks and repair broken hyperlinks.

Q&A

Q: What is the difference between relative URLs and absolute URLs and why is it best to use relative URLs?

A: Absolute URLs list the complete path to a page or file. They contain the protocol, server, folder, and filename (for example, `http://www.microsoft.com/frontpage/default.htm` is the absolute URL to the FrontPage home page on Microsoft's Web site).

Relative URLs contain a partial URL as it relates to the page from which you are creating a hyperlink. FrontPage generates relative URLs for you automatically when you create hyperlinks to pages in your current Web. In addition, when you move pages to other folders in your current Web, FrontPage automatically corrects the relative URLs for you. Relative URLs are portable, meaning that the links in your Webs will still relate to each other if you copy or publish the same pages to another server. In contrast, when you use absolute or base URLs, you need to edit each URL to reflect the new location. This is a tedious and time-consuming task.

Q: Do all browsers support `mailto` hyperlinks?

A: No—if a browser does not support a `mailto` hyperlink, the user receives an error message.

Q: You haven't mentioned anything about the Target Frame field in the Create Hyperlink or Edit Hyperlink dialog box. What is that all about?

A: The Target Frame field applies when you want to link to a page that appears in a frameset. It tells your browser on which frame in the frameset to display the page that you are linking to. For more information about framesets, see Chapter 18.

TEN

Composing and Editing Pages

Now that you are thinking about what you want to put on your site, you probably want to start building your own pages. You should have a fairly good idea of the types of pages you want to put in your Web. Roll up your sleeves—it's time to start building those pages. This chapter starts with the basics: working with headings, paragraphs, and text styles.

In this chapter, you

- ❏ Learn about the basic content elements that are contained on a page
- ❏ Use headings to identify the contents on your page
- ❏ Learn about the basic types of paragraph styles and what they are used for
- ❏ Format text and paragraphs to add style without images

Tasks in this chapter:

- ❏ Creating a One-Page Web
- ❏ Entering Headings on a Page
- ❏ Using Normal, Formatted, and Address Paragraphs
- ❏ Using Fonts and Characters
- ❏ Inserting Comments
- ❏ Inserting and Formatting Horizontal Lines and Line Breaks
- ❏ Setting Page Properties
- ❏ Using the Clipboard as a Helper
- ❏ Cutting or Deleting Text
- ❏ Finding and Replacing Text
- ❏ Checking Spelling and Grammar

Creating a One-Page Web

As you read along, you should reproduce the examples in this chapter and the chapters that follow. To create a one-page Web, follow these steps:

1. From the FrontPage Explorer, choose **F**ile | **N**ew | FrontPage **W**eb. The New FrontPage Web dialog box appears.

2. In section 1, choose the **O**ne Page Web radio button.

3. In section 2, enter a name for your new Web in the Choose a **t**itle for your FrontPage web field. The path to your new Web displays beneath the field.

4. To optionally edit the Web's folder name, click the **C**hange button. The Change Location dialog box appears. Edit the path to your Web server if you want to create a Web on TCP/IP port 8080 or if you want to change the folder name for the Web. For additional instructions on these procedures, see Chapter 5, "Lightning-Speed Web Design." Choose OK or press Enter to return to the New FrontPage Web dialog box.

5. Choose OK from the New FrontPage Web dialog box to create your Web.

6. After the Web appears in the FrontPage Explorer, choose the Themes tab. For the time being, select **T**his Web Does Not Use Themes and click the **A**pply button. This creates pages that have a white background and default text and hyperlink colors.

> You learn more about using themes in Chapter 14, "Using FrontPage Style Sheets and Themes."

7. Now select the Folders icon from the FrontPage Explorer's Views list. From the home folder in your Web, double-click the home page (`index.htm` or `default.htm`) to open the page in the FrontPage Editor.

Entering Headings on a Page

Now you have a blank page in front of you, and you are wondering where to start. You can begin your page by entering headings first. Starting this way gives you a feel for the content that you want to include on a page. It is also easier to create bookmarks when there is not much text between headings—you have less to scroll through.

> Learn how to create bookmarks in Chapter 9, "Getting from Here to There."

You can add headings to your page in a number of different ways. One method is to apply the heading formatting to each heading as you enter it on the page. The following example shows how to do this.

Here is one way you can create the headings shown in Figure 10.1:

1. With the insertion point at the upper-left corner of the page, choose Heading 1 from the Change Style drop-down menu in the Format toolbar. (If the Format toolbar is not displayed, choose **V**iew | **F**ormat toolbar.)

2. Enter the following:

   `How to Build a Better Stuffed Potato`

3. Press Enter. By default, the next line is formatted as a normal paragraph. Choose Heading 2 from the Change Style drop-down menu and enter the following:

   `Picking Your Potato`

4. Press Enter and choose Heading 2 again. Enter the following:

   `Making the Gravy`

5. Press Enter and choose Heading 3. Enter the following:

   `From Scratch`

6. Press Enter and choose Heading 3. Enter the following:

   `From a Packaged Mix`

7. Press Enter and choose Heading 3. Enter the following:

   `From a Can (Hey, It's Quick and Easy)`

8. Press Enter and choose Heading 2. Enter the following:

   `Adding Spices`

9. Press Enter and choose Heading 2. Enter the following:

   `What to Top Your Potatoes With`

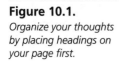

Figure 10.1.

Organize your thoughts by placing headings on your page first.

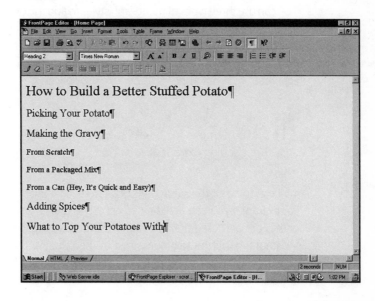

NOTE: When you position the insertion point at the end of a heading and press Enter, the next line is automatically formatted as a normal paragraph. When you position the insertion point at the beginning of a heading and press Enter, the heading moves down one line, and the space it formerly occupied is formatted with the same heading style.

Another way to create the headings on the page is to enter all items as normal text and then use the Change Style drop-down menu in the Format toolbar to reformat the headings appropriately. You can also reformat headings from the Paragraph Properties dialog box, which is discussed in the section "Setting Paragraph Properties," later in this chapter.

Using Paragraph Styles

Learn how to add lists to your pages in Chapter 11, "Organizing Information into Lists." Use tables to enhance your page layout, as discussed in Chapter 12, "Your Tables Are Ready."

In Chapter 6, "What To Do?" you learn how to add tasks to your To Do List in several different ways.

After you enter the headings, enter the content beneath each heading. Look at the section and decide what best conveys the information that you want to include. Sometimes, plain text is all that is necessary. Other times, a list or a table might be more effective in getting the message across. As you enter the content, you can create links to other pages in your Web. You can create new pages as you create the links and add them to your To Do list so you can work on them later.

You can use three types of paragraph styles to add the content to your pages—normal, formatted, and address. A paragraph is a line or a group of contiguous lines that use the same format and are separated in the FrontPage Editor with whitespace. Once you hit the Enter key at the end of a line, you start a new paragraph. The paragraph is separated by what appears to be an extra space.

TIP: You can use line breaks to start a new line in the same paragraph without adding extra space.

You use some of the same methods discussed earlier to add text content to a page. For example, you can use the Change Style drop-down menu in the Format toolbar or the Format I Paragraph command to choose your paragraph style. When you format a paragraph, all the text contained in the paragraph changes to that format. You cannot mix paragraph styles in a paragraph. You can, however, mix character styles in a paragraph; this is discussed later in this chapter.

Using Normal Paragraphs

Normal paragraphs are the meat-and-potatoes paragraphs of your Web page. You use them for most of your content. There are several ways that you can insert a normal paragraph on a page:

❏ Position the insertion point at the end of a heading or another normal paragraph and press Enter. The new line is automatically formatted as a normal paragraph.

❏ Position the cursor at the end of the last item in a list and press Enter twice or use Ctrl+Enter. The new line is formatted as a normal paragraph.

To enter a normal paragraph on your page, follow these steps:

1. Position the insertion point at the end of the first heading, which reads How to Build A Better Stuffed Potato, and press Enter. The new line is formatted as a normal paragraph.

2. Enter the following text. Your page will look as shown in Figure 10.2.

   Stuffed potatoes. Boy, I really like them a lot. And I've
   figured out some great ways to make them, too. If you follow
   the tips I've included on this page, you'll want to have
   stuffed potatoes for dinner every night. Sound boring? Not
   really, because you can top potatoes with just about anything
   you can think of.

Figure 10.2.

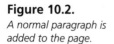

A normal paragraph is added to the page.

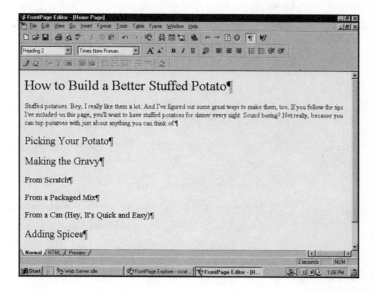

Adding Formatted Paragraphs

Use formatted paragraphs when you need to provide content in a fixed-width format. FrontPage 98 enables you to place tabs within formatted paragraphs, which makes creating formatted text like that shown in Figure 10.3 very easy. Formatted paragraphs are typically used for text-based tables, ASCII art, and code. Figure 10.3 shows three examples of formatted paragraphs. Line breaks split each paragraph into several lines.

Figure 10.3.
Use formatted paragraphs when you need to use fixed-width text with layout.

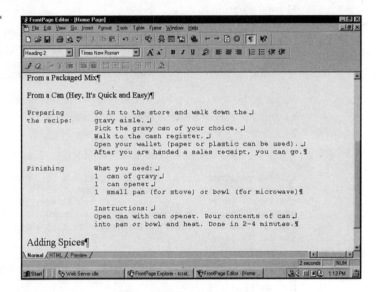

Enter the text shown in Figure 10.3 on your page by using the following steps:

1. Position the insertion point at the end of the heading that reads From a Can (Hey, It's Quick and Easy).

2. Press Enter. The insertion point moves to the beginning of the next line.

3. Choose Formatted from the Change Style drop-down menu on the Format toolbar.

4. Enter the following text:

   Preparing (press Tab key) Go in to the store and walk down the

5. Press Shift+Enter or choose Insert I Break and choose Normal Line Break from the Break Properties dialog box. The insertion point moves to the next line.

6. Enter the following text:

   the recipe: (press Tab key) gravy aisle.

7. Press Shift+Enter to insert another line break at the end of the second line.

8. Enter the remaining text shown in Figure 10.3, adding tabs and line breaks to complete the layout. Line breaks are shown in the figure as arrows at the end of the lines. Where a paragraph follows a line that does not end with a line break, it was created by pressing the Enter key.

Adding Address Paragraphs

An address paragraph formats text in italics. The traditional use for an address paragraph is to place author information at the beginning or the end of a page. Most commonly, this information is placed at the end of a page, as shown in Figure 10.4.

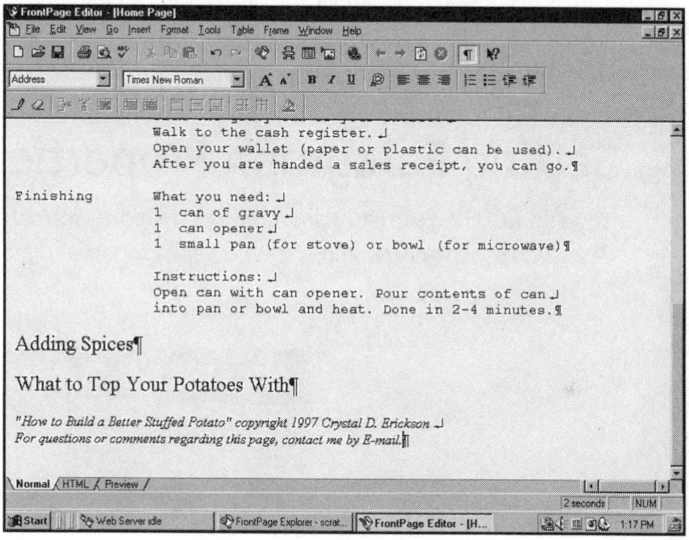

Figure 10.4.

Use address paragraphs to place author information or other italicized content on a page.

In Chapter 19, "Using FrontPage Components," you learn how to create a footer to place at the end of all the pages in your Web.

To insert an address paragraph on a page, use the following steps:

1. Position the cursor on the bottom line in the page, beneath the heading that reads What to Top Your Potatoes With.

2. Choose Address from the Change Style drop-down menu on the Format toolbar.

3. Enter this text:

   "How to Build a Better Stuffed Potato" copyright 1997

   followed by your name.

4. Press Shift+Enter or choose Insert I Break and select Normal Line Break from the Break Properties dialog box.

5. Enter the following:

   For questions or comments regarding this page, contact me by E-mail.

Reformatting Paragraphs

Once you have text or headings on your page, it's very easy to reformat it to another heading or paragraph style. You can reformat a paragraph or heading in a couple of ways.

You can change paragraphs among normal, address, and formatted styles; you can change from paragraphs to headings; or you can change among heading styles—and you can make these changes very easily. To change the formatting of a paragraph or heading, you need only follow these simple steps:

1. Click inside any part of the paragraph or heading that you want to change.
2. Choose the new style of heading or paragraph from the Change Style drop-down menu in the Format toolbar.

Setting Paragraph Properties

You can use the Format I Paragraph command to format a paragraph or heading. When you use this command, the Paragraph Properties dialog box appears (see Figure 10.5).

Figure 10.5.

The Paragraph Properties dialog box provides one way to format the paragraphs on a page.

To format a paragraph or heading from the Paragraph Properties dialog box, follow these steps:

1. Position the insertion point anywhere within the paragraph you want to change.
2. Choose Format I Paragraph. The Paragraph Properties dialog box appears.
3. To select the style of paragraph or heading, use the Paragraph Format list. The choices are Address, Formatted, Heading 1, Heading 2, Heading 3, Heading 4, Heading 5, Heading 6, and Normal.
4. To apply a different style to the paragraph, click the Style button.

Styles use tags that are associated with Cascading Style Sheets and are explained in more detail in Chapter 27, "Using Styles."

5. To specify the alignment of the paragraph or heading, click the Paragraph **A**lignment drop-down menu. The choices are Default, which does not override the paragraph alignment; left, which aligns the paragraph or heading with the left margin of the page or table cell; right, which aligns the paragraph or heading with the right side of the page or table cell; and center, which centers the paragraph or heading to the center of the page or table cell.

6. Click OK to return to the FrontPage Editor. Your selections are applied to the paragraph or heading.

TIP: Use the Align Left, Center, and Align Right buttons on the FrontPage Format toolbar to align paragraphs or headings quickly.

Formatting Your Text

Although FrontPage enables you to format the text in your pages into any font style you have on your system, there's something you should know. When you work with FrontPage, it's all too easy to forget that you aren't working with a word processor or page layout program. You're working with an advanced HTML editor, and a Web page is a slightly different animal. HTML code is basically data that specifies how a page should be displayed, and it's designed so that it's not specific to one computer platform.

When you choose a font in FrontPage, you're choosing a font that resides on your computer. The name of the font appears in the HTML code, but the actual font does not. The main reason things are designed this way is because the HTML language was written to work on many types of operating systems (Windows, Macintosh, UNIX, and so on). The browser that exists on a user's computer interprets the tags and displays the Web pages, using the tags and fonts that are compatible with the browser.

So, in order for the user to see the same font you use in your pages, the user must have a browser that supports the use of different font faces. Not only that, but the font face you used must also reside on the user's system. Now you see where the problem lies— if you use a Windows font for which there is no compatible Macintosh or UNIX version, your page will look quite different to users. They will see the default fonts that their browsers use (usually Times Roman for proportional font and Courier for fixed-width font).

How do you know which fonts are safe to use? As a general rule, it's safe to use the fonts in the following list (examples of the fonts are shown in Figure 10.6):

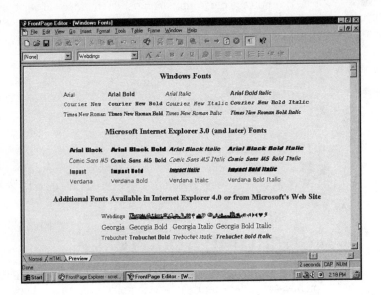

❏ Windows (Windows 3.1, Windows 95, and Windows NT) furnishes the following fonts: Arial (normal, bold, italic, and bold italic), Courier New (normal, bold, italic, and bold italic) and Times New Roman (normal, bold, italic, and bold italic).

❏ Microsoft Internet Explorer 3.0 (or later) is able to display additional fonts that are readily available to those who use this browser. They are Arial Black (normal, bold, italic, and bold italic), Comic Sans MS (normal, bold, italic, and bold italic), Impact (normal, bold, italic, and bold italic), and Verdana (normal, bold, italic, and bold italic).

NOTE: To view Webdings, Georgia, and Trebuchet fonts as they are rendered in your browser, select Preview view in the FrontPage Editor. They will not render correctly when you use the FrontPage Editor in Normal view.

❏ You can download additional fonts from Microsoft's site, some of which are available with Internet Explorer 4.0. Although Windows and Microsoft Internet Explorer come furnished with the previously mentioned fonts, the Web versions come with additional characters. In addition to all the fonts mentioned previously, users can download Webdings, Trebuchet (normal, bold, and italic), and Georgia (normal, bold, italic, and bold italic). These fonts are available in Windows 3.1, Windows 3.11, Windows 95, Windows NT, and Mac format in the section True Type Fonts for the Web. If you use any of these fonts, provide a link to the following Web pages so that the user can download and install them:

You can find the Windows versions of the fonts at

`http://www.microsoft.com/truetype/fontpack/win.htm`

You can find the Mac versions of the fonts at

`http://www.microsoft.com/truetype/fontpack/mac.htm`

After you download the TrueType fonts for the Web, you need to install them on your system. In order to install the new versions of the fonts, you have to delete the old versions. You add and delete fonts to your system from the Windows 95 Control Panel. From your Windows desktop, click My Computer. Then, choose Control Panel and click the Fonts folder. The Fonts dialog box shown in Figure 10.7 appears. To delete fonts, highlight the fonts you want to delete and choose **F**ile | **D**elete. To add new fonts, choose **F**ile | **I**nstall New Font and locate the directory that contains the fonts you want to install.

Figure 10.7.

You can install new fonts from the Fonts dialog box, accessed from the Windows 95 Control Panel.

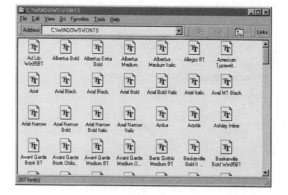

TASK   Using Fonts in the FrontPage Editor

In the FrontPage Editor, the Font dialog box is divided into two tabs. The Font tab enables you to choose a font face, size, and color. As you select your font options, a preview of the result is shown in the lower-right section of the dialog box.

Use the **Fo**rmat | **F**ont command to apply formatting to the text on a page. You can apply formatting to a single character, a word, a group of words, a sentence, a paragraph, or even the entire page. You can also set five traditional HTML character style tags from the Font dialog box, as shown in Table 10.1.

Table 10.1. Character styles in the Font tab of the Font dialog box.

Style	HTML Tag	Typical Use
Emphasis	`<em>`	Select Italic from the Font Style section. Renders text in italics.
Strong	`<strong>`	Select Bold from the Font Style section. Renders text in bold letters.
Underline	`<u>`	Underlines text.
Strikethrough	`<strike>`	Renders text with a line drawn through it. Often used in legal online documents.
Typewriter font	`<tt>`	Renders text in fixed-width format.

To format the fonts on your page, follow these steps:

1. Select the text you want to format. You can select a contiguous area (multiple lines) by using the Shift key and clicking at the start and the end of the area you want to format.

2. Choose Format | Font. The Font dialog box appears. It opens to the Font tab shown in Figure 10.8 by default.

Figure 10.8.

Choose the font you want to use in your pages with the Font tab in the Font dialog box.

You can select italic or bold text from the Format toolbar. Use the Bold button on the Format toolbar or Ctrl+B to apply the `<strong>` tag. Use the Italic button or Ctrl+I to apply the `<em>` tag.

3. Select a font from the Font section. All fonts on your system are shown in the list, but you should stick with those mentioned in the section "Formatting Your Text," earlier in this chapter.

4. From the Font Style section, choose Regular, Italic, Bold, or Bold Italic (not all fonts have all four options).

5. Select a font size from the Size list. The available sizes are Normal, 1 (8 point), 2 (10 point), 3 (12 point), 4 (14 point), 5 (18 point), 6 (24 point), and 7 (36 point). The default size is 3 (12 point).

Use the Increase Text Size or Decrease Text Size buttons on the toolbar to change the size of your text quickly. Each time you click the button, the size of the text increases or decreases by one increment.

Use the Underline button or Ctrl+U to apply the <u> tag.

Use the Text Color button on the Format toolbar to change the color of your text quickly.

6. Select any special effects that you want to apply, such as **U**nderline, Stri**k**ethrough, or **T**ypewriter text.

7. Select the **C**olor of the text from the drop-down menu. Choose Default to use the text color you specify in the Page Properties dialog box (Background tab). To specify a different text color, choose one of 16 predefined colors or select Custom to create a custom text color.

8. Click OK to exit the Font dialog box.

Setting Font Options

You can designate a default proportional and fixed-width font to use in the FrontPage Editor. If you would rather use Arial instead of Times Roman, for example, you can configure the FrontPage Editor to do so. You can also specify what character set you want to use for your pages. For example, if you need a character set that supports special characters for French or Spanish, you can configure FrontPage to do that as well.

NOTE: The font you select in the Font Options dialog box is the default font for the FrontPage Editor only. If you want to see the same font in Web browsers, you must format your page content accordingly. The easiest way to format an entire page to use a specific font is to choose **E**dit I Select All and select your font from the Font drop-down menu in the Format toolbar.

To set font options, follow these steps:

1. Choose **T**ools I **O**ptions. The Options dialog box shown in Figure 10.9 appears. Click the Default Font tab.

Figure 10.9.
You can choose another default proportional and fixed-width font using the Options dialog box.

2. By default, the character set for US/Western European is used. If you need a multilingual character set, choose Multilingual (UTF-8) from the **L**anguage (character set) list.

3. Select your default proportional font from the Default **P**roportional font drop-down menu. The default is Times New Roman.

4. Select your default fixed-width font from the **F**ixed-width font drop-down menu. The default is Courier New.

5. Choose OK to exit the Font Options dialog box.

Using Character Styles

If you don't want to take a chance on different font faces, you can also use several types of character styles that are built in to HTML code (see Table 10.2). These character styles are basically nothing more than variations on one proportional font (usually Times New Roman) and one fixed font (usually Courier New). You can format any text on your page to use a different color, alignment, or font size.

Table 10.2. Character styles in the Special Styles tab of the Font dialog box.

Style	HTML Tag	Typical Use
Citation	`<cite>`	Marks a citation from a book or other published source.
Definition	`<dfn>`	Marks a definition. Usually preceded by a term.
Sample	`<samp>`	Renders sample text or special characters.
Blink	`<blink>`	Causes selected text to blink on and off. Use it sparingly.
Code	`<code>`	Marks computer source code. Rendered as fixed-width text in FrontPage Editor, but is rendered as monospaced text in some browsers.
Variable	`<var>`	Marks a variable used in computer code, equations, or similar work. Usually rendered in italics.
Bold	`<b>`	Renders text as bold. You can also use the Bold button on the FrontPage Editor toolbar.

Style	HTML Tag	Typical Use
Italic	<b>	Renders text as italic. You can also use the Italic button on the FrontPage Editor toolbar.
Keyboard	<kbd>	Marks instructions that a user enters by keyboard. Rendered as fixed-width text in FrontPage Editor; rendered as monospaced text in some browsers.
Superscript	<sup>	Renders text above the normal text baseline by a specified amount.
Subscript	<sub>	Renders text below the normal text baseline by a specified amount.

To apply character styles to your text, follow these steps:

1. Select the text you want to format. You can select a contiguous area (multiple lines) by using the Shift key and clicking at the start and the end of the area you want to format.

2. Choose Format I Font. The Font dialog box appears.

3. Select the Special Styles tab, shown in Figure 10.10.

4. Choose the HTML tag that you want to apply to the selected text. Examples are shown in Figure 10.11.

Figure 10.10.
Choose special styles from the Special Styles tab in the Font dialog box.

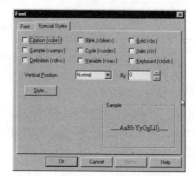

5. To create superscript or subscript text, set the Vertical Position of the text to a value other than Normal. To render superscript text, select Superscript and enter a value in the By field. To render Subscript, select Subscript and enter a negative value in the By field.

6. Click OK to exit the Font dialog box. Your selections are applied to the text.

Figure 10.11.

Examples of the special styles that you can use, as rendered in the FrontPage Editor.

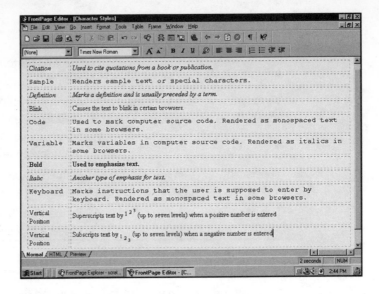

In the following task, you'll add some formatted text to your page so that it looks like the page shown in Figure 10.12. As you can see, you can use character formatting to achieve interesting effects without relying on graphics.

Figure 10.12.

Normal text can be reformatted in interesting ways when you combine different formats.

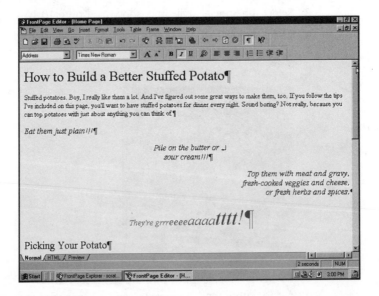

To add special characters and text formatting to your page, follow these steps:

1. Position the insertion point after the first normal paragraph and press Enter. A new paragraph starts.

2. Enter the first line of text:

    `Eat them just plain!!!`

3. Use the Italic button on the Format toolbar to format the text in italics. Increase the size of the text by pressing the Increase Text Size button once.

4. Deselect the text and position the insertion point at the end of the line. Press Enter to place the insertion point on the next line, which uses the same formatting. Center the line with the Center button on the Format toolbar.

5. Enter the following text, inserting a line break (using Shift+Enter or Insert I **B**reak, and choosing Normal Line Break) at the end of the first line:

    `Pile on the butter or`
    `sour cream!!!`

6. Press Enter. The insertion point moves to the next line. Align the text to the right of the page by using the Align Right button on the Format toolbar.

7. Enter the following text, inserting a line break (Shift+Enter) at the end of the first and second lines:

    `Top them with meat and gravy,`
    `fresh-cooked veggies and cheese,`
    `or fresh herbs and spices.`

8. Press Enter. The insertion point moves to the next line. Use the Center button on the Format toolbar to center the text.

9. Enter the following text:

    `They're grrreeeeaaaatttt!`

10. Highlight a portion of the word `grrreeeeaaaatttt` and use the Increase Text Size button to increase the size of the letters. Highlight other sections and increase the size by one level more than the previous selection.

11. Select the text that reads `They're grrreeeeaaaatttt!`.

12. Click the Text Color button on the Format toolbar. Choose red (the first color in the second row) and click OK. The text turns to red.

13. With the same text still selected, choose F**o**rmat I **F**ont. The Font dialog box appears. Click the Sp**e**cial Styles tab.

14. Select B**l**ink and choose OK. The text does not blink in the FrontPage Editor, but it will blink when you view the page in a browser that supports this feature.

15. Choose **F**ile I Preview in **B**rowser to preview the page in a browser that supports blinking text. You are prompted to save your page before the browser opens. Assign the page a title and a URL and choose OK. The page appears in your browser.

Removing Formatting

If you change the format of your text—such as increase or decrease the font size—you can return the text to the default format. Simply select the text and choose Format l **R**emove Formatting or press Ctrl+Space. The text returns to the default format for its paragraph style (normal text for normal paragraphs, italic text for address paragraphs, and preformatted text for formatted paragraphs).

Inserting Special Characters

FrontPage enables you to insert symbols in your pages without using ASCII codes. You can also add comments to your pages that appear in the FrontPage Editor but are not visible in other browsers.

Special characters are items such as trademark, registration, and copyright symbols; accent marks on text; special currency symbols; and common fractions. In the following example, you replace the word copyright with the copyright symbol.

To insert a special character, follow these steps:

1. Scroll to the bottom of the page where you added your copyright statement.
2. Position the insertion point at the beginning of the word copyright.
3. Choose **I**nsert l **S**ymbol. The Symbol dialog box shown in Figure 10.13 appears.

Figure 10.13.
Choose the symbol you want to use from the Symbol dialog box.

4. Select the copyright symbol from the fourth row or use the arrow keys to move through the available symbols.
5. Click **I**nsert. You can also insert a character by double-clicking it. The symbol appears on your page.
6. Click **C**lose to exit the Symbol dialog box.
7. Press the Delete key to remove the word copyright from your page.

Inserting Comments

You can apply comments to your pages to remind you of items that need to be changed or addressed. Comments display in the FrontPage Editor only. If you view the pages in another browser, they are undetectable. In other words, your pages appear as if the comments don't exist on the page.

To insert a comment on your page, follow these steps:

1. Position the insertion point at the end of the heading that reads From Scratch and press Enter. The insertion point moves to the next line.
2. Choose Insert | FrontPage Component. The Insert FrontPage Component dialog box appears. Double-click Comment to open the Comment dialog box shown in Figure 10.14.

Figure 10.14.

You can add comments that are not visible in other browsers with the Insert FrontPage Component dialog box.

3. In the Comment field, enter the following:

   Add the recipe for home-style turkey gravy here.

4. Choose OK. The comment appears on your page in purple text (or the text color you select for your visited link color).

5. To edit the comment, position the cursor over the comment text, where it becomes a pointer that looks like a robot. Double-click the comment text in your page. The Comment dialog box appears, and you can make your changes. Click OK to return to the FrontPage Editor.

   To replace the comment with normal text, click to select the Comment and begin typing.

Inserting a Horizontal Line

You use horizontal lines (traditionally known as horizontal rules) to distinguish the beginning or end of sections on your pages. For example, if you have a page that describes the main sections on your site, you use horizontal lines at the end of each section's description.

To insert a horizontal line into your page, follow these steps:

1. Position the insertion point on the line before which you want to insert the horizontal line. For this example, position the insertion point at the end of the last heading, which reads What to Top Your Potatoes With.

2. Choose Insert I Horizontal Line. A horizontal line appears on your page, using the default settings or the settings you last entered in the Horizontal Line Properties dialog box.

 ## Formatting a Horizontal Line

You can change the appearance of a horizontal line by using the Horizontal Line Properties dialog box. When you edit the appearance of a horizontal line, FrontPage remembers the settings until you close the FrontPage Editor. Any time you insert another horizontal line afterward, the previous settings are used.

To change the appearance of a horizontal line, use the following steps:

1. Double-click the horizontal line on your page or click the line and press Alt+Enter. The Horizontal Line Properties dialog box shown in Figure 10.15 appears.

Figure 10.15.

Specify settings for horizontal lines in the Horizontal Line Properties dialog box.

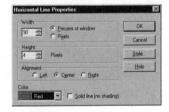

2. Choose any of the following options:

   ❏ *Percent of window.* Choose this option to specify a line that spans across a percentage of the screen. Enter the percent value in the Width field. For the example, enter 90 in the Width field to create a line that spans 90 percent of the screen.

   ❏ *Pixels.* Choose this option to specify a line that spans across a certain number of pixels. Enter the number of pixels in the Width field. If you choose this setting, be sure to keep in mind that some people use 640×480 resolution to browse the Web. Make sure your horizontal line isn't too wide.

   ❏ *Height.* Specify the height of the horizontal line in pixels. For the example, enter 4.

❏ *Alignment.* Choose an alignment for the horizontal line. Available choices are **L**eft, which aligns the line with the left edge of your page; **C**enter, which centers it; and **R**ight, which aligns it with the right side of your page. For the example, leave your line set at the default of **C**enter.

❏ *Solid line (no shading).* Choose this checkbox if you want to create a horizontal line that is the same color as your text.

3. Choose a color for your horizontal line from the Color drop-down menu. Choose Red for the horizontal line you placed on your page.

4. If you want to use a cascading style sheet or Web theme style with your horizontal rules, click the Style button. Styles are explained in more detail in Chapter 27.

5. Choose OK to return to the FrontPage Editor. The settings you choose are applied to the horizontal line and continue to be in effect until you change the settings or exit the FrontPage Editor.

 # Inserting Line Breaks

When you press the Enter key to start a new line on a page, it starts a new paragraph and inserts white space after the preceding paragraph. You can use line breaks to begin a new line without adding whitespace, as you have already learned in the examples for this chapter. You can also use line breaks to enhance the layout of images.

> # TIP:
> To view where the line breaks are on your page, click the Show/Hide button, which shows and hides paragraph marks. This button, which is on by default, has the paragraph mark on it; it is located just to the left of the Create or Edit Link button on the toolbar.

The most common type of line break is the normal line break, which is the default selection in the Break Properties dialog box. You insert a normal line break quickly by pressing Shift+Enter at the point where you want the line break to appear. You have already inserted normal line breaks in the tasks in this chapter. Three other types of line breaks are most commonly used in conjunction with image layout.

To insert a line break, follow these steps:

1. Position the insertion point where you want the line break to appear.

2. Choose **I**nsert | Line **B**reak. The Break Properties dialog box shown in Figure 10.16 appears.

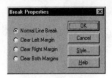

3. Choose one of the following types of line breaks from the dialog box:

   ❑ *Normal Line Break*. This forces a line break without clearing images in the left or right margin. This is the same as pressing Shift+Enter.

   ❑ *Clear Left Margin*. The next line of text moves to the next clear line after an image that appears in the left margin.

   ❑ *Clear Right Margin*. The next line of text moves to the next clear line after an image that appears in the right margin.

   ❑ *Clear Both Margins*. If an image is in either or both margins, the next line of text moves until both margins are clear.

4. Click the **S**tyle button if you want to add different styles to the line break. See Chapter 27 for more information.

5. Click OK. The line break appears on your page.

Setting Page Properties

The page you are creating in this chapter does not use a Web theme. Web themes, which are discussed in more detail in Chapter 14, work in conjunction with cascading style sheet commands to create an organized and consistent appearance in your Web. You can also add backgrounds and color schemes to pages that do not use Web themes. For this, use the Page Properties dialog box, which is discussed in the following tasks.

Keep in mind that some people use certain colors to represent link colors. The standards are blue for links, purple for visited links, and red for active links. You can choose to stay within these color guidelines, but there's nothing wrong with using colors that complement your background and text colors.

TIP: While I'm on the subject of color, here's another tip: Consider how stark contrasts in color can affect people's eyes. You might like how that red text looks on that lime green background, but other people might not like it. If color differences are too drastic, the colors vibrate and cause eyes to tire quickly. For this reason, try not to keep your colors pure. Rather than create a blue that's pure blue (an RGB value of 0,0,255), for example, use a value more like 0,0,204. Rather than use pure white (255,255,255), use a white that has a little bit of gray or other color undertone in it. The goal is to make your pages easy on the eyes.

Setting General Page Properties

You often see color formulas expressed in graphics software as *hue, saturation, and luminance values (HSV)* or as *red, green, and blue values (RGB).*

You use the General tab in the Page Properties dialog box to specify a title for your Web page. In addition, you can assign a base URL to the page, designate a default target frame, or assign a background sound to your page.

The **B**ase Location (or base URL), which is optional, is used to convert any relative URLs that appear on the page into absolute URLs. In this field, you enter the complete, or absolute, URL of the page, including the server name on which it resides. For example, enter the following:

`http://yourserver.com/current-page.htm`

Learn more about default target frames in Chapter 18, "Frames: Pages with Split Personalities."

To complete the options in the General tab of the Page Properties dialog box, use the following steps:

1. With your page open in the FrontPage Editor, choose **F**ile | Page Properties. The Page Properties dialog box appears opened to the General tab, as shown in Figure 10.17.

Figure 10.17.

Use the General tab in the Page Properties dialog box to assign a page title, base location URL, default target frame, or background sound.

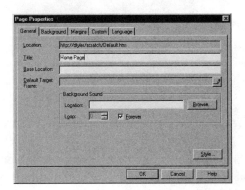

2. To change the title of your page, enter the new title in the **T**itle field.

3. To specify a base location for your page, enter the URL in the **B**ase Location field.

4. To specify the default target frame for a frameset, enter the frame name in the Default Target **F**rame field.

5. To attach a background sound to the page, see Chapter 15, "Working with Images and Sound."

6. To add cascading style sheet properties to the page, click the **S**tyle button. This is covered in more detail in Chapter 27.

7. Click OK to exit the Page Properties dialog box, or click another tab to set more page properties.

Setting Background Properties

You use the Background tab in the Page Properties dialog box to specify the background and text colors that you want to use in your page. Background images can be selected from the current FrontPage Web, from a file on your local or network hard drive, from a page or file on the World Wide Web, or from the FrontPage clip art folder. If you want to use something other than the default background, text, and link colors, you can choose one of 16 predefined colors or create your own.

To specify the background properties for your page, follow these steps:

1. From the Properties dialog box, click the Background tab, shown in Figure 10.18.

Figure 10.18.

Use the Background tab in the Page Properties dialog box to choose your background images and colors and your text and link colors.

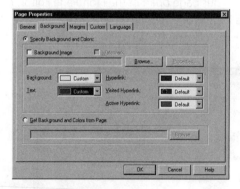

2. The **S**pecify Background and Colors radio button is selected by default. If you want your pages to use the settings from another page, select the **G**et Background and Colors from Page radio button.

You'll create a page that uses custom colors in Chapter 14. You'll also learn how to use this custom page as a style sheet for a Web that does not use themes.

3. The page you are creating now will use a solid background color. If you want to add a background image to a Web page, check the Background **I**mage checkbox. Click the **B**rowse button to locate a background image. The Select Background Image dialog box appears. The steps to selecting an image are discussed in more detail in Chapter 15.

4. To make a background image stationary so that it does not scroll, check the **W**atermark checkbox in the Page Properties dialog box.

5. Now you will change the background color to light yellow. To do this, choose Custom from the Ba**c**kground drop-down menu. In the Color dialog box, enter the following numbers: **R**ed **255**; **G**reen **255**; **B**lue **204**. Choose OK to return to the Page Properties dialog box.

6. Choose Custom from the **T**ext drop-down menu. The Color dialog box appears. Select brown (the first color in the third row of **B**asic colors.) Choose OK to return to the Page Properties dialog box.

7. For this example, leave the **H**yperlink, **V**isited Hyperlink, and **A**ctive Hyperlink colors set to Default. You are able to change them using procedures similar to those outlined in steps 5 and 6.

8. Click OK to exit the Page Properties dialog box, or select another tab to set more page properties.

You can also choose Default from the Background drop-down menu to use the default WWW gray background or choose one of 16 predefined colors for a background color.

Setting Page Margins

By default, the top margin is located at 16 pixels, and the left margin is located at 12 pixels. Sometimes you want to change this. For example, if you create navigation buttons that are located in a narrow frame within a frame set, you probably don't want much wasted space. In that case, you can set the top and left margins at 0, which places the graphics at the extreme upper-left corner of the page. In other cases, where you want to create more whitespace on a page, you can increase the values of the top and left margin settings. These settings are adjusted by using the Margins tab in the Page Properties dialog box, which is shown in Figure 10.19.

Figure 10.19.
Use the Margins tab to adjust the top and left margins of the page.

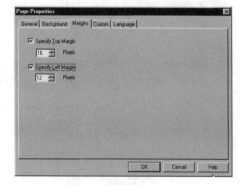

To specify the page margins, follow these steps:

1. To specify a top margin, check the Specify **T**op Margin checkbox. Enter the top coordinate in the Pixels field. The default value is 16 pixels.

2. To specify a left margin, check the Specify **L**eft Margin checkbox. Enter the left coordinate in the Pixels field. The default value is 12 pixels.

3. Choose OK to return to the Page Properties dialog box, or select another tab to set more page properties.

Setting Custom Page Properties

You use the Custom tab, shown in Figure 10.20, to enter system and user meta variables to your pages. Meta variables describe information about the document.

Figure 10.20.

Use the Custom tab to assign system and user meta variables to your page.

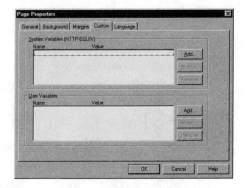

There are two attributes for the META tag. System variables use the HTTP-EQUIV tag and generate special headers that are sent by the server to activate features in the client. You can use this tag to tell when a document expires or how often a document should reload when using client pull to animate a document. *Client pull* uses multiple passes between browser and server to reload several pages in sequence. It gives the appearance that a document is animated, but it can be somewhat slow. User variables use the NAME attribute. You can use these variables to designate the author of a page or search key terms for Web spiders and robots.

For more information about the META tag, refer to the Meta-Meta Page at the Web Developer's Virtual Library. You can find it at the following URL:

```
http://www.stars.com/Location/Meta/
```

To set Custom page properties, follow these steps:

1. To add system variables to your page (HTTP-EQUIV tag), use the **S**ystem Variables (HTTP-EQUIV) section.

    To add a system variable, click the **A**dd button. The System Meta Variable (HTTP-EQUIV) dialog box appears. Add the meta variable name in the **N**ame field and its value (if applicable) in the **V**alue field. Click OK to return to the Page Properties dialog box.

NOTE: If you want to edit or remove a system or user variable, highlight the variable you want to change or delete. Click **M**odify to change an existing meta variable or **R**emove to delete an existing meta variable from the list.

2. To specify user variables, use the **U**ser Variables section.

   To add a user variable, click the **A**dd button. The User Meta Variable dialog box appears. Add the user meta variable name in the **N**ame field and its value (if applicable) in the **V**alue field. Click OK to return to the Page Properties dialog box.

3. Click OK to exit the Page Properties dialog box, or select another tab to specify more page properties.

Setting Language Properties

When you create a page in a specific language, you select the type of HTML character encoding used to generate the text on the pages. The encoding type you select uses a table of numbers that equates with characters in a character set. You can specify a different type of encoding for saving and loading your pages.

You specify language properties using the Language tab in the Page Properties dialog box, which is shown in Figure 10.21.

Figure 10.21.

Use the Language tab to select what language you want to use for the HTML encoding on your page.

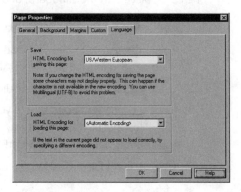

To set the language properties from the Language tab, follow these steps:

1. From the Save drop-down menu, select the language encoding that you want to use when you save the Web page. The default selection is US/ Western European. Choose <none> if you want to remove the `charset` meta tag from your Web page. The page will use the current character set when you save the page in this case. Choose Multilingual (UTF-8) if some of the

characters on your page do not display properly due to characters not being available in the new encoding.

2. From the Load drop-down menu, select the language encoding that you want to use when you load the Web page. The default selection is <Automatic Encoding>. Choose Multilingual (UTF-8) or US/Western European if the page does not appear to load correctly.

Undoing Mistakes

FrontPage has a multiple-level Undo function. This means that you can undo several steps. When you choose the Undo command from the Edit menu, it lists the command or action that it will undo when you use the command.

To undo an action, choose **E**dit | **U**ndo (Ctrl+Z) or click the Undo button in the Standard toolbar for each step that you want to undo. Choose **E**dit | **R**edo (Ctrl+Y) or click the Redo button in the Standard toolbar for each undo that you want to place back on your page.

Using the Clipboard as a Helper

If the hot list or other page you create is so long that you have to scroll to read all of it, you might want to split it into several pages. To do this, you can cut the text from one page, place it in the clipboard, and paste it into another page.

To copy and paste text and images to and from the clipboard, follow these steps:

1. Select the text or image you want to copy. To select all the content on your Web page, choose **E**dit | Select A**l**l (Ctrl+A).

2. Choose **E**dit | **C**opy (Ctrl+C) or click the Copy button on the toolbar.

3. Place the insertion point where you want to paste the text or image. You can place the insertion point anywhere on the current page or on another page that is opened in the FrontPage Editor.

4. Choose **E**dit | **P**aste (Ctrl+V) or click the Paste button on the toolbar.

TIP: You can also use the **E**dit | Paste **S**pecial command to specify how you want to paste text into your Web page. When you choose this command, the Convert Text dialog box enables you to paste the selected text as **O**ne formatted paragraph, multiple **F**ormatted paragraphs, **N**ormal paragraphs, or Normal paragraphs with line **b**reaks.

Cutting or Deleting Text

You have two ways to delete text. One method places the text into the clipboard for pasting into another location. The other method deletes the text from the page without placing it into the clipboard.

To delete text from a page and place it into the clipboard, use the **E**dit I Cu**t** command or click the Cut button. To delete text from a page without placing it into the clipboard, choose **E**dit I Cle**a**r or press the Delete key.

You can also delete the character before the insertion point by pressing the Backspace key for each character you want to delete. To delete text after the insertion point, press the Delete key for each character you want to delete.

 ## Finding and Replacing Text

Suppose that you want to edit the recipe in Figure 10.22 to make stuffed tomatoes instead of stuffed potatoes. You can quickly find every instance of potato, potatoes, or potatos. To find text, do the following:

1. Choose **E**dit I **F**ind (Ctrl+F). The Find dialog box shown in Figure 10.22 appears.

Figure 10.22.
Use the Find dialog box to find a word or phrase in your page.

2. In the Fi**n**d What field, enter the word or phrase that you want to find.
3. From the Direction section of the dialog box, choose whether you want to search **U**p or **D**own from the current insertion point.
4. Choose Match **w**hole word only to limit the text to words that match only the whole word you specify. Choose Match **c**ase to limit the text to words that match the capitalization of the word you specify.
5. To find the next match, click **F**ind Next.
6. Click Cancel to exit the Find dialog box.

You realize that what you said about petunias actually applies to daffodils. Instead of retyping everything, you can use the Replace command. To replace text, do the following:

1. Choose **E**dit I R**e**place (Ctrl+H). The Replace dialog box shown in Figure 10.23 appears.

Figure 10.23.
Use the Replace dialog box to find and replace a word or phrase on your page with another word or phrase.

2. In the Find what field, specify the text that you want to replace.

3. In the Replace with field, specify the text you want to use to replace the text you are searching for.

4. Click **R**eplace to replace the most recently found text with the replacement text. Click **F**ind Next to find the next occurrence. This enables you to choose which instances of the text you want to change. Click Replace **A**ll to replace all instances of the text.

5. Click Cancel to exit the Replace dialog box.

 ## Spell-Checking a Page

It is always a good idea to spell-check your pages before they go out to the public. FrontPage has a built-in spell-checker at your disposal. The spell-checker starts at the beginning of the page and checks the spelling of each word. When a spelling error is found, it is displayed in the Not in Dictionary field in the Spelling dialog box. If the spelling resembles a word in the standard dictionary, replacement words are suggested. To use the spell-checker, use the following steps:

You can also do an across-the-web spell check. See Chapter 34, "Testing and Publishing Your Webs," for further information.

1. Choose **T**ools | **S**pelling (F7) or click the Check Spelling button.

2. To correct a spelling error, click one of the proposed corrections in the Suggestions field or edit the Change To field. Click Change to change a single instance of the spelling error. Click Change All to change all instances of the spelling error. The error or errors are corrected, and the next spelling error is displayed.

3. The spell-checker might indicate that a word is misspelled when actually it is spelled correctly. This might be because the word it found does not exist in the dictionary. If you do not want to place the word in your custom dictionary, you can tell the spell-checker to ignore it. Click Ignore to ignore a single instance of the word. Click Ignore All to ignore all instances of the word. You might want to place words that are used on other pages in your custom dictionary. Simply click the Add to Custom Dictionary button.

4. Choose Cancel to exit the Spelling dialog box.

Using the Thesaurus

The thesaurus enables you to search for other words that have the same meaning as words on your page. You can use the thesaurus to find a word that means the same as a word you select or that means the opposite.

To use the thesaurus, follow these steps:

1. Highlight the word for which you want to find an alternative.
2. Choose **T**ools I **T**hesaurus or press Shift+F7. The Thesaurus dialog box appears.
3. Select a replacement word from the dialog box.
4. Choose OK or press Enter to exit the dialog box.

Workshop Wrap-Up

Once you have an idea of the information you want to include on your Web, entering content into your pages is very simple. Starting with basic headings helps you organize your thoughts. You can use character styles and formatting to add your content. Using different character styles, you can add emphasis to areas on your Web page. After the content is complete, you can use the FrontPage spell-checker to verify that your content is spelled correctly.

Your text can be more than simple text. You can use color, change the alignment, increase or decrease the font size, select different formats, and even insert special characters.

Next Steps

As you'll quickly learn, Web pages can be far more than text and headings. You'll learn some additional techniques in the following chapters:

❏ To use lists to organize your page content, see Chapter 11, "Organizing Information into Lists."

❏ Chapter 12, "Your Tables Are Ready," tells you how to organize text and images in tables.

❏ In Chapter 13, "Real-Life Examples II: Keeping It Plain and Simple," you learn how to create basic Web pages that combine Web navigation, hyperlinks, lists, and tables, and that use consistent Web colors throughout the Web.

Q&A

Q: Why do the headings get smaller as the numbers get larger, and the character styles get larger as the numbers get larger?

A: The reason the headings get smaller as their numbers get larger is that they correspond to hierarchical logic. Typically, your page title is displayed in Heading 1, topics beneath it in Heading 2, topics beneath them in Heading 3, and so on. Text styles increase in size as their designations increase because it is most logical. A small number indicates a small font size; a large number indicates a large font size.

Q: Are there any rules regarding what font size to use following a heading?

A: Not really, except that you might want to use a heading that is at least the same size or larger than the text beneath it. Normal paragraphs use a default font size of 3 (12 point), which means that Headings 1 through 4 look all right with it. If you use smaller headings, such as Heading 5 or Heading 6, you might want to decrease the font size.

Q: Can I change the default size of the font in the FrontPage Editor?

A: Although you can change the default fonts you use, you cannot set the default font size. You must set the font size or use the Increase Font Size or Decrease Font Size buttons on the toolbar to change the size of your text.

ELEVEN

Organizing Information into Lists

Do you have links to sites that you want to point people to? Have you written a great paper that shows people how to build, install, or complete something? Lists are among the best ways to organize information. They help information stand out clearly. You can use several types of lists in your pages, and this chapter shows you how to construct each of them.

Working with Numbered Lists

Numbered lists are used to place items in a definite order. They are good for describing steps or procedures. In its most basic form, the FrontPage Editor begins a numbered list with the number 1 and numbers the remaining items in the list for you automatically. If you want to change the appearance of the numbered list by adding large or small Roman numerals, large letters, or small letters, you can do that as well, but browsers handle these other attributes differently. Preview your pages in different browsers to view the differences.

Creating a Numbered List

Top Ten lists are popular on the Web. Obviously, many people like to use numbered lists. I have my own Top Ten list, shown in Figure 11.1. You can create this list yourself by following a few easy steps.

Figure 11.1.

Use numbered lists when you need to arrange items in a specific order.

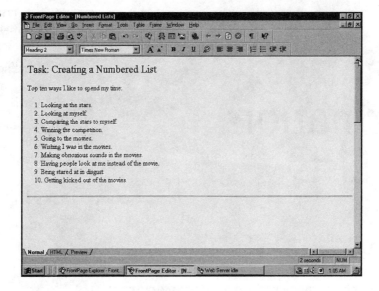

Numbered lists are usually rendered as paragraphs separated by whitespace and prefixed by numbers.

To create a numbered list, do the following:

1. Position the insertion point on a new line. Choose Normal from the Change Style drop-down menu in the Format toolbar. Enter the following text:

    `Top ten ways I like to spend my time:`

2. Press Enter. The insertion point moves to the beginning of the next line.

3. Choose Numbered List from the Change Style drop-down menu in the Format toolbar or click the Numbered List button on the Format toolbar. FrontPage enters the first number for you automatically.

4. Enter the first item in the list (you can replace these examples with your own list items if you prefer):

    `Looking at the stars.`

5. Press Enter at the end of each line and add the additional list items:

```
Looking at myself.
Comparing the stars to myself.
Winning the competition.
Going to the movies.
Wishing I was in the movies.
Making obnoxious sounds in the movies.
Having people look at me instead of the movie.
Being stared at in disgust.
Getting kicked out of the movies.
```

6. At the end of the last item, press Enter twice or use Ctrl+Enter to complete the list.

7. Choose Insert | Horizontal Line to end the section.

Creating a Nested Numbered List

By default, FrontPage starts numbered lists with the number 1 and adds all the list items at the same level. Sometimes you need to create nested lists—that is, multilevel lists—to arrange content. You can use the Increase Indent and Decrease Indent buttons to create a nested list.

To modify the list you created in the last task, "Creating a Numbered List," follow these steps:

1. Position the insertion point at the end of the list item that reads `Looking at the stars.` and press Enter. The insertion point moves to the next line and starts a new list item.

2. Press the Increase Indent button on the Format toolbar twice. The insertion point indents, moves to the next line, and starts a new number sequence.

3. Enter two more list items, pressing Enter at the end of the first and second lines. Your list will look as shown in Figure 11.2 when you are finished:

```
My favorite constellations.
The best time to go out.
Great ways to see stars.
```

4. Position the insertion point at the end of the line that reads `My favorite constellations.` Press Enter to begin a new list item.

5. Press the Increase Indent button on the Format toolbar twice. The list indents to a new level.

6. Enter the following three list items. When you reach the end of the last item, your list should look like Figure 11.3.

```
The Big Dipper
Orion
The Pleiades
```

Figure 11.2.
You create a nested numbered list using the Increase Indent and Decrease Indent buttons on the Format toolbar.

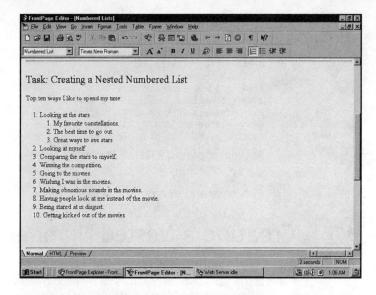

Figure 11.3.
A third level is added to the numbered list.

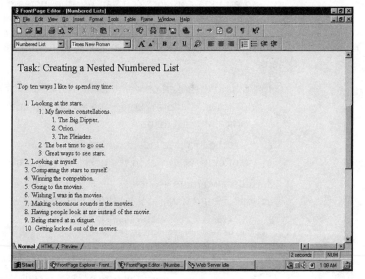

Changing the Numbered List Type

Look at the numbered list in Figure 11.3. A multilevel list is sometimes arranged with numbers and letters to designate the levels, as in an outline. How can you do that?

In FrontPage, the default is to use numbers in a numbered list, but you can assign other attributes to them. For example, you can specify large letters, small letters, large Roman numerals, or small Roman numerals in a numbered list. To do this, you use the Format I Bullets and Numbering command.

To change the numbered list type, use the following steps:

1. Position the insertion point anywhere within the `Looking at the stars.` list item.

2. Choose Format I Bullets and Numbering. The List Properties dialog box appears. Click the Numbers tab, shown in Figure 11.4.

3. Select the Large Roman Numerals list type (third type in the first row, labeled I, II, III) and choose OK. All list items in the first level change to large Roman numerals.

Figure 11.4.

Use the List Properties dialog box to select the type of numbered list you are creating.

You can also open the List Properties dialog box by positioning the insertion point at the beginning of a list item. To change the list properties of all list items in a single-level list, or of one level in a nested list, right-click and choose List Properties from the pop-up menu. To change the list properties of one item in a list, right-click and choose List Item Properties from the pop-up menu.

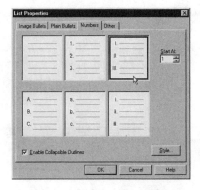

4. Position the insertion point at the beginning of the list item that reads `My favorite constellations.`

5. Choose Format I Bullets and Numbering. The List Properties dialog box appears and defaults to the Numbers tab.

6. Select the Large Letters list type (first type in the second row, labeled A, B, C) and choose OK. All list items in the second level change to large letters. Your list should look as shown in Figure 11.5.

Figure 11.5.
The numbered list now contains three different number types.

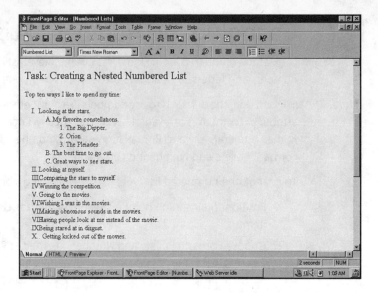

TASK Changing the Starting Number

You might want to begin a numbered list with a different number. For example, if you're writing instructions on how to complete a process, you enter a few steps in a numbered list. Then, you use a graphic to illustrate a point before you continue with the instructions. You want the list that follows the table to pick up where the preceding numbered list left off. Figure 11.6 shows what the list looks like before you change the number.

Figure 11.6.
By default, all numbered lists begin with the number 1.

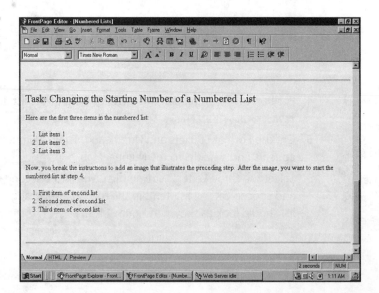

To change the starting number of a numbered list, follow these steps:

1. Position the insertion point anywhere within the list item that you want to change.

2. Choose Format I Bullets and Numbering or right-click and choose List Properties from the pop-up menu. The List Properties dialog box appears, opened to the Numbers tab.

3. In the Start At field of the Numbers tab, enter the new starting number for the list. In the example shown, you enter the number 4.

4. Choose OK. The starting number of the list changes, as shown in Figure 11.7.

Figure 11.7.

You change the starting number of the list in the Numbered tab of the List Properties dialog box.

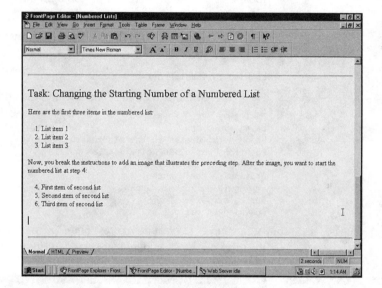

Working with Bulleted Lists

You use bulleted lists when you do not need to list items in a specific order. Many people use bulleted lists to display links to their favorite sites, and there are many other applications for them as well. Bulleted lists are usually rendered as paragraphs separated by whitespace and prefixed by filled or unfilled circles or squares. Different browsers display the bullets differently. For example, some browsers render bullets exactly the way you see them in FrontPage. Others render all bullets as solid circles, regardless of the bullet type you specify. Others render level 1 bullets as shaded circles, level 2 bullets as shaded diamonds, and level 3 bullets as shaded squares, regardless of the bullet you specify. WYSIWYG is WYSIWYG only to a point when it comes to bulleted lists.

Creating a Bulleted List

Bulleted lists are created using similar procedures as those mentioned for numbered lists. You use the same list items from the previous tasks in the following example.

To create a bulleted list, use the following steps:

1. Position the insertion point on a new line. Enter the following text:

   ```
   Ways I like to waste my time:
   ```

2. Press Enter. The insertion point moves to the beginning of the next line.

3. Choose Bulleted List from the Change Style drop-down menu in the Format toolbar or use the Bulleted List button on the Format toolbar. FrontPage enters the bullet for you automatically.

4. Enter the first item in the list (you can replace these examples with your own list items if you prefer):

   ```
   Looking in the mirror.
   ```

5. Press Enter at the end of each line and add the additional list items:

   ```
   Poking my eye.
   Using eye drops.
   Using metal dishes in the microwave.
   Painting Australian animals on my wall.
   Reading comic books.
   Writing on comic books.
   Trying to sell comic books.
   Eating my hair.
   Coughing up hairballs.
   ```

6. At the end of the last item, press Enter twice or use Ctrl+Enter to complete the list. Your list should look as shown in Figure 11.8.

Figure 11.8.
Use bulleted lists to present a list of items that don't need to be arranged in a specific order.

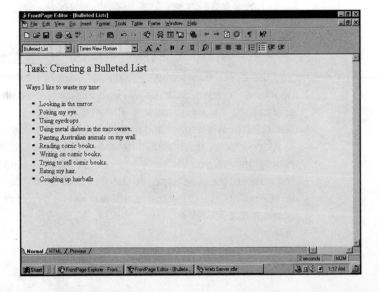

Creating a Nested Bulleted List

You create nested bulleted lists using the same basic procedures as those for a nested numbered list. When you create nested bulleted lists, each level in the list is represented by a different bullet type:

1. Position the insertion point at the end of the list item that reads `Looking in the mirror.` and press Enter. The insertion point moves to the next line and starts a new list item.

2. Click the Increase Indent button on the Format toolbar twice. The insertion point indents, moves to the next line, and changes the bullet to an unfilled circle.

3. Enter two more list items, pressing Enter at the end of each line:

   `My favorite features`
   `The best time to look in the mirror`

4. Add the last item in the list:

   `Great ways to see myself`

5. Position the insertion point at the end of the line that reads `My favorite features`. Press Enter to begin a new list item.

6. Click the Increase Indent button on the Format toolbar twice. The list indents to a new level, and the bullet changes to a square.

7. Enter the following three list items. When you reach the end of the last item, your list should look as shown in Figure 11.9:

   `Eyes`
   `Nose`
   `Pores`

Figure 11.9.

The bulleted list now contains three levels.

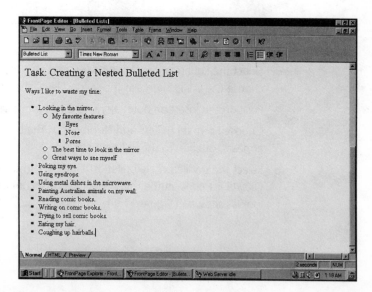

Changing the Bulleted List Type

When you create nested bulleted lists, each level automatically receives a different bulleted type. If you want to change the bullets in the list, you can select one of two types of bullets—plain bullets or image bullets.

Using Plain Bullets

Plain bullets (solid circles, unfilled circles, and squares) are used by default when you create a bulleted list. You can select a different type of plain bullet, but keep in mind that browsers render bullet types differently.

To change the bulleted list type, follow these steps:

1. Position the insertion point anywhere within the list item that reads My favorite features.

2. Choose Format I Bullets and Numbering. The List Properties dialog box appears, opened to the Plain Bullets tab shown in Figure 11.10.

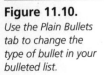

Figure 11.10.
Use the Plain Bullets tab to change the type of bullet in your bulleted list.

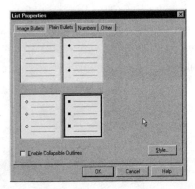

3. Select the square bullets list type (second type in the second row) and choose OK. All list items in the second level change to square bullets.

4. Position the insertion point anywhere within the list item that reads Eyes.

5. Choose Format I Bullets and Numbering. The List Properties dialog box appears, opened to the Bulleted tab.

6. Select the unfilled circle bullet list type (first in the second row) and choose OK. All list items in the third level change to unfilled circles. Your list should look as shown in Figure 11.11.

Figure 11.11.

Now, the bulleted list uses bullet types that you specify.

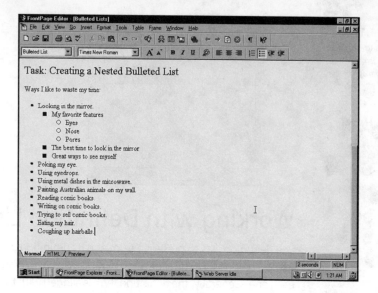

TASK Using Image Bullets

Plain bullets can be boring, and fortunately FrontPage 98 offers an easy way to add images for bullets. Image bullets add more color and interest to your page, and you can also use a tasteful animated GIF to highlight the top levels of each bulleted list.

To use image bullets, follow these steps:

1. Position the insertion point anywhere within the list item that reads Looking in the mirror.

2. Choose Format I Bullets and Numbering. The List Properties dialog box appears. Click the Image Bullets tab, shown in Figure 11.12.

3. Select the type of image you want to use as follows:

   ❏ To use the bullet images from your current theme, select the Use images from current theme radio button. Choose OK. The page updates with the bullets used in the theme. For more information on themes, see Chapter 14, "Using FrontPage Style Sheets and Themes." Because you are not using themes in this page, select the next option.

   ❏ If you are not using themes in your Web but you want to use images for bullets, select the Specify image radio button. Click the **B**rowse button to open the Select Image dialog box. Choose an image from your current Web, from the World Wide Web, or from your Clip Art folder, and choose OK to insert the image on your Web page. For more information on inserting images into your pages, see Chapter 15, "Working with Images and Sound."

Figure 11.12.
Use the Image Bullets tab to use images for the bullets in your lists.

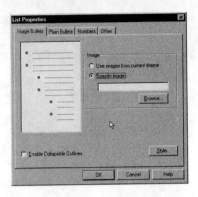

Working with Definition Lists

Use definition lists to present a term and its definition, such as in a glossary. You also use definition lists to provide a list of items when you want to include a description for each one. Generally, the definition term is aligned with the left margin of the page and its definition is indented.

Most browsers display definition lists in the same way. The amount of indentation of the definition may vary slightly.

Using a Definition List

It is very easy to create a definition list in FrontPage. You format the first list item as a defined term. Pressing the Enter key formats the next item as a definition. Pressing the Enter key again starts a new term, followed by a new definition, and so on.

To create a definition list, follow these steps:

1. Position the insertion point on your page and enter the following text:

   `The different types of lists you can use in your pages are:`

2. Press Enter. The insertion point moves to the next line.

3. Choose Defined Term from the Change Style drop-down menu in the Format toolbar. Enter the following term:

   `Numbered Lists`

4. Press Enter to add the definition. The insertion point moves to the next line. The Change Style drop-down menu shows the line formatted Definition. Enter the following text:

   `Used when the list must be arranged in a definite order.`

5. Press Enter to add the next defined term:

   `Bulleted Lists`

6. Press Enter again to add the next definition:

    `Used when the list does not have to be arranged in a definite order.`

7. Continue to add the remaining list items, pressing Enter at the end of each line:

    Term: `Definition List`

    Definition: `Used to display a list of terms and their`
                  `definitions.`

    Term: `Directory List`

    Definition: `Used to list the contents of a directory. Primarily`
                  `used by programmers and not widely supported by`
                  `browsers.`

    Term: `Menu List`

    Definition: `Used to list the contents of a menu or short items`
                  `(20 characters or less). Primarily used by program-`
                  `mers and not widely supported by browsers.`

8. At the end of the last list item, press Enter twice or use Ctrl+Enter to end the list. When you finish, your list should look as shown in Figure 11.13.

Figure 11.13.
A definition list shows a list of terms and their definitions.

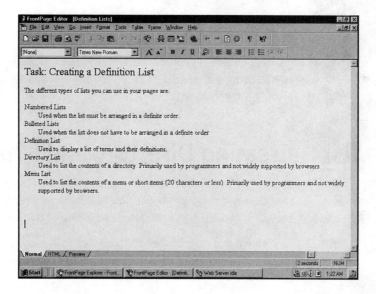

Working with Directory and Menu Lists

FrontPage supports two more types of lists: directory lists and menu lists. As you learned in the previous definition list task, they were intended for programmers and are not used very often anymore. Many browsers do not support them well. Directory lists typically list the contents of a directory. Similarly, menu lists display the contents of a menu or short items of twenty characters or less. Figure 11.14 shows examples of both types of lists.

Figure 11.14.

Directory and menu lists look similar to bulleted lists in the FrontPage Editor, but many browsers no longer support them. Where possible, use bulleted lists instead.

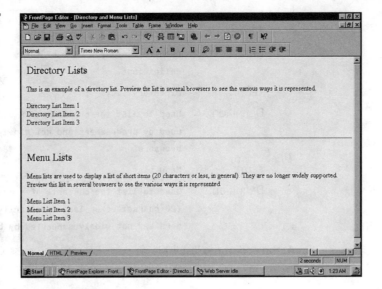

 NOTE: Some browsers do not recognize directory or menu lists. It is safer to use a bulleted list or numbered list instead. In the FrontPage Editor, directory and menu lists appear with bullets. Some browsers, however, do not display bullets for these lists.

TASK Creating Directory and Menu Lists

In the FrontPage Editor, directory lists display with bullets. Note that other browsers may display directory lists with bullets. Because they are not widely supported by browsers, consider using bulleted lists in lieu of these list types.

To create a directory or menu list, use the following steps:

1. Place the insertion point at the beginning of the line on which you want to create the list.

2. Choose Directory List or Menu List from the Change Style drop-down menu on the Format toolbar.

3. Enter a list item.

4. Press Enter to add additional items.

5. Press Enter twice to end the list.

Editing Lists

You can easily change one type of list to another, insert new items in a list, or delete list items.

Changing the List Type

If you change your mind about how you want to present your lists, you can change the list type easily. Here are some notes and pointers about changing list types:

❏ Basic numbered lists convert to bulleted lists, and bulleted lists to numbered lists, with no problem.

❏ Nested bulleted lists and nested numbered lists retain their level structure, but you need to change one level at a time to change the list type.

❏ You can use a combination of bullets and numbers in a nested list.

❏ When you change from any other type of list to a definition list, all the list items become formatted as definitions—not as terms. You can easily change the definitions to terms by selecting them all and choosing Defined Term from the Change Style drop-down menu in the Format toolbar.

To change the list type, follow these steps:

1. Position the insertion point anywhere within the list you want to change.

2. Choose a new list type from the Change Style drop-down menu in the Format toolbar or right-click and choose List Properties from the pop-up menu. From the List Properties dialog box, select the Bulleted or Numbered tab to change the style of your list and click OK.

Deleting Lists or List Items

To delete a list or a list item from a page, do the following:

1. Select the list or list item that you want to delete. To select a list, move the pointer to the selection bar next to the list and double-click; the entire list is selected. To select a list item, place the pointer over the number or bullet of the item and double-click; the item is selected.

2. Choose **E**dit | Cle**a**r or press the Delete key.

Inserting List Items

To insert list items, just place the insertion point where you want to insert the new item and press Enter. A new number, bullet, or term is started for you. Enter the new list item as you usually do.

Enabling Collapsible Outlines

Microsoft Internet Explorer 4.0 and other browsers that support Dynamic HTML enable users to collapse or expand an outline list. This is accomplished through a Dynamic HTML list attribute named `dynamicoutline`. You can apply this attribute from within the List Properties dialog box.

To enable collapsible outlines, follow these steps:

1. Click within any list item in the list you want to make collapsible.
2. Choose **F**ormat I Bullets and **N**umbering. The List Properties dialog box opens to the tab that is appropriate for the list you are editing.
3. Check the Enable Collapsible Outlines box in the Image Bullets, Plain Bullets, Numbers, or Other tab.
4. Choose OK.

Workshop Wrap-Up

Organizing your information in lists is easy. The hardest part is thinking of the information that you want to include. Keep in mind that lists can appear differently in your visitors' browsers. While you develop your site, have a few different browsers on hand to check the appearance of your pages.

In this chapter, you learned how to format information in different types of lists. You learned how to create basic and nested lists and how to change their appearances by specifying different bullet and numbering types. You also learned how to prepare yourself for new list tags coming down the road by examining how to add an extended attribute to a list.

Next Steps

In Chapter 15, you learn how to add images and animation to your pages. You learn how to make images appear as though they float on your pages by using transparent GIFs. Read on to learn how to use color and images effectively. You even get tips on how to create your own images.

To learn more about creating page content, refer to the following chapters:

❏ See Chapter 9, "Getting from Here to There," to learn how to add and edit the hyperlinks in your Web pages.

❏ See Chapter 10, "Composing and Editing Pages," to learn how to add and edit paragraphs, text, and headings.

❏ See Chapter 12, "Your Tables are Ready," to learn how to add and format tables and use them for page layout.

Q&A

Q: How do people make bulleted lists that use graphics? I see them all the time.

A: When you choose a FrontPage theme, bullet graphics are added automatically for you. If your page does not use a theme, you can customize the bullet graphic by using the Image Bullets tab in the List Properties dialog box.

Q: How do I increase the indent in a definition list? When I position the insertion point in the list and click the Increase Indent button, the list doesn't move.

A: To increase the indentation of a definition list, select all the items in the list (terms and definitions) and then click the Increase Indent button. To select the entire definition list, position your cursor anywhere in the left margin of the definition list and double-click.

TWELVE

Your Tables Are Ready

FrontPage 98 supports tables and table attributes to the fullest. Using tables, you can really control the layout of a page in many ways, placing content and images where you want them. Well... sort of.

Browsers handle tables differently. Some older browsers don't recognize tables at all; they leave your hard layout work laying in the dust, displaying a jumble of text and images. You should keep several different browsers around to test your tables as you design them and make compromises when you can.

There is good news, though. The latest versions of Internet Explorer and Netscape handle tables quite well. Each of these browsers has its own nifty little tricks up its sleeve. When designing pages to view in Netscape 4.0 and Internet Explorer 4.0, you can specify different colors for individual cells. Internet Explorer adds even more flexibility in how you can view tables. You have the capability of specifying a separate background image for each cell as well. Tables are the way to go if you want to create a fancy layout.

What Makes Up a Table?

A table has several elements, and to understand them is to understand the terminology needed to create them. Figure 12.1 shows an example of a basic table.

Figure 12.1.
The basic elements of a table are rows, columns, cells, and borders.

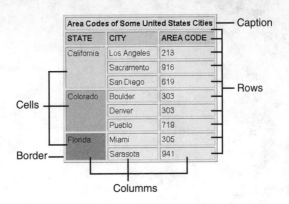

You see the following elements in Figure 12.1:

❏ *Rows and columns*. A table usually consists of multiple rows and columns. Rows run horizontally and columns run vertically.

❏ *Cells*. Each data field in a table is called a cell, which can sometimes be referred to as a data cell. Cells used for table headings are called *header cells*.

❏ *Captions*. The table caption is a title or description of the contents of the table. Typically, it is located immediately above the table.

❏ *Borders*. A table can be created with or without a border. It can appear on all sides of the table or on selected sides through the use of extended attributes.

Setting the Basic Table

You enter a basic table in your page first by choosing the Table I Insert Table command. This command invokes the Insert Table dialog box, from which you can specify several table attributes.

Inserting a Table

By default, FrontPage creates a table that contains two rows and two columns. The remaining settings default to those that you entered last.

I explain what cell padding and cell spacing do later in this chapter, in the section titled "Using the Insert Table Dialog Box."

You can specify several different values for your basic table. Follow these steps:

1. Place the insertion point on the line on which you want to insert the table.

2. Choose Table I Insert Table. The Insert Table dialog box shown in Figure 12.2 appears.

Figure 12.2.

Choose the table settings in the Insert Table dialog box.

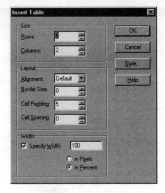

You can insert a table with up to five columns and four rows by using the Insert Table button on the Standard toolbar. Click the button and a grid appears. Click the cell that corresponds with the lower-right cell in the table you want to insert. The table appears on your page with the same settings last set in the Table Properties dialog box.

To learn more about styles and cascading style sheets, see Chapter 27, "Using Styles."

3. Enter the settings for your table. Each setting is described in the following sections.

TIP: You can preview your settings by clicking the Apply button in the Table Properties dialog box.

4. To add custom styles to your table, click the **S**tyle button.

5. When all table settings are entered, click OK to create the table.

Using the Insert Table Dialog Box

The Insert Table dialog box enables you to specify the number of rows and columns your table contains. You also can specify how the table aligns on the page and choose a table width in percentage of screen or pixels. You can specify the overall cell padding and cell spacing values in this dialog box, too.

Rows and Columns

You set the number of rows or columns in the Size section of the Insert Table dialog box. First, enter the number of rows in the **R**ows field or use the up and down arrows to select a value from 1 to 100. Then, enter the number of columns in the **C**olumns field or use its up and down arrows to select a value from 1 to 100. Figure 12.3 shows a table that contains five rows and three columns.

Table Alignment

The Alignment setting is the first in the Layout section of the Insert Table dialog box. This setting is not for the alignment of the contents within the cells; it controls how the entire table is aligned on your page.

Figure 12.3.

A basic table with five rows and three columns.

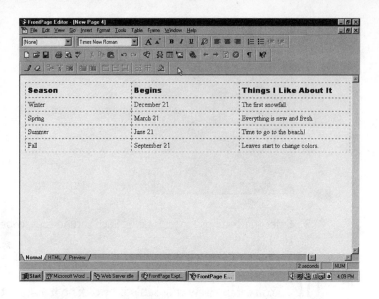

NOTE: If you want to design tables that display fairly consistently in several browsers, you need to make some compromises. Some browsers don't recognize the right-alignment setting and align the table to the left side of the page instead.

To choose a table alignment, select one of the following options from the **A**lignment drop-down list box in the Layout section of the dialog box:

❏ *Default* aligns the table to the position that was specified when the table was created.

❏ *Left* aligns the table to the left edge of your page.

❏ *Right* aligns the table to the right of your page. This choice is not recognized in some browsers.

❏ *Center* aligns the table to the center of your page.

Figure 12.4 shows examples of left, center, and right alignment applied to the table in our example. The Alignment setting won't be noticeable unless the table width is set to a value of less than 100 percent.

Border Size

The Border Size setting controls the width of the border that appears around the outer edge of the table. Many people use tables to enhance page layout, placing graphics and text in fixed areas of the page. Most commonly, the tables used in this manner don't have borders; using them would detract from the effect of the layout. When you specify a border of 0, the FrontPage Editor displays the borders of the table and cells in dotted lines. Not to worry—this is just a guide for you to place your content in the cells. When you view the table in other browsers, you won't see those border designations. Figure 12.5 shows the table from Figure 12.3 with borders added.

Figure 12.4.

Tables aligned to the left, center, and right of a page.

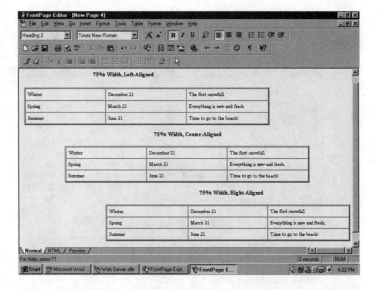

Figure 12.5.

Borders of varying widths are added to the tables.

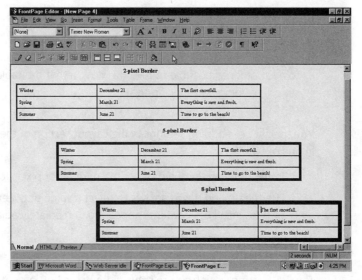

The Border Size setting is found in the Layout section of the Insert Table dialog box. To set the border size, you can do one of two things:

❑ Enter a value in the **B**order Size field of the Layout section in the dialog box.

❑ Use the up and down arrows to select a value between 0 and 100 pixels.

Cell Padding

The Cell Padding setting controls how far from the edge of the cell's border its contents appear. To see what I mean, compare the top table in Figure 12.6 to the middle table, which does not use cell padding.

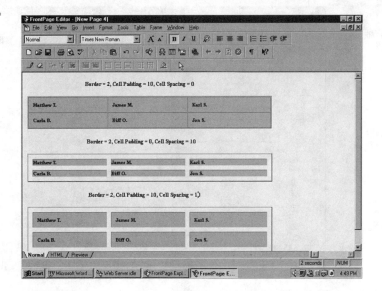

TIP: For text content, you probably want to use cell padding and cell spacing to improve the appearance of your tables. If you want graphics to get as close to each other as possible to give the illusion that the table is one solid graphic, set cell padding and spacing to 0.

You specify Cell Padding settings in the Layout section of the Insert Table dialog box in one of two ways:

❑ In the Cell Padding field, enter the number of pixels for cell padding.

❑ Use the up and down arrows to select a value between 0 and 100. A value of 0 results in cell contents appearing immediately adjacent to its borders.

Cell Spacing

The Cell Spacing setting controls the width of the borders between cells (the row and column dividers, so to speak). Refer to Figure 12.6, where the center and bottom tables have cell spacing added. Compare them to the top table, which does not.

To set cell spacing, you use one of the following two methods:

❏ In the Cell **S**pacing field, enter the number of pixels for cell spacing.

❏ Use the up and down arrows to select a value between 0 and 100. A value of 0 results in no borders between cells.

Changing Table Width

You can format tables to different widths by using the Width section of the Insert Table dialog box. Figure 12.7 shows some examples of different table widths that are aligned to the left of the page. You set table width in percentage of screen or in pixels. You can also uncheck the Specify **W**idth button to create a table that is sized based on the content within the table.

Figure 12.7.

These tables use various width settings as configured in the Insert Table dialog box.

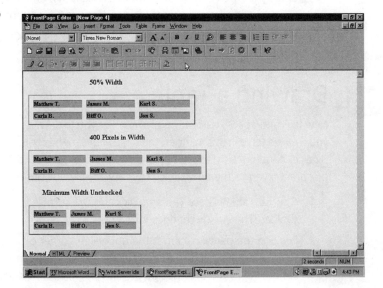

TIP: In most cases, you want to specify the table width in percentage of screen because users might have their browser windows sized other than maximized. Also, some users browse the Internet in 640×480 resolution, whereas others use 800×600 or 1024×768. If you specify the width in percentage of screen, the table resizes to accommodate a user's browser window.

On the other hand, if you're adding graphics to your tables, pixel settings help you visualize the table layout before the graphics are inserted. You should note, however, that when users resize their browser windows or view them in a different resolution, portions of your table might not be visible. Perhaps a good rule of thumb here is to size your pixel table width for 640×480 resolution and size your graphics accordingly. You should be fairly safe with that setting in most cases.

To specify table width, follow these steps:

1. Enable the Specify **W**idth checkbox in the Width section (it is checked by default). Uncheck this box if you want to create a table that automatically sizes to accommodate the contents within it.

2. Select the in Pi**x**els or in **P**ercent radio button.

3. Specify the percentage or number of pixels in a whole number. You don't need to add a percent sign or decimal point for percent value.

4. Continue specifying other table properties or click OK to exit the Insert Table dialog box.

Drawing a Table

New to FrontPage 98 is a feature that enables you to draw a table on your page. When you create a table in this manner, the table aligns to the center of the page. The border size, cell padding, and cell spacing settings that were last used in the Insert Table dialog box are applied to the new table. To draw a table on your page, follow these steps:

1. Choose T**a**ble I Draw Ta**b**le or click the Draw Table button on the Table toolbar. The cursor changes into a pencil.

2. Position the pencil cursor at the upper-left corner of where you want your table to appear. Click and drag to the lower-right corner of your new table. An outline of a table appears on your page, as shown in Figure 12.8.

3. To add rows to your table, position the pencil cursor inside, but not touching, the left or right edge of the table. Click and drag to the opposite side of the table. Release the mouse when the dotted line that represents your new row attaches itself to the left and right borders of the table, as shown in Figure 12.9. A new row appears in your table.

4. To add a column to your table, position the pencil cursor inside, but not touching, the top or bottom edge of the table. Click and drag to the opposite side of the table. Release the mouse when the dotted line that represents your new column attaches itself to the top and bottom borders of the table, as shown in Figure 12.10. A new column is added to the table.

Figure 12.8.

Draw the outline of your table first.

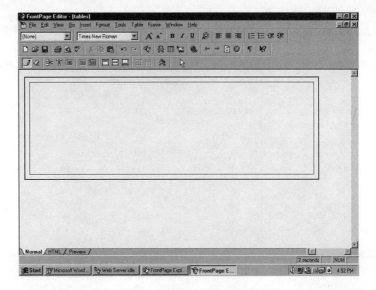

Figure 12.9.

Drawing a row in your table.

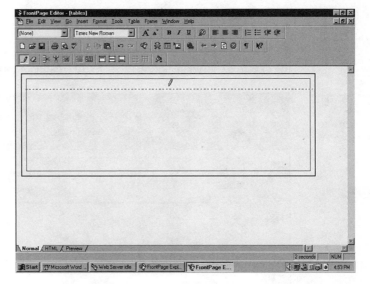

5. Continue adding rows and columns, using the procedures outlined in steps 3 and 4.

6. To exit table drawing mode, click the Draw Table button on the Table toolbar again to toggle it off. You can also press the Escape key or click once outside the table to exit table drawing mode.

Figure 12.10.
Drawing a column in your table.

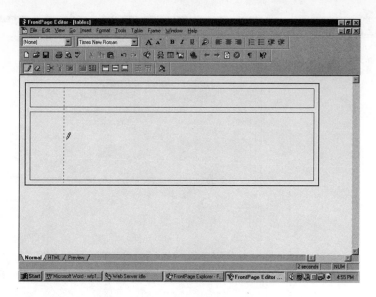

TASK Creating a Basic Table

If you want to create your own table, create a new page in the FrontPage Editor. Use the example shown in Figure 12.11 to try creating a table yourself.

Figure 12.11.
Insert a table with three rows and two columns.

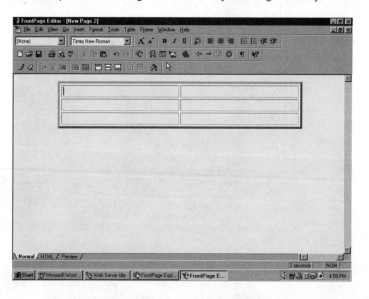

To insert the table, follow these steps:

1. Place the cursor on the line before the location where you want to insert the table. Choose Table I Insert Table. The Insert Table dialog box appears.

2. Specify the following settings:

   Rows: 3
   Columns: 2
   Alignment: Center
   Border Size: 5
   Cell Pa**d**ding: 3
   Cell **S**pacing: 3
   Specify **W**idth: 75 in **P**ercent

3. Click OK to create the table. The table appears on your page.

Setting Table Background and Border Properties

You can apply table background colors, border colors, and background images to tables within the Table Properties dialog box or from the Tables toolbar, which is new to FrontPage 98. The FrontPage Editor updates the display of all table properties as you design the table.

The upper section of the Table Properties dialog box, shown in Figure 12.12, contains many of the settings that you entered when you created your table. The lower section of the dialog box contains the Custom Background section, where you specify background and border settings for the table.

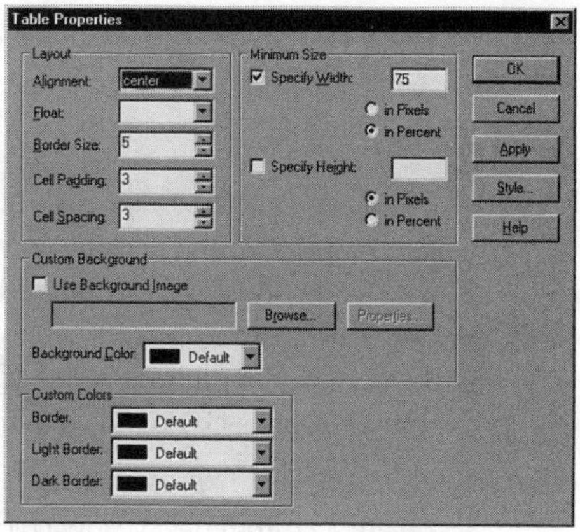

Figure 12.12.

Assign background and border colors to your tables in the Table Properties dialog box.

To specify table background and border properties, follow these steps:

1. Position the insertion point anywhere within the table. Right-click and choose Table Properties from the pop-up menu. The Table Properties dialog box appears.

2. To choose how you want text to flow around the table, choose one of the following options from the Float drop-down menu:

❑ *Default*. Text will not flow around the table.

❑ *Left*. The table is positioned against the left page margin, and text appears between the table and the right page margin.

❑ *Right*. The table is positioned against the right page margin, and text appears between the table and the left page margin.

3. To use a background image in the entire table, check the Use Background Image checkbox in the Custom Background section. The Browse button is enabled.

4. Click the Browse button. The Select Background Image dialog box appears.

5. To insert `Book\Chap12\Project Files\bg01.gif` from the CD-ROM that accompanies this book, click the Make a hyperlink to a file on your local computer button that appears at the right of the URL field in the Select Background Image dialog box. The Select File dialog box appears.

6. Use the Look in drop-down menu to locate the drive and directory in which the image appears. Double-click the filename or highlight the file and choose Open. You return to the Table Properties dialog box.

7. To use a solid background color for your table, choose a color from the Background Color drop-down menu. If you choose Default, the table background is the same as your page background. You can also choose one of 16 predefined colors. For this example, select Custom from the Background Color drop-down menu to create a custom color. The Color dialog box appears.

To learn other ways that you can insert images into your pages or tables, see Chapter 15, "Working with Images and Sound."

TIP: You can also apply a background color to a selected table or a group of selected cells using the Background Color button in the Tables toolbar. Choose View | Table Toolbar if the tables toolbar is not displayed. Select the table or cells that you want to apply the background color to and select the Background Color button. Define your color in the Color dialog box and choose OK. The background color in the table or cell changes.

8. Create a custom pale yellow color by entering the following values in the Color dialog box:

Red 255 Green 255 Blue 204

9. Choose OK to return to the Table Properties dialog box. The color swatch in the Background Color field turns to light yellow.

10. In a similar manner, repeat steps 6 through 8 to select border colors for the table, using the color formulas that follow. The Border setting in the Custom Colors section of the dialog box applies to a solid border around the table. The Light Border and Dark Border colors apply if you want the table border to have a three-dimensional appearance.

   For the Light Border color, choose Custom and create a color of **R**ed **204 G**reen **204** Bl**u**e **153** (a very light olive green). Click OK to return to the Table Properties dialog box. Click the **A**pply button to preview the color in your table.

   For the Dark Border color, choose Custom and create a color using **R**ed **153 G**reen **102** Bl**u**e **51**, which creates a reddish brown color. Click OK to return to the Table Properties dialog box.

11. Click OK to close the Table Properties dialog box and apply the settings to the table. Your table should now look as shown in Figure 12.13.

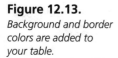

Figure 12.13.
Background and border colors are added to your table.

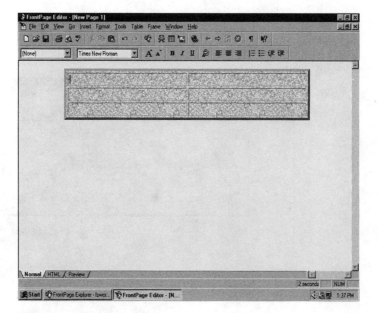

Adding Content in Tables

After you place your table on your page, it's easy to place text, images, FrontPage components, or forms in the cells. The procedures to add content into tables are the same as those used to enter content on a page that doesn't have tables.

Entering Text in Your Tables

Start first with a basic text table to learn how easy it is to enter content into tables. Enter the following text into your table or make up your own example.

To enter text into your table, follow these steps:

1. Place the insertion point inside the left cell in the second row. Enter **STATE**.
2. Press the Tab key to move to the right cell in the second row. Enter **CITY**.
3. Press the Tab key again. Enter `California`.
4. Tab to move to the right cell in the third row. Enter `Los Angeles`.
5. Press the Tab key again. FrontPage adds a new row to the table. Tab again and enter `Sacramento` in the second cell in the fourth row.
6. Press the Tab key again. FrontPage adds a new row to the table. Enter `Colorado`.
7. Press Tab and enter `Boulder`.
8. Press Tab twice and enter `Denver`. When you're done, your table should look like Figure 12.14.

Figure 12.14.
Text is added to the table.

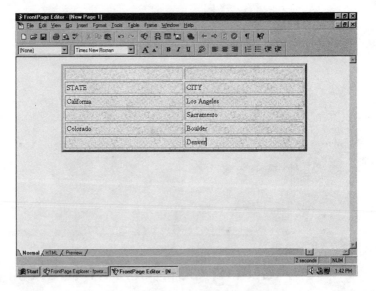

Inserting an Image in a Table

Many times, tables are used to lay out text and images on a Web page because they offer more control over where images are placed. You'll learn more about this in a later example. For now, add an image to the first row of your table. Follow these steps:

1. Position the insertion point in the right cell in the first row and choose Insert I Image. The Image dialog box appears.

2. Click the Make a hyperlink to a file on your computer button. The Select File dialog box appears.

3. Use the Look in drop-down menu to locate `Book\Chap12\Project Files\skyline.gif` on the CD-ROM that accompanies this book. Double-click the filename or highlight the file and choose Open. The image appears in your table.

4. Position the insertion point in the left cell in the first row. Choose Heading 2 from the Change Style drop-down menu on the Format toolbar. Enter `United States Cities`. When you're done, your table should look like the one in Figure 12.15.

Figure 12.15.
A heading and image are added to the first row in the table.

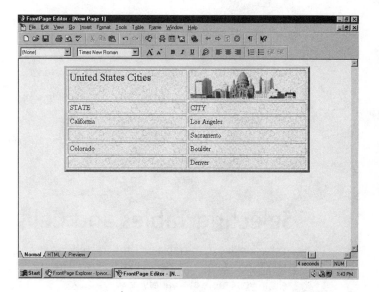

 ## Inserting a Table Within a Table

You also can create a *nested table*—a table within a table. It is sometimes easier to create more complex tables using this approach. In the example shown in Figure 12.16, the original table contained four rows and three columns. A second table is inserted into the second cell in the fourth row. The table that is inserted has Border Size set to 0 and a width of 100 percent.

Figure 12.16.

You can create more complex tables by inserting tables within tables.

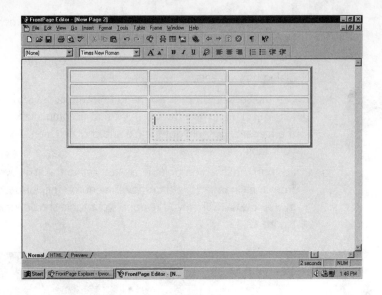

To insert a table within a table, follow these steps:

1. Place the insertion point within the cell in which you want the table inserted.

2. Choose Table I Insert Table.

3. Specify the table properties as outlined in the section "Using the Insert Table Dialog Box," earlier in this chapter.

4. Click OK to insert the table within the selected cell.

Selecting Tables and Cells

You're looking at the table you just created and saying, "So, what's the big deal? Just looks like a standard table to me!" As you are about to learn, you can reformat the cells in your table in a variety of ways.

You can apply cell formatting to a single cell or to multiple cells at once. To do this, you need to select the cells first. You can select a group of cells, an entire row or column, or the entire table.

Selecting Cells

To apply cell formatting to cells, you select only the cells you want to apply the formatting to before you choose the Edit I Properties or Cell Properties command. You can apply cell formatting to a single cell by clicking in the cell you want to format and applying your command. There are several ways that you can select multiple cells.

After you merge or split cells, it can be a bit confusing about how to select them. See the section "Notes on Selecting Split or Merged Rows," later in this chapter.

To select multiple cells, follow these steps:

1. Place the insertion point in the first cell you want to select.
2. Choose Table I Select Cell. The cell appears in an inverse highlight.
3. To select additional cells, hold down the Shift key. You can drag the mouse to select a range of contiguous cells or click any remote cell to add it to the selection.

TIP: You can also select a contiguous range of cells by clicking inside the first cell you want to select. Then, drag to select multiple cells in the same or adjacent rows or columns. Release the mouse button when you complete your selection.

 ## Selecting Rows

You can select an entire row or multiple rows at a time. A good example for doing this is formatting all the cells in the row as header cells.

To select an entire row, use one of these methods:

❑ Place the insertion point in one of the cells in the row you want to select and choose Table I Select Row.

❑ Position the insertion point outside the left edge of the table, where it becomes a selection pointer. Click to select the table row. You can drag the arrow to select additional contiguous rows.

 ## Selecting Columns

If you want to change the width of an entire column of cells, you can select one or more columns using one of these methods:

❑ Place the insertion point in one of the cells in the row you want to select and choose Table I Select Column.

❑ Position the insertion point above the top edge of the table, where it becomes a selection pointer. Click to select the table column. You can drag the arrow to select additional contiguous columns.

 ## Deleting Tables and Cells

To delete a table from your page, you need to select the entire table. To select the entire table, use one of these methods:

❏ Place the insertion point in one of the cells in the row you want to select and choose Table I Select Table.

❏ Select all rows and columns in the table using any of the methods mentioned in the sections "Selecting Rows" and "Selecting Columns," earlier in this chapter.

It's pretty easy to delete cells from your table. Actually, all you have to do is select the cells, rows, or columns you want to delete and press the Delete key or use the Delete Cells button in the Table toolbar. You can also use the Table I Delete Cells command.

Working with Cells

After you select your cells, you use the Cell Properties dialog box, shown in Figure 12.17, to change the properties of the cells. This dialog box enables you to set the properties of a single cell or a group of selected cells in your table. Just as you can assign a background color or image to an entire table, you can also assign a background color or image to individual cells. The settings you can choose from are described in the following sections.

Figure 12.17.
The Cell Properties dialog box enables you to reformat your cells in a variety of ways.

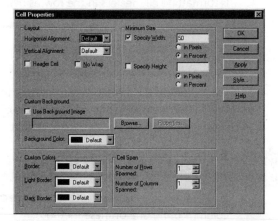

Using the Cell Properties Dialog Box

Use the Cell Properties dialog box to specify properties for your cells. To open the Cell Properties dialog box, follow these steps:

1. Select the cell or cells that you want to change, as described in the section "Selecting Cells," earlier in this chapter.

2. Choose Table I Cell Properties or right-click and choose Cell Properties from the pop-up window. The Cell Properties dialog box appears.

Specifying Cell Layout

You set horizontal alignment in the Layout portion of the Cell Properties dialog box. You can choose left, center, or right alignment. The first row of the table in Figure 12.18 shows examples of these alignments.

Figure 12.18.

Contents of cells can be aligned horizontally and vertically.

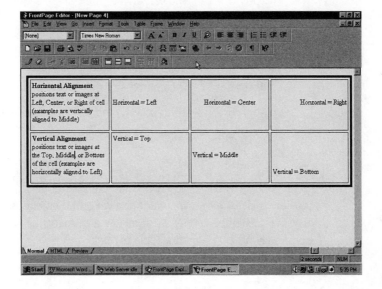

To specify horizontal alignment, follow these steps:

1. In the Layout section's Horizontal Alignment drop-down list box, choose one of the following options:

Default	The contents of the cell are aligned to the left.
Left	The contents of the cell are aligned to the left.
Right	The contents of the cell are aligned to the right.
Center	The contents of the cell are aligned to the center.
Justify	The contents of the cell are positioned equally between the right and left borders of the cell.

2. Click **A**pply if you want to preview the results before applying the command.

3. Click OK to apply the setting to your cells.

You also set vertical alignment in the Layout portion of the Cell Properties dialog box. You can choose to align the contents of your cell at the top, middle, or bottom sides of the cell. Refer to the second row of Figure 12.17 for examples of these types of alignments.

To specify vertical alignment, follow these steps:

1. In the Layout section's **V**ertical Alignment drop-down list box, choose one of the following options:

Default	The contents of the cell are aligned to the middle.
Top	The contents of the cell are aligned to the top.
Middle	The contents of the cell are aligned to the middle.
Baseline	The contents of the cell are aligned to the baseline of the text. The baseline matches the tallest text in the row that contains the selected cell.
Bottom	The contents of the cell are aligned to the bottom.

2. Click **A**pply if you want to preview the results before applying the command.

3. Click OK to apply the setting to your cells.

TIP: You can apply vertical alignment commands very quickly from the Table toolbar. Select the cells you want to align and then choose Align Top (for top alignment), Center Vertically (for middle alignment), or Align Bottom (for bottom alignment) from the Table toolbar.

Specifying Cell Width

You can specify a minimum cell width for each column in your table. When you specify cell width, select the entire column of cells so that they are all formatted in the same width. To specify minimum cell width, follow these steps:

TIP: To adjust cell widths very quickly and easily, position your cursor above the column divider that you want to adjust. The cursor turns into a bidirectional arrow. Move the divider to the left or right to adjust the width.

You can adjust cell height in a similar manner. Position your cursor above the row divider that you want to adjust. The cursor turns into a bidirectional arrow. Move the divider up or down to adjust the height.

NOTE: It is best to format cell widths before you split and merge cells.

1. Position your cursor above the column that you want to format. Click to select all cells in the column. You can also click and drag to select multiple adjacent columns or Shift+click to select columns that are not adjacent to each other.

2. Choose Table I Cell Properties or right-click and choose Cell Properties from the pop-up menu. The Cell Properties dialog box appears.

3. In the Minimum Size section, check the Specify Width checkbox. Enter a value in the field and choose In Pixels (for a pixel width) or In Percent (for percentage of table width). If you leave the Specify Width checkbox unchecked, the cells expand to fit the contents.

Choosing Cell Backgrounds and Borders

The procedures to choose cell background colors and images are the same as those discussed in the section "Setting Table Background and Border Properties," earlier in this chapter. The only difference is that you can apply these properties to any cell or group of cells within your table. Each cell in your table can have a different background color, image, or border color if you so choose.

To assign background and border colors to individual cells, simply select the cells that you want to change and select background and border colors as indicated in the earlier section "Setting Table Background and Border Properties."

Creating or Removing Header Cells

It's typical to assign the top row and the first column in your table as header cells. Figure 12.19 shows a table where the top row is formatted as header cells. Header cells appear in bold text, and the contents are aligned to the center.

NOTE: When you format cells as header cells, the contents of the cell become what appears to be emphasized (or bold) text. You won't be able to use the Bold button on the Format toolbar to remove the bold formatting from the header cell. You need to convert the header cells back to normal cells for this. You can also italicize, underline, or use fixed-width font in a header cell.

To change selected cells into header cells, enable the Header Cell checkbox in the Layout section of the Cell Properties dialog box. To remove header cell formatting, disable the Header Cell checkbox.

Figure 12.19.

The header cells in the first row enable you to distinguish what the contents of the cells represent.

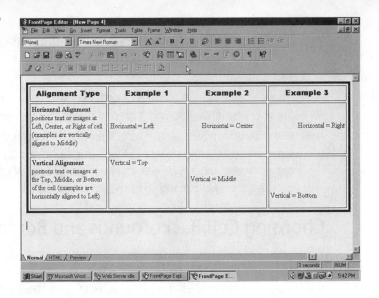

Changing Tables

As you work with your tables, you sometimes need to insert additional cells, rows, and columns. The following tasks describe the procedures to add additional cells and how to split and merge cells to create advanced tables.

Inserting Rows and Columns

You also can insert new rows or columns into your tables by using the Insert Rows or Columns dialog box.

To insert new columns using the Insert Rows or Columns command, follow these steps:

1. Select the column before or after the location where you want to insert the new column.

2. Choose Table | Insert Rows or Columns. The Insert Rows or Columns dialog box appears.

3. Select the Columns radio button.

4. In the Number of Columns field, enter the number of columns you want to insert and choose whether you want to insert the new columns to Left of selection or Right of selection.

5. Click OK to insert the columns.

To insert new columns using the Insert Columns button in the Table toolbar, follow these steps:

1. Select one or more columns before which you want the new column or columns to appear. The number of columns you select is equal to the number of columns that will be added to your table.

2. Select the Insert Columns button on the Table toolbar. The new column or columns appear before (to the left of) your selection.

To insert new rows using the Insert Rows or Columns command, follow these steps:

1. Select the row before or after the location where you want to insert the new row.

2. Choose Table | Insert Rows or Columns. The Insert Rows or Columns dialog box appears.

3. Select the **R**ows radio button.

4. In the Number of **R**ows field, enter the number of rows you want to insert and choose whether you want to insert the new rows **A**bove selection or **B**elow selection.

5. Click OK to insert the rows.

To insert new rows using the Insert Rows button in the Table toolbar, follow these steps:

1. Select one or more rows before which you want the new row or rows to appear. The number of rows you select is equal to the number of rows that will be added to your table.

2. Select the Insert Rows button on the Table toolbar. The new row or rows appear before your selection.

NOTE: When you insert rows or columns in your table, the new row uses the same number of cells as the row that you select to insert before or after. This is important to keep in mind when you insert new rows in tables that have split and merged cells.

Inserting a Cell

You can insert a new cell into your table. When you do this, the contents of the other cells shift over. You might need to reformat cell widths in that row to compensate. Sometimes you want this shifting to happen, but you might be better off splitting the cell that appears before the cell you want to insert. That way, your table layout isn't affected.

To insert a cell, follow these steps:

1. Position the insertion point at the point where you want to insert the new cell.

2. Choose Table I Insert Cell. A new cell appears in the table, and the contents of the table shift over.

Splitting Cells

Splitting cells is the opposite of merging cells. You can split a cell into multiple rows or columns. Figure 12.20 shows an example of this. The top table, which has two columns and two rows, was split using the Split Cells command. The first column in the first row was split into three columns, and the second column in the second row was split into five rows. The bottom table of Figure 12.20 shows the results.

Figure 12.20.
Cells can be split into multiple rows or columns.

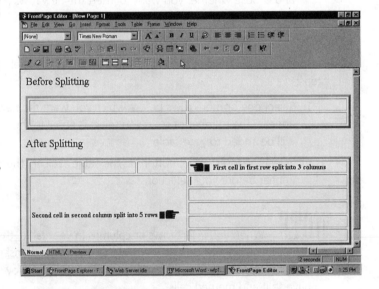

If you want to split a cell into both rows and columns, you can insert another table within that cell. See the section "Inserting a Table Within a Table," earlier in this chapter.

To split a cell, follow these steps:

1. Select the cell or cells you want to split.

2. Choose Table I Split Cells or select the Split Cells button from the Table toolbar. The Split Cells dialog box appears.

3. To split the cell into columns, choose Split Into Columns. In the Number of Columns field, enter the number of columns that you want to split the cell into.

To split the cell into rows, choose Split Into **R**ows. In the Number of **R**ows field, enter the number of rows that you want to split the cell into.

4. Click OK. The cells you selected are split as specified.

TIP: You can also use the Draw Table button or the Table | Draw Table command to split rows and columns in your table.

 Spanning and Merging Cells

You can make a cell or group of cells span more than one row or column. Select an entire row, an entire column, or a range of contiguous cells, as shown in the top table in Figure 12.21, and choose the Table | **M**erge Cells command or select the Merge Cells button from the Table toolbar. The bottom table shows what the cells look like after they are merged.

Figure 12.21.
You can merge cells for advanced layout.

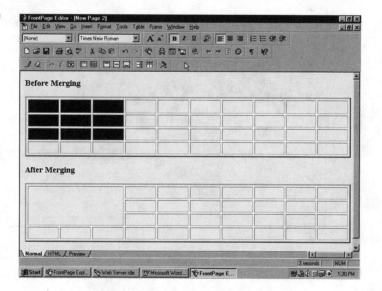

TIP: If you want to remove a dividing line between a table row or column, use the Eraser button on the Table toolbar. Click the Eraser button, then click and drag the eraser over the boundary line you want to remove. The boundary line turns red. When you release the mouse button, the line disappears and the cells that were once divided by the line are merged into one cell.

Notes on Selecting Split or Merged Rows

After you split cells, it sometimes can be a little confusing as to how to select them. How do you find out which row the big area is in? How do you select the smaller cells to the right of that big cell?

Figure 12.22 shows how you find out. Position the insertion point at the left edge of the table near the row you want to select. The cursor becomes a small arrow. Click to select the row.

Figure 12.22.

Selecting rows after splitting.

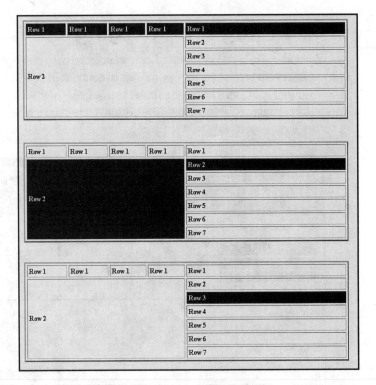

As you can see in the top table of Figure 12.22, the first row (which contains the cell that you split into columns) is still intact as a row.

Now look at the center table in the figure. The second row contains that big cell. To select it and its corresponding cell in the second column, place the mouse at the left side of the table, directly opposite the cell in the second row of the second column.

To select the cells in rows 3 through 7 of the table, position the mouse at the left side of the table, directly opposite the cell or cells you want to select. Click to select the row. The bottom table in Figure 12.22 shows this.

A similar situation occurs with the cells that were split into columns. The first column contains the big cell and first cell in the first row because those were the cells that were there originally. The second through fourth columns (the ones you split) don't have any additional cells associated with them in the example. All three of these cells are selected in the center table shown in Figure 12.23. The fifth column is still intact as a column, as shown in the bottom table of Figure 12.23.

Figure 12.23.
Selecting columns after splitting.

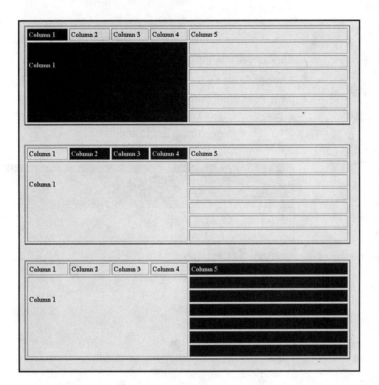

TASK Distributing Rows and Columns Evenly

You can use the Distribute Rows Evenly or Distribute Columns Evenly commands to create rows and columns of even width or height.

To distribute rows or columns evenly, follow these steps:

1. Select the rows or columns that you want to distribute evenly.
2. Choose **T**able | Distribute Ro**w**s Evenly or **T**able | Distribute Columns Evenl**y**. The cells in the row or column are set at equal heights or widths.

TIP:

You can also distribute rows and columns evenly from the Table toolbar. Select the rows or columns and then choose Distribute Rows Evenly or Distribute Columns Evenly from the Table toolbar.

Converting Tables to Text

New to FrontPage 98 is the capability of converting from tables to text. When you convert a table to text, the data that was once contained in a cell is reformatted into a normal paragraph.

To convert a table to text, follow these steps:

1. Click anywhere inside the table that you want to convert.

2. Choose Table I Convert Table to Text. The cells in your table appear on your page as normal paragraphs, with data from each cell appearing on a separate line. Figure 12.24 shows a portion of the table from Figure 12.15 after it has been converted to text.

Figure 12.24.

The table from Figure 12.15 after being converted to text. The contents of each cell convert into separate normal paragraphs.

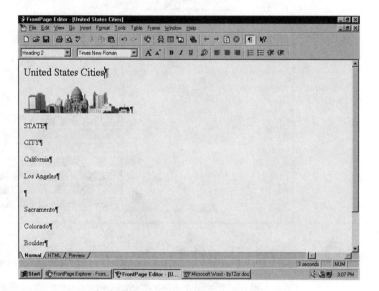

Converting Text to Tables

Just as you can convert tables to text, you can also go the other way. The upper part of Figure 12.25 shows three rows of text. Tabs separate the elements in each row. The lower part of Figure 12.25 shows what the text looks like after it is converted into a table.

To convert text to a table, follow these steps:

1. Select the text that you want to convert into a table.

2. Choose Table I Convert Text to Table. The Convert Text to Table dialog box appears.

3. Choose how you want to convert the table to text, based on how the items in your text are separated:

   ❏ Choose **P**aragraphs if each line of text appears on a separate line.

   ❏ Choose **T**abs if you have separated the data for each cell by tabs.

   ❏ Choose **C**ommas if the data for each cell is separated by commas.

   ❏ Choose **O**ther if the data for each cell is separated by another indicator, and enter the indicator that separates each item in the **O**ther field.

4. Choose OK. The text converts into a table.

Figure 12.25.

Use the Convert Text to Table command to convert multiple lines of text into a table.

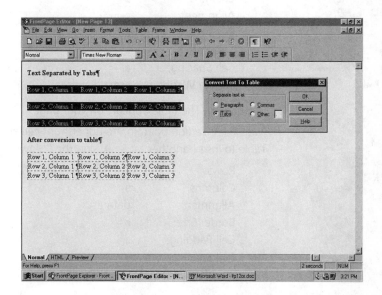

 # Adding and Selecting Table Captions

Tables don't always have captions, but in some cases, captions are necessary. They help you point out what the table is about. When you apply a caption to a table, it actually becomes part of the table instead of a separate line of text. Generally, a table caption uses one line.

To add a caption to a table, follow these steps:

1. Position the insertion point anywhere within the table.

2. Choose **T**able | Insert **Ca**ption. The insertion point moves to a center location above the table, where you can type the table caption. If your table uses a background image, the caption uses the same image as a background.

To select a table caption, move the pointer to the left of the table caption and click to select it.

Building a Fancy Table

Build a quick example of a table that combines some of what you've learned here:

1. Create a new page. Format the first line as Heading 2 and enter something like `Building A Fancy Table`.

2. Choose Table I Insert Table to insert a new table. Assign it the following properties:

Rows:	2
Columns:	2
Alignment:	Center
Border Size:	5
Cell Pa**d**ding:	0
Cell **S**pacing:	0
Specify **W**idth:	600 in Pixels

3. Choose OK. The table appears on your page.

4. Place the insertion point in the upper-right cell and choose Table I Insert Table to insert another table. Assign the following properties to it:

Rows:	1
Columns:	3
Alignment:	default
Border Size:	0
Cell Pa**d**ding:	0
Cell **S**pacing:	0
Specify **W**idth:	300 in Pixels

5. Choose OK. The second table appears within the first.

6. Click in the first cell in the table that you inserted into the first row. Choose Table I Select C**e**ll. Press the Shift key and click in the third cell in the inserted table. You should now have two cells selected in the inserted table.

7. Choose Table I **S**plit Cells. The Split Cells dialog box appears. Choose Split into **R**ows and enter 2 in the Number of **R**ows field. Choose OK to split the cells.

 8. The following graphics are located in the `Book\Chap12\Project Files` folder on the CD-ROM that accompanies this book. Choose the Insert I Image command to insert them into the new table. Use the Make a hyperlink to a file on your computer button to insert the images into the table within the table as follows:

Insert `small1.gif` (the New image) into the top cell in the first column.

Insert `small2.gif` (the Hot image) into the bottom cell of the first column.

Insert `small3.gif` (the Guest Book image) into the top cell of the third column.

Insert `small4.gif` (the Send Email image) into the bottom cell of the third column.

Insert `medium1.gif` (the Really Cool Links image) into the middle cell.

9. Position the insertion point in the lower-left cell of the main table. Insert `large1.gif` into this cell.

10. Click in the left cell in the top row of the table. Choose Table I Select Cell. Shift-click to select the right cell in the second row.

11. Right-click and choose Cell Properties from the pop-up menu. The Cell Properties dialog box appears.

12. From the Background Color section, create a custom color of **R**ed **204 G**reen **204** B**lu**e **255**. Choose OK twice to return to the FrontPage Editor.

13. Position the insertion point anywhere within the table and right-click. Choose Table Properties from the pop-up menu. The Table Properties dialog box appears.

14. From the Custom Colors section, choose Blue from the Border drop-down menu. Click OK to return to the FrontPage Editor.

When you're finished, your table should look like Figure 12.26. You can assign links to the images in the upper-right portion of the main table, and you can add text to the other cells in the table to describe the things you are linking.

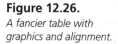

Figure 12.26.

A fancier table with graphics and alignment.

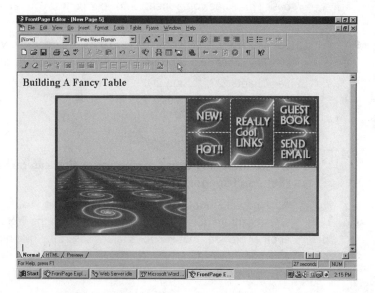

Workshop Wrap-Up

I hope I've started the wheels turning now. I think you can see from what you've learned in this chapter that tables aren't just for data any more. They go a long way in dressing up your pages and can sometimes compensate for using image maps on your pages.

You've covered a lot of ground in this chapter. You learned what tables are and the many ways you can use them. You built a basic table and applied table properties to it. Then, after learning the many ways in which you can format cells, you got a taste of building a more advanced table, complete with graphics. You also learned ways in which you can give your tables a fresh look for those users with Internet Explorer for browsers. Well done—you deserve a hearty pat on the back!

Next Steps

In the next chapter, you begin to develop a Web site, using many of the techniques you learned in this section of the book. You begin to plan your Web site while developing a welcome screen, home pages, and navigation pages.

For information that relates to this chapter, refer to the following chapters:

❏ See Chapter 15, "Working with Images and Sound," for procedures on how to add images to pages. The same principles can apply to tables.

❏ Chapter 19, "Using FrontPage Components," teaches you how to place basic FrontPage components into your pages. You can also insert FrontPage Components into your tables.

❏ See Chapter 21, "Quick and Easy Forms," to learn how to develop a form. Like any other item on your page, you can insert forms into tables as well.

❏ See Chapter 27, "Using Styles," to learn how to apply cascading style sheet properties to your tables.

Q&A

Q: Are there any other compromises that can be made for browsers that don't support tables very well?

A: One workaround is to build your table as you usually do and then make a screen capture of it while viewing the table in the FrontPage Editor or another browser that supports tables. Insert the graphic of the table onto your page instead of the actual table.

For browsers that don't support graphics or for folks who have graphics turned off, create a text alternative of your table on another page. Use formatted paragraphs or typewriter font to neatly align the contents of the page. Then, provide a link to the text version on the page that contains your original table.

Q: I inserted a table at the very beginning of my page, and now I want to add text up there. I can't figure out how to do that because my cursor won't go above the table. Help!!!

A: Position your cursor at the beginning of the top-left cell in the table and press Ctrl+Enter. A new line appears above your table.

Q: I'm using a background that puts a really neat design at the left side of my page. I used the Increase Indent button to position my text beyond that border, but some browsers put the text at the beginning of the page over the border. How can I fix that?

A: Put your page contents in a table. Create a table that contains one row and two columns and spans 100 percent of the page width. Create a spacer graphic that is as wide as or slightly wider than the design on the left side of your background. This spacer graphic doesn't have to be that tall—even one pixel will do. After you insert the spacer graphic into the left table cell, use the Make Transparent button on the Image Toolbar to add transparency so it doesn't show.

Q: I formatted my tables for 50 percent width and aligned them to the right side of my page. Now I want to put text on my page at the left side of the table, but I can't. What gives?

A: Tables are an entity unto themselves. The table might be formatted to display in a portion of your screen, but the areas to the right and left are also a part of that table. What you can do is insert another table on your page that spans 100 percent page width and has one row and two columns. Uncheck the Specify **W**idth button to expand the columns to fit their contents as necessary. Next, reformat your original table for 100 percent width. Cut or copy it to the clipboard and paste it in one of the cells in the new table. Then, you can add your text in the other empty cell.

THIRTEEN

Real-Life Examples II: Keeping It Plain and Simple

In the previous chapters, you learned how to add basic content to your pages. Now it's time for you to get started on your own Web site. Every site begins with an idea of the topics or products that you want to focus on. You begin building your idea in the FrontPage Explorer, starting your site with one of the Web templates. More than likely, if you're building your site from the ground up, you start with an empty Web or a one-page Web.

You can add pages to your Web with the templates provided with FrontPage or with templates that you create yourself. As you add your pages, you can easily add them to your navigation bars in the FrontPage Explorer's Navigation view. Eventually, your site begins to grow.

Creating a One-Page Web

When you begin a Web site, you start with an empty Web template or with the one-page Web template. The only difference between the two templates is that the one-page template automatically creates a blank home page in your Web.

NOTE: Completed examples of the pages discussed in this chapter are located in the `Book\Chap13\Examples` folder on the CD-ROM that accompanies this book.

To create a one-page Web, follow these steps:

1. From the FrontPage Explorer, choose **F**ile I **N**ew I FrontPage **W**eb. The New FrontPage Web dialog box appears, as shown in Figure 13.1.

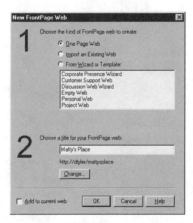

Figure 13.1.
Use the New FrontPage Web dialog box to create a one-page Web.

2. Choose the **O**ne Page Web radio button.
3. In the Choose a **t**itle for your FrontPage web field, enter a title for your Web, such as `Matty's Place`, which is used for the example in this chapter.
4. The URL for your Web appears beneath the title. In the example shown, the URL defaults to `http://servername/mattysplace`.

See Chapter 30, "Using the FrontPage Personal Web Server," or Chapter 31, "Using the Microsoft Personal Web Server," to learn how to change your default home page name.

NOTE: To change the server or Web folder name, or to select SSL connections, click the **C**hange button. The Change Location dialog box appears. Edit the path to your server as necessary and choose OK to return to the New FrontPage Web dialog box.

You will add a theme to your Web in Chapter 20, "Real-Life Examples III: Dressing Up Your Webs."

5. Choose OK. FrontPage creates the Web and places a blank home page in the Web's root folder. The filename for the homepage, by default, is `index.htm` for the FrontPage Personal Web Server or `default.htm` for the Microsoft Personal Web Server.

6. Choose the Themes icon in the Views pane. For the time being, choose the This **W**eb Does Not Use Themes button, as shown in Figure 13.2. Click **A**pply.

Figure 13.2.

*From Themes view, choose This **W**eb Does Not Use Themes.*

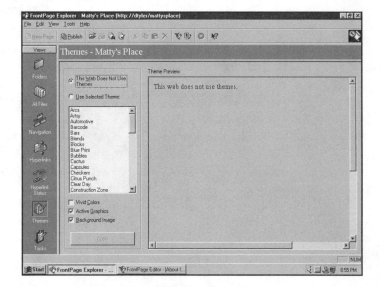

TASK

Adding Navigation Bars

You learned how to add pages to your navigation system in Chapter 8, "Designing Your Web Navigation." You will review the steps again in this chapter for your own Web site. Matty's Place, the example Web used in this chapter, is a Web site that contains several pages that focus on publicizing and promoting a highly popular (and fictitious) comic strip and related merchandise. The site consists of four main sections that you can use as a guideline to create your own Web site:

Main	The main section of the Web contains pages that help the user navigate through the site more easily. The pages included in this site include an About the Site page, a table of contents, a What's New page, a search page, and a guest book.
Matty's Gang	The pages in this section provide information about the characters in the Matty's Gang comic strip. These pages

demonstrate basic techniques, such as lists and tables. Replace the pages in this section with pages that focus on the main topic in your Web site or with several sections that focus on different areas of interest.

Cool Stuff   The pages in the Cool Stuff section demonstrate advanced features, such as animation and using FrontPage components as an alternative to navigation bars.

Discussion   The Discussion section demonstrates how you can add a discussion group to your Web site.

NOTE: Matty's Place, the site that is featured in the Real Life Examples chapters in this book, utilizes many features that are compatible with Internet Explorer 4.0. Because some of these features may not be compatible with other browsers, there are two additional versions of the site included on the CD-ROM. One site is designed so that it will be compatible with older browsers, and the other is designed to present the site in a frameset. Comments are provided on pages when techniques are important for you to learn. These additional samples are located in the `Book\Chap29\Examples` folder on the CD-ROM that accompanies this book.

To design the navigation bars for your site, switch to Navigation view in the FrontPage Explorer. Create four pages in the navigation pane as follows:

1. From the FrontPage Explorer, click the Navigation icon in the Views pane. You switch to Navigation view, and the home page appears in the navigation pane.

2. Right-click the home page in the navigation pane and choose Rename from the pop-up menu. Relabel the page `Matty's Place`. Press Enter to assign the new label.

3. With the page still selected, press the New Page button. FrontPage asks whether you want to create navigation bars. Choose **Y**es.

4. A new page appears in Navigation view. Press the New Page button three more times to create three additional pages.

5. Repeat step 2 to relabel the four new pages to sections that you want to create in your Web. Remember to keep the names fairly brief, because the text you enter here is that which appears on the navigation buttons. For Matty's Place, the sections are named as follows, as shown in Figure 13.3:

   ```
   Main
   Matty's Gang
   ```

Cool Stuff
Discussion

6. Choose the Folders icon in the Views pane. You switch to Folders view.

7. Highlight the root folder in your Web. Choose File | New | Folder. Name the new folder `main`.

8. Click the `main.htm` page in the Web's root folder and move it into the new `main` folder. Select the page in the main folder and rename the page `index.htm`.

9. Repeat steps 7 and 8 to create a new folder named `gang` (or a name that suits your main topic of interest). Move the page from the root folder into this new folder and rename the page `index.htm`.

10. Repeat steps 7 and 8 to create a new folder named `coolstuff`. Move the page from the root folder into the `coolstuff` folder and rename the page `index.htm`.

11. Repeat steps 7 and 8 to create a new folder named `discussion`. Move the `discussi.htm` page from the root folder into this new folder and rename the page `index.htm`. Figure 13.4 shows the new folders listed in the All Folders pane of Folders view.

Figure 13.3.

Add new pages in the navigation pane and assign brief names that describe the sections in your Web.

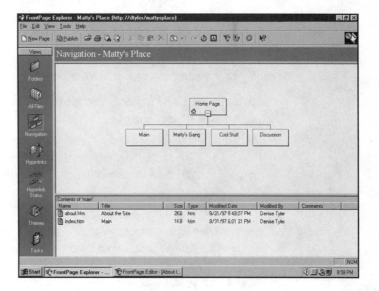

Figure 13.4.

Add four new folders in your Web to hold the pages in each section.

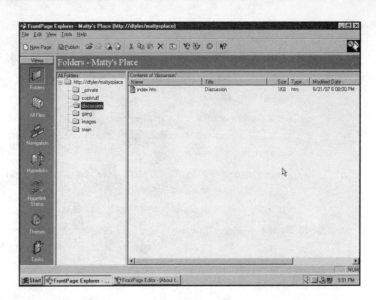

 Setting Your Shared Borders

As you learned in Chapter 8, you can add navigation bars to your pages by using the shared borders commands or by using the Insert | Navigation Bar command in the FrontPage Editor. In the following steps, you will configure shared borders that will be used by default for all the pages in your Web site.

To configure shared borders for your Web, follow these steps:

1. From the FrontPage Explorer, choose Tools | Shared Borders. The Shared Borders dialog box appears.

2. In the Borders to include section, check Top, Left, and Bottom, as shown in Figure 13.5. The top border will be used for the banner image, the left border for navigation bars, and the bottom border for copyright and contact information.

3. Choose OK. FrontPage applies the default shared border settings to your pages. When you open or create new pages, the default shared borders will automatically be added to your Web pages.

Figure 13.5.

Create top, left, and bottom shared borders to contain your banner, navigation buttons, and copyright information, respectively.

Describing Your Site

Your users will find it helpful if you include a page that provides a general overview of the pages that are included on your site. In the following task, you will create an About the Site page that serves this function. You will begin with one of the page templates provided with FrontPage 98, and you will then customize the content on the page.

To create your About the Site page, follow these steps:

1. From the FrontPage Explorer, choose **T**ools | Show FrontPage **E**ditor. The FrontPage Editor opens, and a new page appears in the FrontPage Editor. You can close this page, using the **F**ile | **C**lose command.

2. Choose **F**ile | **N**ew (Ctrl+N). The New dialog box appears.

3. Double-click the Wide Body with Headings template. The page appears in the FrontPage Editor.

4. In Chapter 20, you will assign a theme to your Web. In order for the page template to use the colors and fonts used in a Web theme, you have to remove the text formatting that is already applied to the page. Choose **E**dit | Select A**l**l (Ctrl+A); then choose F**o**rmat | **R**emove Formatting. All the content on the page changes to the default font.

5. Select the text in the first row of the table that reads `Main Heading Goes Here`. Edit the text to read `About the Site`. Use the Change Style drop-down menu to change the text to `Heading 2`.

6. Replace each of the lines that read `Section Heading Goes Here` with the names of the sections that you will include in your Web site. Use the Change Style drop-down menu to change each of the headings to `Heading 3`.

    For Matty's Place, these sections are named as follows:
    ```
    Main Section
    Matty's Gang
    Cool Stuff
    Discussion
    ```

7. Select the Main Section heading and click the Create or Edit Hyperlink button. Create a hyperlink to the `main/index.htm` page in your current Web.

8. Select the heading for the main topic in your Web (in this case, Matty's Gang). Click the Create or Edit Hyperlink button. Create a hyperlink to the home page in the main topic section of your Web (in this case, `gang/index.htm`).

9. Select the Cool Stuff heading. Click the Create or Edit Hyperlink button. Create a hyperlink to the `coolstuff/index.htm` page in your current Web.

10. Select the Discussion heading. Click the Create or Edit Hyperlink button. Create a hyperlink to the `discussion/index.htm` page in your current Web.

11. In the cell beneath each heading, describe the contents that will appear in each of the sections in your Web. At this point, your page should look similar to Figure 13.6.

Figure 13.6.

The About the Site page briefly describes the contents in each section in the Web and links to the home page in each of the main sections.

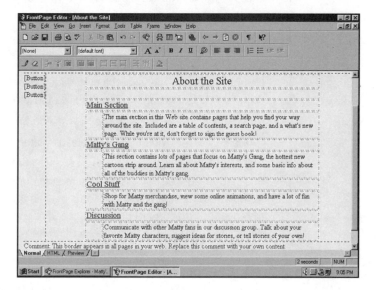

TIP: To add additional rows to the table, press the Tab key when the insertion point is in the last cell in the last row of the table. For rows that contain section headings, select both cells in the new row and merge them together with the Table | Merge Cells command. These procedures are discussed in more detail in Chapter 12, "Your Tables Are Ready."

12. Choose File | Save (Ctrl+S) or click the Save button on the Standard toolbar. The Save As dialog box appears.

13. From the list of folders in your current Web, double-click the `main` folder. Then enter the following information in the dialog box:

    URL: `about.htm`

    Title: `About the Site`

14. Choose OK to save your page to the Web.

15. Return to the FrontPage Explorer with the Show FrontPage Explorer button on the Standard toolbar. Click the Navigation icon in the Views pane.

16. From the Files pane at the bottom of the screen, double-click to select the Main folder. Drag the About the Site page into the navigation pane and release it when it attaches to the Main page in the navigation pane, as shown in Figure 13.7.

Figure 13.7.

As you add new pages to your Web, include them in the navigation pane.

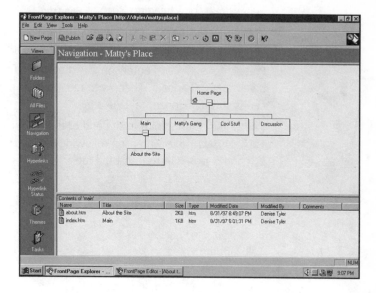

Creating a Page Template

TASK

If you foresee a number of pages in your site that will require the same layout or have the same type of content in them, you can create a page template. Matty's Place, for example, contains several pages that describe the characters in the comic strip. Each character information page includes a paragraph or two about the character, a table of biographical information, and a cartoon image of the character.

A template that includes the basic layout is shown in Figure 13.8. To create a similar template, follow these steps:

1. From the FrontPage Editor, choose the New button on the Standard toolbar. A new blank page appears in the FrontPage Editor.

2. Choose **T**able | **I**nsert Table. The Insert Table dialog box appears.

3. Enter the following settings and choose OK to insert the table on the page:

   Rows: 1
   Columns: 2
   Alignment: Center
   Border Size: 0
   Cell Pa**d**ding: 5

Cell Spacing: **5**

Specify **W**idth: **95**, in Percent

4. Position the insertion point inside the left cell in the table. Choose Heading 2 from the Change Style drop-down menu on the Format toolbar. Enter some generic text for a heading, such as **Heading**.

5. With the insertion point at the end of the heading, choose **I**nsert | Horizontal **L**ine. A horizontal line appears beneath the heading.

6. Press Enter again and enter some text to mark a place where an introductory paragraph will appear. Then, with the insertion point at the end of the text, choose **I**nsert | Horizontal **L**ine again.

7. With the insertion point at the end of the second horizontal line, choose T**a**ble | **I**nsert Table. Enter the following settings in the Insert Table dialog box and choose OK to insert the table:

Rows: **7**

Columns: **2**

Alignment: Center

Border Size: **2**

Cell Pa**d**ding: **2**

C**e**ll Spacing: **2**

Specify **W**idth: **100**, in Percent

8. Right-click inside the table and choose Table Properties from the pop-up menu. Enter the following additional properties in the Table Properties dialog box and choose OK to apply the settings:

Light Bord**e**r: Custom, **R**ed **255**, **G**reen **102**, B**l**ue **51**

Dar**k** Border: Maroon

9. Position the cursor over the left row in the new table and click to select the seven cells in the first column. Press Alt+Enter to open the Cell Properties dialog box. Enter the following settings and choose OK to apply them:

Hea**d**er Cell: Checked

Backgrou**n**d Color: Custom, **R**ed **255**, **G**reen **255**, Blue **204**

Specify **W**idth: 25, in Percent

10. If the labels in the table will be common from page to page, enter them in the left column. The table can be used to list hyperlinks to your favorite sites, product information, or other information that is pertinent to your Web pages. In the case of Matty's Place, the table lists information about each of the characters in the comic strip, as shown in Figure 13.8.

Figure 13.8.

Create page templates for pages that will contain similar content or require similar layouts.

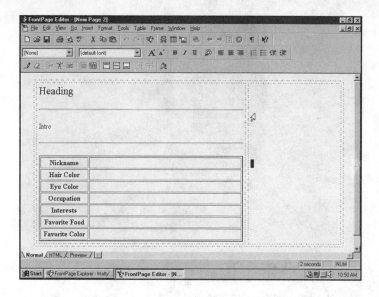

11. To save your page as a template, choose **F**ile I **S**ave (Ctrl+S) or click the Save button on the Standard toolbar. The Save As dialog box appears.

12. In the **U**RL field, enter a filename of 8 characters or less and enter a title for the template in the **T**itle field. In the case of Matty's character template, the following information is entered:

    URL: `mattchar.htm`
    Title: `Matty's Place Character Template`

13. Click the As Template button at the bottom of the Save As dialog box. The Save As Template dialog box shown in Figure 13.9 appears. The information in the **T**itle and **N**ame fields is already filled in for you, based on the information you entered in step 12. Enter a description for the template in the **D**escription field.

14. Choose OK to save the template. The next time you choose the **F**ile I **N**ew command in the FrontPage Editor, your template is available in the New dialog box, as shown in Figure 13.10.

Figure 13.9.

Use the Save As Template dialog box to enter a description for your page template.

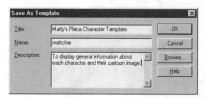

Figure 13.10.
Your new page template becomes available in the New dialog box in the FrontPage Editor.

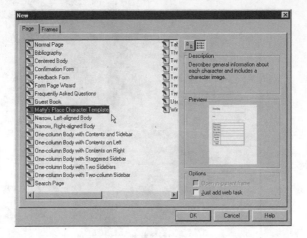

Adding More Content to Your Site

As you've learned so far in this chapter, you can use your own custom templates or those that are provided with FrontPage 98 to build up the content in your site. As you add pages to your site, be sure to also add navigation button labels in the FrontPage Explorer's navigation pane.

NOTE: Pages from Matty's Place are included on the CD-ROM that accompanies this book, in the `Book\Chap13\Examples` folder. You can use these pages as a guide to create and build up your own site in a similar manner.

To begin Matty's Place, several different character pages were created with the custom page template that was completed in the section "Creating a Page Template," earlier in this chapter. To create a page from your template, you simply choose the **File | N**ew command from the FrontPage Explorer and select the page template from the New dialog box, as shown in Figure 13.10. Seven pages were created from the template and saved into the `gang` folder in the Web. Figure 13.11 shows an example of one of the pages.

After the pages are created and saved to the Web, navigation button labels are added in the FrontPage Explorer's navigation pane. To add a page to the navigation bar, click and drag a file from the Files pane at the bottom of Navigation view into the navigation pane. Release the mouse button when the page attaches itself to the page on the previous level (the parent page), as shown in Figure 13.12. For more information on this, refer to Chapter 8.

Figure 13.11.

An example of a page created with the custom page template.

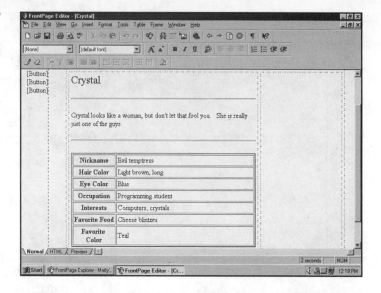

Figure 13.12.

To add the new pages to the navigation bars, click and drag a file from the Files pane into the navigation pane in the FrontPage Explorer's Navigation view.

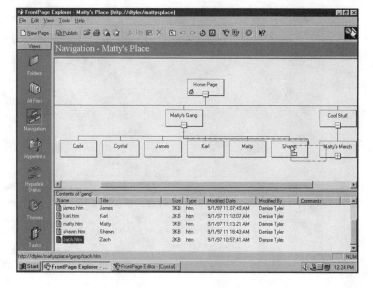

The Matty's Merch page, shown in Figure 13.13, provides links to products that can be ordered from the site's online catalog. This page began with a normal page template. You can easily create a new blank page by selecting the New button in the FrontPage Editor's standard toolbar. Three product pages were created from the custom page template, and links to the pages were added to the Matty's Merch page. A new folder named merchandise was added beneath the coolstuff folder in the Web, and the new pages were saved into this folder. Finally, as Figure 13.14 shows, the pages were added to the navigation pane in the FrontPage Explorer.

Figure 13.13.

The Matty's Merch page provides hyperlinks to the products pages in the Web.

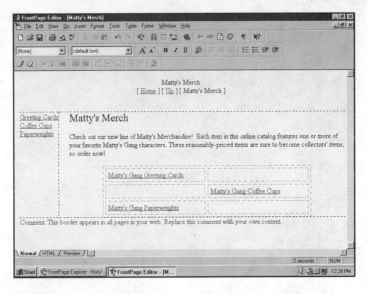

Figure 13.14.

The products pages and their index page are added to the Cool Stuff section in the navigation pane.

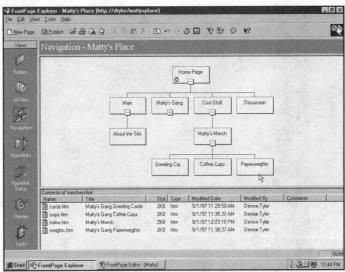

You learn how to create various kinds of lists in Chapter 11, "Organizing Information into Lists."

Because readers of the comic strip want to know more about their hero Matty, the makers of the site decided to expand upon his interests. First, a links page provides hyperlinks to other pages on the World Wide Web that relate to Matty's interests. In addition, there are several pages that explain various interests that Matty himself has, and why he is interested in them. These pages primarily demonstrate the use of different types of lists. You can find these additional pages in the gang folder in the

Web. In the navigation pane, they appear beneath the Matty page, as shown in Figure 13.15.

`animals.htm`	Definition list
`cars.htm`	Numbered list
`hunting.htm`	Nested and expandable numbered list
`links.htm`	Nested, bulleted list of hyperlinks to other sites on the World Wide Web
`movies.htm`	Expandable, bulleted list
`pinball.htm`	Bulleted list

Figure 13.15.

Matty's Interests pages appear in the Matty's Gang section of the Web.

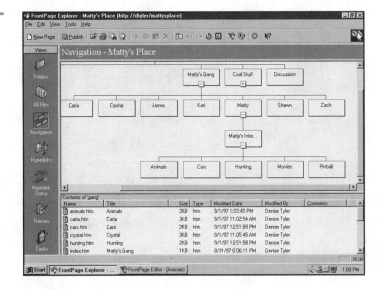

A Summary of the Pages in Matty's Place

Matty's Place already contains the beginnings of 24 pages. Based on the techniques you learned in the chapters in this section, your pages contain text navigation bars, horizontal rules, hyperlinks to other pages in your Web and to sites on the World Wide Web, different types of lists, and tables.

The pages in Matty's Place are summarized in Table 13.1, which shows the folder each page appears in, the filename, page description, and its location in the navigation pane shown in Figure 13.16.

Figure 13.16.

Matty's Place pages as they appear in the navigation pane in the FrontPage Explorer.

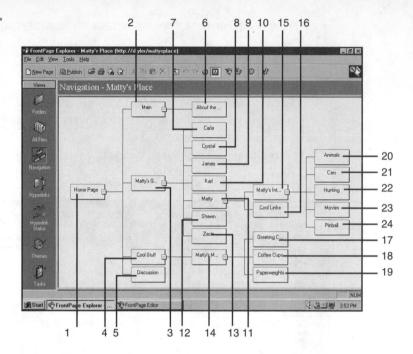

Table 13.1. Pages in Matty's Place.

Number	Filename	Page Description
		Root Folder
1	index.html	Matty's Place Home Page
		Coolstuff Folder
4	index.htm	Cool Stuff section home page
		Coolstuff/Merchandise Folder
17	cards.htm	Matty's Gang Greeting Cards
18	cups.htm	Matty's Gang Coffee Cups
14	index.htm	Matty's Merch section home page
19	weights.htm	Matty's Gang Paperweights
		Discussion Folder
5	index.htm	Discussion section home page
		Gang Folder
20	animals.htm	Animals (Matty's Interests section)
7	carla.htm	Carla (Matty's Gang section)
21	cars.htm	Cars (Matty's Interests section)

Number	Filename	Page Description
8	crystal.htm	Crystal (Matty's Gang section)
22	hunting.htm	Hunting (Matty's Interests section)
3	index.htm	Matty's Gang section home page
15	interests.htm	Matty's Interests section home page
9	james.htm	James (Matty's Gang section)
10	karl.htm	Karl (Matty's Gang section)
16	links.htm	Cool Links (Matty's Interests section)
11	matty.htm	Matty (Matty's Gang section)
23	movies.htm	Movies (Matty's Interests section)
24	pinball.htm	Pinball (Matty's Interests section)
12	shawn.htm	Shawn (Matty's Gang section)
13	zach.htm	Zach (Matty's Gang section)
	Main Folder	
6	about.htm	About the Site
2	index.htm	Main Section home page

Workshop Wrap-Up

Using the techniques that you learned in this chapter, you are well on the way to creating your Web site. Your pages contain lists, tables, and text navigation bars. You learned how to add pages to your Web using existing templates or templates that you create yourself. You also learned how to add your pages to your navigation bars and how to use shared borders to place the navigation bars onto designated regions in your pages.

Next Steps

Admittedly, the pages that you created in this chapter need some dressing up, and that is precisely what you will learn how to do in the chapters that follow. You'll continue with your Web project by adding themes, images, animation, active content, and FrontPage components to your site. You'll learn these techniques in the following chapters:

❑ In Chapter 14, "Using FrontPage Style Sheets and Themes," you'll convert these plain and simple pages into pages with graphic backgrounds, navigation buttons, and different font faces and colors.

❏ In Chapter 15, "Working with Images and Sound," you'll learn how to add images to your pages and how to add a background sound that plays when the page opens in a Web browser.

❏ In Chapter 16, "Working with Animation and Active Content," you'll learn how to apply animated text, page transitions, and more to your Web pages.

❏ In Chapter 17, "Integrating with Other Editors," you'll learn how to configure other editors to open and edit other types of content in your Web pages.

❏ In Chapter 18, "Frames: Pages with Split Personalities," you'll learn how to create and configure framesets.

❏ In Chapter 19, "Using FrontPage Components," you'll learn how to insert and configure several different components that help make your Web site design easier.

❏ In Chapter 20, "Real-Life Examples III: Dressing Up Your Webs," you'll apply all the techniques you learn in the preceding chapters to the Matty's Place Web site.

Q&A

Q: Is there any way to easily tell whether a page has not been added to my navigation bars?

A: Yes. Choose All Files view in the FrontPage Explorer. The fourth column in All Files view is labeled Orphan. If Yes appears in this column, the associated page has not yet been added to the navigation pane and will not appear in the navigation bars. If No appears in this column, the page has been added and will appear in the navigation bars.

Q: Can I add pages from other Web sites into the navigation bars?

A: No. In order for a page to be added to a navigation bar, it must exist in your current Web.

Q: I added an expandable list to one of my pages, but nothing happens when I double-click the list in my browser. Did I do something wrong?

A: In order for expandable lists to work correctly, the browser that you view the page in must support Dynamic HTML. Internet Explorer 4.0 does support this feature.

P A R T

III
Advanced Techniques

FOURTEEN

Using FrontPage Style Sheets and Themes

FrontPage provides two ways to assign background images and text colors to your pages. The first method creates pages that are consistent regarding the background images and text and hyperlink colors you use in your Web pages, and it is compatible with most browsers. The second method uses FrontPage Themes to take the appearance of your Web pages a step farther. Themes create a consistent appearance with the banner images, navigation buttons, horizontal rules, button images, font faces, font sizes, and font colors used throughout your Web site. Using cascading style sheet properties and many of the latest and hottest Web technologies, your Web pages use professionally designed image and color combinations with a minimum of effort.

In this chapter, you

- ❏ Learn how to develop and use FrontPage style sheets that are compatible with most browsers
- ❏ Assign a FrontPage style sheet to another page in your Web
- ❏ Learn about FrontPage themes and how to assign them to your entire Web or to specific pages in your Web
- ❏ Review the features that are unavailable or enhanced when you use FrontPage themes

Tasks in this chapter:

- ❏ Using FrontPage Style Sheets
- ❏ Assigning a FrontPage Style Sheet to Another Page
- ❏ Enabling Warnings Before You Apply a Theme
- ❏ Switching to Themes View
- ❏ Choosing a Theme
- ❏ Applying a Theme to a Page

Using FrontPage Style Sheets

The advantage of using the Page Properties dialog box to assign page properties to your Web pages is that the properties you select can be displayed in any browser that supports images and different font and hyperlink colors (which is most of them nowadays).

NOTE: To differentiate between the two kinds of style sheets that FrontPage uses, I will refer to the method that is compatible with more browsers as a *FrontPage style sheet*. The style sheets used with themes are *cascading style sheets*, which are discussed in more detail later in this chapter and in Chapter 27, "Using Styles."

To create a FrontPage style sheet, follow these steps:

> If you need further assistance on creating an empty Web, refer to Chapter 5, "Lightning-Speed Web Design."

1. From the FrontPage Explorer, use the **F**ile | **N**ew | FrontPage **W**eb command to create an empty Web in which you can practice. Name your Web **Style Sheets**.

2. Choose **V**iew | **T**hemes or click the Themes icon in the Views pane to switch to Themes view in the FrontPage Explorer. Select the This **W**eb Does Not Use Themes radio button and click **A**pply.

3. Choose **T**ools | Show FrontPage **E**ditor or use the Show FrontPage Editor button to open the FrontPage Editor. The FrontPage Editor opens and a blank page appears.

4. Choose **F**ile | Page Proper**t**ies. The Page Properties dialog box appears, opened to the General tab.

5. Enter `Web Style Sheet` in the **T**itle field.

6. Click the Background tab, shown in Figure 14.1. Here, you assign the background image and text and hyperlink colors for your page.

7. To specify a background image for your page, check the Background **I**mage checkbox. Click the **B**rowse button. The Select Background Image dialog box appears.

8. To insert a background image from your clip art folder, select the **C**lip Art button. From the category list at the left of the Microsoft Clip Gallery 3.0 dialog box, select the Web Backgrounds category, as shown in Figure 14.2. Double-click on one of the light backgrounds to assign it to your page.

Figure 14.1.

Use the Background tab to assign a background image or color and text colors to Web pages that do not use themes.

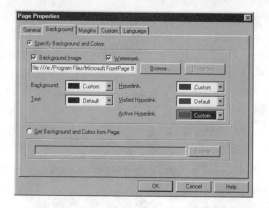

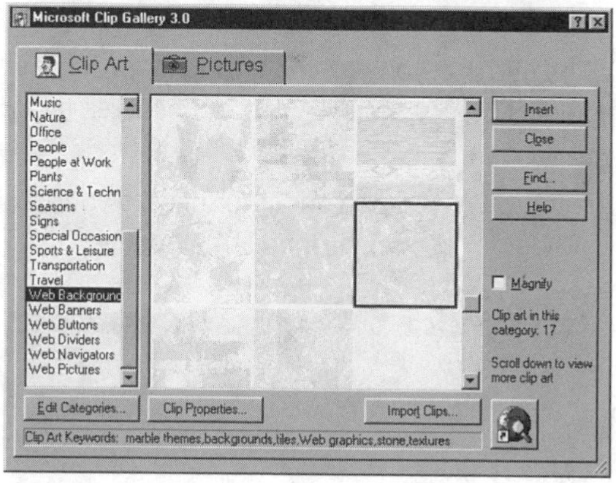

Figure 14.2.

Select a background image from the Web Backgrounds category in the Microsoft Clip Gallery.

9. To make the background image a watermark (a stationary background image that does not scroll), check the **W**atermark checkbox.

10. From the **T**ext drop-down menu, choose Custom to create a custom text color for your Web page. Use the Color dialog box, shown in Figure 14.3, to create a custom color of **R**ed **51**, **G**reen **0**, Bl**u**e **0**. This is a very deep maroon color. Choose OK to return to the Page Properties dialog box.

Figure 14.3.

Create a custom color for your text and hyperlinks in the Color dialog box.

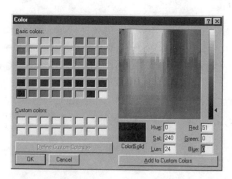

11. In a similar manner, repeat step 10 to select the following colors for the hyperlinks on your pages:

Hyperlink   Choose Custom, and create a custom color of **R**ed **0**, **G**reen **0**, **B**lue **204**.

Visited Hyperlink   Leave this set at the default color of dark purple.

Active Hyperlink   Choose Custom and create a custom color of **R**ed **204**, **G**reen **0**, **B**lue **0**.

12. Click OK to exit the Page Properties dialog box. The background image appears on your page.

13. Choose **F**ile | **S**ave (Ctrl+S) or click the Save button in the Standard toolbar. The Save As dialog box appears.

14. The title that you entered in step 2 appears in the **T**itle field. From the list of folders in your current Web, double-click the _private folder. Then enter **webstyle.htm** in the **U**RL field.

15. Choose OK to save your style sheet to your Web. The Save Embedded Files dialog box shown in Figure 14.4 appears.

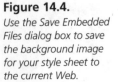

Figure 14.4.
Use the Save Embedded Files dialog box to save the background image for your style sheet to the current Web.

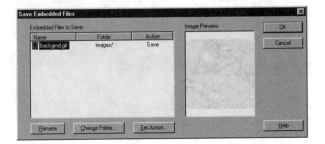

16. Highlight the filename in the Embedded Files to Save list. The **R**ename button activates. Press **R**ename and rename the background image **backgrnd.gif**. Press Enter or click outside the bounding box to rename the file.

17. With the filename still highlighted, press the **C**hange Folder button. Double-click the images folder to select it. If there are no images in your images folder, choose OK to save your background into this folder. If other images already exist in this folder, highlight one of the filenames and then choose OK. You return to the Save Embedded files dialog box. The Folder column displays images/ as the folder to which your image is saved.

18. Choose OK. Your background image is saved to the `images` folder, and your style sheet is saved to the `_private` folder.

19. Choose **F**ile | **C**lose to close the Web Style Sheet page. An example of this style sheet is furnished in the `Book\Chap14\Examples` folder on the CD-ROM that accompanies this book.

Assigning a FrontPage Style Sheet to Another Page

Now that you have created your own FrontPage style sheet, you can easily assign it to another page. You use the Background tab in the Page Properties dialog box to accomplish this task as well. In the following task, you will create a new page based on one of the FrontPage page templates. You will assign the style sheet that you created in the previous task to this Web page.

To assign your style sheet to another page, follow these steps:

1. From the FrontPage Editor, choose **F**ile | **N**ew (Ctrl+N). The New Page dialog box appears.

2. Double-click the One-column Body with Contents and Sidebar page template or highlight the template name and choose OK. The new page appears in the FrontPage Editor.

3. Choose **F**ormat | Bac**k**ground. The Page Properties dialog box opens to the Background tab shown in Figure 14.1.

4. Choose the **G**et Background and Colors from Page radio button. The choices in the Specify Background and Colors section of the dialog box are disabled.

5. Click the B**r**owse button. The Current Web dialog box opens.

6. Double-click the `_private` folder to select it, then double-click the `webstyle.htm` page to assign your style sheet. You return to the Page Properties dialog box.

7. Click OK. The properties you assigned to your style sheet are assigned to your current page. Optionally, save your practice page to your Web.

You assign your Web style sheet to each of the pages in your Web on an individual basis. If you later decide to change the look of your Web pages, you can open the `private/webstyle.htm` page and change the background image, background color, and text and hyperlink colors. When you resave the page to your Web, all pages that are linked to your FrontPage style sheet will change their appearance automatically.

Using Themes with Your FrontPage Webs and Pages

New to FrontPage 98 is the capability of adding Web themes to your entire Web site or to individual pages. Using Themes view in the FrontPage Explorer, you can apply banner images, navigation buttons, horizontal rule images, bullet images, and font faces and colors to all the pages in your Web site. If you get tired of the way your Web looks, simply change the look by applying a different theme. With the click of a few buttons and in a matter of moments, your Web site looks entirely different. You can also apply a theme to a single page from within the FrontPage Editor.

Though some of the features of FrontPage themes are viewable in only the most current and up-to-date Web browsers, they offer several advantages. Your pages display a consistent appearance, using the same graphics and fonts throughout the site. Each of the dozens of available themes is professionally designed, and the images and fonts are coordinated to work well together.

You use Themes view in the FrontPage Explorer to apply a theme to your entire Web. There are over fifty themes from which you can choose. Each theme gives your Web site a consistent appearance throughout all the pages. To apply a theme to a single Web page, use the **F**ormat | **T**heme command in the FrontPage Editor.

 TASK

Enabling Warnings Before You Apply a Theme

Because themes change the way fonts and images appear in your pages, FrontPage 98 issues a warning before you permanently apply a theme to your Web. When you initially apply a theme to your Web, you may receive the following message:

```
Applying a theme to a FrontPage Web will change the way
fonts, colors, bullets, and lines appear in all pages.
This will permanently replace some of the existing
formatting information. Do you want to apply the theme?
```

Choose **Y**es to apply your theme or **N**o to cancel the procedure. You can enable or disable this warning through the Options dialog box as follows:

1. From the FrontPage Explorer, choose **T**ools | **O**ptions. The Options dialog box appears, opened to the General tab shown in Figure 14.5.

2. To disable the warning, uncheck the box that reads Warn before permanently **a**pplying themes. Check the box again to enable the warning.

3. Choose OK to exit the Options dialog box and update the setting.

Figure 14.5.

The Options dialog box allows you to enable or disable a warning before you apply themes to your Web.

 # Switching to Themes View

Using themes, you can quickly select a graphical theme that is used throughout your entire Web. This gives your site a consistent appearance with a minimum of work. Each theme uses its own style of banner images, navigation buttons, horizontal rules, and bullets. In addition, various font faces, sizes, and colors are assigned to complement the graphics you select. The themes gallery contains dozens of themes from which you can choose.

To switch to Themes view, follow one of these procedures:

❑ From the FrontPage Explorer, choose **V**iew | **T**hemes.

❑ Click the Themes icon in the Views pane along the left side of the FrontPage Explorer workspace.

 # Choosing a Theme

Once you enter Themes view, you'll see the screen shown in Figure 14.6. If you choose to use themes in your Web, select the name of the theme you want to assign to your Web from the left pane. As you highlight one of the names in the Themes list, a preview of the theme appears in the Theme Preview pane at the right.

You can also select to use vivid colors in your text or graphics, to use graphics that animate or change state when the user moves his or her mouse over the button, or to apply or remove a background image.

To apply a theme to your entire Web, follow these steps:

1. To configure your Web to use standard FrontPage style sheets or to remove the theme from your current Web, select the This **W**eb Does Not Use Themes radio button. The Theme Preview displays a gray page and text that reads This web does not use themes. Click the **A**pply button to apply this setting to your Web.

2. To apply a theme to all the pages in your Web, choose the **U**se Selected Theme radio button. For this example, select the Arcs theme shown in Figure 14.6. A preview of the theme you select appears in the Theme Preview pane.

Figure 14.6.

Use Themes view in the FrontPage Explorer to assign a Web theme to all of the pages in your Web.

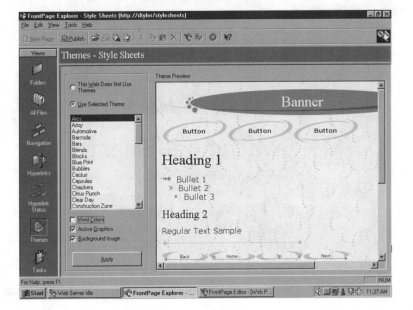

NOTE: Themes are applied to all pages, unless the This **W**eb Does Not Use Themes option is selected or a page is configured to use its own theme. This may include pages that you have already configured with standard FrontPage style sheets. To revert to your FrontPage style sheet, open the pages you want to change in the FrontPage Editor. Use the **F**ormat | **T**heme command to set each page to not use themes, as discussed in "Applying a Theme to a Page," later in this chapter.

3. Use the right scrollbar in the Theme Preview to move up or down in the preview window. This enables you to view all the graphic and text elements that will be used in the theme.

4. If you want to use brighter text colors in your Web, check the Vivid **C**olors checkbox. The brighter colors generally apply to the headings and link colors on your pages.

5. To use static graphics for your navigation buttons, uncheck the Active **G**raphics checkbox. Check this option if you want to use animated graphics in your navigation buttons. Hover buttons and animated GIFs are used with active graphics.

NOTE: *Hover buttons* are small Java applets that are not compatible with all browsers. They are discussed in more detail in Chapter 16, "Working with Animation and Active Content." Other browsers may have difficulty displaying the static graphic and text navigation bars as well. NCSA Mosaic, for example, did not render graphic navigation buttons and the superimposed text for them.

Preview the pages that use Web themes in your favorite browsers to make sure they display properly. If they do not, you can use standard FrontPage style sheets, discussed in "Using FrontPage Style Sheets," earlier in this chapter. Develop your own navigation bars on individual pages and include them on your Web pages with Include Page components. This FrontPage component is discussed in more detail in Chapter 19, "Using FrontPage Components."

6. To use a solid background color for your Web pages, uncheck the **B**ackground Image checkbox. Checking this option applies a background image that is compatible with the banner and navigation images in your Web.

7. Click **A**pply to apply the theme to all the pages in your Web that are configured to use the default Web theme. FrontPage will automatically apply the theme to any new pages you create. The FrontPage Explorer copies several files into your Web, which you can find in the _themes folder and subfolders.

NOTE: If you reassign a different theme to a Web that has already had a theme applied to it, you will need to refresh your Web to view the files associated with the new theme. Choose **V**iew | **R**efresh (F5) from the FrontPage Explorer to update the files in your Web. You should then be able to see the new files listed in Folders or All Files view.

 ## Applying a Theme to a Page

There may be cases where you want to apply a different theme to a page or section of pages in your Web. You can override the default theme setting for a page from within the FrontPage Editor. Choose the **F**ormat | **T**heme command from the FrontPage Editor to apply a theme to your active page.

To apply a unique theme to a page in your Web, follow these steps:

1. From the FrontPage Editor, open the page that you want to change.

2. Choose **F**ormat I **T**heme. The Choose Theme dialog box shown in Figure 14.7 appears.

Figure 14.7.

Use the Choose Theme dialog box in the FrontPage Editor to apply a theme to a single page in your Web.

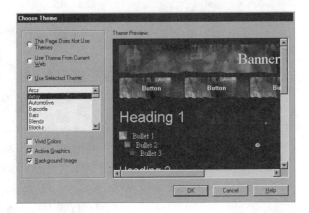

3. Select one of the following options for your current page:

   ❏ To remove the theme from the current page so that you can use a standard FrontPage style sheet, check the **T**his Page Does Not Use Themes radio button.

   ❏ To reassign the theme that you selected for your entire Web, check the Use Theme From Current **W**eb checkbox.

   ❏ Choose the **U**se Selected Theme radio button if you want to use the current Web theme with different options (Vivid **C**olors, Active **G**raphics, or **B**ackground Image), or if you want to use an entirely different theme for this page. Select the theme from the Theme list and view the preview of the theme in the Theme Preview pane.

4. Choose any of the following options for your active page (as described in "Choosing a Theme," earlier in this chapter):

   ❏ If you want to use brighter text colors in your Web, check the Vivid **C**olors checkbox.

   ❏ To use static graphics for your navigation buttons, uncheck the Active **G**raphics checkbox.

   ❏ To use a solid background color for your Web pages, uncheck the **B**ackground Image checkbox.

5. Choose OK. FrontPage applies the theme to your active page.

Notes About Themes

When you use Themes in your FrontPage Webs, many of the text styles and heading styles that you insert on your pages will automatically use the font faces and colors defined in the cascading style sheets used by your Web or page theme. This is true of the following text elements:

❑ Body text (the font used for Normal paragraphs on your pages)

❑ Hyperlink text (the color and style of the text used for a hyperlink that the user has not yet followed)

❑ Visited hyperlink text (the color and style of the text used for a hyperlink that the user has visited)

❑ Active hyperlink text (the color and style of the text used for a hyperlink that the user is in the process of navigating to)

❑ Heading 1 through Heading 6 (the color and style of the text used for all heading styles on your pages)

If you use the Paragraph Properties dialog box to format a paragraph, you see the following results:

❑ When you choose Normal paragraphs, the selected text will use the body font defined in the theme.

❑ When you choose Address paragraphs, the selected text will use an italicized version of the body font defined in the theme.

❑ When you choose Formatted paragraphs, the selected text uses a fixed-width font such as Courier.

When you use Themes in your Web pages, you will be unable to change hyperlink colors through the Page Properties dialog box. The Background tab will be unavailable, as shown in Figure 14.8. To change the colors of your hyperlinks, you will need to edit the cascading style sheets associated with your themes. See "Files Associated with Themes," later in this chapter, to learn which files contain the properties you need to edit.

Setting Page Properties with Themes

If the active page has a Web or page theme assigned to it, the Background tab in the Page Properties dialog box is unavailable. If you prefer to use FrontPage style sheets instead of cascading style sheets, configure your Web or current page so that it does not use themes. You can then specify background colors, images, text, and hyperlink colors by using the Page Properties dialog box in the FrontPage Editor.

Figure 14.8.

When your Web page uses themes, the Background tab in the Page Properties dialog box will be unavailable.

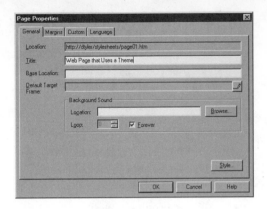

Using Bulleted Lists with Themes

When you use bulleted lists in your pages, the List Properties dialog box shown in Figure 14.9 enables you to use the bullet images that are applicable to your current theme or another image that you specify. For more information about bulleted lists, refer to Chapter 11, "Organizing Information into Lists."

Figure 14.9.

You can use the bullet images from your current theme or select another bullet image.

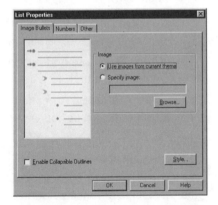

Using Themes with Discussion Webs

In Chapter 24, "Real-Life Examples IV: Adding Interactivity," you work with the Discussion Web Wizard. You have the option of choosing a theme for the pages that the Discussion Web Wizard creates, providing that you are creating the discussion group in a new FrontPage Web. If you are adding the discussion Web to an already existing Web, the Discussion Web Wizard does not prompt you to select another theme.

When you configure the submission form in your Discussion group, you are asked to provide a URL for a style sheet in your Web in the Options for Discussion Form Handler dialog box shown in Figure 14.10. This dialog box and its options are explained in more detail in Chapter 23, "Configuring Form Handlers." If a theme has been applied to your Web, the URL that you enter in the **G**et background and colors from page field will have no effect on your discussion articles.

Figure 14.10.

*When you use themes, discussion group articles will use the same theme that you set for your Web. The **G**et background and colors from page field in the Options for Discussion Form Handler dialog box has no effect.*

Using Horizontal Lines with Themes

When you insert a horizontal line on a Web page that has a theme applied to it, the image used for your Web theme appears. If you double-click on the horizontal line to change its properties, you will notice that the Width, Height, and Color fields in the Horizontal Line Properties dialog box are disabled. However, you will be able to change the alignment of the horizontal line to **L**eft, C**e**nter, or **R**ight, as shown in Figure 14.11.

Figure 14.11.

When themes are applied to your Web pages, you cannot change the width, height, and color of a horizontal line.

Saving Pages with Themes as Templates

In Chapter 5, you learned how to create templates from your pages. Depending on how you assigned the theme, you will achieve different results when you use the template to create new pages in a Web.

❑ To create a page template that uses the theme assigned to the Web that you are creating new pages for, first create the content of your page template. Use the **F**ormat | **T**heme command in the FrontPage Editor to assign the Use Theme from Current **W**eb option in the Choose Theme dialog box. Then save your page template as outlined in Chapter 5. When you use the template to create new pages for a Web, the page template will use whichever theme you have assigned to your current Web.

❑ To create a page template that will always use a specific theme, regardless of the theme that you select for a Web, choose the **U**se Selected Theme option in the Choose Theme dialog box before you save your template.

Using Page Banners with Themes

When you use the **I**nsert I FrontPage **C**omponent command to insert a page banner on your page, you select whether your banner appears as an image or as text. This is set in the Page Banner Properties dialog box shown in Figure 14.12. Either selection (Images or Text) uses the properties associated with the theme applied to your active page. If the current page does not have a theme assigned to it, the page banner inserts the page title as large, bold text.

Figure 14.12.

When you insert page banners on a page that has a theme, the banner uses the images and fonts associated with the theme. If no theme is applied, the page title appears as large, bold text.

Using Themes with Framesets

If you want to assign a different theme to each of the frames in your frameset, you have to assign them through the FrontPage Editor, as outlined in "Applying a Theme to a Page," earlier in this chapter. Generally, the main frame in your frameset will use the default Web theme, and navigation areas in your frameset can use another compatible theme.

Using Themes with Background Images

When your page has a theme applied to it, the **F**ormat I Bac**k**ground command is disabled. You will not be able to use the Image toolbar to apply image effects to the background image.

Workshop Wrap-Up

With FrontPage 98, you have two ways to attain a consistent appearance throughout all the pages in your Web site. You can use FrontPage style sheets to assign common background images or colors and text and hyperlink colors to your Web pages. This type of style sheet offers the advantage of being compatible with most browsers. You can also use FrontPage themes to apply professionally designed banner graphics, navigation buttons, bullets, horizontal rules, and font faces and colors to your Web pages. Though some theme elements are compatible with fewer browsers, you can recommend that the user download a browser, such as Internet Explorer 4.0, that is capable of displaying all the features that Web themes utilize.

Next Steps

In the next chapter, you will learn how to add images and sound to your Web pages and how to use and manage your clip art using the new Microsoft Clip Gallery. To learn more about topics that relate to themes and style sheets, refer to the following chapters:

❏ Refer to Chapter 8, "Designing Your Web Navigation," to learn about navigation bars and page banners used with your themes.

❏ See Chapter 19, "Using FrontPage Components," to learn how you can use the Include Page component to design navigation bars that are compatible with more browsers.

❏ See Chapter 27, "Using Styles," to learn how to develop and use your own cascading style sheets and how to customize styles throughout your Web site.

❏ See Appendix D, "About Theme-Related Cascading Style Sheets," for information about the CSS selectors and properties used in your themes.

Q&A

Q: Can I use themes in such a manner that each of the main sections in my Web uses a different theme?

A: You can assign a Web theme in the FrontPage Explorer that will be applied to your entire Web. However, if you want other pages to use different themes, you'll have to apply them on a page-by-page basis. You cannot, for example, assign a different Web theme to all pages in a single folder at once.

Q: Can I customize the graphics in a theme?

A: You can, but you shouldn't change the cascading style sheets unless you are familiar with how to format cascading style sheet files and assign properties. Appendix D gives a complete list of the files associated with themes and the theme elements that each property sets. The easiest way to replace the graphics is to replace the existing images in your Web with new graphics that use the same filename. This way you won't need to touch the existing .css files.

Don't be discouraged if you cannot figure out CSS coding. You can use familiar dialog boxes to create your own cascading style sheets also. See Chapter 27 to learn how to create your own cascading style sheets.

FIFTEEN

Working with Images and Sound

When I first started browsing the Internet, the Web didn't offer too much in the way of graphics. As a person who enjoys the visual side of electronic media and communications, I quickly lost interest and didn't get back on the Web for quite a while. As a person who did a lot of reading during the day at work, it wasn't fun for me to spend my leisure time reading as well.

Graphics and multimedia are running rampant on the Web now, and people are taking notice. We're able to design past that standard WWW-gray background color. We can use tiled background images, specify custom colors, use images for links, and even place animations in the pages. The Web is becoming the way I like it! Obviously, a lot of us out here enjoy a graphical environment. Give us flash and give us style, but do it in a manner that doesn't tie up our modems too long or distract us, okay?

Images: To Be or Not To Be?

Eighty percent or more of the people who use the Internet use graphical browsers. This percentage should increase even more in the near future; however, that doesn't necessarily mean that all the people who use graphical browsers actually view the graphics. Some people don't like the added download time and turn the feature off if they can.

How do you keep these people happy? One way is to keep your pages lean and mean and your graphics small. It doesn't take a person with a 56KB modem very long to download that 300KB animated header graphic you're so proud of. It takes a *long* time to download a header graphic of that size on a slower modem. Whether you use GIF or JPEG images (you'll learn about the differences between them in "Using Images in Your Pages," later in this chapter), try to limit the total page size (including the images) to 50KB or less.

TIP:
When you open a page in the FrontPage Editor, an estimate of how long it takes to download your current page appears in the right portion of the status bar.

There are several ways that you can economize on the size of your graphics. Here are some ideas:

❑ Reduce the dimensions of your images. It's not often that you need an image that consumes the entire browser screen. If you do, try to economize your image using another method.

❑ Rather than create a border around your image, crop out that extra space. Use the horizontal and vertical spacing settings in the Image Properties dialog box to increase the amount of space between the image and the contents on your page.

❑ Use JPEG compression on photographic-quality or high-resolution graphics. JPEG compression produces files that are generally much smaller than GIF files.

❑ If your GIF image contains only a few colors, reduce the image's palette so that it includes only the colors contained in the image. A 256-color palette adds a lot of extra "weight" to an image that contains only a handful of colors.

There is a great utility available that helps put your images on a diet. Check out Ulead PhotoImpact GIF/JPEG Smart Saver, which you can download from the page shown in Figure 15.1. It lets you view the original image beside a preview while you adjust palettes for GIFs or compression for JPEGs. This enables you to get the best quality image at the smallest file size possible. You can download a trial version of this utility, along with free animation files and trial versions of other Web-related image software, at Ulead's Web site:

`http://www.ulead.com`

Figure 15.1.

Ulead's PhotoImpact GIF/JPEG Smart Saver enables you to preview your Web images while you adjust settings to achieve the smallest file size possible.

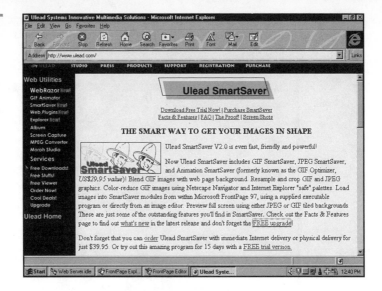

Using Images in Your Pages

Web pages usually use one of two image formats—GIF or JPEG. FrontPage can also import several other types of common image formats, but it converts them to one of these two formats. When FrontPage sees an image that uses 256 or fewer colors, it automatically converts the file to GIF format. Images that use more than 256 colors are converted to JPEG.

GIF Images

GIF images are best used for gray-scale photographs, cartoon-type images, small icons, buttons, bars, dividers and bullets, and small-to-medium-sized header graphics, providing that the file size doesn't get too large. If your image uses only a few colors or has large areas of solid color, the GIF format may be your best choice. Here are some of the things you can do with GIF images:

❏ GIF images can be *interlaced*—rendered on your screen in progressive steps. The image appears blocky at first, but at least something appears on the page fairly quickly. As the image is downloaded to a local computer, the blockiness gives way to a clear image.

❏ You can designate transparent areas in a GIF image, giving the appearance that the image is floating on the background of your page.

❏ GIF images can be animated. After creating a series of images that differ slightly, as shown in Figure 15.2, you can assemble them into one file with a GIF animation utility. You insert an animated GIF file the same way you do an ordinary GIF. Only browsers that support animated GIFs can display the animation. Browsers that don't support animated GIFs display the first frame of the animation as a still image.

Figure 15.2.
You can create several frames that differ slightly and assemble them with a GIF animation utility to create an animated GIF file.

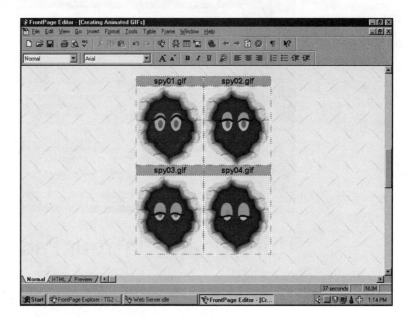

Appendix B, "FrontPage Reference," points you to some shareware and retail programs that enable you to build animated GIF files.

JPEG Images

JPEG images are generally used to display photographic quality images in a greatly reduced file size by using various compression schemes. In most cases, a true-color JPEG image that uses good- to high-quality compression is smaller than a 256-color image of the same dimension, yet it contains more colors. Colors are reduced by applying image compression, but you won't see a lot of difference if you use compression settings wisely.

The compression settings you choose vary from program to program. Some programs, for example, have you choose the amount of compression in percentages, with lower values indicating best quality. For example, if you specify **10%** compression, the file is compressed to 90 percent of maximum quality. In other programs, you specify compression levels in percentages with 100 percent quality being best. In these cases, you can use 60 to 85 percent quality (depending on the richness of the image). Photographs and images with a lot of color differences can withstand a higher amount of compression than images with many solid areas. Other programs, such as Adobe Photoshop and Fractal Design Painter, give a range of choices, such as low, good, and high or low, medium and high. Don't choose low, because it causes too much deterioration.

TIP: Don't recompress a compressed JPEG image. If you think your image might need to be modified again at some point, keep a true-color version of it on your hard drive (TIF, TGA, true-color PCX, true-color BMP, and so on). Make the changes to the original and compress again.

TASK

Inserting an Image on Your Page

You use the Image dialog box, shown in Figure 15.3, to insert an image onto your pages. The Image dialog box enables you to insert images in several ways. You can insert graphics files into your pages from your currently opened Web, from a drive on your local computer, or from a network drive. You can also insert images from the World Wide Web or from the FrontPage clip art folder. New to FrontPage 98 is the capability of acquiring an image with a scanner, digital camera, or other TWAIN-compatible device.

To insert an image on your page, use the following steps:

1. Move the insertion point to the place where you want to insert the image.
2. Choose Insert | Image. The Image dialog box shown in Figure 15.3 appears.

Figure 15.3.
Use the Image dialog box to insert an image on your page.

❏ To select an image from your current Web, select the folder in which the image appears from the list of folders in your current Web. Double-click the name of the image you want to insert or highlight the image and choose OK to insert the image.

❏ To select an image from your local or network hard drive, click the Select a file on your computer button that appears at the right of the URL field. From the Select File dialog box, use the Look in drop-down menu to locate the drive and directory in which the image appears. Double-click the filename or highlight the file and choose OK to insert the image.

❏ To select a background from the World Wide Web, enter the absolute URL of the image in the **U**RL field or choose a URL from the drop-down menu. Click OK to insert the image.

❏ To use your browser to locate an image on your local or network computer or on the World Wide Web, click the Use your web browser to select a page or file button that is located at the right of the **U**RL field. Use your browser to navigate to the image you want to insert. When the image appears in your browser window, return to the FrontPage Editor, where its URL appears in the **U**RL field. Click OK to insert the image.

❏ To select a background from the clip art folder, select the **C**lip Art button. The Microsoft Clip Gallery 3.0 dialog box appears. The next section, "Using the Clip Gallery," tells you how to use the Microsoft Clip Gallery.

❏ To acquire an image from a digital camera, scanner, or other TWAIN-compatible device, click the **S**can button. For further information, see "Using Your Scanner or Digital Camera with FrontPage," later in this chapter.

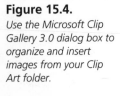

When you insert an image from the World Wide Web, the image is inserted from its location on the World Wide Web instead of being imported into your Web. Use this if you have a limited amount of space on your server but still want to use images from elsewhere on the World Wide Web.

Using the Clip Gallery

When you select the Clip Art button in the Image dialog box, the Microsoft Clip Gallery 3.0 dialog box shown in Figure 15.4 appears. This Clip Gallery enables you to organize and retrieve clip art, images, sounds, video clips, and animation files from the clip art folder on your local or network hard drive. You can also download additional clip art from Microsoft's Web site.

Figure 15.4.

Use the Microsoft Clip Gallery 3.0 dialog box to organize and insert images from your Clip Art folder.

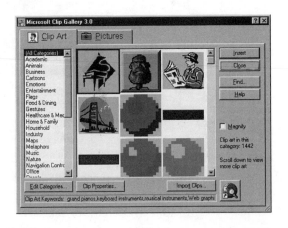

The Clip Gallery enables you to work with several types of images and multimedia files. You use the Clip Art tab, shown in Figure 15.4, to insert vector-based image formats onto your pages. These types of images are created with draw programs such as Adobe Illustrator, CorelDRAW, Micrografx Designer, Fractal Design Expression, and others. Vector-based images are those that save your images as a series of shapes that you can rescale without losing clarity. When you insert a vector-based image format into your page, FrontPage automatically converts the image to GIF or JPG when you save your page.

The Clip Gallery supports the following vector-based file formats:

CGM Computer Graphics Metafile file format

CDRCorel Draw file format

DRW Micrografx Designer file format

EPSEncapsulated PostScript files

WMF Windows Metafile format

WPG Word Perfect Graphics file format

You use the Pictures tab in the Clip Gallery to insert pixel-based or raster graphics. This tab is shown in Figure 15.5. Raster images are typically created with paint programs such as Microsoft Image Composer, Adobe Photoshop, Fractal Design Painter, Ulead PhotoImpact, Corel PhotoPaint, and images obtained from scanners and digital cameras.

Figure 15.5.

Use the Pictures tab in the Microsoft Clip Gallery to insert images created with paint programs or acquired from your scanner or digital camera.

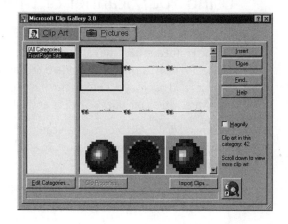

The Clip Gallery supports the following raster-based file formats:

BMP	Windows Bitmap file format
GIF	Compuserve GIF file format
JPG	JPEG File format

PCD	Photo CD File Format
PCX	Zsoft Paintbrush format
TIF	Tagged Image File Format

To insert an image from the Clip Gallery, follow these steps:

1. From the FrontPage Editor, position the insertion point where you want to insert the image on your page.

2. Choose Insert | Image or click the Insert Image button on the Standard toolbar. The Image dialog box appears.

3. Click the Clip Art button. The Microsoft Clip Gallery 3.0 dialog box appears.

NOTE: You can also open the Microsoft Clip Gallery by choosing the Insert | Clipart command. When you open the Clip Gallery in this manner, two additional tabs appear in the Clip Gallery: Sounds and Videos.

4. Select the Clip Art or Pictures tab and select an image category from the categories list in the left portion of the dialog box.

5. Double-click the file you want to place on your page or select the file and choose Insert.

Using Your Scanner or Digital Camera with FrontPage

New to FrontPage 98 is the capability of acquiring an image from a TWAIN-compatible device. TWAIN is an industry standard that acts as a type of plug-in with many different graphics and page layout programs. It is used to communicate with input and output hardware, which includes scanners and digital cameras.

The Image dialog box contains a Scan button that starts up your TWAIN-compatible scanner or digital camera software. To acquire an image from your scanner or camera, follow these steps:

1. From the FrontPage Editor, position the insertion point where you want to insert the image on your page.

2. Choose Insert | Image or click the Insert Image button on the Standard toolbar. The Image dialog box appears.

3. Click the Scan button. The Camera / Scanner dialog box shown in Figure 15.6 appears.

4. Click the Source button to select your TWAIN device. The Select Source dialog box shown in Figure 15.7 appears. It displays a list of the TWAIN-compatible sources installed on your computer.

Figure 15.6.

The Camera / Scanner dialog box lets you choose your TWAIN device and initialize its software.

Figure 15.7.

Choose your device from the Select Source dialog box.

5. Highlight the source you want to use and click Select. You return to the Camera / Scanner dialog box.

6. Click **A**cquire. This starts up the software associated with your camera or scanner. If your software enables you to customize the settings for your image before you scan, choose an option that gives you a lower DPI Setting, such as 72 or 75. These are the settings normally used for on-screen images. Some scanning software also enables you to specify a size in pixels, as Figure 15.8 shows. If you set the dimensions and DPI settings of your image before you scan it, you will not need to modify the image in FrontPage 98 or your image editing software.

Figure 15.8.

Reduce the size of your scanned image before you scan.

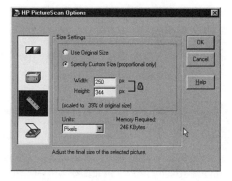

7. After you scan your image using the steps you normally follow, you return to the Image dialog box. The URL displays the path to a temporary file in your

Microsoft FrontPage directory. For the time being, leave this path as it is. You will have the opportunity to rename the file when you save it. Choose OK to place the scanned image on your page.

8. Make any modifications to your image in the Image Properties dialog box, as noted in the next task.

TIP: Your scanned image is saved in GIF format by default, which is sometimes not suitable for photographic quality. Use the Image Properties dialog box to convert your scan to JPEG format before you save your page and your image to your FrontPage Web. If you forget this step, your scan will be converted to 256 colors or less. Once the extra colors are taken away, you'll have to scan the image again to get them back!

9. When you save your page, the Save Embedded Files dialog box lists your scanned image using a filename similar to photo.1.gif or photo.1.jpg in the Embedded Files to Save list. To rename the file, click the **R**ename button. To change the folder to which the image is saved, use the **C**hange Folder button. Then click OK to save the image to your Web.

Setting Image Properties

After you insert an image on your page, you can specify several properties for the image. You use the Image Properties dialog box to change the image type, specify alternative representations, assign video properties, and change the appearance of the image.

Open the Image Properties dialog box by using one of the following methods:

- ❑ Click the image you want to change and choose **E**dit I Image Properties.
- ❑ Click the image you want to change and press Alt+Enter.
- ❑ Left-click the image you want to change. Then, right-click the mouse and choose Image Properties from the pop-up menu.

Setting General Image Properties

The General tab in the Image Properties dialog box is shown in Figure 15.9. It is used to change the image type, specify alternative low-resolution and text representations for the image, and specify a default link or target frame when the image is used as a navigation button.

Figure 15.9.

Use the General tab in the Image Properties dialog box to alter the image type, specify alternative representations, and designate a link or target frame.

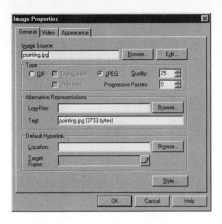

To set general image properties, follow these steps:

1. From the Image Properties dialog box, select the General tab (default).

2. To change the image from what is currently on the page, enter the new image name in the Image **S**ource field or use the **B**rowse button to select another image from the Image dialog box. After you select your image, choose OK to return to the Image Properties dialog box.

3. To edit the current image, click the **E**dit button. Your image editor opens with the current image displayed.

If you don't have an image editor configured, you will receive a message indicating so. For more information on configuring an image editor, see Chapter 17, "Integrating with Other Editors."

4. You can change an image from GIF to JPEG, and from JPEG to GIF, in the Image Properties dialog box.

   To convert the image from JPEG to GIF, select the **G**IF radio button. If you want the GIF image to be interlaced (progressively rendered on the page while the user downloads it), select the **I**nterlaced button. To add transparency to the image, see "Using Transparent Images," later in this chapter

   To convert the image from GIF to JPEG, select the **J**PEG radio button. Set the compression quality in the **Q**uality field (60 to 85 percent are suitable settings). If you want your JPEG image to render on your page in progressive steps, enter the number of steps in the Progressive Passes field.

5. If the file size of your image is large and takes a while to download, you can use a smaller low-resolution image in its place while your "real" image loads. To specify an alternative low-resolution image for the current image, enter its relative URL in the Alternative Representations, Lo**w**-Res field or use the Low-Res **B**rowse button to choose an image in the Image dialog box. Click OK from the Image dialog box to return to the Image Properties dialog box.

6. If individuals have graphics turned off in their browsers, they will not be able to tell where navigation buttons are supposed to take them. You can use an

alternative text representation to provide this information. By default, the name of the image and its file size are entered in this field, but you can modify it to display the same text that your navigation button includes. Enter the text you want to display in the Alternative Representations, Te**x**t field.

7. If you are using the image as a navigation button, enter the relative URL of the page in your current Web, or enter the absolute URL of a page on the World Wide Web in the **L**ocation field of the Default Hyperlink section. You can also use the Default Hyperlink Br**o**wse button to create a link using the Edit Hyperlink dialog box. Choose OK after you create your link to return to the Image Properties dialog box.

8. If the page to which you are linking is supposed to display in a frameset, enter the name of the frame in the **T**arget Frame field. For more information, see Chapter 18, "Frames: Pages with Split Personalities."

9. To add custom style properties to your image, click the **S**tyle button. See Chapter 27, "Using Styles," for more information.

10. Click OK to exit the Image Properties dialog box or choose another tab to add more image properties.

Setting Image Appearance Properties

You use the Appearance tab in the Image Properties dialog box (shown in Figure 15.10) to specify image alignment, border thickness, horizontal and vertical spacing, and image size.

Figure 15.10.
Use the Appearance tab to set image alignment, border thickness, horizontal and vertical spacing, and alternate display size.

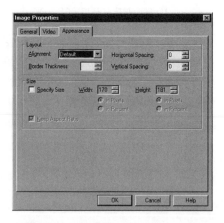

To change video appearance, use the following steps:

1. From the Image Properties dialog box, select the Appearance tab.

2. From the **A**lignment drop-down menu in the Layout section, choose one of the following options; examples of alignment types are shown in Figure 15.11:

❏ *LEFT.* Aligns the image to the left of the text. Good for wrapping text around an image.

❏ *RIGHT.* Aligns the image to the right of the text. Another choice for wrapping text around an image.

❏ *TOP.* Aligns the top of the image with the text.

❏ *TEXTTOP.* Aligns the top of the image with the top of the tallest text in the line.

❏ *MIDDLE.* Aligns the middle of the image with the text.

❏ *ABSMIDDLE.* Aligns the middle of the image to the middle point of the top and bottom text in the line.

❏ *BASELINE.* Aligns the bottom of the image with the baseline of the current text line.

❏ *BOTTOM.* Aligns the bottom of the image with the text.

❏ *ABSBOTTOM.* Aligns the bottom of the image with the bottom of the current line.

❏ *CENTER.* Aligns the bottom of the image to the center of the current line.

Figure 15.11.

Examples of image alignment types.

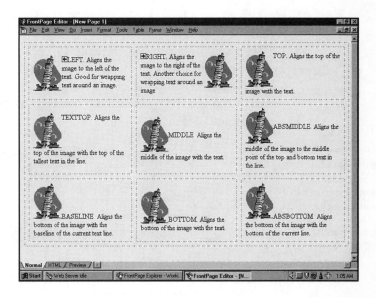

3. In the **B**order Thickness field, enter a value, in number of pixels, for how wide you want a border to be. This draws a solid border around the image. Don't make your border too wide. Most professional Web designers avoid them entirely—anything wider than 2 pixels might be overkill!

4. The horizontal and vertical spacing settings specify the number of pixels of whitespace between your image and the text on your page. Use the Horizontal Spacing and **V**ertical Spacing settings to enter the amount of space, in pixels, that.you want between your image and other page content.

5. You can stretch the image to fit a larger or smaller area, if you desire. To do so, check the **S**pecify Size checkbox. Enter the width in the **W**idth field and choose whether the entry represents a width in pixels or percent of screen. Enter the height in the **H**eight field and choose whether the entry represents a height in pixels or percent of screen. If you check the Keep Aspect Ratio checkbox, entering a value in the **W**idth or **H**eight field will automatically change the other dimension to keep the image in its proper proportion.

TIP: See "Resizing Your Image," later in this chapter, for another method that you can use to resize your images.

6. Choose OK to exit the Image Properties dialog box or select another tab to set more image properties.

TASK Using the Image Toolbar

The Image toolbar, shown in Figure 15.12, provides several different buttons that enable you to modify the images on your pages. The Image toolbar should automatically appear at the bottom of your FrontPage Editor workspace whenever you click on an image. If it does not, choose the **V**iew | **I**mage Toolbar command from the FrontPage Editor.

Figure 15.12.

The Image toolbar provides commands that let you make changes to the images on your Web pages from within FrontPage 98.

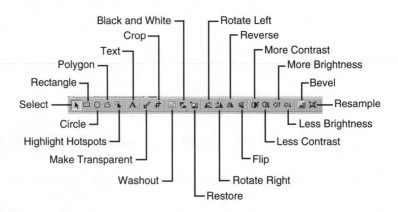

There are many commands on the Image toolbar that are not available in the FrontPage menus. The majority of these commands enable you to make modifications to the images on your Web pages from within the FrontPage Editor.

To modify your image using the Image toolbar, click the image that you want to modify. The Image toolbar appears at the bottom of the FrontPage Editor workspace. The following sections outline the modifications that you can make.

Adding Text to GIF Images

You can add a text label to a GIF image, as shown in Figure 15.13. If the image on your page is a JPEG image, FrontPage informs you that the image will be converted to GIF format. This reduces the number of colors in the image and also can increase its byte size. If you want to add text labels to JPG images, use an image editing program, such as Microsoft Image Composer or Adobe Photoshop.

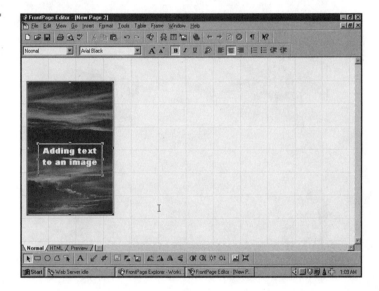

Figure 15.13.
Adding a text label to an image.

To add a text label to a GIF image, follow these steps:

1. Click the image that you want to add the text label to.
2. Click the Text button on the Image toolbar. A bounding box appears on the image, with the cursor centered within the bounding box.
3. Enter the text label. The bounding box resizes to accommodate the text you enter. Adjust the height of the bounding box to display additional lines of text.
4. From the Format toolbar, use the Change Font drop-down menu to change the font face and the Increase Text Size or Decrease Text Size buttons to change the size of the font. Use the Text Color button in the Format toolbar to change the color of the text.

5. To use the text for a hyperlink, choose the Create or Edit Hyperlink button in the Standard toolbar or press Enter when the text label is selected. The Create Hyperlink dialog box appears, and you can create your hyperlink.

Making a Color in a GIF Image Transparent

You can select one of the colors in a GIF image as a transparent color. This enables your page background to show through the image and gives the appearance that the image is floating on your page. Figure 15.14 shows an example.

Figure 15.14.
Creating a transparent image.

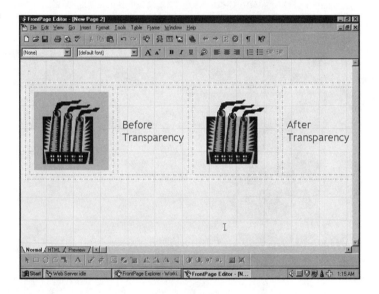

To add a transparent color to a GIF image, follow these steps:

1. Click the image that you want to add transparency to.

2. Click the Make Transparent button on the Image toolbar. The cursor changes to the Make Transparent pointer.

3. Click the color in the image that you want to make transparent. All the pixels that use that color "disappear" from your image, enabling the background color to show through.

4. To remove image transparency, repeat steps 1 through 3 to select the same color. The original color is restored.

You can also remove image transparency by unchecking the Transparent checkbox in the Type section of the Image Properties dialog box.

Cropping Your Image

You can crop wasted space from the outer edges of your image by using the Crop button on the Image toolbar. You can also use the Crop button to crop an image so that it contains a smaller area in a picture, as shown in Figure 15.15. This helps reduce the file size of your image.

Figure 15.15.
An image before and after cropping.

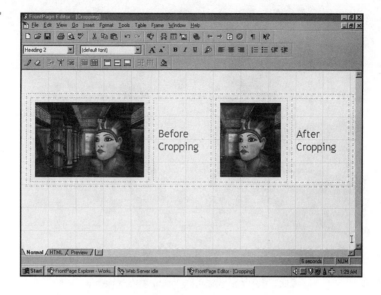

To crop your image, follow these steps:

1. Click the image that you want to crop.
2. Click the Crop button on the Image toolbar. A rectangular outline appears on your page, with resize handles at the corners and centers.
3. Resize the crop rectangle to surround the area in the image that you want to retain.
4. Click the Crop button again. The portion of the image that appeared outside the outline is removed.

Creating a Washed-Out Image

Sometimes when you try to add text to an image, it is difficult to find a text color that shows up well against the colors in your image. This usually occurs when the colors in your image are in the middle range, rather than being light or dark. You can use the Washout button in the Image toolbar to create a washed-out version of your image. This lightens your image and gives it a more pastel appearance, as shown in Figure 15.16. This makes it easier to add text to your image.

Figure 15.16.

An image before and after washing out.

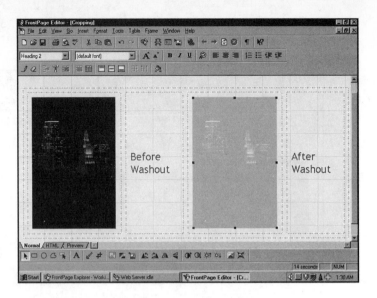

To create a washed-out image, follow these steps:

1. Click the image that you want to change.

2. Click the Washout button on the Image toolbar. The colors in the image change to colors that are more pastel in appearance.

Converting Your Image to Black and White

Black-and-white images can sometimes be quite effective on Web pages. You can also use black-and-white images as alternative low-resolution images that display in your Web pages until the color versions are able to load.

To create a black-and-white image, follow these steps:

1. Click the image that you want to change.

2. Click the Black and White button on the Image toolbar. The image changes to black and white, using dithering to approximate the tones in the original image.

Changing the Orientation of Your Image

Four buttons on the Image toolbar enable you to change the orientation of your image. You can rotate your image 90 degrees clockwise or counterclockwise or flip your image horizontally or vertically. Examples of each are shown in Figure 15.17. These changes can be made with the following steps:

Figure 15.17.

Changing the orientation of your image.

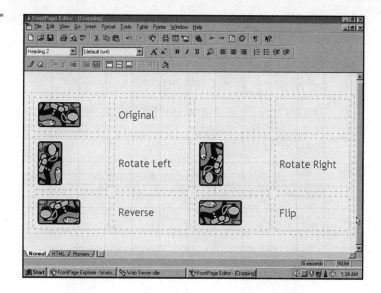

1. Click the image that you want to change.

2. Click one of the following buttons on the Image toolbar:

   ❏ Click the Rotate Left button to rotate your image 90 degrees counterclockwise.

   ❏ Click the Rotate Right button to rotate your image 90 degrees clockwise.

   ❏ Click the Reverse button to flip your image horizontally (side to side).

   ❏ Click the Flip button to flip your image vertically (top to bottom).

Changing Contrast and Brightness

Use the Contrast and Brightness buttons to increase or decrease the amount of contrast between light and dark areas in your image or to lighten or darken it. You may need to select the command more than once to achieve the effect you desire.

To adjust contrast or brightness in your image, follow these steps:

1. Click the image that you want to change.

2. Click one of the following buttons on the Image toolbar:

   ❏ Click the More Contrast button to increase the contrast between the light and dark areas in your image.

   ❏ Click the Less Contrast button to decrease the contrast between the light and dark areas in your image.

❑ Click the More Brightness button to lighten your image.

❑ Click the Less Brightness button to darken your image.

Beveling Your Image

You can use the Bevel button on the Image toolbar to create a beveled button or image very quickly! (See Figure 15.18.) Use this in combination with the Text button to create navigation buttons for your pages.

Figure 15.18.

Creating a beveled image.

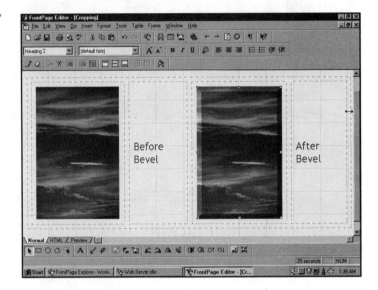

To bevel an image, follow these steps:

1. Click the image that you want to change.

2. Click the Bevel button on the Image toolbar. The outer edges of the image change, making the image appear as if it is projecting outward from your page.

Resizing Your Image

You can adjust the size of your image if it is too large. Though you can also increase the size of an image by resizing it, this can sometimes cause pixels to appear quite blocky. After you resize your image, it is also a good idea to resample your image, to "set" the new dimensions of the image.

TIP: When you resize an image, it changes the dimensions of the file as it appears on your page, but it does not change the byte size of the file. If you reduce the dimensions in the Size field, use the Resample button on the Image toolbar to convert your image to that final size. That way, there is no excess download time!

To resize the image, follow these steps:

1. Drag one of the resize handles, or small black boxes that surround the image. When you position your mouse over one of these resize handles, arrows indicate the direction to drag the mouse for resizing.

    When you drag any of the corner handles, as shown in Figure 15.19, the image changes in height and width. When you drag one of the center handles, the image changes in width or height only as indicated by the directional arrow.

2. After you resize your image, click the Resample button (the last button in the Image toolbar) to set the new image size.

Figure 15.19.
Resizing an image.

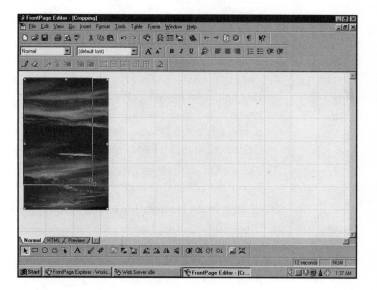

Restoring Your Image

As long as you have not saved any of the revisions you made to your image, you can use the Restore button on the Image toolbar to restore your image to its original state.

To restore your image to its original appearance, click the Restore button. You can also undo one action at a time if you choose **E**dit | **U**ndo Edit Image (Ctrl+Z) from the FrontPage Editor.

Adding Images and Sound to a Page

Now it's time for some fun. You will take some of what you have learned and place some images and animations on your pages. Earlier in this chapter, you created a style sheet that used a grey brick background. You use that style sheet to create this page; additional images and animations are added to the page:

1. From the FrontPage Editor, choose **F**ile | **N**ew. Create a new page based on the Normal Page template.

2. Choose F**o**rmat | **T**heme. The Choose Theme dialog box appears. Select the **T**his Page Does Not Use Themes radio button and click OK.

3. If your new page displays shared borders, click **T**ools | Shared **B**orders. From the Page Borders dialog box, choose the Set for this **p**age only radio button and uncheck all the shared border options. Choose OK to return to the FrontPage Editor.

4. Choose **F**ile | Page Proper**t**ies. The Page Properties dialog box appears.

5. Click the Background tab. Check the Background **I**mage checkbox and click the **B**rowse button. The Select Background Image dialog box appears.

6. Choose the Select a file on your computer button located at the right of the **U**RL field. Use the Select File dialog box to locate the `Light_Grey_Brick.gif` image in the `Book\Chap15\Project Files` folder on the CD-ROM that accompanies this book. Double-click the filename or highlight the file and choose OK to return to the Page Properties dialog box.

7. Choose OK again to exit the Page Properties dialog box and return to the FrontPage Editor. The background appears on your page.

8. Choose **I**nsert | **I**mage. The Image dialog box appears.

9. Choose the Select a file on your computer button located at the right of the **U**RL field. Use the Select File dialog box to locate the `brikwall.gif` image in the `Book\Chap15\Project Files` folder on the CD-ROM that accompanies this book. Double-click the filename or highlight the file and choose OK to place the image on your page.

10. Center the image with the Center button on the Format toolbar. Your page should now look as shown in Figure 15.20.

Figure 15.20.

A home page graphic is inserted in your page.

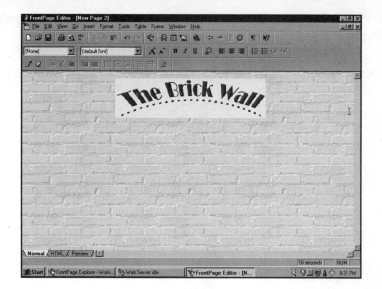

11. Click to select the image. From the Image toolbar, select the Make Transparent pointer. Click the white background in the image to make it transparent. The image now appears to be floating on your page.

12. Choose **I**nsert I **I**mage. The Image dialog box appears again. Choose the Select a file on your computer button located at the right of the **U**RL field. Use the Select File dialog box to locate the spy.gif image in the Book\Chap15\Project Files folder on the CD-ROM that accompanies this book. This is an animated GIF that already has transparency added to it. It looks as though eyes are peeking at you through a hole in the brick wall. Double-click the filename or highlight the file and choose OK to place the image on your page.

13. Center the image with the Center button on the Format toolbar. At this point, your page should look like Figure 15.21.

14. Choose **F**ile I **S**ave (Ctrl+S) or click the Save button on the Standard toolbar. The Save As dialog box appears.

15. Enter The Brick Wall Home Page in the **T**itle field. Enter index.htm (or your default home page name) in the URL field. Choose OK to save the page.

16. When the Save Embedded Files dialog box appears, use Shift+Click to highlight all three image filenames in the Embedded Files to Save list. Click the **C**hange Folder button.

17. From the Change Folder dialog box, double-click the images folder in your current Web. If other images already appear in your images folder, click one of the images. Then choose OK to select the new folder. You return to the Save Embedded Files dialog box.

Figure 15.21.

A transparent GIF, AVI file, and animated GIF are added to your page.

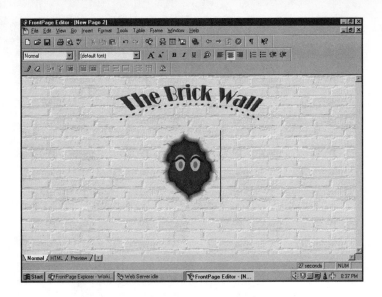

18. Choose OK to save your Web page and images to your current Web.

19. Choose the preview tab in the FrontPage Editor. The eyes peeking through the brick wall animate and blink at you.

Adding a Background Sound

The Brick Wall Home Page needs some spicing up. A MIDI file called `jazzy.mid` in the `Book\Chap15\Project Files` folder on the CD-ROM accompanying this book contains a jazzy tune. Insert this sound file on the page.

TIP: If you want to create your own music for your Web pages, check out Band In a Box, by PG Music. This program is what the name implies—a band within your computer. You can select from a wide variety of song styles, enter chords, change the instruments that make up the song, and automatically generate a soloist part for the song. After you create the song, you can generate a MIDI file for your Web site. Download a play-only demo of the program at the following URL:

`http://www.pgmusic.com/index.html`

To add a background sound to your page, follow these steps:

1. Return to the Normal view in the FrontPage Editor. Choose **F**ile I Page Proper**t**ies. The Page Properties dialog box appears, opened to the General tab.

2. Click the Browse button in the Background Sound field. The Background Sound dialog box appears.

3. Choose the Select a file on your computer button located at the right of the URL field. The Select File dialog box appears.

4. Choose Midi Sequencer (*.mid) from the Files of type drop-down menu. Then, locate jazzy.mid in the Book\Chap15\Project Files folder on the CD-ROM that accompanies this book. Double-click the filename or highlight it and choose OK to return to the Page Properties dialog box.

5. By default, the background sound plays indefinitely. This MIDI file is quite long. To change the setting, uncheck the **F**orever checkbox and enter 1 in the L**o**op field. This plays the sound file once.

6. Save the page to your Web again using the **F**ile | **S**ave command. When the Save Embedded files dialog box appears, click OK to save the sound file to the home folder in your Web. Use the Preview tab to preview your page again, and you will hear the sound file.

TASK Creating an Auto Thumbnail

Sometimes, you can't avoid placing large images in your Web, especially if you worked hard to create some graphics for your Web site. You have an alternative in FrontPage 98. Using the Auto Thumbnail command, you can place a thumbnail version of a large image on your Web page. FrontPage 98 creates a small version of your image and automatically creates a link to the larger file.

To create an auto thumbnail of an image, follow these steps:

1. Use the **I**nsert | **I**mage command to place the large image file on your Web page, as shown in Figure 15.22.

2. Click the image and choose **T**ools | **A**uto Thumbnail (Ctrl+T). The image reduces substantially in size, as shown in Figure 15.23.

3. Choose **F**ile | **S**ave (Ctrl+S). When the Save Embedded Files dialog box appears, you will see two images with similar names. One filename is for the original larger image that you inserted in your page. For example, the filename that I inserted in step 1 was pharoahess.jpg. The filename for the thumbnail has _small appended to it. In this case, the thumbnail image is named pharoahess_small.jpg. Save both these images to your Web. The thumbnail automatically creates a hyperlink to the larger image file. When the user clicks on the thumbnail, the larger image opens in his or her browser.

Figure 15.22.

Place the larger image on your page first to create your auto thumbnail.

Figure 15.23.

After you choose the Auto Thumbnail command, a smaller version of the image appears on your page.

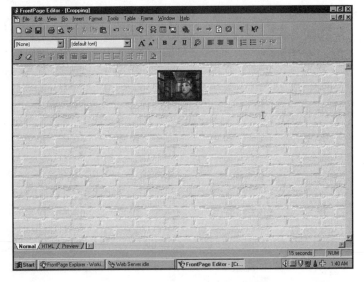

TASK

Setting Auto Thumbnail Options

The Options dialog box in the FrontPage Editor enables you to set default options for your auto thumbnails. You can specify a default width or height for your thumbnails, set border thickness, or create a beveled edge.

To set default options for your auto thumbnails, follow these steps:

1. From the FrontPage Editor, choose **T**ools I **O**ptions. The Options dialog box appears, opened to the Auto Thumbnail tab shown in Figure 15.24.

Figure 15.24.

Use the Auto Thumbnail tab in the Options dialog box to configure default settings for your auto thumbnails.

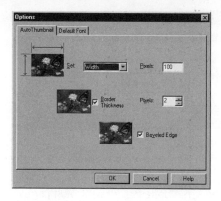

2. From the **S**et drop-down menu, choose one of the following options for sizing your auto thumbnail:

   ❏ Choose Width if you want to create auto thumbnails that are always the same Width. Enter the number of pixels of width in the **P**ixels field. When FrontPage creates the thumbnail, the width will always be the value you enter in the Pixels field. The height will be sized appropriately to create a proportionally correct miniature of your original.

   ❏ Choose Height if you want to create auto thumbnails that are always the same height. Enter the number of pixels of height in the **P**ixels field. When FrontPage creates the thumbnail, the height will always be the value you enter in the Pixels field. The width will be sized appropriately to create a proportionally correct miniature of your original.

   ❏ Choose Shortest side if you want to create auto thumbnails where the shortest side (height or width) will be the value you enter in the **P**ixels field. The other dimension will be sized appropriately to create a proportionally correct miniature of your original.

   ❏ Choose Longest side if you want to create auto thumbnails where the longest side (height or width) will be the value you enter in the **P**ixels field. The other dimension will be sized appropriately to create a proportionally correct miniature of your original.

3. If you want a border around your thumbnail, check the **B**order Thickness checkbox. Enter the width of the border in the Pi**x**els field at the right of the checkbox. If you do not want a border around your thumbnail, uncheck the **B**order Thickness option.

4. To automatically create a beveled edge around your thumbnail, check the Be**v**eled Edge checkbox. Uncheck this option to create a flat thumbnail. You cannot adjust the width of the bevel.

5. Choose OK to configure your new settings. They take effect the next time you choose the Auto Thumbnail command.

Workshop Wrap-Up

Graphics, when used effectively, can really make a page. On the other hand, when graphics aren't used properly, they can break a page. The best way to learn how to use graphics effectively is to carefully examine pages that catch your eye. You'll find lots of "picks of the week" on the Web—check them out for various ideas. How were colors used on the page? What was it about the page that caused you to explore it? Try to apply the same principles to your own pages.

In this chapter, you learned how to insert image files onto your Web pages and how to modify them from within the FrontPage Editor. You learned how to add text to images, how to create auto thumbnails that link to larger images, and how to use the Microsoft Clip Gallery. You'll have the opportunity to work with images further in Chapter 20, "Real-Life Examples III: Dressing Up Your Webs."

Next Steps

In the next chapter, you'll learn how to add animation, hover buttons, and other active content onto your pages. Using some great new features available in FrontPage 98 and Internet Explorer 4.0, you can add page transitions, animated text, and more to your Web pages. For further information about working with images, refer to the following chapters:

- ❏ To learn how to create a clickable image that uses hotspots to link to other pages, refer to Chapter 9, "Getting from Here to There."
- ❏ To learn how to configure image editors that open automatically when you select an image file, see Chapter 17, "Integrating with Other Editors."
- ❏ For information on using images in frames, see Chapter 18, "Frames: Pages with Split Personalities."
- ❏ See Chapter 20, "Real-Life Examples III: Dressing Up Your Webs," for more hands-on experience in working with images.

Q&A

Q: I put an animated GIF on my page and then I made it transparent in the FrontPage Editor. It doesn't animate anymore. What's wrong?

A: When you make an image transparent in FrontPage, it saves the image over the previous version with the transparent data in it. Animated GIFs are a special type of GIF file—there are actually multiple images (called frames) within that single file, and they are grouped together as one image in a special way. Think of an animated GIF as an electronic flip-book. When you add transparency to an animated GIF, you are adding the transparency only to the first frame. FrontPage (and many other graphics programs, for that matter) doesn't know how to recognize the additional frames in an animated GIF, so it just writes the first frame with the transparent data in it. The remaining frames no longer exist after you save the image.

To make transparent GIFs, you need to break apart that special GIF file into separate frames again, add the transparency to each frame, and then rebuild the animated GIF. If you're creating the animation from scratch, add the transparency to each frame before you compile it into an animated GIF file. This sounds like a lot of work, but that's what it takes to make an animation of any kind.

Q: Can I put my own graphics in the Microsoft Clip Gallery?

A: Yes. You can use the Import Clips button in the Clip Gallery to import clip art, pictures, sounds, and videos into your Clip Gallery. You can also choose the Connect to Web for additional clips button in the Clip Gallery to download additional clip art from Microsoft's Web site.

Q: Can a user click an animated GIF or AVI file to go on another page?

A: You can assign an animated GIF or AVI file as a link as you do any other image. Click the image, click the Create or Edit Link button, and away you go!

SIXTEEN

Working with Animation and Active Content

Static graphics are nice, but motion scattered here and there adds interest to your site. FrontPage 98 provides all sorts of bells and whistles that help in that regard. You can insert videos on your pages, create buttons that change appearance when a mouse hovers over or clicks them, animate banner advertisements, and create scrolling text in marquees. Add animated text and page transitions to your page using Dynamic HTML, a feature supported by Internet Explorer 4.0. Your user can also search through your Web site using a search component that is very easy to configure. Keep track of how many times your page is accessed with the new Hit Counter component.

In this chapter, you'll learn how to add several types of active content to your pages. Ranging from the simple to the sophisticated, these features add excitement to your pages!

In this chapter, you

- ❏ Insert a video file into a Web page
- ❏ Learn about hover buttons
- ❏ Learn how to use the banner ad manager
- ❏ Add a marquee to your pages
- ❏ Learn how to create and configure a search form that uses the FrontPage Search component
- ❏ Use the Hit Counter component
- ❏ Animate the text on your pages using Dynamic HTML
- ❏ Add page transitions to your Web pages

Tasks in this chapter:

- ❏ Inserting Videos and Setting Video Properties
- ❏ Inserting a Hover Button
- ❏ Using the Banner Ad Manager
- ❏ Inserting a Marquee
- ❏ Creating and Configuring a Search Form
- ❏ Adding a Hit Counter
- ❏ Formatting Animation Text
- ❏ Adding Page Transitions

Inserting Videos and Setting Video Properties

You insert videos with the Insert | Video command. After you insert the video on your page, set its properties through the Image Properties dialog box. The CD-ROM furnished with this book includes an AVI file for you to practice with. The file is located in the Books\Chap16\Project Files directory and is named campfire.avi.

To insert a video on your page, follow these steps:

1. From the FrontPage Editor, create or open a new page on which to place the video file.

2. Position the insertion point on your page where you want to insert the video.

3. Choose Insert | Active Elements | Video. The Video dialog box shown in Figure 16.1 appears.

Figure 16.1.
Use the Video dialog box to choose a video file to insert in your page.

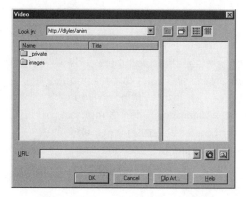

4. To insert a video from a local or network drive, click the Select a file on your computer button located to the right of the URL field. Use the Look in box in the Select File dialog box to locate the campfire.avi file on the CD-ROM that accompanies this book. Double-click the filename or highlight it and choose OK. The video appears on your page. You can also insert a video using the following methods:

   ❏ To insert a video from your current Web, select the Web from the Look in drop-down menu. Double-click on the folder names in your Web to locate the folder in which the video resides. Double-click the video file (.avi extension) that you want to insert on your page. The video appears on your page.

❏ To insert a video from the World Wide Web, click the Use your web browser to select a page or file button located to the right of the URL field or enter the URL of the video you want to insert and choose OK. The video appears on your page.

❏ To insert a video from the Microsoft Clip Gallery, select the **C**lip Art button. The Microsoft Clip Gallery 3.0 dialog box appears. Use the Videos tab to select your video and choose Insert to place the video on your page.

For further information about the Microsoft Clip Gallery, refer to Chapter 15, "Working with Images and Sound."

By default, the video plays once as soon as the video is downloaded to the user's computer. You can adjust the settings of the video from the Image Properties dialog box. To set video properties, follow these steps:

1. Right-click on the video and choose Image Properties from the pop-up menu. The Image Properties dialog box appears, opened to the Video tab shown in Figure 16.2.

Figure 16.2.

Set the video properties with the Video tab in the Image Properties dialog box.

2. Use the **V**ideo Source field to insert a video onto your page from within the Image Properties dialog box. Enter the relative URL of the video file in your current Web or use the **B**rowse button to insert a file through the Video dialog box. Click OK to return to the Image Properties dialog box.

3. Check the **S**how Controls in Browser button to display VCR type controls beneath the video on your page. This enables the user to start and stop the video when he or she chooses. If you do not select this option, the video will automatically begin to play as soon as it downloads.

4. Use the Repeat section to specify how many times you want the video file to play.

    ❏ To play the video once (default), enter **1** in the **L**oop field.

    ❏ To play the video more than once, enter the number of times you want the video to play in the **L**oop field. Check the **F**orever checkbox if you want the video to play indefinitely. Select this option for the `campfire.avi` video on your page.

5. By default, there is no delay between each successive play of the video. If you want to add a delay between each time the video plays, enter the number of milliseconds for the delay in the Loop **D**elay field. You do not need an entry here if you play the video once.

6. Choose how you want the video to start. If you want the video to start as soon as the page opens, check **O**n File Open. If you want the video to start when the user clicks the mouse, choose On **M**ouse Over.

7. Click OK to exit the Image Properties dialog box. The video appears on your page, as shown in Figure 16.3.

8. Click the Preview tab at the bottom of the FrontPage Editor workspace to preview your video.

Figure 16.3.

The video appears on your page. Use the Preview tab in the FrontPage Explorer to view the video in action.

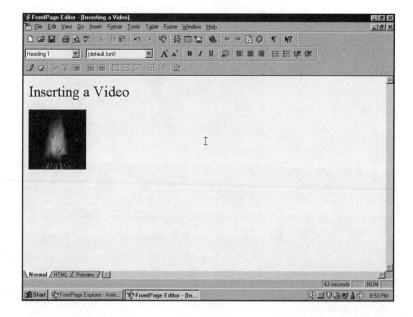

Inserting a Hover Button

In Chapter 8, "Designing Your Web Navigation," and Chapter 14, "Using FrontPage Style Sheets and Themes," you were introduced to hover buttons. Hover buttons are sometimes used when you specify active graphics for your themes. When you position your mouse over a hover button, it changes its appearance. The button also changes appearance again when you click it.

Hover buttons are actually small Java applets that FrontPage automatically generates and configures. The Java applet incorporates settings that you select in the Hover Button dialog box. No coding is necessary.

NOTE: Internet Explorer 3.0 and later will support hover buttons. Note, however, that not all browsers support Java applets. Test your pages in several different browsers or provide links for users to download browsers that are compatible with the features on your pages.

1. Position the insertion point where you want the hover button to appear.
2. Choose Insert | Active Elements | Hover Button. The Hover Button dialog box shown in Figure 16.4 appears.

Figure 16.4.

Use the Hover Button dialog box to configure the properties for your hover button.

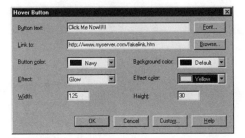

3. In the Button text field, enter the text that you want to appear on the button. For the example, enter `Click Me Now!!!!!`.
4. Click the Font button to open the Font dialog box. Here, you select the font you want to use for your text. Select the following settings for your practice button:

Font	MS Sans Serif
Font style	Bold
Size	14
Color	Blue

5. Choose OK to return to the Hover Button dialog box.

6. In the **L**ink to field, enter the relative URL to the page or file in your current Web that you want to link to. You can also enter the path to a file on your local or network hard drive, or the absolute URL to a file on the World Wide Web. For this example, enter `http://www.myserver.com/fakelink.htm`.

NOTE:
Use the **B**rowse button to use the Select Hover Button Hyperlink dialog box to locate the page or file to which you want to link. This is similar to the Create Hyperlink dialog box discussed in Chapter 9, "Getting from Here to There."

7. If you want to associate a sound with your hover button, click the Cust**o**m button. The Custom dialog box shown in Figure 16.5 appears.

Figure 16.5.
Use the Custom dialog box to assign sounds and custom images to your hover button.

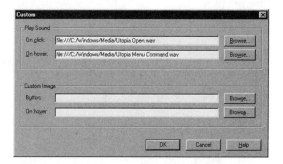

8. In the Play Sound section, set the following properties:

On **c**lick	Click the **B**rowse button to locate a sound that plays when the user clicks the hover button. You can choose a sound from your current Web, a local or network hard drive, or from the World Wide Web. For example, choose the Select a file on your computer button and locate the C:\Windows\Media\Utopia Open.wav file on your hard drive.
On hover	Click the Bro**w**se button to locate a sound that plays when the user positions the mouse cursor over the button. For example, choose the Select a file on your computer button and locate the C:\Windows\Media\Utopia Menu Command.wav file on your hard drive.

9. The button you create in this example will use a solid background. Choose OK to exit the Custom dialog box and skip to step 11.

   If you prefer to use a custom button, use the Custom Image section in the Custom dialog box and select your images in the following fields:

Button	Click the Browse button to locate the image that appears when the button is in its normal state. You can choose an image from your current Web, a local or network hard drive, or from the World Wide Web.
On hover	Click the Browse button to locate the image that appears when the mouse cursor hovers over the button.

10. Choose OK to exit the Custom dialog box. You return to the Hover Button dialog box.

11. To create a hover button with a solid color background, select a color from the Button color drop-down menu. For this example, choose Navy.

12. Use the Background color drop-down menu to choose a background color for your hover button. Note that you cannot make the background of a hover button transparent, so you want to select or create a color that is close to or compatible with your page background. Choose from one of 16 default Windows system colors or select Custom to choose or create a color from the Color dialog box. After you select or create your color, choose OK to return to the Hover Button dialog box.

13. From the Effect drop-down menu, select a visual effect that will display when the user hovers over the button. For this example, choose Glow.

   The effects are as follows:

Color fill	Changes the button color to the color you specify in the Effect color drop-down menu.
Color average	Changes the button color to an intermediary color between your button color and the color you specify in the Effect color drop-down menu. For example, if your button color is red and the effect color is blue, color average changes the button to purple when the mouse cursor hovers over it.
Glow	Causes the middle portion of the button to change to the color you specify in the Effect color drop-down menu, creating a glowing effect.

Reverse glow	Causes the outer portions of the button to change to the color you specify in the Effect color drop-down menu.
Light glow	Causes the middle portion of the button to glow as if a light is shining on it.
Bevel out	Causes the button to appear raised when the mouse hovers over it.
Bevel in	Causes the button to appear "depressed" when the mouse hovers over it.

14. From the Effect color drop-down menu, choose the effect color that will be used with the color fill, color average, glow, or reverse glow effect. Choose Yellow for this example.

15. Enter the pixel width of your hover button in the **W**idth field and its pixel height in the Heigh**t** field. Remember to make the buttons wide enough to fit all the button text on your buttons. You can also reduce the font size to fit the button label. If you have selected an image for your hover button, the width and height should match the dimensions of your image. For this example, enter **125** in the **W**idth field and **30** in the Heigh**t** field.

16. Choose OK to exit the Hover Button dialog box. The button appears on your page.

17. Choose **F**ile | Preview in **B**rowser to view your hover button in a browser that supports Java applets (such as Internet Explorer 3.0 or later or Netscape Navigator 3.0 or later). When you move your mouse over the button, the center of the button turns yellow. Figure 16.6 shows an example.

Figure 16.6.

When the mouse hovers over the button, the effect displays.

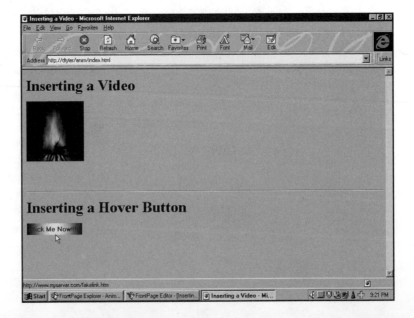

Using the Banner Ad Manager

Have you ever navigated to a Web page and noticed animated banners that display advertisements for other sites? Typically, these banners display a series of different images with transition effects between them. With FrontPage 98 and its Banner Ad Manager, you can easily create these types of banners for your Web pages.

The Banner Ad Manager works with a series of images. Generally, you should choose images that are approximately the same size. You size your banner ad based on the widest and tallest dimensions of your image collection. If other images in your banner are smaller, they are centered both horizontally and vertically within the space allocated for the banner. The space that is not covered by your image displays a neutral gray background color.

The CD-ROM that accompanies this book contains three images for you to experiment with: `banner01.jpg`, `banner02.jpg`, and `banner03.jpg`, located in the `Book\Chap16\Project Files` folder. These images measure 450 pixels wide and 75 pixels high. Use these images to build your own banner ad.

To insert a banner ad on your Web page, follow these steps:

1. Position the insertion point where you want your banner to appear.

2. Choose **I**nsert I Active **E**lements I **B**anner Ad Manager. The Banner Ad Manager dialog box shown in Figure 16.7 appears.

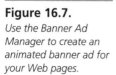

Figure 16.7.

Use the Banner Ad Manager to create an animated banner ad for your Web pages.

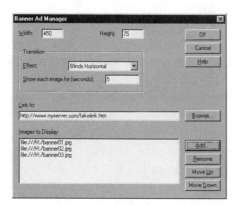

3. In the **W**idth field, enter the pixel width of your banner. The value you set here should be as wide as the widest image that you place in your banner ad. For this example, enter **450**.

4. In the Heigh**t** field, enter the pixel height of your banner. The value you set here should be as high as the tallest image that you place in your banner ad. For this example, enter **75**.

5. In the Transition section, choose one of the following effects from the **E**ffect drop-down menu:

None	The images in your banner display in sequence without any effects between them.
Blinds Horizontal	Creates a horizontal blind effect between each image. Choose this option for the banner you are creating in this example.
Blinds Vertical	Creates a vertical blind effect between each image.
Dissolve	Dissolves out the previous image while the next image dissolves in.
Box In	Replaces the outer edges of the previous image first and moves inward toward the center of the image.
Box Out	Replaces the inner portion of the previous image first and moves outward toward the borders.

6. In the **S**how each image for (seconds) field, enter the number of seconds that you want each banner to appear stationary. Make sure this value is long enough for the user to view information on the banner. Enter **5**.

7. In the **L**ink to field, enter the URL of the page or file that the user will navigate to if he or she clicks on the banner image. Use the **B**rowse button to locate a page or file in your current Web, on your local or network hard drive, or on the World Wide Web. For this example, enter **http://
www.myserver.com/fakelink.htm**.

8. To add a series of images to your banner ad, click the **A**dd button. The Add Image for Banner Ad dialog box appears. You can select an image from your current Web, from the World Wide Web, from a file on your local computer, or from your clip art folder. For this example, choose the Select a file on your computer button and insert banner01.jpg, banner02.jpg, and banner03.jpg, in sequence, from the Book\Chap16\Project Files folder on the CD-ROM that accompanies this book. Choose OK to return to the Banner Ad Manager.

9. To change the order in which the images appear in your banner, highlight the image you want to move and press the Move **U**p or Move **D**own button. To remove an image from the banner, choose the **R**emove button.

10. Choose OK to place the banner ad on your Web page.

11. Save the page to your Web. Use the Preview tab in the FrontPage Editor or choose the **F**ile I Preview in **B**rowser command to preview your page in a browser of your choosing. The banner displays each of the three images in sequence, with a transition between each of them. Figure 16.8 shows an example at the bottom of the page.

Figure 16.8.

The banner displays three images in sequence, with a transition effect between each image.

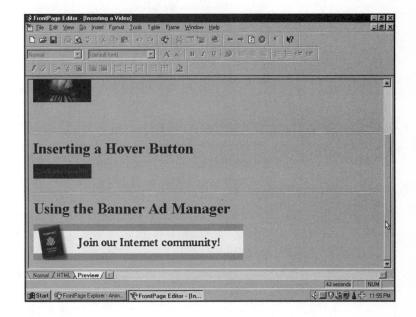

Adding a Marquee to Your Pages

Marquees are an Internet Explorer invention. They scroll text across your pages in a number of ways. You can view marquees in Internet Explorer 2.0, 3.0, and 4.0. Marquees are not yet supported in Netscape Navigator and Netscape Communicator.

Inserting a Marquee

You use the **I**nsert I Active **E**lements I Marqu**ee** command to place a marquee on your page.

To set the properties of the marquee you entered on your page, use the Marquee Properties dialog box. To complete the dialog box, follow these steps:

1. Position the insertion point where you want the marquee to appear.

2. Choose **I**nsert I Active **E**lement I Marqu**ee**. The Marquee Properties dialog box shown in Figure 16.9 appears.

Figure 16.9.

Configure the settings for your marquee in the Marquee Properties dialog box.

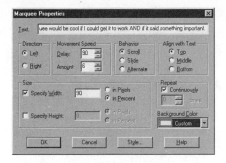

3. In the **T**ext field, enter the text that you want to appear in the marquee. For example, enter the following:

   ```
   This marquee would be cool if I could get it to work AND if it said
   something important.
   ```

4. From the Direction section, select the direction that you want the marquee to scroll. The default is Le**f**t, which scrolls the marquee from the right to the left of your screen. To make the marquee scroll from left to right, select **R**ight. For this example, use the default setting of Le**f**t.

5. Choose your movement speed settings in the Movement Speed section of the dialog box:

   Delay   Specifies the number of milliseconds after which the marquee begins to move. The default setting is 90 milliseconds. Increase the setting if the marquee scrolls too soon when your page is loaded. Leave this setting at the default for this example.

   Amo**u**nt   Specifies the number of pixels by which the marquee moves each time it is drawn on the page. The default value is 6. For faster marquees, increase the number. For slower marquees, decrease the number. Leave this setting at the default for this example.

6. Choose how you want the marquee to behave from the Behavior section.

   Scroll   If you select this option, the marquee begins on one side of the page, scrolls toward the other side, and moves completely off the page again. This is similar to a stock ticker. Use this option for your sample marquee.

   Slide   Choose this option to create a marquee that slides in from one side of the screen and stops

	once it reaches the opposite marquee window border.
Alternate	Choose this option to create a marquee that alternates between the marquee window borders. The text of the marquee remains on the screen at all times. Make sure that your marquee window is wide enough to contain all the marquee text.

7. From the Align with Text field, choose how you want the text in the marquee to align with other text on the same line (if any). T**o**p aligns the marquee to the top of normal text. **M**iddle aligns the marquee with the middle of the text, and **B**ottom aligns the marquee with the bottom of the text. Use the default setting of T**o**p for your example marquee.

8. By default, the size of the text in the marquee determines its size. You can alter the size of the marquee in the Size section.

   To specify a different width for the marquee, check the Specify **W**idth checkbox. Enter a value in the number field and choose in Pi**x**els (for a width in pixels) or in **P**ercent (for a width in percentage of browser window width). To specify a different height for the marquee, check the Specify Hei**g**ht checkbox and enter values. For this Page marquee, set the width to 90 percent. Leave the height at the default setting.

9. By default, the marquee repeats continuously. To change this setting, uncheck the **C**ontinuously checkbox located in the Repeat section and enter the number of times you want the marquee to repeat in the Times field. Leave this at the default setting for this page marquee.

10. By default, the background color of the marquee is the same as that used on your page. To specify a different background color, select it from the Background **C**olor drop-down menu. For this Page's marquee, choose Custom and create a custom color of **R**ed **204**, **G**reen **255**, and **B**lue **255** (a light blue color). Choose OK to return to the Marquee Properties dialog box.

11. If you want to apply a different font or font color for your marquee, click the **S**tyle button. The properties you set in the Style dialog box are discussed in more detail in Chapter 27, "Using Styles."

NOTE: If you do not select a style as mentioned in step 11, you can use the Change Font, Increase Text Size, Decrease Text Size, and Font Color buttons on the Format toolbar to change the appearance of the text in the marquee.

12. Choose OK to apply the settings to the marquee. The marquee appears on your page.

13. Use the Preview tab in the FrontPage Editor to view the marquee (see Figure 16.10). You should see the text scrolling across the screen.

Figure 16.10.

The marquee appears on your page in the FrontPage Editor. You can view its animation by choosing the Preview tab.

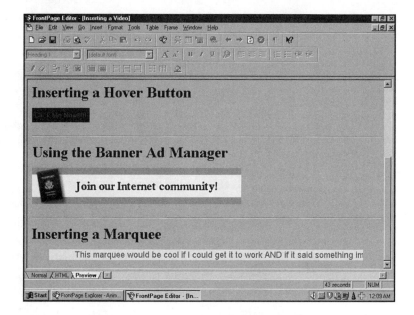

Using the Search Component

If your site is very large, including a search form in your Web site enables visitors to find topics of interest quickly and easily. The FrontPage Editor offers a Search Page template in the New dialog box that you can use. If you don't want to create a search form on its own page, you can also place it on another page in your Web.

There's really no hard and fast rule for where to put a search form in your Web. The following list offers some ideas:

❏ You can place a WebBot search component on your home page so that users can find it right away.

❏ You can include a search form on your table of contents page.

❏ If your Web site contains several child Webs, you can place several WebBot search components on a single page and place the page in your root Web.

The Search component in FrontPage 98 creates a list of links to pages containing one or more words—that is, the *search term*—entered by the user in the search form. The results returned to the user list pages in which his or her search term appears. The list can also include the file's date and size and the score for the quality of the search term's match.

Creating and Configuring a Search Form

You can create a search form that searches your entire Web site, a portion of it, or only discussion articles. Figure 16.11 shows a slightly modified example of the search page template that is provided with FrontPage 98.

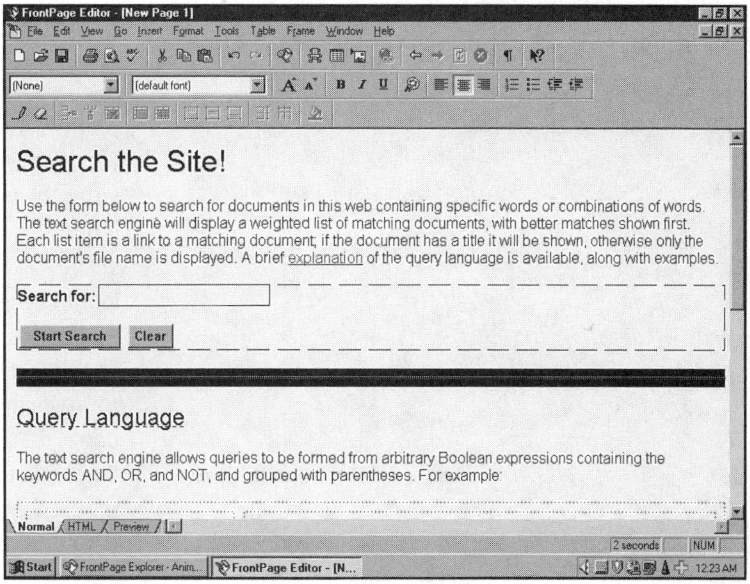

Figure 16.11.

FrontPage 98 provides a Search Page template that you can customize for your own use.

![Screenshot of FrontPage Editor showing the Search Page template with "Search the Site!" heading, search form, and "Query Language" section]

To create a search form, follow these steps:

1. Design the page on which you want to insert the WebBot search component.
2. Position the insertion point where you want to place the Search component.
3. Choose Insert | Active Elements | Search Form. The Search Form Properties dialog box shown in Figure 16.12 appears.

Figure 16.12.

Use the Search Form Properties dialog box to configure your search form.

4. Configure the following properties in the Search Form Properties tab:

Label for Input	Enter the label that you want to appear before the text input field on the search form. The default text is Search for:.
Width in Characters	Enter the width in characters of the input field or select the default of 20. Note that this doesn't limit the length of text the user can enter in the field; rather, it limits the width of the text entry box. Take care not to make the width too wide for the page.
Label for "**S**tart Search" Button	Enter the text you want to appear on the Start button or accept the default of Start Search.
Label for "Cl**e**ar" Button	Enter the text you want to appear on the Clear button or accept the default of Reset.

5. Click the Search Results tab, shown in Figure 16.13. Here, you choose whether the search bot searches through your entire Web site or through a discussion group. You also specify the information that returns to the user after he or she presses the Start Search button on the search form.

In the Word List to Search field, enter one of the following terms:

❑ Enter **All** to allow users to search through all the pages in your current Web, with the exception of pages that are stored in hidden folders (those preceded by an underscore).

❏ Enter the name of the directory in which discussion group articles are stored to search a single discussion group. If you want to search a discussion group, its directories begin with an underscore (for example, `_discgrp`).

Figure 16.13.
Use the Search Results tab to identify which pages the search bot will search and to configure the results that return to the user after the search is complete.

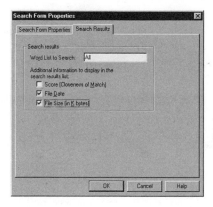

6. In the Additional information to display in the search results list section, you choose additional information that returns to the user after he or she presses the Start Search button. Select one or more of the following checkboxes:

Score (Closeness of **M**atch)	Indicates the quality of the match to the text the user enters.
File **D**ate	Reports the date and time of the document that matches the user's search entry. The date reported is the date the document was last modified.
File Size (in **K** bytes)	Reports the size of the matching document in kilobytes.

7. Choose OK to accept your selections and return to the FrontPage Editor.

8. Choose **F**ile | **S**ave (Ctrl+S) or click the Save button to save the page to your Web. Then choose **F**ile | Preview in **B**rowser to test the search page and verify that it works properly on your server. Note that the FrontPage Server Extensions have to be installed and running on the server on which your page resides in order for the search form to work properly.

 # Adding a Hit Counter

Some people like to track how popular their pages are. One way to easily tell how many times a certain page is accessed is to place a Hit Counter on your page. Hit Counters place a "page odometer" of sorts on your Web page. Each time your page is accessed, the counter on the odometer increments by one.

If you have your Web pages stored on a FrontPage-enabled Web site, you can use the new Hit Counter component to quickly and easily place a Hit Counter on your page. The steps to add a Hit Counter are as follows:

1. Position the insertion point where you want the Hit Counter to appear.

2. Choose Insert I Active Elements I Hit Counter; alternatively, choose Insert I FrontPage Component, select Hit Counter from the Insert FrontPage Component dialog box, then choose OK. The Hit Counter Properties dialog box shown in Figure 16.14 appears.

Figure 16.14.
Use the Hit Counter Properties dialog box to place or configure a Hit Counter on your Web page.

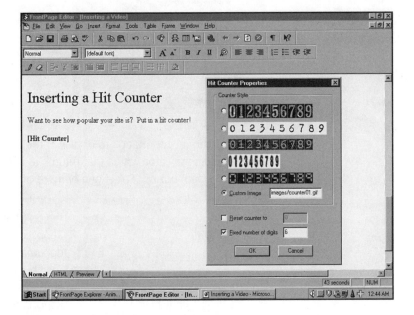

3. From the Counter Style section, select one of five number styles for your page odometer; or, use steps 4 through 8 to use a custom image for your counter.

4. To use a custom image for your page counter, switch to the FrontPage Explorer. Select the folder into which you want to import the image (for example, the images folder in your Web).

5. Choose File I Import. The Import File to FrontPage Web dialog box appears.

6. Click Add File. The Add File to Import List dialog box appears. Use the Look in box to locate the drive and directory in which the Book\Chap16\Project Files\counter01.gif image appears. It is furnished on the CD-ROM that accompanies this book. Double-click the image file to place it in the import list. You return to the Import File to FrontPage Web dialog box.

7. To import the image into the folder, choose OK. The FrontPage Explorer imports the file into your Web.

8. Return to the Hit Counter Properties dialog box. Check the Custom Image radio button and enter the path to the image file in your current Web (for example, `images/counter01.gif`).

9. There are cases when you want to start your counter with a specific number. For example, if the URL for the page changes in any way, the counter will reset back to `0`. You can start the counter at a specific number if you check the **R**eset counter to checkbox. Enter the starting number for the page counter in the Reset counter to field.

10. By default, the page counter displays only the number of digits that is required to display the number of hits on your page. For example, if your page has 534 hits, the page counter displays `534` in three digits. If you want your counter to display a fixed number of digits, such as `000534`, check the **F**ixed number of digits checkbox. Enter the number of digits that you want your counter to use in the number field (for example, `6`).

11. Choose OK to place the counter on your page. The Hit Counter component appears on your page and displays text that reads `[Hit Counter]`.

12. The Hit Counter does not appear in the FrontPage Editor's Preview tab. Save your page to the Web and choose **F**ile I Preview in **B**rowser. Select the browser in which you want to view your Web page. The FrontPage Server Extensions must be installed on the server for the Hit Counter to work properly.

Formatting Animation

You can also apply text animations to your Web pages. Text animations go a step farther than marquees, because you can animate your text in a greater number of ways. Text animations use Dynamic HTML, currently supported by Internet Explorer 4.0. Other Web browsers that support Dynamic HTML can also display them. Browsers that do not support text animation display static text instead of the text animation.

NOTE: Text animations will display in the FrontPage Editor's Preview tab only if you have Internet Explorer 4.0 installed on your system.

To add animation effects to text, follow these steps:

1. Select the text that you want to animate. In the example shown in Figure 16.15, the text that reads `Animate it!!!` is selected.

2. Choose Format I Animation and select one of the following animation effects from the slide-out menu shown in Figure 16.15:

Off	Disables page transitions on the current page.
Fly from **B**ottom	The text you select flies in from the bottom of the browser window.
Fly from **L**eft	The text you select flies in from the left side of the browser window.
Fly from **R**ight	The text you select flies in from the right side of the browser window.
Fly from **T**op	The text you select flies in from the top of the browser window.
Fly from Bottom-L**e**ft	The text you select flies in from the bottom-left corner of the browser window.
Fly from Botto**m**-Right	The text you select flies in from the bottom-right corner of the browser window.
Fly from To**p**-Left	The text you select flies in from the top-left corner of the browser window.
Fly from Top-Rig**h**t	The text you select flies in from the top-right corner of the browser window.
Fly from Top-Right B**y** Word	The text you select flies in one word at a time from the top-right corner of your browser window.
Fly from Bottom-Right By Word	The text you select flies in one word at a time from the bottom-right corner of your browser window.
Drop In By Word	The text you select scrolls in to your browser window from the top, one word at a time.
Spiral	The text you select loops in to your browser window from the top-right corner in a spiraling effect.

Do your site visitors a favor—don't apply any of the "By Word" text animation effects to your entire page!!!

| Zoom **In** | The text you select initially appears small and gradually increases in size. |
| Zoom **Out** | The text you select initially appears large and gradually decreases in size. |

3. If you have Internet Explorer 4.0 or later installed on your system, click the Preview tab in the FrontPage Editor to preview the text effect. To preview the effect in another browser that supports Dynamic HTML, choose **F**ile | Preview in **B**rowser and select another browser.

Figure 16.15.

*Use the Format |
Animation slide-out
menu to select a text
animation effect.*

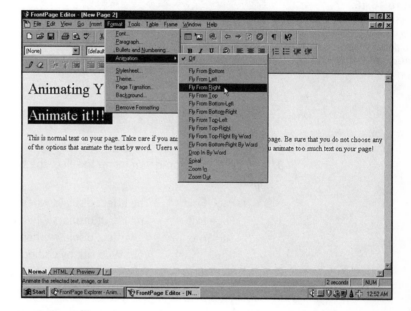

Adding Page Transitions

One of the nice new features of FrontPage 98 is the capability of adding page transitions that display effects when you navigate from one page to another in your Web. Page transitions use Dynamic HTML, which is currently supported by Internet Explorer 4.0.

The page transition you select is applied to your active page. When the user opens a page that has a page transition applied to it, the contents of the page display after the selected effect is completed.

NOTE: Page transitions will display in the FrontPage Editor's Preview tab only if you have Internet Explorer 4.0 installed on your system.

To add a page transition to your page, follow these steps:

1. In the FrontPage Editor, open the page to which you want to add a transition.
2. Choose Format I Page Transition. The Page Transitions dialog box shown in Figure 16.16 appears.

Figure 16.16.

Use the Page Transitions dialog box to select a transition effect to be associated with an event.

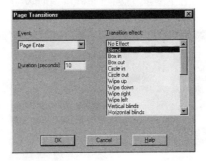

3. Use the **E**vent drop-down menu to select the type of transition you want to apply:

Page Enter	The effect displays when a user visits your active page.
Page Exit	The effect displays when a user leaves the active page.
Site Enter	The effect displays when a user initially enters your Web site by visiting the active page.
Site Exit	The effect displays when a user exits your Web site from the active page.

4. Select one of the effects from the **T**ransition effect list. There are several transitions from which to choose, including box effects, circle effects, wipes, blinds, checkerboards, dissolves, splits, strips, and random effects. If you choose No Effect, any transition that was previously applied to your page is removed.
5. In the **D**uration (seconds) field, enter the number of seconds that you want the transition to last.
6. Choose OK to apply the effect to your page.
7. If Internet Explorer 4.0 is installed on your system, click the Preview tab in the FrontPage Editor to preview the effect. You can also choose **F**ile I Preview in **B**rowser and select Internet Explorer 4.0 or another browser that supports Dynamic HTML.

Workshop Wrap-Up

As you can see, FrontPage 98 provides a lot of bells and whistles that make your pages come alive with movement. Using video, hover buttons, banner advertisements, marquees, animated text, and page transitions, you go beyond static page content and add areas of interest to your pages. Your site visitors can also search through your Web quickly and easily with the addition of a Search component. Keep track of the number of times your pages have been visited with the Hit Counter.

A closing few words of advice—don't overdo the amount of animated areas that you add to your pages. Too much movement can be distracting. You may find it more effective if you use animation on your pages when you want to draw attention to a specific area in your Web or to a specific section on the page. The eye is automatically drawn to the movement, and if your page contains too much of it the user will not know where to look first!

Next Steps

In the next chapter, you learn how to use FrontPage 98 in conjunction with other types of software. You can import documents created by other programs into your FrontPage Webs and configure editors so that you can open files in their native applications from within FrontPage. You'll also learn how you can work with different types of file formats in FrontPage 98.

Refer to the following chapters for more information about active content and animation:

- ❏ See Chapter 20, "Real-Life Examples III: Dressing Up Your Webs," to learn how to incorporate animation and active content into your Web.
- ❏ See Chapter 25, "Using Java Applets and Netscape Plug-Ins," to learn how to add multimedia elements using these popular Web technologies.
- ❏ See Chapter 28, "Working with ActiveX and Scripts," to learn how to add ActiveX controls to your Web pages.

Q&A

Q: I inserted a Hit Counter on my Web page. It works fine on my local computer, but when I place it on my ISP's server it doesn't appear on the page. What's wrong?

A: Your ISP may not have the FrontPage Server Extensions installed. Check with your ISP to see whether your Web site is FrontPage-enabled.

Q: I'd like to add transparency to my AVI file. Is that possible?

A: The AVI file format does not support transparency. If you want a transparent animation, you need to create an animated GIF file.

Q: My hover buttons work fine in some Java-enabled browsers but not in others. Why?

A: Each browser may interpret Java a little differently. It's always a good idea to keep several different browser types on hand so that you can test how each browser reacts to the features you put on your pages.

Q: I tried to view my animated text and my page transitions in Internet Explorer 3.0, and I couldn't see anything. Did I do something wrong?

A: Animated text and page transitions use a relatively new Web technology called Dynamic HTML. This is a capability that was introduced in Internet Explorer 4.0. Versions prior to that will not be able to display animated text and page transitions.

SEVENTEEN

Integrating with Other Editors

Sometimes you need to work with content other than HTML format. For example, you might want to use a text editor to edit text or ASCII files that are located in your Web. You might want to touch up a graphic. You might want to convert a word processing document, spreadsheet, or presentation into Web pages. You can open many types of documents in FrontPage. You can also configure FrontPage to open other types of editors when you click the file you want to edit. This chapter shows you how.

In this chapter, you

- ❏ Open and insert text files, word processing documents, spreadsheets, databases, and other types of files into your Web
- ❏ Configure FrontPage to use other editors in conjunction with the FrontPage Editor
- ❏ Learn about other options for incorporating documents created with other Microsoft applications

Tasks in this chapter:

- ❏ Inserting Files into Pages
- ❏ Opening Files in the FrontPage Editor
- ❏ Opening and Inserting Text Files
- ❏ Configuring Editor Associations in the FrontPage Explorer
- ❏ Opening Files from the FrontPage Explorer
- ❏ Working with RTF Files

Inserting Files into Pages

Although it's nice to be able to include many types of documents on your Web site, you have the worry of keeping track of helper applications. FrontPage 98 enables you to insert several types of files in your Web pages. FrontPage automatically converts the file types shown in Table 17.1 into HTML format when you open them.

Table 17.1. File formats supported in FrontPage.

File Type	Extensions
HTML files	*.htm, *.html
Hypertext templates	*.htt
Preprocessed HTML	*.htx, *.asp
Microsoft Excel Worksheet	*.xls, *.xlw
Rich text format	*.rtf
Text files	*.txt
Windows Write	*.wri
Word 6.0/95 for Windows and Macintosh	*.doc
Word Asian Versions 6.0/95	*.doc
Word 4.0–5.1 for Macintosh	*.mcw
Word 2.x for Windows	*.doc
Word for MS-DOS 3.x–5.x	*.doc
Word for MS-DOS 6.0	*.doc
Word 97	*.doc
WordPerfect 5.x	*.doc
WordPerfect 6.x	*.wpd, *.doc
Works 3.0 for Windows	*.wps
Works 4.0 for Windows	*.wps

It's very easy to insert another file type into your pages. You use the Insert | File command in the FrontPage Editor. The steps are as follows:

1. In the FrontPage Editor, open or create a page in which you want to insert a file.

2. Choose Insert | File. The Select File dialog box shown in Figure 17.1 appears.

Figure 17.1.

Use the Select File dialog box to insert an HTML document into another Web page.

3. From the Files of **t**ype drop-down menu, choose the file format that you want to insert in your page. In the example shown, Word 97 documents in the current folder are selected.

4. Use the Look **i**n box to locate the file you want to insert. Select the file and click OK. FrontPage inserts the file at the current insertion point.

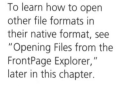

Opening Files in the FrontPage Editor

The file formats listed in Table 17.1 can also be opened in the FrontPage Editor. When you open any of the supported file types in the FrontPage Editor, they are automatically converted into HTML format for you.

To learn how to open other file formats in their native format, see "Opening Files from the FrontPage Explorer," later in this chapter.

To open a file from the FrontPage Editor, follow these steps:

1. From the FrontPage Editor, choose **F**ile | **O**pen (Ctrl+O) or use the Open button on the Standard toolbar. The Open dialog box shown in Figure 17.2 appears.

Figure 17.2.

Use the Open dialog box to open non-HTML files in the FrontPage Editor. This automatically converts the files into HTML format.

2. Choose the Select a file on your computer button located at the right of the **U**RL field. The Select File dialog box appears.

3. From the Files of **t**ype drop-down menu, choose the file format that you want to open.

4. Use the Look **i**n box to locate the file you want to open. Select the file and click OK. The file you selected opens in the FrontPage Editor, in HTML format.

Opening and Inserting Text Files

When you open or insert a text file into your page, FrontPage 98 enables you to select one of four ways to format the text before it converts to HTML format. The options are available in the Convert Text dialog box shown in Figure 17.3.

Figure 17.3.
The Convert Text dialog box appears when you open or insert a text file in the FrontPage Editor.

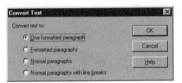

The following are the options you can select from the Convert Text dialog box:

❑ **O**ne formatted paragraph, an example of which is shown in Figure 17.4, places the contents of the entire text file into a single formatted paragraph. Formatted text, such as Courier, is used to format the paragraphs. Line breaks are inserted at the end of each line.

❑ **F**ormatted paragraphs, an example of which is shown in Figure 17.5, inserts the text file in multiple paragraphs. Formatted text, such as Courier, is used to format the paragraphs. Line breaks are inserted at the end of each line within a paragraph.

❑ **N**ormal paragraphs, an example of which is shown in Figure 17.6, inserts the text file in multiple normal paragraphs. The default font for normal paragraphs is Times New Roman or the default body font used in the theme you select for your Web or page. There are no line breaks inserted at the end of each line.

❑ Normal paragraphs with line **b**reaks, an example of which is shown in Figure 17.7, inserts the text file in multiple normal paragraphs. The default font is Times New Roman or the default body font used in the theme you select for your Web or page. Line breaks are inserted at the end of each line, retaining the layout of the original text file.

Figure 17.4.

One formatted paragraph.

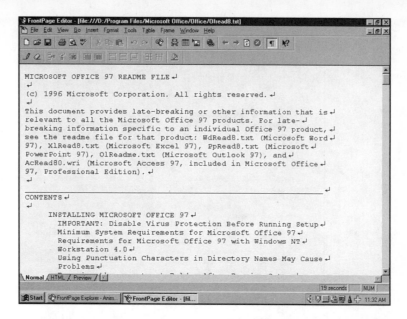

Figure 17.5.

Formatted paragraphs.

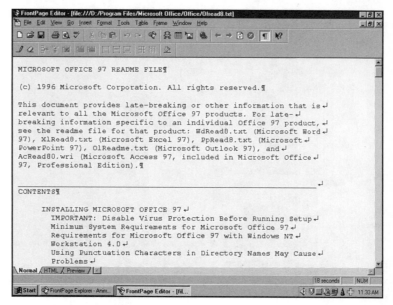

Figure 17.6.

Normal paragraphs.

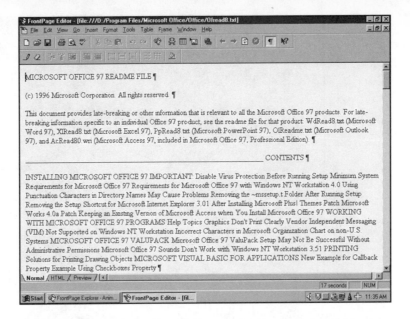

Figure 17.7.

Normal paragraphs with line breaks.

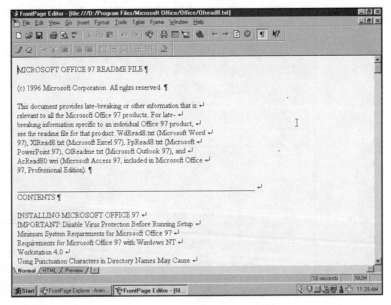

To open a text file from the FrontPage Editor, follow these steps:

1. From the FrontPage Editor, choose **F**ile I **O**pen (Ctrl+O) or use the Open button on the Standard toolbar. The Open dialog box appears.

2. Choose the Select a file on your computer button located at the right of the **U**RL field. The Select File dialog box appears.

3. From the Files of **t**ype drop-down menu, choose Text Files (`*.txt`).

4. Use the Look **i**n box to locate the file you want to open. Select the text file and click OK. The file you selected opens in the FrontPage Editor, in HTML format.

Configuring Editor Associations in the FrontPage Explorer

You can use the FrontPage Explorer to open any file in your Web. When you open a file from the FrontPage Explorer, the file will open in its native application, providing that you have an editor association configured in FrontPage.

If you don't have an editor associated with a file type, the Save As dialog box appears when you double-click a file in the FrontPage Explorer. You can use the Save As dialog box to save the file to a directory on your local or network hard drive.

By default, FrontPage 98 configures the following editors during installation:

File Type	Associated Editor
`.htm`	FrontPage Editor
`.html`	FrontPage Editor
`.htx`	FrontPage Editor
`.asp`	FrontPage Editor
`.css`	Notepad (Text Editor)
`.idc`	FrontPage Database Connection Wizard
`.cdf`	FrontPage Channel Definition Wizard
`.`	Notepad (Text Editor)

If you install Microsoft Image Composer 1.5 (which also installs Microsoft GIF Animator) in addition to FrontPage 98, the following graphics formats are automatically configured for you:

File Type	Associated Editor
`.gif`	Image Composer
`.jpg`	Image Composer

If you import files of other types into your FrontPage Webs, you can configure editor associations for them as well. For example, you can import Office 97 documents into your FrontPage Webs and configure editor associations for Word documents (`.doc`), Excel worksheets (`.xls` and `.xlw`), and Access database files (`.mdb`). If you click on any file that uses these extensions, the associated editor will open, and you can edit your file in its native format.

To configure an editor association in the FrontPage Explorer, follow these steps:

1. From the FrontPage Explorer, choose **T**ools I **O**ptions. The Options dialog box appears.

2. Click the Configure Editors tab, shown in Figure 17.8. A list of the file types and their associated editors appears.

3. To add an editor association, click the **A**dd button. The Add Editor Association dialog box shown in Figure 17.9 appears.

Figure 17.8.

Use the Configure Editors tab in the Options dialog box to associate file extensions with other editors.

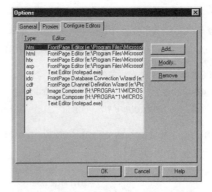

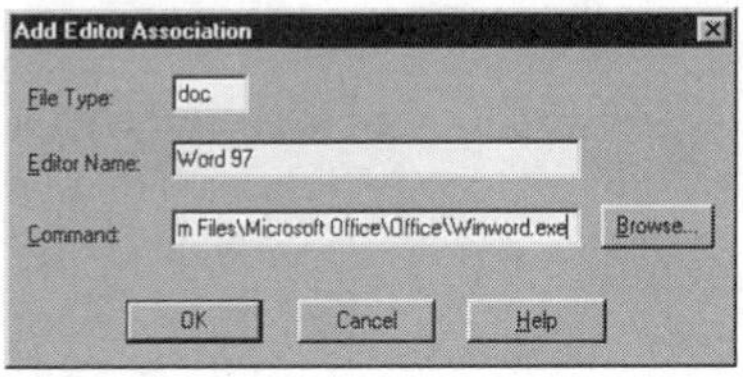

Figure 17.9.

Add a new editor association with the Add Editor Association dialog box.

4. Enter the file extension that you want to assign in the File Type field. You do not need to precede the extension with a period. For example, if you want to configure an editor association for your Word 97 documents, enter **doc**.

5. In the **E**ditor Name field, enter the application that opens when you select a file that uses the extension you are configuring. The example shows Word 97 in this field.

6. Click the **B**rowse button located at the right of the Command field. The Browse dialog box shown in Figure 17.10 appears. Use the Look in box to locate the drive and directory on your local computer in which the executable file for your editor is located.

Figure 17.10.

Use the Browse dialog box to locate the executable file that will run when you open the associated file type.

7. Double-click the executable file or highlight the filename and click **O**pen. You return to the Add Editor Association dialog box.

8. Choose OK to add the editor association. You return to the Options dialog box, and the editor is added to the list.

9. Choose OK to exit the Options dialog box when all your editors have been added.

NOTE: Use the **M**odify button in the Configure Editors tab to modify an editor association. You can change the name and command line for a file type. The **R**emove button in the Configure Editors tab will remove an editor association from the list.

Opening Files from the FrontPage Explorer

After you configure your editor associations, you can open associated files from the FrontPage Explorer. To open the file, use one of the following methods:

❏ From the FrontPage Explorer's Folders view or All Files view, double-click the filename that you want to open.

❏ Right-click on the filename you want to open and click **O**pen.

The associated editor opens, and the file appears in the editor window. After you modify the file, save it from within the configured editor. When you return to the FrontPage Explorer, you will see the updated file in your Web.

Working with RTF Files

Most Windows word processing programs enable you to save your document to rich text format (RTF). The one drawback to rich text format files, however, is that they usually don't retain the nice layout that you spent so much time with in your word processor. For example, if your original document uses multiple columns, you lose them when converting to RTF. You can add tables to the Web page version of your document to add back columns.

Figure 17.11 shows a Word document that was saved in rich text format. When you view the RTF file in Word 97, the layout retains its formatting and font faces. However, HTML formats font faces and styles a little differently. Compare the RTF file that you see in Word to the one you see in Figure 17.12. This is a screen shot of the same area of the page after it is opened in FrontPage and converted to HTML. As you can see, the two versions are quite similar, but there are some differences in heading sizes and in layout. After you open an RTF file in the FrontPage Editor, you may need to make some changes in formatting.

Figure 17.11.
The rich text format document as it appears in a word processor.

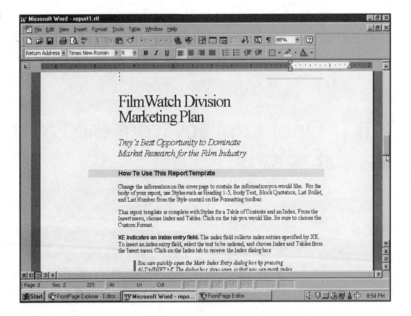

Figure 17.12.

After converting to HTML format in FrontPage, the text retains most of the original formatting.

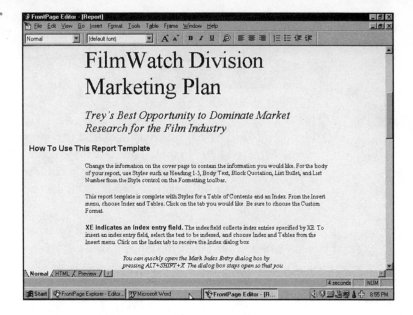

To open a rich text format document from the FrontPage Explorer, follow these steps:

1. From the FrontPage Explorer, right-click the filename and choose Open **W**ith from the pop-up menu. The Open with Editor dialog box shown in Figure 17.13 appears.

Figure 17.13.

Use the Open With Editor dialog box to open a page or file in your Web with a specific editor.

2. From the list of configured editors, highlight FrontPage Editor and choose OK. The Open File As dialog box shown in Figure 17.14 appears.

3. Select **R**TF from the Open As list. If you choose HT**M**L or **T**ext, all the formatting code contained in the document appears in your Web page.

Figure 17.14.

From the Open File As dialog box, choose RTF format.

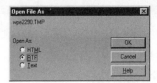

TIP: If your original RTF file contains graphics, they may appear larger or smaller after you open your file in the FrontPage Editor. If this occurs, open your images in a graphics editor and check the dots per inch setting at which the graphic was saved. Graphics convert best if their dpi setting is 72.

4. Choose **F**ile | Save **A**s (Ctrl+A) to save your document in HTML format. In the **U**RL field, enter a filename for your Web page. Enter its title in the **T**itle field.

5. Choose OK to save your new page to the Web.

You also can use the **I**nsert | **F**ile command to insert an RTF document into any Web page. When you choose this option, FrontPage automatically converts your RTF file into HTML format. Here are the steps:

1. From FrontPage, open or create a page in which to insert the text file.

2. Position the insertion point where you want the RTF file to appear.

3. Choose **I**nsert | **F**ile. The Select File dialog box appears.

4. From the Files of **t**ype drop-down menu, choose Rich Text Format (*.rtf).

5. Locate the drive and directory where the RTF file is located.

6. Highlight the page that you want to open and click **O**pen. FrontPage converts the RTF document to HTML format and inserts it at your insertion point. Any graphics that are contained in the RTF document are converted to GIF or JPEG format, as appropriate.

7. Save the page to your current Web with the **F**ile | **S**ave command. Assign it a title and a URL.

Integrating with Office 97

Office 97 gives you the capability of creating Web pages without learning HTML. You can create hyperlinks from one type of Office document to another. A portion of Office 97's Internet capabilities lies in its ActiveWeb features. You are able to author and view documents in their native formats. When you use Microsoft Outlook, an integral part of Office 97, you enter a URL or UNL address in your document and it automatically creates a link to a file or site.

You can convert your Office documents into HTML format at the click of a button. However, you don't have to convert to HTML—you can use files in native Office 97 formats as well. This enables you to analyze and edit the data as you usually do. Using Web Find Fast, a Web administrator can create a full context index and an organized catalog of documents on the site. For corporate intranet users, this is a boon to site development.

Microsoft Office 97 uses ActiveX technology to work seamlessly with common Web browsers. ActiveX technology is built into Internet Explorer 3.0 and employed in other browsers through plug-ins. You can share Office documents through FTP services. For those who do not use Microsoft Office, you can distribute the appropriate viewers that enable the user to view and print Office 97 documents.

Working with Word Processing Files

Word 97 provides custom templates to design Web pages. An Online Layout View makes your Web text easy to read. You can use colored and textured backgrounds and animated text effects. You can also insert and play inline videos within Word. Marquees, backgrounds, horizontal lines, and bullets can appear in your Word documents. The Web Page Wizard provides graphical themes for your Web pages.

NOTE: Users of Office 95 or Word 95 can also take advantage of Internet technology. You can find a current version of the Word 95 viewer at the following URL:

`http://www.microsoft.com/msword/internet/viewer/`

Table 17.1, earlier in this chapter, lists several other word processing formats that you can open in FrontPage. When you open any of these file types in FrontPage, the file is first converted to rich text format and then into HTML format before it opens in FrontPage. Documents that contain multiple columns in your word processing program will need to be touched up. To display multiple columns in a Web page, you need to manually insert content into tables.

HTML pages are meant to be viewed in multiple platforms, and for that reason, the formatting is very basic. (It's getting there, though, thanks to the cascading style sheet tags that you will learn about in Chapter 27, "Using Styles.") When you design a word processing document that you feel is destined for the Web, lay out your content in tables rather than using the word processor to format the column layout.

You have another way around these differences. Most word processors have viewers that the user can download. They enable the user to view and print the word processing document in its native format. Provide a link to download the appropriate viewer in your site.

Working with Spreadsheet Software

Excel 97 includes many new enhancements for Web page creation and integration. Web Queries enable you to pull information from your Web site directly into your Excel worksheets. The Internet Assistant Wizard, shown in Figure 17.15, converts spreadsheets and charts into Web pages.

Figure 17.15.

Use the Internet Assistant Wizard in Excel 97 to convert your spreadsheets and charts into Web pages.

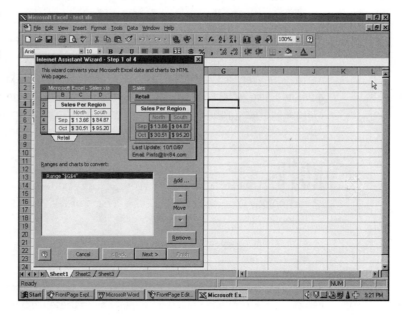

When working with Excel worksheet files from within FrontPage 98, simple tables and chart graphics will convert into HTML format without a problem. If your worksheet contains advanced features, such as macros and scripts, the Insert I File command may fail. Use the Save as HTML command in Microsoft Excel 97 to export your spreadsheet and then import that page into your FrontPage Web.

Figure 17.16 shows an example of a simple table that was created by opening an Excel worksheet in FrontPage. If your Excel spreadsheets contain charts, they are formatted into GIF format by default.

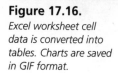

Figure 17.16.

Excel worksheet cell data is converted into tables. Charts are saved in GIF format.

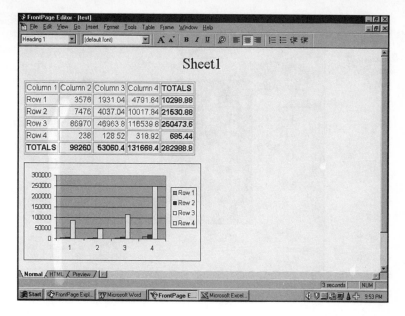

You also can import an Excel spreadsheet into your Web in its native format. Provide a link to it on another page, so that the user can download the appropriate viewer from Microsoft's Web site. You can download the current viewer from the following URL:

`http://www.microsoft.com/msexcel/internet/viewer/`

Working with PowerPoint 97

Microsoft PowerPoint 97 contains built-in converters and viewers that work in conjunction with Internet Explorer 3.0 and above. Using the PowerPoint Animation Player for ActiveX, you can publish your presentations on the Internet. The Web pages can contain animation and narration. New templates contain bullets, buttons, backgrounds, and other enhancements for Web page development. PowerPoint's Save as HTML Wizard, shown in Figure 17.17, translates your presentations into HTML format. You can make presentations interactive by assigning action settings to graphics, text, and buttons.

If you use PowerPoint 95, you can obtain Internet Assistant for PowerPoint 95 to enhance the use of PowerPoint presentations in your Web. It converts PowerPoint presentations into a series of consecutively numbered HTML files and provides navigation between them. The presentation screens are converted to graphics that are placed on each page. You can download this utility from

`http://www.microsoft.com/mspowerpoint/internet/ia/`

Figure 17.17.

Use PowerPoint 97's Save as HTML Wizard to save your presentation files in HTML format.

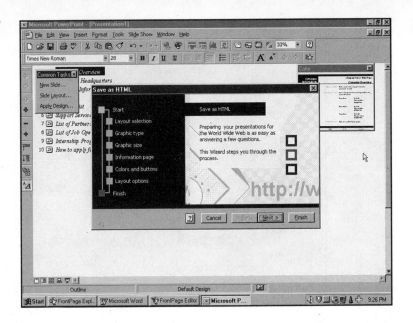

You also can import a PowerPoint presentation into your Web and provide a link to it on another Web page. Likewise, provide a link to the following URL so that users can download the PowerPoint Viewer:

`http://www.microsoft.com/msoffice/mspowerpoint/internet/viewer/`

If your PowerPoint presentation includes animated effects, check out what is available in the PowerPoint Animation Player for ActiveX. Internet Explorer 3.0 provides built-in ActiveX support. You can download the PowerPoint Animation Player for ActiveX from

`http://www.microsoft.com/powerpoint/internet/player/default.htm`

Working with Database Software

Using Access 97, you can convert your data and reports to HTML, enabling you to share them across your intranet or the World Wide Web. You can then use Access to publish datasheet and reports as well as Web pages. You can also use Access to create applications that display HTML documents in forms. With the Publish to the Web Wizard, shown in Figure 17.18, you can automate the design of dynamic Web pages that integrate with your database. This wizard enables you to create database files and Web pages that integrate through Internet Database Connector (IDC) files or Active Server Pages.

can download the Internet Assistant for Microsoft Access 95 from the
on Microsoft's site:

`rosoft.com/access/internet/ia/default.htm`

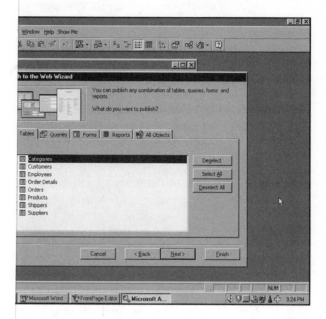

hop Wrap-Up

FrontPage works with a wide variety of file formats. You can import just about any type
of file into your Web, as well as recommend helper applications or viewers to visitors
to your site. You can open these files by configuring editors in FrontPage. You can
open and insert text or rich text format and other word processing documents in your
Web documents directly, and you can save them in standard HTML format to your
Web. FrontPage also converts Excel spreadsheet data into tables.

In this chapter, you learned how to work with types of files other than HTML. You
learned how to configure FrontPage to open an editor associated with a specific file
type by clicking the file that you want to edit. You also learned about using other
Microsoft Office documents in your Web.

Next Steps

In the next chapter, you'll learn how to design and incorporate framesets into your
Web sites. Framesets are another way that you can simplify the navigation in your Web
site. You use framesets to divide your browser window into multiple pages—some
display navigation bars and others display the content in your site.

To learn more about working with other types of content, refer to the following chapters:

❏ Refer to Chapter 15, "Working with Images and Sound," to learn how to insert graphics into your Web pages.

❏ See Chapter 28, "Working with ActiveX and Scripts," to learn how ActiveX components can enhance your Web pages.

Q&A

Q: What should I do if my word processor doesn't export to rich text format, and I don't have a viewer available to view files in their native format?

A: Most Windows word processors have this option. If yours does not, it might be necessary for you to convert your word processing document into text format instead. When you save your document, select Text format (sometimes called ASCII text). If your word processor has an option to save as Text with Layout, line breaks are inserted to format the document properly.

Q: Is there any way that I can import spreadsheet data from another spreadsheet program if I don't have Excel?

A: One thing to check—your spreadsheet software might allow you to export your spreadsheet into Excel format. Try this first. If that is not an option, open your spreadsheet software and select the cells you want to place into a Web page. Copy them into your clipboard using Ctrl+C. Then, position the insertion point on the page you have opened in FrontPage. Use Ctrl+V to paste the cells onto your page.

EIGHTEEN

Frames: Pages with Split Personalities

No doubt you have browsed the Web and come across some sites that display several pages in a single browser window. Some sections in the browser provide navigation links to other pages on the site. When you click the hyperlinks, the page that you link to opens in another portion of the browser window, and the navigation area remains on the screen. You no longer have to use your Back button to return to the navigation area, because it's always there.

More than likely, the site uses framesets to achieve that effect. You can think of a frame as multiple pages in one. It really is what the title of this chapter implies: a page with a split personality. Each region of a framed page displays a separate page that is scrollable, just like any other Web page. The most common way to use framesets is to develop pages that enable users to find their way through a Web site without getting too lost.

FrontPage 98 enables you to create and edit your framesets in WYSIWYG mode. In addition, you can edit the HTML code associated with your framesets directly. This chapter shows you how to create and edit your own framesets and how to add content into the frames.

Not All Browsers Are Frame-Compatible

Frames offer you great flexibility in displaying pages. Don't let your Web site rely totally on that flexibility, however. Many people use browsers that are not compatible with frames. Others use different browsers at different times for various reasons. For example, a user might prefer the way one browser views mail and newsgroups over another, and that choice might not have frame compatibility.

Be considerate to those out there who do not have frame-compatible browsers or who do not use them all the time. Provide alternatives for navigating to the pages that you display within the frames. FrontPage 98 provides a very easy way to create an alternate content page. If a browser that is not frame-compatible encounters a page with a frameset, the alternate content page displays instead. You can create a Web page that enables the user to navigate to other pages in your site instead of receiving a `This site uses frames but your browser does not support them` message.

Frames Terminology

Figure 18.1 shows four pages loaded into a frameset. This frameset is used in the support site for this book. A *frameset* is a special kind of page. Its function is to divide the browser window into multiple sections, called *frames*. You assign the frameset a URL, just as you would any other page. When a user navigates to the frameset with a frame-compatible browser, the frameset opens in the browser first. The browser window then gets divided into frames.

Figure 18.1.
A frameset displays multiple pages in a single screen.

Next, the frame-compatible browser loads other pages from your Web site into the frames in the frameset. To accomplish this, you assign a *source URL* to each of the frames in your frameset. The source URL identifies the URL of the page or file in your current Web that loads into a frame when the frameset opens. Without a source URL, each of the frames in your frameset would initially be empty, and the user would have nowhere to go.

The source URL can belong to a page, a file, or another frameset in your Web. In the example shown in Figure 18.1, you see four individual pages displayed in the frameset:

❏ The *source URL* for the left frame is a navigation bar that displays the main sections in the Web site. When a user clicks on any of the navigation buttons in the left frame, a change occurs in the top frame.

❏ The top frame displays one of several tables of contents that list the pages in each section of the Web. For example, if the user clicks the Links button in the left frame, the top frame displays a list of the pages in the Links section, as shown in Figure 18.2.

Figure 18.2.

The left frame causes changes in the contents frame on the top.

❏ When the user clicks on any of the links in the top frame, a change occurs in the largest, or main, frame in the frameset. (See Figure 18.3.)

❏ The bottom frame displays links to the Microsoft FrontPage home page and the Internet Explorer download area. This page always remains in the bottom frame, enabling the user to download a recommended browser at any time while viewing pages in the site.

Figure 18.3.

The contents frame on the top causes changes in the main frame beneath it.

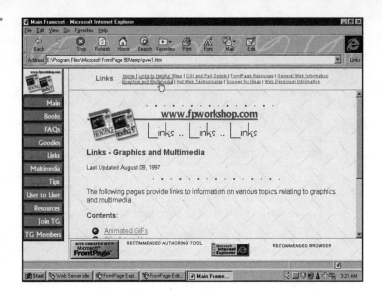

You can configure a hyperlink to display another frameset within one of the frames. For example, you might want to open a discussion group in the main frame of your frameset, which then causes the main frame to divide into two frames instead of one. In cases such as these, the main frame is called a *parent frame*, and the discussion group frames are *child frames*.

To configure hyperlinks to cause changes in another frame, you need to assign a *target frame* name to a page or a hyperlink. When you assign a *default target frame* to a page, each hyperlink on the page will load the target page into the frame you assign in the default target frame field. You can override this setting by assigning a *target frame* to a hyperlink. You'll learn more about assigning default target frames and target frames later in this chapter.

 ## Creating Your Practice Web

When you create framesets, you create hyperlinks between multiple pages in a Web site. For this reason, you must have a Web opened in the FrontPage Explorer while you create your framesets.

 To follow the examples in this chapter, create a one-page Web. Name the Web **Framesets** and do not use themes or shared borders. Examples of the completed project are provided on the CD-ROM that accompanies this book. They are located in the Book\Chap18\Examples folder.

Briefly, the steps to create the Web are as follows:

1. Choose **F**ile | **N**ew | FrontPage **W**eb from the FrontPage Explorer. Choose the One Page Web radio button, enter **Framesets** in the Choose a title for your FrontPage web field, and click OK.

2. Choose the Themes icon from the Views pane in the FrontPage Explorer. If necessary, select This **W**eb Does Not Use Themes and click **A**pply. The Apply button will be disabled if this setting is already applied to your Web.

3. Choose **T**ools | Shared **B**orders. Verify in the Shared Borders dialog box that all border options are unchecked and click OK.

Creating a Frameset from a Template

FrontPage 98 provides several frameset templates. You select one of them from the FrontPage Editor. When you highlight the name of a frameset template, a preview of the layout of the frames appears in the New dialog box. If you don't see a frameset that is laid out quite exactly as you would like, have no fear. You can modify any frameset to suit your purposes. Start out with a frameset that appears close to the one you'll need.

To create a simple two-frame frameset from a template, follow these steps:

In this example, you will start with a simple two-frame frameset. Later, I'll show you how to add another frame to the frameset and make modifications to it.

1. Open the Frames tab in the New dialog box, using one of the following methods:

   ❏ Choose F**r**ame | **N**ew Frames Page.

   ❏ Choose **F**ile | **N**ew (Ctrl+N) and click the Frames tab in the New dialog box, as shown in Figure 18.4.

Figure 18.4.

Use the Frames tab in the New dialog box to select a frame template.

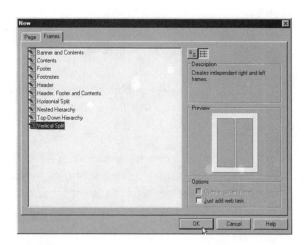

2. From the list of frame templates, choose Vertical Split. This creates a frameset that contains two frames that appear side by side.

3. Choose OK. The FrontPage Editor screen displays two frames, as shown in Figure 18.5. Each of the pages contains three buttons:

Figure 18.5.

Two frames display in the FrontPage Editor. Each frame contains three buttons.

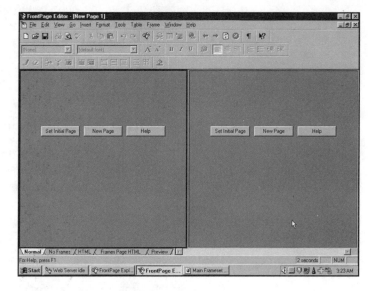

❏ Use the Set Initial Page button in one of the frames to select the page that initially loads in that frame when the browser first opens the frameset. Use the Create Hyperlink dialog box to select a page from your current Web or to create a new one.

NOTE: You can also assign the initial page by clicking in the frame you want to assign the initial page to and choosing Frame I Set Initial Page.

❏ Use the New Page button in one of the frames to create a new page that loads into that frame. This creates a blank page in your frameset.

NOTE: To create a new frame page that is based on a page template, choose File I New (Ctrl+N). Select your page template from the New dialog box and verify that the Open in current frame button in the lower-right corner of the New dialog box is checked. Choose OK to create a new page in the selected frame.

❏ Use the Help button to display the Getting Started with Frames topic from the FrontPage 98 Help file.

 ## Adding Another Frame to the Frameset

If you decide that you need another frame in your frameset, you can add another frame to it without having to start again. You use the Split Frame command in the Frame menu to split a frame into two rows or two columns. In the following example, you'll divide the left frame into two rows, making a total of three frames in your frameset.

To add another frame, follow these steps:

1. Click in the right frame in your frameset.
2. Choose Frame I Split Frame. The Split Frame dialog box appears.
3. To split the frame into two rows, choose the Split into Rows radio button and click OK. Now you have two frames in the right portion of your frameset, making a total of three frames in your frameset.

 ## Deleting a Frame from a Frameset

You also can delete frames from a frameset. If your current frameset has four frames, for example, and you want to change it so that your pages display in three frames, you can use the Delete Frame command in the Frames menu to delete the frame.

NOTE: You need to reassign any default target link or target link settings that point to the frame you deleted.

To delete a frame, follow these steps:

1. Click in the frame you want to delete.
2. Choose Frame I Delete Frame. The frame is removed from your frameset.

 ## Assigning Frames Page Properties

By default, your frameset displays two pixels of "padding" between each of the frames in your frameset when they are displayed in a browser. In addition, the borders in the frameset are visible. Some people don't like to display borders in a frameset, and browsers such as Internet Explorer enable you to create borderless frames that appear much smoother and more seamless than those with borders. To adjust the default settings, you need to configure your Frames Page Properties.

To configure Frames Page Properties, follow these steps:

1. From the FrontPage Editor, choose Frame I Frames Page Properties. The Page Properties dialog box appears, opened to the Frames tab shown in Figure 18.6.

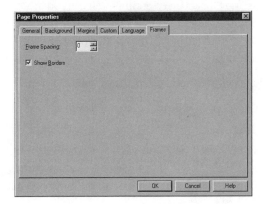

Figure 18.6.
Use the Frames tab in the Page Properties dialog box to adjust the amount of space between each frame and to turn borders on or off.

2. Use the **F**rame Spacing field to specify the number of pixels that you want to add between the frames in your frameset. For this example, specify 0.

3. Check the Show **B**orders checkbox if you want the borders between each frame in your frameset to display. Uncheck this option to create borderless frames that remove the display of borders between each frame. Borderless framesets have a much cleaner appearance, but this feature is not supported by all browsers. For the frameset that you are creating in this example, uncheck the Show **B**orders checkbox.

4. Click OK to assign the properties to your frames page. The border lines disappear from view.

About Frame Properties

Next, you want to assign properties to each of the *frames* in your frameset. You not only have to give each of the frames in your frameset a name, but you can also set sizing and scrolling properties and margin settings. The Frame Properties dialog box, shown in Figure 18.7, enables you to configure these settings.

The Options section in the Frame Properties dialog box determines whether the current frame is resizeable and whether scrollbars display in the frame.

❏ The **R**esizeable in Browser checkbox determines whether the user can resize the frames in his or her browser. By default, this option is checked, and it's a good rule to leave it that way. The user can position the dividing lines between the frames to accommodate the content in your pages. If you do not want your frames to be resizeable, uncheck the **R**esizeable in Browser checkbox.

TIP: To quickly resize one of the frames in the FrontPage Editor, click and drag the frame border and release the mouse when the frame is properly sized to hold your page contents.

Figure 18.7.
Use the Frame Properties dialog box to configure the settings for each frame in your frameset.

❑ Use the Show Scroll**b**ars drop-down menu to choose how you want to display scrollbars in your frames. The default selection is If Needed, which displays scrollbars along the left or bottom edges of a frame if the contents of the page are too wide or too long to display in the frame. Again, it's generally a good idea to leave this setting as is. You can optionally choose Never if you want to completely disable the scrollbars in a frame or choose Always if you want to display scrollbars whether or not they are required.

The Frame Size section in the Frame Properties dialog box enables you to set the width of a frame when there are two or more columns in your frameset or the height of a frame when there are two or more rows in your frameset. There are three types of width or height settings from which to choose:

❑ Use the Pixel setting when you want the width or height of your frame to always be the same width or height in pixels. This is the most likely choice when your frame contains navigation buttons or graphics. If, for example, your left frame contains navigation buttons that are 100 pixels wide, choose Pixels from the Width drop-down menu and enter **100** in the **W**idth field. Add an additional 25 pixels to your width or height if you think that a scrollbar will be required along the right or bottom side of the frame.

❏ Use the Percent setting when you want the width or height of your frame to always be a percentage of full browser width or height. If, for example, you want the left navigation frame to always consume 20 percent of the browser width and the top and main frames to take up the remaining 80 percent, do the following: Choose Percent from the Width drop-down menu, enter **20** in the left frame's **W**idth field, and enter **80** in the top and main frame's **W**idth field.

❏ The Relative setting is used in conjunction with either the Pixel or Percent setting to size any remaining frames to the space that is available after you define pixel or percent width or height for other frames in your frameset. If you set the left frame to use a width of 100 pixels, the top and main frames automatically are set to Relative, and they take up the remaining area in the browser window.

But suppose you have *three* columns in your frameset, as shown in Figure 18.8. The frame in the left column has a width of 100 pixels. You want the middle column to be 1/3 the remaining width and the right column to be 2/3 the remaining width. Choose Relative for the frame in the middle column and specify **1** in the Width field. Choose Relative for the frame in the right column and specify **2** in the Width field.

Figure 18.8.
The Relative width setting enables you to divide the remaining browser width into one or more frames.

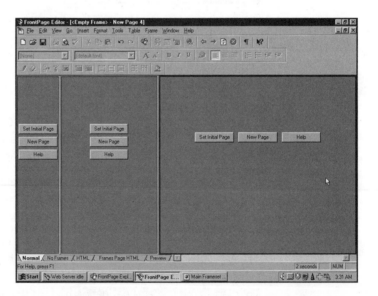

The Margins section in the Frame Properties dialog box enables you to set the width and height of the margins between the frame borders and the content that displays within each of the frames. This adds extra whitespace between the borders and the content on your pages.

❏ To set the amount of space between the left and right borders of a frame and the contents of your page, increase or decrease the value in the Width field.

❏ To set the amount of space between the top and bottom borders of a frame and the contents of your page, increase or decrease the value in the Height field.

The Initial Page field enables you to specify the page that gets loaded into the frame when it first opens. In most cases, you initially want to load a page from within your own Web site. You can use the Browse button to select a page from the Edit Hyperlink dialog box.

❏ To load a page that already exists in your Web, select the page that you want to load from the list of pages in your current Web.

❏ To create a new page, choose the Create a new page button located at the right of the URL field. Select the page template that you want to use and save the page to your Web, as outlined in Chapter 5, "Lightning-Speed Web Design."

Assigning Frame Properties

Now you'll assign properties to each of the frames in your sample frameset. You will use the left frame to display links to the main sections in your Web site. The top frame will contain tables of contents of the pages within each of the sections. The main pages in your Web will load into the main frame in the frameset.

To assign properties to each frame, follow these steps:

1. Click in the left frame in the frameset.

2. Choose Frame | Frame Properties or right-click and choose Frame Properties from the pop-up menu. The Frame Properties dialog box appears.

3. Enter the following settings for the left frame:

Name:	left
Resizeable in Browser:	Checked (default)
Show Scrollbars:	If Needed (default)
Column Width:	125 Pixels
Margins	Width:	0
Margins	Height:	0
Initial Page:	Click the Browse button. Select the Create a new page button located to the right of the URL field. Choose the Normal Page template and then click OK. You return to the Frame Properties dialog box.

4. Choose OK to apply the settings to the left frame. A blank source URL page appears in the left frame in your frameset.

5. Click in the top frame in the frameset.

6. Choose Frame I Frame Properties or right-click and choose Frame Properties from the pop-up menu. The Frame Properties dialog box appears.

7. Enter the following settings for the top frame:

Name:	**top**
Resizeable in Browser:	Checked (default)
Show Scroll**b**ars:	If Needed (default)
Column **W**idth:	1, Relative
Heigh**t**:	20, Percent
Margins I **W**idth:	0
Margins I Hei**g**ht:	0
Initial **P**age:	Click the Browse button. Select the Create a new page button located to the right of the **U**RL field. Choose the Normal Page template and then click OK. You return to the Frame Properties dialog box.

8. Choose OK to apply the settings to the top frame. A blank source URL page appears in the top frame in your frameset.

9. Click in the bottom-right frame in the frameset.

10. Choose Frame I Frame Properties or right-click and choose Frame Properties from the pop-up menu. The Frame Properties dialog box appears.

11. Enter the following settings for the bottom-right frame:

Name:	**main**
Resizeable in Browser:	Checked (default)
Show Scroll**b**ars:	If Needed (default)
Column **W**idth:	1, Relative
Heigh**t**:	1, Relative
Margins I **W**idth:	0
Margins I Hei**g**ht:	0
Initial **P**age:	Click the Browse button. Select the Create a new page button located to the right of the **U**RL field. Choose the Normal Page template and then choose OK. You return to the Frame Properties dialog box.

12. Choose OK to apply the settings to the bottom-right frame. A blank source URL page appears in the main frame in your frameset. Your screen should now look as shown in Figure 18.9.

Figure 18.9.

Each of the frames in your frameset are configured, and blank source URL pages appear in each frame.

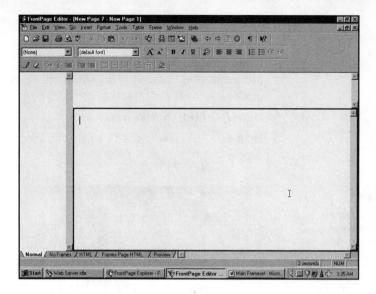

TASK Adding Content to the Left Frame

The left frame in the frameset contains links to the table of contents pages that display in the top frame. For purposes of demonstration, this page will be very simple, containing only text hyperlinks for now. You can replace the text links with navigation buttons later.

To add content to the left frame in your frameset, follow these steps:

1. Click in the left frame in your frameset. The insertion point is ready for you to add content.

TIP: If you prefer to edit the content of a framed page in a full browser window, click in the frame you want to edit and choose Frame | **O**pen Page in New Window. The content of your framed page appears in a full window in the FrontPage Editor.

2. Enter the lines of text, pressing Shift+Enter at the end of each line to insert a normal line break:

```
Home
Main
Interests
Links
```

3. Format the text in any way you choose. I selected all the text on the page and chose Arial from the Change Font drop-down menu in the Format

toolbar. I used the Decrease Text Size button on the Format toolbar once to reduce the size of the text.

4. Choose F**r**ame I **S**ave Page. The Save As dialog box appears, displaying a preview of your frameset in the right portion, as shown in Figure 18.10. The preview shows the left frame selected.

5. In the **U**RL field, enter `sections.htm`.

6. Enter `Main Sections` in the **T**itle field and choose OK. The page is saved to your Web.

Figure 18.10.

The Save As dialog box displays a preview of your frameset in the right portion.

TASK Adding Content to the Top Frame

The left frame in your frameset will remain onscreen while the hyperlinks within it display different pages in the top frame in the frameset. You will add the hyperlinks to your pages later in this chapter. Now you will add the content for the source URL of the top frame.

1. Click in the top frame in your frameset. The insertion point is ready for you to add content.

2. You want to provide links to the pages that you place in the main section in your Web here. Enter the following text in the top frame in your frameset:

   `What's New? ¦ Table of Contents ¦ Search ¦ Guest Book`

3. Format the text in any way you choose. Again, I selected all the text on the page and chose Arial from the Change Font drop-down menu in the Format toolbar.

4. Choose F**r**ame I **S**ave Page. The Save As dialog box appears, and this time the top frame is highlighted in the frameset preview.

5. Enter `maintoc.htm` in the **U**RL field and `Main TOC for Frameset` in the **T**itle field. Choose OK to save the page to your Web. It should look similar to Figure 18.11.

Figure 18.11.

The Main TOC for Frameset page lists all of the pages in the Main section of your Web.

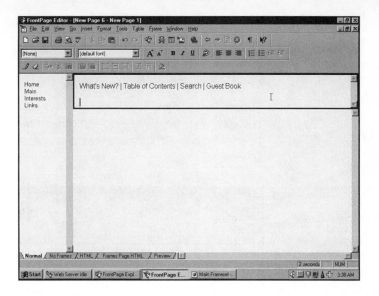

You'll need a second table of contents page to place in the top frame in your frameset. This page will list the pages in the Interests section in your Web. To create this page, follow these steps:

1. With the insertion point in the top frame, select **F**ile | **N**ew (Ctrl+N). Select the Normal Page template from the New dialog box. Verify that the Open in **c**urrent frame checkbox is checked and choose OK. A new blank page appears in the top frame.

2. Enter the following text in the new page (you can replace these interests with your own if you choose):

   `Web Design ¦ Graphics Development ¦ Music ¦ Multimedia ¦ Movies ¦ Sci Fi`

3. Format the text in any way you choose.

4. Choose F**r**ame | **S**ave Page. The Save As dialog box appears. Enter **interests-toc.htm** in the **U**RL field and **Interests TOC for Frameset** in the **T**itle field. Choose OK to save the page to your Web. Figure 18.12 shows an example of this page.

The third table of contents page for the top frame in your frameset will list pages that contain links to other sites on the World Wide Web. To create this page, follow these steps:

1. With the insertion point in the top frame, select **F**ile | **N**ew (Ctrl+N). Select the Normal Page template from the New dialog box. Verify that the Open in **c**urrent frame checkbox is checked and choose OK. A new blank page appears in the top frame.

2. Enter the following text in the new page (you can replace these with your own links pages if you choose):

   Links about Web Design ¦ Links about Graphics ¦ Links about Movies

3. Format the text in any way you choose.

4. Choose Frame I Save Page. The Save As dialog box appears. Enter **links-toc.htm** in the URL field and **Links TOC for Frameset** in the Title field. Choose OK to save the page to your Web. Figure 18.13 shows an example.

Figure 18.12.

The Interests TOC for Frameset page lists all of the pages in the Interests section of your Web.

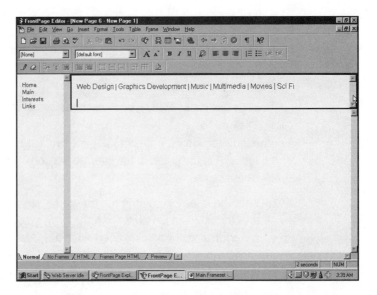

Figure 18.13.

The Links TOC for Frameset page lists all of the pages in the Links section of your Web.

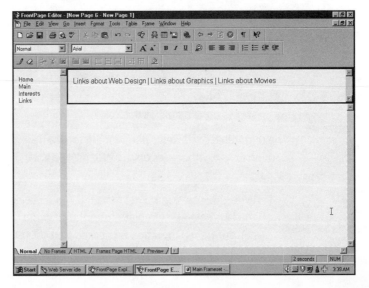

Creating the Page for the Main Frame

Now you enter some content in the source URL page for the main frame. This frame can contain a welcome splash screen that welcomes users to your site, a page that highlights some of the main pages in your Web, or a catchy animation that attracts the attention of your visitors. For purposes of this chapter, you will just add some text that reminds you what you can put on this page:

1. Click in the main frame in your frameset. The insertion point is ready for you to add content.

2. Choose Insert | FrontPage Component. The Insert FrontPage Component dialog box appears.

3. From the Select a component list, choose Comment and click OK. The Comment dialog box appears.

4. Enter the following text in the Comment box:

   ```
   This page is the source URL for the main frame in the frameset.
   It can contain an introductory graphic, welcome message, or
   home page contents. When you create graphics for this page or
   any page which displays in the main frame of the frameset,
   remember that the page will not be displayed in a full browser
   window. Size your graphics accordingly.
   ```

5. Choose OK. The Comment appears on your page, as shown in Figure 18.14.

Figure 18.14.
Enter a comment on the main page to remind you what to place on the source URL page for the main frame.

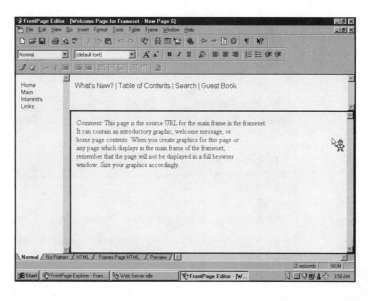

6. Choose Frame | Save Page. The Save As dialog box appears, with the main frame highlighted in the frameset preview. Enter `welcome.htm` in the URL field and `Welcome Page for Frameset` in the Title field. Choose OK to save the page to your Web.

Creating the Alternate Content Page

There is still one more page to create—the alternate content page that gets displayed when users do not use frame-compatible browsers. This page displays in a full browser window, because it is the page that displays when the user is not using a frame-compatible browser.

In FrontPage 98, it is very easy to add content to your alternate content page. The alternate content that displays in lieu of the frameset is actually embedded within your frameset page. To see this, click the Frames Page HTML tab in the FrontPage Editor. The HTML code that starts with the `<noframes>` tag and ends with the `</noframes>` tag is your alternate content. Figure 18.15 shows an example of this.

Figure 18.15.

The alternate content that appears in lieu of the frameset is embedded within the HTML code for your frameset.

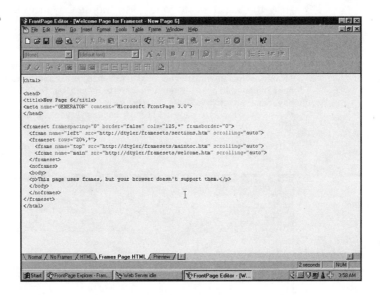

If you click the No Frames tab in the FrontPage Editor, you can view and edit the alternate content page in WYSIWYG format. By default, the page displays the following text:

`This page uses frames, but your browser doesn't support them.`

It's not a very friendly greeting to present to users who want to see your site, is it? Just imagine how they feel when someone e-mails them the URL to your site and tells them how great your site is. Then when users navigate to your site without a frame-compatible browser, they receive this message. So much for the interest!

You'll learn more about creating an alternate content page in Chapter 20, "Real-Life Examples III: Dressing Up Your Webs."

Instead, add some content that enables users to navigate to the pages in your Web. It's much more friendly, because it enables them to see what your site has to offer.

Adding a Default Target Frame to a Page

Now you need to learn how to tie all these pages together so that your Web pages load in the correct frames when a user clicks your hyperlinks. Before I get into showing you how to do this, I need to explain the difference between default target frames and target frames.

Notice that the left frame in your frameset contains text for four hyperlinks. All but one of those hyperlinks (the Home hyperlink) will display a table of contents in the top frame in your frameset.

The quickest and easiest way to instruct the frameset to load target pages into the same frame is to assign a *default target frame* to the page that contains the hyperlinks. You assign a default target frame through the General tab in the Page Properties dialog box. When you assign a default target frame to a page, it basically tells the frameset, "When the user clicks any link on this page, load the page that he or she is navigating to into this other frame."

A *target frame*, on the other hand, is what you apply to the Home hyperlink on the page. Because it goes somewhere other than the default target frame, it's just a "plain old target frame." Target frames tell the browser, "When the user clicks only this link on this page, load the page that he or she is navigating to in this *different* frame." You learn how to assign them in "Assigning Target Frames to Hyperlinks," later in this chapter.

To assign a default target frame to the Main Sections page in the left frame, follow these steps:

1. With the frameset opened in the FrontPage Editor, click in the left frame. Choose File | Page Properties or right-click and choose Page Properties from the pop-up menu. The Page Properties dialog box appears, opened to the General tab.

2. Click the Change Target Frame button located at the right of the Default Target Frame field. The Target Frame dialog box shown in Figure 18.16 appears.

3. Notice the frameset preview at the left side of the dialog box. To assign the top frame as the default target frame, click the top frame in the frameset preview. The word top appears in the Target Setting field at the bottom of the dialog box.

4. Choose OK to return to the Page Properties dialog box and choose OK again to set the default target frame for the page.

Figure 18.16.
*Use the Target Frame
dialog box to choose
the frame in which the
hyperlink will load
the page.*

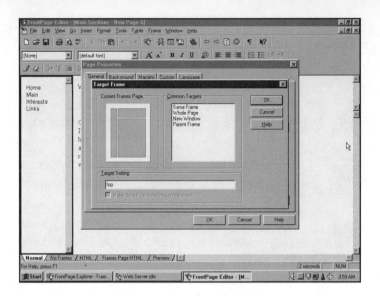

5. Choose Frame | Save Page to update the page to your Web.

6. Use steps 1 through 5 in a similar manner to choose the main frame as a default target frame for the pages that load in the top frame. You need to choose File | Open (Ctrl+O) to open the two pages that are not currently displayed in the top frame. Use the Page Properties dialog box to assign the `main` frame as the default target frame. Update each of the pages to your Web using the Frame | Save Page command. Apply these steps to the following pages:

`interests-toc.htm`	Interests TOC for Frameset
`links-toc.htm`	Links TOC for Frameset
`maintoc.htm`	Main TOC for Frameset

 TASK

Assigning Target Frames to Hyperlinks

Sometimes it's not enough to assign a default target frame to a Web page. There may be cases where you want to load one or more of the links on a page in a different frame in your frameset. There are other times that you want to load a target page in a full browser window instead.

The Home hyperlink in the left frame is a good example of this. Let's assume that the home page in your Web is supposed to display in a full browser window instead of within your frameset. When the user clicks on the Home hyperlink in the left frame, you want to remove the frameset from the browser window to display the home page outside of the frameset.

In cases such as these, you assign a target frame to the *hyperlink* instead of to the page. The target frame setting assigned to the hyperlink overrides the default target frame assigned to the page. To assign a target frame to a hyperlink, follow these steps:

1. With your frameset opened in the FrontPage Editor, select the text in the left frame that reads Home.

2. Click the Create or Edit Hyperlink button on the Standard toolbar. The Create Hyperlink dialog box appears.

3. Notice that Page Default (top) appears in the **T**arget Frame field. This is because you assigned a default target frame in the previous task. To assign a different target frame, click the Change Target Frame button at the right of the **T**arget Frame field. The Target Frame dialog box appears.

4. This time, you do not want to select one of the frames in your frameset to load in the home page. Notice that there are other options listed in the **C**ommon Targets section in the dialog box:

Same Frame	When you choose this option, the **T**arget Setting field displays a target frame of _self. This loads the page to which you are hyperlinking in the same frame that the hyperlink you are following appears in.
Whole Page	When you choose this option, the **T**arget Setting field displays a target frame of _top. This removes the frameset from the current browser window and displays the target page in a full browser window. If any of the hyperlinks in your frames navigate to other sites on the World Wide Web, you want to select this option.
New Window	When you choose this option, the **T**arget Setting field displays a target frame of _blank. This loads the page to which you are hyperlinking in a new browser window and keeps your frameset in the original browser window.
Parent Frame	When you choose this option, the **T**arget Setting field displays a target frame of _parent. This loads the page to which you are hyperlinking in the parent frame if the hyperlink that you are following appears on a child frame.

5. From the **C**ommon Targets list, highlight Whole Page. The Target Setting field displays a target frame name of _top.

6. The **M**ake default for hyperlinks on the page button is enabled, but unchecked. Because your current page already has a default target frame assigned, leave this option unchecked. Use this option if you have not yet specified a default target frame for the current page.

7. Choose OK to return to the Create Hyperlink dialog box.

8. Enter the URL for your home page in the URL field or select your home page from the list of pages in your current Web.

9. Choose OK to complete the hyperlink. The home page will load in a full browser window instead of displaying in the frameset.

10. Choose Frame I Save Page to update the page to your Web.

TASK

Saving Your Frameset

All the content pages have been saved to your Web, but you still need to save your frameset page. To do this, follow these steps:

1. Choose File I Save (Ctrl+S). The Save As dialog box appears, and the entire frameset in the preview is highlighted. This indicates that you are going to save the frameset instead of one of the frames pages.

2. Enter `Frameset for My Web Site` (or something a little more imaginative, if you desire) in the Title field and `frameset.htm` in the URL field.

3. Choose OK. The frameset is saved to your Web.

Workshop Wrap-Up

In this chapter, you learned how to give your pages multiple personalities by using framesets. With FrontPage 98, you started with a simple page template and added another frame to it. You learned how to add pages to your framesets and how to create hyperlinks that load pages into specific frames in your frameset. You even learned how to create a page that displays for those who do not use frame-compatible browsers. Now that you know what frames are and what they do, it is time to hit the ground running and develop more framesets of your own.

Next Steps

More challenging projects with frames await. In Chapter 20, you design another frameset for your Web site. Soon, the pages you design throughout this book will be displayed in a frameset. For related topics, refer to the following chapters:

❏ See Chapter 19, "Using FrontPage Components," to learn how to create navigation bars that you can use in the main pages of your frameset. Include the navigation bars on your pages with Include Page components.

❏ In Chapter 20, "Real-Life Examples III: Dressing Up Your Webs," you add a frameset and navigation to your Web site.

Q&A

Q: Can I put anything I want into framesets?

A: More or less, yes. You can insert picture presentations, animations, video files, Java applets, forms (such as those used in the discussion groups), and even links to your favorite sites.

Q: When I divide pages into frames, how large should I make the graphics?

A: The resolutions most commonly used when browsing the Web are 640×480 and 800×600, with the latter being most common. You can choose the **F**ile I Preview in **B**rowser command to display your frameset in any of these resolutions. Use a screen capture program to take a screen shot of the frameset exactly as it appears in your browser at each resolution. That way, you can determine the exact measurements for your graphics. The hard part is deciding whether you want to design your graphics for 640×480 resolution or for 800×600 resolution. It is probably best to design for 640×480 resolution.

Q: How many frames can I put in a page?

A: As many as you want. Remember, though, that some users display pages at lower resolutions. You do not want to use so many frames that the content of your pages becomes unreadable. If your framesets contain many sections, check them out at 640×480 resolution before you put them on the Web. If you find it difficult to view many frames in that resolution, your visitors will also. Either reduce the number of frames or recommend that your visitors use a higher resolution, such as 800×600 or higher.

NINETEEN

Using FrontPage Components

As your Web grows—and it will—it becomes difficult to keep track of the content that you want to include on your pages. You find yourself using the same contact information or navigation links repeatedly on your pages. At times, you forget about a page or a graphic that you wanted to place on your site on a certain date, only to remember it weeks later. You forget to add new pages to your table of contents, and it soon becomes incomplete. When you move your Web site, you must change all the pages that have your contact information on them.

There is an easier way to handle these situations. FrontPage's components help automate your pages so that you can keep these situations well under control.

What Is a Component?

Through the use of *FrontPage components,* FrontPage enables even novice Web page designers to use advanced features that are usually handled with scripts. These components are basically custom-made scripts that are configured to perform certain tasks. With FrontPage, you just need to plug in the variables that each component requires, and you are on the way to automating your pages.

Creating the Web for This Chapter

The `Book\Chap19\Project Files` folder on the CD-ROM furnished with this book includes some files for you to work with. Create a new Web in the FrontPage Explorer. Import the files into your Web as follows:

1. From the FrontPage Explorer, choose **F**ile | **N**ew | FrontPage **W**eb. The New FrontPage Web dialog box appears.
2. Choose the From **W**izard or Template radio button. Highlight Empty Web.
3. In the Choose a **t**itle for your FrontPage web field, enter `Components`. Click OK. The Web appears in the FrontPage Explorer.
4. From the Views pane, select the Folders icon. Highlight the root folder in your Web and choose **F**ile | **I**mport. The Import File to FrontPage Web dialog box appears.
5. Click **A**dd File. The Add File to Import List dialog box appears.
6. Locate the `Book\Chap19\Project Files` directory on the CD-ROM that accompanies this book. Highlight the following files:

navbar.htm	footer.htm	index.htm
calendar.htm	tocbot.htm	oct97.htm
nov97.htm	dec97.htm	jan98.htm
feb98.htm	mar98.htm	apr98.htm
may98.htm	jun98.htm	jul98.htm
aug98.htm	sep98.htm	oct98.htm
nov98.htm	dec98.htm	

Other FrontPage components are discussed elsewhere in this book. Refer to Chapter 18, "Frames: Pages with Split Personalities," for an example of using the FrontPage Comment component. Refer to Chapter 16, "Working with Animation and Active Content," for examples of the Hit Counter. In Chapter 26, "Using Your Own HTML," you learn how to use the Insert HTML component.

7. Click **O**pen. You return to the Import File to FrontPage Web dialog box. Choose OK to import the files.
8. After the Web pages import into your Web, select the `images` folder from the All Folders pane in Folders view. Choose **F**ile | **I**mport again. The Import File to FrontPage Web dialog box appears.
9. Click **A**dd File. The Add File to Import List dialog box opens to the same directory in which the Web pages were located.
10. Highlight `winter.gif`, `spring.gif`, `summer.gif`, and `fall.gif` and click **O**pen. They appear in your import list.
11. Click OK. The graphics appear in your images directory. You're all set to complete the tasks in this chapter.

Including Pages Within Pages

The navigation bars generated with themes sometimes contain features that are not compatible with older browsers. The Include Page component is a handy alternative to use if you do not want to assign shared borders and automatic navigation bars to your pages. You use the Include Page component to insert the content of one Web page into another. The Web page can contain images, animation, sound, and any other elements you normally place onto pages. Any content that you use repeatedly, such as navigation bars, footers, logo graphics, and copyright information can be placed on multiple pages with an Include Page component. You change only the original file, and any page that includes the original file is automatically updated for you.

Using the Include Page component is straightforward. It involves only a few steps:

1. From the FrontPage Editor, choose **F**ile | **O**pen (Ctrl+O), or use the Open button on the Standard toolbar. The Open dialog box appears.

2. From the list of pages in your Web, double-click `calendar.htm` (the Calendar page). The page opens in the FrontPage Editor.

3. Position the insertion point at the end of the heading in the second cell that reads `Here's What's Happening This Month!`

4. Choose **I**nsert | Front**P**age Component. The Insert Front**P**age Component dialog box appears.

5. Highlight Include Page and click OK. The Include Page Component Properties dialog box appears, as shown in Figure 19.1.

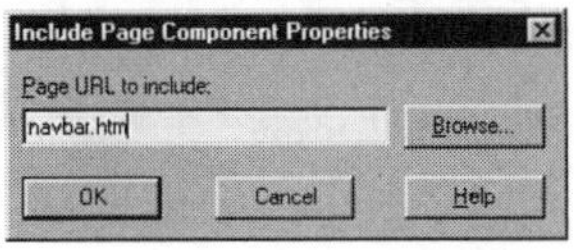

Figure 19.1.

Include the contents of another page with the Include Page Component Properties dialog box. The contents of the referenced page appear in your current page.

6. Click the **B**rowse button. The Current Web dialog box appears. Locate the `navbar.htm` page that you imported into your Web. Double-click the filename to assign it to the Include Page component. You return to the Include Page Component Properties dialog box.

NOTE: The **B**rowse button is not highlighted if you don't have a Web open in the FrontPage Explorer.

TIP: Consider placing navigation bars and other included content in your Web's _private directory. This directory serves as a storage area for pages and content to which you do not want to provide public access.

7. Choose OK to exit the Include Page Component Properties dialog box. The navigation bar appears on your page.

8. Choose **F**ile | **S**ave (Ctrl+S) or click the Save button to save your calendar page.

TIP: The following are tips for this task:

❏ To assign a different page to your Include Page component, move your mouse over the Include Page component until it turns into a cursor shaped like a robot. Double-click the component to reopen the Include Page Component Properties dialog box.

❏ To edit the contents of the included page, right-click on the Include Page component that you want to edit. Choose Open *webpage.htm* from the pop-up menu shown in Figure 19.2, where *webpage.htm* is the URL of the page that you included in the component. Make the changes to the originating page and save it to your Web. Use the **V**iew | **R**efresh command in the Standard toolbar to view the updates on any pages that are opened in the FrontPage Editor.

To follow hyperlinks on an included page, position the mouse over the hyperlink you want to follow and press Ctrl+Click. FrontPage opens the page in a new window.

Inserting Content at Specified Times

The Scheduled Include Page component is similar to the standard Include Page component, except that you can specify a date range in which the page appears in your Web. You prepare your pages beforehand and specify the date when they are posted to your Web. The page displays on your site until the end date specified in the Scheduled Include Page component.

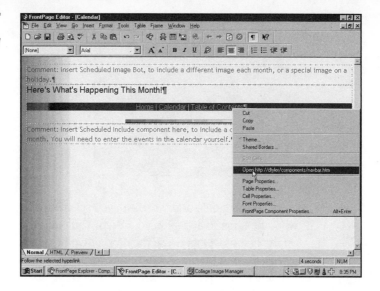

In the following example, you place a calendar table into your Calendar page on the
first day of each month. Each calendar table can contain hyperlinks to pages that
describe the events you add to the days on the calendar.

To configure a Scheduled Include Page component, follow these steps:

1. Position the insertion point at the end of the comment that appears in the
   bottom frame in the table.

2. Choose **I**nsert I Front**P**age Component. The Insert FrontPage Component
   dialog box appears.

3. Highlight Scheduled Include Page and choose OK. The Scheduled Include
   Page Component Properties dialog box appears, as shown in Figure 19.3.

4. Enter the URL of a page in your current Web in the **P**age URL to include
   field, or click the **B**rowse button to select a page from the Current Web
   dialog box. After you select the file, choose OK to return to the Scheduled
   Include Page Component Properties dialog box. For the example in this task,
   assume that it is nearing October 1997 and you want to use the calendar for
   that month. Enter `oct97.htm`.

Figure 19.3.

Use the Scheduled Include Page Compo-nent Properties dialog to place the contents of a page into your Web at a specified time.

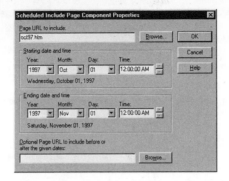

5. In the **S**tarting date and time field, you specify the date and time that you want the page to appear in your Web. You want the newsletter to appear on the first of October. Use the drop-down menus in the Year, Month, and Day fields, and the slider in the Time field, respectively, to enter the following date and time:

   ```
   1997 Oct 01 12:00:00 AM
   ```

6. In a similar manner, use the sliders in the **E**nding date and time field to specify an end date as follows:

   ```
   1997 Nov 01 12:00:00 AM
   ```

7. You can also add a page URL that is displayed before or after the Scheduled Include page. For example, you could create a page that says `Calendar coming soon` and title it `soon.htm`. Then you can display this page before or after the Scheduled Include Page component. If you do not specify an alternate page, the user receives an error message indicating that the scheduled page does not appear on the site. Enter the URL of an alternate page in your current Web in the **O**ptional Page URL to include before or after the given dates field, or click the Bro**w**se button to select one from your currently opened Web.

8. Repeat steps 2 through 7 to configure a Scheduled Include Page component for additional calendar pages, if desired. For example, you can add all the Scheduled Include components for the remainder of the year and all of next year on the page, configuring each for the proper date range. When November 1 arrives, the Scheduled Include Page component that places the November 1997 calendar on your page takes effect.

9. Click OK. If the current date falls between the dates you entered in the Scheduled Include Page Properties dialog box, the `oct97.htm` page appears in the bottom cell of the table, as shown in Figure 19.4. If you create the page before or after the Scheduled Include Page date and time, you see either the alternate page or the following text:

   ```
   [Expired Scheduled Include Page]
   ```

Figure 19.4.

When the current date falls between those you specified in the Scheduled Include Page component, the included page appears on your current page.

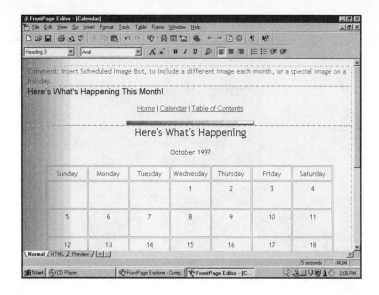

NOTE: If you see [Expired Scheduled Include Page] during the time period specified by the Scheduled Include Page component, the page that you included might not exist in your current Web. Verify the name of the included file or check to see whether a file by that name exists in your current Web.

TASK Inserting Images at Specified Times

The Scheduled Image component is similar to the Scheduled Include Page component, except that it places an image on a page during a specified time period. Use it to display, for example, calendar graphics or an image of the week. The same rules and cautions applicable to a Scheduled Include Page component apply here.

You can insert a Scheduled Image component anywhere on a page. Note that you cannot apply image formatting to a scheduled image after it is placed on your page, because you cannot access the Image Properties dialog box. Apply image transparency or hotspots to an image before you place it on the page with a Scheduled Image component. You can, however, place an image on a Web page and use a Scheduled Include Page component instead.

To insert a scheduled image on a page, use the following steps:

1. Position the insertion point at the end of the comment in the top table cell.
2. Choose **I**nsert I Front**P**age Component. The Insert FrontPage Component dialog box appears.

3. Highlight Scheduled Image and choose OK. The Scheduled Image Properties dialog box appears, as shown in Figure 19.5. It is similar to the Scheduled Include Page Component Properties dialog box.

Figure 19.5.

Use the Scheduled Image Properties dialog box to place a scheduled image on your page.

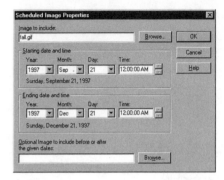

4. Enter the URL of an image in your current Web in the **I**mage to include field or click the **B**rowse button to select an image from the currently opened Web. For this example, highlight `fall.gif` and choose OK. You return to the Scheduled Image Properties dialog box.

5. In the **S**tarting date and time field, you specify the date and time that you want the image to appear in your Web. In this case, you want the image to appear on the first day of fall (`sept 21`). Use the Year, Month, and Day drop-down menus and the Time sliders to enter the following date:

   `1997 Sep 21 12:00:00 AM`

6. In a similar manner, use the sliders in the **E**nding date and time field to specify the first day of winter:

   `1997 Dec 21 12:00:00 AM`

7. If you want, add an image URL that is displayed before or after the sched-uled image in the **O**ptional Image to include before or after the given dates field. Enter the URL of an image in your current Web or click the Bro**w**se button to select one from the currently opened Web.

8. Click OK. If you open the page in the FrontPage Editor during the time period specified by a Scheduled Image component, you see the image specified in the component, as shown in Figure 19.6. If you create the scheduled image before the scheduled date, you see either the alternate image or the following text:

   `[Expired Scheduled Image]`

Figure 19.6.

When the current date falls between the dates you configured in the Scheduled Image Properties dialog box, the image appears on your page.

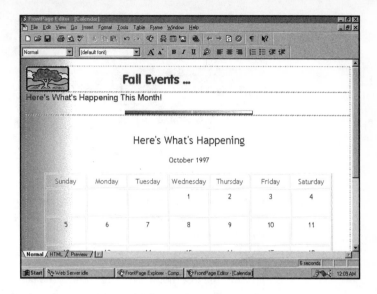

TASK   Using Substitution Components

If you are familiar with word processors, you might be aware of the concept of fields. Fields enable you to set up a form letter or a master mailing label, placing variable names in certain locations. The fields are replaced with data set up in a database or in another word processing document.

The Substitution component works almost the same way, although the variables that it places on pages are settings that you apply to your current Web. It enables you to place on your pages the names of generic variables whose contents are replaced with values specified in the Web configuration settings.

In this task, you complete a footer that can be inserted into several pages. The footer is designed to substitute your actual contact information with the values specified in Web settings. Use the following steps:

1. From the FrontPage Editor, choose **F**ile | **O**pen. The Open dialog box appears.

2. From the list of pages in your current Web, double-click the Included Footer page (footer.htm). The page opens in the FrontPage Editor.

3. If you cannot see the line break marks on the page, click the Show/Hide button on the Standard toolbar. The line breaks and paragraph marks appear on your page.

4. Click just before the line break in the first line.

5. Add a space and choose **I**nsert | Front**P**age Component. The Insert FrontPage Component dialog box appears.

6. Highlight Substitution and click OK. The Substitution Component Properties dialog box appears, as shown in Figure 19.7.

Figure 19.7.

Use the Substitution Components Properties dialog box to place variable names on your pages.

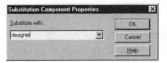

7. In the **S**ubstitute with field, enter a variable name that describes the variable that you want to insert. This text should not contain any spaces or colons. For this example, enter the following text and choose OK to return to the FrontPage Editor:

   `designer`

8. Position the insertion point after the word `contact` on the second line. Add a space and choose **I**nsert | Front**P**age Component again.

9. Highlight Substitution and click OK. The Substitution Page Component Properties dialog box appears. In the **S**ubstitute with field, enter `webmaster` and click OK. The second Substitution component appears on your page. If the configuration variable exists in your Web settings, the value set for it appears on the page instead.

NOTE: Four configuration variables are standard to every Web or page created in FrontPage:

`Author`	Replaced with the name of the author who created the page. The author name is based on the name as entered in the FrontPage Server Administrator or with the **T**ools	Permissions command, where spaces are not allowed in the name.
`ModifiedBy`	Replaced with the name of the author who most recently modified the page.
`Description`	Replaced with a description of the current page as entered in the Comments field of the Properties dialog box.
`Page-URL`	Replaced with the page URL of the page.

You can view the values of each configuration variable from the FrontPage Explorer. Highlight the page whose properties you want to view and choose **E**dit | Properties.

Adding Configuration Variables

Substitution components need configuration variables associated with them. In this chapter, you learn how to add general configuration variables in your Web settings.

NOTE: To add a configuration variable to your Web settings, you need to have access to the Web as an administrator. If you use FrontPage on your own personal computer, you established administrator status when you installed FrontPage under the typical installation procedures, through the FrontPage Server Administrator.

Now you need to add the configuration variable for the `designer` and `webmaster` Substitution components to your Web:

1. Open the FrontPage Explorer. Choose **T**ools | **W**eb Settings. The FrontPage Web Settings dialog box appears.

2. Click the Parameters tab.

3. Click the **Ad**d button. The Add Name and Value dialog box appears, as shown in Figure 19.8.

Figure 19.8.

Use the Add Name and Value dialog box to add the configuration variable for the Substitution component to the Web.

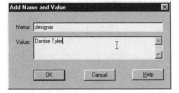

4. In the Name field, enter `designer`.

5. In the Value field, enter your name. Click OK to exit the Add Name and Value dialog box. The variable appears in the Parameters tab of the Web Settings dialog box.

6. Click the **Ad**d button again. Enter `webmaster` in the Name field and your e-mail address in the Value field.

7. Click the **A**pply button in the Web Settings dialog box.

8. Click OK to exit the dialog box and return to the FrontPage Explorer. The configuration variables become an option that you can select from the drop-down menu in the Substitution Component Properties dialog box.

9. Return to the footer page in the FrontPage Editor and click the Refresh button on the Standard toolbar. FrontPage asks whether you want to save

the changes to the included footer. Answer **Y**es. When the page refreshes, you see the configuration variables you entered in the footer in place of the Substitution components, as shown in Figure 19.9.

Figure 19.9.

The configuration variable information now appears in place of the Substitution components.

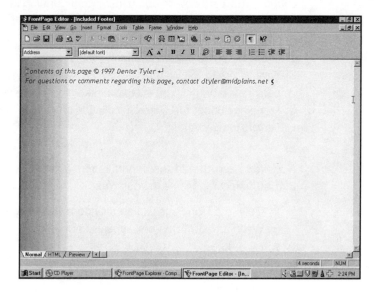

 ## Generating an Automatic Table of Contents

The Table of Contents component enables you to generate a list of the pages that appear in your Web site automatically. Any pages in your Web that appear beneath that page are listed in the table of contents in a hierarchical manner using nested lists. You can include—or not include—pages that cannot be reached by following links from the page you designate as the starting point for your table of contents.

Multiple Table of Contents components can appear on a single page, each generating contents that begin at a different page. When you generate a table of contents using the Table of Contents component, it inserts a generic heading and three dummy links on your page.

To insert a table of contents on a page, do the following:

1. From the FrontPage Editor, choose **F**ile | **O**pen (Ctrl+O), or choose the Open button on the Standard toolbar. The Open dialog box appears.

2. Double-click the `tocbot.htm` page (Table of Contents component). The page opens in the FrontPage Editor.

3. This page is blank at the present time. Insert a Table of Contents component on this page to see how it works. Position the insertion point at the upper-left corner of the page.

4. Choose **I**nsert | Table of C**o**ntents. The Table of Contents Properties dialog box appears, as shown in Figure 19.10.

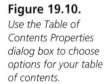

Figure 19.10.

Use the Table of Contents Properties dialog box to choose options for your table of contents.

5. In the **P**age URL for Starting Point of Table field, type the name of the page from which you want to begin generating the table of contents, or click the **B**rowse button to choose a page from the currently opened Web. By default, the table of contents begins with the home page in your current Web. You can also assign another page from which to start the table of contents. For example, if you have several links pages that originate from a page titled `links.htm`, you can begin the table of contents with that originating page.

6. In the Heading **S**ize field, select a heading size for the first entry in the table of contents. The default size is 2. Choose none if you do not want a heading to appear.

7. Select one or more of the following options:

   ❏ *Show each page only **o**nce.* Keep this box checked to list pages that can be reached from more than one page only once in the table of contents. Uncheck it if you want to show the page each time a link to it appears.

   ❏ *Show pages with no incoming hyper**l**inks.* If you want to include orphan pages—that is, pages that cannot be reached by clicking links in your pages—check this option. However, this might produce links to pages to which you do not want users to navigate, such as header and footer pages that are placed on your pages with Include Page components. The table of contents does not include links to any pages placed in your `_private` directory. Uncheck this option for your sample table of contents page.

   ❏ ***R**ecompute table of contents when any other page is edited.* If your Web site is fairly small, it is safe to check this option. Doing so causes the table of contents to regenerate each time you add new pages or move them to new directories. If you leave this option unchecked, you can regenerate the table of contents by opening and saving the page that contains the Table of Contents component.

8. Click OK to exit the dialog box. The Table of Contents component appears on your page, showing three dummy links. Figure 19.11 shows an example.

9. Choose **F**ile | **S**ave (Ctrl+S) or click the Save button to save your table of contents page to your Web.

Figure 19.11.

In the FrontPage Editor, the table of contents appears to be incomplete.

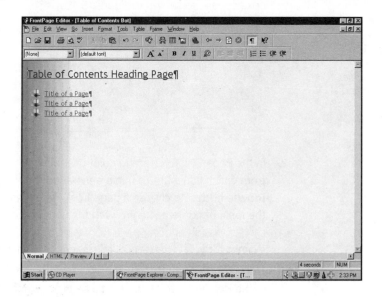

To view the table of contents in your browser, choose **F**ile | Preview in **B**rowser. The Preview in Browser dialog box appears. From the **B**rowser list, select the browser that you want to use to preview the table of contents. Select a **W**indow Size (Default, 640×480, 800×600, or 1024×768). Then click **P**review. The page opens in your browser.

The browser loads the table of contents page, and you can see each page listed, beginning with the page that you specified in the Table of Contents Properties dialog box. The pages are listed in the table of contents by their titles, as shown in Figure 19.12.

NOTE: If you have difficulties viewing the table of contents page in your browser, one of two things may remedy this situation. First, verify that the table of contents page and other open pages in the FrontPage Editor are saved to your current Web. Second, resave the table of contents page if you have added or changed any pages since you last saved it. This causes the Table of Contents component to regenerate the page list. Check in the FrontPage Explorer's Outline view to see whether the pages appear beneath the table of contents page. If they do, you should be able to view them in your browser as well.

Figure 19.12.

When you view the table of contents in a Web browser, the titles of the pages appear.

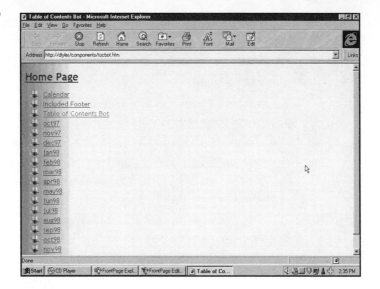

TASK

Indicating When a Page Was Last Revised

The Timestamp component helps you and visitors to your site keep track of the date when a page was most recently updated—manually or automatically. In most cases, you specify manual updating. Sometimes, however, you might want to specify automatic updating.

TIP: Include a Timestamp component at the beginning of your pages. This tells users whether your pages have changed since their last visit.

You should still have the table of contents page opened in your browser. That's as good a place as any to add a Timestamp component.

To place a Timestamp component on your page, follow these steps:

1. Click the Table of Contents component on the page and press Ctrl+Enter. The insertion point moves to the beginning of the page.

NOTE: You can use Ctrl+Enter to reach the beginning of a page any time there is a component placed on your page right at its beginning.

2. On the top line in the page, enter some text that appears before the timestamp. For example, enter

   `This page was last updated on`

   followed by a space.

3. Choose **I**nsert | **T**imestamp. The Timestamp Properties dialog box page appears, as shown in Figure 19.13.

4. In the Display field, choose one of the following options:

   ❏ *Date this page was last **e**dited*. Choose this option if you usually edit the page manually. This is the most common way to specify a timestamp.

   ❏ *Date this page was last **a**utomatically updated*. Choose this option if the page includes any features that are generated automatically. Examples include tables of contents, discussion group articles, or guest book pages in which users' comments are inserted automatically. Select this option for your table of contents page.

5. In the Date **F**ormat field, choose the format for displaying the date on your pages from the drop-down menu.

6. If you also want to specify the time when your page was last updated, choose a time format from the **T**ime Format drop-down menu.

7. Click OK. The timestamp appears on your page, as shown in the top line in Figure 19.13. The timestamp regenerates any time you regenerate the Web or save the table of contents page to your Web.

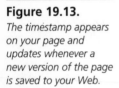

Figure 19.13.

The timestamp appears on your page and updates whenever a new version of the page is saved to your Web.

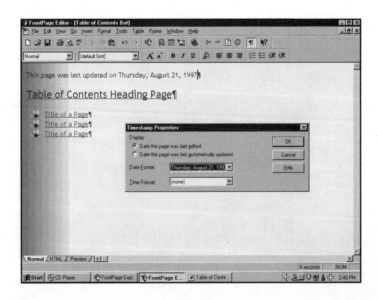

Inserting Page Banners

The Page Banner component works in conjunction with Navigation view to place an image or text page banner on your Web page. The page banner displays the text that you assign to the page in the navigation pane. Page banners are automatically added to your pages if you have shared borders configured to display them. If you do not use shared borders on a page, you can place a page banner anywhere on your page.

If your Web or page uses themes, the page banner uses the image and font properties associated with the theme. On pages that do not use themes, the page title appears on the page in bolded text.

To add a page banner to a Web page, follow these steps:

1. Verify that the page that you want to insert the banner into appears in the navigation pane in the FrontPage Explorer's Navigation view. For further instructions on working with Navigation view, refer to Chapter 8, "Designing Your Web Navigation."

2. Open the page that you want to add the banner to in the FrontPage Editor. Position the insertion point where you want the page banner to appear.

3. Choose **I**nsert | Front**P**age Component. The Insert FrontPage Component dialog box appears.

4. Highlight Page Banner and choose OK. The Page Banner Properties dialog box shown in Figure 19.14 appears.

5. Choose one of the following options for your page banner:

   ❏ Choose **Im**age to insert a page banner that uses the banner image defined by your current theme. If your Web page does not use themes, this selection has no effect.

   ❏ Choose **T**ext to insert a page banner that uses only text. The font properties for the text are defined by the theme used in your Web or page.

6. The page banner appears on your page, using the label that you assigned in the FrontPage Explorer's Navigation view. An example is shown in Figure 19.14. Choose **F**ile | **S**ave (Ctrl+S) or click the Save button to save your page to the Web.

Figure 19.14.

The page banner uses the label that you assign in the FrontPage Explorer's Navigation view.

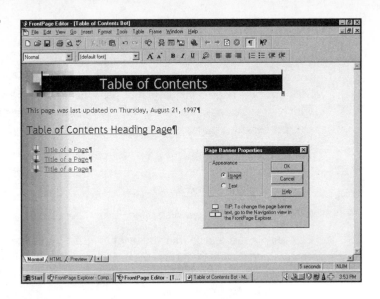

Workshop Wrap-Up

Now you have solutions to the problems described at the beginning of this chapter. You can use FrontPage components to resolve the issues quickly and easily. Components enable you to avoid repetitive typing of links or other text, schedule Web content, and automatically keep track of all the pages in your Web. Your Web creation tasks are greatly simplified, and making changes to your Web site in the future requires less time to complete.

In this chapter, you learned about the basic components available to you in FrontPage. Using them, you can automate your pages in several different ways. You learned how to include content from one page in another, schedule content and images to appear in your Web at specified times, generate a table of contents automatically, use and apply configuration variables to your Webs, and advise yourself and others when changes were last made to your pages. Automating your pages in this manner involves only a few steps, and it makes your work much easier down the road.

Next Steps

In the next chapter, you combine what you have learned in the chapters in this section. You apply some of the techniques to your Web site project, adding images, animation, framesets, and FrontPage components to your Web. For more information about the topics discussed in this chapter, refer to the following additional chapters:

❏ Refer to Chapter 8, "Designing Your Web Navigation," to learn how to add pages to your navigation system.

❏ Refer to Chapter 14, "Using FrontPage Style Sheets and Themes," to learn how to apply themes to your Web pages.

❏ See Chapter 23, "Configuring Form Handlers," to learn how to use and configure the FrontPage components that handle forms.

Q&A

Q: Can I use these components without using the FrontPage Explorer?

A: Many of the components rely on links to pages that exist in the current Web. This means the FrontPage Explorer must be open to the Web that holds the pages with which you are working.

Q: How do these components work if my service provider does not have the FrontPage Server Extensions?

A: When you publish your pages to your Web site, the pages are saved in HTML format. You should keep a copy of your pages in your FrontPage Web if you plan to make changes to them, because the Server Extensions files on your personal Web server contain files that retain configuration settings for your FrontPage components.

Q: I put a Timestamp in a footer and used the Include Page component to place it on several pages. When I changed some of the pages that included the footer, the dates were not updated. In fact, the dates weren't there at all! What happened?

A: The Timestamp updates when you change a page. In this case, however, the timestamp is tied to the footer—not to the page on which it is included. If you place a Timestamp on your pages with an Include Page component, the date does not change unless you save the footer again. This might place an incorrect date on all the pages in which the timestamp is included. Rather than use an Include Page component to place a Timestamp on several pages, place the timestamp on each page individually.

Q: I put a header graphic and some navigation links into an Include Page component. Can I use this as a bookmark?

A: Yes! Click the Include Page component to select it and choose Edit | Bookmark. Assign the bookmark name in the Bookmark dialog box and choose OK. You can also apply bookmarks to images, page banners, Scheduled Image components, and Scheduled Include components.

Q: I inserted a logo at the beginning of my page by using an Include Page component. I want to add something before it. I cannot place the cursor at the beginning of the page now. How do I do that?

A: To place the cursor before the Include Page component, select the Include Page component so that it appears in inverse video. Then press Ctrl+Enter. This places the cursor on a new line above the Include Page component. The new line is formatted as a normal paragraph.

TWENTY

Real-Life Examples III: Dressing Up Your Webs

Imagine adding features such as Java applets, page transitions, hover buttons, and automatic navigation bars without programming! As you've learned in the chapters in this section, it's very easy to do. Now you have a chance to apply what you've learned to a "real" Web site.

In Chapter 13, "Real-Life Examples II: Keeping It Plain and Simple," you followed some examples in the Matty's Place Web site to help you learn how to build and construct a Web site of your own. In this chapter, you will use the pages from Matty's Place to learn how to add images, animation, and sound to your pages. The techniques you learn in this chapter will show you some of the ways that FrontPage 98 can help your pages come alive with color, motion, and sound.

In this chapter, you

- ❏ Choose a theme for Matty's Place Web site
- ❏ Add a splash screen, background sound, animated text, and a hit counter to Matty's Place home page
- ❏ Customize the top, left, and bottom page borders
- ❏ Add images to the pages in the Matty's Place Web site
- ❏ Create a clickable image and add a marquee and page transition to Matty's Gang page
- ❏ Create a table of contents page for the Web site

Tasks in this chapter:

- ❏ Importing the Matty's Place Web Pages
- ❏ Choosing Your Web Theme
- ❏ Completing the Home Page
- ❏ Revising Your Page Borders
- ❏ Inserting Images
- ❏ Completing Matty's Gang Page
- ❏ Adding a Table of Contents

Importing the Matty's Place Web Pages

If you haven't started your Web yet and want to practice with the examples from the Matty's Place Web site, the CD-ROM that accompanies this book includes a set of files as they are listed at the end of Chapter 13. The files are located in the `Bool\Chap13\Examples` folder on the CD-ROM that accompanies this book. You can create a new Web and import these files into your Web as follows:

1. From the FrontPage Explorer, choose **F**ile | **N**ew | FrontPage **W**eb. The New FrontPage Web dialog box shown in Figure 20.1 appears.

Figure 20.1.

Use the Import an Existing Web radio button in the New FrontPage Web dialog box to import the Matty's Place pages into a new FrontPage Web.

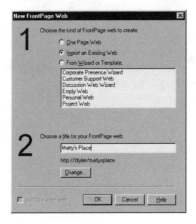

2. Select the **I**mport an Existing Web radio button.

3. In the Choose a **t**itle for your FrontPage Web field, enter `Matty's Place`.

4. Choose OK. The first screen of the Import Web Wizard appears.

5. Select the From a source directory of files on a local computer or network radio button.

6. Click the **B**rowse button beneath the **L**ocation field. Use the Browse for Folder dialog box to locate the directory on your CD-ROM that contains the Matty's Place pages. You will find them in the `Book\Chap13\Examples` folder on the CD-ROM that accompanies this book.

7. Click the **B**rowse button beneath the **L**ocation field. Use the Browse for Folder dialog box to locate the directory on your CD-ROM that contains the Matty's Place pages. You will find them in the `Book\Chap13\Examples` folder on the CD-ROM that accompanies this book. Double-click to select the folder and choose OK to return to the Import Web Wizard screen.

8. Check the Include **s**ubfolders checkbox. Then click Ne**x**t to continue to the Edit File List screen shown in Figure 20.2. A list of 27 pages appears in the import list, three of which are in a hidden borders folder in the Web.

Figure 20.2.
A list of 27 pages from Matty's Place appears in the Edit File List screen. Three of these pages are from a hidden borders folder.

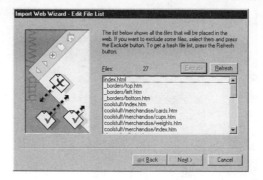

9. Choose Ne**x**t to continue. FrontPage 98 informs you that the wizard has all the answers. Choose Finish to import the pages into your new Web.

10. After you import the pages, you need to add the pages to the navigation pane in the FrontPage Explorer. Use Figure 13.16 (from Chapter 13) as a guide to recreate the navigation tree.

 # Choosing Your Web Theme

The pages that you created in Chapter 13 were exactly that—plain and simple. The only command that you issued to keep them that way was to not apply a theme to your Web. Now, just as easily, you can change the entire appearance of all those pages with a couple of mouse clicks. You can apply a theme to all pages in your Web that do not have settings applied to individual pages.

For Matty's Place, I used the Bubbles theme, which suits the Matty's Place comic strip very well. To apply a theme to your Web site, follow these steps:

1. Open your Web (or the Matty's Place Web) in the FrontPage Explorer.

2. Choose the Themes button in the Views pane. You switch to Themes view.

3. Choose the Bubbles theme, shown in Figure 20.3. Select the following additional options:

Vivid **C**olors
Active **G**raphics
Background Image

4. Click **A**pply. FrontPage asks whether you want to apply the theme, because it permanently replaces some of the existing formatting information. Choose **Y**es. The theme files are imported into your Web.

Figure 20.3.

Choose the Bubbles theme for Matty's Place and apply vivid colors, active graphics, and background image.

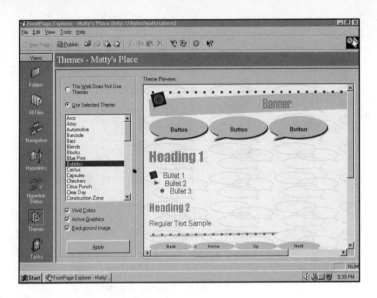

 TASK

Completing the Home Page

You haven't addressed your home page yet. In this task, you will add a splash screen, a background sound, some animated text, and a hit counter to your home page.

To complete the home page, follow these steps:

1. From the FrontPage Explorer, double-click the home page in the root folder of your Web to open it in the FrontPage Editor. The page appears in the FrontPage Editor. Shared borders appear at the top, left, and bottom of the page, and the insertion point appears in the main section of the page.

2. Choose Insert I Image. The Image dialog box appears.

3. Click the Select a file on your computer button located at the right of the URL field. The Select File dialog box appears.

4. Use the Look in box to locate `mattys-home.gif` on the CD-ROM that accompanies this book. You will find this file in the `Book\Chap20\Project Files` directory on the CD-ROM. Double-click the file to insert the image on the Matty's Place home page.

5. Center the image with the Center button on the Format toolbar. Then click the image to open the Image toolbar.

6. Choose the Make Transparent button from the Image toolbar. Click on the white area in the image to make white the transparent color.

7. Press the Home key to position the insertion point before the image. Press the Enter key, then the up arrow to center the insertion point on the line above the image.

8. Choose Heading 1 from the Change Style drop-down menu in the Format toolbar and enter `Welcome to Matty's Place`.

9. Immediately after you enter the text, choose Format I Animation I Fly From Bottom-Right by Word. If you have Internet Explorer 4.0 installed on your computer, you can use the Preview tab in the FrontPage Explorer to preview the text animation. You see the heading fly in to the page one word at a time.

10. Return to normal view in the FrontPage Explorer. Position the insertion point at the end of the heading you just entered and press Enter. The next line is automatically centered and formatted as a normal paragraph.

11. Enter `You are visitor number` followed by a space. Choose Format I Animation I Off to turn off text animation on this line.

12. Choose Insert I FrontPage Component. The Insert FrontPage Component dialog box appears.

13. Double-click Hit Counter to open the Hit Counter Properties dialog box.

14. Select your favorite counter style image from the dialog box. I selected the third set of numbers, which are orange on a black background. Check the Fixed number of digits checkbox and leave the number of digits set to the default of 5.

15. Choose OK to place the page counter on your home page. In the FrontPage Editor, the area for the hit counter displays as text surrounded by brackets. To view the hit counter, save the page to your Web using the File I Save (Ctrl+S) command. When the Save Embedded Files dialog box appears, choose the Change Folder button to save the image to the images folder in your Web and choose OK.

16. Choose the Preview tab or the File I Preview in Browser command to preview the page in your Web browser. The hit counter appears on your page, as shown in Figure 20.4.

17. Return to normal view in the FrontPage Editor and choose File I Page Properties. The Page Properties dialog box appears, opened to the General tab.

18. Use the Browse button in the Background Sound section to select `mattys.mid` from the `Book\Chap20\Project Files` folder on the CD-ROM that accompanies this book. Uncheck the Forever checkbox and enter 1 in the Loop field to play the MIDI file once. Choose OK to exit the Page Properties dialog box.

19. Choose File I Save (Ctrl+S) to save the page to your Web again. When the Save Embedded Files dialog box appears, choose OK to save the sound file to the root folder in your Web. Choose the Preview tab to preview the sound file on the page.

Figure 20.4.

An image, animated text, and a hit counter have been added to your home page.

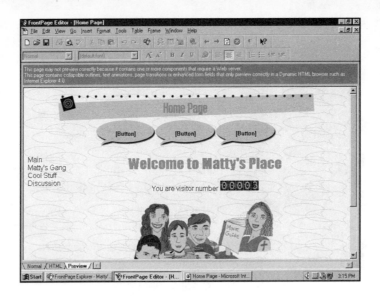

TASK

Revising Your Page Borders

There are a couple of things that you need to do with the page borders. First, the pages will look more balanced if the top border used text navigation instead of navigation buttons. Likewise, the left navigation border will appear more balanced if it used graphic navigation buttons rather than text. You also need to add some content in the bottom shared border.

To change the shared borders, follow these steps:

1. Switch to normal view in the FrontPage Editor. With the home page still open, click the top shared border. It becomes surrounded by a bounding box.

2. Click on the row of navigation buttons in the top border. Press Alt+Enter to open the Navigation Bar Properties dialog box.

3. From the Orientation and appearance section, select the Te**x**t radio button and choose OK. The graphic navigation buttons turn to text navigation buttons.

4. Click the left shared border to select it. Press Alt+Enter to open the Navigation Bar Properties dialog box again. This time, select B**u**ttons from the Orientation and appearance section and choose OK. The navigation bar in the left border changes to graphic navigation buttons.

5. Click the bottom shared border. The comment on the page is highlighted and ready for you to enter the content for the bottom border. Typically, you include copyright information in the footer of the page.

6. Choose Address from the Change Style drop-down menu in the Format toolbar. Enter the following line of text, replacing *name* with your name or the name of your company:

   `Page contents copyright 1997, ` *name*

7. Press Shift+Enter to insert a line break and begin a new line. Enter trademark information (if applicable). Where trademark symbols appear in the following line, use the Insert I Symbol command in the FrontPage Editor to insert the trademark symbol from the Symbol dialog box. An example of trademark information follows:

   `Matty's Place{tm} and Matty's Gang{tm} are trademarks of Matty's Press.`

8. Press Shift+Enter again to insert a line break and begin a new line. Enter the following text, replacing *webmaster* with the e-mail address of the person responsible for the page content.

   `For questions or comments regarding this page, contact ` *webmaster*`.`

9. Select the text of the e-mail address you just entered and choose the Create or Edit Hyperlink button on the Standard toolbar. The Create Hyperlink dialog box appears.

10. In the URL field, enter `mailto:` followed by the e-mail address that you highlighted, as in the following example:

    `mailto:webmaster@mattysplace.com`

11. Choose OK to create the hyperlink. You return to the FrontPage Editor. Your page should now look as shown in Figure 20.5.

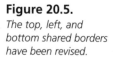

Figure 20.5.

The top, left, and bottom shared borders have been revised.

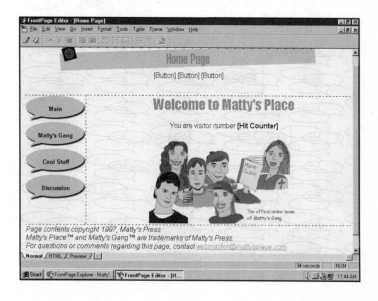

12. Choose **F**ile I **S**ave (Ctrl+S) or click the Save button on the Standard toolbar. The changes that you made to the shared borders on the home page will apply to all pages that use the Web default shared borders.

13. You're satisfied with the left and bottom page borders on the home page, but you want to remove the page banner. To do this, you need to assign shared borders for the home page only. From the FrontPage Editor, choose **T**ools I Shared **B**orders. The Page Borders dialog box appears.

14. In the Borders to include section, select the Set for this **p**age only radio button. Uncheck the **T**op checkbox and choose OK. The page banner is removed from the home page. Figure 20.6 shows the home page in Preview mode.

15. Choose **F**ile I **S**ave (Ctrl+S) or click the Save button on the Standard toolbar. The home page is saved to your Web.

Figure 20.6.
The top shared border is removed from the home page only.

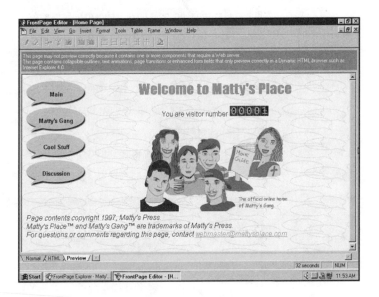

Inserting Images

There are some pages in the Gang and Cool Stuff sections in the Web to which you need to add images. You will find it easier to add the images if you import all the image files into your Web first. These image files are located in the `Book\Chap20\Project Files` folder on the CD-ROM that accompanies this book. To import the files into the Matty's Place Web, follow these steps:

1. From the FrontPage Editor, choose the Show FrontPage Explorer button on the Standard toolbar.

2. From the FrontPage Explorer, choose the Folders icon in the Views pane. Select the `images` folder from the All Folders list.

3. Choose **F**ile | **I**mport. The Import File to FrontPage Web dialog box appears.

4. Click the Add File button. The Add File to Import List dialog box appears.

5. Use the Look **i**n box to locate the `Book\Chap20\Project Files` folder on the CD-ROM that accompanies this book. Highlight the following files and choose **O**pen to return to the Import File to FrontPage Web dialog box. Note that these images are already saved as transparent GIFs where appropriate:

```
card.gif
carla.gif
crystal.gif
cup.gif
hunting.gif
james.gif
karl.gif
matty.gif
mattys-gang.gif
shawn.gif
weight.gif
zach.gif
```

6. Choose OK from the Import File to FrontPage Web dialog box to import the images into your images folder.

7. Return to the FrontPage Editor. Use the **F**ile | **O**pen (Ctrl+O) command or the Open button on the Standard toolbar to open `carla.htm` from the `gang` folder.

8. Click in the right cell in the table. Choose **I**nsert | **I**mage. Double-click the `images` folder, then double-click `carla.gif` to insert the image on the page. Figure 20.7 shows an example of the page.

9. Click the Align Top button on the Tables toolbar to align the image to the top of the right cell.

10. Choose **F**ile | **S**ave (Ctrl+S) or click the Save button on the Standard toolbar to save the page to the Web.

11. Repeat steps 7 through 10 to insert the remaining character images on the associated pages in the `gang` folder:

`crystal.htm`	insert `crystal.gif`
`james.htm`	insert `james.gif`
`karl.htm`	insert `karl.gif`
`matty.htm`	insert `matty.gif`
`shawn.htm`	insert `shawn.gif`
`zach.htm`	insert `zach.gif`

Figure 20.7.

Insert an image for each character into the right cell in the table.

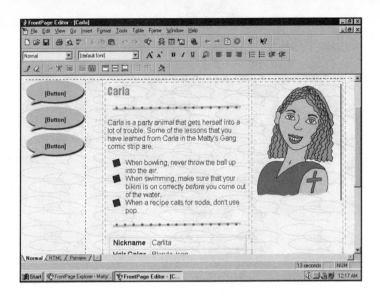

TIP: To quickly open other pages within the same section of the Web, use Ctrl+Click to navigate to one of the pages listed in the top navigation bar. The page opens in the FrontPage Editor.

12. Repeat steps 7 through 10 to insert the product images on the associated pages in the `coolstuff/merchandise` folder. To these pages, add one additional step. Choose the Background Color button on the Tables toolbar to change the background color of the right cell in the table to black (the first color in the last row of the Color dialog box, which is selected by default). Figure 20.8 shows an example of one of these pages. Insert the following:

`cards.htm`	insert `card.gif`
`cups.htm`	insert `cup.gif`
`weights.htm`	insert `weight.gif`

13. Repeat steps 7 through 10 to insert `hunting.gif` into the left cell (next to the numbered list) on the `hunting.htm` page from the `gang` folder. An example is shown in Figure 20.9.

14. Open the `index.htm` page in the `coolstuff/merchandise` folder. Insert `card.gif`, `cup.gif`, and `weight.gif` on this page, as shown in Figure 20.10. Use the Background Color button in the Tables toolbar to change the background color of each of the cells to black. Click the Save button on the Standard toolbar to save your page to the Web.

Figure 20.8.

Insert an image for each product into the right cell in the table and change the background of the cell to black.

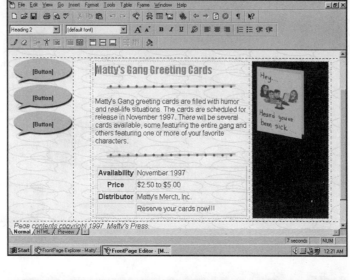

Figure 20.9.

Insert `hunting.gif` *into the left cell on the Hunting page.*

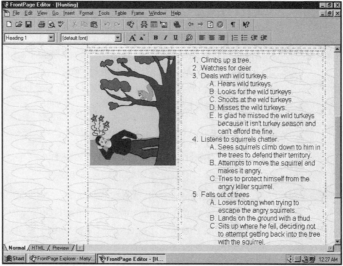

Figure 20.10.

Insert three product images into the table on the Matty's Merch page.

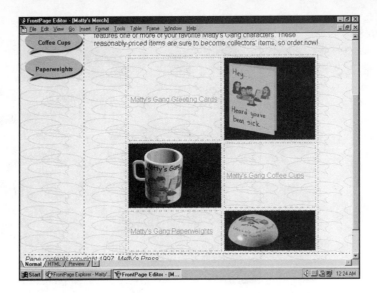

 ## Completing Matty's Gang Page

The Matty's Gang page serves as a gateway to information about all the characters in the Matty's Gang comic strip. You will insert an image onto this page and create an image map. When the user clicks on a character in the image map, the page that describes that character will open in his or her browser. The page will also include a marquee and a page transition.

To complete the Matty's Gang page, follow these steps:

1. From the FrontPage Editor, choose **F**ile I **O**pen (Ctrl+O) or click the Open button. The Open dialog box appears.

2. Locate `index.htm` in the gang folder and double-click the file to open it. The Matty's Gang page appears in the FrontPage Editor. Center the insertion point in the first line of the page with the Center button on the Format toolbar.

3. Choose **I**nsert I Active **E**lements I **M**arquee. The Marquee Properties dialog box appears.

4. In the **T**ext field, enter `Click your favorite character or one of the buttons at the left to learn more about your favorite Matty's Gang member!`.

5. Enter or select the following additional settings for the marquee and then choose OK to place the marquee on your page:

Direction:	Left
Delay:	`90`
Amount:	`6`

Behavior:	Scroll
Align with Text:	Top
Specify Width:	500 in Pixels
Specify Height:	30 in Pixels
Repeat:	Continuously
Background Color:	Custom, Red: 255 Green: 204 Blue: 0

6. Choose Insert | Image. The Image dialog box appears.

7. Double-click the `images` folder and then double-click `mattys-gang.gif` to insert the file on your page.

8. Click the image to open the Image toolbar. Use the Make Transparent button to make white the transparent color.

9. Choose the Polygon button in the Image toolbar. Start at the lower-left corner of the image and draw a polygon hotspot around the left person in the front row (Matty). When you complete the hotspot, the Create Hyperlink dialog box appears. Create a hyperlink to `matty.htm` in the gang folder.

10. In a similar manner, create hotspots around each of the additional characters in the image. The hotspots you create should link to the following pages in the `gang` folder:

Female with brown hair:	`crystal.htm`
Male in green shirt:	`karl.htm`
Male in orange striped shirt:	`james.htm`
Male in purple hat and shirt:	`shawn.htm`
"The movie guide":	`zach.htm`
Female with blonde hair:	`carla.htm`

11. Choose Format | Page Transition. The Page Transitions dialog box appears. Enter or choose the following settings:

Event:	Page Enter (default)
Transition effect:	Random dissolve
Duration (seconds):	10

12. At this point, your page should look like the one in Figure 20.11. Choose File | Save to save your page. When the Save Embedded Files dialog box appears, click the Change Folder button to save `mattys-gang.gif` to the `images` folder in your Web. Then choose File | Preview in Browser to preview the page in a Web browser that supports dynamic HTML (such as Internet Explorer 4.0). To see the effect, click one of the hyperlinks to another page and then return to the Matty's Gang page. The Matty's Gang page fades out when you navigate from it and fades back in when you navigate back to it.

Figure 20.11.

Hotspots, a marquee, and a page transition are added to the Matty's Gang page.

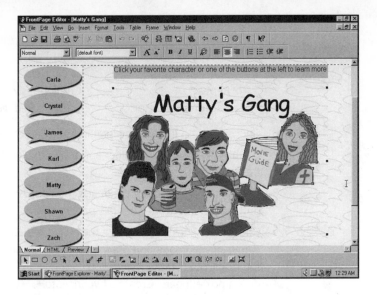

 Adding a Table of Contents

It's always a nice idea to put a table of contents on your site. This table of contents can list all the pages that link from the home page in your Web. You can also include *orphan pages*, those that are unreachable from any other page in the table of contents.

To create a table of contents for Matty's Place, follow these steps:

1. From the FrontPage Editor, choose **F**ile | **N**ew (Ctrl+N). The New dialog box appears.

2. Double-click the Table of Contents template. A new table of contents page appears in the FrontPage Editor.

3. Modify the introductory paragraph on the page as you see appropriate. For example, you might want to change the first sentence to reflect the name of the page from which the table of contents originates. In addition, if you decide that you do not want to show pages with no incoming hyperlinks, you may want to remove the last sentence, stating that unreachable files are shown at the bottom of the list.

4. Double-click the Table of Contents component on the page. The Table of Contents Properties dialog box appears.

5. The entry in the **P**age URL for Starting Point of Table defaults to `index.htm` in the root directory of your Web. If your home page has a different name (such as `index.html`, `default.htm`, `intro.htm`, or another default name), you need to change this entry. Use the **B**rowse button to select the file in your

current Web from which the table of contents will originate. In the case of Matty's Place, choose Home Page (`index.html` in the Web's root folder).

6. Leave the Heading Size at the default of 3. For additional options, select Show each page only **o**nce. Leave the other two options unchecked.

7. Choose OK to configure the Table of Contents component.

8. Scroll down to the bottom of the page and remove the first two lines beneath the second horizontal line, leaving only the line that reads `Revised:` `Current Date`, where the current date is the date that you created the Table of Contents page.

9. Double-click the date to open the Timestamp Properties dialog box. Select the Date this page was last automatically updated radio button. This updates the date on the Table of Contents page whenever you add new pages to your Web and the list of pages in your site is regenerated.

10. Choose a date format and a time format (if desired) to suit your preferences.

11. Choose OK to configure the timestamp. Your page should look similar to Figure 20.12.

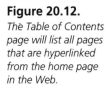

Figure 20.12.

The Table of Contents page will list all pages that are hyperlinked from the home page in the Web.

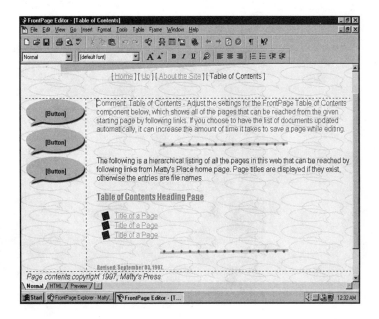

TIP: You can copy the line that includes the timestamp into your clipboard and paste it into the same location on other pages in your Web to add a timestamp to your other pages very quickly. Remember, however, to change the display option back to Date this page was last edited for those pages that you will edit manually.

12. Choose **F**ile I **S**ave (Ctrl+S) or click the Save button on the Standard toolbar. The Save As dialog box appears.

13. Double-click the main folder in your Web. Then enter the following information:

    URL: `contents.htm`
    Title: `Table of Contents`

14. Choose the Show the FrontPage Explorer button in the Standard toolbar and select the Navigation icon from the Views pane. Drag the `contents.htm` folder from the main folder in the Files pane into the navigation pane. Release your mouse button when the page attaches itself to the Main page, as shown in Figure 20.13.

Figure 20.13.
Add the Table of Contents page to the navigation pane.

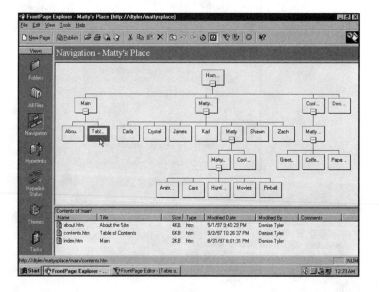

Workshop Wrap-Up

Used effectively, images and animation can really spice up a Web site, and in this chapter you learned how to add color and motion to your pages. You started off by assigning a theme to your site and choosing regions of your page in which to display banners, text, and graphic navigation buttons. Next, you added a splash screen, animated text, background sound, and a hit counter to your home page. Images were added to other pages where they were appropriate. You created an image map that navigates users to other sections of the Web site and spiced up the page with a page transition—*all without a lick of programming!*

Next Steps

I've reserved some of the other techniques that you learned in this section for the next Real-Life Examples chapter. In Chapter 24, "Real-Life Examples IV: Adding Interactivity," you will add a discussion group to your Web site. This discussion group will use a frameset to display the articles in the discussion. In conjunction with the discussion group frameset, you will also learn how to remove the shared borders from the associated pages and how you can use page banners and Include Page components to design similar navigation bars on the pages.

Q&A

Q: Can I apply more than one page transition to a single page? For example, can I use one page transition when I enter a page and another when I leave a page?

A: Yes. You can apply one of each type of page transition to the page (Page Enter, Page Exit, Site Enter, and Site Exit) and assign a different transition to each. The transition changes depending on how the user enters and exits the page.

Q: I put a timestamp on the bottom border in my page, but the timestamp didn't update when I made changes to my What's New (or other) page. Did I do something wrong?

A: The timestamp changes only when the page that it was originally inserted on is changed. Actually, the timestamp is on your bottom border and will update only when you change the border. You need to remove the timestamp from the page border and place the timestamp on the What's New (or other) page instead.

PART

IV

Working with Forms

TWENTY-ONE

Quick and Easy Forms

Everyone has filled out countless forms—order forms, registration forms, personal information forms, surveys, and so on. Even when you enter a message or article in a discussion, you are using a form. Essentially, whenever information is exchanged, it is done through a form.

Designing a form can be tedious, especially if you want to ask many questions. Laying out the form and aligning the fields is a task in itself. It could take you hours to complete the form.

Have no fear. In FrontPage, creating forms is a breeze. The Form Page Wizard does most of the work for you. It takes care of the layout and enables you to present questions in several categories. You think of a question, pick the category that best handles how you want to present it, assign a few variables, and away you go. You can design your form in a matter of minutes.

Examining the Form Page Wizard

The Form Page Wizard is a gem. You use it to design just about any type of form you can think of. If you know the type of form you want to design and the questions or responses you need, the rest is absolutely simple.

To edit the types of fields contained in the forms that the Form Page Wizard generates, see Chapter 22, "Adding and Editing Form Fields."

Refer to Chapter 5, "Lightning-Speed Web Design," to learn how to create a new FrontPage Web.

When you create a form with the Form Page Wizard, you begin on a new page. After you complete the form, you can add additional content to it or copy its contents to the clipboard to paste into another page. To create a form with the Form Page Wizard, follow these steps:

1. From the FrontPage Explorer, create or open a Web in which to save your pages. Choose **T**ools I Show FrontPage Editor or use the Show FrontPage Editor button to open the FrontPage Editor.

2. From the FrontPage Editor, choose **F**ile I **N**ew (Ctrl+N). The New Page dialog box appears, opened to the Page tab.

3. From the list of templates in the Page tab, double-click Form Page Wizard. The introductory screen of the Form Page Wizard appears.

Introducing the Form Page Wizard

The first screen of the Form Page Wizard, shown in Figure 21.1, is an introductory screen. It explains what the Form Page Wizard does. You navigate forward and backward through the wizard by using the navigation buttons at the bottom of each dialog box.

Figure 21.1.
The introductory screen of the Form Page Wizard.

Click the Cancel button to leave the Form Page Wizard without creating the page. Click the **B**ack button to review the questions or choices that you made in previous screens. Click the **F**inish button to generate the page with the content you have chosen up to that point. Click the **N**ext button to proceed to the next step.

NOTE: In some cases, you cannot go back unless you assign a name to the group of fields for the question on which you are working. You can go back and review the question after you assign the name.

Naming a Form Page

On the second screen of the Form Page Wizard, shown in Figure 21.2, you enter a URL for the page and a page title. After you enter the name, you proceed to add questions to the form.

Figure 21.2.
Enter a page URL and a page title.

Adding Questions

The third screen of the Form Page Wizard, shown in Figure 21.3, appears next. You use this screen to add, modify, remove, or rearrange the order of questions. The steps to create each type of question are described in more detail in the page projects in this chapter. In brief, these are the basic procedures you use to add a question to a form:

Figure 21.3.
You can add, modify, remove, or rearrange questions.

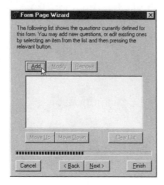

1. Click the **A**dd button shown in Figure 21.3. The screen shown in Figure 21.4 appears.
2. Choose a question type and enter a prompt or question. The types of questions you can add are described in Table 21.1.
3. Configure the options for the form fields to the question on the appropriate screen.

Figure 21.4.

Choose the type of question you want to ask and enter a question in this screen.

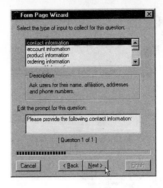

4. To enter another question, repeat steps 1 through 3.

5. Click **N**ext to continue with the Form Page Wizard after you have added all your questions to the list. You proceed to the "Choosing How to Display Your Questions" task, described later in this chapter.

Table 21.1. Types of questions in the Form Page Wizard.

Question Type	Description
Contact information	Prompts the user for contact information, such as name, postal address, work and home phone numbers, fax number, and e-mail address
Account information	Prompts the user for a username and password
Product information	Prompts the user for a product name, platform and version number (for software products), serial number, model, and product code
Ordering information	Displays an order form and prompts the user for billing and shipping information
Personal information	Prompts the user for name, age, height, weight, ID number, hair color, and eye color
One of several options	Prompts the user to select one of several options presented on the form
Any of several options	Prompts the user to select one or more options from several presented on the form
Boolean	Prompts the user for a yes/no, true/false, or similar response
Date	Prompts the user for a date in *mm/dd/yy*, *dd/mm/yy*, or free format
Time	Prompts the user for a time entry (*hh:mm:ss*) in am/pm format, 24-hour format, or free format

Question Type	Description
Range	Prompts the user for a single response in a scale ranging from bad to good, 1 to 5, or disagree strongly to agree strongly
Number	Prompts the user for a numerical response
String	Prompts the user for a brief single-line text response
Paragraph	Prompts the user for a multilined or lengthy text response

Modifying Questions

You also modify questions from the screen shown in Figure 21.3. To modify a question, do the following:

1. From the screen shown in Figure 21.3, highlight the question that you want to modify.

2. Click the **M**odify button. The question's option screen appears, and you can modify the question.

Removing Questions

You can remove questions from your form design with the screen shown in Figure 21.3. To remove a question from the list, use the following steps:

1. From the screen shown in Figure 21.3, highlight the question that you want to remove.

2. Click the **R**emove button. The question is removed from the list.

NOTE: To remove all the questions from the list, click the Clear List button.

Reordering Questions

You can use the Move **U**p and Move **D**own buttons in the screen shown in Figure 21.3 to rearrange the order of your questions as follows:

1. From the screen shown in Figure 21.3, highlight the question that you want to move.

2. Click the Move **U**p or Move **D**own button to change its location in the list.

Choosing How to Display Your Questions

After you complete your question list, select how you want to present it, using the screen shown in Figure 21.5.

Figure 21.5.

Choose how you want to present your questions.

To present your questions, follow these steps:

1. Select a format for displaying your questions. Choose one of the following options:

   as normal **p**aragraphs
   as a nu**m**bered list
   as a b**u**lleted list
   as a **d**efinition list

2. Choose whether you want a table of contents included on your form. If your form is lengthy, choose **y**es. Links to the questions are listed at the top of the page. When the user clicks the link, the page jumps to the appropriate question.

NOTE: You must edit the table of contents manually to reflect the questions on your form.

3. Choose how you want your form fields displayed. By default, the form fields are displayed in table cells, which makes layout of your form much easier and more flexible. To display the form fields as formatted paragraphs, uncheck the use **t**ables to align form fields checkbox.

4. Click **N**ext to proceed to the next screen.

Storing Your Responses

The screen shown in Figure 21.6 asks how you want to retrieve the information from the form.

Figure 21.6.

Choose the output option.

To specify how you want to retrieve the information, follow these steps:

1. Choose how you want to handle the input from the form. You can store the responses in one of three ways:

   ❏ *save results to a **w**eb page.* When you choose this option, the results from the form are stored on your site in Web page format, using an `.htm` extension.

   ❏ *save results to a **t**ext file.* When you choose this option, the results of the form are stored on your site in text format, using a `.txt` extension.

   ❏ *use custom CGI **s**cript.* When you choose this option, the results of the form are passed to a custom CGI script for further processing.

2. **E**nter the base name of the results file. This is the name of the Web page, text file, or CGI script where you store the responses of the form. Don't include the extension in your entry here because the extension is added automatically based on your selection in step 1. The full name of the results file is displayed below the data entry field.

3. Click **N**ext to continue with your form.

Finishing the Form

The screen shown in Figure 21.7 is the final screen in the Form Page Wizard. Here, you simply click **F**inish to create your form. Your page appears in the FrontPage Editor window. At this point, you can save it to your Web or you can copy it to the clipboard and paste it into another page in your Web.

Figure 21.7.
The final screen in the Form Page Wizard.

Creating a Guest Book

Now that you know the basics about how to create a form, try some of your own. This first example creates a simple guest book page by adding two questions with the Form Page Wizard. The first question asks the user to rate your Web site by choosing one response in a scale. Then, the user adds comments in a paragraph field on the page. Figure 21.8 shows a complete example of this guest book.

Figure 21.8.
This simple guest book page uses range and paragraph questions.

A completed example of the Guest Book form is included on the CD-ROM that accompanies this book. It is located in the `Book\Chap21\Examples` folder.

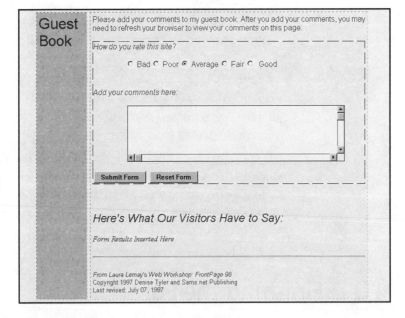

After creating the page, I moved the form fields into tables, changed the page properties, and changed the font to Arial. I also added an Include WebBot after the heading that reads `Here's What Our Visitors Have to Say.`

To create a simple guest book page, follow these steps:

1. From the FrontPage Explorer, create or open a Web in which to save your page. Choose **T**ools | Show Fro**n**tPage Editor or use the Show FrontPage Editor button to open the FrontPage Editor.

2. From the FrontPage Editor, choose **F**ile | **N**ew (Ctrl+N). The New Page dialog box appears, opened to the Page tab.

3. From the list of templates in the Page tab, double-click Form Page Wizard. The Form Page Wizard introductory screen appears.

4. Click **N**ext to continue to the next screen. The screen shown in Figure 21.2 appears.

5. In the Page **U**RL field, enter `guestbook.htm`.

6. In the Page **T**itle field, enter `Guest Book`.

7. Click **N**ext to continue to the next screen. The screen shown in Figure 21.3 appears. You are now ready to add your questions to the page.

Asking a Range Question

You want to know what visitors think of your site. One easy way to obtain this answer is to ask a range question. You can tell at a glance how you're doing. Figure 21.9 shows three questions and the form fields generated by a range question.

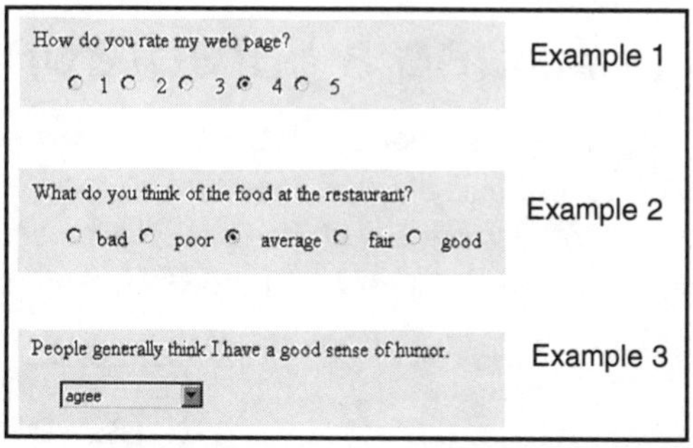

Figure 21.9.
Range questions show a scale of 1 to 5, bad to good, or strongly disagree to strongly agree. You can use radio buttons or drop-down menus.

> How do you rate my web page?
> ○ 1 ○ 2 ○ 3 ● 4 ○ 5   Example 1
>
> What do you think of the food at the restaurant?
> ○ bad ○ poor ● average ○ fair ○ good   Example 2
>
> People generally think I have a good sense of humor.   Example 3
> [agree ▾]

To add a range question to the guest book page, use the following steps:

1. From the screen shown in Figure 21.3, click the **A**dd button.

2. Select the **t**ype of input to collect for this question. Choose **R**ange.

3. **E**dit the prompt for this question. Here, you enter the question you want to ask of the user. Enter `How do you rate this site?`.

4. Click **N**ext to configure the form fields for this question.

5. How should the user provide an answer? The guest book page shown in Figure 21.8 uses the second option (Bad, Poor, Average, Fair, Good). Refer

to Example 2 in Figure 21.9 for similar answers. The other options from which you can choose include the following:

❑ *On a scale of **1** to 5*. The user chooses from one of five choices, labeled with numbers 1 to 5, as shown in Example 1 of Figure 21.9.

❑ *From disagree strongly to agree strongly*. The user chooses from one of five choices, labeled from disagree strongly to agree strongly, as shown in Example 3 of Figure 21.9.

6. Choose from the following presentation options:

❑ *Mid-range choice is default*. Select this option for your Guest Book form. This makes `Average` the default choice in the group of radio buttons on the form, as in Example 2 of Figure 21.9.

❑ *Use drop-down menu instead of radio buttons*. If you choose this option, the list is displayed in a drop-down menu list, as in Example 3 of Figure 21.9.

Each value returned by the form must have a unique variable name. If your form results file returns more than one response in the same category, check the form field properties as discussed in Chapter 22. You probably have duplications in your form field properties.

7. Enter the name of a **v**ariable to hold this answer. Here, you assign a brief and descriptive variable name for this question. This variable name is sent to the form handler with the value selected by the user, as a name/value pair. There is no default name, and this field must be completed before leaving the screen. Enter `Rating`.

8. Click **N**ext to add another question or proceed with the form.

Asking a Paragraph Question

The guest book also includes an area where the user can add comments about your site. Generally, you hope that users enter something more than a single line of text. To encourage such cases, use a paragraph question when you need a multiline response. Figure 21.10 shows an example of a paragraph question on a page.

Figure 21.10.
Use a paragraph question when several lines of text are required for a response.

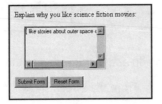

To complete a paragraph question, follow these steps:

1. From the screen shown in Figure 21.3, click the **A**dd button.

2. Select the **t**ype of input to collect for this question. Choose Paragraph.

3. **E**dit the prompt for this question. Enter `Add your comments here:`.

4. Click **N**ext to configure the form field for this question.

5. Enter the name of the variable to hold the answer. Enter `Comments`.

6. Click **N**ext to proceed with the form.

TASK Completing the Guest Book

After you complete your list of questions, you see the screen shown in Figure 21.5. To complete the guest book, follow these steps:

1. From the screen shown in Figure 21.3, click the **N**ext button. The screen shown in Figure 21.5 appears.

2. How should the list of questions be presented? Choose as normal **p**aragraphs.

3. Would you like a Table of Contents for this page? Because the form is brief, choose n**o**.

4. The use t**a**bles to align form fields checkbox is checked by default. You can leave this selection as is.

5. Click **N**ext to continue. The screen shown in Figure 21.6 appears.

6. How do you want to handle the input generated by users when they submit a form? You want the users' comments to be included on a Web page on your site. Choose save results to a **w**eb page.

7. **E**nter the base name of the results file. Here, you enter the name of the Web page that stores the users' responses. The results should be sent to a different page. The appropriate file extension is added to this name automatically. Enter `guestlog`.

8. Click **N**ext to proceed to the final wizard screen.

9. Click **F**inish to create your form. The form appears in the FrontPage Editor window. You can use the form as is or customize it with tables, graphics, and fonts in any way you choose. After you complete the page, choose **F**ile | **S**ave (Ctrl+S) to save the form to a folder in your Web.

Creating an Online Order Form

If you want to sell your products online, you can easily create an online ordering form. The example shown in Figure 21.11 features contact information, ordering information, and boolean (yes or no, true or false) questions. After creating the page, I moved the form fields into tables, changed the page properties, and changed the font to Arial.

Figure 21.11.

Contact information, ordering information, and boolean questions are used in this online order form.

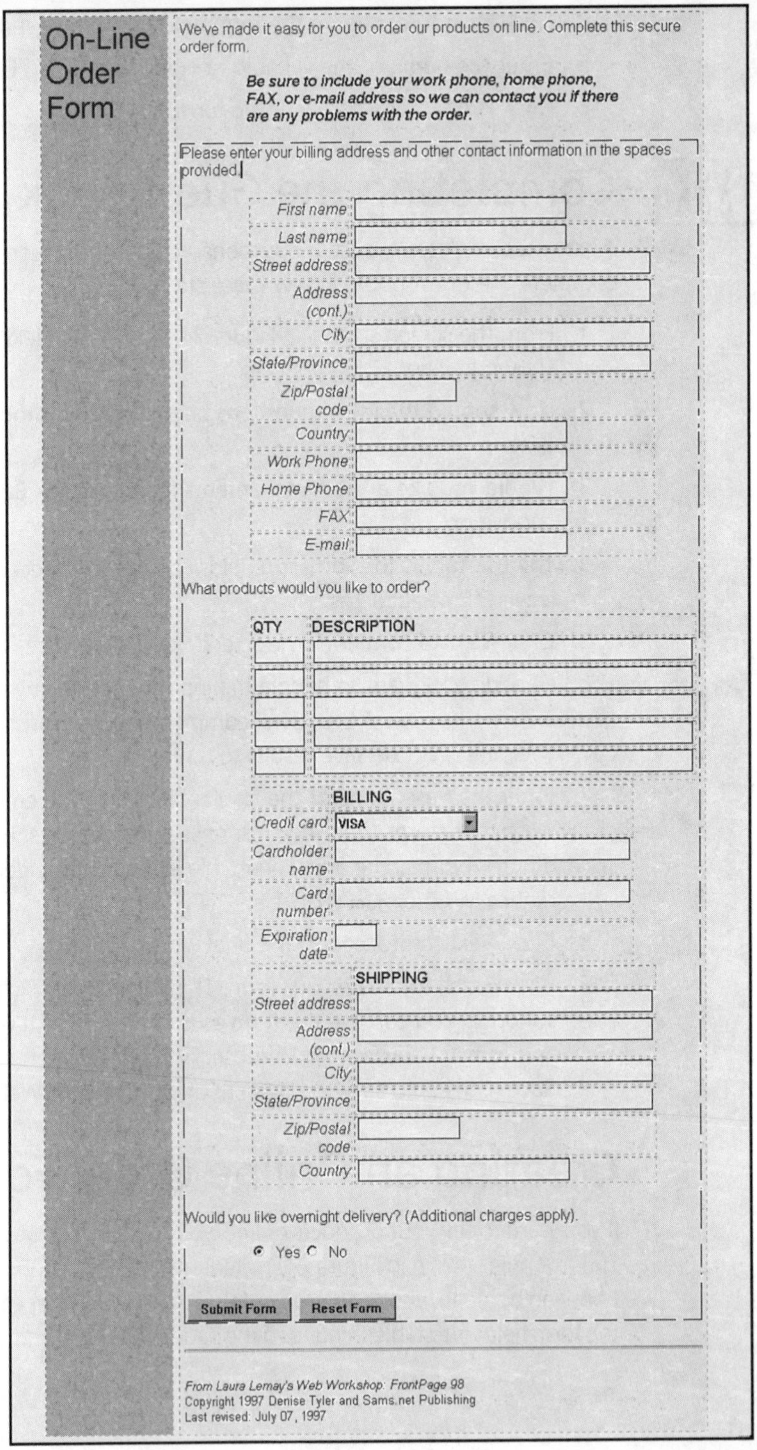

On-Line Order Form

We've made it easy for you to order our products on line. Complete this secure order form.

Be sure to include your work phone, home phone, FAX, or e-mail address so we can contact you if there are any problems with the order.

Please enter your billing address and other contact information in the spaces provided.

First name:
Last name:
Street address:
Address (cont.):
City:
State/Province:
Zip/Postal code:
Country:
Work Phone:
Home Phone:
FAX:
E-mail:

What products would you like to order?

QTY	DESCRIPTION

BILLING

Credit card: VISA
Cardholder name:
Card number:
Expiration date:

SHIPPING

Street address:
Address (cont.):
City:
State/Province:
Zip/Postal code:
Country:

Would you like overnight delivery? (Additional charges apply).

⊙ Yes ○ No

Submit Form   Reset Form

From Laura Lemay's Web Workshop: FrontPage 98
Copyright 1997 Denise Tyler and Sams.net Publishing
Last revised: July 07, 1997

To create the online order form shown in Figure 21.11, follow these steps:

1. From the FrontPage Explorer, create or open a Web in which to save your page. Choose **T**ools I Show Fro**n**tPage Editor or use the Show FrontPage Editor button to open the FrontPage Editor.

2. From the FrontPage Editor, choose **F**ile I **N**ew (Ctrl+N). The New Page dialog box appears.

3. Choose Form Page Wizard and click OK. The Form Page Wizard introductory screen appears.

4. Click **N**ext to continue to the next screen. The screen shown in Figure 21.2 appears.

5. In the Page **U**RL field, enter `order.htm`.

6. In the Page **T**itle field, enter `On-Line Order Form`.

7. Click **N**ext to add a question to the form.

The contact information fields are displayed in text boxes. To learn how to edit these fields, see Chapter 22.

Figure 21.12.
You can request different types of contact information.

Asking a Contact Information Question

Use a contact information question when you need to know how to contact the person filling out your form. Information request forms often ask for contact information. Figure 21.12 shows examples of the fields available for contact information.

Please provide the following contact information: Example 1

Name	John Smith
Title	President
Organization	Smith Home Builders
Street address	886 Main Street
Address (cont.)	Suite 205
City	Capital City
State/Province	MS
Zip/Postal code	02134
Country	USA
Work Phone	213-555-1212
Home Phone	213-555-4545
FAX	213-555-1216
E-mail	bsmith@smithco.com
URL	http://www.smithco.com/~b

Please enter your first and last name in the fields provided: Example 2

First name	Randy
Last name	Taylor

Please enter your first name, middle initial, and last name in the fields provided: Example 3

First name	Beverly
Last name	Johnson
Middle initial	N

To complete a contact information question, do the following:

1. From the screen shown in Figure 21.3, click the **A**dd button.

2. Select the **t**ype of input to collect for this question. Choose Contact Information.

3. **E**dit the prompt for this question. Enter `Please enter your billing address and other contact information in the spaces provided.`

4. Click **N**ext to configure the form fields for this question.

5. Choose the items to collect from the user:

   ❏ *Full*. The user enters his or her name in a single field, as in Example 1 of Figure 21.12.

   ❏ *First, last*. The user enters his or her name in two separate fields, as in Example 2 of Figure 21.12. Select this option to create your online ordering form.

   ❏ *First, last, middle*. The user enters his or her first name, last name, and middle initial in three separate fields, as in Example 3 of Figure 21.12.

6. Check or uncheck the boxes to include the contact information that you want to obtain. For your ordering form, choose **P**ostal Address, **W**ork Phone, Ho**m**e Phone, FA**X**, and **E**-Mail Address. The other options from which to choose include **T**itle, **O**rganization, and Web Add**r**ess (URL). See Figure 21.12 for examples.

TIP: It is most efficient—for you and for the person filling out the form—to ask for no more information than you need in response to a question.

7. Enter the base name for this group of **v**ariables. Leave this at the default name of `Contact`.

8. Click **N**ext to add another question.

Asking an Ordering Information Question

Use an ordering information question when you want users to order products online. You can create order forms easily. Figure 21.13 shows examples of the fields for this type of question.

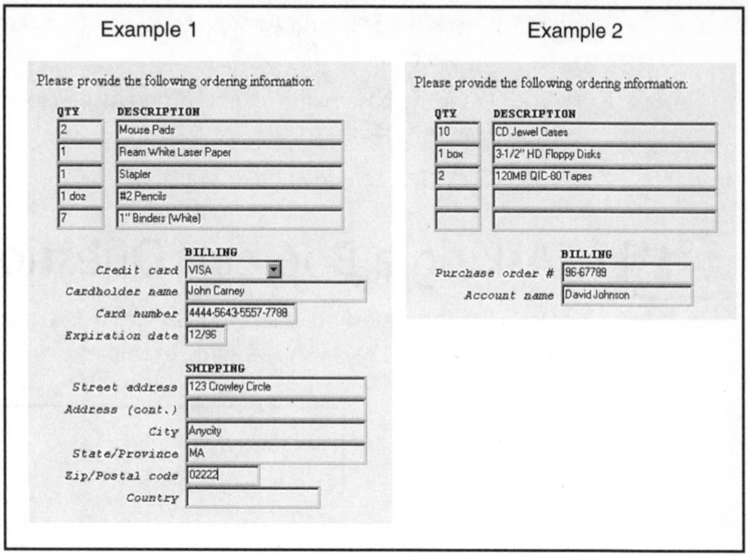

Figure 21.13.

*Use ordering informa-
tion in an online
order form.*

To complete an ordering information question, choose the data that you want to collect from the user.

1. From the screen shown in Figure 21.3, click the **A**dd button.

2. Select the **t**ype of input to collect for this question. Choose Ordering Information.

3. **E**dit the prompt for this question. Enter `What products would you like to order?`.

4. Click **N**ext to configure the form fields for this question.

5. If you want to include an order form on your page, complete the following items:

   ❏ *List of products and quantities*. Check this option to include an order form on the page.

   ❏ *Maximum number*. This is the number of lines in the order form. Leave this value set at the default of 5 lines.

6. Check B**i**lling Information to ask for the method of payment and choose the type of field for billing information:

   ❏ *Credit card*. Choose this option. The name of the cardholder and the card's number and expiration date are entered in text fields, as in Example 1 of Figure 21.13.

   ❏ *Purchase order*. If you choose the Purchase Order option, the user enters a purchase order number and account name in text boxes, as in Example 2 of Figure 21.13.

To learn how to edit a
drop-down menu field,
see Chapter 22.

7. Check the **S**hipping Address checkbox to include shipping information fields on the order form.

8. Enter the base name for this group of **v**ariables. Leave this at the default name of Ordering.

9. Click **N**ext to add another question.

Asking a Boolean Question

Use a boolean question when you want to ask a question that requires an either/or response. Figure 21.14 shows some examples.

Figure 21.14.
Boolean questions can be answered with checkboxes or radio buttons.

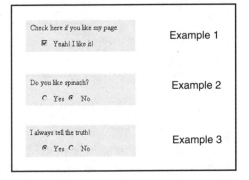

To complete a boolean question, follow these steps:

1. From the screen shown in Figure 21.3, click the **A**dd button.

2. Select the **t**ype of input to collect for this question. Choose **B**oolean.

3. **E**dit the prompt for this question. Enter Would you like overnight delivery? (Additional charges apply).

4. Click **N**ext to configure the form fields for this question.

5. Select the type of response area that you want to include in the form:

   ❏ *Checkbox*. The user checks or unchecks a checkbox to enter the response (see Example 1 of Figure 21.14).

   ❏ *Yes/no radio buttons*. Choose this option to provide Yes and No radio buttons (see Example 2 of Figure 21.14).

   ❏ *True/false radio buttons*. The user chooses between a Yes and a No radio button (see Example 3 of Figure 21.14).

6. Enter a **v**ariable name for holding this answer. There is no default name. Enter Overnight.

7. Click **N**ext to proceed with the form.

Completing the Form

After you complete your list of questions, you see the screen shown in Figure 21.5. To complete the online ordering form, follow these steps:

1. From the screen shown in Figure 21.3, click **N**ext. The screen shown in Figure 21.5 appears.

2. How should the list of questions be presented? Choose as normal **p**aragraphs.

3. Would you like a Table of Contents for this page? Because the form is brief, choose N**o**.

4. Leave the use t**a**bles to align form fields option checked.

5. Click **N**ext to continue. The screen shown in Figure 21.6 appears.

6. How do you want to handle the input generated by users when they submit a form? You want the data from this form to be compatible with a database or spreadsheet program. Choose save results to a **t**ext file.

7. Enter the base name of the results file. Enter `Ordering`.

8. Click **N**ext to proceed to the final wizard screen.

9. Click **F**inish to create your form. The form appears in the FrontPage Editor window.

After you complete the form, review the form fields to customize them further, as discussed in Chapter 22. You also need to verify the settings of the form handler, using the procedures outlined in Chapter 23, "Configuring Form Handlers."

Creating Charlie's Astrological Data Page

Charlie's Astrological Data page, shown in Figure 21.15, uses personal information, date, time, and string questions to complete the form. It's designed to direct the user to another form on or from the confirmation page when he submits his chart data. From the second form (not shown), the user selects the type of chart he wants to have done and completes the billing information. This reduces the amount of form fields on one page and makes it easier to complete.

To create Charlie's Astrological Data page, follow these steps:

1. From the FrontPage Explorer, create or open a Web in which to save your page. Choose **T**ools | Show Fro**n**tPage Editor or use the Show FrontPage Editor button to open the FrontPage Editor.

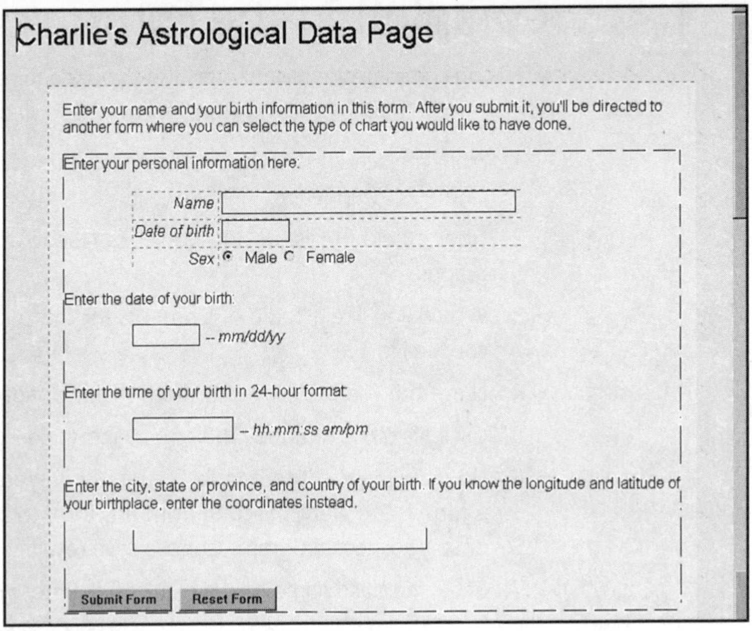

Figure 21.15.

Charlie's Astrological Data page uses personal information, date, time, and string questions.

Charlie's Astrological Data Page

Enter your name and your birth information in this form. After you submit it, you'll be directed to another form where you can select the type of chart you would like to have done.

Enter your personal information here.

Name :
Date of birth :
Sex : ⦿ Male ○ Female

Enter the date of your birth:

-- mm/dd/yy

Enter the time of your birth in 24-hour format:

-- hh:mm:ss am/pm

Enter the city, state or province, and country of your birth. If you know the longitude and latitude of your birthplace, enter the coordinates instead.

[Submit Form] [Reset Form]

2. From the FrontPage Editor, choose **F**ile | **N**ew (Ctrl+N). The New Page dialog box appears.

3. Choose Form Page Wizard and click OK. The Form Page Wizard introductory screen appears.

4. Click **N**ext to continue to the next screen. The screen shown in Figure 21.2 appears.

5. In the Page **U**RL field, enter `astro.htm`.

6. In the Page **T**itle field, enter `Charlie's Astrological Data Page`.

7. Click **N**ext to continue to the next screen. The screen shown in Figure 21.3 appears. You are now ready to add your questions to the page.

Asking for Personal Information

You can ask for personal information in your forms, including age, sex, height, weight, ID number, and hair and eye color. Figure 21.16 shows examples of the fields.

Figure 21.16.

You can request several types of personal information.

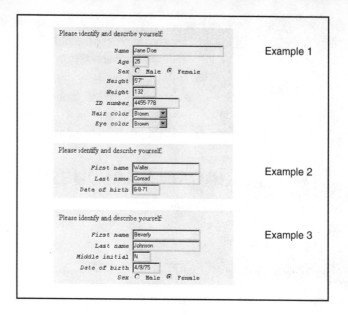

To complete a personal information question, use the following steps:

1. From the screen shown in Figure 21.3, click the **A**dd button.

2. Select the **t**ype of input to collect for this question. Choose Personal Information.

3. **E**dit the prompt for this question. Enter `Enter your personal information here:`.

4. Click **N**ext to configure the form fields for this question.

5. Choose the data items to collect from the user. Verify that the **N**ame option is checked. If you do not want to request a name in this section of the form, uncheck the option. The options are

   ❏ *Full.* The user enters his name in a single text field, as in Example 1 of Figure 21.16. Select this option for your page.

   ❏ *First, last.* The user enters his first and last names in individual fields, as in Example 2 of Figure 21.16.

   ❏ *First, last, middle.* The user enters his first name, last name, and middle initial in individual fields, as in Example 3 of Figure 21.16.

6. Uncheck the Ag**e** checkbox for this page. Although a date of birth is entered in this form, it uses a different format. For reference, the following selections are available for reporting age:

   ❏ *Years old.* The user enters his age in years, as in Example 1 of Figure 21.16.

   ❏ *Date of birth.* The user enters his date of birth, as in Example 2 of Figure 21.16.

7. Check or uncheck the additional types of information that you want to request. For this page, choose only **S**ex. The other options are Heig**h**t, **W**eight, ID nu**m**ber, Hair c**o**lor, and E**y**e color. Examples are shown in Example 1 of Figure 21.16.

8. Enter the base name for this group of **v**ariables. Leave this field at the default name of `Personal`.

9. Click **N**ext to add another question.

Asking a Date Question

A date question asks the user for a date—a calendar date, not the romantic kind. The user can enter a date response in one of three ways. Figure 21.17 shows some examples.

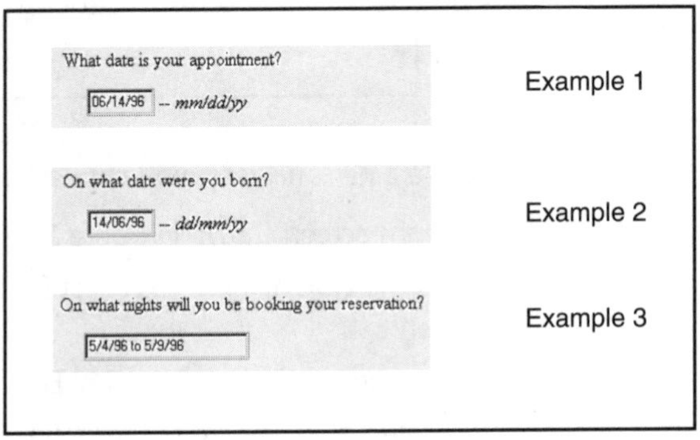

Figure 21.17.
Users can enter dates in three ways.

What date is your appointment? `06/14/96` -- *mm/dd/yy*	Example 1
On what date were you born? `14/06/96` -- *dd/mm/yy*	Example 2
On what nights will you be booking your reservation? `5/4/96 to 5/9/96`	Example 3

To complete a date question, do the following:

1. From the screen shown in Figure 21.3, click the **A**dd button.

2. Select the **t**ype of input to collect for this question. Choose Date.

3. **E**dit the prompt for this question. Enter `Enter the date of your birth:`.

4. Click **N**ext to configure the form fields for this question.

5. How should the user provide an answer? Select one of the following options:

   ❏ *mm/dd/yy*. The user enters his or her response followed with AM or PM, as shown in Example 1 of Figure 21.17.

   ❏ *dd/mm/yy*. The user enters his or her response in 24-hour format, as shown in Example 2 of Figure 21.17. Choose this option for Charlie's page.

   ❏ *Free Format*. The user enters the date in a form of his or her choosing, as shown in Example 3 of Figure 21.17.

6. Enter the name of a **v**ariable to hold this answer. There is no default name. Enter **DOB**.

7. Click **N**ext to add another question.

Asking a Time Question

A time question asks the user for a specific time. Figure 21.18 shows some examples.

Figure 21.18.

You can enter the time in 12-hour, 24-hour, or free format.

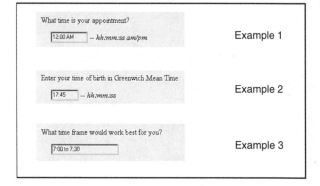

To complete a time question, follow these steps:

1. From the screen shown in Figure 21.3, click the **A**dd button.

2. Select the **t**ype of input to collect for this question. Choose **T**ime.

3. **E**dit the prompt for this question. Enter `Enter the time of your birth in 24-hour format.`

4. Click **N**ext to configure the form fields for this question.

5. How should the user provide the answer? Your options follow:

   ❏ *hh:mm:ss—am/pm.* The user enters the response in 12-hour format, followed by AM or PM, as shown in Example 1 of Figure 21.18.

   ❏ *hh:mm:ss—24-hour clock.* The user enters the response in 24-hour format, as shown in Example 2 of Figure 21.18. Choose this option for Charlie's page.

   ❏ *Free format.* The user enters the response of his or her choice, as shown in Example 3 of Figure 21.18.

6. Enter the name of a variable to hold this answer. There is no default name. Enter **TOB**.

7. Click **N**ext to add another question or proceed with the form.

Asking a String Question

Ask for a string response when you need a single line of text input from the user. A typical question is `Enter your pet's name in the space below.`. Figure 21.19 shows an example.

Figure 21.19.

Use a string question when a single-line text response is sufficient.

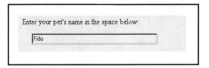

To complete a string question, do the following:

1. From the screen shown in Figure 21.3, click the **A**dd button.

2. Select the **t**ype of input to collect for this question. Choose **S**tring.

3. **E**dit the prompt for this question. Enter `Enter the city, state or province, and country of your birth. If you know the longitude and latitude of your birthplace, enter the coordinates instead.`

4. Click **N**ext to configure the form fields for this question.

5. The default length of the text field is 50 characters, which you keep for this form. To specify a different length, check the Set Maximum Length checkbox and enter a new maximum number.

6. Enter the name of a **v**ariable to hold this answer. There is no default value. Enter `POB`.

7. Click **N**ext to add another question or proceed with the form.

Completing the Form

After you complete your list of questions, you see the screen shown in Figure 21.5. To complete the online ordering form, follow these steps:

1. From the screen shown in Figure 21.3, click **N**ext. The screen shown in Figure 21.5 appears.

2. How should the list of questions be presented? Choose as normal **p**aragraphs.

3. Would you like a Table of Contents for this page? Because the form is brief, choose N**o**.

4. Leave the use t**a**bles to align form fields option checked.

5. Click **N**ext to continue. The screen shown in Figure 21.6 appears.

6. How do you want to handle the input generated by users when they submit a form? Choose save results to a **t**ext file.

7. Enter the base name of the results file. Enter `astrolog`.

8. Click **N**ext to proceed to the final wizard screen.

9. Click **F**inish to create your form. The form appears in the FrontPage Editor window.

Creating a Site Registration Page

You typically use registration pages to register for an event or to gain access to a protected Web site. The latter is the case for this page. It contains a form in which a user enters his or her name, password, and beta site ID to gain access to a protected beta Web site. It uses an account question and a number question.

For the example shown in Figure 21.20, I made some minor modifications to the layout of the form. I added two rows to the table that contains the account question. The number question and form buttons go in the same table. A graphic appears in place of the page title.

Figure 21.20.

The site registration page features account information and number questions.

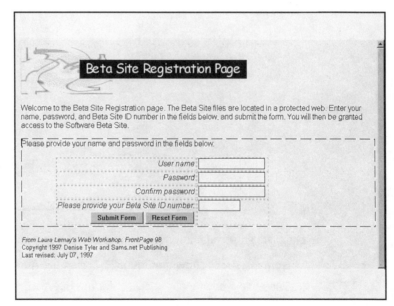

You need to reconfigure your form, as well as the site registration page provided in the `Book\Chap21\Project Files` folder on the CD-ROM, to use a Registration WebBot as a form handler if you want to use it on a FrontPage server. This page must be located in the root Web of the server in order to function properly. See Chapter 33, "Designing Private Webs," for more information on Registration WebBots and pages.

To create the site registration page shown in Figure 21.20, follow these steps:

1. From the FrontPage Explorer, create or open a Web in which to save your page. Choose **T**ools I Show FrontPage Editor or use the Show FrontPage Editor button to open the FrontPage Editor.

2. From the FrontPage Editor, choose **F**ile I **N**ew (Ctrl+N). The New Page dialog box appears.

3. Choose Form Page Wizard and click OK. The Form Page Wizard introductory screen appears.

4. Click **N**ext to continue to the next screen. The screen shown in Figure 21.2 appears.

5. In the Page **U**RL field, enter `sitereg.htm`.

6. In the Page **T**itle field, enter `Beta Site Registration Page`.

7. Click **N**ext to continue to the next screen. The screen shown in Figure 21.3 appears. You are now ready to add your questions to the page.

Asking an Account Information Question

Use an account information question to obtain a username and password. Account information questions are often used on registration forms, such as those used to gain access to a protected Web. Figure 21.21 shows examples of the options available for account information.

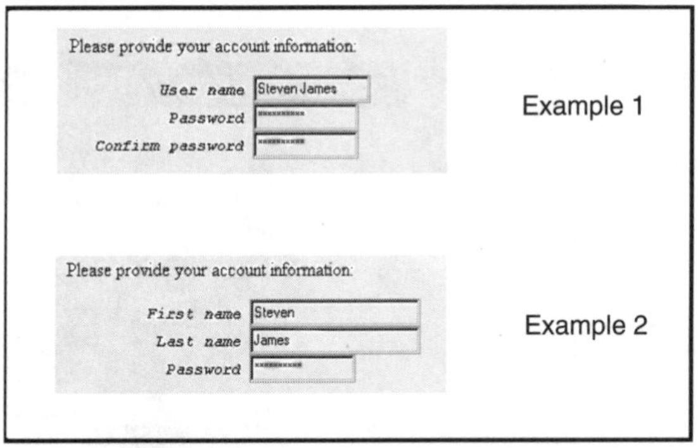

Figure 21.21.

Account information questions ask for a user's name and password.

To complete an account information question, use the following steps:

1. From the screen shown in Figure 21.3, click the **A**dd button.

2. Select the **t**ype of input to collect for this question. Choose Account Information.

3. **E**dit the prompt for this question. Enter `Please provide your name and password in the fields below:`.

4. Click **N**ext to configure the form fields for this question.

5. Select how to include username information on your form. If you do not want to include a username, uncheck the **u**sername option. Your options follow:

❑ *As single field*. The user types his full name, as in Example 1 of Figure 21.21.

❑ *As first and last name fields (for WebBot Registration component)*. Choose this option for your registration page. You always make this choice when you use the Registration WebBot to create a registration form for a protected Web. Refer to Example 2 of Figure 21.21.

6. Choose how you want to receive password information. If you do not want to include password information, uncheck the Password option.

❑ *Require confirmation (must type in twice)*. Choose this option. The user confirms his password in a separate field, as in Example 1 of Figure 21.21.

❑ *Don't require confirmation*. If you do not require confirmation, the user enters his password once, as in Example 2 of Figure 21.21.

7. Enter the base name for this group of **v**ariables. Leave this variable at the default name of `Account`.

8. Click **N**ext to add another question.

Asking a Number Question

Use a number question when you need numerical input from the user. Figure 21.22 shows some examples.

Figure 21.22.
You can specify the length of a numerical response. You can also specify a currency symbol.

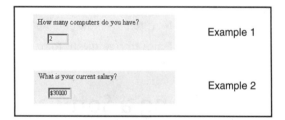

To complete a number question, follow these steps:

1. From the screen shown in Figure 21.3, click the **A**dd button.

2. Select the **t**ype of input to collect for this question. Choose Number.

3. **E**dit the prompt for this question. Enter `Please provide your Beta Site ID number:`.

4. Click **N**ext to configure the form fields for this question.

If you need a numerical value that is longer than ten characters or you need an alphanumeric entry, use a string question instead.

5. The default length of the numerical response is five characters. To set it for 10 characters (the maximum) for your form, check the **S**et maximum length checkbox and set the value to `10`.

6. Check the Set currency **p**refix box if you want to allow additional space for a currency symbol. Enter the currency symbol in the designated field. Leave this option unchecked for your form.

7. Enter the name of a **v**ariable to hold this answer. There is no default name. Enter `BetaID`.

8. Click **N**ext to proceed with the form.

 ## Completing the Form

After you complete your list of questions, you see the screen shown in Figure 21.5. To complete the registration page, follow these steps:

1. From the screen shown in Figure 21.3, click **N**ext. The screen shown in Figure 21.5 appears.

2. How should the list of questions be presented? Choose as normal **p**aragraphs.

3. Would you like a Table of Contents for this page? Because the form is brief, choose N**o**.

4. Leave the use **t**ables to align form fields option checked.

5. Click **N**ext to continue. The screen shown in Figure 21.6 appears.

6. How to you want to handle the input generated by users when they submit a form? Choose save results to a **t**ext file.

7. Enter the base name of the results file. Enter `sitelog`.

8. Click **N**ext to proceed to the final wizard screen.

9. Click **F**inish to create your form. The form appears in the FrontPage Editor window.

Creating a Software Registration Page

The software registration page, shown in Figure 21.23, enables a user to register a software product online. This form utilizes product information, one of several options, and any of several options questions.

To create the software registration page shown in Figure 21.23, follow these steps:

1. From the FrontPage Explorer, create or open a Web in which to save your page. Choose **T**ools I Show Fro**n**tPage Editor or use the Show FrontPage Editor button to open the FrontPage Editor.

2. From the FrontPage Editor, choose **F**ile I **N**ew (Ctrl+N). The New Page dialog box appears.

Figure 21.23.

Product information, one of several options, and any of several options questions appear in this software registration form.

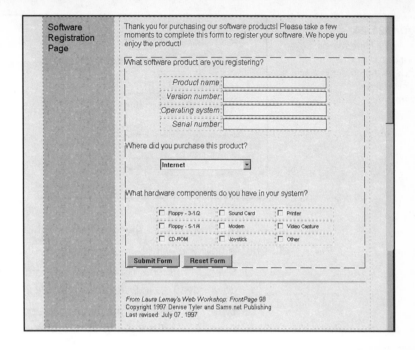

3. Choose Form Page Wizard and click OK. The Form Page Wizard introductory screen appears.

4. Click **N**ext to continue to the next screen. The screen shown in Figure 21.2 appears.

5. In the Page **U**RL field, enter `softreg.htm`.

6. In the Page **T**itle field, enter `Software Registration Page`.

7. Click **N**ext to continue to the next screen. The screen shown in Figure 21.3 appears. You are now ready to add your questions to the page.

 ## Asking a Product Information Question

Use a product information question to obtain warranty or registration information on a product. A form for this type of question might be a software registration form or a warranty service request. Figure 21.24 shows the options available.

To complete a product information question, follow these steps:

1. From the screen shown in Figure 21.3, click the **A**dd button.

2. Select the **t**ype of input to collect for this question. Choose Product Information.

3. **E**dit the prompt for this question. Enter `What software product are you registering?`.

Figure 21.24.

Use product information questions to register software or request warranty service information.

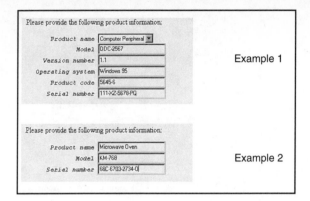

4. Click **N**ext to configure the form fields for this question.

5. Choose how you want to receive the product name:

   ❏ *S*elect from menu. Users can select from a list of products in a drop-down menu, as in Example 1 of Figure 21.24.

   ❏ *T*ype it in. Users type the name of the product, as in Example 2 of Figure 21.24. Choose this option for your form.

6. Check or uncheck the information you want to request on the product. Choose **P**latform and version (for software products) and **S**erial number. Leave **M**odel and Product co**d**e unchecked.

7. Enter the base name for this group of **v**ariables. Leave this at the default name of Product.

8. Click **N**ext to add another question.

 # Asking a One-of-Several-Options Question

Ask a one-of-several-options question when you want the user to choose one response from a list of choices. An example of a question in this category is What is your favorite color?. Figure 21.25 shows examples of the options for this question.

To complete a one-of-several-options question, follow these steps:

1. From the screen shown in Figure 21.3, click the **A**dd button.

2. Select the **t**ype of input to collect for this question. Choose One of several options.

3. **E**dit the prompt for this question. Enter Where did you purchase this product?.

Figure 21.25.

A one-of-several-options question enables you to obtain responses through drop-down menus, a series of radio buttons, or a scrollable menu list.

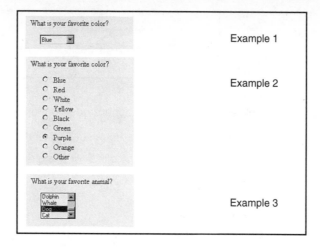

4. Click **N**ext to configure the form fields for this question.

5. Enter the labels for the **o**ptions, one on each line. Enter the following items:

```
Internet
Mail Order
Department Store
Software Specialty Store
Direct from Manufacturer
Other or gift
```

6. Select how you want to display the list:

   ❏ *Drop-down menu.* The list is displayed in a drop-down menu, as in Example 1 of Figure 21.25. Select this option for your form.

   ❏ *Radio buttons.* The list is displayed in a series of radio buttons, as in Example 2 of Figure 21.25.

   ❏ *List.* The list is displayed in a scrollable menu list, as in Example 3 of Figure 21.25.

7. Enter the name of a **v**ariable to hold this answer. There is no default variable name for this question. Enter **Purchase**.

8. Click **N**ext to add another question.

Asking an Any-of-Several-Options Question

Ask an any-of-several-options question when you want to provide one or more choices from a list of several. Figure 21.26 shows an example of the output that you receive.

Figure 21.26.

An any-of-several-options question enables the user to make multiple choices. You can display the checkboxes in a single column or in multiple columns, as shown here.

To complete an any-of-several-options question, do the following:

1. From the screen shown in Figure 21.3, click the **A**dd button.

2. Select the **t**ype of input to collect for this question. Choose Any of several options.

3. **E**dit the prompt for this question. Enter `What hardware components do you have in your system?`.

4. Click **N**ext to configure the form fields for this question.

5. Enter the labels for the choices that you want to include in the scrolling text box on the form. Keep these fairly short if you want to display them in multiple columns. Enter the following values:

   ```
   Sound Card
   CD ROM Drive
   Tape Backup
   Modem
   5-1/4 Floppy Drive
   3-1/2 Floppy Drive
   Other
   Video Capture Board
   Joystick
   ```

6. Check the **U**se multiple columns to present the options checkbox. If you do not check the box, the choices are arranged in a single column.

7. Enter the base name for this group of **v**ariables. The default name is Option. Enter `Hardware`.

8. Click **N**ext to add another question or proceed with the form.

Completing the Page

After you complete your list of questions, you see the screen shown in Figure 21.5. To complete the software registration page, follow these steps:

1. From the screen shown in Figure 21.3, click **N**ext. The screen shown in Figure 21.5 appears.

2. How should the list of questions be presented? Choose as normal **p**aragraphs.

3. Would you like a Table of Contents for this page? Because the form is brief, choose n**o**.

4. Leave the use tables to align form fields option checked.

5. Click **N**ext to continue. The screen shown in Figure 21.6 appears.

6. How to you want to handle the input generated by users when they submit a form? Choose save results to a **t**ext file.

7. Enter the base name of the results file. Enter `orderlog`.

8. Click **N**ext to proceed to the final wizard screen.

9. Click **F**inish to create your form. The form appears in the FrontPage Editor window.

Workshop Wrap-Up

You can design forms quickly and easily with the Form Page Wizard. Start with a list of questions and decide how you want to display them. The wizard does the rest.

 In this chapter, you learned how to design several customized, interactive forms using the FrontPage Form Page Wizard to ask a variety of questions. Based on your selections, the wizard tailors your form so that you can gather information from visitors to your site. Completed examples of the pages in this chapter are located in the `Book\Chap21\Examples` folder on the CD-ROM that accompanies this book.

Next Steps

The next three chapters teach you more about forms. In them, you learn to edit your form fields and assign form handlers to them:

❏ To learn more about the fields in your form, see Chapter 22, "Adding and Editing Form Fields."

❏ In Chapter 23, "Configuring Form Handlers," you learn how to assign and configure form handlers to process the data in your forms.

Q&A

Q: I designed a form and put it on my Web site, but it does not do anything when I try to test it. What is happening?

A: If you assigned a form handler to your form, check whether the FrontPage Server Extensions or custom scripts have been installed on your remote server. You might need to coordinate this with the server administrator at your site. Refer to Chapter 2, "About the FrontPage Server Extensions," for more information.

Q: Which is the better choice to use when I specify a results file— Web pages or text files?

A: Generally, it is more efficient to store your results files as text files. When you store them in a Web page, it requires extra time for the server to process and format the results. You can find more information on the different types of results files in Chapter 23.

Q: Are boolean questions stored as 1s and 0s or as True and False?

A: When a user responds to a boolean question, the names and values that you specify in the form field properties dialog box are reported back to you.

If, for example, you create a question that asks, `Do you like cats?` and specify a checkbox with a name of `likecats`, an initial value of `ON`, and an initial status of `not checked`, the results appear as follows if the user checks the box:

`likecats  ON`

If the same question is asked using a Yes/No radio button with a group name of `likecats`, a Yes radio button that is initially selected, and a No radio button that is initially deselected, the results appear as follows if the user selects No:

`likecats  No`

You learn more about configuring form fields in Chapter 22.

TWENTY-TWO

Adding and Editing Form Fields

In Chapter 21, "Quick and Easy Forms," you learned how to generate a form using the FrontPage Form Page Wizard. The wizard created the form by prompting you with a series of questions. The form fields and the layout were handled automatically.

What if you want to create your own layout, add additional form fields, or edit the content of the forms that you designed with the wizard? This chapter shows you how to do that. You learn how to work with the elements that make up a form.

What Every Form Needs

Every form has some basic elements within it. Form fields are the areas where users enter data. Each form field has a name so that the data can be arranged by category. Every form has a button that users press to submit information to your site. Finally, every form also has a form handler—a set of instructions that tells your server how to process the information that users submit.

Form Fields

When you ask users a question or need input from them, they enter their responses in a form field. For example, the form in Figure 22.1 includes examples of all the form fields. You see, from top to bottom, a text box, a scrolling text box, a checkbox, radio buttons, a drop-down menu, and two pushbuttons. You insert these form fields on your page with the Insert I Form Field command.

Figure 22.1.

Users enter data into your form with form fields.

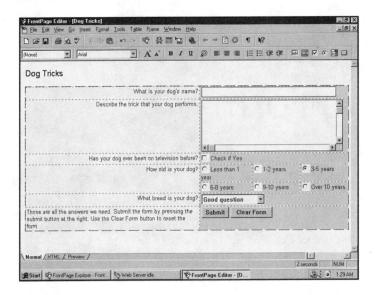

Whenever you insert a form field on a page, you automatically create a form. If you enable the Show/Hide button on the Standard toolbar, the form fields are surrounded by a dashed box. This shows you the area of the page where the form appears.

Form Field Names

Each form field is assigned a name through its respective Properties box, as shown in Figure 22.2. The text box in the first cell of the column has a name of DogName. This name and the value entered by the user are passed first to the form handler and then to you through the use of *name/value pairs*.

Buttons

Unless you place a button on your page, the form cannot do anything. A form must contain, at a minimum, a button that the user clicks to submit the information to you. Most forms include a second button that enables the user to reset or clear the data from the form fields already completed. These buttons are shown at the bottom of the form in Figure 22.1.

Figure 22.2.

Each form field has a name that is matched with the user's value. Together, they make up a name/value pair.

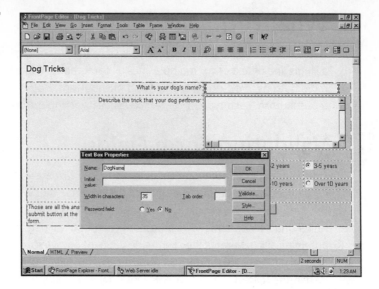

Form Handlers

You learn more about results files in Chapter 23, "Configuring Form Handlers."

After you design a form, you need to assign a form handler to it. You do that with the Form Properties dialog box, shown in Figure 22.3. The form handler resides on the same server as your Web. It accepts the data that the user enters on the form and processes it in some way. Then, it passes the results on to you.

Figure 22.3.

Every form requires a form handler, which is assigned in the Form Properties dialog box.

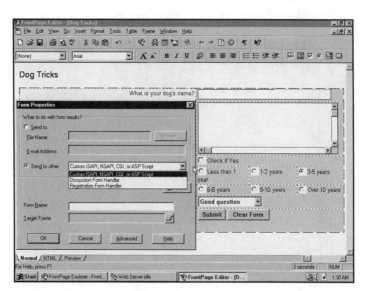

You learn more about the types of form handlers that you can use in Chapter 23.

What Form Fields Do

HTML enables you to place several types of form fields on a page. There are fields for a single line of text or for multiple lines or paragraphs. You also can use checkboxes, radio buttons, drop-down menus, and pushbuttons. You can even use an image as a pushbutton. Each type of form field requests an input from the user.

Validating Form Fields

FrontPage provides commands that let you easily validate your form fields. When you validate a field, you assign parameters that must be met when the user responds to the form field. For example, you can instruct a text box field to accept letters only, rather than alphanumeric responses. When you validate a form field, FrontPage automatically generates the client-side VBScript or JavaScript that performs the form field validation when the data is submitted by the user. As you design each type of form field in the following tasks, you'll learn how to validate the form fields as well.

Designing the Dog Tricks Form

In this chapter, you'll design a simple form and learn to validate the form fields. The form is shown in the preceding figures—the Dog Tricks page.

You start by creating the table shown in Figure 22.4. Insert your form fields in the right column of the table.

Figure 22.4.
Start by adding a table to your page.

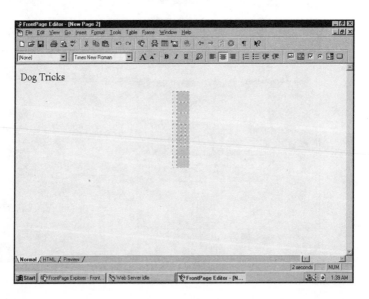

NOTE: Your table will not have borders as shown in the figure. Borders were added so that the screen shot clearly shows the cells in the table.

To begin the form, follow these steps:

1. From the FrontPage Editor, use the New button on the Standard toolbar to create a new normal page. A blank page appears in the FrontPage Editor.

2. With the insertion point at the beginning of the page, choose Heading 2 from the Change Style drop-down menu on the Format toolbar. Enter **Dog Tricks**.

3. Choose Table | Insert Table. The Insert Table dialog box appears. Specify the following settings and choose OK. The table appears in the center of your page.

Rows:	6
Columns:	2
Alignment:	Center
Border Size:	0
Cell Pa**d**ding:	2
Cell **S**pacing:	0
Width:	Uncheck Specify **W**idth checkbox

4. Position the insertion point over the top of the first column, where it becomes a selection arrow pointing downward. Click to select the first column of cells.

5. Press Alt+Enter or right-click and choose Cell Properties from the pop-up menu. The Cell Properties dialog box appears.

6. Assign the following settings in the Cell Properties dialog box. Click OK to exit the Color and Cell Properties dialog boxes. The cells turn to a light yellow color.

Hori**z**ontal Alignment:	Right
Vertical Alignment:	Top
Background **C**olor:	Custom: **R**ed **255** **G**reen **255** **B**lue **204**

7. Position the insertion point inside the bottom cell in the first column. Choose Table | Select C**e**ll and then press Alt+Enter. In the Cell Properties dialog box, change its Hori**z**ontal Alignment setting to Left. Choose OK to apply the setting.

8. Position your mouse above the second column of cells, where it becomes a selection arrow pointing downward. Click to select the cells and press Alt+Enter. The Cell Properties dialog box appears.

9. Set the following settings in the Cell Properties dialog box and choose OK to exit the Color dialog box and the Cell Properties dialog box. The cells change color to a light orange.

    Vertical Alignment: Top
    Background **C**olor: Custom: **R**ed **255 G**reen **204** Blue **153**

10. Click inside the fourth cell in the second column. Choose Ta**b**le I **S**plit Cells. The Split Cells dialog box appears. Select Split into **R**ows. In the Number of **R**ows column, enter **2**. Choose OK. The row is split into two rows.

11. Click inside the fourth cell in the second column again. Choose Ta**b**le I Se**l**ect Cell. Shift-click to select the cell beneath it.

12. Choose Table I Split Cells. The Split Cells dialog box appears. Select Split into **C**olumns and, in the Number of **C**olumns field, enter **3**. Then choose OK. Your table should now look as shown in Figure 22.4, except that yours won't have borders.

Requesting Single-Line Text Input

You're going to insert the first text box on your page to define the area of the form. Then, you'll cut and paste the table into the form area and cut and paste the text box into the table. This way, all the form fields you place in the table are contained in the same form.

Use a single-line text input form field when you expect a brief response from the user or when you request a password. The maximum number of characters allowed in a single-line text input field is 256.

To place a one-line text box on your form, use the following steps:

1. Position the insertion point at the end of the heading that reads `Dog Tricks`.

2. Choose **I**nsert I Form Fiel**d** I One-Line **T**ext Box or click the One-Line Text Box button on the Forms toolbar. The text box appears on your page.

3. Click inside the table and choose Ta**b**le I Select **T**able. Use Ctrl+X to cut the table into your clipboard.

4. Click the right side of the text box in the form. Paste your table into the form area using Ctrl+V. The table is now inside your form.

5. Click to select the text box. Use Ctrl+X to cut the text box into your clipboard.

6. Click in the orange cell in the first row. Paste the text box into the cell using Ctrl+V. Your page should look as shown in Figure 22.5.

7. Click inside the yellow cell in the first row. Enter **What is your dog's name?**.

8. Click to select the text box and press Enter. The Text Box Properties dialog box shown in Figure 22.6 appears.

Figure 22.5.

The table is moved inside the form, and the text box is moved into the table.

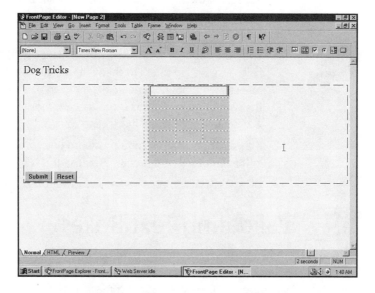

Figure 22.6.

Properties are added into the text box with the Text Box Properties dialog box.

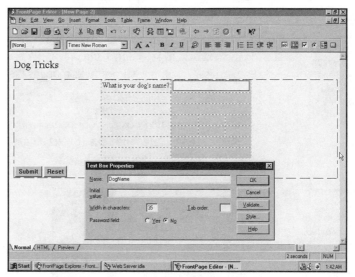

9. In the **N**ame field, enter a name that describes the user's response. This name coincides with the name/value pair reported to the form handler. In the example shown in Figure 22.6, the question asks the user the name of his or her dog. Enter **DogName**.

10. If you want your text box to have a default value when the form initially appears on the page, enter the text in the Initial **v**alue field. For example, you could enter a default entry of `Fido` here (but you won't). This text appears in the form field and is passed on to the form handler unless the user changes it. The user must delete the default value and enter a new value.

11. Enter the width, in characters, for the text box in the **W**idth in characters field. This setting refers to the width of the text box on the page; it doesn't reflect the number of characters that can be entered into it. Make sure that the width of the text box is not too wide for the screen. The default width is 20 characters. Increase this setting to `35`.

12. If this text box is used for a password entry, you select the **Y**es radio button in the Password field section. Because this is not a password field, select **N**o.

13. Click OK. The settings are applied to your text box.

Validating Text Boxes

FrontPage provides commands that enable you to easily validate the form fields that you use with database files. When you validate a form field, FrontPage automatically generates the client-side VBScript or JavaScript that performs the form field validation when the data is submitted by the user.

You can change any property for the text box after it appears on your page by double-clicking the text box, by selecting it and pressing Alt+Enter, or by choosing **E**dit I Form Field Properties. Any of these procedures reopens the Text Box Properties dialog box.

To validate a text box, follow these steps:

1. Double-click the text box on your page. From the Text Box Properties dialog box, choose **V**alidate. The Text Box Validation dialog box, shown in Figure 22.7, appears.

You can also validate any form field by right-clicking the field and choosing Form Field Validation from the pop-up menu.

Figure 22.7.

Text boxes and scrolling text boxes are validated with the Text Box Validation dialog box.

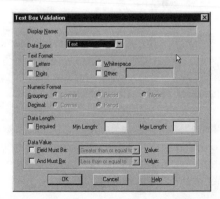

2. In the Data **T**ype field, select the type of data to which you want to constrain the text input from the user. By default, the selection is No Constraints. When this option is selected, many of the other options in the dialog box are disabled. You can choose one of four options from the Data **T**ype drop-down menu:

   ❑ *No constraints*. The user can enter any type of text string.

   ❑ *Text*. The user must enter text. Select this option for your DogName text field.

   ❑ *Integer*. The user must enter a whole number.

   ❑ *Number*. The user must enter any type of number.

3. The Display **N**ame field enables when you select an integer or number from the Data Type drop-down menu. Here, you specify the name that refers to the text field in validation warning messages. It is used when the Name field in the Text Box Properties is different from the label that the user sees on the form. For example, if your numerical form field is named UserIDNumber in the Text Box Properties dialog box, you can assign a display name of **User ID**.

4. The Text Format section enables when you specify a Data **T**ype of text. From the Text Format field, select one or more of the following options. For your DogName field, you want to allow anything but numbers in the response:

   ❑ **L**etters. The field can contain alphabetic characters. Select this option.

   ❑ **D**igits. The field can contain numeric characters. Do not select this option.

   ❑ **W**hitespace. The field can contain whitespace, such as spaces, tabs, carriage returns, and line feeds. Select this option in case the dog's name contains more than one word.

   ❑ **O**ther. Check this option to enter other types of characters that are allowed (commas, hyphens, and other punctuation marks). Select this option and add an apostrophe and a hyphen in the **O**ther field.

5. The Numeric Format section enables when you specify a Data **T**ype of integer or number. From the **G**rouping field, choose one of the following:

   ❑ *Comma*. Commas are permissible in the number, such as **123,456,789**.

   ❑ *Period*. Periods are permissible in the number, such as **1456.56** or **127.0.0.1**.

   ❑ *None*. No punctuation is permissible. The number must be entered similar to the following: **1234567689**.

6. The Decimal field in the Numeric Format section enables when you specify a Data Type of number. You specify the punctuation character that you want to use for a decimal point. You can't use the same character that you used for the Grouping field in step 5. Choose one of the following:

   ❏ *Comma*. A comma character is allowed in the number, such as **123,456,789**.

   ❏ *Period*. A period character is allowed in the number, such as **127.0.0.1** or **1234.56**.

7. In the Data Length field, you specify the data length required for the text box. This applies to any data type selected in step 2. If you require a minimum or maximum length, or both, check the **R**equired checkbox. Then, specify the minimum length in the M**i**n Length field and the maximum length in the M**a**x Length field. For your DogName text box, enter **35** in the M**a**x Length field. This restricts the response to 35 characters or less.

8. The Data Value section specifies additional parameters for the text box. Check the **F**ield Must Be option if you require specific input from the user. Then, select one of the following options from the drop-down menu. Finally, enter a representative value in the **V**alue field. You won't select any of these options for the DogName field in your form.

   ❏ *Less than*. Choose this if the value entered in the text box must be less than the number you specify in the Value field. Example: Less than **5**.

   ❏ *Greater than*. Choose this option if the value entered by the user must be greater than the number you specify in the Value field. Example: Greater than **0**.

   ❏ *Less than or equal to*. Choose this option if the value entered by the user must be less than or equal to the number you specify in the Value field. Example: Less than or equal to **10**.

   ❏ *Greater than or equal to*. Choose this option if the value entered by the user must be greater than or equal to the number you specify in the Value field. Example: Greater than or equal to **1**.

   ❏ *Equal to*. Choose this option if the value entered by the user must be equal to the value you specify in the Value field. Example: Equal to **7**.

   ❏ *Not equal to*. Choose this option if the value entered by the user should not equal the value you specify in the Value field. Example: Not equal to **7**.

9. The And Must **B**e field of the Data Value section adds a second condition to the data value constant. The choices are the same as listed previously. Use this option to check whether the value entered by the user meets more than

one condition. For example, if you want to check that the user's entry falls between 1 and 10, inclusive, you set the Field Must Be and And Must **B**e fields as follows:

❏ Field Must Be Greater than or equal to 1

❏ And Must Be Less than or equal to 10

10. Your settings should look as shown in Figure 22.7. Choose OK to apply the settings to your text box.

Requesting Multiline Text Input

Use the **I**nsert | Form Fiel**d** | **S**crolling Text Box command to insert a multiline or paragraph text box field on your form. Figure 22.8 shows a scrolling text box added to your form.

Figure 22.8.

Scrolling text boxes are used for lengthy text responses.

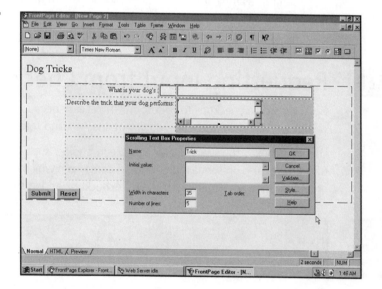

To place a scrolling text box on your form, do the following:

1. Position the insertion point in the yellow cell in the second row. Enter
   Describe the trick that your dog performs:.

2. Position the insertion point in the orange cell in the second row. Choose **I**nsert | Form Fiel**d** | **S**crolling Text Box or click the Scrolling Text Box button on the Forms toolbar. The scrolling text box appears in the cell.

3. Click to select the scrolling text box and then press Alt+Enter. The Scrolling Text Box Properties dialog box appears.

4. In the **N**ame field, enter a name for the scrolling text field. This name coincides with the name/value pair that is reported to the form handler. Enter `Trick`.

5. If you want the scrolling text box to have a default value when the form initially appears on the page, enter the text in the Initial **v**alue field. Leave this blank for your form field.

6. In the **W**idth in characters field, enter a width for your scrolling text box. Like the text box field, this is a screen width, not the number of characters it can contain. The default width is 20 characters. Enter `35`, the same width as the text box.

7. Enter the height of the scrolling text box in the Number of **l**ines field. The default height is 2 lines. Increase this to `5`.

8. Press the **V**alidate button and notice that the scrolling text box uses the same validation screen as the text box, discussed previously. Leave all the settings as they are. No validation script is written for the scrolling text box.

9. Click OK to exit the Text Box Validation dialog box. You return to the Scrolling Text Box Properties dialog box. Choose OK to apply the settings.

Requesting Input from Checkboxes

Next, you add a checkbox to your form. This is easy because checkboxes don't need validation—they're either checked or not checked and that's it.

Use checkboxes to give the user a boolean choice, such as Yes/No or True/False. Checkboxes also present a multiple list of items from which the user can select single or multiple choices. Figure 22.9 shows a checkbox added to your form.

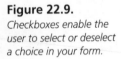

Figure 22.9.
Checkboxes enable the user to select or deselect a choice in your form.

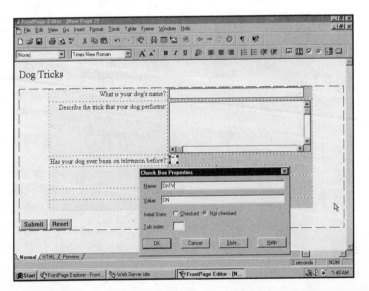

TIP: Checkboxes are often arranged in groups. You can place the first one on your form and copy it and its label to your clipboard. Then, you can paste in the additional checkboxes and edit the properties of the copies. This saves you a few extra steps, and it helps you visualize the layout.

To place a checkbox on your form, follow these steps:

1. Click in the yellow cell in the third row. Enter **Has your dog ever been on television before?**.

2. Click in the orange cell in the third row and choose Insert l Form Field l Check Box, or click the Checkbox button on the Forms toolbar. The checkbox appears in the table.

3. Click to select the checkbox and press Alt+Enter. The Checkbox Properties dialog box appears.

4. In the **N**ame field, enter a name for the checkbox field. This name coincides with the name/value pair that is reported to the form handler. Enter **OnTV**.

5. In the **V**alue field, enter a value for the checkbox. It is easiest to enter a value that makes sense when you receive the results for the form. Usually, you enter the value that represents the checked state of the checkbox. Leave it set at the default of **ON**.

6. In the Initial State field, select either the **C**hecked or **N**ot checked radio button. Leave the option set at the default setting of **N**ot Checked.

7. Choose OK. The settings are applied to your checkbox.

8. Position the insertion point after the checkbox. Enter **Check if Yes**.

 # Requesting Input from Radio Buttons

Radio buttons are similar to checkboxes in that they give the user a boolean choice. Typically, radio buttons are arranged in a group and assigned a group name. The user selects only one option from the group. The group name and the value assigned to each selected button are sent to the form handler after the user submits the form. Figure 22.10 shows a group of six radio buttons entered into the divided cells on the right side of the table.

To place radio buttons on your form, do the following:

1. Position the insertion point in the yellow cell in the fourth row. Enter **How old is your dog?**.

Figure 22.10.

Radio buttons give the user a boolean choice. They typically are arranged in groups, and usually one button of the group is selected.

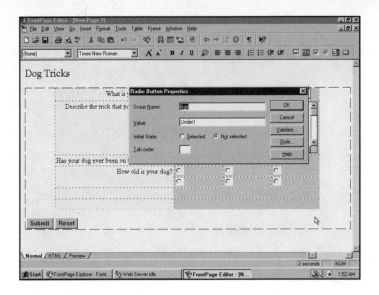

2. Click inside the orange cell in the first column of the fourth row. Choose Insert | Form Fie**l**d | **R**adio Button or click the Radio Button button on the Forms toolbar. The radio button appears in the cell.

3. Double-click the radio button to open the Radio Button Properties dialog box.

4. In the Group **N**ame field, enter a name for the group of radio buttons. This name is assigned to all the radio buttons in the group, and it coincides with the name/value pair that is reported to the form handler. Enter **Age**.

TIP:
Inserting radio buttons is one time when copying the first button and pasting copies to your form really helps. You can keep the group name consistent if you enter the properties for the first radio button and copy additional radio buttons on the page.

5. In the **V**alue field, enter a value for the individual radio button. You want the first radio button to represent a choice of less than 1 year. Enter **Under1**.

6. In the Initial State field, select either the **S**elected or N**o**t selected radio button. Leave the initial state set at the default value of N**o**t Selected.

7. You'll notice at this point that the **V**alidate button is disabled. That's because the validation settings apply to radio buttons that are in a group. Choose OK at this point to apply the settings to the first radio button.

8. Click the radio button to select it. Use Ctrl+C to copy it into your clipboard.

9. Paste one radio button into each of the remaining five split cells. You now have six buttons with the same settings in your table. You'll edit the settings in the following two steps.

10. Click immediately after each button and add the labels shown below. Use Figure 22.1 as a guide if necessary:

```
Less than 1      1-2 years      3-5 years
6-8 years        9-10 years     Over 10 years
```

11. For each of the five additional radio buttons, double-click to open its Radio Button Properties dialog box. Change the **V**alue and Initial State settings, as shown in Table 22.1. The first item is already complete.

Table 22.1. Settings for radio buttons.

Label	Value	Initial State
Less than 1	Under1	Not Selected
1-2 years	1-2	Not Selected
3-5 years	3-5	Selected
6-8 years	6-8	Not Selected
9-10 years	9-10	Not Selected
Over 10 years	Over10	Not Selected

 # Validating Radio Buttons

Radio buttons typically are arranged in groups, as you have just seen. When you develop your pages with the Form Page Wizard, the Name field in the Radio Button Properties dialog box typically displays the group name as part of the radio button name—something like Age_1, Age_2, Age_3, and so on. This not only looks a little confusing to the user, but the name isn't the same as the prompt that the user responded to on the page. You can use the Radio Button Validation dialog box, shown in Figure 22.11, to return to the user a display name that matches what the user sees.

For your Dog Tricks page, you don't need to do validations. The steps required to validate a radio button are as follows:

1. Double-click the radio button you want to validate and choose **V**alidate from the Radio Button Properties dialog box. The Radio Button Validation dialog box appears.

2. To specify a different display name, check the Data **R**equired checkbox (this is not checked by default). The Display **N**ame field enables.

Figure 22.11.

You can specify a different radio button name to be returned to the user in the Radio Button Validation dialog box.

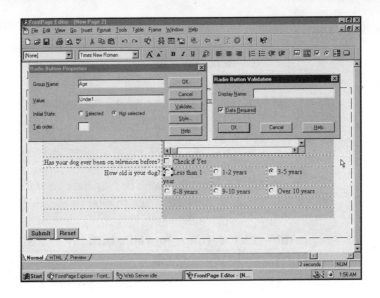

3. Enter the display name that you want to return to the user in the Display **N**ame field.

4. Choose OK to apply the validation settings.

Providing a Menu of Choices

Menus present the user with lists of defined choices. Items are displayed in either a drop-down list or a scrolling list. You can configure a drop-down menu list to permit single or multiple selections. You'll add a single-selection drop-down list to your form.

Figure 22.12.

Drop-down lists contain a list of selections from which the user can choose. They can be configured for single or multiple selections.

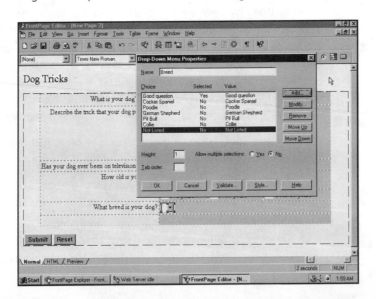

To place a drop-down menu on your form, use the following steps:

1. Click in the yellow cell in the fifth row. Enter **What breed is your dog?**.

2. Click in the adjacent orange cell and choose Insert I Form Field I **D**rop-Down Menu, or click the Drop-Down Menu button on the Forms toolbar. A drop-down menu appears in the cell.

3. Double-click the drop-down menu to open the Drop-Down Menu Properties dialog box.

4. In the **N**ame field, enter a name for the drop-down menu field that appears on your page. This name coincides with the name/value pair that is reported to the form handler. Enter **Breed**.

To enter the first choice in the drop-down menu, use the following steps:

1. Select **A**dd. The Add Choice dialog box appears.

2. In the **C**hoice field, enter the name of the item. For your first choice, enter **Good question**.

3. Usually, the menu choice name you enter in step 2 is sent to the form handler along with its value (selected or not selected). You can specify an optional value to be sent to the form handler in place of the choice name. To do this, check the Specify **V**alue checkbox and enter the optional value in the field beneath the option. (You won't need this option for your form.)

4. In the Initial State field, select either the **S**elected or **N**ot Selected radio button. The default value is **N**ot Selected. Change this value to Selected for the choice you just added.

5. Click OK. The menu item appears in the Drop-Down Menu Properties dialog box.

6. Repeat steps 1 through 5 to add the additional choices shown in Table 22.2 to your drop-down menu. When you're done, your Drop-Down Menu Properties settings should look as shown in Figure 22.12.

Table 22.2. Drop-down menu choices.

Choice	Initial State
Cocker Spaniel	**N**ot Selected
Poodle	**N**ot Selected
German Shepherd	**N**ot Selected
Pit Bull	**N**ot Selected
Collie	**N**ot Selected
Not Listed	**N**ot Selected

7. After you complete your choice list, use the Allow multiple selections field to specify whether you want to allow multiple responses from the user. Choose **Y**es if you want to permit multiple selections from the drop-down menu. Choose N**o** for single selections. Select N**o** for your Dog Tricks form.

8. In the He**i**ght field of the Drop-Down Menu Properties dialog box, enter the number of rows that the drop-down menu list should display. Leave the value set at the default of 1 row.

9. If you want to rearrange the order of your choices, highlight the choice you want to move and then click Move **U**p or Move **D**own, as required. The item is relocated as specified.

10. Choose OK to apply all the settings to the drop-down list.

Based on the He**i**ght and Allow multiple selections settings, the drop-down menu can appear in several ways. Table 22.3 shows how most browsers display a drop-down menu based on your choices.

Table 22.3. Drop-down menu appearances.

Height	Multiple	Appearance
1	No	Displays as a drop-down list
1	Yes	Displays as a scrollable list with half-height arrows
2 or above	No	Displays as a scrollable list with half-height arrows
2 or above	Yes	Displays as a scrollable list with half-height arrows (may be difficult to use unless the list height is sufficient to display all or most items in the drop-down menu list)

Validating Drop-Down Menus

When you validate a drop-down menu, you have one or two options to select, depending on whether your drop-down menu allows single or multiple choices. To validate a drop-down menu, follow these steps:

1. Right-click the drop-down menu that you want to validate and choose Form Field Validation from the pop-up menu. The Drop-Down Menu Validation dialog box shown in Figure 22.13 appears.

Figure 22.13.

Validate your drop-down menus in the Drop-Down Menu Validation dialog box.

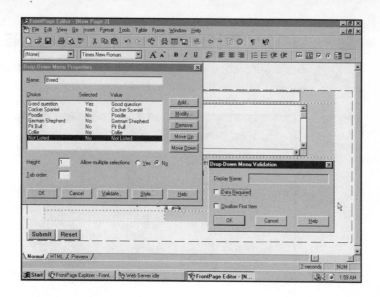

2. In the Display **N**ame field, enter a field name that should be returned to the user in validation warnings. This name is used if the form field's internal name is different from what you want to return to the user.

3. Select the Data **R**equired checkbox if you require at least one selection from this field.

4. If you configured your drop-down menu to allow multiple selections, you see two options that are not present for single-selection drop-down menus:

   ❏ *Minimum Items.* Select this option if you want the user to select a minimum number of choices, and add the minimum number in the M**i**nimum Items field.

   ❏ *Maximum Items.* Select this option if you want the user to select not more than a maximum number of choices, and add the maximum number in the M**a**ximum Items field.

5. Select **D**isallow First Item if you don't want the first item to be selected by the user. For example, if you use the first item in the drop-down menu to display an instruction to the user rather than a choice, you can select Disallow First Item to prohibit the user from entering the instruction as a choice.

6. Click OK to apply the validation settings.

TASK Inserting Buttons on Forms

You use pushbutton fields to submit or reset the data that the user enters in form fields. You can insert more than one pushbutton on a form, as Figure 22.14 shows.

Figure 22.14.

Pushbuttons are used to submit or clear the data from the form.

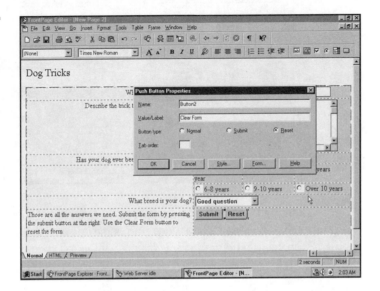

FrontPage provides three types of pushbuttons that forms can use: **No**rmal buttons, **S**ubmit buttons, and **R**eset buttons. Use **No**rmal buttons when you want to write custom scripts to process your forms (such as JavaScripts and ActiveX scripts).

To place a pushbutton on your form, follow these steps:

1. Click inside the bottom yellow cell. Enter **Those are all the answers we need. Submit the form by pressing the submit button at the right. Use the Clear Form button to reset the form.**

2. Click in the bottom orange cell. Choose **I**nsert | Form Fiel**d** | **P**ush Button twice to insert two pushbuttons in the cell.

3. Double-click the left pushbutton. The Pushbutton Properties dialog box appears.

4. In the **N**ame field, enter a name for the pushbutton. This name coincides with the name/value pair that is reported to the form handler. Enter **Button1**.

5. In the **V**alue/Label field, enter a value for the pushbutton. By default, the value `Button` appears as a label for a normal button. `Submit` appears as a label for a submit button, and the value `Reset` appears as a label for a reset button. Leave the value set at the default of `Submit`.

6. Select the type of button that you want to insert. The choices are **N**ormal (used with custom scripts), **S**ubmit (used to submit the form), and **R**eset (used to clear the form). Choose **S**ubmit.

7. Click OK. The settings are applied to the button.

8. Double-click the second button and assign the following settings in the Pushbutton Properties dialog box:

Name:	Button2
Value/Label:	Clear Form
Button Type:	**R**eset

9. Click OK. The settings are applied to the second button.

10. To complete the form, choose **E**dit | Select All. Select Arial from the Change Font drop-down menu. Reduce the size of the font by clicking the Decrease Font Size button once.

11. Choose **F**ile | **S**ave (Ctrl+S) or click the Save button on the Standard toolbar. The Save As dialog box appears. The **T**itle field should read Dog Tricks, and the **U**RL field should read dogtrick.htm. Choose OK to save the page.

 ## Using Image Form Fields

If you write custom form handlers, you can use graphics (image form fields) to submit data entered on your forms. Any image can be a button on a form. When a user submits a form by clicking an image field, FrontPage passes the coordinates from the image's coordinate system to the form handler. The WebBots do not use this coordinate information, so you must create a custom form handler with a language such as CGI, JavaScript, or VBScript to process the coordinates.

To place an image form field on your form, do the following:

1. From the FrontPage Editor, choose **I**nsert | Form Fiel**d** | **I**mage. The Image dialog box appears.

2. Locate an image as follows:

   ❑ To insert an image from the current Web, choose the Current Web tab. Locate the folder in which your image is located. Select the image and choose OK.

   ❑ To insert an image from a file on your local or network hard drive, click the Other Location tab. Choose the From File radio button and click the **B**rowse button to locate the image. Select the image and choose **O**pen. The image appears on your page.

❏ To insert an image from the World Wide Web, click the Other Location tab. Choose the **F**rom Location radio button and enter the URL of the image in the field. Then, click OK to return to the FrontPage Editor. The image appears on your page.

3. Double-click the image to open the Image Form Field Properties dialog box.

4. To change the image properties, click the Image **P**roperties button. The Image Properties dialog box appears. Set image properties as indicated in Chapter 10, "Composing and Editing Pages," and choose OK. You return to the Image Form Field Properties dialog box.

5. Enter a name for the image form field in the **N**ame field.

6. Click OK to apply the settings to your image form field.

Using Hidden Form Fields

Use hidden form fields to pass information from one form to another. For example, the product data sheet that you created with the Corporate Presence Web Wizard (see Chapter 7, "Real-Life Examples I: Using What You've Got") contains an information request form. This information request form uses a hidden form field to pass the name of the product to the results file and to the confirmation form that is sent to the user.

You can use hidden form fields in other ways as well. Suppose that your first form has a question such as `How long ago did you read this book?` and that the user responds `16 days`. A custom script looks at that value and determines that the user read the book within the last month. The CGI script returns a hidden form field from the first form to the user in a second page that says `You read your favorite book in the last 1 month`.

To create a hidden form field, do the following:

1. Click anywhere inside a form that appears on your page.

2. Right-click and choose Form Properties from the pop-up menu. The Form Properties dialog box appears.

3. In the Hidden Fields area, click the **A**dd button. The Name/Value Pair dialog box appears.

4. Enter a name for the hidden form field in the **N**ame field.

5. Enter a value to associate with the name in the **V**alue field. The value can be any text string.

6. Click OK to close the Name/Value Pair and Form Properties dialog boxes.

To modify a hidden form field, follow these steps:

1. Click anywhere inside a form that appears on your page.
2. Right-click and choose Form Properties from the pop-up menu. The Form Properties dialog box appears.
3. In the Form Properties dialog box, select the field to change from the Hidden Fields section.
4. Click the **M**odify button. The Name/Value Pair dialog box appears.
5. Edit the values in the **N**ame field or the **V**alue field.
6. Click OK to close the Name/Value Pair and Form Properties dialog boxes.

To delete a hidden form field, use the following steps:

1. Click anywhere inside a form that appears on your page.
2. Right-click and choose Form Properties from the pop-up menu. The Form Properties dialog box appears.
3. In the Form Properties dialog box, select the field to change from the Hidden Fields section.
4. Click the **R**emove button. The hidden form field is removed from the list.
5. Click OK to close the Hidden Form Field and Form Properties dialog boxes.

Workshop Wrap-Up

You already learned how to create forms quickly by using the Form Page Wizard. In this chapter, you learned how to add and validate your own form fields and edit their properties. There now remains one major step in designing your forms, which you learn about in the next chapter.

In this chapter, you learned about the various form fields that you can use. You learned how to insert them in your Web pages and how to configure each type of field. You learned how to use form field validations to validate the user's entries.

Next Steps

In the next chapter, you learn how to assign a form handler to your forms and what the runtime WebBots do. You learn different ways to configure your forms. You can also find related information in the following chapters:

❏ See Chapter 24, "Real-Life Examples IV: Adding Interactivity," to learn how to configure a discussion group easily. The steps outlined in this chapter help you edit the form fields created in your discussion groups.

❏ Chapter 5, "Lightning-Speed Web Design," discusses how to create pages from the FrontPage page templates. Several of these pages include forms that are already made for you. This includes the Confirmation Form, Feedback Form, Guest Book, Search Page, and User Registration Page.

Q&A

Q: Can I design any form from scratch and not use the templates or the Form Page Wizard?

A: As you learned in this chapter, it's quite easy to do. You might find the Form Page Wizard a lot quicker, especially when it comes to laying out a long form.

Q: I don't like the way my form looks. What is the easiest way to delete it and start over again?

A: There are a couple of ways in which you can delete a form from a page. For example, delete every object on the form and use the Backspace or Delete key to delete the form. To delete a form field, use the Delete or Backspace key. Alternatively, position the cursor in the upper-left corner of the form, where it turns into a selection pointer. Double-click to select the entire form and cut the page to the clipboard, or use the Del key to delete the form from the page.

Q: When I do validations on text fields, can I set up a number to contain both commas and periods, in case a user enters a number such as 12,557.95?

A: Yes. In the Data Type field, specify Number. In the Numeric Format Grouping field, specify Comma. In the Numeric Format Decimal field, specify Period. That should do it!

TWENTY-THREE

Configuring Form Handlers

In the previous two chapters, you learned how to design forms for your Web pages. The only thing that remains is to assign a form handler to your form. FrontPage 98 provides several types of form handlers, one of which is the Save Results component. This component enables you to process the results on general forms, such as a guest book, survey page, feedback form, or other form of a general nature.

Why are the FrontPage form handling components so special? They save you the bother of having to write a custom form handler yourself. Scout the shelves in your local bookstore, and you'll see rows of books on CGI, Perl, Java, JavaScript, VBScript, and countless other languages that can be used with your Web pages. With these scripting languages, you can add functionality to your Web pages—if you want to get into programming, that is.

For those who don't want to learn all those other programming techniques, you have the FrontPage components to fall back on, which are really nothing more than custom CGI scripts designed to work with the FrontPage Server Extensions—like the plug-and-play of Web pages.

The Purpose of Results Files

It might help you figure out what's going on here if you know what a results file is. In Chapter 21, "Quick and Easy Forms," and Chapter 22, "Adding and Editing Form Fields," you learned how to design forms and configure the form fields. Each of the fields on your form accepts input from a user. When the user presses the Submit button to process the form, the form handler extracts the data that the user entered in the form fields and sends that data to you. The data is saved into a *results file* that can be stored on your Web site or sent to you by e-mail.

The file formats you can select for your results files are shown in Table 23.1. A results file can be saved as an HTML page or as a text file. Text results files are a better choice in many cases, because the server does not have to take additional time to format the user's responses into HTML code. In addition, text files can be delimited by spaces, tabs, or commas and input into database software. When you want the user's responses to be placed directly on a page in your Web, such as for a guest book, choose one of the HTML file formats.

Results files cumulate user responses as they are received. Each response received from a user is combined with previous responses into one file. You can select whether the most recent results are placed at the beginning or end of the results file.

Table 23.1. File formats for results files.

Format	Description
HTML	The user's responses are saved to an HTML file, with the user's responses saved as normal paragraphs.
HTML definition list	The responses are saved to an HTML file, with form field entries saved in a definition list. The field names are formatted as terms, and the user's responses are formatted as definitions.
HTML bulleted list	The responses are saved to an HTML file, with form field entries saved in a bulleted list.
Formatted text within HTML	The responses are saved to an HTML file, with the user's responses saved as formatted paragraphs.
Formatted text	The responses are saved to a text file, with line breaks separating each response.

Format	Description
Comma-separated text file	Choose Text database using comma as a separator to save the user's responses in a comma-separated text file. Responses in the results file are enclosed by quotation marks.
Tab-delimited text file	Choose Text database using tab as a separator to save the user's responses to a tab-delimited text file. Each response entered by the user will be separated by a tab. This is the most common choice for text files that will be used with database file formats.
Space-delimited text file	Choose Text database using space as a separator to save the user's responses to a space-delimited text file.

NOTE: If you choose one of the first four options shown in Table 23.1, be sure to specify a results filename that ends with `.htm` or `.html`. If you select one of the last four options, specify a filename with a `.txt` extension.

Creating the Web for This Chapter

In the previous two chapters, you learned how to create forms using the Forms Page Wizard and how to add and configure your own form fields. In this chapter, you'll assign a form handler to a slightly modified version of the Dog Tricks form that you created in the previous chapter. The main difference between the two forms is that the version in this chapter does not use any special font formatting and can be used with themes. The revised page and an associated confirmation page are located in the `Book\Chap23\Project Files` folder on the CD-ROM that accompanies this book.

From the FrontPage Explorer, create an Empty Web and use the **F**ile | **I**mport command from the FrontPage Explorer to import `dogtrick.htm` and `tricks-conf.htm` into the Web's home folder. Use Themes view to select a light theme for your Web.

Assigning the Save Results Component to a Form

The Save Results component is the general-purpose form handler in FrontPage. It is used for many types of forms. Survey forms, guest books, information forms, and online ordering forms are some examples of what you can do with a Save Results component. Figure 23.1 shows the new Dog Tricks form. All the form fields on the Dog Tricks page have already been configured and are ready to go.

Figure 23.1.

You can use the Save Results component for forms of a general nature, such as the Dog Tricks form.

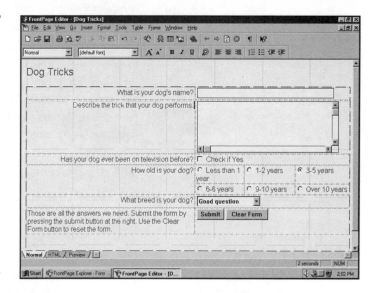

FrontPage 98 provides a few other form handling components that serve special functions. See Chapter 24, "Real-Life Examples IV: Adding Interactivity," to learn more about the Discussion Form Handler. In Chapter 33, "Designing Private Webs," you learn about the Registration Form Handler.

When you assign the Save Results component as a form handler, it gathers information from the form and stores it in a variety of Web page and text formats.

To assign the Save Results component as a form handler for a form, follow these steps:

1. From Folders view in the FrontPage Explorer, double-click the `dogtrick.htm` page to open it in the FrontPage Editor.

2. Right-click anywhere inside the form (the area enclosed by dashed lines).

3. Choose Form Properties from the pop-up menu to open the Form Properties dialog box, shown in Figure 23.2.

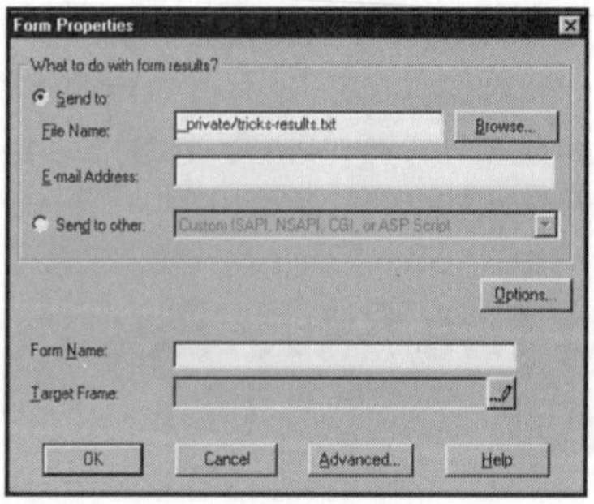

Figure 23.2.

Use the Form Properties dialog box to assign a form handler to your form.

4. Choose the first of the following three options to configure the results file for your form:

   ❏ To save the user's responses to a page in your current Web, select the **S**end to radio button. Enter the relative URL of the page in your current Web or use the **B**rowse button to select a page from the Current Web dialog box. Choose OK to return to the Form Properties dialog box after you select your file. If the file does not already exist in your Web, FrontPage 98 automatically creates the file for you. Enter `_private/tricks-results.txt` in this field.

   ❏ To save the user's responses to a page in your root Web (such as when you are configuring a registration form for a private Web), enter a server-relative URL that points to a file in your `_vti_log` folder in the root Web. You learn how to save a registration form to your root Web in Chapter 33.

   ❏ To save the user's responses to a file on your local or network hard drive, enter the complete path to the file (for example, `c:\web_results\users\user-results.txt` or `c:\web_results\users\user-results.htm`).

NOTE: Saving results to files on a local or network hard drive is appropriate for intranet applications. If your Web resides on a server that is hosted by an Internet Service Provider, you should not save form results to a file or folder on your local or network hard drive. You may not be online when users process the form, so you'll want to save your results to a file on your remote Web site.

5. By default, the form results are saved to a comma-delimited text file, which can be imported into many database programs. The form field names are listed along with the information entered by the user. If you want to change any of these options, click the **O**ptions button to open the Options for Saving Results of Form dialog box. Choose the File Results tab shown in Figure 23.3.

6. From the upper section of the File Results dialog box, enter or select the following options:

   File Name. This field contains the path to the file you selected in step 3. You can use the **B**rowse button in the File Results tab to change your selection, if desired.

Figure 23.3.

Use the File Results tab in the Options for Saving Results of Form dialog box to configure the name and file format for the results file.

File Format. Choose the file format for your results file. For your Dog Tricks form, use the default selection of Text database, using a comma as a separator. Other file format options are listed in Table 23.1.

Include field names. Check this option to include the form field names with the user's responses in the results file. Uncheck this option to create a results file without headers, which you can import directly into a database program. Leave this option checked for your Dog Tricks form.

Latest Results at End. Disabled when you choose a text file format. When checked, form results are added to the end of the page each time a user responds to the fields on your form. When not checked, the most recent form results appear at the top of the Web page.

7. If you want to create a second results file that uses a different file format, complete the items in the Optional Second File section. The options you select in this area are similar to those described in step 5.

8. Choose OK to exit the Options for Saving Results of Form dialog box. You return to the Form Properties dialog box.

9. If your form results are to be sent to a frame in a frameset, enter the name of the frame in the Target Frame field. For more information about framesets, refer to Chapter 18, "Frames: Pages with Split Personalities." Leave this option blank for your Dog Tricks form.

10. Click the **A**dvanced button to configure any hidden form fields for your form. These are discussed in more detail in Chapter 22. Skip this step for now.

Configuring Confirmation Page Options

Now you can assign the custom confirmation page to your form. By default, FrontPage 98 generates a generic confirmation page that displays the information that the user entered into the form fields. This lets the user know that his or her information was received and processed by the form handler and that the data is on its way to you. You can create your own confirmation pages as well. The steps to creating a confirmation page are described in the section "Confirming Pages," later in this chapter. After you create your confirmation page, you use the Confirmation Page tab in the Options for Saving Results of Form dialog box to assign your custom confirmation page to the form handler.

To assign your custom confirmation page, follow these steps:

1. From the Form Properties dialog box, click the Options button. The Options for Saving Results of Form dialog box appears.

2. Click the Confirmation Page tab, shown in Figure 23.4.

Figure 23.4.

Use the Confirmation Page tab in the Options for Saving Results of Form dialog box to assign and configure your confirmation page.

3. Enter the URL of a page in your current Web or click the **B**rowse button to select a page from the Current Web dialog box. For your Dog Tricks page, either type `tricks-conf.htm` in this field or click the **B**rowse button and select this page to assign it. Choose OK to return to the Confirmation Page tab.

4. You can also specify a validation failure page. This is a page that you create and send to the user when he or she enters information that does not meet the criteria that you specify for the form field. Enter the URL of a page in your current Web or choose the Bro**w**se button to select a page from your current Web. Choose OK to return to the Confirmation Page tab. The Dog Tricks form does not use form field validation (discussed in Chapter 22), so you can skip this step.

 # Configuring Saved Fields Options

By default, all the form fields on your page are saved to the results file. You can use the Saved Fields tab in the Options for Saving Results of Form dialog box to customize the form fields that are saved in your results file. You can change the order of the fields, select subsets of fields, or save additional information with your results file.

To configure your saved field options, follow these steps:

1. From the Options for Saving Results of Form dialog box, click the Saved Fields tab, shown in Figure 23.5.

Figure 23.5.

Use the Saved Fields tab in the Options for Saving Results of Form dialog box to select the information you want to include in your results file.

2. All the fields that appear on your form are listed in the Form Fields to Save list. If you leave this list blank, all the form fields on your page will be written in the order in which they appear on the form. You can change the order of the fields to list the user's responses in a different order from that which appears on the form. List each field name you want to receive on a separate line and in the order you want each to appear in your results file. For the Dog Tricks form, leave these settings as they are.

3. From the Additional information to save section, choose **D**ate and User **n**ame for your Dog Tricks form. The options you can select are as follows:

    Time. Includes the time that the user submitted the form.

    Date. Includes the date that the user submitted the form.

    Remote Computer Name. Includes the user's IP address in the results file.

    User name. Includes the user's name in the results file.

    Browser type. Includes information about the user's browser. This is very handy information to track if you want to make sure you are designing your pages for the right browsers!

4. Choose OK to exit the Options for Saving Results of Form dialog box.

5. Choose OK to exit the Form Properties dialog box. Your confirmation page is configured.

6. Choose **File | S**ave (Ctrl+S) to save the Dog Tricks page to your Web. You can now preview and test the form in your browser.

At this point, when you test your form, you should see the custom confirmation page appear after you press the Submit button. Note, however, that the data you entered in the form will not yet appear in the confirmation page, because you still have to configure the confirmation field components on that page. You will complete these steps in the section "Confirming Pages," later in this chapter.

To test your form, make sure that the FrontPage Server Extensions are running on your server. Use the **F**ile I Preview in **B**rowser command to select the browser you want to preview your page in; then press the Preview button. The form opens in your browser.

Enter some responses in your form, as shown in Figure 23.6. Then press the Submit button. Your browser may issue a security warning that you are about to send information over the Internet. Choose Yes or OK to continue. If your form is configured properly, you should see the custom confirmation page appear in your browser, as shown in Figure 23.7.

NOTE: If you receive a message that the `_vti_bin/shtml.dll` file does not exist on your server, it could mean one of two things. Either you do not have your server running on your local computer, or your ISP or remote server does not have the FrontPage Server Extensions installed. Contact your server administrator to resolve this problem.

Figure 23.6.

Enter some responses into your Dog Tricks form and press the Submit button.

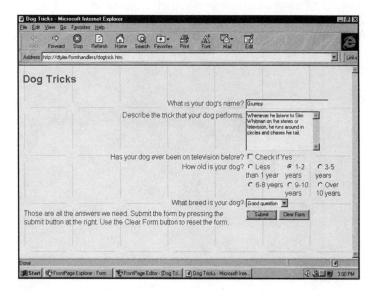

Figure 23.7.
If your form is working properly, the confirmation page should display in your browser after you submit the form.

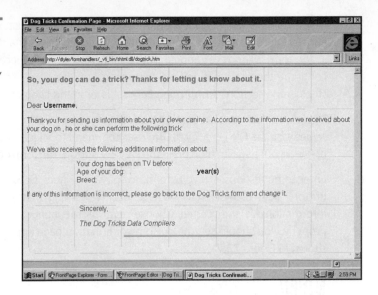

To view your results file, go to the FrontPage Explorer and choose **T**ools I **W**eb Settings. Click the Advanced tab in the FrontPage Web Settings dialog box. In the Options section, check Show documents in **h**idden directories and click OK. When FrontPage asks whether you want to refresh the Web, answer **Y**es.

Double-click the `tricks-results.txt` file located in the `_private` directory in your Web. The file should open in Notepad or the editor that you have configured to open text files. An example of the file is shown in Figure 23.8. If you configured your results file to be saved in HTML format, you can open it in the FrontPage Editor.

Figure 23.8.
Open your text results file in Notepad or the editor you have configured for text files.

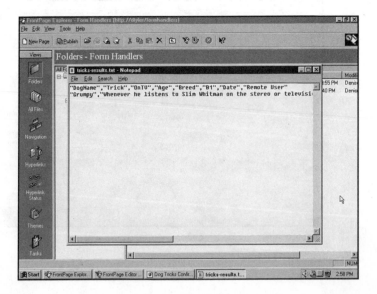

Configuring Your Mail Server in FrontPage 98

In order to send your form results to an e-mail address, you need to configure the FrontPage 98 Server Extensions to understand how to reach an SMTP mail server. If your Web site will reside on a FrontPage Web hosted by an Internet Service Provider, your ISP will need to set up this configuration on its end as well.

To test this feature on your own Windows 95 system, however, you need to add an entry to the `frontpg.ini` file that is located in your `c:\windows` folder (by default). To add the configuration, follow these steps:

1. From the Windows 95 Start menu, choose the Windows Explorer.

2. Locate your Windows installation directory (`c:\windows`, by default). Double-click the `frontpg.ini` file in that directory to open the file in Notepad.

3. Scroll down until you find the section that begins with the following code:

   `[FrontPage 3.0]`

4. Position the insertion point at the end of the last line in that section and press Enter. Add the name of your SMTP mail server, replacing the mail server name shown below with your mail server name. To configure an e-mail program, add the second line, revising the path to the executable file for your e-mail program appropriately:

   ```
   SMTPHost=mail.servername.com
   SendMailCommand=d:\Eudora\Eudora.exe
   ```

5. Choose File | Save to save the file to your hard drive, then choose File | Exit to close NotePad. The change will take effect the next time you start FrontPage.

 # Sending Form Results to an E-Mail Address

Sometimes, you may have a need to obtain form results right away. In these cases, you can configure your form handler to send form results to you by e-mail. By default, e-mail results files are saved as formatted text. The form field names are listed along with the information entered by the user. You will need to use the Options button in the Form Properties dialog box to configure additional options for your e-mail results file.

To send the results file to an e-mail address, configure the form handler as follows:

1. Right-click anywhere inside the form (the area enclosed by dashed lines).

2. Choose Form Properties from the pop-up menu to open the Form Properties dialog box.

3. To configure the form to send the user's responses to an e-mail address, enter the e-mail address you want to send the results to. The following is an example:

```
webmaster@dogtricks.com
```

4. To configure additional options, click the **O**ptions button to open the Options for Saving Results of Form dialog box. Choose the E-mail Results tab shown in Figure 23.9.

Figure 23.9.

Use the E-mail Results tab to configure options for an e-mail results file.

5. The e-mail address you entered in step 3 appears in the E-mail **A**ddress to Receive Results field. Revise this address if necessary.

6. Use the E-mail **F**ormat drop-down menu to select a file format for your E-mail results file. The default choice is Formatted text. Other options are listed in Table 23.1.

7. In the E-mail Message Header section, enter or choose the following options:

*S*ubject Line. Enter the text that should appear in the subject line of the e-mail message you receive. This should be descriptive so that you recognize that it is results from a form on your Web site. For example, enter `Dog Tricks Results File`.

*Form Field N*ame. Check this option if you want the subject line to contain information that the user entered in one of the form fields on your page. For example, the subject line of your e-mail message could contain the name of the user's dog. Check the Form Field **N**ame option and enter `DogName` in the field to test this option if you prefer.

*R*eply-to Line. Enter the text that should appear in the reply-to line of the e-mail message you receive. If, for example, you want to automatically forward a copy of an e-mail message to another person or company, uncheck the Form Field Na**m**e option and enter the e-mail address in the Reply-to Line field. Leave this field blank if you don't want to generate an automatic reply.

Form Field Name. Check this option if you want the reply-to line to contain information that the user entered in one of the form fields on your page (for example, one of the fields on your form might contain the user's e-mail address). Enter the name of the form field in which the user enters this information.

8. Configure the Confirmation Page and Saved Fields tabs as outlined earlier in this chapter in the sections "Configuring Confirmation Page Options" and "Configuring Saved Fields Options."

9. Choose OK to exit the Options for Saving Results of Form dialog box. You return to the Form Properties dialog box.

10. Click the Advanced button to configure any hidden form fields for your form. These are discussed in more detail in Chapter 22.

11. Choose OK to exit the Form Properties dialog box. Your form is configured.

12. Save the page to your Web using the **F**ile I **S**ave (Ctrl+S) command or the Save button on the Standard toolbar.

To test your form, make sure that the FrontPage Server Extensions are running on your server. Use the **F**ile I Preview in **B**rowser command to select the browser you want to preview your page in; then press the **P**review button. The form opens in your browser.

Again, enter some responses in your form and press the Submit button. If your form is configured properly, you should see the custom confirmation page appear in your browser. The form results are sent to the e-mail address you specified.

Confirming Pages

When users send a response from a form to your site, it's nice to send them a thank you with a confirmation form. It lets users know that their information was received. The confirmation form can also include details about what you'll do with the information after you get it. For example, if you created a survey form, you can inform users that once the survey is complete and tabulated, you'll post the results on your site. The confirmation page can also be as simple as acknowledging that you received the information.

Figure 23.10 shows a confirmation page for the form that you are working with in this chapter. The areas contained in bracketed text are placed there with Confirmation Field components. These components work at runtime and require processing from the server to insert the replacement text. It extracts information from the originating form and places the data on the confirming page.

Figure 23.10.

Confirmation fields, which confirm responses from the user, are placed into pages with the Confirmation Field component.

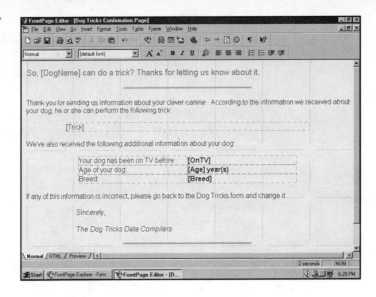

To configure the Dog Tricks confirmation form, follow these steps:

1. From the FrontPage Editor, choose **F**ile | **O**pen (Ctrl+O) or click the Open button on the Standard toolbar. The Open dialog box appears.

2. From the list of files in your current Web, double-click `tricks-conf.htm` to open it. The page appears in the FrontPage Editor.

3. Highlight the text in the top heading that reads `your dog`.

4. Choose **I**nsert | Front**P**age Component and choose Confirmation Field from the Insert FrontPage Component dialog box. Choose OK. The Confirmation Field Properties dialog box shown in Figure 23.11 appears.

Figure 23.11.

Enter a confirmation field in a page by using the Confirmation Field Properties dialog box.

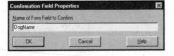

5. In the **N**ame of Form Field to Confirm field, enter `DogName`. When the user receives the confirmation, his or her dog's name appears in the Confirmation Field component's place.

6. Choose OK. The name of the field is inserted into your confirmation form, surrounded by brackets.

7. Position the insertion point in the first table. Repeat steps 4 through 6 to insert a confirmation field named `Trick`.

8. Position the insertion point in the top-right cell in the second table. Repeat steps 4 through 6 to insert a confirmation field named onTV.

9. Position the insertion point just before the text that reads year(s) in the middle-right cell in the second table. Repeat steps 4 through 6 to insert a confirmation field named Age.

10. Position the insertion point in the bottom-right cell in the second table. Repeat steps 4 through 6 to insert a confirmation field named Age.

11. Choose **F**ile I **S**ave (Ctrl+S) to save the confirmation page to your Web.

Open the submission form in your Web browser again, using the **F**ile I Preview in **B**rowser command. Enter some information in the form fields and resubmit the form. This time, the information you submitted with the form appears in place of the confirmation page, as shown in Figure 23.12.

Figure 23.12.
The Confirmation Field components place the data entered into the form fields into the confirmation form.

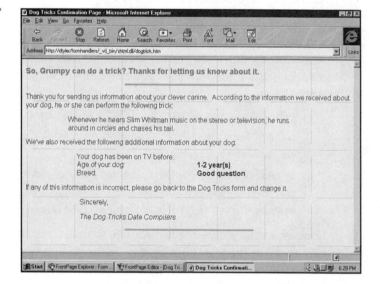

How to Assign Custom ISAPI, NSAPI, CGI, or ASP Scripts

One of the options you have if your Internet service provider does not have the FrontPage Server Extensions installed is using a custom ISAPI, NSAPI, CGI, or ASP script to process your forms. CGI (Common Gateway Interface) scripts are typically platform-dependent, and they reside on your service provider's server. You need to coordinate usage of CGI scripts with them. ISAPI (Internet Server Application Programming Interface) is an interface developed by Process Software and Microsoft Corporation.

NSAPI (Netscape Server Application Programming Interface) is an interface developed by Netscape Communications Corporation and runs only on Netscape servers. ASP scripts work with Active Server Pages, a component of Microsoft Internet Information Server 3.0 or later, and the Microsoft Personal Web Server with Active Server Extensions.

You might want to include advanced features in your form, such as automatically entering the results in a database or spreadsheet or tabulating totals in an online ordering form. In that case, some programming of your own is definitely in order. What's important to learn here is how to configure your FrontPage form to use that custom script. In the following task, you will configure an example for a CGI script. The steps to configure other scripting languages are similar.

Using Custom Scripts

A form and script are usually developed in concert with each other. The script contains information on how to handle each of the form fields in the form, along with other instructions for the server. You can find several good examples of CGI scripts you can use, along with the HTML pages associated with them, at the following sites on the Web:

❑ Matt's Script Archive has several good forms with features similar to those some of the components accomplish. You can find his site at `http://worldwidemart.com/scripts/`.

❑ Selena Sol's Public Domain CGI Script Archive also offers some creative examples of how you can use CGI scripts with forms, scripts, and Web page examples. The URL for this site is `http://www.selena.mcp.com/`.

However, even if you use ready-made CGI scripts, you can still expect to spend some time on them. The CGI scripts must be tweaked in many cases to get them up and running on your own site. You might also need to check with your service provider to see whether you can use custom CGI scripts on your site—and if so, where you are allowed to place them. Sometimes, CGI scripts must be assigned a `.cgi` extension to be recognized on the server; other times, they have to be placed in a specific directory to function properly. These particulars should be coordinated with your ISP before you configure your form. At that time, ask your service provider how to assign permissions for the form. It may already have a "frequently asked questions" page on its site that deals with these issues.

If all this sounds confusing, don't feel bad. CGI scripts are not something you can learn to work with in a few minutes; if you find you're still scratching your head after a few days of working with them, you aren't the first. Several good resources on the Web for learning all about CGI scripts are listed in Appendix B, "FrontPage Reference."

Configuring a Form to Use ISAPI, NSAPI, CGI, or ASP Scripts

You assign an ISAPI, NSAPI, CGI, or ASP script to your FrontPage form in much the same way as you assign any of the other form handling components—with the Form Properties dialog box. Here are the steps:

1. Right-click anywhere inside the form and choose Form Properties from the pop-up menu to open the Form Properties dialog box.

2. In the What to do with form results? section, check the Se**n**d to other radio button. The drop-down menu defaults to Custom ISAPI, NSAPI, CGI, or ASP Script.

3. Click **O**ptions to configure the form handler. The Options for Custom Form Handler dialog box shown in Figure 23.13 appears.

Figure 23.13.

Assign a custom ISAPI, NSAPI, CGI, or ASP script to your form in the Options for Custom Form Handler dialog box.

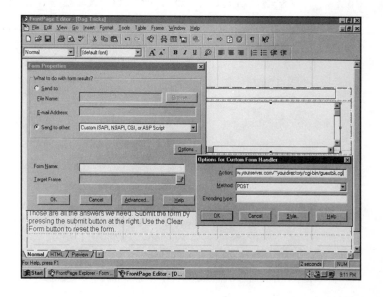

4. In the **A**ction field, enter the absolute URL of the form handler. For example, if your form handler is named `guestbk.cgi` and it resides in the `/cgi-bin` subdirectory of your Web site, the absolute URL might look something like this:

`http://www.yourserver.com/~yourdirectory/cgi-bin/guestbk.cgi`

5. In the **M**ethod field, enter the method the form handler needs to process the form. If you're using one of the examples from either of the sites mentioned earlier, you can see which method was used by examining the

HTML page example provided with the CGI script. You typically have one of the following options:

POST (default). This method passes the name/value pairs to the form handler as input.

GET. This method encodes the name/value pairs of the form and assigns the information to a server variable called QUERY_STRING.

6. In the Encoding **t**ype field, enter the default encoding method used for the form. If you leave this field blank, the following encoding method is used by default:

   `application/x-www-form-urlencoded`

7. Click OK to close each of the Settings for Custom Form Handler and Form Properties dialog boxes.

Assigning a Form to a Frame

You can display forms in tables or frames much as you can any other type of content. To display a form in a table, create the form by using the Form Page Wizard or build your own as you've learned in this section. You can copy the form into the clipboard and paste it into a table, or you can insert the form into another page with an Include component.

You can also configure forms to direct their output to a frame. The steps are as follows:

1. Right-click anywhere inside the form and choose Form Properties from the pop-up menu to open the Form Properties dialog box.

2. Click the Choose Target Frame button located at the right of the **T**arget Frame field. Select the frame into which you want to load the form from the frameset preview on the left side of the Target Frame dialog box, or choose another frame from the Common Targets list. Choose OK to return to the Form Properties dialog box.

3. Click OK to close the Form Properties dialog box.

Workshop Wrap-Up

You should now know the basics about designing forms in FrontPage. If you want to learn more about writing your own scripts, see the online sources listed in Appendix B.

In this chapter, you learned how to configure FrontPage's runtime components—the backbone of form handling in FrontPage. You learned why you need the FrontPage Server Extensions to use the components covered in this chapter and how they enable you to add interactivity to your site without programming. You learned about results files and how to store them in your site in several different formats. You also learned how to configure your FrontPage forms to use the IDC files generated by the Database Connector Wizard and how to assign custom ISAPI, NSAPI, and CGI scripts to your forms. You should now have an understanding of what really makes these forms tick.

Next Steps

If the built-in features of FrontPage aren't enough for you, get ready for an introduction into some exciting Web technologies that can take you in just about any direction. If you want to add pizzazz to your site, read on. You'll learn how to add multimedia, native document viewing, and even more interactivity into your site by using Java, JavaScript, Netscape Plug-Ins, ActiveX, and VBScript. With these Web technologies, the sky is the limit.

Other options you can use as an alternative to FrontPage components and CGI scripts are discussed in the following chapters:

❏ See Chapter 24, "Real-Life Examples IV: Adding Interactivity," to learn how to use the Discussion Web Wizard and how to configure the Discussion component.

❏ Consult Chapter 2, "About the FrontPage Server Extensions," to learn more about what the FrontPage Server Extensions do and why the FrontPage form handling components require them.

Q&A

Q: I designed my form, I've got everything configured, and my Internet service provider has the FrontPage Server Extensions installed. Is there anything else I need to know about forms?

A: Believe it or not, after three chapters, you've finally reviewed all the commands that you need to process general forms using the FrontPage form handling components. If you want to go beyond what you've learned, you can get even more interactivity if you write custom routines yourself.

Q: Where should I put the results files?

A: It's best to put them in a location where your table of contents can't find them. If your service provider has the FrontPage Server Extensions installed, the most likely place is the `_private` directory, because your Table of Contents component doesn't look there. Browsers can't find that one, either.

Q: If I place more than one form on a single Web page, do the results go to the same file?

A: You can configure them to go to different files, just as you could if they were on separate pages. Of course, if you want all the forms on a single page to point to one results file, you can do that too!

TWENTY-FOUR

Real-Life Examples IV: Adding Interactivity

The Discussion Web Wizard helps you create a discussion group for an existing Web or for a new Web. A discussion group is similar to a bulletin board system. It enables users to read, post, and reply to messages on your Web site. These messages are called *articles*.

The Discussion Web Wizard is quite simple to use and is briefly described later in this chapter.

In this chapter, you

- ❏ Create and configure a discussion group for Matty's Place
- ❏ Review all the pages associated with the discussion group
- ❏ Create a guest book that stores results on a separate page
- ❏ Add a search page to your site

Tasks in this chapter:

- ❏ Using the Discussion Web Wizard
- ❏ Reviewing Pages in the Discussion Folder
- ❏ Configuring the Discussion
- ❏ Reviewing Discussion Pages in the _private Folder
- ❏ Reviewing Pages in Hidden Discussion Folders
- ❏ Creating a Guest Book
- ❏ Creating the Guest Book Log Page
- ❏ Creating the Guest Book Confirmation Page
- ❏ Testing Your Guest Book
- ❏ Creating a Search Page
- ❏ Adding the New Pages to Your Navigation Bars

Using the Discussion Web Wizard

The steps to add a full-featured discussion to Matty's Place are as follows:

NOTE: A completed version of the Web you create in this chapter is located in the `Bool\Chap24\Examples` folder on the CD-ROM that accompanies this book.

1. Use the **F**ile I **O**pen FrontPage Web command to open your Matty's Place Web.

2. From the FrontPage Explorer, choose **F**ile I **N**ew I FrontPage **W**eb. The New FrontPage Web dialog box appears.

3. Select the From **W**izard or Template radio button and highlight Discussion Web Wizard.

4. Check the **A**dd to current Web checkbox at the lower-left section of the dialog box.

5. Choose OK to start the Discussion Web Wizard. The first screen appears.

6. The first screen introduces you to the Discussion Web Wizard. Click **N**ext to continue.

7. From the second screen, choose all the following features for your discussion group (the Submission form is automatically created for you):

Table of Contents	Creates a table of contents page that lists all articles in the discussion group
Search Form	Creates a search form that enables the user to search through all discussion group articles for a word or group of words
Threaded **R**eplies	Arranges the table of contents in a list that keeps all related articles together
C**o**nfirmation Page	Creates a confirmation page that returns to the user after he or she submits an article to the discussion group

8. Click **N**ext. On the third screen, enter the following information:

Descriptive **t**itle	`Matty's Discussion`
Folder **n**ame	`_mattdis` (the folder name must be preceded by an underscore)

9. Click **N**ext. You are asked to choose a set of input fields for the discussion submission form:

Subject, Comments	The user enters or chooses the subject of the article and enters the article text in the Comments field. Select this option for Matty's Discussion.
Subject, C**a**tegory, Comments	The user enters or chooses a subject and category for the article and enters the article text in the Comments field.
Subject, **P**roduct, Comments	The user enters or chooses a subject and the name of a product, and enters the article text in the Comments field.

10. Click **N**ext. You are asked whether the discussion group will take place on a protected Web. Choose N**o**, anyone can post articles to create a public discussion group.

11. Click **N**ext. You are asked how you want to sort the articles in the discussion. Choose **O**ldest to newest (default) to list the articles in chronological order with the most recent articles listed at the bottom.

12. Click **N**ext. You are asked whether you want the table of contents page to be the home page for the Web. Choose N**o**.

13. Click **N**ext. You are asked what information should be returned by the Search form. Choose Subject, Size, **D**ate.

14. Click **N**ext. You are asked whether you want to use framesets in your discussion. Select Dual interface. This displays the discussion group in frames if the user's browser supports them, or in a full browser window if the user is not using a frame-compatible browser.

15. Click **N**ext. You are informed that the wizard has received all the answers. Click **F**inish to generate the discussion group.

16. After you create your discussion group, seven new pages appear in the root folder of your Matty's Place Web. The pages associated with the discussion group begin with the prefix `mattdis`. Highlight these files and move them to the `discussion` folder in your Web, as shown in Figure 24.1.

Figure 24.1.

The Discussion Web Wizard adds seven pages to the root folder in your Web. Move them into the discussion *folder in the Web.*

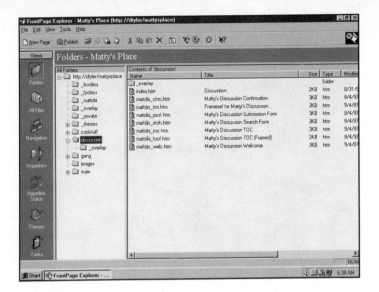

 TASK

Reviewing Pages in the Discussion Folder

The seven pages that you just moved into the discussion folder in your Web are the main pages of the discussion group. They include a confirmation page, the discussion submission form, a frameset page, a search page, framed and not-framed versions of a table of contents, and a Welcome page. The following sections describe what you need to complete on each page.

Matty's Discussion Confirmation

A user receives Matty's Discussion Confirmation page (mattdis_cfrm.htm) when he or she submits an article to the discussion. This page, shown in Figure 24.2, contains one Confirmation Field component named subject. The confirmation field returns the subject of the article in the confirmation form. There is a link on this page that tells the user to refresh the main page to see the new article appear in the list.

Frameset for Matty's Discussion

The frameset for the discussion, shown in Figure 24.3, contains two rows and one column. The upper frame is named contents, and it initially loads the Matty's Discussion TOC (Framed) page. In this frame, a table of contents lists all articles in the discussion group. The lower frame in the frameset initially loads the Matty's Discussion Welcome page into it, but when a user clicks on an article from the contents frame, the article appears beneath it in this lower frame. If the user is not viewing your Web in a frame-compatible browser, the Matty's Discussion TOC page is displayed in lieu of the frameset.

Figure 24.2.

The Discussion Confirmation Form contains one Confirmation Field component.

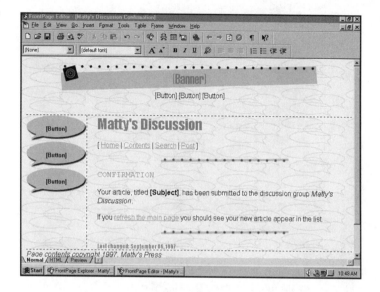

Figure 24.3.

The frameset for your discussion contains two frames. The upper frame displays a table of contents of the articles in your discussion, and the lower frame displays the articles.

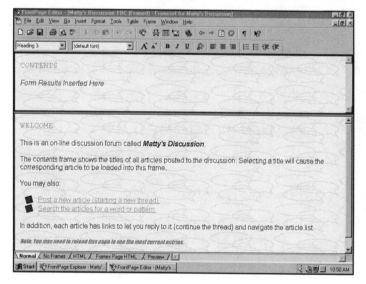

Matty's Discussion Submission Form

The Discussion Submission Form, shown in Figure 24.4, contains several form fields. You can add some of the other fields shown here to your discussion's confirmation form, if you like.

Figure 24.4.

The Discussion Submission Form is used to post and reply to articles in your discussion.

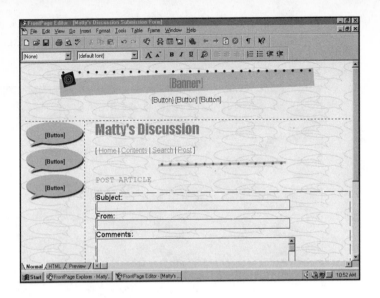

To review the settings for a Discussion form handler, follow these steps:

1. Right-click anywhere in the form and choose Form Properties from the pop-up menu. The Form Properties dialog box appears.

2. The Send to other radio button is selected, and Discussion Form Handler should appear in the drop-down menu.

3. Click **O**ptions to configure the Discussion form handler. The Options for Discussion Form Handler dialog box appears. By default, it opens to the Discussion tab.

Configuring the Discussion

Use the Discussion tab of the Options for Discussion Form Handler dialog box, shown in Figure 24.5, to configure the discussion and its table of contents arrangement. The steps to configure the Discussion form handler follow:

1. Enter `Matty's Discussion` in the Title field. This title appears on the main pages and articles in your discussion.

2. In the Director**y** field, the relative path to the discussion folder appears. In this case, the path is `../_mattdis`.

3. In the Table of contents layout section, complete the following:

   ❏ *Form fields.* In this section of the dialog box, enter the fields you want to appear at the top of the discussion articles, separating each with a space. Based on the selections you chose in the Discussion Web Wizard, `Subject` and `From` already appear for you in this field.

❏ *Time.* If you select this option, the table of contents includes the time an article was written.

❏ *Date.* If you select this option, the table of contents includes the date an article was written. This is selected for you.

❏ *Remote computer name.* If you select this option, the table of contents includes the remote computer name of the article's author.

❏ *User name.* If you select this option, the table of contents includes the name of the article's author.

❏ *Order newest to oldest.* Uncheck this option to sort the articles in the order in which they were created, but check it to place the most recent articles at the top of the table of contents.

4. When you add a discussion group to a Web that uses themes, as is the case in Matty's Place, the entry in the Get background and colors from page (optional) field is irrelevant. If the Web does not use themes, you can use a FrontPage style sheet for page backgrounds. The style sheet is located in the _private folder in your Web, and the relative URL of the style sheet is listed in the Get background and colors from page (optional) field; or use the Browse button to select a page from your current Web site.

5. Click the Article tab to continue with the article settings.

Figure 24.5.

Use the Discussion tab to configure your discussion articles.

Configuring the Discussion Articles

You use the Article tab, shown in Figure 24.6, to configure the articles in the discussion.

To configure your articles, follow these steps:

1. To configure the discussion articles, click the Article tab in the Options for Discussion Form Handler dialog box.

Figure 24.6.
Use the Article tab to assign a header and footer to your discussion articles.

2. Enter the URL of the article header in the URL of **H**eader to Include field, or use the **B**rowse button to select a page from your current Web site.

3. Enter the URL of the article footer in the URL of **F**ooter to Include field, or use the Bro**w**se button to select a page from your current Web site.

4. From the Additional information to include section, select any or all of the following items to include on each discussion article:

    ❏ *Time.* If you select this option, the article includes the time it was written.

    ❏ *Date.* If you select this option, the article includes the date it was written.

    ❏ *Remote computer name.* If you select this option, the article includes the remote computer name of its author.

    ❏ *User name.* If you select this option, the article includes the author's name.

5. Select another tab in the Options for Discussion Form Handler dialog box or choose OK to assign the Discussion form handler properties to your form.

Configuring the Discussion Confirmation Page

Use the Confirmation Page tab of the Options for Discussion Form Handler dialog box, shown in Figure 24.7, to configure the confirmation page and validation failure page for the Discussion form handler. The steps follow:

1. In the URL of **c**onfirmation page (optional) field, enter the name of the page that you use to confirm the user's submission to your discussion. Enter the URL or use the **B**rowse button to select a page from your current Web.

Figure 24.7.

Use the Confirmation Page tab to configure the confirmation page and validation page for your discussion.

You learn how to validate form fields in Chapter 22, "Adding and Editing Form Fields."

2. Use the URL of **v**alidation failure page (optional) field to specify the page that is returned to the user when the form fields do not meet validation requirements. Enter the URL or use the Bro**w**se button to select a page from your current Web.

3. Click OK to apply the form handler settings to your form.

Matty's Discussion Search Form

The Search page for Matty's Discussion, shown in Figure 24.8, is configured to search through the articles in the discussion. This is done by assigning the discussion group's directory (_mattdis) in the Search Results tab of the Search Form Properties dialog box. The Word List to Search field instructs the Search Form component to search through the pages in the _mattdis folder in your Web.

Figure 24.8.

The Search Form component is configured to keep track of only the articles in the discussion.

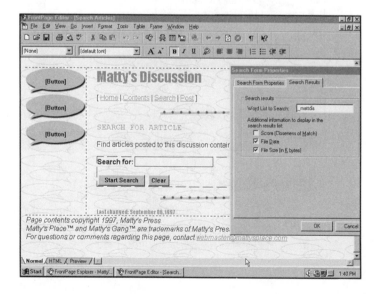

The default settings for the Search Form component on this page are as follows (you can edit any settings you want, except the Word List to Search directory):

Label for input:	Search for:
Width in Characters:	20
Label for "**S**tart Search" Button:	Start Search
Label for "**C**lear" Button:	Reset
Wo**r**d List to Search:	_mattdis
Additional Information to Display:	File **D**ate and File Size (in **K** bytes)

Matty's Discussion TOC

The Matty's Discussion TOC page (`mattdis_toc.htm`), shown in Figure 24.9, displays if a user is not using a frame-compatible browser. It displays a list of the articles on your site. The page contains an Include Page component beneath the line that reads `Note: you may need to reload this page to see the most recent additions`. The Include Page Component places the `_mattdis/tocproto.htm` page into the Table of Contents. There are no changes to make to this page.

Figure 24.9.

The Matty's Discussion TOC page displays when a user is viewing your site with a browser that does not support frames.

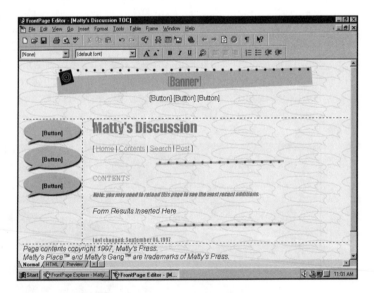

Matty's Discussion TOC (Framed)

The Matty's Discussion TOC (framed) Page isn't much to look at. Initially, it contains only the word CONTENTS, beneath which is an Include Page component that places the contents of `_mattdis/tocproto.htm` into the page.

NOTE: Because this page appears in the discussion group frameset, you need to use the **T**ools I Shared **B**orders command in the FrontPage Editor to remove all borders from the following pages:

Matty's Discussion TOC (Framed)

Matty's Discussion Welcome

Included Article Footer for Matty's Discussion

Included Article Header for Matty's Discussion

Included Footer for Matty's Discussion

Included Header for Matty's Discussion

_mattdis Discussion Page

_mattdis/tocproto.htm

Matty's Discussion Welcome

The Matty's Discussion Welcome page, shown in Figure 24.10, welcomes the user to the discussion and provides links to post an article to the site or search the site for a word or phrase. There are two links on this page that the user follows to post a new article to the discussion and to search the articles for a word or pattern.

Figure 24.10.

The Matty's Discussion Welcome page provides links to post an article and search the discussion articles for a word or phrase.

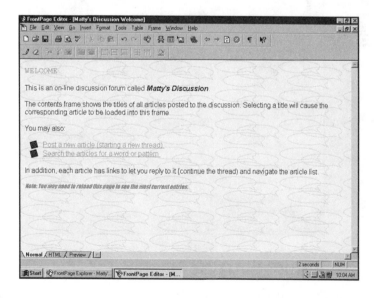

Reviewing Discussion Pages in the _private Folder

The Discussion Web Wizard also placed five pages in the _private folder in your Web. These pages are used to assign page backgrounds and colors to the files associated with your discussion group. In addition, the header and footer pages provide navigation bars for the pages that display in the frameset. The headers and footers are placed on your discussion pages through the use of Include Page components that are automatically configured for you. The following sections describe the items that you need to complete.

Included Article Footer for Matty's Discussion

The Included Article Footer for Matty's Discussion (shown in Figure 24.11) contains a timestamp that places the date that the page was last automatically updated on the page. By default, the timestamp uses a date format and does not include the time. To change the date and time styles, double-click the timestamp and choose a new date and time configuration. Click OK to return to the FrontPage Editor.

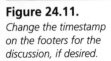

Figure 24.11.

Change the timestamp on the footers for the discussion, if desired.

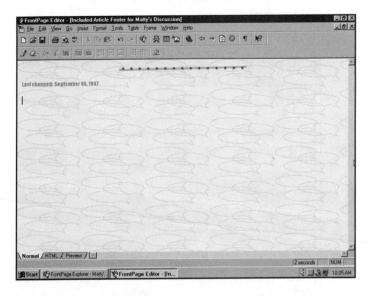

Included Article Header for Matty's Discussion

The Included Article Header for Matty's Discussion page, shown in Figure 24.12, appears on all the discussion group articles. This navigation bar enables the user to navigate to the Home page, the Discussion Contents page, the Search page, and the

Discussion Submission Form. In addition, the user can reply to a post and navigate to the next, previous, and top messages in the discussion group.

Figure 24.12.
The Included Article Header appears on all the discussion group articles.

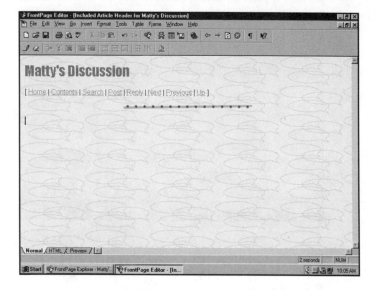

Included Footer for Matty's Discussion

The Included Article Footer for Matty's Discussion page is identical to that shown in Figure 24.11.

Included Header for Matty's Discussion

The Included Header for Matty's Discussion page is shown in Figure 24.13. This header appears on all the main pages in the discussion and enables the user to navigate to the Home page, the discussion group table of contents, the Discussion Search Form, and the Discussion Submission Form. There are no changes to make to this page.

Web Colors

The Matty's Discussion Web Colors page assigns page background and text colors to discussion Web pages that do not use themes. As is the case for Matty's Place, this page is not used. You can optionally use the **T**ools I Shared **B**orders command to remove the default page borders from this page.

Figure 24.13.

The Included Header for Matty's Discussion page appears on all the main pages in the discussion group.

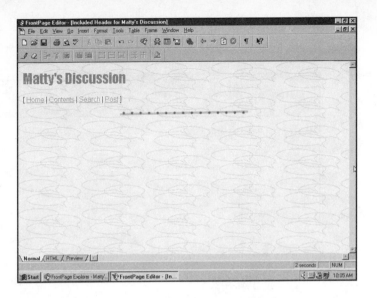

 # Reviewing Pages in Hidden Discussion Folders

There are a couple of additional pages that reside in hidden folders in your FrontPage Web. To display these pages, choose **T**ools | **W**eb Settings and check the Show documents in **h**idden directories checkbox in the Advanced tab of the FrontPage Web Settings dialog box. Then click OK. When FrontPage asks whether you want to refresh the Web, choose **Y**es. The _mattdis folder appears in your Web, and you can view the pages discussed in the following sections.

_mattdis Discussion Page (_mattdis/toc.htm)

The Discussion page is shown in Figure 24.14 and is the table of contents for the articles in your discussion. You'll want to change the title from Contents for _mattdis to Contents for Matty's Discussion. You'll probably also want to change the font style to Arial and reduce the size by clicking the Decrease Indent button once.

Beneath the heading is an Include Page component. As a user submits articles or replies to your discussion, his or her titles are added to the _mattdis/tocproto.htm page. Eventually, you will see a list of articles on this page. The list of articles is compiled each time a user submits an article to your discussion group.

Figure 24.14.

The contents of the included page won't show until after a user enters an article in your discussion.

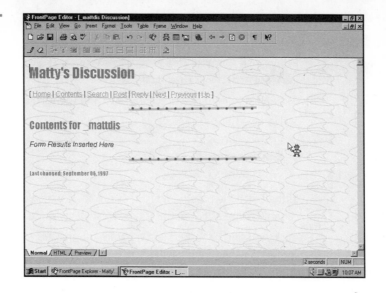

_mattdis/tocproto.htm (_mattdis/tocproto.htm)

When you open the page, you'll see text that reads Form Results Inserted Here. This is a Form Insert Here WebBot component, which is used with the Save Results WebBot when you specify a results file. It acts as a placeholder for the next group of data submitted by a form. The Form Insert Here WebBot component is not configurable.

TASK Creating a Guest Book

The forms you create in this chapter will utilize the FrontPage form handlers, which means that in order to test them you need to have the FrontPage Personal Web Server, Microsoft Personal Web Server, or Internet Information Server running with the FrontPage Server Extensions installed. The first form you complete will be a guest book. Use the Form Page Wizard to create a new form.

To complete your guest book, follow these steps:

1. Choose **F**ile | **N**ew (Ctrl+N). The New Page dialog box appears. Select the Form Page Wizard and choose OK.

2. When the introductory screen appears, click **N**ext to continue.

3. In the Page **T**itle field, enter Matty's Place Guest Book. In the Page **U**RL field, enter guestbk.htm. Click **N**ext to continue.

FrontPage 98 provides a Guest Book page template that you can select from the New dialog box in the FrontPage Editor. The Guest Book page template places the users' comments on the same page on which the guest book form is located.

4. Click the **A**dd button and choose to add a contact information question. For the prompt, enter something like the following:

   `Let us know who you are! We'd appreciate it if you could at least add your name and location to the list. Contact information is optional.`

5. Click **N**ext to continue and choose to add the following fields:

   > **N**ame—full
   > **P**ostal address
   > **E**-mail address
   > Web add**r**ess (URL)

6. In the Enter the base name for this group of **v**ariables field, leave the variable name as `Contact` and click **N**ext to continue.

7. Click **A**dd and choose to add a paragraph question. For the prompt, enter something like the following:

   `Tell us what you think of the site. Your comments will be added to our Guest Book log.`

8. Click **N**ext to continue. In the Enter the name of a **v**ariable to hold this answer field, enter `Comments`.

9. Click **N**ext to advance to the Presentation Options screen. You are asked how you want to present the form. Choose to present the list of questions as normal paragraphs. Choose No for a Table of Contents and select to align form fields in tables.

10. Click **N**ext to continue. In the output options screen, choose Save results to a **w**eb page. In the Enter the base name of the results file, enter `guestlog` (the `.htm` extension is automatically assumed and not necessary).

11. Click **N**ext to proceed to the final screen and then click **F**inish to generate the form; it should look like the one shown in Figure 24.15.

Editing the Form and the Form Fields

You need to edit the form fields on the guest book page a little. Some of the fields are not necessary, so you can delete them. You can also check the settings of the form fields on the page.

To edit the form and the form fields, follow these steps:

1. Remove the top line on the page that reads `This is an explanation of the purpose of the form.`

Figure 24.15.

Your guests will use portions of this form to add their comments to your page.

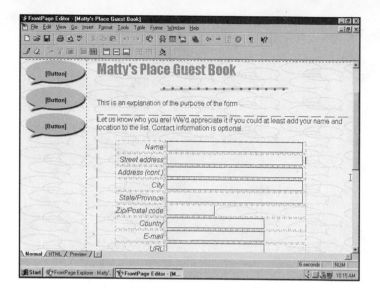

2. From the Contact Information section, position your cursor at the left of the table to select the six rows that begin with Street address and end with Country. Choose Table | Delete Cells. You should have Name, E-mail, and URL remaining in the top table.

3. Click the Name text box and press Alt+Enter. The Text Box Properties dialog box appears. In the Name field, enter Name. Choose OK to return to the FrontPage Editor.

4. In the same manner, assign the following words to each of the properties in their respective Text Box Properties dialog boxes:

   E-mail text box: should read Email
   URL text box: should read URL

5. Click the scrolling text box and press Alt+Enter. The Scrolling Text Box Properties dialog box appears. Verify that the width is set to 35 and the number of lines is 5. Choose OK to return to the FrontPage Editor. When you're finished, your form should look like the one shown in Figure 24.16.

6. Scroll to the bottom of the form and delete the line that reads Copyright information goes here. The timestamp on this page is already configured correctly to update the timestamp whenever you edit the page manually.

7. Choose File | Save to save the page to your Web.

Figure 24.16.
The form is edited slightly to better suit the application.

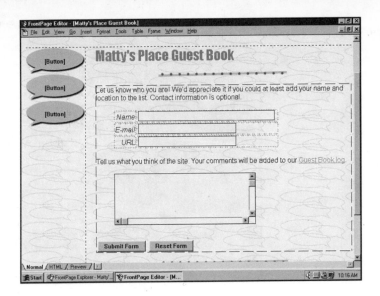

Configuring the Guest Book Form Handler

Now you have to assign a form handler to your form. To do this, follow these steps:

1. Position your cursor anywhere in the form. Right-click and choose Form Properties from the pop-up menu. The Form Properties dialog box appears.

2. The File **N**ame field defaults to `http://servername/mattysplace/guestlog.htm`, based on information you added in the Forms Page Wizard. Edit this to read `guestlog.htm`.

3. Choose the **O**ptions button. The Options for Saving Results of Form dialog box appears, opened to the File Results tab.

4. Click the Confirmation Page tab. In the URL of **c**onfirmation page (optional) field, enter `gstcfrm.htm` and click OK.

5. Click OK to exit the Form Properties dialog box. Your form is configured.

6. Choose **F**ile | **S**ave (Ctrl+S). The Save As dialog box appears.

7. Double-click the main folder in your Web. Enter `guestbk.htm` in the **U**RL field and `Matty's Place Guest Book` in the **T**itle field. Then choose OK to save the page to the Web.

 ## Creating the Guest Book Log Page

When you configured the Save Results component for your guest book, you assigned a form results page of `guestlog.htm`. This page is created automatically the first time a user submits his or her comments to your site. You'll include the `guestlog.htm` page on a new page, which is titled `Matty's Place Guest Book Log`.

Follow these steps to create the page:

1. From the FrontPage Editor, choose **F**ile | **N**ew. The New dialog box appears.

2. Double-click Normal Page. A blank page appears in the FrontPage Editor.

3. Choose Heading 2 from the Change Style drop-down menu in the Format toolbar and enter `Matty's Place Guest Book Log`.

4. Press Enter to position the insertion point on the next line. Enter `This page was last updated on` followed by a space.

5. Choose **I**nsert | **T**imestamp. The Timestamp Properties dialog box appears.

6. Choose Date this page was last **a**utomatically updated. Select the date and time formats of your choice and choose OK. The timestamp appears on your page.

7. Choose **I**nsert | Horizontal **L**ine. A horizontal line appears on the next line.

8. Press Enter to position the insertion point on the next line. Enter `Here are the entries from our guests:`.

9. Choose **I**nsert | Front**P**age Component. The Insert FrontPage Component dialog box appears.

10. Double-click Include Page. The Include Page Component Properties dialog box appears.

11. In the **P**age URL to include field, enter `guestlog.htm` and then click OK to return to the FrontPage Editor. The Include Page component places text on your page that reads `[guestlog.htm]` because the page does not yet exist in your Web. When you receive entries from your visitors, all the guest log entries appear on the page in this location.

12. Press the Home key and then Enter to position the insertion point on the next line. Choose **I**nsert | Horizontal **L**ine. Your page should now look like Figure 24.17.

13. Choose **F**ile | **S**ave (Ctrl+S) or click the Save button on the Standard toolbar. The Save As dialog box appears.

14. Double-click the main folder in your Web. Enter `readbook.htm` in the **U**RL field and `Matty's Place Guest Book Log` in the **T**itle field. Choose OK to save the page.

15. Return to the Matty's Place Guest Book page (`guestbk.htm`). Above the scrolling text box is a line that reads (in part) `Your comments will be added to our Guest Book log`. Highlight the words `Guest Book log` and choose the Create or Edit Hyperlink button on the Standard toolbar.

16. Double-click the main folder and then double-click `Matty's Place Guest Book Log` (`readbook.htm`). The link is created.

Figure 24.17.

The Guest Book Log page displays the comments that the users enter into your Guest Book.

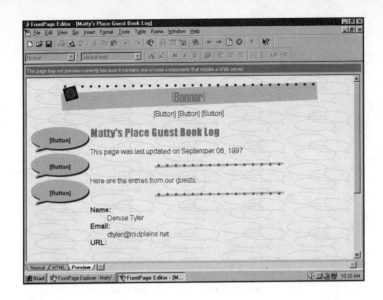

17. Choose File I Save (Ctrl+S) or use the Save button on the Standard toolbar to save the Matty's Place Guest Book page to your Web.

Creating the Guest Book Confirmation Page

You want to thank your site visitors for submitting their comments to your guest book and also let them know they can view their comments if they go to the My World Guest Book Log and refresh the page in their browsers. Create a simple confirmation page as follows:

1. Use the New button on the Standard toolbar to create a new page.

2. On the first line, choose Insert I Horizontal Line. A horizontal line appears on your page.

3. Press Enter to move the insertion point to the next line. Enter `Hey,` followed by a space.

4. Choose Insert I FrontPage Component and double-click Confirmation Field to open the Confirmation Field Properties dialog box. In the Name of Form Field to Confirm field, enter `Name` and choose OK.

5. Add a comma after the Confirmation Field WebBot. Press Enter to move the insertion point to the next line. Enter the following:

```
Thanks for adding your comments to our guest book! The following
information will appear in the guest book log. You can view your entry in
```

the Guest Book Log page. Note that you may need to refresh your browser to see your comments.

6. Choose T**a**ble | **I**nsert Table. The Insert Table dialog box appears. Enter the following settings and choose OK to insert the table on your page:

   Rows: 4
   Columns: 2
   Alignment: Center
   Border Size: 0
   Cell Pa**d**ding: 2
   Cell **S**pacing: 2
   Specify **W**idth: 90 in **P**ercent

7. In the left column of the table, enter (from top row to bottom row): Name, E-mail, URL, and Comments.

8. Drag the border line between the two columns of cells to increase the size of the right column. Click inside the top cell in the right column.

9. Choose **I**nsert | Front**P**age Component and double-click Confirmation Field. In the Name of Form Field to Confirm field, enter Name. Choose OK or press Enter to place the confirmation field on your page.

10. Select the confirmation field you just inserted on your page and copy it into your clipboard, using Ctrl+C. Paste a copy of the confirmation field into the three remaining cells in the table, using Ctrl+V.

11. Double-click each of the confirmation bots in the second, third, and fourth rows; revise the confirmation field to read Email (for the second row), URL (for the third row), and Comments (for the fourth row).

12. Press Ctrl+Enter to position the insertion point on the line beneath the table. Choose **I**nsert | Horizontal **L**ine.

13. Highlight the words Guest Book Log in the text above the table and click the Create or Edit Hyperlink button. From the list of open pages in the Create Hyperlink dialog box, double-click Matty's Place Guest Book Log (readbook.htm). The link to your guest book log is created.

14. Choose **F**ile | **S**ave (Ctrl+S) or click the Save button on the Standard toolbar. From the Save As dialog box, double-click the main folder. Then enter the following information and choose OK to save the page:

   U**R**L: gstcfrm.htm
   T**i**tle: Guest Book Confirmation Page

Figure 24.18 shows an example of the page.

Figure 24.18.

The Guest Book Confirmation Page returns to the user after he or she submits an article to your discussion.

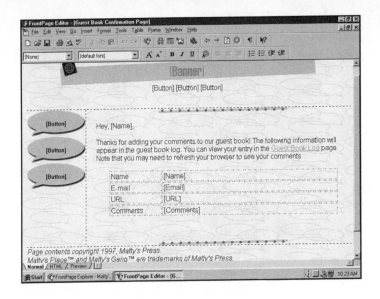

TASK

Testing Your Guest Book

Open your Matty's Place Guest Book page (guestbk.htm in the main folder) in the FrontPage Editor if it is not still open. Then, with your server running, choose **F**ile | Preview in **B**rowser. Select a browser and resolution and click **P**review.

Add a sample entry in the form fields, as shown in Figure 24.19. Then click the Submit Form button. You should see the Guest Book Confirmation Page shown in Figure 24.20. Click the link to the Guest Book Log page, and you should see your entry in the My World Guest Book Log page, as shown in Figure 24.21.

Figure 24.19.

Your visitors first navigate to the My World Guest Book page and enter their comments.

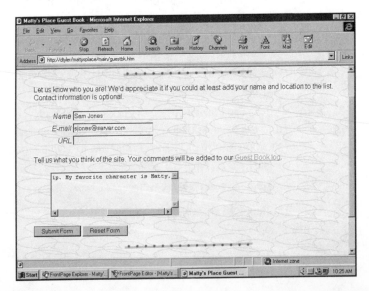

Figure 24.20.
*After comments
are entered, the
user receives a
confirmation page.*

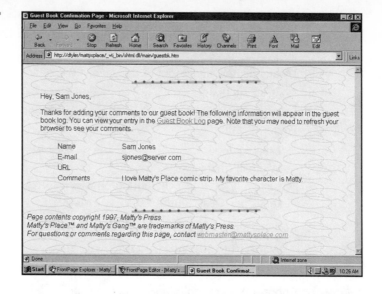

Figure 24.21.
*The comments they
enter are stored in
guestlog.htm and
included on the My
World Guest Book
Log page.*

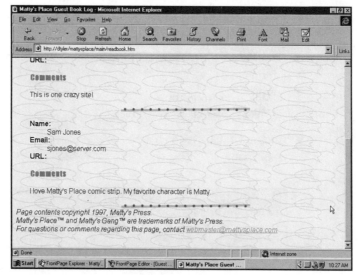

TASK Creating a Search Page

You use the Search Page template to create a search page for Matty's Place. To complete the search form, follow these steps:

1. Choose **F**ile | **N**ew (Ctrl+N) and double-click Search Page. The Search Page template opens in the FrontPage Editor.

2. Scroll down to the bottom of the page and remove the line that reads Author information goes here and the copyright line below it. Leave the timestamp line.

3. Modify the text and layout of the page, if you desire.

4. Double-click the Search component on the page to open the Search Form Properties dialog box. The following settings are entered in the Search Form Properties tab:

Label for Input:	Search for:
Width in Characters:	20
Label for "**S**tart Search" button:	Start Search
Label for "**C**lear" button:	Clear

5. Click the Search Results tab and choose or enter the following settings:

Wo**r**d List to Search:	All
Additional Information:	File **D**ate and File Size (in **K** bytes)

6. Choose OK to return to the FrontPage Editor.

7. Choose **F**ile | **S**ave (Ctrl+S) or click the Save button on the Standard toolbar. The Save As dialog box appears.

8. Double-click the main folder in your Web and enter the following information:

URL:	search.htm
Title:	Search Matty's Place

9. Choose OK to save the page to your Web. Figure 24.22 shows an example of the page.

Figure 24.22.

The Search Page now contains an introduction, a Search component, and information on how to use the query language.

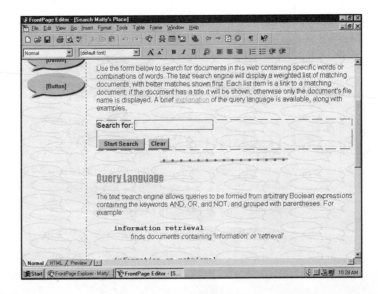

Adding the New Pages to Your Navigation Bars

You need to add some of the new pages that you added in this chapter to your navigation bars. To complete the additions, follow these steps:

1. Choose Tools | Show FrontPage Explorer or click the Show FrontPage Explorer button on the Standard toolbar to return to the FrontPage Explorer.

2. Click the Navigation icon in the Views pane to switch to Navigation view.

3. In the files pane, select the `discussion` folder in your Web. Click and drag the following pages, in this order, and place them beneath the Discussion page in Navigation view:

`mattdis_post.htm`	Matty's Discussion Submission Form
`mattdis_srch.htm`	Matty's Discussion Search Form
`mattdis_toc.htm`	Matty's Discussion TOC

4. Relabel the three pages in Navigation view, as shown in Figure 24.23:

   Post Article
   Search Articles
   Contents

Figure 24.23.

Add the Discussion Submission Form, Search Form, and Table of Contents to the navigation pane.

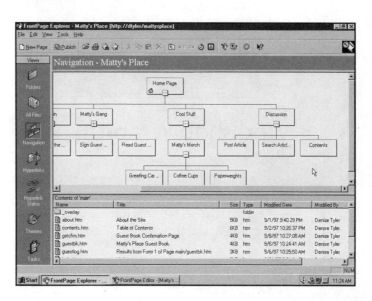

5. In the files pane, select the `main` folder in your Web. You can use the Up One Level button in the Standard toolbar to navigate back one level in the files pane and then double-click the main folder to display the pages. Click and

drag the following pages, in this order, and place them to the right of the Table of Contents page:

search.htm	Search Matty's Place
guestbk.htm	Matty's Place Guest Book
readbook.htm	Matty's Place Guest Book Log

6. Relabel the three pages in Navigation view, as shown in Figure 24.24.

```
Search the Site
Sign Guest Book
Read Guest Book
```

Figure 24.24.
Relabel the new pages in the navigation pane to Search the Site, Sign Guest Book, and Read Guest Book.

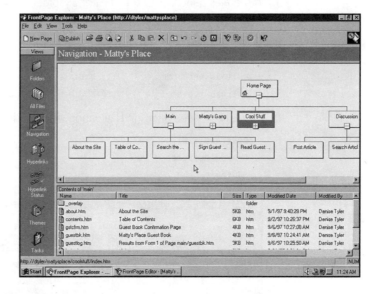

Workshop Wrap-Up

In this chapter, you added interactivity and enhanced features to your site, using FrontPage's form handlers. You added a discussion group to your site, a guest book complete with confirmation page and a separate page for the users' entries, and a search page so users can search through your entire site for words or phrases. You added the new pages to your navigation bars and learned how to test your guest book form.

Next Steps

The chapters in Part VI, "Publishing and Maintaining Your Webs," discuss how to maintain your Web site, how to work with the FrontPage Server Extensions, and how to test and publish your Web site.

❏ In Chapter 25, "Using Java Applets and Netscape Plug-Ins," you learn how to add Java applets and Netscape plug-ins to your Web pages.

❏ In Chapter 26, "Using Your Own HTML," you learn how to modify and add HTML code to your pages and how to design a floating frame.

❏ In Chapter 27, "Using Styles," you learn how to create your own cascading style sheets.

❏ In Chapter 28, "Working with ActiveX and Scripts," you learn how to insert ActiveX controls and scripts in your pages.

❏ In Chapter 29, "Real-Life Examples V: Using Browser-Specific Features," you combine these features into Matty's Place and make a final check of the pages in your site.

Q&A

Q: Can I configure a Search component to place its results on a different page rather than on the same page?

A: At the present time, no. The Search component places the results on the same page.

Q: Can I create a discussion group that has a different section for each topic, instead of using multiple topics in the same discussion?

A: Yes, you can, but remember that you'll be adding several pages to your Web site for each discussion when you do. Your Web will be easier to maintain if you create multiple subjects in a single discussion group. On the other hand, if the discussion gets a lot of articles, it can be easier to locate specific subjects if you create several smaller discussion groups. Start with one and see how it goes!

Q: What's the best way to trim a discussion down when the article count gets too high?

A: One way to do it would be to periodically go through the discussion articles and select the best of the lot. Place the best articles on another Web page in an archive area or zip the pages into a file and provide a link to download the zip files of past articles.

PART

V

Still More Advanced Techniques

TWENTY-FIVE

Using Java Applets and Netscape Plug-Ins

One of the hottest Web technologies is Java, a general-purpose programming language developed by Sun Microsystems. Java is a versatile programming language. Using it, you can write small programs, called *applets*, and attach them to your Web pages. These applets can do a wide variety of things, such as display multimedia elements, online games, and animation; process and display data; include an online chat on your site; and much more.

If you've been a part of the World Wide Web for a while, you also know that the most widely used browser is Netscape Navigator. When you use Netscape Navigator 2.0 or later, or a compatible browser such as Internet Explorer 3.0 or later, you can use plug-ins to display multimedia elements, view documents in their native formats, add RealAudio files to your pages, and add a host of other features into your pages.

FrontPage 98 features built-in support for both of these Web technologies. Using commands in the Insert menu, you can add Java applets and Netscape plug-ins to your pages very easily. This chapter will give you a couple of examples to follow.

Adding Java to Your Pages

You need a few things to include a Java applet on your page, one of the most important of which is the permission to use it. If you've written the applet yourself, permission is not an issue. If the applet was written by someone else, do some checking to see whether you have permission to use an applet freely or to find the requirements for obtaining the rights to use it. Sometimes, the requirements are nothing more than providing a link to the author's site or including a mention of trademark or copyright information on your page. Other times, you must purchase the rights to use the applet.

Basically, a Java applet begins with source code, which is nothing more than a text file with a series of commands written in Java. Figure 25.1 shows an example of the source code written for the example used in this chapter. Many applications enable you to develop source code using point-and-click interfaces, including Sun Microsystem's Java Development Kit, Microsoft's Visual J++ (shown in Figure 25.1), Kinetix Hyperwire (a division of Autodesk), Symantec's Visual Café and Visual Café Pro, and Borland's JBuilder.

Figure 25.1.

You compile Java source code with a Java compiler.

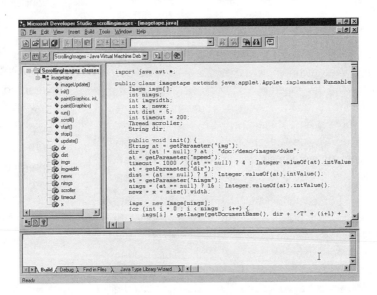

This source code file isn't what you need to put on your Web, however. After you develop the source code, it must be compiled into a Java *class* file, which combines the classes in your source file with the interpreter. You reference the path to this class file in the Java Applet Properties dialog box. Along with the class file, you need to know the path to any images, sounds, and other elements that are associated with the Java applet. Finally, you need to know which parameters you have to add to your Web pages. Many times, when you download a Java applet from the Web or use a sample provided with your Java compiler, the parameters and values you need to insert into your page are listed on a Web page, as shown in Figure 25.2.

Figure 25.2.

The parameters you need to insert in your Web page are sometimes indicated on Web pages provided with the sample applet.

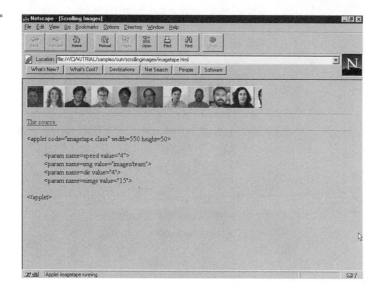

When you insert a Java applet into your page, it is downloaded from the Web server to the user's computer. The user's browser interprets the class file and runs it on his or her computer.

NOTE: For additional reference on Java, check out *Teach Yourself Java 1.1 in 21 Days, Second Edition* by Laura Lemay and Charles L. Perkins, published by Sams.net (ISBN #1-57521-142-4).

 # Importing a Java Class File

For this simple example of how to add a Java applet to a page, I used one of Sun Microsystem's Java applet samples and imported the necessary files into my Web. This sample is available in its Java Development Kit as well as in Microsoft Visual J++. Called Image Tape (or Scrolling Images), the applet scrolls a series of small images across your screen.

 For this applet, I created an `images` directory in my Web. I also created a `classes` folder and imported the Java applet's class file into it. The class file and the associated images are located in the `Book\Chap25\Project Files` folder on the CD-ROM that is furnished with this book.

After the source code was compiled into a class file, I imported Sun Microsystem's ImageTape applet as follows:

1. Open or create a Web in the FrontPage Explorer. Select the home directory of your Web from the All Folders pane in Folders view. Choose **F**ile I **N**ew I **F**older to create a new folder named `classes`.

2. From the All Folders view, click the `classes` folder to select it.

3. Choose **F**ile I **I**mport. The Import File to FrontPage Web dialog box appears.

4. Click **A**dd File. The Add File to Import List dialog box appears.

5. Locate the drive and directory in which the `imagetape.class` file appears, as shown in Figure 25.3. Highlight the file and click **O**pen. You return to the Import File to FrontPage Web dialog box, and the class file appears in the Import list.

Figure 25.3.

Use the Add File to Import List dialog box to add the class file to your current Web.

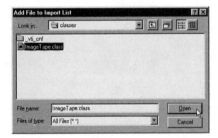

6. Click OK to import the class file into your `classes` directory.

7. From the All Folders view, select the `images` folder in your Web. (This folder is created automatically when you create a new Web.) Choose **F**ile I **I**mport.

8. From the Import File to FrontPage Web dialog box, click the **A**dd File button. Locate the `images\team` folder for the ImageTape applet. Highlight `t1.gif` through `t15.gif`, as shown in Figure 25.4, and click **O**pen. The images appear in your import list.

Figure 25.4.

You must also import any multimedia elements that are referenced by the Java applet.

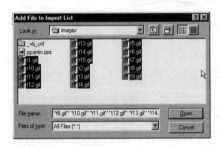

9. Click OK to import the images into your `images` folder.

Inserting and Configuring a Java Applet

With the class files and images imported into the Web, you can insert the Java applet into your Web page. To insert the ImageTape Java applet, follow these steps:

1. From the FrontPage Explorer, choose **T**ools | Show FrontPage **E**ditor or use the Show FrontPage Editor button on the toolbar to open the FrontPage Editor.

2. Create or open a new page in which to insert the Java applet.

3. Choose **I**nsert | **A**dvanced | **J**ava Applet or click the Insert Java Applet button on the Advanced toolbar. The Java Applet Properties dialog box shown in Figure 25.5 appears.

Figure 25.5.

Configure the settings for your Java applet in the Java Applet Properties dialog box.

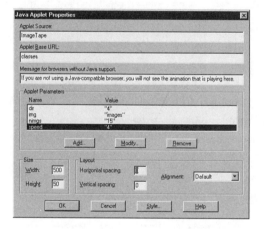

4. In the Applet **S**ource field, enter the name of the Java applet source file. In this case, enter **ImageTape** (upper and lower case is important here, because it must match the parameters specified by the Java class file). You don't need to add the `.class` extension to this name.

5. In the Applet **B**ase URL field, enter the URL of the folder that contains the Java applet source file. You imported the applets into your classes folder. Enter `classes` here.

6. In the Messa**g**e for browsers without Java support field, enter the HTML to display in Web browsers that do not support Java applets. Enter **If you are not using a Java-compatible browser, you will not see the animation that is playing here.**

7. For this applet, you need to enter four applet parameters. To add an applet parameter, click the A**d**d button. The Set Attribute Value dialog box shown in Figure 25.6 appears.

Figure 25.6.

You enter the applet parameters in the Set Attribute Value dialog box.

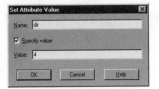

NOTE: Each Java applet has parameters that are particular to the applet. You need to consult the documentation for the Java applet to configure these parameter names properly.

8. The first parameter specifies the direction that the images scroll. Enter the parameter name **dir** in the **N**ame field. In the Value field, enter **4**.

9. Click OK. The entries appear in the Applet Parameters field of the Java Applet Properties dialog box.

10. The second parameter specifies the directory in which your images appear. Click the A**d**d button. For the parameter name, enter **img**. For its value, enter **images**. Click OK to return to the Java Applet Properties dialog box.

11. The third parameter specifies the number of images that you want to scroll across the screen. Click the A**d**d button. For the parameter name, enter **nimgs**. For its value, enter **15**. Click OK to return to the Java Applet Properties dialog box.

12. The fourth parameter specifies the speed at which you want the images to scroll. Click the A**d**d button. For the parameter name, enter **speed**. For its value, enter **4**. Click OK to return to the Java Applet Properties dialog box. The parameters appear in the Applet Parameters list of the Java Applet Properties dialog box, as shown in Figure 25.5.

13. Next, you enter values in the Size portion of the Java Applet Properties dialog box. In the **W**idth field, enter **500**. In the Heigh**t** field, enter **50**.

14. In the Hori**z**ontal spacing field, enter the number of pixels you want between the Java applet and the nearest text. Leave this setting at the default of **0** for this example.

15. In the **V**ertical spacing field, enter the number of pixels you want between the Java applet and the line above or below the current line. Leave this setting at the default of **0** for this example.

16. To specify how you want the applet to align with other text on your page, choose a setting from the **A**lignment drop-down menu. For this example, choose `Default`. The available choices are as follows:

Default	The applet appears in the left margin of the page.
Left	Places the applet in the left margin and wraps the text that follows along the control's right side.
Right	Places the applet in the right margin and wraps the text that follows along the control's left side.
Top	Aligns the top of the applet with the text.
Texttop	Aligns the top of the applet with the top of the tallest text in the line.
Middle	Aligns the middle of the applet with the text.
Absmiddle	Aligns the applet with the middle of the current line.
Baseline	Aligns the applet to the baseline of the current line.
Bottom	Aligns the bottom of the applet with the text.
Absbottom	Aligns the applet with the bottom of the current line.
Center	Aligns the applet to the center of the page.

17. Use the **S**tyle button to add cascading style sheet properties to the applet, if desired. For more information about cascading style sheet properties, see Chapter 27, "Using Styles."

18. Click OK to exit the Java Applet Properties dialog box. A representation of the applet appears on your page, as shown in Figure 25.7.

Figure 25.7.
A representation of the Java applet appears on your page.

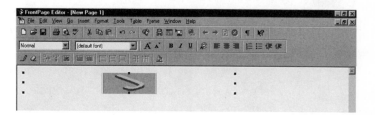

19. Choose **F**ile | **S**ave (Ctrl+S). The Save As dialog box appears. In the **T**itle field, enter `Sun Microsystem's Image Tape Applet`. In the **U**RL field, enter `imgtape.htm`.

20. Choose OK to save your page to the Web.

21. Choose **F**ile | Preview in **B**rowser. The Preview in Browser dialog box appears. Select your favorite Java-enabled browser from the **B**rowser list. In the **W**indow Size field, select a resolution for the preview. Then click the **P**review button. The Java applet loads into your browser and animates the images.

Working with Netscape Plug-Ins

Plug-ins are software modules that integrate into Web browsers. With plug-ins, you can add animation, multimedia, online games, calendar programs, and interactivity to your Web pages. In addition, many applications offer plug-ins so that you can view documents in their native formats. There are many plug-ins available.

In Chapter 17, "Integrating with Other Editors," you learned about a plug-in that adds PowerPoint presentations to your Web pages. I'll use that plug-in as an example in this chapter.

 ## Importing a Netscape Plug-In into Your Web

When you insert a plug-in into your page, you actually insert the data file that the plug-in program plays. In the case of this example, the data file is a PowerPoint animation file. When the user opens the page that contains this animation, his or her browser checks to see whether the appropriate plug-in is installed. If it is not, the browser asks whether the user wants to download it.

To insert a Netscape plug-in, follow these steps:

 NOTE: If you want to view the PowerPoint animation that is provided in the Book\Chap25\Project Files folder on the CD-ROM for the following example, you need to download and install the PowerPoint Animation Player from the following URL:

http://www.microsoft.com/powerpoint/internet/player/default.htm

For a viewer that is compatible with PowerPoint 97 animations, visit the following page:

http://www.microsoft.com/powerpoint/internet/viewer

1. From the FrontPage Explorer, create or open a Web in which to create a page. Select the images folder from the All Folders pane in Folders view.

2. From the FrontPage Explorer, choose File | Import. The Import File to Web dialog box appears.

3. Click the Add File button. The Add File to Import List dialog box shown in Figure 25.8 appears.

Figure 25.8.

Import the PowerPoint animation into your Web using the Add File to Import List dialog box.

4. Locate `Book\Chap25\Project Files\ppanim.ppz` (the PowerPoint presentation file) on the CD-ROM that accompanies this book. After you locate the file, click **O**pen. You return to the Import File to FrontPage Web dialog box.

5. Click OK. The animation appears in the `images` directory in your Web.

Inserting a Netscape Plug-In into Your Page

After you import the PowerPoint animation into your Web site, you can insert it into a Web page as follows:

1. From the FrontPage Explorer, choose **T**ools I Show Fro**n**tPage Editor or use the Show FrontPage Editor button to open the FrontPage Editor.

2. Create or open a page in which to insert the PowerPoint animation file. Position the insertion point where you want the presentation to appear.

3. Choose **I**nsert I **A**dvanced I **P**lug-In or click the Insert Plug-In button on the Advanced toolbar. The Plug-In Properties dialog box shown in Figure 25.9 appears.

Figure 25.9.

Configure the settings for your plug-in in the Plug-In Properties dialog box.

4. In the **D**ata Source field, enter the URL or file location of the data that you want to display in the plug-in. In this case, that data is the PowerPoint animation you imported into your Web. Enter `images/ppanim.ppz`.

   Optionally, click the **B**rowse button. The Select Plug-In Data Source dialog box appears.

   ❏ To select the plug-in data source from your current Web, locate the folder in which the plug-in appears. Highlight the file and click OK to return to the Plug-In Properties dialog box.

   ❏ To select the plug-in data source from your local or network hard drive, click the Select a file on your computer button. Use the Select File dialog box to locate the drive and directory in which the file appears. Highlight the file and click OK to return to the Plug-In Properties dialog box.

   ❏ To insert a plug-in data source from the World Wide Web, enter the URL for the plug-in data source in the URL field or choose the Use your web browser to select a page or file button. After you locate the plug-in file with your browser, return to the FrontPage Editor, where the path to the plug-in appears in the URL field. Choose OK to return to the Plug-In Properties dialog box.

5. In the **M**essage for browsers without Plug-In support field, enter the HTML text to display in Web browsers that do not support plug-ins. Here, enter something like `If you're using a browser that supports Netscape plug-ins and don't see a PowerPoint presentation playing here, you need to download the files listed below.` You can provide links on your page to ensure that the user finds the correct plug-in.

6. In the Heigh**t** field, enter the height of the plug-in in pixels. For this example, enter `300`.

7. In the **W**idth field, enter the width of the plug-in in pixels. For this example, enter `400`.

8. Check the Hide **P**lug-In checkbox if you don't want a visual representation of the plug-in to appear on the page. You can choose this option if you use a plug-in to insert a sound on your page. In that case, you do not want a visual representation. Leave this option unchecked for the example.

9. Use the Layout's **A**lignment drop-down menu to specify how you want the plug-in to align with other text on your page. For the example, leave it set at the default of `Default`. The following options are available:

Left	Places the plug-in in the left margin and wraps the text that follows along the control's right side.
Right	Places the plug-in in the right margin and wraps the text that follows along the control's left side.
Top	Aligns the top of the plug-in with the text.
Texttop	Aligns the top of the plug-in with the top of the tallest text in the line.
Middle	Aligns the middle of the plug-in with the text.
Absmiddle	Aligns the plug-in with the middle of the current line.
Baseline	Aligns the plug-in to the baseline of the current line.
Bottom	Aligns the bottom of the plug-in with the text.
Absbottom	Aligns the plug-in with the bottom of the current line.
Center	Aligns the plug-in to the center of the page.

10. In the **Bo**rder thickness field, enter the thickness of the border in number of pixels. This sets a black border around the plug-in. For this example, enter **0**.

11. In the Hori**z**ontal spacing field, enter the number of pixels you want between the plug-in and the nearest text. The default is 0. Enter **5** here.

12. In the **V**ertical spacing field, enter the number of pixels you want between the plug-in and the line above or below the current line. For this example, leave this option at the default of 0.

13. Click the **S**tyle button to add cascading style sheet properties to the plug-in, if desired. For more information about cascading style sheets, see Chapter 27.

14. Click OK to exit the Plug-In Properties dialog box. A representation of the plug-in appears on your page, as shown in Figure 25.10.

15. Choose the **F**ile | **S**ave command (Ctrl+S) or click the Save button on the Standard toolbar. The Save As dialog box appears.

16. In the **T**itle field, enter **PowerPoint Animation**.

17. In the **U**RL field, enter **powerpoint.htm**.

18. Choose OK. The page is saved to your Web. Use the **F**ile | Preview in **B**rowser command to preview the animation in a browser that supports plug-ins. The PowerPoint animation appears on the page, sized as you specified in the Plug-In Properties dialog box. An example is shown in Figure 25.11.

Figure 25.10.

The representation of the plug-in appears on your page.

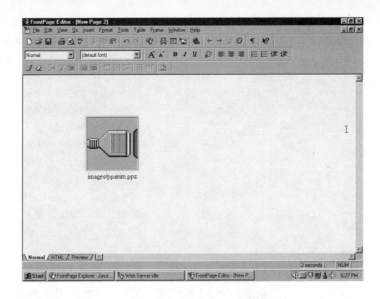

Figure 25.11.

The PowerPoint animation as viewed in a browser that supports Netscape plug-ins.

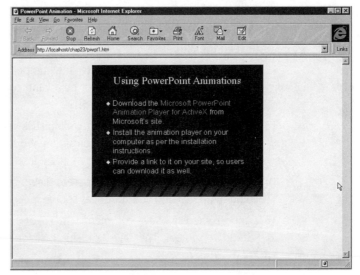

What happens if the user doesn't have the plug-in you used on his or her computer? One solution is to provide a link to the correct plug-in as outlined previously in step 5. However, some browsers automatically locate the source of the plug-in as well. For example, Netscape Navigator displays a dialog box that enables the user to download the appropriate plug-in for the page.

Workshop Wrap-Up

This chapter introduced you to two ways that you can extend the capabilities of your Web pages. Using Java applets and Netscape plug-ins, you no longer need to limit your Web pages to text, images, and animation. You can view documents in their native formats, add extended capabilities such as chats and enhanced multimedia, view Web pages in three-dimensional virtual worlds, and much more. You learned how to add and configure Java applets to your pages and how to set the parameters in your Web pages. You also learned how to insert a plug-in into your pages and what happens when the user doesn't have the right plug-in player.

Next Steps

In the next chapter, you'll learn how to use the HTML Markup component and the HTML view in the FrontPage Editor to add your own HTML code to your Web pages. To learn more about other hot new Web technologies, refer to the following chapters:

❑ See Chapter 27, "Using Styles," to learn how to create your own cascading style sheets that apply consistent fonts and background properties through-out your Web pages.

❑ See Chapter 28, "Working with ActiveX and Scripts," to learn about adding ActiveX controls and scripting languages such as VBScript and JavaScript into your pages.

❑ In Chapter 29, "Real-Life Examples V: Using Browser-Specific Features," you address some of the issues that you need to face when you incorporate new technologies into your Web site.

Q&A

Q: Where can I go to find examples of Java applets or applets that I can use in my pages?

A: A great source for both is Gamelan, which is located at `http://www.gamelan.com`. Before you plop any applet on your page, however, check to see whether you have the rights to use it freely or to find the require-ments to license or purchase the rights.

Q: I'm using a browser that supports Netscape plug-ins, but I don't see the PowerPoint animation in my page. How come?

A: Check to see whether the plug-in is configured properly. For example, in Netscape, you should see the plug-in file `npsurge.dll` installed in your `plugins` directory. The following MIME types are configured for the plug-in:

`application/vnd.ms-powerpoint` for PowerPoint templates (.ppt extension)

`application/x-mspowerpoint` for PowerPoint slide shows (.pps extension)

`application/ms-powerpoint` for PowerPoint presentations (.ppt extension)

`application/mspowerpoint` for PowerPoint animations (.ppz extension)

Q: Can I combine Java applets and plug-ins on the same page?

A: Sure you can. Watch those file sizes, though. If a user has to download many megabytes worth of files to view a page, he or she might decide to go to another page.

Q: I like using all the latest technologies in my pages. What's the best way to put them in my Web so that I can make sure users have the right browsers?

A: One way is to arrange your Web so that all pages that use Java applets are in one section of your Web, plug-ins are in another, ActiveX pages another, and so on. Each section can have a home page that links to all the pages in the section. On that page, you can place a link that enables the user to download the browser that supports the features you use in the section. Advanced Web developers sometimes write scripts that automatically detect what browser is used and load a page that is compatible with the browser.

TWENTY-SIX

Using Your Own HTML

FrontPage contains a lot of built-in features that make your Web designing tasks a lot easier. You need only edit the HTML code in your pages when you choose to, for the most part. But sometimes you need to add other features in your pages that are not supported by the FrontPage Editor.

If you are interested in adding your own HTML code, you have peeked behind the scenes and studied the code that FrontPage generates for you automatically. You feel you really have a handle on things and want to get your hands on the code to fine-tune it and tweak it a little. You might want to add other features that are not supported from within FrontPage 98.

FrontPage enables you to add code in your pages in a couple of ways. One solution is to use the HTML tab, which opens a color-coded HTML editor. There, you can modify the code that FrontPage generates without going through the dialog boxes to modify the code. Another solution is to use the HTML Markup component, which enables you to add HTML code that FrontPage does not directly support and bypasses FrontPage's code-checking features.

In this chapter, you

- ❏ Take a peek at the HTML editor provided with FrontPage
- ❏ Use the HTML Markup component to place into your pages snippets of code that FrontPage does not check for accuracy
- ❏ Learn how to create floating frames using your own HTML code

Tasks in this chapter:

- ❏ Using the HTML Markup Component
- ❏ Creating a Web for Your Floating Frame Tasks
- ❏ Adding a Floating Frame to Your Web Page
- ❏ Naming Your Floating Frame
- ❏ Loading Other Pages in Your Floating Frame

When the FrontPage Features Aren't Enough

The Web is like the weather: Wait five minutes and it will change. As a result, it's hard for browser and Web page editing software programmers to predict what features they'll need to incorporate in their software. It's one of the reasons FrontPage gives you a couple of ways to add extensibility. For those tags that aren't covered in the FrontPage Editor, you can use the HTML Markup component or the **H**TML tab to enter code manually.

Using the HTML Tab

When you want to view or edit your HTML code, choose the HTML tab in the FrontPage Editor. This editor is a color-coded HTML editor, where HTML tags are displayed in purple, attributes are displayed in red, attribute values are displayed in blue, and page content is displayed in black. An example of a Web page displayed in the HTML tab is shown in Figure 26.1.

Figure 26.1.

The HTML tab is a color-coded HTML editor from which you can modify your HTML code.

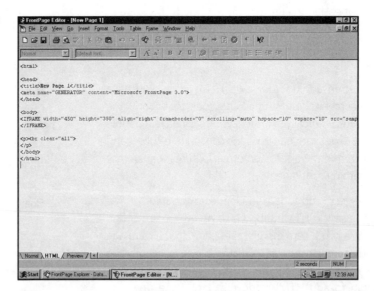

From the HTML tab, you can add or modify any code that you choose. Some find it quicker to modify settings from this window, rather than re-enter settings in the FrontPage dialog boxes. You can also use copy (Ctrl+C) and paste (Ctrl+V) commands to copy code from other HTML editors and insert it into HTML view. When you are finished editing the code, choose OK to return to the WYSIWYG FrontPage Editor.

Using the HTML Markup Component

What happens if you insert code that the FrontPage Editor does not directly support? FrontPage 98 fields the code, and it handles the situation automatically for you. When you return to the FrontPage Editor, you see small yellow rectangles on your page with question marks in them. These are HTML Markup components, which you will use in this task.

What the HTML Markup components do is enable you to enter "snippets" of code that the FrontPage Editor doesn't write itself. The code that is contained in HTML Markup components is not checked for accuracy. FrontPage lets you do the thinking there and figures you've got it right.

The HTML Markup component is really quite simple to use. Here's basically what you do:

1. Create as much as you can in the FrontPage Editor's Normal tab. After all, it's easy to use, and you can get a good idea of what your page layout looks like.

2. From the Normal tab, position the insertion point where you want to add additional features by using code.

3. Choose Insert | FrontPage Component and then double-click Insert HTML. The HTML Markup dialog box, shown in Figure 26.2, appears.

Figure 26.2.

Insert HTML code into your page with the HTML Markup dialog box.

4. Enter the code you want to include on the page in the HTML Markup dialog box or cut and paste it from other editors.

5. Choose OK. FrontPage then inserts the code into your Web page. If you view your page in HTML view, you will see green text that marks the start point and end point of the code that you placed in the HTML Markup component.

6. To edit the code in the HTML Markup component, switch to HTML view. Edit the code that lies between the `webbot bot="HTMLMarkup" startspan` and `webbot bot="HTMLMarkup" endspan` tags.

What Are Floating Frames?

I'll give you an example of a feature that is supported by Internet Explorer 3.0 and later, but is not supported in the FrontPage Editor. By learning how to create a floating frame, you learn how to use the HTML Markup component and HTML view to add code to your pages.

Floating frames were introduced in Internet Explorer 3.0. They differ in some respects from a standard frameset, which you learned about in Chapter 18, "Frames: Pages with Split Personalities." Standard framesets have the advantage of being compatible with more browsers, but alas—many people don't like them. Not only are you somewhat limited in how your page can be laid out, but frames can sometimes detract from a Web page's appearance.

Floating frames provide a bridge between a standard Web page and a frameset. They are similar to standard framesets in that they enable the contents of another Web page to be displayed in a defined space; but that is where the similarity ends. A floating frame can appear anywhere within a Web page—even within tables and forms. Figure 26.3 shows a floating frame placed in the right cell of a table. With floating frames, contents of other pages can appear just about anywhere imaginable, much like placing images on your pages. Gone are the boundaries that confine frame placement within a designated portion of your browser window.

Figure 26.3.

A floating frame can appear anywhere on a Web page. Here, Internet Explorer 3.0 displays a floating frame in the right cell of a table.

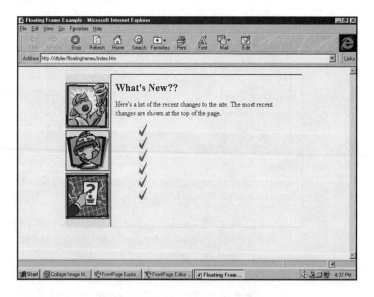

Floating frames differ from standard framesets in the following ways:

❏ One or more floating frames can be placed *anywhere* on a Web page. You can place a floating frame anywhere that an image can be placed.

❏ The browser window is not divided into different frames. Instead, areas within your Web page are defined as frames. This enables more flexibility in page design, especially when used in conjunction with tables.

❏ Floating frames use the IFRAME tag in Microsoft Internet Explorer 3.0 or later.

❏ One drawback to floating frames is that you cannot specify an alternative content source. Normal framesets enable you to designate a page, which displays in lieu of the frameset when a frame-compatible browser is not detected; the IFRAME tag does not. When a browser that does not support floating frames comes across a page that includes them, it is as if nothing exists in that portion of the page; no contents appear there at all. So, if you decide to incorporate floating frames in your pages, provide a means to display alternative content for browsers that do not support them.

The Anatomy of Floating Frames

Microsoft Internet Explorer 3.0 utilizes the IFRAME tag to define a floating frame. You can add floating frame tags to your Web pages by using HTML view in the FrontPage Editor or by inserting the code into HTML Markup components. The IFRAME tag uses the attributes and values listed in Table 26.1.

Table 26.1. Attributes for the IFRAME tag.

Attribute	Value	Description
ALIGN	LEFT	Aligns the floating frame to the left margin of the page. This is the default value if no alignment is specified.
ALIGN	RIGHT	Aligns the floating frame to the right margin of the page.
FRAMEBORDER	0	Creates a borderless floating frame, giving it a seamless look.
HEIGHT	*n*	Defines the height of the floating frame in pixels. See also WIDTH attribute.
HEIGHT	*n%*	Defines the height of the floating frame in percentage of browser window. See also WIDTH attribute.

continues

Table 26.1. continued

Attribute	Value	Description
HSPACE	*n*	Defines the size of the margin around the horizontal (top and bottom) sides of the frame, in pixels. See also VSPACE attribute.
NAME	*framename*	Assigns a name to the floating frame. This name can be referenced as a target frame when creating links to pages that should appear within the floating frame.
SCROLLING	AUTO	Creates a floating frame that contains scrollbars as necessary.
SCROLLING	NO	Creates a floating frame that does not contain scrollbars.
SCROLLING	YES	Creates a floating frame that contains scrollbars on the right and bottom sides of the frame.
SRC	*url*	Defines the URL that is loaded into the floating frame when the page first opens. The URL should be relative to the folder in which the floating frame resides.
VSPACE	*n*	Defines the size of the margin around the vertical (left and right) sides of the frame, in pixels. See also HSPACE attribute.
WIDTH	*n*	Defines the width of the floating frame in pixels. See also HEIGHT attribute.
WIDTH	*n%*	Defines the width of the floating frame in percentage of browser window. See also HEIGHT attribute.

The following code example shows the syntax of all the commands listed in Table 26.1. The code creates a floating frame named mainframe. It measures 450 pixels wide and 350 pixels high. The floating frame is aligned to the left margin of the page and does not display borders. Ten pixels of space will appear between the floating frame and the top, bottom, and side contents of your page. The page whatsnew.htm from your current Web will display in the floating frame when the page first opens:

```
<iframe width=450 height=350 align=left frameborder=0 hspace=10 vspace=10
➥name=mainframe src="whatsnew.htm">
</iframe>
<!--webbot bot="HTMLMarkup" endspan -->
```

Creating a Web for Your Floating Frame Tasks

To complete the tasks in this chapter, you'll need to create an empty Web in which to save the pages. You will also need to import a sample content page from the `Book\Chap26\Project Files` folder on the CD-ROM that accompanies this book (or you can create your own if you wish). To create the Web, follow these steps:

1. From the FrontPage Explorer, choose **F**ile I **N**ew I Front Page **W**eb. The New FrontPage Web dialog box appears.

2. Select the From Wizard or **T**emplate radio button and choose Empty Web from the list of available templates.

3. In the Choose a **t**itle for your FrontPage web field, enter **Floating Frames**.

4. Choose OK. FrontPage creates the Web.

5. Click the Folders icon in the Views pane to switch to Folders view. Highlight the home folder in the Web.

6. To import the sample Web pages from the CD-ROM that accompanies this book, choose **F**ile I **I**mport. The Import File to FrontPage Web dialog box appears.

7. Click **A**dd File. The Add File to Import List dialog box appears.

8. Use the Look in box to locate the following files in the `Book\Chap26\Project Files` folder on the CD-ROM that accompanies this book. Highlight the filenames and choose **O**pen. You return to the Import File to FrontPage Web dialog box.

   ```
   faqs.htm
   index.htm
   links.htm
   whatsnew.htm
   ```

9. Click OK. The files are imported into the home directory of your Web.

10. Highlight the `images` folder in your Web. To import the images from the CD-ROM that accompanies this book, choose **F**ile I **I**mport. The Import File to FrontPage Web dialog box appears.

11. Click **A**dd File. The Add File to Import List dialog box appears.

12. Use the Look in box to locate the following files in the `Book\Chap26\Project Files` folder on the CD-ROM that accompanies this book. Highlight the filenames and choose **O**pen. You return to the Import File to FrontPage Web dialog box.

    ```
    checkmrk.jpg
    faqs.gif
    links.gif
    news.gif
    ```

13. Click OK. The images are imported into the images directory of your Web.

Adding a Floating Frame to Your Web Page

Figure 26.4 shows the page to which you will add the floating frame. Three images appear in the left cell in the table on the page. When the user clicks any of the images, the associated page will display in a cell in the right side of the table.

Figure 26.4.

You will add your floating frame to the right cell in this table.

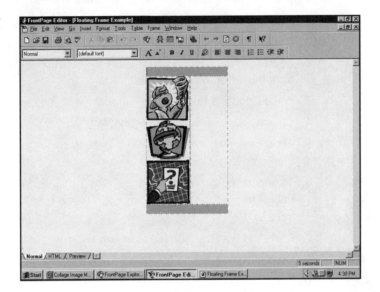

Although you can enter or edit HTML code directly from FrontPage by using the **V**iew I **H**TML command, FrontPage checks the code you enter for compatibility with the tags supported by the FrontPage Editor. FrontPage checks the accuracy of your code and makes any changes in syntax that it feels are necessary. Sometimes, however, it may change things in such a way that your code may not work in certain browsers. If you add your code in an HTML Markup component, you can avoid this. The FrontPage Editor does not verify or modify the code you insert within an HTML Markup component.

In the following task, a basic floating frame that measures 450 pixels wide and 350 pixels high is defined on the page. The floating frame displays the What's New page within the right cell in the table when the page first opens.

To create the floating frame on the Floating Frame Example page, follow these steps:

1. From the FrontPage Explorer, double-click the `index.htm` page in your Web's home directory to open it in the FrontPage Editor.

2. Click in the right cell of the second row in the table.

3. Choose Insert | FrontPage Component. The Insert FrontPage Component dialog box appears.

4. Double-click Insert HTML. The HTML Markup dialog box shown in Figure 26.5 appears.

5. To define a basic floating frame that measures 450×350 pixels and displays the whatsnew.htm page within it, enter the following code in the HTML Markup dialog box:

```
<iframe width=450 height=350 src="whatsnew.htm">
</iframe>
```

6. Choose OK. To view the code that you placed in the HTML Markup component, click the HTML tab in the FrontPage Editor. The code in the HTML Markup component appears as follows (edited for clarity, and also shown in Figure 26.6). The first and last lines in the following code example are displayed in green text in HTML view. Tags are displayed in purple, attributes in red, and values in blue.

```
<!--webbot bot="HTMLMarkup" startspan -->
<iframe width=450 height=350 src="whatsnew.htm">
</iframe>
<!--webbot bot="HTMLMarkup" endspan -->
```

7. Click the Normal tab in the FrontPage Editor to return to normal view.

8. Choose File | Save (Ctrl+S) or click the Save button on the Standard toolbar. The page is updated to your current Web.

9. Choose File | Preview in Browser. The Preview in Browser dialog box appears.

10. From the Browser list, select Microsoft Internet Explorer 3.0 (or later). Select the resolution in which you want to preview the page from the Window Size field.

11. Choose OK. The floating frames appear on the page in your browser window. You see the What's New page appear in your floating frame, as shown in Figure 26.4.

Figure 26.6.
The code you entered for your floating frame appears between starting and ending tags in HTML view.

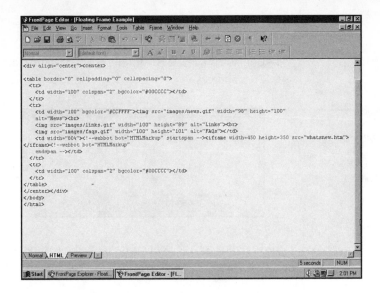

 # Naming Your Floating Frame

Now you know how to construct a basic floating frame. The next thing you need to do is configure the frameset so that when the user clicks the images on your page, it loads the appropriate page into the floating frame. To do this, you must name your floating frame. This is easily done by adding the name attribute to your floating frame definition. You can do this in HTML view in the FrontPage Editor.

In the following example, you assign a name of mainframe to your floating frame:

1. Choose the HTML tab in the FrontPage Editor. You switch to HTML view, where you can edit your code manually.

2. To name your floating frame, add the name attribute and a name for the frame to your HTML code in the HTML Markup dialog box. If your floating frame is defined in pixels, the code should be similar to the following:

```
<!--webbot bot="HTMLMarkup" startspan -->
<iframe width=450 height=350 name=mainframe src="whatsnew.htm">
</iframe>
<!--webbot bot="HTMLMarkup" endspan -->
```

 # Loading Other Pages in Your Floating Frame

The basic steps to load a page into a floating frame are similar to those used when you link to pages in a standard frameset. You'll find it easier to create the links, though, if the pages already exist in your current Web. The steps to creating a link to a page that displays in a floating frame are briefly described here.

In the following example, you will use the three images on your page to create hyperlinks that load the correct page into the floating frame. Follow these steps:

1. Choose the Normal tab in the FrontPage Editor to switch to normal view.

2. Click the top image in the left cell of the table and click the Create or Edit Hyperlink button on the Standard toolbar. The Create Hyperlink dialog box appears.

3. From the list of current pages in your Web, highlight whatsnew.htm. The URL appears in the **U**RL field.

4. Click the Change Target Frame button located to the right of the Target Frame field. The Target Frame dialog box shown in Figure 26.7 appears.

Figure 26.7.

Use the Target Setting field in the Target Frame dialog box to assign your floating frame to the page.

5. Because this is not a standard frameset, a frameset preview will not appear in the Current Frames Page section of the Target Frame dialog box. Instead, you enter the name of the floating frame in the Target Setting field at the bottom of the dialog box. Enter **mainframe** in the **T**arget Setting field.

6. Because the other two images on your page will also load pages into the mainframe floating frame, check the **M**ake default for hyperlinks on the page checkbox. You will not need to assign a target frame to the other image hyperlinks on the page.

7. Choose OK. You return to the Create Hyperlink dialog box, and Page Default (mainframe) appears in the Target Frame field. Choose OK to create the hyperlink.

8. Click the middle image in the left cell. Choose the Create or Edit Hyperlink button. From the list of pages in your current Web, highlight `links.htm`. Notice that `Page Default (mainframe)` already appears in the **T**arget Frame field. Choose OK to create the hyperlink.

9. Click the bottom image in the left cell. Choose the Create or Edit Hyperlink button. From the list of pages in your current Web, highlight `faqs.htm`. Again, `Page Default (mainframe)` already appears in the **T**arget Frame field. Choose OK to create the hyperlink.

10. Choose **F**ile | **S**ave (Ctrl+S) or click the Save button on the Standard toolbar to save your page to the current Web.

11. Choose **F**ile | Preview in **B**rowser, and select Internet Explorer 3.0 or later. You may need to use the Refresh button in Internet Explorer to load the most recent version of your page into the browser. Now when you click the images in the left cell in the table, the associated page displays in the right cell in the table, as shown in Figure 26.8.

Figure 26.8.
When you click the images in the right cell, the target page displays in the left cell in the table.

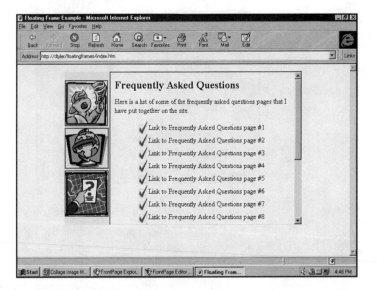

Workshop Wrap-Up

As you've learned in this chapter, it's very easy to customize and use your own HTML code in your Web pages. Besides learning how to use the HTML Markup component and the HTML view in the FrontPage Editor, you have also learned a little bit about floating frames. Note, however, that floating frames are currently supported only by

Internet Explorer 3.0 or later. Other browsers will display blank areas where the floating frames are supposed to appear. If you plan to use floating frames on your site, either provide alternate content for other browsers or use them on a site where you are certain that everyone will browse your pages using Internet Explorer (such as in an Intranet environment).

Next Steps

In the next chapter, you will learn how to customize the look of your pages by creating your own cascading style sheets. By configuring your own custom styles in user-friendly dialog boxes, you can create pages that use consistent fonts, colors, backgrounds, margin settings, and more throughout all the pages in your Web site.

To learn more about working with your own HTML code, refer to the following chapters:

❑ See Appendix B, "FrontPage Reference," for a list of sites that can help you with your own HTML code.

❑ Appendix C, "HTML Quick Reference," outlines a list of the tags that are supported directly by FrontPage 98. If a tag does not appear on the list, you can add it with the HTML Markup component or by entering your code in HTML view.

Q&A

Q: Are you saying that it's actually best to do as much as I can in the FrontPage Editor and then add the rest with the HTML Markup Component or the HTML window?

A: I find it to be the simplest way, but you might learn different tips and tricks as you become more familiar with entering your own code. If you can see what you get while you're working on it, why not use that to your advantage while you develop your page?

Q: Can I add VBScript and Java Script code using the HTML Markup bot and HTML view?

A: Sure you can—but you can also add scripting with the Script Wizard. This is discussed in more detail in Chapter 28, "Working with ActiveX and Scripts."

TWENTY-SEVEN

Using Styles

If you elect not to use themes in your Web, you can still take advantage of the power of cascading style sheets. You can build your own style sheets using commands and dialog boxes in the FrontPage Editor. Cascading style sheets enable you to precisely control the way fonts, colors, and images appear on your pages.

What Are Cascading Style Sheets?

Cascading style sheets form a new and developing Web technology that helps you specify text and page formatting options similar to those that you design in a word processing or page layout program. You achieve precise control over the formatting of text in your Web pages, specifying properties such as text color, font face, letter and line spacing, font weight, and more. The properties you specify can be assigned to an entire site, a single page, or an element on a page.

The themes that you are already familiar with from preceding chapters use cascading style sheet tags to achieve their special looks. The cascading style sheets associated with themes are referred to as *external style sheets*. They are linked to each of the pages in your Web through HTML commands located in the header of each page.

To apply a custom style sheet for a single Web page, you create an *embedded style sheet*. Embedded style sheets are similar to external style sheets, except that the cascading style sheet properties apply only to the current page. You can also apply cascading style sheet properties to any element on a page. When you apply a property in this manner, you use an *inline style*. This chapter primarily shows you how to create embedded style sheets and how to apply inline styles to your pages.

Creating an Embedded Style Sheet

An embedded style sheet is a set of CSS selectors, properties, and values that are built in to a single Web page. The CSS rules that you specify in an embedded style sheet override or add to the rules that are specified in an external style sheet.

You can create an embedded style sheet with the **F**ormat | **S**tylesheet command in the FrontPage Editor. To create an embedded style sheet, follow these steps:

1. From the FrontPage Editor, create a new page, or open the page that you want to create an embedded style sheet within.

2. Choose **F**ormat | **S**tylesheet. The Format Stylesheet dialog box shown in Figure 27.1 appears. Initially, the dialog box displays the following CSS code:

```
<style>
<!--
-->
</style>
```

Figure 27.1.

The Format Stylesheet dialog box contains the code used to define your embedded style sheet.

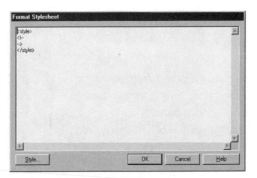

3. Position the insertion point at the end of the second line and press Enter to begin a new line.

4. Enter a selector for which you want to define a style.

   ❑ Enter a selector such as **H1**, **body**, or **address** (or similar tags, as shown in Table 27.1) to assign a style to a standard HTML tag.

   ❑ To create a special style, you define a class selector. The class selector can be a variation of a standard HTML tag (for example, **H1.red**, **H1.blue**, and **H1.green** are selectors for three different level 1 headings colored red, blue, and green). You can also create class selectors that define specific types of text on your pages (such as **.quotations**, **.notes**, or **.tips**).

❏ To create an ID selector, which is usually used on a per-element basis, precede the selector name with a pound sign (such as **#footer** or **#price**).

5. Press the spacebar to follow your selector name with a space and then press the *Style* button. The Style dialog box shown in Figure 27.2 appears.

Figure 27.2.
Use the Style dialog box to choose the properties and values that will be used for the style selector.

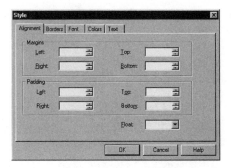

6. Complete your selections in the Style dialog box as indicated in the section "Using the Style Dialog Box," later in this chapter.

7. Choose OK to return to the Format Stylesheet dialog box.

8. Repeat steps 4 through 7 to add additional selectors, properties, and values to your style sheet, placing each selector on a new line. After you define all your selectors, press OK to return to the FrontPage Editor.

Table 27.1. HTML tags you can use as selectors.

HTML Tag	Description
a:link	Hyperlink text
a:visited	Visited hyperlink text
a:active	Active hyperlink text
address	Address paragraphs
applet	Java applet
b	Bold text
blink	Blinking text
body	Body text or background properties
br	Line break
caption	Table caption
cite	Citation text

continues

Table 27.1. continued

HTML Tag	Description
code	Code text
dd	Definition
dfn	Definition text
dir	Directory list
dt	Defined term
em	Emphasized text
h1	Heading 1
h2	Heading 2
h3	Heading 3
h4	Heading 4
h5	Heading 5
h6	Heading 6
hr	Horizontal rule
I	Italic text
img	Image
input	Checkbox, pushbutton, hidden form field, image form field, radio button, text box
kbd	Keyboard text
marquee	Marquee
menu	Menu list
ol	Numbered list
option	Drop-down menu
pre	Preformatted paragraphs
s	Strikethrough text
samp	Sample text
strike	Strikethrough text
strong	Strong (or bold) text
sub	Subscript text
sup	Superscript text
table	Table
tbody	Table body
td	Data cell in table

HTML Tag	Description
textarea	Scrolling text box
tfoot	Table footer
th	Header cell in table
thead	Table header
tt	Typewriter text
u	Underlined text
ul	Bulleted list
var	Variable text

 # Using the Style Dialog Box

Use the Style dialog box to select the properties and values that apply to a style selector. There are several different tabs in the Style dialog box, enabling you to control almost every aspect of a font. You can also apply some of the properties and values to images. The tabs in the Style dialog box are described in the following sections.

Setting Alignment

The Alignment tab in the Style dialog box, shown in Figure 27.3, specifies margins, padding, and text wrapping properties of an element such as an image, Java applet, or plug-in. The alignment settings specify border margins and padding around the element and how text and other content wrap around the element. Examples are shown in Figure 27.4.

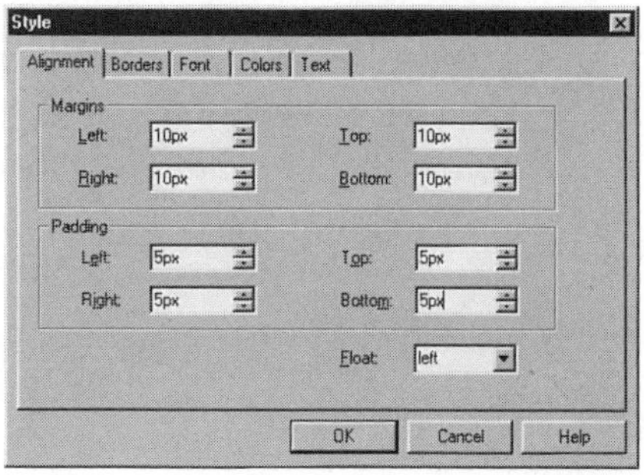

Figure 27.3.

Use the Alignment tab to specify margins, padding, and how text wraps (or floats) around an image or other page element.

Figure 27.4.

Examples of alignment settings applied to an image.

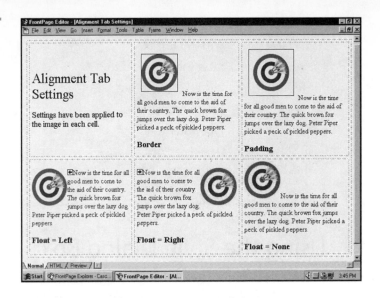

To specify the alignment settings, follow these steps:

1. Click the Alignment tab in the Style dialog box. This tab is shown in Figure 27.3.

2. To specify the distance between the borders of an element and the edges of an element, enter or choose a unit of measurement (shown in Table 27.2) for the following settings in the Margins section:

Left	Defines the width of the left margin
Right	Defines the width of the right margin
Top	Defines the height of the top margin
Bottom	Defines the height of the bottom margin

3. To specify the amount of space between the borders of the selected element and the content of the element, enter or choose a unit of measurement (shown in Table 27.2) for the following settings in the Padding section:

Left	Defines the amount of padding between the left border and the content of the element
Right	Defines the amount of padding between the right border and the content of the element
Top	Defines the amount of padding between the top border and the content of the element
Bottom	Defines the amount of padding between the bottom border and the content of the element

4. To specify how surrounding text wraps around the selected element, choose one of the following settings from the **F**loat drop-down menu:

none	Turns off text wrapping
left	Surrounding text wraps along the left side of the selected element
right	Surrounding text wraps along the right side of the selected element

Table 27.2. Units of measurement.

Unit	Example	Description
%	**5%**	5 percent
cm	**1cm**	1 centimeter
em	**5em**	5 ems, or 5 times the height of the element's font
ex	**5ex**	5 x-heights, or 5 times the height of the letter *x* in the selected font
in	**.2in**	.2 inches
mm	**10mm**	10 millimeters
pc	**12pc**	12 picas
pt	**16pt**	16 points
px	**25px**	25 pixels

Choosing Border Styles, Colors, and Widths

The Borders tab in the Style dialog box, shown in Figure 27.5, enables you to set colors and widths around a selected page element, such as an image, Java applet, plug-in, table, or table cell. Examples of Border settings are shown in Figure 27.6.

Figure 27.5.

Use the Border tab to specify the type of border that appears around an image or page element.

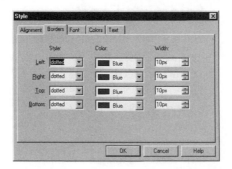

Figure 27.6.

*Examples of border
settings applied
to an image.*

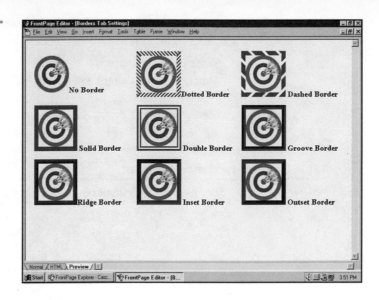

To specify border properties, follow these steps:

1. Click the Borders tab in the Style dialog box.

2. From the **L**eft, **R**ight, **T**op, or **B**ottom drop-down menu, select one of the following border styles: none, dotted, dashed, solid, double, groove, ridge, inset, or outset.

3. From the **L**eft, **R**ight, **T**op, or **B**ottom Color drop-down menu, choose Default to use the default color scheme or Custom to create a custom color, or choose one of 16 predefined colors.

4. From the **L**eft, **R**ight, **T**op, or **B**ottom Width drop-down menu, enter a number followed by **em** (for ems), **ex** (for x-height), or **px** (for pixels). You can also choose a pixel measurement or select thick, medium, or thin from the drop-down menu.

Selecting Fonts

You use the Font tab, shown in Figure 27.7, to specify a primary font and a secondary font, as well as its size. The primary font is used if the user has it installed on his or her system. The secondary font is used if the primary font does not reside on a user's system. Generally, if you select a specific primary font, you want to select a generic font for the secondary font. Generic font families are supported by several different browsers. You need to view generic font styles by using the Preview tab in the FrontPage Editor or by choosing the **F**ile I Preview in **B**rowser command to view in a browser that supports cascading style sheets. Examples of generic font families are shown in Figure 27.8.

Figure 27.7.

Use the Font tab to select font faces and size for your text.

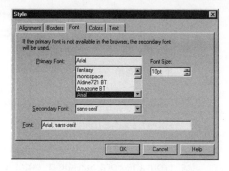

Figure 27.8.

Examples of generic font families.

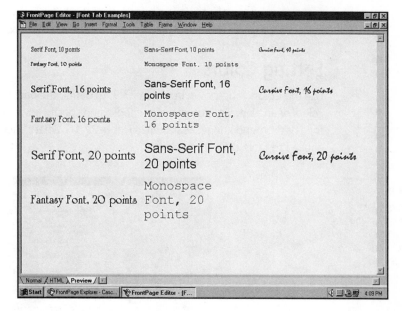

To specify a font and font size for an element, follow these steps:

1. Click the Font tab in the Style dialog box.

2. From the **P**rimary Font list, choose the font face that you want to use for the style, or select one of the following generic family fonts:

serif	Renders a serif font, such as Times New Roman
sans-serif	Renders a sans-serif font, such as Arial or Helvetica
cursive	Renders a cursive font, such as Zapf-Chancery
fantasy	Renders a fantasy font, such as Western
monospace	Renders a monospace font, such as Courier

3. From the *Secondary Font* drop-down menu, select an alternative font to be used if the primary font does not reside on the user's system. The selections are the same as those listed in step 2.

4. If you want to specify more than two fonts, you can enter additional fonts in the **F**ont field. It is generally a good idea to complete the list with a generic family name. Separate each font or font family name with a comma, as shown in the following example:

   ```
   Verdana, Arial, sans-serif
   ```

5. From the Font S**i**ze field, enter a value in points (example **12pt**) or use the spin dial to select a font size or one of the following values: `larger`, `smaller`, `xx-large`, `x-large`, `large`, `medium`, `small`, `x-small`, or `xx-small`.

Setting Colors

Use the Colors tab, shown in Figure 27.9, to define the background and foreground colors of an element. You can also choose and specify advanced positioning options for a background image, as shown in Figure 27.10, where background properties are applied to table cells.

Figure 27.9.

Use the Colors tab to define background and foreground colors or properties for background images.

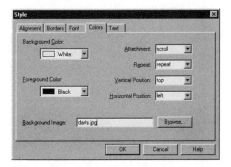

To assign background and foreground colors and properties, follow these steps:

1. Click the Colors tab in the Style dialog box.

2. From the Background **C**olor drop-down menu, select the color that you want to apply to the background of the element (such as page body or table cell). Choose Default to use the default color scheme, choose Custom to create a custom color, or choose one of 16 predefined colors. If you are going to use a background image, create or choose a background color that closely matches it.

Figure 27.10.

*Examples of background
repeats and horizontal
or vertical positions.*

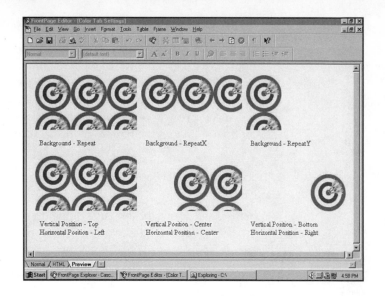

3. From the **F**oreground Color drop-down menu, select the color that you want
   to apply to the foreground text on the element (such as page body text or
   the text in the table cell). Choose Default to use the default color scheme,
   choose Custom to create a custom color, or choose one of 16 predefined
   colors.

4. From the **B**ackground Image field, use the Browse button to select a
   background image from the Image dialog box. You can select an image
   from your current Web, from the World Wide Web, or from your local or
   network hard drive. Choose OK to return to the Style dialog box after you
   select your image.

5. From the **A**ttachment drop-down menu, select one of the following options:

   scroll   Attaches the background image to the selected element so
                that the image and the element move together when the
                page is scrolled horizontally
   fixed   Attaches the background image to the page so that the
                image does not move when the page is scrolled

6. From the **Re**peat drop-down menu, select one of the following options:

   repeat   Tiles the image horizontally and vertically
   repeat-x   Tiles the image horizontally, but not vertically
   repeat-y   Tiles the image vertically, but not horizontally
   no repeat   Does not tile the image

7. From the **V**ertical Position drop-down menu, select one of the following options:

top	Aligns the top of the background image with the top of the selected element or page
center	Aligns the vertical center of the background image with the vertical center of the selected element or page
bottom	Aligns the bottom of the background image with the bottom of the selected element or page

8. From the **H**orizontal Position drop-down menu, select one of the following options:

left	Aligns the left edge of the background image with the left edge of the selected element or page
center	Aligns the horizontal center of the image with the horizontal center of the selected element or page
right	Aligns the right edge of the background image with the right edge of the selected element or page

Assigning Text Properties

Use the Text tab in the Style dialog box, shown in Figure 27.11, to assign additional text properties to a style. These settings include how a font is aligned and rendered and how much indentation and line spacing to use (see Figure 27.12).

Figure 27.11.

Use the Text tab to specify text alignment, weight, indentation, and spacing.

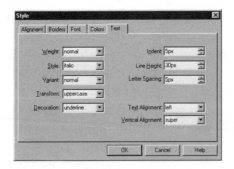

To set text properties, follow these steps:

1. Click the Text tab in the Style dialog box.

2. From the **W**eight drop-down menu, select one of the following:

normal	Selected element will use the same weight as the default font on the page
bold	Creates a font that is heavier than the default font on the page

bolder	Creates a font that is much heavier than the default font on the page
lighter	Creates a font that is lighter than the default font on the page
x00 (100 thru 900)	Specifies an absolute value that does not relate to the default font on the page; the greater this value, the heavier the font

Figure 27.12.
Examples of Text settings.

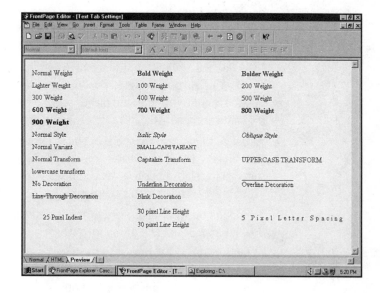

3. From the **S**tyle drop-down menu, select how you want the text to slant. Choose one of the following:

normal	Text displays normally
italic	Text displays in italics
oblique	Text displays in oblique (slanted)

4. From the V**a**riant drop-down menu, select one of the following:

| normal | Text displays normally |
| small-caps | Text displays in small uppercase letters |

5. From the **T**ransform drop-down menu, select one of the following:

none	Text displays normally
capitalize	Text displays the initial letter of each word with a capital letter
uppercase	Text displays all letters in uppercase
lowercase	Text displays all letters in lowercase

6. From the **D**ecoration drop-down menu, select one of the following:

none	Text displays normally
underline	A line appears beneath the text
overline	A line appears above the text
line-through	A line appears through the text (similar to strikethrough)
blink	The text blinks

7. To define the amount of indentation that the text uses, use the **In**dent drop-down menu. Enter a number and unit of measurement or use the spin dial to select a positive or negative value in pixels. Negative values outdent text. Units are the same as those listed in Table 27.2, earlier in this chapter.

8. To define the amount of distance between the baselines in each line of text, use the Line **H**eight drop-down menu. Enter a positive number and unit of measurement or use the spin dial to select a positive value in pixels. Units are the same as those listed in Table 27.2, earlier in this chapter.

9. To define the amount of space between letters, use the Letter **Sp**acing drop-down menu. Enter a positive number and unit of measurement or use the spin dial to select a positive value in pixels. Units are the same as those listed in Table 27.2, earlier in this chapter.

10. To define horizontal alignment of the text, use the Te**x**t Alignment drop-down menu. Select one of the following:

left	Aligns text to the left
center	Aligns text to the center
right	Aligns text to the right
justify	Justifies text across entire width of the page or element

11. To define vertical alignment of the text, use the **V**ertical Alignment drop-down menu. Select one of the following:

baseline	Aligns the baseline of the text to the baseline of the text in the parent element
sub	Subscripts the text in relation to the parent text
super	Superscripts the text in relation to the parent text
top	Aligns the top of the text to the tallest element on the line
text-top	Aligns the top of the text to the top of the parent text
middle	Aligns the middle of the text with the middle of the parent text
bottom	Aligns the bottom of the text to the lowest element on the line
text-bottom	Aligns the bottom of the text to the bottom of the parent text

Using Inline Styles

To assign a selector to a single element on your page, you use an inline style. You assign inline styles through the Class tab in the Style dialog box. This tab appears only when you choose the Style button from one of the Properties dialog boxes listed in Table 27.3.

To assign a class selector or ID selector to an element on your page, follow these steps:

1. Select the text or other page element to which you want to apply an inline style.

2. Open the applicable Properties dialog box, using one of the following methods: Choose **E**dit | Proper**ti**es, right-click and choose the appropriate Properties command from the pop-up menu or press Alt+Enter.

NOTE: You can sometimes assign a style selector when you place elements on your page. For example, the Insert Table dialog box contains a Style button. The commands shown in Table 27.3 are the commands you choose to insert each type of page element on your page. You may need to select the element and open its respective Properties dialog box to access the Style button in some cases.

3. Click the **S**tyle button in the related dialog box. In the example shown in Figure 27.13, the Style button in the Image Properties dialog box is clicked. The Style dialog box opens to the Class tab.

4. To assign a class selector to the page or element, enter the name of the class selector that you have defined in an external or embedded style sheet. Select an existing style from the list or enter the name of a new style in the box.

   To assign an ID selector to the element, enter the name of the ID selector that you have defined in an external or embedded style sheet.

5. To edit the properties of a class selector or ID selector *for the current inline occurrence only*, use the other tabs in the Style dialog box to change the settings. The other tabs are discussed in the section "Using the Style Dialog Box," earlier in this chapter.

6. Choose OK to exit the Style dialog box and choose OK again to return to the FrontPage Editor.

Figure 27.13.

Use the Class tab in the Style dialog box to assign a class selector or an ID selector to a page element.

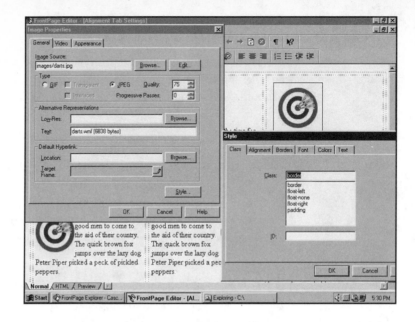

Table 27.3. Dialog boxes from where you can add styles.

Dialog Box	FrontPage Editor Command
ActiveX Control Properties	Insert I Advanced I ActiveX Control
Break Properties	Insert I Line Break
Bullets and Numbering (Image Bullets tab)	Format I Bullets and Numbering
Bullets and Numbering (Numbers tab)	Format I Bullets and Numbering
Cell Properties	Table I Cell Properties
Check Box Properties	Insert I Form Field I Check Box
Create Hyperlink	Edit I Hyperlink (for a new hyperlink)
Drop-Down Menu Properties	Insert I Form Field I Drop-Down Menu
Edit Hyperlink	Edit I Hyperlink (for an existing hyperlink)
Font (Font tab)	Format I Font
Font (Special Styles tab)	Format I Font
Format Stylesheet	Format I Stylesheet

Dialog Box	FrontPage Editor Command
Frame Properties	Frame I Frame Properties
Horizontal Line Properties	Insert I Horizontal Line
Image Properties	Insert I Image
Insert Table	Table I Insert Table
Java Applet Properties	Insert I Advanced I Java Applet
List Properties (Image Bullets tab)	Right-click on a list item and choose List Properties from the pop-up menu, or press Alt+Enter.
List Properties (Numbers tab)	Right-click on a list item and choose List Properties from the pop-up menu, or press Alt+Enter.
List Properties (Other tab)	Right-click on list item and choose List Properties from the pop-up menu, or press Alt+Enter.
Marquee Properties	Insert I Active Elements I Marquee
Options for Custom Form Handler	Choose Send to Other in the Form Properties dialog box and click the Options button.
Page Properties (General tab)	File I Page Properties
Paragraph Properties	Format I Paragraph
Plug-In Properties	Insert I Advanced I Plug-In
Push Button Properties	Insert I Form Field I Push Button
Radio Button Properties	Insert I Form Field I Radio Button
Scrolling Text Box Properties	Insert I Form Field I Scrolling Text Box
Table Properties	Table I Table Properties
Text Box Properties	Insert I Form Field I One-Line Text Box

Workshop Wrap-Up

In this chapter, you learned how to create embedded style sheets and how to apply inline styles to selected page elements. You learned about the HTML tags that you can apply cascading style sheet properties to and the dialog boxes from which you can create inline styles. You saw examples of many of the cascading style sheet properties and how they affect your pages.

Next Steps

In the following chapter, you learn how to add ActiveX controls to your Web pages and how to use the Script wizard in the FrontPage Editor. You can learn more about topics that relate to cascading style sheets in the following chapters:

❏ In Chapter 8, "Designing Your Web Navigation," you learn how to design a navigation system that applies navigation bars and banners which use cascading style sheet properties.

❏ In Chapter 14, "Using FrontPage Style Sheets and Themes," you learn how to choose a theme for your Web. Themes use special cascading style sheets that also specify images for navigation buttons and banners.

❏ In Appendix D, "About Theme-Related Cascading Style Sheets," you learn about the selectors, properties, and values that are used in your Web themes.

Q&A

Q: It looks like external style sheets and embedded style sheets contain just about the same information in the beginning of the page. Can I use an embedded style sheet for an external style sheet?

A: No, there are a couple of minor differences between the two types of files. External style sheets are saved with a `.css` extension and contain CSS rules without surrounding HTML tags. Microsoft's Web site contains information about how to use and implement cascading style sheets with Internet Explorer, as well as links to other sites with technical information. You can start with the following URL:

`http://www.microsoft.com/iesupport/content/css/default.htm`

You can also find additional information about cascading style sheets in *Laura Lemay's Web Workshop: Designing with Style Sheets, Tables, and Frames,* by Molly E. Holzschlag. This book is published by Sams.net (ISBN 1-57521-249-8).

Q: Let's say I have an external style sheet that assigns properties to all the pages in the Web. Then I use an embedded style sheet on a page and, in addition to that, apply inline styles to some of the page elements. Which one is "the boss" in this type of arrangement?

A: In general, the properties that you assign in an external style sheet take the lowest priority. If you then use an embedded style sheet in a page and assign new or different properties to a selector that was defined in the Web's external style sheet, those in the embedded style sheet *should* take precedence. Likewise, styles that you specify as inline styles *should* take precedence over both external and embedded style sheets. This is partly why they call them *cascading* style sheets.

I say they *should* take precedence with reservation, however. Much of the way a style sheet is rendered depends on how the browser parses and interprets the information. As with any new and developing Web technology, you should always test your cascading style sheets and pages in several different browsers to see how they appear.

TWENTY-EIGHT

Working with ActiveX and Scripts

Microsoft has developed another technology that has heated up the action in the browser war. ActiveX controls are reusable components that add special functions to your Web pages. What makes them different, however, is that you can use the same controls in software programs. This enables content developers to create Web pages and applications that work together. Nice stuff. With ActiveX, you can add form fields, enhanced navigation controls, animation and multimedia, credit card transactions, spreadsheet calculations, database communications, and more to your Web pages. Thousands of ActiveX controls are published by many third-party software vendors. These components run on Intel hardware, running Windows software. Internet Explorer 3.0 and later have ActiveX technology built into the browser. Other browsers can add ActiveX capabilities through the use of plug-ins.

FrontPage also enables you to insert scripts into your pages, using either VBScript or JavaScript. This is sometimes necessary to make some of the ActiveX controls work. For example, if you insert ActiveX form fields, such as text boxes, drop-down menus, and pushbuttons on your page, the script tells the browser what to do after the user pushes the button on the page.

Adding ActiveX to Your Pages

As with any other element that you can download from the Internet, you should verify that you have the right to use an ActiveX control. Some of these controls are available as freeware, whereas others are available on a commercial basis. Appendix B, "FrontPage Reference," lists some online sources where you can check out many ActiveX controls that are available for preview or for use. The following URL on Microsoft's Web site hosts a gallery of ActiveX controls:

```
http://microsoft.com/activeplatform/default.asp
```

 # Inserting an ActiveX Control

You insert an ActiveX control on your page in one of two ways. You use the following method when an ActiveX control exists on your system. When you encounter a page that contains an ActiveX control, you are given the option of downloading it. When you do, the controls are installed in your Windows system directory. They're also registered in the system registration database. FrontPage examines your system to see what ActiveX controls you have available and enables you to select one of them from a drop-down list.

To insert an ActiveX control that exists on your system, follow these steps:

1. From the FrontPage Editor, choose **I**nsert I **A**dvanced I **A**ctiveX Control, or use the Insert ActiveX Control button on the Advanced toolbar. The ActiveX Control Properties dialog box shown in Figure 28.1 appears.

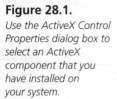
Figure 28.1.
Use the ActiveX Control Properties dialog box to select an ActiveX component that you have installed on your system.

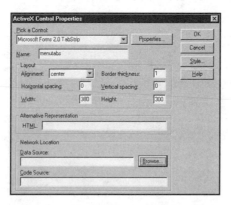

2. If you click the drop-down menu in the **P**ick a Control field, a list of all the ActiveX controls that are installed on your system appears. Assume, for example, that you have the Microsoft Web Browser Control installed on your system.

Some of the controls on your machine may be OCX controls that have not yet been fully upgraded to ActiveX protocol.

3. Click the Properties button. Two windows appear.

4. The Edit ActiveX Control window, shown on the left of Figure 28.2, displays the ActiveX control within it. From this window, you can resize the ActiveX control, if necessary, and preview some of the property settings for the control.

5. A Properties dialog box, shown on the right in Figure 28.2, contains a table editor that lists all the ActiveX control's properties and the current values set for each property. These properties are specific to each ActiveX control. When you highlight a property, you can enter its value or choose one of several values from a drop-down menu located at the top of the Properties box.

6. After you set the properties for your ActiveX control, click OK in the Edit ActiveX Control window. You return to the ActiveX Control Properties dialog box.

Figure 28.2.

The ActiveX control appears in the Edit ActiveX Control window. You use the Properties dialog box to define the parameters for a control that is installed on your system.

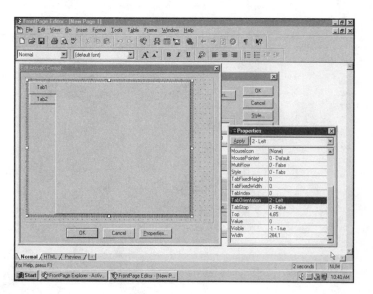

NOTE: When possible, obtain a reference document for the control you are inserting. The reference document should tell you the legal settings for each property, the events that can be implemented when the user clicks a control, and other methods that are particular to the control. ActiveX components often come with a Help file that contains this information.

When an ActiveX control is installed on your system, FrontPage obtains its class ID from your Windows registry. If you don't have a particular ActiveX control installed on your system but you know its class ID, you can insert it on your page. The class ID is a very long 128-bit string that identifies the name and version number of the ActiveX control that you are inserting. This number is assigned by the creator of the ActiveX control.

To insert an ActiveX control that does not exist on your system, follow these steps:

1. From the FrontPage Editor, choose **I**nsert I **A**dvanced I **A**ctiveX Control, or use the Insert ActiveX Control button on the Advanced toolbar. The ActiveX Control Properties dialog box shown in Figure 28.1 appears.

2. Enter the class ID for the control in the **P**ick a Control field. This is a number that is unique to each control and looks similar to the following example:

   EAE50EB0-4A62-11CE-BED6-00AA00611080

3. Click the Properties button. The Object Parameters dialog box shown at the left of Figure 28.3 appears.

Figure 28.3.

Use the Object Parameters dialog box to add parameters for controls that do not exist on your system. The parameters are entered in the Edit Object Parameter dialog box.

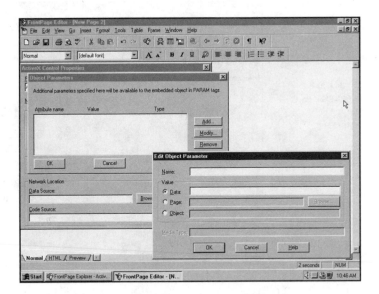

4. To add a parameter name and value, click the **A**dd button. The Edit Object Parameter box shown on the right in Figure 28.3 appears.

5. Enter the parameter name in the **N**ame field and its value in the **V**alue field.

6. Choose one of the following parameter types for the control you are adding:

   Data   Specifies that the parameter value should be interpreted as data. Enter the data into the **D**ata field.

Page	Specifies that the parameter value should be interpreted as the URL of a file. Enter the relative or absolute URL of the file in the **P**age field.
Object	Specifies that the parameter value should be interpreted as the name of another ActiveX control on the current page. Enter the name of the other control (as entered in the **N**ame field of its ActiveX Control Properties dialog box) in the **O**bject field.
Media Type	Enabled when the parameter type is Data or Page. Enables you to specify a MIME (Multipurpose Internet Mail Extension) type for the parameter.

7. Click OK to exit the Object Parameters dialog box. You return to the ActiveX Control Properties dialog box.

After you select a control using either of these methods, you complete the entries in the ActiveX Control Properties dialog box as follows:

1. In the **N**ame field, enter an optional name to use when referring to the ActiveX control within a script on the current page.

2. To specify how you want the ActiveX control to align with other text on your page, choose one of the following from the **A**lignment drop-down menu in the Layout section:

left	Places the ActiveX control in the left margin and wraps the text that follows along the control's right side.
right	Places the ActiveX control in the right margin and wraps the text that follows along the control's left side.
top	Aligns the top of the ActiveX control with the text.
Ttexttop	Aligns the top of the ActiveX control with the top of the tallest text in the line.
middle	Aligns the middle of the ActiveX control with the text.
absmiddle	Aligns the ActiveX control with the middle of the current line.
baseline	Aligns the ActiveX control to the baseline of the current line.
bottom	Aligns the bottom of the ActiveX control with the text.
absbottom	Aligns the ActiveX control with the bottom of the current line.
center	Aligns the ActiveX control to the center of the current line.

3. In the Border thic**k**ness field of the Layout section, enter the number of pixels in thickness that you want for the border around the control. This sets a black border around the control.

TIP: Try not to make your borders too thick if you elect to use them. In most cases, a border thickness of 1 or 2 pixels is sufficient.

4. In the Horizontal spacing field of the Layout section, enter the number of pixels you want between the ActiveX control and the nearest text. If there is no text on the same line as the control, you can leave this value at the default setting of 0.

5. In the **V**ertical spacing field of the Layout section, enter the number of pixels you want between the ActiveX control and the line above or below the current line. If there is no other text above or below the control, you can leave this value at the default setting of 0.

6. In the **W**idth field of the Layout section, enter the width of the ActiveX control in pixels.

7. In the Height field of the Layout section, enter the height of the ActiveX control in pixels.

TIP: You can size the width and height visually in the layout window of the ActiveX control and then use the **W**idth and Height fields in the ActiveX Control Properties dialog box to fine-tune the settings.

8. In the Alternate Representation, HTML field, enter the text that you want to appear when the user is not using a browser that supports ActiveX. If you leave this field blank, the user won't see anything in place of the control.

NOTE: Many sites offer Java applets that perform similar functions to ActiveX controls. One such site is Gamelan, which you will find at the following URL:

`http://www.gamelan.com`

9. In the Network Location field, enter the following parameters:

Data Source   Specify the URL of a file that contains the runtime parameters for the control. Click **B**rowse to locate the file in your current FrontPage Web, the World Wide Web, or your local or network hard drive.

Code Source   Specify the URL that Web browsers should use to download the ActiveX control when the page is loaded. This field is optional but recommended. A typical entry looks something like this:

```
http://www.codesite.com/activex/mycontrol.ocx#Version=2,55,0,1092
```

NOTE:
The code source file you specify here uses the codebase attribute. This entry enables the user to download the ActiveX control if it doesn't already exist on his or her system. If the user doesn't have the ActiveX control installed and you don't specify a value in this field, the user won't be able to view the ActiveX controls on your page.

The code source (or codebase entry, in HTML terms) also contains the version number of the control. If there is a more recent version of the control at the source URL, it is downloaded to the user's system. This ensures that the most current version of the ActiveX control is used.

In order to download an ActiveX control, the user must set security levels to enable downloading of ActiveX controls. These settings are found by choosing the **V**iew I **O**ptions command in Internet Explorer. For IE 3.0 and 4.0, select the Security tab in the Options dialog box and set the security level to Medium.

10. To change the style of an ActiveX control, click the **S**tyle button. The Style dialog box appears (see Figure 28.4). You can learn more about styles in Chapter 27, "Using Styles."

Figure 28.4.
Use the Style dialog box to change an ActiveX control.

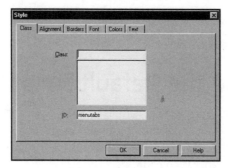

11. Click OK to exit the ActiveX Control Properties dialog box. A representation of the control appears on your page as a solid gray box.

Each time you insert an ActiveX control on your page, FrontPage adds code into your HTML page that is enclosed by an `<object>` tag. This tag defines the ActiveX control or controls that you inserted on your page. The code includes the ActiveX control's class ID, the settings you define in the layout section of the ActiveX Control Properties dialog box, and the properties that you set with the Properties table editor or Name/Value Pair dialog box. The properties you set are those indicated by the `param name` and `value` tags.

You can view and edit additional parameter names and values in the code as necessary by choosing the HTML tab in the FrontPage Editor. In Figure 28.5, for example, the HTML code for the Microsoft Forms 2.0 `Tab Strip ActiveX` control was edited to specify a total of 4 tabs (`TabsAllocated` parameter), and the `Items` and `Names` parameter values were changed to `Main`, `Links`, `Topics`, and `Help`. The code now looks something like this (edited slightly for clarity):

```
<object classid="clsid:EAE50EB0-4A62-11CE-BED6-00AA00611080"
    width="380"
    height="300"
    align="center"
    id="menutabs"
    border="1"
    <param name="ListIndex" value="0">
    <param name="Size" value="10022;7985">
    <param name="Items" value="Main;Links;Topics;Help;">
    <param name="TabOrientation" value="2">
    <param name="TipStrings" value=";;;;">
    <param name="Names" value="Main;Links;Topics;Help;">
    <param name="NewVersion" value="-1">
    <param name="TabsAllocated" value="4">
    <param name="Tags" value=";;;;">
    <param name="TabData" value="2">
    <param name="Accelerator" value=";;">
    <param name="FontName" value="Arial">
    <param name="FontCharSet" value="0">
    <param name="FontPitchAndFamily" value="2">
    <param name="FontWeight" value="0">
    <param name="TabState" value="3;3">
</object>
```

 TASK

Setting the Default Script Language

In some cases, FrontPage generates VBScript or JavaScript for you automatically. For example, when you validate form fields as discussed in Chapter 22, "Adding and Editing Form Fields," FrontPage 98 writes the associated VBScript or JavaScript and inserts it into your Web page.

Figure 28.5.

Edit the code in the FrontPage Editor's HTML tab, if necessary.

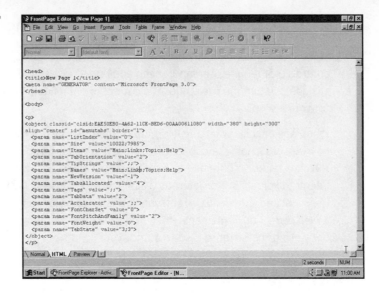

You need to configure your Web settings so that FrontPage knows which language to use when it generates these scripts. You can choose your default scripting language from the FrontPage Web Settings dialog box. To specify your default scripting language, follow these steps:

1. From the FrontPage Explorer, choose **T**ools | **W**eb Settings. The FrontPage Web Settings dialog box appears.

2. Choose the Advanced tab, shown in Figure 28.6.

3. In the Validation Scripts section, choose JavaScript or VBScript from the Language drop-down menu.

4. Click OK to exit the Web Settings dialog box, or click Apply to add more Web settings.

Figure 28.6.

Use the Advanced tab in the FrontPage Web Settings dialog box to choose the scripting language for scripts that FrontPage generates automatically.

Adding a Script to Your Pages

Some ActiveX controls, such as form fields, buttons, labels, tab strips, and similar controls that require user input, need additional code that defines what is supposed to happen when the user chooses a control or enters data into it. For this, you need to write a script.

FrontPage enables you to develop VBScript and JavaScript for your pages in a couple of ways. VBScript is a subset of Microsoft's Visual Basic programming language. VBScript code is contained within your Web page and can be read by Microsoft Internet Explorer 3.0 or later, as well as other browsers. JavaScript is derived from LiveScript and is similar to Java in syntax. This scripting language also can appear within a Web page. You implement either of these scripting languages by using dialog boxes or by using the Script Wizard to author your scripts.

NOTE:

The intent here isn't to show you how to write a complete script using JavaScript or VBScript, because that can get quite involved. This chapter shows you how to use the Script Wizard or the Script dialog box to enter the scripts in your pages.

It will help if you have knowledge of the JavaScript or VBScript programming languages. For additional references on these programming languages, check out the books mentioned in the section "Workshop Wrap-Up," later in this chapter.

 TASK

Inserting a Script into Your Page

When you insert a script on your page, you choose whether you want to use JavaScript or VBScript. You cannot use both languages on the same page.

An inline script is embedded in the page and runs when the page is displayed in a browser. If you're familiar with either scripting language, you can insert a script into your page with the Script dialog box as follows:

1. Position the insertion point on your page where you want the script to appear.
2. Choose **I**nsert | **A**dvanced | Scrip**t**. The Script dialog box shown in Figure 28.7 appears.
3. Select the scripting language you want to write your script in. To write a script using **V**BScript, select the VBScript radio button. To write a script using **J**avaScript, select the JavaScript radio button.

Figure 28.7.

You can enter your script manually in the Script field in the Script dialog box.

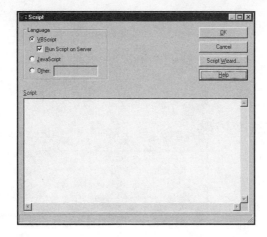

4. If you want to run your VBScript on Internet Information Server, check the **R**un Script on Server checkbox. Your page may need to be saved to your Web with an `.asp` (Active Server Pages) extension. If you leave this option unchecked, the script will run on the client computer when the user browses to your page.

5. In the **S**cript pane, enter the script.

6. Choose OK to place the script in your page.

Creating a Script with the Script Wizard

When you use the List view in the Script Wizard, you can write only event scripts. The interface enables you to select objects and associated events. Next, you pick an action that is done when the event takes place. The Script Wizard generates the JavaScript or VBScript for you automatically:

1. Position the insertion point on your page where you want the script to appear.

2. Choose **I**nsert | **A**dvanced | **S**cript. The Script dialog box appears.

3. Select the scripting language you want to write your script in. To write a script using **V**BScript, select the VBScript radio button. To write a script using **J**avaScript, select the JavaScript radio button.

4. Click the Script **W**izard button. The Script Wizard opens.

Selecting an Event Handler

When you first open the Script Wizard, you see a screen similar to that shown in Figure 28.8. You use the Script Wizard's List view to write event scripts. Event scripts perform actions when a user selects a control on your page.

Figure 28.8.

Use the List view in the Script Wizard to generate event scripts.

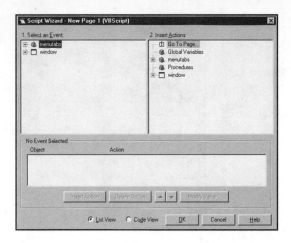

You see three panes in the Script Wizard's List view. The first pane is labeled 1. `Select` an `Event`. This is the event pane. You see a hierarchical view of the events that are available to choose from, including the events that are applicable to the ActiveX controls that are inserted on your page.

The first thing you want to do in the Script Wizard is select an event handler. You can't go anywhere else without doing that.

To select an event handler, follow these steps:

1. In the Select an **E**vent field, click the plus sign (+) beside the `window` object or ActiveX control (such as the `menutabs` control shown in Figure 28.9) to expand the tree. A list of the events that you can apply to the object appears, listed in alphabetical order by ID name.

2. Highlight the event that you want to apply an action to. For example, in Figure 28.9, the event handler that performs an action when the user clicks the mouse is selected.

After you select an event handler, a couple of things occur. The **S**cript pane waits for you to select an action for the event. In this case, the Script Wizard is waiting for you to select an action to occur when the user clicks the `menutabs` control, as indicated by the prompt above the bottom pane in the Script Wizard. In addition, the Insert Action button located at the bottom of the Script Wizard enables.

Next, you insert an action that takes place when the user selects the option. That's where it gets interesting (and where you need some additional references). You choose an action from the action pane, labeled 2. `Insert` **A**ctions. The actions listed in this pane are specific to the ActiveX controls included on your page.

Figure 28.9.

Select an event handler from the event pane.

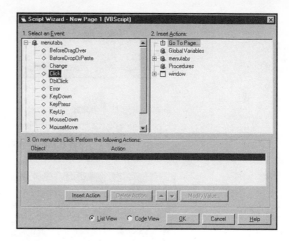

Selecting an Action

You select an action to perform from the action pane. The list of actions varies, depending on the control you are using. To give you a simple example of how to insert an action, I'll show you the Go To Page action. This action takes the user to another page or property in your script. You can also use this action to play a sound file when the user clicks a button.

To insert a Go To Page event, follow these steps:

1. In the action pane of the Script Wizard (labeled 2. `Insert Actions`), select Go To Page.

2. Click the Insert Action button at the bottom of the Script Wizard. The Go To Page dialog box shown in Figure 28.10 appears.

Figure 28.10.

To jump to a page, enter the URL in the Go To Page dialog box.

3. You can choose one of three options at this point:

   ❑ Enter the URL of the page you want to go to in the Enter a Text String field and choose OK. You return to the Script Wizard.

   ❑ To jump to a predefined variable, property value, or value that is not a simple constant, click the Custom button. The Go To Page dialog box shown in Figure 28.11 appears. Enter a single-word value in the Enter a single value or variable name field and choose OK to return to the Script Wizard.

❏ To change the color of a page or object, click the Color button. The color dialog box shown in Figure 28.12 appears. Select a color and choose OK to return to the Script Wizard.

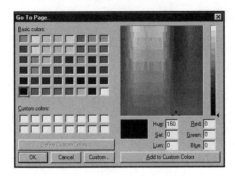

Inserting Global Variables

If your script uses global variables, you can add them to your script using the Global Variables selection in the action pane. When you insert a global variable, the Script Wizard places it at the beginning of the HTML code for the script. In VBScript, a global variable uses the form `dim` *variablename.* In JavaScript, global variables use the form `var` *variablename.*

To insert a new global variable, follow these steps:

1. Right-click anywhere in the Insert **A**ctions section of the Script Wizard.

2. Choose New Global Variable from the pop-up menu. The New Global Variable dialog box shown in Figure 28.13 appears.

3. In the Enter the new global variable name field, enter the name of the variable.

4. Click OK. The variable name appears beneath the Global Variables heading in the action tree.

To edit a global variable, follow these steps:

1. From the Insert **A**ctions field, highlight the global variable that you want to edit.

2. Choose Edit from the pop-up menu. The Edit Global Variable dialog box appears.

3. Enter a new declaration name for the variable.

4. Click OK. The new variable name appears beneath the Global Variables heading in the action tree.

To delete a global variable, follow these steps:

1. From the Insert **A**ctions field, highlight the global variable that you want to delete.

2. Choose Delete from the pop-up menu. The variable is removed from the action tree.

Inserting New Procedures

To define a new procedure in your script, select the Procedure option in the action pane. Procedures are added at the beginning of your script. In VBScript, procedures use the form `sub Proceduren()`. In JavaScript, procedures use the form `function Proceduren()`.

To insert a new procedure, follow these steps:

1. Right-click anywhere in the action pane of the Script Wizard.

2. Choose New Procedure from the pop-up menu.

3. Select an action or actions for the procedure from the action pane field.

4. Click the Insert Action button to add the action to the procedure.

Using the Code View in the Script Wizard

You can use the Code view in the Script Wizard to edit your code manually. To switch the Script Wizard to Code view, select the Co**d**e View radio button at the bottom of the Script Wizard screen. You can add events and actions to your script by double-clicking items in the action pane. Then, you can edit the script for the action in the **S**cript pane at the bottom of the Script Wizard screen. Code view is shown in Figure 28.14.

Figure 28.14.

Use Code view in the Script Wizard to manually edit the code in your scripts.

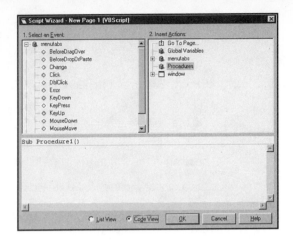

Workshop Wrap-Up

In this chapter, you learned how to add ActiveX controls to your pages. You also learned the basics of how to use the Script Wizard to write event code for the controls you place on your pages. Admittedly, further reference is required for this chapter. Coding in JavaScript and VBScript requires knowledge that is beyond the scope of this book and is better covered by books that focus on each topic. However, using either of these scripting languages, you can extend the functionality of your Web pages with customized menus, active multimedia content, and more. Through the use of these Web technologies, you can create pages the way the big guys do.

Next Steps

To begin your adventures with JavaScript and VBScript, check out the following books published by Sams.net:

❑ *Laura Lemay's Web Workshop: JavaScript.* Laura Lemay and Michael Moncur. ISBN: 1-57521-141-6.

❑ *JavaScript Unleashed.* Richard Wagner *et al.* ISBN: 1-57521-118-1.

❑ *Teach Yourself JavaScript in 21 Days.* Arman Danesh. ISBN: 1-57521-073-8.

❑ *Teach Yourself VBScript in 21 Days.* Keith Brophy and Timothy Koets. ISBN: 1-57521-120-3.

Q&A

Q: Are there any other online development tools available for ActiveX Controls?

A: The ActiveX Control Pad, which is available from Microsoft's Web site, contains control references for many of Microsoft's ActiveX controls. In addition to using many of the same features and the Script Wizard mentioned in this chapter, it includes the HTML Layout Control. This control makes it much easier to layer controls and images on your pages. You can download the ActiveX Control Pad from the following URL:

```
http://www.microsoft.com/workshop/author/cpad/
```

Q: Are there any other online resources available where I can learn more about the ActiveX controls that are available?

A: Additional references are listed in Appendix B.

TWENTY-NINE

Real-Life Examples V: Using Browser-Specific Features

Matty's Place awaits for you to add some of the features that you learned about in this section. In this chapter, you'll learn how to customize the theme for your Web and add feature-rich multimedia to your Web site. You'll also wrap up those loose ends in the Web site by adding content to the index pages in each of the sections in your Web, as well as completing the site with a What's New page.

In this chapter, you

- ❏ Create a new, custom theme for Matty's Place
- ❏ Learn what you can edit in the cascading style sheet files and how to add the files to your custom themes folder
- ❏ Apply the new custom theme to your Web
- ❏ Add an embedded style sheet and an inline style to a page that uses a theme
- ❏ Review some applications that help you create feature-rich multimedia for the Web
- ❏ Add a PowerPoint 97 animation file to Matty's Place
- ❏ Wrap up the loose ends in the Web

Tasks in this chapter:

- ❏ Creating a Custom Theme
- ❏ Adding the New Files to the Theme
- ❏ Updating Your Web Theme
- ❏ Adding an Embedded Style Sheet
- ❏ Adding an Inline Style
- ❏ Adding Matty's Notebook Page

NOTE: If you followed along with the examples in Chapter 24, "Real-Life Examples IV: Adding Interactivity," you should be up to speed and have all the files on your system to continue the project at this point. If you did not create the examples in that chapter, you can find a complete set of files on the CD-ROM that accompanies this book. You can create a new Web as outlined in Chapter 24, but instead, import the `mattysplace` Web files from the `Book\Chap24\Examples` folder instead of the `Book\Chap20\Examples` folder.

TASK Creating a Custom Theme

If you feel adventurous, you can create your own themes. An easy way to do this is to make a copy of a theme that uses fonts and colors similar to the theme that you want to create. Then you can add your own images and modify the cascading style sheet files for your new `themes` folder. This and the following tasks step you through this process.

To make a copy of a `themes` folder, follow these steps:

1. From the Windows 95 Explorer, locate the Microsoft FrontPage 98 installation folder and expand the tree to locate the `themes` folder beneath that. The default installation path will be `c:\Program Files\Microsoft FrontPage\themes`.

2. Select the `bubbles` folder (or the folder that you selected for your Matty's Place Web theme) and choose **E**dit | **C**opy (Ctrl+C).

3. Now select the `themes` folder and choose **E**dit | **P**aste (Ctrl+V). A folder named `Copy of bubbles` appears in the `themes` folder.

4. Rename the new folder `mattys` (or another folder name that contains eight characters or less). This folder will be used to store the cascading style sheets and graphics for your theme, as shown in Figure 29.1.

5. Rename the `bubbles.inf` file in the `mattys` folder to `mattys.inf`. Choose **F**ile | **O**pen to open the file in Notepad and edit the title line to read `Title=Matty's Place`. Save the revised file using **F**ile | **S**ave and exit Notepad.

6. Rename the `bubbles.utf8` file in the `mattys` folder to `mattys.utf8`. Choose **F**ile | **O**pen to open the file in Notepad and edit the title line to read `Title=Matty's Place`. Save the revised file using **F**ile | **S**ave and exit Notepad.

Figure 29.1.

Use Windows Explorer to create a folder named mattys *in the FrontPage 98* themes *folder.*

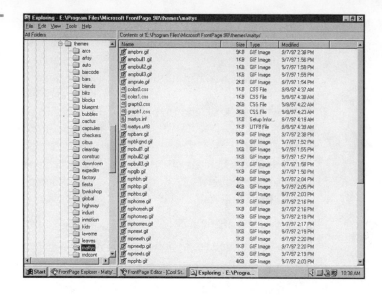

You have just created a theme that will appear in Themes view in the FrontPage Explorer. Now you can use Notepad to edit the cascading style sheet files in this folder. Appendix D, "About Theme-Related Cascading Style Sheets," lists all the selectors used in these files. Use this appendix as a guide if you want to create new graphics or change the font faces used in your theme.

Editing the Cascading Style Sheet Files

There are five cascading style sheet files associated with a theme. The filenames are theme.css, color0.css, color1.css, graph0.css, and graph1.css. You can open these files from the Windows Explorer and edit them in Notepad, as shown in Figure 29.2.

The selectors, properties, and values for these cascading style sheet files are described in more detail in Appendix D. It's important to remember that when you edit the cascading style sheet files, you should limit your changes to the properties that already exist in the cascading style sheet files for the themes. If you add properties, you will affect the way the themes appear on your pages. In general, you can change the following properties:

❏ Font family names

❏ Font colors

❏ Graphics filenames

   Use filenames of 8 characters or less. Graphics listed in the graph1.css file can be static or animated GIFs. If you want to use transparent GIFs, you must apply image transparency in your image editing program. Graphics must be saved in GIF format and conform to the following sizes:

Banner images	600w×60h pixels
Global navigation bar buttons	95w×20h pixels (should be a solid color and very plain in appearance)
Home, Next, Prev, and Up buttons	100w×20h pixels
Horizontal rules	300w×10h pixels
Level 1 bullets	20w×20h pixels
Levels 2 and 3 bullets	12w×12h pixels
Navigation buttons	140w×60h pixels
Textured background	15KB maximum

❑ Vertical alignment

Can be top, middle, or bottom, only where specified in the original files

❑ Horizontal alignment

Can be left, center, or right, only where specified in the original files

Figure 29.2.

Use Notepad or another text editor to edit the cascading style sheet files for your new theme.

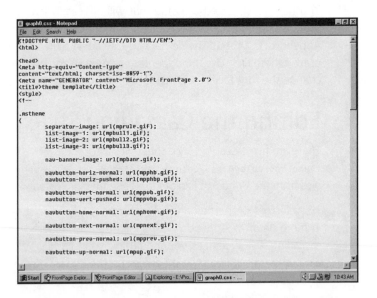

Adding the New Files to the Theme

TASK

When you add your new graphics files and cascading style sheet files to your theme, do not place them in your Web. You need to place them in the themes folder within your Microsoft FrontPage installation folder.

There are several new files for the Matty's Place theme located in the `Book\Chap29\Project Files` folder on the CD-ROM that accompanies this book. The cascading style sheet files on the CD-ROM have been revised to point to the new graphics listed in Table 29.1. Besides the cascading style sheet files and other information files, the graphics mentioned in each of the cascading style sheet files are furnished.

Table 29.1. Images in the New Matty's Place Theme.

Images	theme.css	graph0.css	graph1.css
Top navigation bar	mpglb.gif		
Background image	mpbkgnd.gif		
Horizontal rule		mprule.gif	amprule.gif
Level 1 bullet		mpbull1.gif	ampbull1.gif
Level 2 bullet		mpbull2.gif	ampbull2.gif
Level 3 bullet		mpbull3.gif	ampbull3.gif
Navigation banner		mpbanr.gif	ampbnr.gif
Horizontal button—normal		mpphb.gif	mphbs.gif
Horizontal button—hovered			mphbh.gif
Horizontal button—pushed		mpphbp.gif	mphbp.gif
Vertical button—normal		mppvb.gif	mpvbs.gif
Vertical button—hovered			mpvbh.gif
Vertical button—pushed		mppvbp.gif	mpvbh.gif
Home button—normal		mphome.gif	mphomes.gif
Home button—hovered			mphomeh.gif
Home button—pushed			mphomep.gif
Next button—normal		mpnext.gif	mpnexts.gif
Next button—hovered			mpnexth.gif
Next button—pushed			mpnextp.gif
Prev button—normal		mpprev.gif	mpprevs.gif
Prev button—hovered			mpprevh.gif
Prev button—pushed			mpuprevp.gif
Up button—normal		mpup.gif	mpups.gif
Up button—hovered			mpuph.gif
Up button—pushed			mpupp.gif

To add the images and new cascading style sheet files to your `mattys` folder, follow these steps:

1. From the Windows 95 Explorer, locate the Microsoft FrontPage 98 installation folder and expand the tree to locate the `themes` folder beneath that. The default installation path will be `c:\Program Files\Microsoft FrontPage\themes`.

2. Select the `mattys` folder. Delete all the files that currently exist in the folder (you will replace them with the files on the CD-ROM).

3. Locate the Matty's Place graphics and CSS files in the `Book\Chap29\Project Files\Theme Files` folder on the CD-ROM that accompanies this book. There are 45 files in all. Copy them into your `mattys` folder in the Microsoft FrontPage `themes` directory.

Updating Your Web Theme

Now for the moment of truth. You want to apply your new graphics to your Web. Using a custom theme is no different than using one of the themes that are furnished with FrontPage. Your new Matty's Place theme will appear in Themes view along with the rest of the themes.

You should apply the following steps to apply your new Web theme. They should also be performed any time you make changes to the cascading style sheet files or images in your Microsoft FrontPage themes folder.

To apply your new Matty's Place theme to your Web, follow these steps:

1. If you have the FrontPage Explorer open, close it and restart FrontPage. This will reset the items in Themes view and display the correct images in the Matty's Place theme.

2. Open Matty's Place Web in the FrontPage Explorer and choose the Themes icon from the Views pane.

3. Choose This **W**eb Does Not Use Themes and then click **A**pply to remove all the old graphics from your Web themes folders.

4. Next, choose the Matty's Place theme in your `themes` folder. The new graphics appear in the Theme Preview at the right of Themes view, as shown in Figure 29.3. Select Vivid **C**olors, Active **G**raphics, and **B**ackground Image for options, and click **A**pply. FrontPage imports the custom theme files into your Web.

Figure 29.3.

Your new theme appears in the FrontPage Explorer's Themes view.

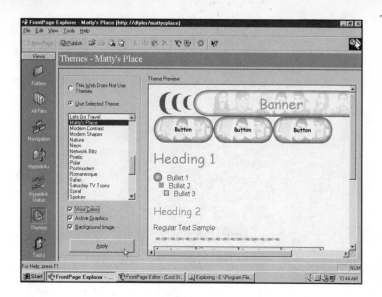

TASK

Adding an Embedded Style Sheet

When you want to make changes to a single page, you can create an embedded style sheet that changes the cascading style sheet properties on that page only. For a simple example, let's say you want to change the color of all the headings on the About the Site page. Rather than selecting each heading and using the Color button on the format toolbar, you can create an embedded style sheet that replaces all the Heading 2 and Heading 3 text with a different color.

To modify the headings on the About the Site page, follow these steps:

1. From the FrontPage Editor, choose **F**ile I **O**pen (Ctrl+O) or click the Open button on the Standard toolbar. The Open dialog box appears.

2. Double-click the main folder; then double-click about.htm to open the page.

3. Choose F**o**rmat I **S**tylesheet. The Format Stylesheet dialog box appears.

4. Position the insertion point after the second line of code in the dialog box and press Enter. The insertion point moves to the next line.

5. Enter **h2** followed by a space.

6. Click the **S**tyle button. The Style dialog box appears.

7. Click the Colors tab. From the **F**oreground Color drop-down menu, select Maroon.

8. Choose OK. You return to the Format Stylesheet dialog box.

9. Highlight the code that reads `h2 { color: rgb(128,0,0) }` and copy it into your clipboard using Ctrl+C. Paste it into the next line using Ctrl+V.

10. Change the `h2` in the new line of code to read **h3**. The code in the Format Stylesheet dialog box now reads as follows, as shown in Figure 29.4:

```
<style>
<!--
h2 { color: rgb(128,0,0) }
h3 { color: rgb(128,0,0) }
-->
</style>
```

11. Choose OK to return to the FrontPage Editor. The headings on the page turn to maroon.

Figure 29.4.

Add code for the embedded style sheet in the Format Stylesheet dialog box.

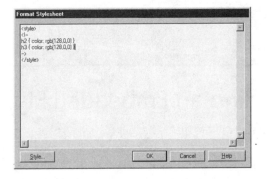

TASK   Adding an Inline Style

You've just seen that the embedded style sheet overrides the heading properties that were originally assigned to the theme cascading style sheet (the external style sheet). Now you can override the property of both the external and embedded style sheets with an inline style. For example, suppose you want to change the color of the Main Section heading in the table, which is only one of the level 3 headings.

To apply an inline style to the heading, follow these steps:

1. Choose Format | Stylesheet. The Format Stylesheet dialog box appears.

2. Position the insertion point after the following lines of code and press Enter; the insertion point moves to the next line:

```
<style>
<!--
h2 { color: rgb(128,0,0) }
h3 { color: rgb(128,0,0) }
```

3. Enter **h3.red**, followed by a space.

4. Click the **S**tyle button. The Style dialog box appears.

5. Click the Colors tab. From the **F**oreground Color drop-down menu, select Red.

6. Choose OK. You return to the Format Stylesheet dialog box. The code on the page now reads as follows, as shown in Figure 29.5:

```
<style>
<!--
h2 { color: rgb(128,0,0) }
h3 { color: rgb(128,0,0) }
h3.red { color: rgb(255,0,0) }
-->
</style>
```

Figure 29.5.

Add an additional selector for the inline style in the Format Stylesheet dialog box.

7. Choose OK again to return to the FrontPage Editor.

8. Select the Main Section heading in the table. Right-click and choose Paragraph Properties from the pop-up menu. The Paragraph Properties dialog box appears.

9. Click the Style button. The Style dialog box appears, opened to the Class tab. Click the red class to place this class in the **C**lass field.

10. Choose OK to return to the Paragraph Properties dialog box and OK again to return to the FrontPage Editor. The heading turns to red.

Adding Content to Your Cool Stuff Pages

The Cool Stuff in Matty's Web is also meant to display pages that contain animations, Java applets, or Netscape plug-ins, or any other pages that use multimedia-related files. Typically, these types of files consume a lot of bandwidth, so it's nice to isolate them and warn users that download times in this section will be high.

There are enough options for Web-based multimedia to make your head spin. Rather than tell you about all of them and their capabilities, I'll let some of the applications speak for themselves. The following are three multimedia-related tools that I find particularly impressive:

❏ Macromedia Flash 2, the current version of a program formerly known as FutureSplash Animator, is one of my personal favorites. It uses vector-based graphics to create compact animations that download quickly and stream into your browser. The tools you use to create animations are extremely intuitive and a *lot* of fun to use. Flash 2 animations can also be used to create extremely creative interfaces for your Web site. They are inserted on your Web pages as an ActiveX control or as a Netscape plug-in. In most cases, you'll want to use the latter option so that the animation can be viewed in any browser that supports Netscape plug-ins. This includes Internet Explorer 3.0 and above.

To check out the power and capabilities of Macromedia Flash 2, go to Macromedia's Web site, shown in Figure 29.6. If you download the trial version from Macromedia's site, be sure to step through all the tutorials to see the full power of what this program can do. The home page for Flash 2 is located at the following URL:

`http://www.macromedia.com/software/flash`

Be sure also to check out the demos at the following URL:

`http://www.macromedia.com/shockzone/edge/flash`

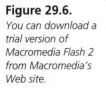

Figure 29.6.
You can download a trial version of Macromedia Flash 2 from Macromedia's Web site.

❏ Many Web developers use Macromedia Director to produce Shockwave files. Though Director is a high-end program that produces interactive multimedia for a wide range of applications, Shockwave is a very popular format on the Web. Like Flash 2, its "little sibling," Shockwave animations are streamed into your browser through the use of a plug-in. File sizes and download times aren't quite as economical as Flash 2, but the results are very impressive. Check out Shockzone, located at the following URL, for more information about Director 6 and for some real-life examples of what you can do with Shockwave on the Web (see Figure 29.7):

`http://www.macromedia.com/shockzone/edge/`

Figure 29.7.

Learn more about Shockwave and Director 6 at Shockzone, located on Macromedia's Web site.

❏ Put a little Java in your cup. A list of Java-related books is provided in Appendix B, "FrontPage Reference." If you don't want to get into hands-on programming, there are several Java authoring tools that enable you to create Java applets without touching code. One such example is Kinetix Hyperwire, which you can preview from the Kinetix Web site shown in Figure 29.8. By "wiring" different modules together, you create Java applets that offer feature-rich interactive multimedia. Product information, a trial version, and samples are located at the following URL:

`http://www.ktx.com/hyperwire`

Figure 29.8.

On the Kinetix Web site, you can obtain product information, obtain a trial version, and view samples of Hyperwire files.

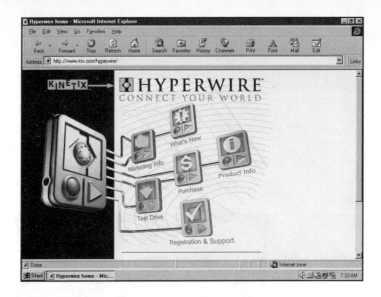

TASK Adding Matty's Notebook Page

Microsoft Office users have PowerPoint at their disposal, which helps create animations and presentations for the Web. The Matty's Notebook page includes a PowerPoint 97 animation file that you can insert on your page as an ActiveX control or as a Netscape plug-in. In this case, let's use the latter option to make the page compatible with more browsers.

If you don't have PowerPoint 97 or the PowerPoint Animation Player that is compatible with PowerPoint 97 animation files, you need to download and install the plug-in in order to view the animation in your browser. A self-extracting installation file, `PPView97.exe`, is available from Microsoft's Web site at the following URL (see Figure 29.9):

`http://www.microsoft.com/mspowerpoint/internet/viewer/viewer32.htm`

To insert the PowerPoint 97 animation on your page, follow these steps:

1. Open the Matty's Place Web in the FrontPage Explorer.
2. Choose the Folders icon from the Views pane to switch to Folders view.
3. Select the `images` folder in your Web and choose **F**ile I **I**mport. The Import File to FrontPage Web dialog box appears.
4. Click the **A**dd File button. The Add File to Import List dialog box appears.

5. Use the Look **i**n box to locate `matty.pps` in the `Book\Chap29\Project Files` folder on the CD-ROM that accompanies this book. Double-click the file to place it in the import list.

Figure 29.9.

Download PowerPoint Viewer 97 from Microsoft's Web site to view the animation in the following task.

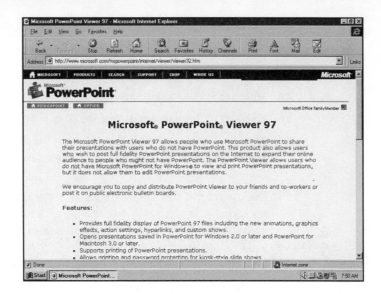

6. Choose OK. The presentation file is imported into your Web.

7. Choose **T**ools | Show FrontPage **E**ditor or click the Show FrontPage Editor button on the Standard toolbar. The FrontPage Editor opens with a new page.

8. In the event that the plug-in does not navigate the user to the correct URL, it is always a good idea to provide a link on your page that will take the user to the correct page. Choose the Center button on the Format toolbar to align the insertion point to the center of the page. Enter the following text:

   ```
   You will need the PowerPoint Animation Player to view the animation on
   this page.
   ```

9. Select the text that reads `PowerPoint Animation Player` and click the Create or Edit Hyperlink button. The Create Hyperlink dialog box appears.

10. In the URL field, enter the following URL and choose OK to return to the FrontPage Editor; the link appears on your page:

    ```
    http://www.microsoft.com/mspowerpoint/internet/viewer/viewer32.htm
    ```

11. Press Enter and Choose **I**nsert | **A**dvanced | **P**lug-In. The Plug-In Properties dialog box appears.

12. Click the **B**rowse button near the **D**ata Source field. The Select Plug-In Data Source dialog box appears.

13. Double-click the `images` folder; then double-click `matty.pps` to insert the plug-in file on your page.

14. In the Message for browsers without Plug-In support field, enter `You need to view this PowerPoint Animation file with a browser that supports Netscape plug-ins. Please be patient while the animation file downloads.`

15. Enter `360` in the Height field and `480` in the Width field.

16. Choose OK. A representative of the plug-in appears on your page.

17. To play a background sound throughout the entire presentation, choose **F**ile | Page Proper**t**ies. The Page Properties dialog box appears, opened to the General tab.

18. Use the Browse button in the Background Sound section to open the Background Sound dialog box. Double-click the `mattys.mid` file in your Web's root folder to assign the sound to your page. Choose OK to exit the Page Properties dialog box.

19. Choose **F**ile | **S**ave (Ctrl+S) or click the Save button on the Standard toolbar. The Save As dialog box appears.

20. Double-click the `coolstuff` folder in your Web. Then enter `notebook.htm` in the **U**RL field and `Matty's Notebook` in the **T**itle field. Choose OK to save the page. Your page should look as shown in Figure 29.10. The navigation buttons will be added after you add your page to the Cool Stuff section in the FrontPage Explorer's Navigation view.

Figure 29.10.

The PowerPoint Animation file is added to your Web page.

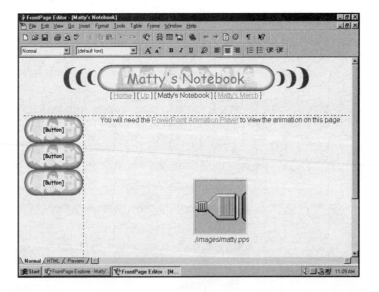

21. Choose **F**ile | Preview in **B**rowser and select a browser that supports Netscape plug-ins. If you have installed and configured the PowerPoint

Animation 97 player, you should see the plug-in appear on your page, as shown in Figure 29.11.

Figure 29.11.

View the PowerPoint animation in a browser that supports Netscape plug-ins.

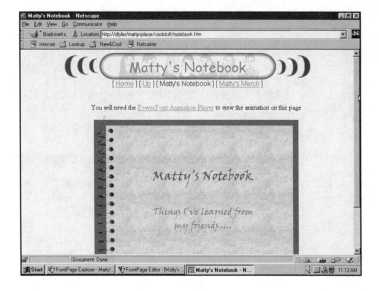

In relation to pages that use browser-specific features or external plug-ins or ActiveX controls, it's nice to inform your users what they will need to take the best advantage of your site. You can create a Related Downloads page, such as that shown in Figure 29.12. This will inform the user why he or she needs certain files and provide a central location for the links.

Figure 29.12.

Create a Related Downloads page that provides links to download recommended browsers, plug-ins, ActiveX controls, and other files that your users will need.

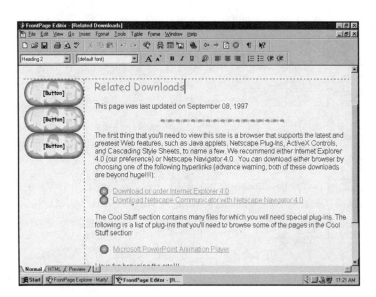

Wrapping Up the Loose Ends

As you add pages to your Web, remember to add appropriate pages to your navigation bars. Make sure that you also complete the content on any new pages that you create from Navigation view. Recall that you added some pages in Navigation view in Chapter 13, "Real-Life Examples II: Keeping It Plain and Simple." There is currently no content on the Cool Stuff, Main, and Discussion pages, so you need to add something there.

The Main Section index page (`main/index.htm`) is shown in Figure 29.13. It contains a brief description of each of the pages in the Main Section, as well as links to navigate to the pages. A timestamp is also included at the top of the page.

Figure 29.13.

Add links to the main pages in your Web on the Main Section index page.

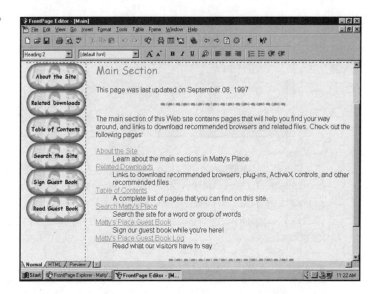

Likewise, the Cool Stuff section index page (`coolstuff/index.htm`) contains links to the pages in the Cool Stuff section (see Figure 29.14). As you add more content to your own pages, don't forget to add hyperlinks on this page.

The Discussion index page (`discussion/index.htm`) contains links to the discussion submission form, the table of contents, and the search page for the discussion. This page is shown in Figure 29.15.

Finally, you'll want to add a What's New page to your Web site. The What's New page lists the latest additions to your Web site and informs your site visitors about the most recent additions and the latest news. An example of a What's New page is shown in Figure 29.16.

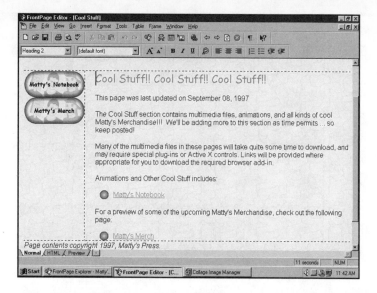

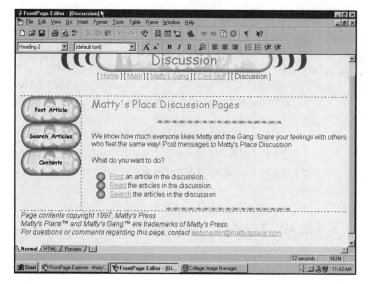

Figure 29.16.

Add a What's New page that informs users of the recent changes to your Web site.

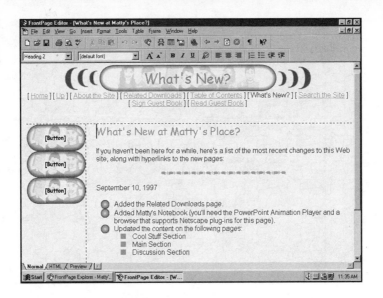

Workshop Wrap-Up

In this chapter, you learned how to customize the style sheets for your Web site. You reviewed some applications that help you create feature-rich multimedia for your Web sites and inserted a PowerPoint 97 animation into the Matty's Place Web site. You also reviewed how to wrap up the loose ends in your site by creating the content for the index pages. Examples of the final Matty's Place files are included in the Book\Chap29\Examples folder on the CD-ROM that accompanies this book. The CD-ROM also includes a couple of other versions of the Web site—one that uses framesets and another that uses Include Page components to place navigation bars on the Web pages.

Next Steps

In Part V, "Still More Advanced Techniques," you will learn more about the FrontPage Personal Web Server and the Microsoft Personal Web Server. You'll also learn how to take that final step and publish your own Web site to a remote server!

❑ In Chapter 30, "Using the FrontPage Personal Web Server," you learn how to configure the FrontPage Personal Web Server.

❑ In Chapter 31, "Using the Microsoft Personal Web Server," you learn how to configure the Microsoft Personal Web Server.

❑ In Chapter 32, "Administering Your Webs," you learn how to perform tasks that are common to both personal Web servers.

❑ In Chapter 33, "Designing Private Webs," you learn how to create registration forms and private Web sites and how to configure your Web as an Internet Explorer 4.0 channel.

❑ In Chapter 34, "Testing and Publishing Your Webs," you learn how to get your pages out to the Web!

Q&A

Q: I'm having problems getting the Netscape plug-In to display in my browser. What could be the problem?

A: If you are using a beta version of a browser, there may be some notes in the beta release that explain what features are not yet supported in the browser. If you are using a final-release browser, check the Help files or any Options dialog boxes that explain how to install and configure plug-ins and other browser helpers. Most browsers provide an Options dialog box, or something similar, that enables you to specify MIME types. For example, Netscape's Preferences dialog box, shown in Figure 29.17, provides a setting for applications in its Navigator category. The MIME type for the PowerPoint 97 animation is `application/pps`.

Figure 29.17.

If you are having problems viewing plug-ins in your browser, check to see whether the plug-in has been configured in your browser.

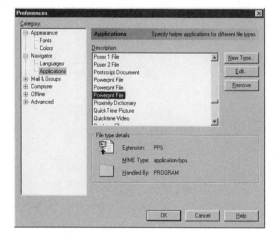

Q: I made an embedded style sheet that changes some of the selectors on my Web style sheet, but the changes didn't appear when I viewed them in my browser. What could the problem be?

A: Again, check the release of your browser. Beta versions typically include a list of known problems. Because cascading style sheets are an up-and-coming Web technology, browsers will also handle these tags a bit differently. If your updates display properly in the FrontPage Editor, but you see variations in your browser, the differences may relate to the way the browser parses the files and handles cascading and inheritance. For further information about cascading style sheets, check out *Laura Lemay's Web Workshop: Designing with Style Sheets, Tables, and Frames,* Sams.net Publishing, ISBN 1-57521-249-8.

P A R T

VI

Publishing and Maintaining Your Webs

THIRTY

Using the FrontPage Personal Web Server

FrontPage 98 enables you to create and manage Webs with or without the use of a Web server. However, there is an increasing number of features that require that you have a FrontPage-compatible Web server running to test or operate them. This includes creating a navigation system, using themes, and using the form handling components. By installing a FrontPage-compatible Web server on your local or network computer, you can take full advantage of all the features that FrontPage has to offer.

FrontPage 98 is furnished with two personal Web servers, each with different capabilities. This chapter discusses the FrontPage Personal Web Server, one of the two servers furnished with FrontPage 98. In Chapter 31, "Using the Microsoft Personal Web Server," you'll learn about the second personal Web server.

For many users, the FrontPage Personal Web Server is more than adequate in its capabilities. Most people who use FrontPage to design their personal Web sites will find it so. This chapter examines the capabilities and the shortcomings of the FrontPage Personal Web Server. You'll also learn when you will need to use a more robust server to fulfill your needs.

Knowing Whether This Server Is Right for You

The FrontPage Personal Web Server is exactly that—a *personal* Web server. It enables you to create, manage, and test Web sites that incorporate the majority of features found in FrontPage. You can use this server to navigate through and test the pages in your Webs or even to demonstrate your Web sites to customers. There are many limitations to using this server in an online situation, however. This server is not capable of medium-to-heavy traffic. It is designed to provide a platform on which you can design and test your pages before they are published to your intranet or World Wide Web site. Table 30.1 shows at a glance the capabilities of the FrontPage Personal Web Server.

Table 30.1. FrontPage Personal Web Server capabilities.

Feature	Supported?
Number of Webs	18, including root Web
Active Server Pages	No
Custom CGI scripts	No
FTP services	No
Gopher services	No
High-traffic sites	No
IDC database files/scripts	No
ISAPI interface	No
Multihoming	No
NSAPI interface	No
NTLM authentication	No
Secure Socket Layer (SSL) communications	No

Table 30.1 is not really as bleak as it appears. For the average home user, the FrontPage Personal Web Server is more than sufficient to develop and test Web pages. This server enables you to create and manage 18 Webs—the root Web and 17 child Webs beneath it. Using this server, you can create and test Web sites that use all the FrontPage components, Java applets, Netscape plug-ins, ActiveX controls, and scripting languages, such as VBScript or JavaScript. You can develop Active Server Pages, specify custom CGI scripts as form handlers, and provide links to FTP and Gopher sites, but these features cannot be fully tested while running the FrontPage Personal Web Server.

The Microsoft Personal Web Server, discussed in Chapter 31, supports FTP, multihoming, NTLM authentication, custom CGI scripts, and IDC files and scripts. For information about Microsoft Internet Information Server, check out *Microsoft Internet Information Server 3 Unleashed*, by Arthur Knowles, published by Sams.net (ISBN 1-57521-271-4).

The FrontPage Personal Web Server is designed for very light traffic. If you want to test features such as custom CGI scripts or Internet Database Connector (IDC) files and scripts, you'll need to move up to the Microsoft Personal Web Server or another more robust server platform, such as Microsoft Internet Information Server running on Windows NT Server 4.0. This latter server enables you also to employ or test advanced features, such as multihoming, Secure Socket Layer communications, NTLM authentication, and Active Server Pages.

Installing FrontPage 98 with the FrontPage Personal Web Server

To install the FrontPage Personal Web Server, choose the **C**ustom installation option when you run FrontPage 98 Setup. Figure 30.1 shows the setup screen in which this choice is presented. After you select the **C**ustom installation option, select the **M**icrosoft FrontPage Personal Web Server checkbox, as shown in Figure 30.2. To install the Server Extensions in addition to the Personal Web Server, select the Server **E**xtensions checkbox.

Figure 30.1.
To install the FrontPage 98 Personal Web Server, select Custom installation during setup.

Figure 30.2.
Custom installation options enable you to install the FrontPage 98 Personal Web Server and the FrontPage 98 Server Extensions.

NOTE: The FrontPage Personal Web Server and FrontPage Server Extensions are automatically updated to the FrontPage 98 version when you upgrade from a previous version of FrontPage.

You can install both personal Web servers on your system. If the Microsoft Personal Web Server has already been installed to Port 80, the FrontPage Personal Web Server will be installed to Port 8080. To run the FrontPage Personal Web Server in this case, specify a server name, such as `http://myservername:8080`, when you browse the Webs created with the FrontPage Personal Web Server.

Using FrontPage 98 with Previous Versions of FrontPage

The FrontPage 98 Server Extensions are backward-compatible, and they will work with Webs created with earlier versions of FrontPage. All the features found in FrontPage 1.1 and FrontPage 97 function properly when you use the FrontPage 98 Server Extensions.

Earlier versions of the FrontPage Server Extensions do not support tasks such as adding navigation bars and themes to your Webs. In addition, if you attempt to use the FrontPage 98 Explorer to delete a folder that is located on a FrontPage 1.1 server, you might encounter an error message that says the pages cannot be removed. Microsoft suggests trying one of two methods to remedy this situation:

❏ Upgrade the FrontPage 1.1 Server to the FrontPage 98 Server Extensions and then use the Delete command in the FrontPage 98 Explorer to delete the folder from the upgraded server.

❏ Access the Web content on the FrontPage 1.1 Server using telnet, FTP, or the operating system's file management software to delete the folder. Then use the **T**ools | **R**ecalculate Hyperlinks command in the FrontPage Explorer to update the links in the Web.

FrontPage Personal Web Server File Locations

When you install the FrontPage Personal Web Server on a system running the Windows 95 or Windows NT 4.0 operating system, the default directories are as follows:

❏ The default installation directory for the FrontPage Personal Web Server executable file is `c:\FrontPage Webs\Server`. The file is named `vhttpd32.exe`.

❏ The default installation directory for the configuration files is `c:\FrontPage Webs\Server\conf`. Files with a `.cnf` extension are the configuration files used by the Server Extensions. The original configuration file uses an `.org` extension, and the most recent backup copy of the configuration file uses a `.bak` extension. Here, you find access configuration files (`access.cnf`, `access.org`, and `access.bak`), Web server configuration files (`httpd.cnf`, `httpd.org`, and `httpd.bak`), and server resource files (`srm.cnf`, `srm.org`, and `srm.bak`). You'll also find a configuration file for the mime types used on your server (`mime.typ`).

❏ The `c:\FrontPage Webs\Server\icons` directory contains icon files that you can use for several different file types.

❏ The default installation directory for your server log files is `c:\FrontPage Webs\Server\logs`.

How Your File Directories Relate to the Web Server

When you install the FrontPage Personal Web Server on your local computer, the content files for your root Web are located, by default, in the following directory on your local hard drive:

`c:\FrontPage Webs\Content`

When you create child Webs with the FrontPage Explorer, a directory for each child Web is placed beneath the root Web. For example, if you create a Web named `personalweb`, its home page might have a name as follows:

`c:\FrontPage Webs\Content\personalweb\index.htm`

In many cases, you can easily browse your Web content by entering this filename into your browser's URL field. However, when you browse a file on your hard drive, the FrontPage Server Extensions will not function. If your pages contain features that require the FrontPage Server Extensions, you won't be able to test them fully. Therefore, you need to enter the URL of the file as it should be when it is running on your local server. First, you need to determine your server name.

Finding the Name of Your Web Server

When you install the FrontPage Server Extensions on your local computer and start the FrontPage Explorer the first time, the program searches for the name of your server. Normally, the name returned is the name of your local computer as configured in Network Properties. You can use other names to identify your server. To determine the names or IP address you can use, run the TCP/IP Test Utility that is furnished with FrontPage. To run this utility, follow these steps:

1. From the FrontPage Explorer, choose **H**elp I **A**bout Microsoft FrontPage Explorer. The About FrontPage Explorer dialog box appears.

2. In the About FrontPage Explorer dialog box, click **N**etwork Test. The FrontPage TCP/IP Test dialog box shown in Figure 30.3 appears.

Figure 30.3.

The FrontPage TCP/IP Test checks all your network connections and reports server names and IP addresses you can use.

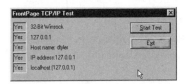

3. If you normally connect to a remote server while online, dial in to your Internet Service Provider. If you do not, some values will not be reported during the test.

4. Click the **S**tart Test button. Up to four values that you can use for your server name may be returned as follows:

    127.0.0.1, which is the IP address for localhost (the server on your local computer).

    Host name (for example, myserver), where the name is configured in Network Properties for your local computer or your Internet Service Provider.

    IP address (for example, 255.255.1.1), where the numbers are the IP address that you have configured in Network Properties (configured from Windows 95 or Windows NT Control Panel) for your local computer or your Internet Service Provider.

    localhost, which runs the FrontPage Server Extensions on your local computer.

5. Click E**x**it to return to the About FrontPage Explorer dialog box.

6. Click OK to return to the FrontPage Explorer.

You should be able to use any of the reported addresses as part of the URL when you browse your Webs with the FrontPage Server Extensions running in the background. Typically, localhost and 127.0.0.1 are used to run the Server Extensions on your local computer. Use these values when you are not connected to an Internet Service Provider or network server. Use the host name and IP address values to connect to a network server or Internet Service Provider.

When you want to browse your local computer with the FrontPage Server Extensions running, replace the `c:\FrontPage Webs\Content` portion of the filename with `http:` followed by your server name. Use backslashes as you normally do when entering Web URLs. The URL to the `c:\FrontPage Webs\personalweb\index.htm` file instead becomes a URL that looks something like this:

```
http://servername/personalweb/index.htm
```

What Is Unique About the FrontPage Personal Web Server?

To determine whether you are using the FrontPage Personal Web Server, look on the bottom of your screen at the taskbar. If you see a button that displays the Web Server status, such as the `Web Server Idle` status message shown in Figure 30.4, you are running the FrontPage Personal Web Server. For the most part, the majority of the FrontPage features function the same from one server to the next. However, there are some tasks that are unique to the FrontPage Personal Web Server. The following sections cover these tasks.

Figure 30.4.

When you run the FrontPage Personal Web Server, a Web Server status button is located in your Windows 95 taskbar.

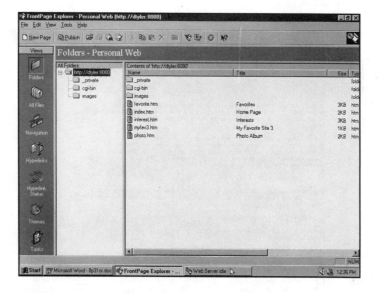

 # Changing the Default Home Page Name

If you browse to the home page of your Web by entering the Web name followed by a slash (for example, **http://myweb/**), you might see a list of files rather than your home page. This situation is caused when you name your home page other than that which

FrontPage expects to see. By default, the FrontPage Personal Web Server uses a home page (or welcome page) name of `index.htm`. Your remote server might require that you use a home page with a different filename, such as `index.html`, `welcome.htm`, or `default.htm`. You can configure FrontPage to use a different home page name if you want. The name you configure for a default home page name is used for all Webs.

If you installed FrontPage with its default settings, you can find the configuration file in which you change your default home page name in the following directory:

`c:\FrontPage Webs\server\conf\srm.cnf.`

Within this file is a section in which you specify your directory index (or home page name), as you can see in Figure 30.5. To specify a directory index file other than `index.htm`, remove the pound sign before the line that reads `DirectoryIndex index.htm` and revise the filename to reflect the home page designation that you want to use. It should look similar to the last line shown here:

```
# DirectoryIndex: Name of the file to use as a pre-written HTML
# directory index. This document, if present, will be opened when the
# server receives a request containing a URL for the directory, instead
# of generating a directory index.
#
DirectoryIndex index.html
```

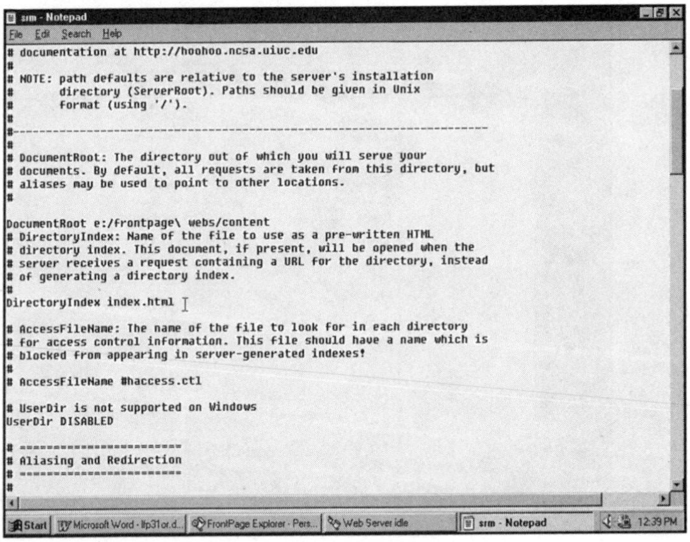

Figure 30.5.

Change the default directory index (home page) name by editing the `srm.cnf` configuration file in Notepad or WordPad.

For corporate intranet development, you can configure the FrontPage Personal Web Server to allow multiple Web administrators and authors. This enables you to assign teams of individuals to develop portions of your intranet Webs.

Administering Your FrontPage Personal Web Server Webs

When you use the FrontPage Personal Web Server, you use standard dialog boxes to administer your FrontPage Webs. This includes adding, changing, or removing users. You must have administrator status to authorize another end user, author, or administrator. To add users to your Web, follow the steps in the next section.

Adding Users to Your Web

When you use the FrontPage Personal Web Server, you add users to your Web through the Permissions dialog box. To add administrators, authors, or end users to your Web, follow these steps:

1. From the FrontPage Explorer, choose **T**ools I **P**ermissions. The Permissions dialog box appears. If you are changing permissions for a child Web, the dialog box opens to the Settings tab, as shown in Figure 30.6.

Figure 30.6.

Use the Settings tab in the Permissions dialog box to assign unique permissions for a child Web.

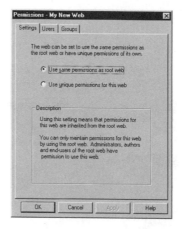

2. Select one of the following options for your Web permissions:
   - ❏ Select the Use **s**ame permissions as root web radio button to configure the child Web to inherit the same settings as those used for the root Web.
   - ❏ Select the Use **u**nique permissions for this web radio button if you need to configure unique administrators, authors, or end users for a child Web. You should also select this option to create a child Web that allows only registered users to gain access to the Web, as outlined further in Chapter 33, "Designing Private Webs."

3. Click **A**pply.

4. Click the Users tab, shown in Figure 30.7. Then click the Add button to open the Add User dialog box shown in Figure 30.8.

Figure 30.7.

The Users tab in the Permissions dialog box enables you to configure users for a Web.

5. Use the **O**btain list from drop-down menu to select the domain on which your user list is stored. This defaults to <Local> when you are using the FrontPage Personal Web Server on a standalone system.

6. From the Users tab, you can add, modify, or remove users as follows:

   ❏ To add a user, click the A**d**d button. The Add Users dialog box shown in Figure 30.8 appears. Enter the new user's name in the Add Name**s** field. Proceed to step 5.

Figure 30.8.

Add a user to your Web with the Add Users dialog box.

   ❏ To edit access permissions for an existing user, highlight the username you want to edit and click the **E**dit button. The Edit Users dialog box shown in Figure 30.9 appears. Proceed to step 5.

Figure 30.9.

Edit existing user information with the Edit Users dialog box.

❑ To remove a user, highlight the user you want to remove and click the **R**emove button. The user is removed from the user list. You cannot remove the original administrator whose name was configured during installation of FrontPage.

7. Select the user's level of access as follows:

For more information about configuring private (or restricted) Webs, see Chapter 33.

❑ If you are adding or editing an end user to the current registered (protected) Web, select the **B**rowse this web radio button. End users are allowed only to browse the Web.

❑ If you are adding or changing the user to an author for the current Web, select the Au**t**hor and browse this web radio button. Authors are allowed to create and delete pages.

❑ If you are adding or changing the user to an administrator for the current Web, select the Ad**m**inister, author, and browse this web radio button. Web administrators can add and delete Webs and pages, designate other administrators, authors, and end users, and restrict end users from accessing certain portions of the Web site.

8. Click OK to return to the Users tab in the Permissions dialog box.

9. From the Users tab in the Permissions dialog box (see Figure 30.7), select the type of Web that you are configuring:

❑ If the current Web is one that allows access to all end users, choose the Everyone has **b**rowse access radio button.

❑ If the current Web is a protected Web to which only registered users can gain access, choose the **O**nly registered users have browse access radio button.

10. Click OK. The user is added to your Web.

 # Restricting IP Addresses

With the FrontPage Personal Web Server, you can also specify access to your Web by IP address. This enables an individual or a group of people sharing IP addresses to gain access to your Web at different levels. This option is not available if you are using the Microsoft Personal Web Server.

1. From the FrontPage Explorer, choose **T**ools | **P**ermissions. The Permissions dialog box appears, open to the Settings tab.

2. Choose one of the following options for your Web permissions:

   ❏ Select the Use **s**ame permissions as root web radio button to configure the child Web to inherit the same settings as those used for the root Web.

   ❏ Select the Use **u**nique permissions for this web radio button if you need to configure different administrators, authors, or end users for a child Web.

3. Click **A**pply.

4. Click the Computers tab, shown in Figure 30.10. Add, modify, or remove an IP address as follows:

   ❏ To add an IP address, click the A**d**d button. The Add Computer dialog box shown in Figure 30.11 appears. Enter the IP address in the IP **M**ask fields. To add a group of computers, enter a wildcard (asterisk) character in place of a specific group. Some sample entries are **196.135.0.1** or **196.135.*.***, with each number entered in a separate field in the dialog box.

   ❏ To edit an existing IP mask, highlight the IP mask you want to edit and click the **E**dit button. The Edit Computer dialog box shown in Figure 30.12 appears. Proceed to step 5.

   ❏ To remove an IP mask, highlight the IP mask you want to remove and click the **R**emove button. The IP mask is removed from the user list.

5. Select the level of access for the IP mask as follows:

   ❏ If you are adding or editing an IP mask for the current registered (protected) Web, select the **B**rowse this web radio button.

   ❏ If you are adding or changing the IP mask for an author of the current Web, select the **A**uthor and browse this web radio button.

   ❏ If you are adding or changing the IP mask for an administrator of the current Web, select the A**d**minister, author, and browse this web radio button.

6. Click OK to return to the Computers tab in the Permissions dialog box.

7. Click OK. The computer is added to your Web.

Figure 30.10.

Use the Computers tab in the Permissions dialog box to add IP mask accessibility to your Web.

Figure 30.11.

Use the Add Computer dialog box to add an IP mask setting to your Web.

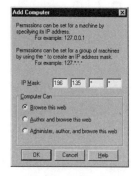

Figure 30.12.

Use the Edit Computer dialog box to edit an existing IP mask configuration.

TASK Changing Passwords

When you use the FrontPage Personal Web Server, an administrator or author can change his or her password through the Change Password dialog box. This option is disabled when you use the Microsoft Personal Web Server (discussed in Chapter 31). In order for the password to be changed, the existing password must be known.

To change the password for a Web user, follow these steps:

1. From the FrontPage Explorer, choose **T**ools | C**h**ange Password. The Change Password for *(name)* dialog box, shown in Figure 30.13, appears.

Figure 30.13.

Change the password for a user in your Web in the Change Password for (name) dialog box.

2. Enter the old password in the **O**ld Password field.

3. Enter the new password in the **N**ew Password field and confirm it again in the **C**onfirm Password field. Spaces are not allowed.

4. Click OK. The password is updated for the user.

Workshop Wrap-Up

In this chapter you learned some of the features and limitations of the FrontPage Personal Web Server. The FrontPage Personal Web Server enables you to test pages that feature all the FrontPage features, with some exceptions. For most who use FrontPage 98 to develop personal Web sites, the FrontPage Personal Web Server might be sufficient for most of their needs. However, to test more advanced features, such as custom CGI scripts, Active Server Pages, and database connection, a more robust server might be necessary.

You learned how to install the FrontPage Personal Web Server and where you can find the files after installation. You also learned some of the differences in how you change the home page name, add users, and administer this server with the FrontPage Server Administrator.

Next Steps

In the next chapter, you'll learn some of the features and functions of the Microsoft Personal Web Server, which is a more robust server that enables you to create and test database connectivity and more.

The following articles in the Microsoft Knowledge Base offer additional information about using the FrontPage Personal Web Server and the FrontPage Server Administrator with FrontPage 98. You can view these articles at Microsoft's Web site by entering the URL following each article title:

❏ Err Msg: No Server on Port <Port Number> at <Server Name> (Q150684)

   `http://www.microsoft.com/kb/articles/q161/1/54.htm`

❏ Err Msg: Timed Out While Trying to Connect to a Server (Q150680)

   `http://www.microsoft.com/kb/articles/q150/6/80.htm`

❏ FrontPage: Basic Troubleshooting Utilities (Q143093)

http://www.microsoft.com/kb/articles/q143/0/93.htm

❏ FrontPage: Browsing Web Returns List of Files (Q143104)

http://www.microsoft.com/kb/articles/q143/1/04.htm

❏ FrontPage: Error "Unable to open ..." and "404 Not Found" (Q143089)

http://www.microsoft.com/kb/articles/q143/0/89.htm

❏ FrontPage Personal Web Server Supports Standard CGI Only (Q151042)

http://www.microsoft.com/kb/articles/q151/0/42.htm

❏ How to Assign a Document Other Than index.htm as Default Page (Q150681)

http://www.microsoft.com/kb/articles/q150/6/81.htm

❏ How to Create an Alias for FrontPage Personal Web Server (Q151541)

http://www.microsoft.com/kb/articles/q151/5/41.htm

❏ How to Delete a Disk-Based Web (Q162240)

http://www.microsoft.com/kb/articles/q162/2/40.htm

❏ How to Upgrade the FrontPage Server Extensions (Q161845)

http://www.microsoft.com/kb/articles/q161/8/45.htm

❏ Personal Web Server Can't Bind to Port 80 (Q149843)

http://www.microsoft.com/kb/articles/q149/8/43.htm

❏ Switching from FrontPage Personal Web Server to Microsoft PWS (Q161418)

http://www.microsoft.com/kb/articles/q161/4/18.htm

❏ Using NCSA or CERN Image Maps with Personal Web Server Upgrade (Q151567)

http://www.microsoft.com/kb/articles/q151/5/67.htm

❏ WebBot Browse-Time Components Don't Function on a Disk-Based Web (Q160227)

http://www.microsoft.com/kb/articles/q160/2/27.htm

❏ When to Use FrontPage Personal Web Server Versus Microsoft PWS (Q161417)

http://www.microsoft.com/kb/articles/q161/4/17.htm

❏ Why Are There Two Versions of the Personal Web Server? (Q161150)

http://www.microsoft.com/kb/articles/q161/1/50.htm

Q&A

Q: Can I develop pages that use custom scripts, Active Server Pages, or database connectivity when I use the FrontPage Personal Web Server?

A: Yes, you can design pages that incorporate these features. However, you will not be able to test them fully before you publish them to the server on which they will reside. If you prefer to test your pages before doing so, the Microsoft Personal Web Server might be a better choice for you.

Q: Are there any limitations as to how many pages I can place in my Web when I use the FrontPage Personal Web Server?

A: I tested the FrontPage Personal Web Server with a Web that contained over 1,000 pages. Although it took quite some time for the Web to open, all pages were listed in the FrontPage Explorer. Tasks such as moving files and folders, using the Verify Links commands, and those that automatically changed page URLs did not perform quite up to the norm. If you expect to create a large site and want to use the FrontPage Personal Web Server, consider placing general content in the root Web and add child Webs for topic-specific content. Remember that you can design only 17 child Webs while using the FrontPage Personal Web Server.

THIRTY-ONE

Using the Microsoft Personal Web Server

In this chapter, you

- ❏ Learn where the files are located
- ❏ Learn how to configure and administer the Microsoft Personal Web Server
- ❏ Start and stop the Microsoft Personal Web Server
- ❏ Start, stop, and configure the WWW and FTP servers
- ❏ Administer the WWW and FTP servers
- ❏ Learn where you can go for additional help

Tasks in this chapter:

- ❏ Displaying Your Web Home Page
- ❏ Starting and Stopping the Microsoft Personal Web Server
- ❏ Starting and Stopping the WWW or FTP Servers
- ❏ Administering the Microsoft Personal Web Server
- ❏ Administering the WWW Server
- ❏ Administering the FTP Server
- ❏ Configuring Your Users
- ❏ Viewing Online Documentation

The FrontPage Personal Web Server enables you to create and test pages that use most of FrontPage 98's built-in features. However, you might find it beneficial to use the Microsoft Personal Web Server instead of or in addition to the FrontPage Personal Web Server. The Microsoft Personal Web Server operates under Windows 95 only. It offers additional capabilities over the FrontPage Personal Web Server, enabling you to test extended features such as custom CGI scripts, FTP services, ISAPI features, and pages that use Internet Database Connector files. You can also install Microsoft Active Server Pages, a component of Internet Information Server 3.0. The server speed is much improved over the FrontPage Personal Web Server, and the limitation of 18 Webs per server is gone.

Learning Whether the Microsoft Personal Web Server Is Right for You

The Microsoft Personal Web Server is furnished as part of the FrontPage Bonus Pack. It offers several enhancements over the FrontPage Personal Web Server, one of which is increased speed in performing server tasks. In addition to faster processing, you don't have the limitation of being able to create only 18 Webs as you do with the FrontPage Personal Web Server.

The Microsoft Personal Web Server includes many of the capabilities that are found in the Microsoft Internet Information Server, which is furnished with Windows NT 4.0 Server. Among these capabilities are support of custom CGI scripts, FTP services, Internet Database Connector (IDC) files, multihoming, ISAPI interface, and increased user access security through NTLM authentication.

NTLM is an authentication scheme used by Windows NT, the Microsoft Internet Information Server, Microsoft Peer Web Services for NT Workstation 4.0, and the Microsoft Personal Web Server for Windows 95.

Additionally, this personal Web server also offers the capability of remote administration through the use of Web-based administration pages. Table 31.1 summarizes the capabilities of the Microsoft Personal Web Server.

Table 31.1. Microsoft Personal Web Server capabilities.

Feature	Supported?
Active Server Pages	Yes (with Active Server Pages installed)
Custom CGI scripts	Yes
FTP services	Yes
Gopher services	No
High traffic sites	No
IDC Database files/scripts	Yes
ISAPI interface	Yes
Multihoming	Yes
NSAPI interface	No
NTLM authentication	Yes
Secure Socket Layer (SSL) communications	No

Installing the Microsoft Personal Web Server

When you insert the FrontPage 98 CD-ROM into your CD-ROM drive, the FrontPage 98 setup program initially checks to see whether a Web server exists on your system. If you do not yet have a server, setup asks whether you would like to install the Microsoft Personal Web Server. Choose Yes to install it.

You also can install the Microsoft Personal Web Server by following these steps:

1. Insert the FrontPage 98 CD-ROM into your CD-ROM drive. The FrontPage 98 setup screen appears.

2. Select the Microsoft Personal Web Server for Windows 95 option. A license agreement screen appears. To continue installation, select I **A**gree.

3. Setup installs several files onto your system, after which a Personal Web Server dialog box appears. You are asked whether you want to restart your computer. Answer **Y**es.

If the Microsoft Personal Web Server is the only server on your system, it is installed to port 80. You can browse Webs on this server by specifying server addresses similar to the following:

```
http://yourserver/
http://yourserver/childweb/
http://yourserver/childweb/webpage.htm
```

If another server has been previously installed on your system, the Microsoft Personal Web Server is installed to port 8080. You can browse Webs on the Microsoft Personal Web Server by specifying a server address as follows:

```
http://yourserver:8080/
http://yourserver:8080/childweb/
http://yourserver:8080/childweb/webpage.htm
```

Microsoft Personal Web Server File Locations

When you install the Microsoft Personal Web Server on your computer, the files and images associated with the server are installed to the following default directories:

❏ The c:\Program Files\docs subdirectory contains documentation and help files.

❏ The c:\Program Files\htmla subdirectory contains Web administration files.

❏ The c:\Program Files\htmlascr subdirectory contains scripts for the Microsoft Personal Web Server.

- ❏ The `c:\Program Files\system` subdirectory contains executable and administration files.
- ❏ Web content is saved to the `c:\Webshare\wwwroot` directory by default.
- ❏ The FTP server files are located in the `c:\Webshare\ftproot` directory.
- ❏ Custom scripts are placed in the `c:\Webshare\scripts` subdirectory.

Setting Microsoft Personal Web Server Properties

You configure the Microsoft Personal Web Server through the Personal Web Server Properties dialog box. From the Windows 95 Start menu, choose Settings and then Control Panel. From the Control Panel group, click Personal Web Server. The Personal Web Server Properties dialog box appears. The following is a brief overview of the screens that you use to administer and configure your Microsoft Personal Web Server.

Displaying Your Web Home Page

When you first open the Personal Web Server Properties dialog box, you see the General tab, shown in Figure 31.1. This dialog box displays the Internet address of the Microsoft Personal Web Server (for example, `http://servername`). Each child Web you create resides in subfolders of this server. To browse a child Web in your Internet browser, enter a URL similar to **http://servername/childwebname**.

Figure 31.1.

Use the Personal Web Server Properties dialog box to access and configure the Microsoft Personal Web Server.

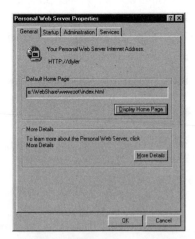

The URL of your default home page (that is, the home page in your server's root Web) is shown beneath the Web server address. To view the default home page in your Web browser, follow these steps:

1. From the Windows 95 Start menu, choose Settings, then Control Panel. The Control Panel group dialog box appears.

2. From the Control Panel group, select Personal Web Server. The Personal Web Server Properties dialog box appears, opened to the General tab.

3. In the Default Home Page section, select the **D**isplay Home Page button. The home page that exists in your root Web opens in your browser.

Starting and Stopping the Microsoft Personal Web Server

To edit the contents of the default home page, choose **F**ile | **O**pen FrontPage Web from the FrontPage Explorer. From the list of Webs on your server, select the root Web. After the root Web appears in the FrontPage Explorer, double-click `default.htm` to open the page in the FrontPage Editor.

The Startup tab in the Personal Web Server Properties dialog box enables you to start and stop the Microsoft Personal Web Server. You also can configure the Personal Web Server to start automatically whenever Windows 95 starts up. The Startup tab also provides an option to include an icon for the Personal Web Server on your Windows 95 taskbar. To access these features, follow these steps:

1. From the Windows 95 Start menu, choose Settings, then Control Panel. The Control Panel group dialog box appears.

2. From the Control Panel group, select Personal Web Server. The Personal Web Server Properties dialog box appears.

3. Select the Startup tab, shown in Figure 31.2.

Figure 31.2.

Use the Startup tab in the Personal Web Server Properties dialog box to start and stop the Microsoft Personal Web Server.

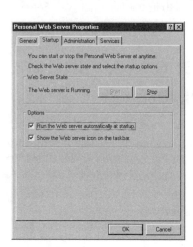

4. In the Web Server State section, a status message that displays the current state of the Personal Web Server appears. You are informed whether the Web server is running or is stopped.

❏ If the Web server is not running, choose **S**tart to start the World Wide Web server.

❏ If the Web server is running, choose **S**top to stop the World Wide Web server.

5. The Options section of the Startup tab enables you to start the Microsoft Personal Web Server automatically when Windows 95 starts up. To enable this option, check the Run the Web server automatically at startup checkbox. If this option is disabled, you will need to start the server manually as outlined in steps 1 through 4.

6. You also can choose to locate an icon for the Microsoft Personal Web Server in your Windows 95 taskbar. To enable this option, check the Show the Web server icon on the taskbar checkbox. With the icon in your taskbar, you can do the following:

   ❏ Double-click the icon to open the Personal Web Server Properties dialog box. You can also open this dialog box if you right-click the icon and choose **P**roperties from the pop-up menu.

   ❏ Right-click and choose **A**dminister to open the Internet Services Administrator Web-Based Server Administration page in your browser.

   ❏ Right-click and choose **H**ome Page to open the home page in the root Web of your server.

7. Select another tab in the Personal Web Server Properties dialog box or choose OK to apply your settings.

 ## Starting and Stopping the WWW or FTP Servers

By default, the WWW server is configured to start automatically when Windows 95 starts. The FTP server does not run by default. You can customize these settings using the Services tab in the Personal Web Server Properties dialog box, shown in Figure 31.3. The display at the bottom of the page tells you the current status of each server. You can tell whether the server is stopped or running and whether the server is started manually or automatically.

To start and stop the WWW or FTP services through the Services tab, follow these steps:

1. From the Windows 95 Start menu, choose Settings, then Control Panel. The Control Panel group dialog box appears.

2. From the Control Panel group, select Personal Web Server. The Personal Web Server Properties dialog box appears.

3. Select the Services tab.

4. In the Services section, highlight the server for which you want to start, stop, or change properties.

   ❏ To start a server that is not running, click the **S**tart button.

   ❏ To stop a server that is running, click the **S**top button.

   ❏ To change the configuration of the WWW server, highlight HTTP from the list and click **P**roperties. The HTTP Properties dialog box appears. To start the HTTP server automatically when Windows 95 starts, select the **A**utomatic (HTTP service starts up automatically) radio button. To start the HTTP server manually, select the **M**anual radio button. Selecting the Change Home Root button or the Change Home Page button opens the WWW Administrator—Directory page, discussed in the section "Administering the Microsoft Personal Web Server," later in this chapter.

   ❏ To change the configuration of the FTP server, highlight FTP from the list and click **P**roperties. The FTP Properties dialog box appears. To start the FTP service automatically, choose the **A**utomatic (FTP Service Starts Up Automatically) radio button. To start the FTP service manually, select the **M**anual button. To change the FTP server's home root directory, select the Change FTP Home **R**oot button.

Figure 31.3.

Use the Services tab in the Personal Web Server Properties dialog box to start, stop, or configure your WWW or FTP server.

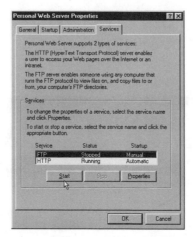

 # Administering the Microsoft Personal Web Server

You use the Administration tab of the Personal Web Server Properties dialog box, shown in Figure 31.4, to administer your Microsoft Personal Web Server. From this tab, you gain access to administration tasks for the WWW and FTP servers, as well as the ability to add users and groups to your server. Use the following steps:

1. From the Windows 95 Start menu, choose Settings, then Control Panel. The Control Panel group dialog box appears.

2. From the Control Panel group, select Personal Web Server. The Personal Web Server Properties dialog box appears.

3. Select the Administration tab.

4. Click the Administration button. The Internet Services Administrator Web-based Server Administration page, shown in Figure 31.5, opens in your browser. From this page, you can administer your WWW and FTP servers and add users and groups to your Webs.

Figure 31.4.

Use the Administration tab of the Personal Web Server Properties dialog box to gain access to administrator tasks.

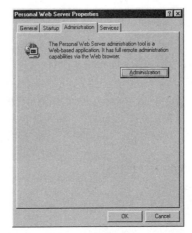

Figure 31.5.

The Internet Services Administrator Web-based Server Administration page enables you to configure your servers and its users.

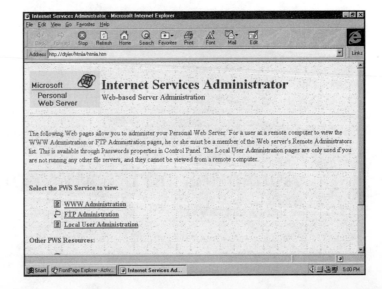

Administering the WWW Server

When you choose to administer your HTTP (or World Wide Web) server, the Administration page shown in Figure 31.6 opens in your browser. This page contains three tabs: Service, Directories, and Logging.

Figure 31.6.

The Service tab on the WWW Administration page.

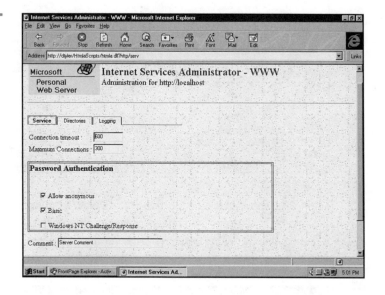

You can administer the Microsoft Personal Web Server remotely from Web-based administration pages that are located on the server.

The Service tab enables you to configure the following items:

- ❑ Connection Timeout (default 600 seconds)
- ❑ Maximum Connections (default 300 connections)
- ❑ Password Authentication, which lets you enable anonymous connections, basic authentication, or Windows NT Challenge/Response authentication
- ❑ Comment, which enables you to configure a server comment message.

The WWW Administrator—Directory page, the top of which is shown in Figure 31.7, lists all directories on your server. You can edit, add, or delete directories from this page:

- ❑ To edit a directory, select the Edit link that is adjacent to the directory you want to edit.
- ❑ To delete a directory, select the Delete link that is adjacent to the directory you want to delete.
- ❑ To add a directory, click the Add link at the bottom-right of the directory list.

Figure 31.7.

The upper portion of the WWW Administrator - Directory page contains a list of all the directories on your server. You can edit, delete, or add directories on this page.

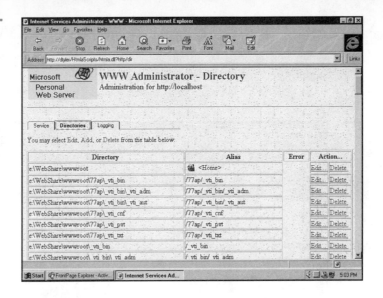

Figure 31.8 shows the lower portion of the WWW Administrator—Directory page. In this section of the page, you find an option to rename the default home page, which is (appropriately) named `Default.htm`. Enter another name in the Default Document field if you need to.

Figure 31.8.

The lower portion of the WWW Administrator - Directory page.

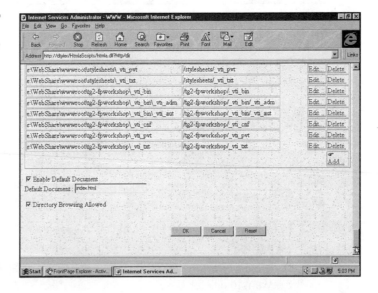

You also have the following options in this portion of the page:

❑ Enable Default Document

❑ Directory Browsing Allowed

The Logging tab, shown in Figure 31.9, lets you enable and disable logging and specify how often you want a log file to be generated. To specify the settings for your logging file, follow these steps:

1. To enable logging, check the Enable logging checkbox, which is checked by default. If you disable the checkbox, no logging file is generated.

2. To automatically open a new log at a specified interval, check the Automatically open new log checkbox. Then, select how you want a new log file to be generated. The options are Daily, Weekly, Monthly, or when the file size reaches a specified number of megabytes.

3. In the Log file directory field, enter the directory in which you want to store your log file, or click the Browse button to locate a directory on your local or network hard drive.

Figure 31.9.

The Logging tab of the WWW Administration page.

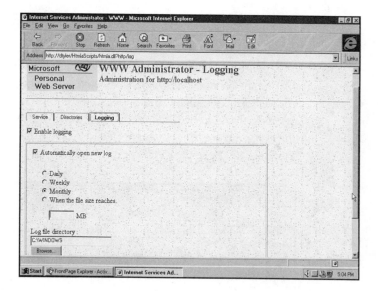

 # Administering the FTP Server

The FTP server included in the Microsoft Personal Web Server enables users to download files from your Web site. You can specify a maximum number of people that are allowed to connect to your download area at a given time, generate activity logs, and configure messages and directories for your FTP server. When you choose to configure your FTP server, the Internet Services Administrator—FTP page appears in your browser. This page contains four tabs: Service, Messages, Directories, and Logging. The Service tab is shown in Figure 31.10.

Figure 31.10.
The Service tab of the FTP Administration page.

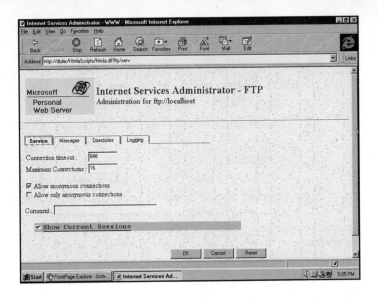

The Service tab enables you to configure the following items: Connection Timeout, Maximum Connections, Allow anonymous connections, Allow only anonymous connections, Comment, and Show Current Sessions. If you select Show Current Sessions, the Current FTP Sessions page, shown in Figure 31.11, appears. It displays the users who are currently connected to your FTP site and enables you to disconnect the users and close the FTP service.

Figure 31.11.
The Current FTP Sessions page displays the users who are connected to your FTP service.

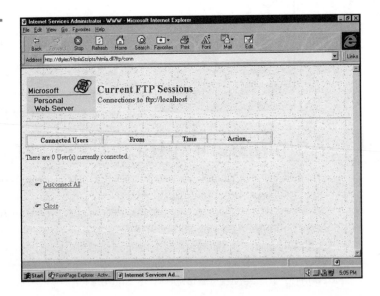

The FTP Administrator—Messages page, shown in Figure 31.12, enables you to configure default messages for your FTP server. You can configure a welcome message, an exit message, and a maximum connections message.

Figure 31.12.

You can configure FTP messages in the FTP Administrator - Messages page.

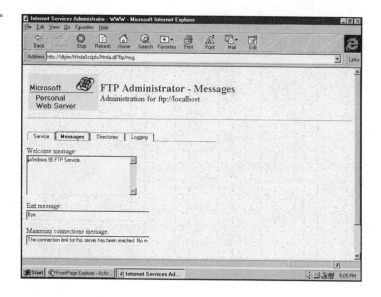

The FTP Administrator—Directory page, shown in Figure 31.13, lists the directories on your FTP server. You can edit, add, or delete directories from this page:

❏ To edit a directory, select the Edit link that is adjacent to the directory you want to edit.

❏ To delete a directory, select the Delete link that is adjacent to the directory you want to delete.

❏ To add a directory, click the Add link at the bottom-right of the directory list.

❏ To select a directory listing style, choose either the Unix radio button or the MS-DOS radio button.

The Logging tab, shown in Figure 31.14, lets you enable and disable logging and specify how often you want a log file to be generated. To specify the settings for your logging file, follow these steps:

1. To enable logging, check the Enable Logging checkbox, which is checked by default. If you disable the checkbox, no logging file is generated.

2. To automatically open a new log at a specified interval, check the Automatically open new log checkbox. Then, select how you want a new log file to be generated. The options are Daily, Weekly, Monthly, or When the file size reaches. The latter refers to a specified number of megabytes.

3. In the Log file directory field, enter the directory in which you want to store your log file, or click the Browse button to locate a directory on your local or network hard drive.

Figure 31.13.

The FTP Administrator - Directory page contains a list of all the directories on your FTP server.

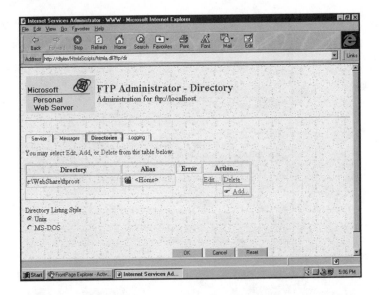

Figure 31.14.

The Logging tab of the FTP Administrator page.

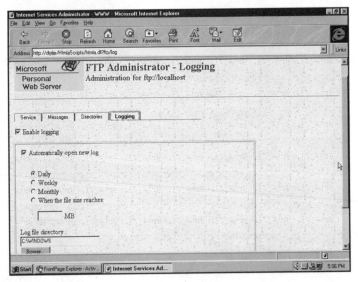

Configuring Your Users

When you choose Local User Administration from the Internet Services Administrator Web-Based Server Administration page, the Internet Local User Administrator page opens. This page consists of three tabs: Users (shown in Figure 31.15), Groups, and User/Group.

Figure 31.15.
The Users tab of the Internet Local User Administrator page.

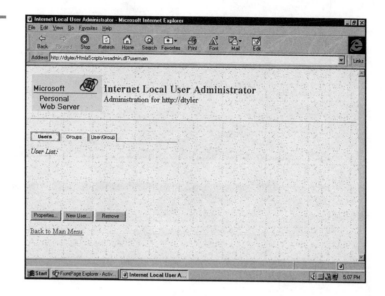

When you use the Microsoft Personal Web Server, you configure users and user groups with Web-based administration pages.

In the Users tab, you edit, add, and remove users from your server:

❏ To add a new user, click the New User button. The page shown in Figure 31.16 appears. Enter the user's name and password in the User Name and User Password fields and then confirm the password in the Confirm Password field. Click the Add button to add the new user.

❏ To edit the properties of an existing user, click the Properties button.

❏ To remove a user, select the user you want to remove and click the Remove button.

The Groups tab, shown in Figure 31.17, enables you to add, remove, or change properties of user groups. From the Groups tab, click the New Group button. This takes you to the Add New Group to Web Server Database page shown in Figure 31.18. Enter a group name in the Group Name field and click Add.

Figure 31.16.

Enter the user's name and password on this page.

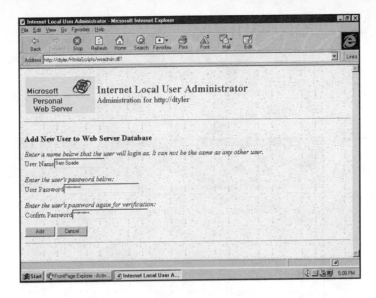

Figure 31.17.

The Groups tab enables you to add, remove, or change properties of user groups.

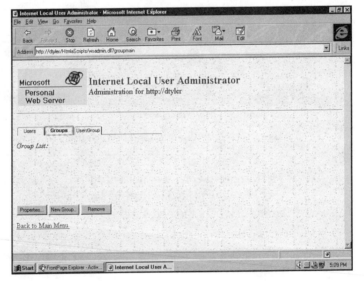

NOTE: You also can configure groups and assign users to them by choosing **T**ools | **P**ermissions from the FrontPage Explorer and selecting the Groups tab in the Permissions dialog box. This tab is not available when you use the FrontPage Personal Web Server.

Figure 31.18.

Add user group names on this page.

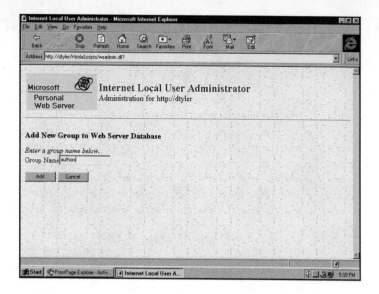

The User/Group tab lets you assign users to any groups you have configured in your Web. This tab takes you to the page shown in Figure 31.19. Highlight a user from the User List, select the group to which you want to add the user, and click the Add user to group button.

Figure 31.19.

You assign users to groups in the User/ Group page.

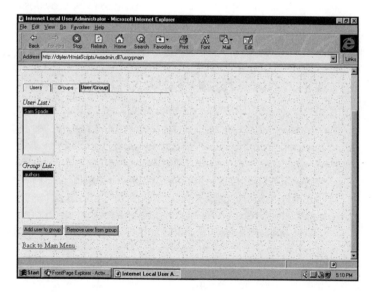

Viewing Online Documentation

Additional information about administering and configuring the Microsoft Personal Web Server is installed to your system. You gain access to this information as follows:

1. From the Windows 95 Start menu, choose Settings, then Control Panel. The Control Panel group dialog box appears.

2. From the Control Panel group, select Personal Web Server. The Personal Web Server Properties dialog box appears, opened to the General tab.

3. To obtain more information about the Microsoft Personal Web Server, select the More Details button. Documentation for the Microsoft Personal Web Server appears in your browser. Choose one of the following three links:

   ❏ The `Getting Started with Personal Web Server` link provides instructions for creating a Web site on your computer, how to start the Personal Web Server, and how to test servers connected to the Internet and your intranet.

   ❏ The `Personal Web Server Administration` link provides instructions for restricting access to your site, information about basic authentication and Windows NT Challenge/Response authentication, and instructions on how to configure user lists and logging.

   ❏ The `FTP Server Administration` link provides instructions for creating an FTP site, configuring its home directory, and restricting access to the FTP site.

Workshop Wrap-Up

In this chapter, you learned the capabilities of the Microsoft Personal Web Server, a Windows 95 server that offers many of the capabilities available in Windows NT's Internet Information Server. When using FrontPage on a system that runs Windows 95, the Microsoft Personal Web Server offers many advantages over the FrontPage Personal Web Server. In addition to the increase in speed and the number of Webs that can reside on the server, you can create and test pages that utilize advanced Web capabilities. You can develop and test pages that incorporate features such as custom CGI scripts, FTP file transfers, and IDC database connection. Those who require compatibility with ISAPI extensions, used with Internet Information Server, will be pleased to know that this server supports those functions as well. As you learned in this chapter, you can configure and administer this server locally or remotely through the use of Web-based server administration pages. You also learned how to locate additional documentation that is installed on your local computer along with the Microsoft Personal Web Server.

Next Steps

In the next chapter, you learn about the new Internet features in Microsoft Word 97 and how you can use this application in conjunction with FrontPage 98. You'll compare the features and capabilities of using either application as a Web page editor.

For additional information about the Microsoft Personal Web Server, check the following articles in the Microsoft Knowledge Base. You can find these articles by navigating to the URLs that follow each document title:

❑ FrontPage: Error "Unable to open ..." and "404 Not Found" (Q143089)

  http://www.microsoft.com/kb/articles/q143/0/89.htm

❑ FrontPage Explorer Doesn't Accept Blank Password (Q163587)

  http://www.microsoft.com/kb/articles/q163/5/87.htm

❑ How to Make a Web Page that Displays Data from a Database (Q161155)

  http://www.microsoft.com/kb/articles/q161/1/55.htm

❑ IDC Queries to Access Fail from IIS 2.0 or MSPWS 1.0 Servers (Q162245)

  http://www.microsoft.com/kb/articles/q162/2/45.htm

❑ Internet Database Connector Wizard Runs on Non-IDC Server (Q160810)

  http://www.microsoft.com/kb/articles/q160/8/10.htm

❑ Memory Leak in FrontPage Extensions on MS Personal Web Server (Q160225)

  http://www.microsoft.com/kb/articles/q160/2/25.htm

❑ Permission Settings Changed After Reinstalling Extensions (Q161847)

  http://www.microsoft.com/kb/articles/q161/8/47.htm

❑ Permissions Not Retained when Web Is Renamed (Q161964)

  http://www.microsoft.com/kb/articles/q161/9/64.htm

❑ Personal Web Server Doesn't Support Multiple Queries in IDC File (Q160809)

  http://www.microsoft.com/kb/articles/q160/8/09.htm

❑ Switching from FrontPage Personal Web Server to Microsoft PWS (Q161418)

  http://www.microsoft.com/kb/articles/q161/4/18.htm

❑ Unable to Complete Transaction on Server with NTLM (Q160618)

  http://www.microsoft.com/kb/articles/q160/6/18.htm

❑ WebBot Browse-Time Components Don't Function on a Disk-Based Web (Q160227)

  http://www.microsoft.com/kb/articles/q160/2/27.htm

❑ When to Use FrontPage Personal Web Server Versus Microsoft PWS (Q161417)

http://www.microsoft.com/kb/articles/q161/4/17.htm

❑ Why Are There Two Versions of the Personal Web Server? (Q161150)

http://www.microsoft.com/kb/articles/q161/1/50.htm

Q&A

Q: Is there any advantage in using the FrontPage Personal Web Server instead of the Microsoft Personal Web Server?

A: If you are upgrading from previous versions of FrontPage, you might feel more at home using the FrontPage Personal Web Server. However, if you're using FrontPage with Windows 95, the Microsoft Personal Web Server does offer many improvements over the FrontPage Personal Web Server. Even if you do not need the additional features that the Microsoft Personal Web Server offers, it is faster, more secure, and more capable in the number of Webs you can create.

Q: What advantages do I have if I use a commercial Web server such as Internet Information Server or one of the Netscape servers?

A: Commercial Web servers are probably much more than the average home user will need. They are designed for much heavier traffic, such as that used on a public Web site or corporate intranet. With a commercial Web server, you can provide many additional features, such as private or public Internet relay chats, newsgroups, and merchant transactions. Commercial Web servers are written for a wide variety of platforms, including Windows 95, Windows NT, UNIX, and more. If you want to move up to a commercial Web server, a list of servers for which the FrontPage Server Extensions are available is listed in Chapter 2, "About the FrontPage Server Extensions."

THIRTY-TWO

Administering Your Webs

As a server administrator, you can get pretty busy keeping track of where pages are located. Sometimes you have to make changes to the Web. You might need to relocate, rename, or remove Webs. New administrators, authors, and end users must be added or removed, and passwords must be changed. These tasks all require administrator authorization.

Running the FrontPage Server Administrator

You use the FrontPage Server Administrator to install, uninstall, and maintain the FrontPage Server Extensions. When you are upgrading from previous versions of FrontPage, the FrontPage 98 Server Administrator will feel very familiar. Server administration is accomplished through the dialog box shown in Figure 32.1.

CAUTION: Be careful if you have older versions of the FrontPage Server Administrator on your hard disk in addition to the FrontPage 98 Server Administrator. For example, if you attempt to manage the FrontPage 98 Server Extensions with the FrontPage 1.1 Server Administrator, you might receive page fault errors. To remedy this situation, use the FrontPage 98 Server Administrator to manage both FrontPage 1.1 and FrontPage 98 Server Extensions.

Figure 32.1.

The FrontPage Server Administrator (Windows version) administers your server through a dialog box.

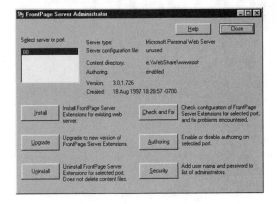

To run the FrontPage Server Extensions, follow these steps:

1. From the Windows 95 Start menu, choose **R**un. The Run dialog box appears.

2. In the **O**pen field, enter the path to the FrontPage Server Administrator executable file or use the **B**rowse button to locate the file on your local or network hard drive. A shortcut to the executable file appears in your FrontPage 98 installation folder. The default installation path to the shortcut for the FrontPage Server Administrator is

   ```
   c:\Program Files\Microsoft FrontPage\FrontPage Server Administrator.Ink
   ```
   The default installation path to the executable file is

   ```
   c:\Program Files\Microsoft FrontPage\version3.0\bin\fpsrvwin.exe
   ```

3. After you select the file in the Browse dialog box, choose **O**pen to return to the Run dialog box. Then choose OK to start the FrontPage Server Administrator.

TASK

Installing the FrontPage Server Extensions

If you have not yet installed FrontPage 98, it is best to install your server software before you do. Then, FrontPage 98 will automatically install the Server Extensions to your server during installation. If you add another server to your computer after FrontPage 98 has been installed on your computer, you can use the Install button in the FrontPage Server Administrator to install the FrontPage Server Extensions to your new server. The FrontPage Server Administrator enables you to install the Server Extensions to the following Windows 95 servers:

FrontPage Personal Web Server
Microsoft Personal Web Server
Netscape Commerce Server
Netscape Communications Server
Netscape Enterprise Server
Netscape FastTrack Server
O'Reilly WebSite Server

To install the FrontPage Server Extensions on a server, follow these steps:

1. Install one of the listed servers on your computer first. A port number will be assigned during installation. The default port number is usually port **80** for the first server you install and port **8080** for a second server. Your server software may also enable you to specify another port number.

2. Start the FrontPage Server Administrator, as outlined in the earlier section "Running the FrontPage Server Administrator." The FrontPage Server Administrator dialog box shown in Figure 32.1 appears.

3. If the port number to which you are installing the Server Extensions appears in the **Se**lect server or port field, highlight the port number to which you want to install the Server Extensions. Information about the server appears at the right of the field. This information lists the server type, a server configuration file (if used), the location of your content directory, authoring status, and version and date of the file. If the server does not appear in the list, proceed to step 4.

4. Click **I**nstall. The Configure Server Type dialog box shown in Figure 32.2 appears.

5. From the **S**erver type drop-down menu, select the type of server that is installed on the port you selected in step 3.

6. Choose OK. If the server requires a configuration file, a Server Configuration dialog box appears. This dialog box varies depending on the server you select:

   ❏ If you are installing the Server Extensions on the FrontPage Personal Web Server, you specify the name of the main server configuration file in the Server Configuration dialog box shown in Figure 32.2. The default installation path to this file is `c:\FrontPage Webs\Server\conf\httpd.cnf`.

   ❏ If you are installing the Server Extensions to the Microsoft Personal Web Server, the Server Configuration dialog box will not appear.

   ❏ If you are installing the Server Extensions to a Netscape server, you need to enter the port number on which the Server Extensions will be installed.

   ❏ If you are installing the Server Extensions to WebSite and are using multihoming, enter the fully qualified domain name for the host that will contain the Server Extensions. Leave the field blank if you are not using multihoming.

7. Choose OK. The Confirmation Dialog shown in Figure 32.3 displays information about your server installation.

Figure 32.2.

Choose your server from the Configure Server Type dialog box.

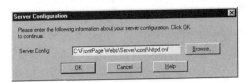

Figure 32.3.

The Confirmation Dialog displays information about your server installation.

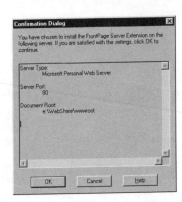

8. Choose OK to continue. The Administrator Setup dialog box may appear, asking you to enter an account name that you will use to identify yourself when authoring and administering your FrontPage Webs. Enter a name in the Name field. This name cannot contain spaces, tabs, or colon characters.

9. Choose OK to install the Server Extensions to the selected server. If the server administrator detects that the port already has a root Web, the existing Webs on the server will be upgraded to the most recent version of the FrontPage Server Extensions that have been installed on your computer. Choose OK to continue.

10. You are notified when installation has completed successfuly. Choose OK to return to the Server Administrator.

Upgrading the FrontPage Server Extensions

When you upgrade to FrontPage 98 from a previous version, your existing content folders may need to be upgraded to use the current version of the FrontPage Server Extensions. For example, if you use Navigation view to open a Web that was created with a previous version of FrontPage, you may receive a message that the Server Extensions used with the Web do not support Navigation view. In cases such as these, you need to upgrade the Server Extensions in your old content directories.

To upgrade the FrontPage Server Extensions on a selected port, follow these steps:

1. Start the FrontPage Server Administrator, as outlined in the earlier section "Running the FrontPage Server Administrator." The FrontPage Server Administrator dialog box appears.

2. From the Select server or port field, highlight the port number on which you want to upgrade the Server Extensions.

3. Click **U**pgrade. The dialog box shown in Figure 32.4 notifies you that the port will be upgraded with the currently installed FrontPage Server Extension software. Choose OK to continue.

Figure 32.4.
The Server Administrator notifies you that the port will be upgraded with the currently installed Server Extensions.

4. You are notified when installation has completed successfuly. Choose OK to return to the Server Administrator.

Uninstalling the FrontPage Server Extensions

Sometimes you may need to uninstall previous versions of the Server Extensions before you install another server. For example, you might have the FrontPage Personal Web Server installed to port 80, and you would rather use the Microsoft Personal Web Server on that port; or you might want to move your server files and content to another directory on your hard drive. To accomplish this, you need to uninstall the Server Extensions before you install or move your server.

When you uninstall the FrontPage Server Extensions from a port, the information about the selected port is removed from the `frontpg.ini` file in your `C:\Windows` directory. The `_vti_bin` folder that holds the server extension executable files is removed from your FrontPage Web, and the `_vti_txt` directory that holds the text index for your FrontPage Web is also removed. Your content files (Web pages, images, and other files that you imported into your Webs) remain unaffected.

To uninstall the FrontPage Server Extensions from a selected port, follow these steps:

1. Start the FrontPage Server Administrator, as outlined in the earlier section "Running the FrontPage Server Administrator." The FrontPage Server Administrator dialog box appears.

2. From the Select server or port field, highlight the port number from which you want to uninstall the Server Extensions.

3. Click Uninstall. The dialog box shown in Figure 32.5 notifies you that the Server Extensions will be uninstalled from the Webs associated with the server, but that your content files will remain. Choose OK to continue. The Server Administrator removes the Server Extensions from the selected port.

Figure 32.5.
When you uninstall the Server Extensions from a port, your content files remain.

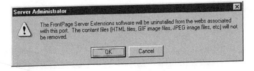

After you uninstall the Server Extensions from the selected port, you can install your new server software. You can also use the Windows Explorer to move your old content directory to a new location or to rename your content folder. If you change the location or name of a previous content folder, you need to change the document root directory using the normal procedures provided with your server.

NOTE: Chapter 31, "Using the Microsoft Personal Web Server," outlines the steps to change the document root directory on the Microsoft Personal Web Server.

To change the document root directory for the FrontPage Personal Web Server, open the `c:\FrontPage Webs\Server\conf\srm.cnf` file in NotePad and edit the path that appears in the following line:

```
DocumentRoot c:/frontpage\ webs/content
```

TASK — Checking and Fixing the FrontPage Server Extensions

If you run into problems with your installation, you can use the Check and Fix feature in the FrontPage Server Administrator to check the configuration files on your selected port and fix problems that it encounters. This process replaces missing FrontPage directories and files. It also ensures that all the executable files are present and the correct permissions have been assigned, and it removes locked files from your Webs. If you are using the Microsoft Personal Web Server (or Internet Information Server on a Windows NT system), you will also be prompted to tighten security.

To check and fix your FrontPage installation, follow these steps:

1. Start the FrontPage Server Administrator, as outlined in the earlier section "Running the FrontPage Server Administrator." The FrontPage Server Administrator dialog box appears.

2. From the Select server or port field, highlight the port number that you want to check.

3. Click Check and Fix. If you are checking the installation on the Microsoft Personal Web Server or on the Internet Information Server, the dialog box shown in Figure 32.6 appears. You are asked whether you want to tighten security as much as possible for all FrontPage Webs. Choose Yes to continue.

4. If there are any files that need to be reinstalled, you will be prompted to insert installation disks. You are notified if the check completes successfully.

Figure 32.6.

If you are checking installation on the Microsoft Personal Web Server or on Internet Information Server, you are asked whether you want to tighten security on your Webs.

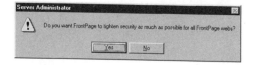

Enabling and Disabling Authoring

You can use the FrontPage Server Administrator to enable or disable authoring on the selected port. You can also select whether Secure Socket Layer (SSL) communication is required for authoring. SSL communication is supported by Internet Information Server as well as other servers; it is not supported by the FrontPage Personal Web Server.

NOTE: Configure your Web server to use SSL *before* you select the SSL option in the FrontPage Server Administrator. If the server is not properly configured before you select the SSL option in the FrontPage Server Administrator, you will not be able to author against the server.

To enable or disable authoring, follow these steps:

1. Start the FrontPage Server Administrator, as outlined in the earlier section "Running the FrontPage Server Administrator." The FrontPage Server Administrator dialog box appears.

2. From the S**e**lect server or port field, highlight the port number that you want to check.

3. Click **A**uthoring. The Enable/Disable Authoring dialog box shown in Figure 32.7 appears.

Figure 32.7.
Use the Enable/Disable Authoring dialog box to configure authoring options on your server.

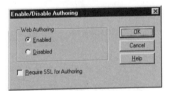

4. To change the status of authoring on your server, choose **E**nabled or **D**isabled from the Web Authoring section.

5. Choose the **R**equire SSL for Authoring checkbox if authors will need to use Secure Socket Layer communications. This causes the Server Extensions to check whether the author has selected the Connect Using SSL checkbox when attempting to connect to Webs on your server.

6. Choose OK to apply the settings.

Adding Administrators

You can use the FrontPage Server Administrator to create or modify administrator names and passwords in your FrontPage Webs. Here are the steps:

1. Start the FrontPage Server Administrator, as outlined in the earlier section "Running the FrontPage Server Administrator." The FrontPage Server Administrator dialog box appears.

2. From the Select server or port field, highlight the port number that you want to check.

3. Click Security. The Administrator Name and Password dialog box shown in Figure 32.8 appears.

Figure 32.8.

Use the Administrator Name and Password dialog box to add an administrator to a Web on your server.

4. In the Web name field, enter the name of the Web to which you want to add an administrator. By default, the root Web is selected. Child Webs must already be configured to use unique permissions as explained in Chapter 30, "Using the FrontPage Personal Web Server."

5. In the Name field, enter the name of the server administrator.

6. Choose OK to continue. The Server Administrator adds the administrator name to the list of administrators for the selected Web.

 Configuring Web Settings

The tasks that follow are general tasks that you can do while using either the Microsoft Personal Web Server or the FrontPage Personal Web Server. These are tasks that you can access through the FrontPage Web Settings dialog box. Follow these steps:

Changing Your Web Name and Title

You can easily change the name and title of your Web by using the Configuration tab in the FrontPage Web Settings dialog box, which is shown in Figure 32.9.

Figure 32.9.

Use the Configuration tab in the FrontPage Web Settings dialog box to change your Web name and title.

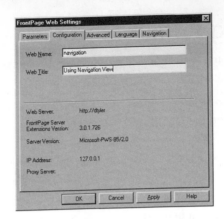

To learn how to use the Parameters tab in the FrontPage Web Settings dialog box, refer to the section "Adding Configuration Variables" in Chapter 23, "Configuring Form Handlers."
To learn how to configure your image map style, refer to Chapter 9, "Getting from Here to There."
To learn how to choose a default scripting language, refer to Chapter 28, "Working with ActiveX and Scripts."

1. From the FrontPage Explorer, choose **T**ools I **W**eb Settings. The FrontPage Web Settings dialog box appears. Choose the Configuration tab.

2. In the Web **N**ame field, enter the new name for your Web. This name cannot contain spaces or punctuation and must conform to the naming conventions of the server on which it resides.

3. In the Web **T**itle field, enter a new title for your Web.

4. Click OK or press Enter to exit the FrontPage Web Settings dialog box, or click Apply to modify additional Web settings.

Displaying Documents in Hidden Directories

There are several FrontPage features that add pages to hidden folders in your Webs. Among these features are themes, hover buttons, and discussion groups. By default, FrontPage is configured so that it does not display these hidden directories in the FrontPage Explorer's Folders View. You can choose to view these hidden directories by following these steps:

1. From the FrontPage Explorer, choose **T**ools I **W**eb Settings. The FrontPage Web Settings dialog box appears.

2. Choose the Advanced tab, shown in Figure 32.10.

3. Check the box beside Show documents in **h**idden directories.

4. Click OK to apply the settings to your Web site and exit, or click **A**pply if you want to change additional Web settings.

5. FrontPage asks whether you want to refresh the Web after the changes are made:

    ❏ Choose **Y**es to refresh the Web and update the directory trees to display the files in hidden directories.

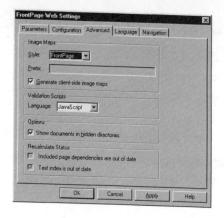

❑ Choose **N**o if you want to view the updated directories at a later time.
The directories will show the next time you open the Web site or if you
choose the **V**iew I **R**efresh (F5) command in the FrontPage Explorer.

Recalculating Your Web Status

You use the Advanced tab in the FrontPage Web Settings dialog box to recalculate
your Web status when page dependencies are out of date or when your Web's text
index is out of date. Common examples of this are if you want to update all Include
Page components in your Web or generate a new text index for your search pages.

To recalculate your Web status, follow these steps:

1. From the FrontPage Explorer, choose **T**ools I **W**eb Settings. The Web Settings
dialog box appears.

2. Choose the Advanced tab, shown in Figure 32.10.

3. In the Recalculate Status section, you see two checkboxes enabled when
your Web needs to be recalculated:

    ❑ *Included page dependencies are out of date*. This option enables when
    Include Page components contained on any page are out of date.

    ❑ *Text index is out of date*. This option enables when FrontPage has a
    text index that is out of date.

4. To apply the settings that you selected in the Advanced tab, click **A**pply if
you want to set additional Web settings, or click OK to exit the Web Settings
dialog box.

Setting Default Web and HTML Encoding Languages

By default, FrontPage 98 uses English as its default Web language and uses US/Western European as its default HTML encoding language. You can change these settings, if necessary, from the FrontPage Web Settings dialog box.

To change Web and HTML encoding languages, follow these steps:

1. From the FrontPage Explorer, choose **T**ools | **W**eb Settings. The Web Settings dialog box appears.

2. Choose the Language tab, shown in Figure 32.11.

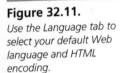

Figure 32.11.
Use the Language tab to select your default Web language and HTML encoding.

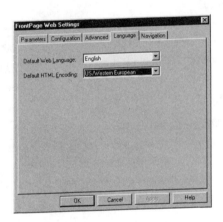

You can configure the FrontPage Explorer to issue warnings when included components and text indexes are out of date. From the FrontPage Explorer, choose **T**ools | **O**ptions and click the General tab in the Options dialog box. Check Warn when **i**ncluded components are out of date or Warn when **t**ext index is out of date and click OK.

3. Use the Default Web **L**anguage drop-down menu to select your default Web language. This is the language used by the FrontPage Server Extensions to return error messages from the Web server to the Web browser. Change this setting to match the language returned by the server to the language you use in your Web pages. The available choices are

   English
   French
   German
   Italian
   Japanese
   Spanish

4. If the pages you create use a different character set from the default set on your computer, you can choose a different character set from the Default HTML **E**ncoding drop-down menu. The default is US/Western European. The available choices are

<None>
Baltic
Central European
Central European (ISO 8859-2)
Cyrillic
Cyrillic (KO18-R)
Greek
Japanese (EUC)
Japanese (JIS)
Japanese (Shift-JIS)
Korean (Wansung)
Multilingual (UTF-8)
Simplified Chinese (GB2312)
Traditional Chinese (Big5)
Turkish
US/Western European

5. To apply the settings that you selected in the Language tab, click **A**pply if you want to set additional Web settings, or click OK to exit the Web Settings dialog box.

NOTE:
To change the character set and the default font that is used in the FrontPage Editor, choose **T**ools I **O**ptions from the FrontPage Editor. Choose the Default Font tab in the Options dialog box. Select a character set from the Language (characters set) list and choose your fonts from the Default **P**roportional font and Default **F**ixed-width font drop-down menus. These settings apply to the fonts used only in the FrontPage Editor. They do not apply to the fonts that you apply to your pages and see in other browsers.

To assign the HTML encoding that is used to save and load a specific page, open the page you want to assign the properties to in the FrontPage Editor. Choose **F**ile I Page Properties and select saving and loading HTML encoding preferences in the Language tab of the Page Properties dialog box.

Setting Default Navigation Button Labels

If you use FrontPage 98 to generate automatic navigation buttons, there are four buttons included in navigation bars that the user clicks to navigate to your home page, the parent level page, the previous page, and the next page. By default, the labels for these respective pages are Home, Up, Back, and Next, respectively. You can modify these labels using the Navigation tab in the FrontPage Web Settings dialog box.

To change navigation labels, follow these steps:

1. From the FrontPage Explorer, choose **T**ools I **W**eb Settings. The Web Settings dialog box appears.

2. Choose the Navigation tab, shown in Figure 32.12.

Figure 32.12.
Use the Navigation tab to select your default Web language and HTML encoding.

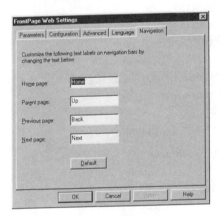

3. Enter the new labels that you want to use in the Ho**m**e page, Par**e**nt page, **P**revious page, and **N**ext page fields, or click the **D**efault button to use the default labels of Home, Up, Back, and Next (respectively).

4. To apply the settings that you selected in the Navigation tab, click **A**pply if you want to set additional Web settings, or click OK to exit the Web Settings dialog box.

Workshop Wrap-Up

FrontPage offers great flexibility, whether you're using it to develop your own personal Web site or using it in a corporate intranet environment. If you're working on your own Web site, you're already granted access permissions to do administrative and authoring tasks. If you need to configure multiple administrators and authors, the capability is there for you to do so. You learned how to maintain and manage your Web sites and how to specify the name of your Web's home pages. You also learned how to assign administrators, authors, and end users to your Web site.

Next Steps

In the next chapter, you'll learn how to create Webs that allow only registered members to browse the contents of a Web and how to deliver content to subscribers that use Internet Explorer 4.0. To learn more about creating and managing your Webs, refer to the following chapters:

❑ Refer to Chapter 30, "Using the FrontPage Personal Web Server," to learn how to install and configure the FrontPage Personal Web Server.

❑ Refer to Chapter 31, "Using the Microsoft Personal Web Server," to learn how to administer the Microsoft Personal Web Server.

❑ See Chapter 34, "Testing and Publishing Your Webs," to learn how to do the final tests and get your Webs online.

Q&A

Q: I installed the Microsoft Personal Web Server on my computer and installed the FrontPage Server Extensions. When I try to administer my page or open the home page on the server, I get a message that says that a connection to the server cannot be established. What's happening?

A: It is possible that your browser is configured to dial into the Internet when needed. If the Connect To dialog box comes up when you attempt to administer the Microsoft Personal Web Server, but you do not want to administer it while online, you can open the administration page by entering the following URL in your browser:

```
http://localhost/htmla/htmla.htm
```

Q: Sometimes when I try to connect to my server, I get a message that says There is no server on port 80 (or 8080) at "servername" (servername being the name of my server). What is wrong here?

A: First, check to see whether your server is running. If the Personal Web Server is running, you will see an icon in your Windows 95 taskbar, or you can verify the status by choosing the Personal Web Server icon from the Windows Control Panel. If the FrontPage Personal Web Server is running, you will see a button in your Windows 95 taskbar. If the server is running when you get that message, you may need to reinstall your FrontPage Server Extensions and perhaps reinstall your server software. Use the procedure outlined in this chapter in the section "Checking and Fixing the FrontPage Server Extensions" to verify your installation.

Q: When I tried to install FrontPage 98 over my existing content directory, I received some messages that said `Cannot open` `C:\Webshare\webname\_vti_pvt\service.lck. No such file or directory.` **What causes this?**

A: You may have deleted the Web indicated by the *webname* section in the URL using the Windows Explorer rather than using the FrontPage Explorer. You should always delete Webs by opening the Web you want to delete in the FrontPage Explorer and choosing the **F**ile | **D**elete FrontPage Web command.

To remedy the situation you are experiencing here, use the Windows Explorer to "rebuild" a Web that uses the same name as the one you cannot open. You can create a copy of an Empty Web or one of the other Webs in your content directory. Rename the copied folder to the same Web name referenced in the error message and then open that Web in the FrontPage Explorer. Choose the **F**ile | **D**elete FrontPage Web command to delete the Web. This will remove all references to this Web from all configuration files.

THIRTY-THREE

Designing Private Webs

Sometimes, you want to create Web sites that provide access to registered members only. FrontPage 98 offers a couple of items that can help you create and deliver content to members of your Web sites. Using the registration form handler, you can restrict access to registered members only. You can also use the Channel Definition Wizard to deliver content to those members who use Internet Explorer 4.0 and who subscribe to certain pages or areas in your Web site. This chapter shows you how to use both features of FrontPage 98.

About the FrontPage Registration Form Handler

In Chapter 23, "Configuring Form Handlers," you learned how to configure form handlers for general forms. There is a special type of form handler, called a *registration form handler*, that enables you to create registration pages so that users can sign up for access to private Web sites.

When you design a protected Web, a user is not allowed to gain access to your Web unless he or she enters a name and password that exists in your Web's authentication database. In order to add his or her name to the authentication database, he or she must complete a registration page, which uses a registration form handler to process the information. This registration page is placed in the root Web on your server and prevents access to the restricted Web unless the name and password is verified against the authentication database.

TASK Creating a Private Web

Before you create and save your User Registration form to your root Web, the Web that you are going to define as registered must exist on the server. First, create a Web on your server named Private Web. This will enable you to test your registration form after you configure it.

To create the private Web, follow these steps:

1. From the FrontPage Explorer, choose **F**ile | **N**ew | FrontPage **W**eb. The New FrontPage Web dialog box appears.

2. Choose the **O**ne Page Web radio button. This creates a Web that has a single blank home page.

3. In the Choose a **t**itle for your FrontPage Web field, enter `Private Web`. The URL listed beneath the Web title displays `http://servername/privateweb`, where *servername* is the name of your server.

4. Choose the **C**hange button if you need to create your Web on a different server. For example, if you need to create the Web on port 8080, specify a server name such as `servername:8080/privateweb` in the Change Location dialog box, shown in Figure 33.1. If you need to connect to the server using the Secure Sockets Layer communications, check the Secure connection required (SSL) checkbox; then click OK to return to the New FrontPage Web dialog box.

5. Choose OK to create your Web. The home page appears in the FrontPage Explorer.

6. Choose **T**ools | **P**ermissions. The Permissions dialog box appears.

7. In the Settings tab, select the Use unique permissions for this Web radio button and click **A**pply.

8. Click the Users tab. From the bottom of the Users tab, shown in Figure 33.2, select the **O**nly registered users have browse access radio button.

9. Choose OK. Your Web is configured as a private Web.

Figure 33.1.
Create a new Web in the FrontPage Explorer. Name your Web **Private Web**.

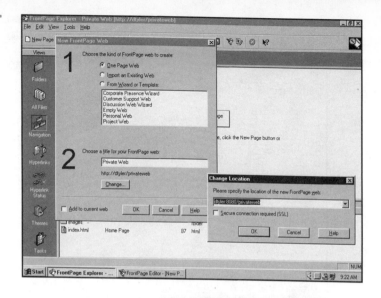

Figure 33.2.
Use the Permissions dialog box to configure your Web so that only registered users have browse access.

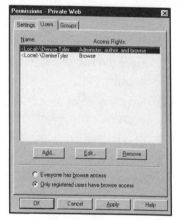

TASK

Creating the Registration Page

To learn how to add authors and administrators to the Web, refer to Chapter 30, "Using the FrontPage Personal Web Server," or Chapter 31, "Using the Microsoft Personal Web Server."

Now that you have a Web created, you can create and save your user registration page. You use the registration form handler when you design a form that registers a user for an event or to gain entry to a protected Web page on your site. Figure 33.3 shows a portion of a user registration page, which you can easily create by selecting the User Registration template from the New dialog box in the FrontPage Editor.

Figure 33.3.
Registration form handlers are used with forms that register a user for an event or a protected Web site.

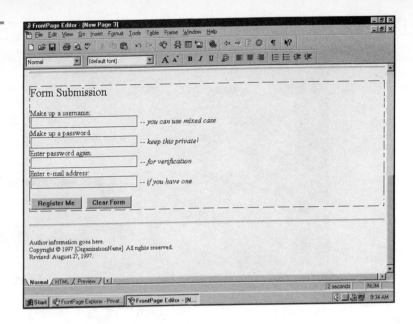

To create a user registration page from a template, follow these steps:

1. From the FrontPage Editor, choose **F**ile | **N**ew (Ctrl+N). The New dialog box appears.

2. From the list of templates, double-click User Registration. A new page appears in the FrontPage Editor. This is the user registration page template.

3. Choose **E**dit | **R**eplace. The Replace dialog box shown in Figure 33.4 appears.

4. In the Fi**n**d what field, enter **[OtherWeb]**. In the Replace with field, enter the name of the private Web that you are creating the registration page for (in this case, **Private Web**).

5. Choose Replace **A**ll. All instances of [OtherWeb] on the registration page change to your Web name. Choose Cancel to exit the Replace dialog box.

Figure 33.4.
Use the Replace dialog box to replace all instances of [OtherWeb] with the name of the private Web you are configuring.

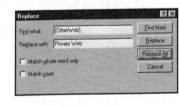

Configuring the Registration Form Handler

The registration page contains four form fields and two pushbuttons. The name of the form field associated with each of the prompts on the page are as follows:

`Make up a username`	Username
`Make up a password`	Password
`Enter password again`	PasswordVerify
`Enter e-mail address`	EmailAddress

Now you need to configure the registration form handler on the user registration page. To do this, scroll down the page until you see the form fields, as shown in Figure 33.3. Then follow these steps:

1. Right-click anywhere within the form (the area enclosed by the dotted lines). Choose Form Properties from the pop-up menu. The Form Properties dialog box appears.

2. Choose the Sen**d** to other radio button if it is not already selected. From the drop-down menu, select Registration Form Handler, as shown in Figure 33.5.

Figure 33.5.

Choose the Registration Form Handler from the Send to Other drop-down menu.

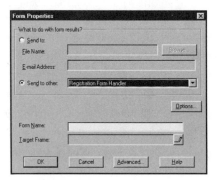

3. Click the **O**ptions button to open the Options for Registration Form Handler dialog box. Choose the Registration tab shown in Figure 33.6.

Figure 33.6.

Use the Registration tab to configure the private Web, the names of the form fields, and the registration failure page.

4. Enter the following information in the Registration tab:

❏ *FrontPage **w**eb name.* Enter the name of the FrontPage Web that the user will be registering for. The path must be relative to the root Web in your server. In this case, the private Web is located one level beneath the root Web, so you enter `privateweb` in this field.

❏ *User **n**ame fields.* Enter the name of the form field or form fields that are used to construct the username. In this case, the user enters his or her name in one form field named `Username`. If he or she enters first and last names in separate fields, separate each form field name with a comma or space (such as `FirstName LastName` or `FirstName,LastName`).

❏ ***P**assword field.* Enter the name of the form field that is used to retrieve the user's password, such as `Password`.

❏ *Password **c**onfirmation field.* Enter the name of the form field that is used to confirm the user's password, such as `PasswordVerify`.

❏ ***R**equire secure password.* Check this option if you require a secure password that contains six or more characters and does not partially match the user's name (such as a username of `jsmith` using a password of `smithy`).

❏ ***U**RL of registration failure page.* Enter the URL of a page that returns to the user if the information entered in the form cannot be registered for the FrontPage Web. If you leave this field blank, FrontPage 98 automatically generates and maintains a registration failure page. Use the **B**rowse button to select a page that already exists in your private Web. Leave this field blank for your example page.

Use the File Results tab in the Options for Saving Results of Form dialog box to configure the name and file format for the results file.

 TASK

Configuring the File Results

Use the File Results tab, shown in Figure 33.7, to configure the results file into which the user registration information is stored. The results file will be saved to the private Web rather than the root Web. By default, the results received from the user registration page are stored in a tab-delimited text file that is stored in the `_private` directory of your private Web. The text file is named `regdb.txt`.

To configure the results file, follow these steps:

1. From the Options for Registration Form Handler, click the File Results tab.

Figure 33.7.

Use the File Results tab to configure the results file that stores the user registration information.

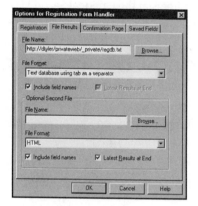

2. From the upper section of the File Results dialog box, enter or select the following options:

File Name
This field contains the absolute URL to the results file that will be located in your private Web. The URL defaults to `http://servername/_privateweb/_private/regdb.txt`. You can use the **B**rowse button in the File Results tab to choose another page or file in your private Web, if desired.

File For**m**at
Choose the file format for your results file. The default format is `Text database using tab as a separator`. Other file format options are listed in Table 23.1 in Chapter 23.

Include field names   Check this option to include the form field names with the user's responses in the results file. Uncheck this option to create a results file without headers that you can import directly into a database program. Leave this option checked for your registration page.

Latest Results at End   Disabled when you choose a text file format. When checked, form results are added to the end of the page each time a user responds to the fields on your form. When not checked, the most recent form results appear at the top of the Web page.

3. If you want to create a second results file that uses a different file format, complete the items in the Optional Second File section. The options you select in this area are similar to those described in step 2.

Configuring Confirmation Page Options

You learned about creating and configuring confirmation pages in Chapter 23. You can create a custom confirmation page for your registration page, if desired, and store this page in your private Web.

To assign a confirmation page, follow these steps:

1. Click the Confirmation Page tab, shown in Figure 33.8.

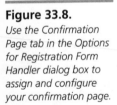

Figure 33.8.

Use the Confirmation Page tab in the Options for Registration Form Handler dialog box to assign and configure your confirmation page.

2. Enter the relative URL or absolute URL of a page in your private Web or click the **B**rowse button to select a page from the Current Web dialog box. When you use the **B**rowse button, the absolute URL of the page that you selected is automatically entered in the URL of confirmation page field.

3. You can also specify a validation failure page. This is a page that you create and send to the user when he or she enters information that does not meet the criteria that you specify for the form field. Enter the URL of a page in your current Web or choose the **B**rowse button to select a page from your current Web. Leave this field blank for your sample form.

Configuring Saved Fields Options

By default, only the Username field is listed when you first open the Saved Fields tab shown in Figure 33.9. You can use the Save All button in this tab to save all fields on your user registration page.

To configure your saved field options, follow these steps:

1. From the Options for Saving Results of Form dialog box, click the Saved Fields tab.

Figure 33.9.
Use the Saved Fields tab in the Options for Registration Form Handler dialog box to select the information you want to include in your results file.

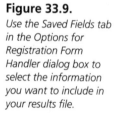
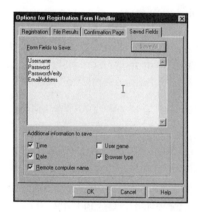

2. By default, the Username field is listed in the Form Fields to Save list. To save all fields on the form, click the Save All button located in the upper-right portion of the dialog box.

3. From the Additional information to save section, choose any or all of the following options:

Time	Includes the time that the user submitted the form
Date	Includes the date that the user submitted the form

Remote Computer Name	Includes the user's IP address in the results file
User **n**ame	Includes the user's name in the results file
Browser type	Includes information about the user's browser

4. Choose OK to exit the Options for Registration Form Handler dialog box. You return to the Form Properties dialog box.

5. Choose OK to exit the Form Properties dialog box. FrontPage 98 informs you that the registration page will work only in the root Web. Choose OK to continue.

Saving the Registration Form to Your Root Web

Keep your registration page open in the FrontPage Editor as you return to the FrontPage Explorer to open the root Web. Then save your registration page into the root Web.

Note, however, that if your private Web is going to reside on a server that is hosted by an Internet Service Provider, you need to coordinate this with your ISP. Your registration page should be saved to the root Web on your ISP's server as well as your own. Therefore, your ISP will have to be informed beforehand that you want to create a private Web on its server. Some ISPs may not allow this, and others may charge additional fees for hosting a private Web.

To save the registration page to the root Web on your local computer's server, follow these steps:

1. From the FrontPage Editor, choose **T**ools | Show Fro**n**tPage Explorer, or choose the Show FrontPage Explorer button on the Standard toolbar.

2. Choose **F**ile | **O**pen FrontPage Web or choose the Open FrontPage Web button on the toolbar. The Getting Started dialog box appears.

3. Open the root Web using one of the following procedures:

   ❑ Double-click <Root Web> (local) if the root Web appears in the list of Webs in the **O**pen an Existing FrontPage Web list. The root Web opens in the FrontPage Explorer.

   ❑ If the root Web does not appear in the Open an Existing FrontPage Web list, click the **M**ore Webs button. The Open FrontPage Web dialog box appears. From the Select a **W**eb server or disk location field, select the server on which your private Web resides. Click the **L**ist Webs button and select <Root Web> from Webs that appear in the FrontPage Webs found at location list. Choose OK. The Root Web opens in the FrontPage Explorer.

4. Choose **T**ools | Show FrontPage **E**ditor or click the Show FrontPage Editor button on the toolbar. You return to the registration page in the FrontPage Editor.

5. Choose **F**ile | **S**ave (Ctrl+S) or click the Save button on the Standard toolbar. The Save As dialog box appears.

6. In the **U**RL field, enter a filename for your registration page. This filename has to be unique to your private Web. Take care that you do not save the registration page over one that already exists for another private Web on the server. For this example, enter `privateweb-reg.htm`.

7. In the **T**itle field, enter `Registration Page for Private Web`.

8. Choose OK. The registration page is saved to your root Web.

Testing Your Registration Page

When you test your registration page, you should see a name and password dialog box that asks you to enter a username and password so that you can gain access to the private Web on your server. To test your form, follow these steps:

1. With your server and the FrontPage Server Extensions running, open your Web browser.

2. Enter the URL for your private Web. Use one of the following examples, replacing *servername* with the name of your server and `index.htm` with the URL of the home page in your Web:

   `http://servername/privateweb/`

   `http://servername/privateweb/index.htm`

   The user registration form should appear, prompting you to enter your user information. Each time thereafter that you first enter the site, you will be prompted to enter your username and password.

About the Channel Definition Wizard

If you've been keeping up with the changes going on in Internet Explorer, you might already be familiar with the features available in the latest release, Internet Explorer 4.0. Included among the bountiful supply of new features is the capability of subscribing to content on a Web site. When pages are updated or added to a site, they can be delivered straight to your desktop. Figure 33.10 shows the Channels pane and the Channel Guide page displayed in Internet Explorer 4.0.

Figure 33.10.

Internet Explorer 4.0 browsers can use the Channels pane to automatically receive updates from sites that they subscribe to.

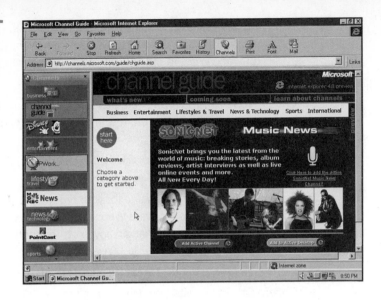

All this is done through *active channels*. A *channel* is a Web site that uses a channel definition file (CDF) to index the site. This CDF file describes the content that is available on your site. A CDF file can contain the following information:

❏ A list of URLs for your site content

❏ Schedules for content updates, from every few minutes to every few weeks

❏ A list of active desktop components

❏ Screensavers

Channels enable you to deliver personalized Web content to users who browse the Internet with Internet Explorer 4.0 or later. When the user receives the content, it is displayed in the Channels pane on the user's desktop.

 ## Turning Your Website into a Channel

You can easily create a CDF file for your site using the Channel Definition Wizard. The Channel Definition Wizard steps you through the process of creating a CDF, which most commonly is stored in your Web's root folder. The Channel Definition Wizard helps you select which folder and subfolders store the pages in your channel. You also assign the pages to which the user will subscribe. Each of the pages that you assign to the channel can be assigned different properties. As you create the CDF file, you can control the content that is delivered to your users through server push technology.

To define your website as a channel, follow these steps:

1. Open the Web that you want to define as a channel in the FrontPage Explorer.

2. Choose **T**ools | **D**efine Channel. The first screen of the Channel Definition Wizard appears.

3. To create a new CDF file, select the Create a new Channel Definition Format file for the current FrontPage Web radio button. To modify an existing file, select the **O**pen an existing CDF file radio button and use the Browse button to select the CDF file from your current Web. Choose OK to return to the Channel Definition Wizard after you select the file.

4. Click Ne**x**t to continue. On the screen shown in Figure 33.11, you are asked to describe your channel. Enter or choose the following information:

When you double-click a CDF filename in the FrontPage Explorer, the Channel Definition Wizard opens the file and enables you to modify its settings.

Title	Enter the title that you want to use when your channel is listed in a user's Web browser. By default, the name of your current FrontPage Web appears here.
Abstract	Enter a brief description of the content in your channel. This text displays in Internet Explorer 4.0 when the user rests the mouse pointer on your channel's logo image or title.
Introduction **P**age	Enter the URL of the page that will display in your user's browser when he or she subscribes to your channel. Use the B**r**owse button to select a page in your current Web and choose OK to return to the Channel Definition Wizard.
Logo Image	Enter the URL or use the B**r**owse button to select an image that identifies your channel in the user's browser. This image must be saved to your Web in GIF format and should be 80 pixels wide and 32 pixels high. If no image is specified, the user's browser displays a default channel logo image.
Icon Image	Enter the URL or use the B**r**owse button to select an image that identifies the pages in your channel. This image should be saved to your Web in GIF format and should be 16 pixels wide and 16 pixels high. If no image is specified, the user's browser displays a default icon image.
Last **M**odified	This field displays the date and time that you started the Channel Definition Wizard or the date and time that you last modified the file.

Figure 33.11.

Use the Channel Description screen to describe your site and specify the starting page, logo image, and icon image that is used in the Channels pane.

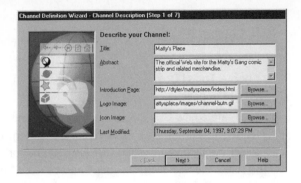

5. Click Next to continue. On the screen shown in Figure 33.12, you specify a folder in your current FrontPage Web that contains the pages in your channel. By default, the root folder in your current Web appears in the Source folder field. Use the Browse button to select a different folder in your Web, if desired. Then choose OK to return to the Channel Definition Wizard. If you want to include all subfolders beneath the folder you selected, check the Include Subfolders checkbox.

Figure 33.12.

Use the Choose Source Folder screen to select the folder that contains the pages and files in your channel.

6. Click Next to continue. A list of the pages that will be included in your channel appears on the screen, as shown in Figure 33.13. To remove pages from the list, highlight the page or pages that you want to remove and click Exclude. To reset the list so that it includes all the original pages listed, click the Restore button.

TIP: If your site is large, you may want to include only key pages in your channel, such as newsletters, what's new pages, tables of contents, and other pages that list new content on your site.

Figure 33.13.
Use the Edit Page List screen to exclude files from the channel.

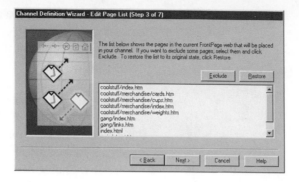

7. Click Ne**x**t to continue. The screen shown in Figure 33.14 appears. This screen enables you to set properties for each of the pages in the list. The pages that you selected in the previous step are listed in the Channel Items box located at the left side of the screen. Use the **D**elete button to remove pages from your channel or the Rest**o**re button to reset the list to its original state.

Figure 33.14.
In the Channel Item Properties screen, enter information for each page or file that you are adding to your channel.

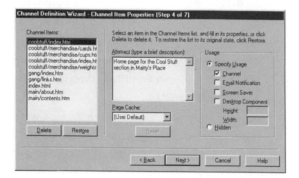

8. To set the properties for one of the pages in your channel, highlight the page that you want to set the properties for. Then complete the following information for each page you want to define:

Abstract — Enter a brief description of the content in your page. This text displays in Internet Explorer 4.0 when the user rests the mouse pointer on your page icon image or title.

Page Cache — Choose how you want to cache your page from the drop-down list. (User Default) caches the page as specified by the user's browser settings. Choose Use Cache to allow the user to download your pages for offline browsing. Choose Don't Use Cache to prevent your pages from being downloaded to the user's computer for offline browsing. The user will have to be connected to your site to browse the pages in your channel.

Specify **U**sage

Choose how you want the page to function in the user's browser. Select `Channel` (default selection) to use the selected page as an item in your channel. Select `Email Notification` to send an e-mail notice to the user when the selected page is modified or updated. Choose `Screen Saver` to enable the selected page as a screen saver on the user's computer. Choose `Desktop Component` to use the selected page as a desktop component on the user's computer. Enter the **H**eight and **W**idth of the desktop component in pixels.

Hidden

Select this radio button to allow the user to download the selected page for offline browsing, but to not list it as a channel item, screen saver, or desktop component.

Reset

Choose this button to restore the Abstract, Page Cache, and Usage selections for the selected page to its original settings.

9. Choose Ne**x**t to continue. On the screen shown in Figure 33.15, describe when to check your FrontPage Web for updated pages. Enter or choose the following information:

From **s**tart date

Enter the date on which you want the user's computer to begin connecting to the current FrontPage Web. The default is `(now)` which instructs the user's computer to connect on the same day he or she subscribes to the channel. To specify a different date, enter the starting date in the format that is correct for your Windows regional settings (such as `10/31/97`).

Until **e**nd date

Enter the date on which the user's subscription should stop connecting to the current FrontPage Web. The default is `(forever)`, which enables the user to connect to the site indefinitely. To specify a different date, enter the ending date in the format that is correct for your Windows regional settings.

C**h**eck every

Choose how often you want the user's computer to connect to your FrontPage Web for updates. Select Days, Hours, or Minutes from the drop-down menu and enter a number in the number field at its left.

For example, if you want the user to connect once a week, enter **7** in the number field and select Days from the drop-down menu.

Delay checks

If you anticipate that there will be many simulta neous connections, you can randomly delay connection times. Enable the **D**elay checks checkbox and enter numbers in the between and and fields. For example, to randomly connect between 2:00 and 4:00 AM, choose Hours from the drop-down menu and enter **2** and **4** in the number fields.

Figure 33.15.

Use the Channel Scheduling screen to define how often your channel is checked for updated pages.

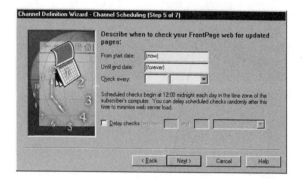

10. You can track how your subscribed users browse your site. The screen shown in Figure 33.16 enables you to log the browsing behavior of your subscribers. If you specify the name of a Log Target URL, usage information is sent from your user's browser to your FrontPage Web the next time the user goes online. The Log Target URL should point to a custom form handler in your current Web that you have created. Use the Browse button to select the custom form handler from your current Web. Skip this step if you have not created or obtained a custom form handler for this purpose.

Figure 33.16.

You can track a user's browsing habits by writing a custom form handler and entering its filename in the Log Target screen. Skip this step if you do not have such a form handler.

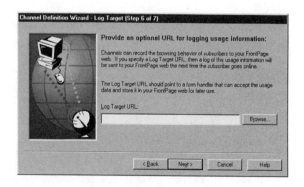

11. Choose Ne**x**t to continue. On the screen shown in Figure 33.17, you are asked to specify a filename for your CDF and to select additional options. Enter or choose the following information:

❏ For **F**ile Name, enter a filename for your channel definition file. By default, the file is saved to your home folder and is named `channel.cdf`. If another file by this name already exists in your home folder, the filename increments to the next number (`channel0.cdf`, `channel1.cdf`, and so on). Although you can use the **B**rowse button to select a different folder, it is recommended that you store CDF files in the home folder in your Web. This ensures compatibility with all browsers that support CDF files.

❏ Choose Place a button on the navigation bar of your home page that allows users to subscribe to this channel to create a Subscribe button on the child-level navigation bars for Webs that use shared borders and navigation bars. If your Web does not use these features, you can create a hyperlink that points to the CDF file.

❏ If you are preparing the CDF file for a Web that is published on a remote server, choose **P**repare for publishing to and enter the complete URL for the server. Once you select this checkbox, your CDF file enables users to subscribe only to the channel in its new location on the remote server, instead of the Web on your local computer.

For example, assume that you are going to publish the Web that currently resides on your local computer to a server that is hosted by an ISP. To configure the CDF file to subscribe to the remote site instead of the site on your local computer, check the Prepare for publishing to checkbox. Assuming that the URL of the home page in your site is `http://www.mattysplace.com/index.html`, enter the following information in the **P**repare for publishing to field:

`http://www.mattysplace.com`

Figure 33.17.

Enter a filename and path for your CDF file. If your Web is going to be published to a server other than that on which you designed the Web, enter the server URL in the Prepare for publishing to field.

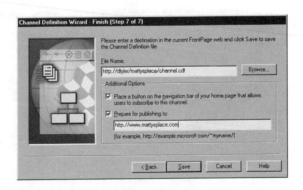

12. Click **S**ave to save your channel definition file to your current Web.

When an Internet Explorer 4.0 user navigates to a site that is defined as a channel, the Subscribe dialog box shown in Figure 33.18 appears. By default, the user is notified when an icon changes and downloads channel content to his or her browser automatically.

To change these settings, the user clicks the **C**ustomize button. The Channel Subscription Wizard asks the user whether he or she wants to download content or only receive notification when the content changes. The user can also select whether to include the channel as a screen saver. If the user asks to receive notification by e-mail, he or she specifies the e-mail address to which notifications are sent. The user also specifies whether to update channel subscription content automatically (daily or upon connection to the Internet), by a custom schedule created by the user, or manually.

Figure 33.18.

When the users navigate to a channel, they are invited to subscribe to it.

Workshop Wrap-Up

FrontPage 98 helps you create sites that are geared for special users. You can use the registration form handler to create sites that are open to registered users only. You can also deliver updated content automatically to users who browse the Web with Internet Explorer 4.0, by creating a channel definition file. You learned how to do both in this chapter.

Next Steps

In the next chapter, you will learn how to give your Web site that final once-over before you publish your pages to the Web. You'll also learn how easy it is to get your Web online! Get ready for the final step—your home page will soon be on the Web.

Q&A

Q: Can I have more than one channel in a Web site?

A: Yes. You can create multiple CDF files that point to different folders in a Web site. For example, you might have updates in one channel, screen savers in another, and desktop components in another. You can also have your users subscribe to a weekly or monthly newsletter on your site.

Q: Can I create a Web site that is partly public and partly private?

A: When you create a private Web site (one that has its permissions set so that only registered users have browse access), the setting applies to all files and folders within a single FrontPage Web. You can create two separate Webs, one public and one private, and create links between the two. However, if your site resides on a server hosted by an ISP, you need to obtain two sites on that server as well. You should also verify that your ISP will allow you to create private Webs before you design the pages.

THIRTY-FOUR

Testing and Publishing Your Webs

It's time to give your Web page that final once-over before you get it out to the Web. You should check your spelling, check your hyperlinks, check your directories—check *everything*. Fortunately, FrontPage keeps in mind everything you have to do from start to finish and offers a few tools that can help you as well!

Hyperlinks at a Glance

When you develop your pages with other types of editors, sometimes you can't tell, at a glance, whether your hyperlinks are working correctly. With FrontPage, you can tell quite easily within the FrontPage Explorer. Choose Hyperlinks view to examine links that enter and exit a page in your Web.

Figure 34.1 shows hyperlinks from and to a Web page as they appear in Hyperlinks view. The current page appears at the center of Hyperlinks view. Pages that link to the current page are displayed at the left. If the current page hyperlinks to other pages or images in your Web, or to other pages on the World Wide Web, those hyperlinks are displayed at the right side of the current page.

When you view your pages in Hyperlinks view, you can expand the tree by clicking on any page icon that has a plus symbol (+) on it. That symbol tells you there are hyperlinks to other pages contained in that page.

Figure 34.1.
Use Hyperlinks view to tell at a glance whether hyperlinks to and from a page are working correctly.

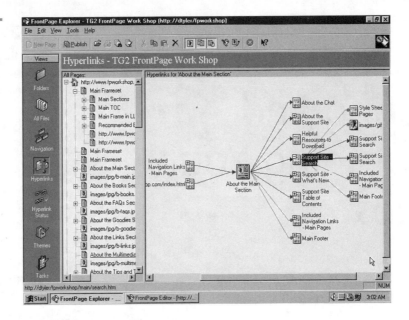

 ## Viewing Hyperlinks Inside Pages

Hyperlinks inside pages are hyperlinks from a page to itself, such as hyperlinks to bookmarks that appear on the same page. In the example shown in Figure 34.2, the search page contains hyperlinks to bookmarks on the page.

Notice also that some of the outgoing hyperlinks are represented by arrows and others by circles. The arrows designate hyperlinks to other pages (either in your Web or to other Webs). The circles represent items that are included in the current page—usually images or content that appears inside Include WebBots.

You can view hyperlinks inside a page by using one of the following methods:

❑ From the FrontPage Explorer, choose **V**iew | Hyperlinks Inside **P**age.
❑ Click the Hyperlinks Inside Page button on the FrontPage Explorer toolbar.

To turn off the display of hyperlinks inside pages, repeat one of those procedures.

Figure 34.2.

*Use **V**iew | Hyperlinks Inside **P**age or the toolbar button to view hyperlinks within a single page.*

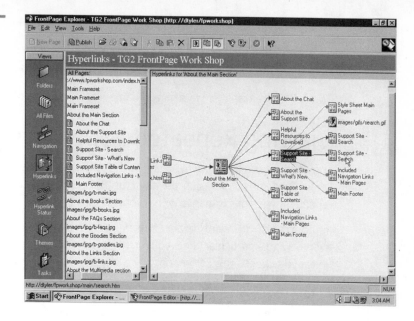

TASK

Viewing Hyperlinks to Images

You can use the FrontPage Explorer's Hyperlinks view to view hyperlinks to images within your current Web site. Hyperlinks to images are displayed with an icon of a picture in a frame, as shown in Figure 34.3.

Figure 34.3.

*View hyperlinks to images in your pages by choosing the **V**iew | Hyperlinks to **I**mages command or toolbar button.*

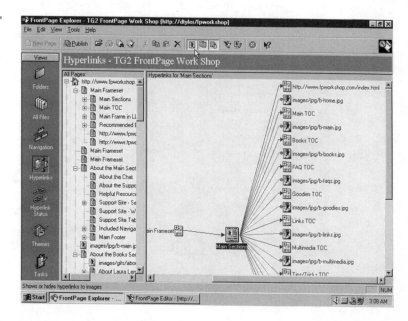

To view hyperlinks to images, use one of the following methods:

❑ From the FrontPage Explorer, choose **V**iew I Hyperlinks to **I**mages.

❑ Click the Hyperlinks to Images button on the FrontPage Explorer toolbar.

To turn off the display of hyperlinks to images, repeat one of those procedures.

Viewing Repeated Hyperlinks

Sometimes more than one hyperlink to the same page appears within your page, as Figure 34.4 shows. You can use the FrontPage Explorer's Hyperlinks view to view repeated hyperlinks to pages within your current Web site.

In most cases, you want to view hyperlinks only once—but if you need to remove hyperlinks to a particular page, you might miss the additional hyperlinks on the page unless you choose this command.

To view repeated hyperlinks, use one of the following methods:

❑ From the FrontPage Explorer, choose **V**iew I **Re**peated Hyperlinks.

❑ Click the Repeated Hyperlinks button on the FrontPage Explorer toolbar.

To turn off the display of repeated hyperlinks, repeat one of those procedures.

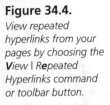

Figure 34.4.

*View repeated hyperlinks from your pages by choosing the **V**iew I **Re**peated Hyperlinks command or toolbar button.*

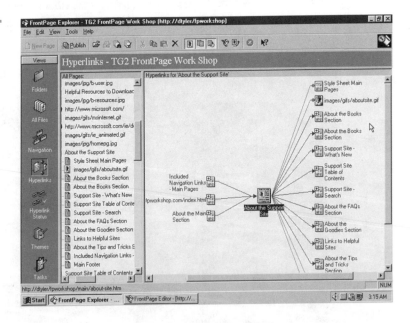

Verifying Hyperlinks

What if you've got hundreds of pages on your site? You don't have to look at them all manually, do you?

Have no fear—there's an easy way to check the hyperlinks on all those pages. Use the **T**ools | **V**erify Hyperlinks command to both verify and repair internal and external hyperlinks.

To verify hyperlinks, follow these steps:

1. Choose **T**ools | **V**erify Hyperlinks. You automatically switch to Hyperlink Status view, and the Verify Hyperlinks dialog box shown in Figure 34.5 appears. Unverified links are shown in the Status column with yellow circles beside them and marked Unknown. Broken hyperlinks are shown in the Status column with red circles beside them and marked Broken.

Figure 34.5.

Use the Verify all hyperlinks button to verify all the hyperlinks in your current Web site.

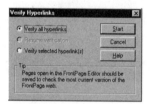

2. Choose one of the following options:
   - ❏ To verify all hyperlinks in your Web, choose the Verify all hyperlinks radio button.
   - ❏ To resume a verify session that has been canceled, click Resume verification.
   - ❏ To verify only some of the hyperlinks in your Web, select the hyperlinks you want to verify and choose the Verify selected hyperlink(s) radio button.

3. If any of the hyperlinks that you select for verification reside on the World Wide Web, connect online to your Internet Service Provider.

4. Click the **S**tart button. FrontPage steps through the hyperlinks in your Web and verifies them one by one. Working external hyperlinks display a green circle beside the word OK, and broken external hyperlinks display a red circle beside the word Broken (see Figure 34.6).

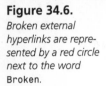

Figure 34.6.
Broken external hyperlinks are represented by a red circle next to the word Broken.

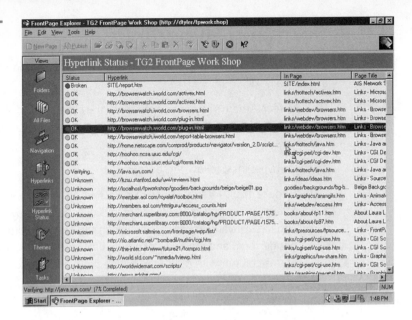

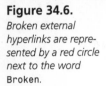 TASK

Fixing Internal and External Hyperlinks

You might have some broken hyperlinks inside your Web, such as hyperlinks you forgot to complete, hyperlinks to pages you might have deleted from your Web, or even hyperlinks from pages imported into your Web that you forgot to edit. You can easily fix them by using the **T**ools | **V**erify Hyperlinks command in the FrontPage Explorer.

TIP: If you've got a lot of broken hyperlinks to view, you can sort the list of broken hyperlinks by one of three categories—Status, Hyperlink (the URL of the page to which you are linking), In Page (the URL of the page in your Web that links to the hyperlink) or Page Title (the page title in your Web that links to the hyperlink). Click the headings above the list of broken hyperlinks in the Hyperlink Status view.

To repair broken internal or external hyperlinks, follow these steps:

1. From the Hyperlink Status view, right-click on a hyperlink in the list that displays as broken. Choose Edit **H**yperlink from the pop-up menu. The Edit Hyperlink dialog box shown in Figure 34.7 appears.

Figure 34.7.

Edit the broken hyperlink in the Edit Hyperlink dialog box. You can repair the hyperlink on any or all pages on which it appears.

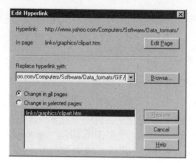

2. The broken URL appears in the Replace hyperlink **w**ith field. Edit the URL, if known, or use the Browse button to select a page from your Web or from the World Wide Web. If the hyperlink resides on the World Wide Web, your browser opens. Navigate to the correct page and then return to the FrontPage Explorer. The correct URL appears in the Edit Hyperlink box.

3. Choose one of the following options:

   ❏ *Change in all pages.* Choose this option to change the hyperlink in all pages on which the broken hyperlink appears.

   ❏ *Change in selected pages.* Choose this option if you want to repair the broken hyperlink on a set of selected pages. Select the pages on which you want to change the hyperlink from the list.

4. Click **R**eplace. FrontPage corrects the hyperlink on the pages you selected.

TIP: Page URLs can change frequently on the Web or become outdated rapidly. If you run the **T**ools I **V**erify Hyperlinks command on a fairly regular basis, you can delete or revise hyperlinks when necessary and keep all the external hyperlinks in your Web site current.

You can also choose to edit the page on which the broken hyperlink appears. This doesn't automatically fix the other hyperlinks on which the same broken hyperlink appears, but it does enable you to verify where you wanted that hyperlink to go. To edit the page on which the hyperlink appears, follow these steps:

1. From the Hyperlink Status view, right-click on a hyperlink in the list that displays as broken. Choose Edit **H**yperlink from the pop-up menu. The Edit Hyperlink dialog box appears.

2. Select the broken internal or external hyperlink you want to repair.

3. Click Edit **P**age. The page opens in the FrontPage Editor, and you can repair the hyperlink in the page.

4. Save the revised page to the Web site.

You might not have the time to repair all your external links in one sitting, so add the tasks to your To Do list. Using this procedure, you won't have to use the Verify Hyperlinks command again. Tasks are added to your To Do list and include the URL that you need to repair as well as the page on which it appears. To add a broken hyperlink to your To Do list, follow these steps:

1. From the Hyperlink Status view, right-click on a hyperlink in the list that displays as broken. Choose Edit **H**yperlink from the pop-up menu. The Edit Hyperlink dialog box appears.

2. Right-click the broken internal or external hyperlink you want to repair and choose Add Task from the pop-up menu. The New Task dialog box appears.

3. Enter the name of the person to which you want to assign the task in the **A**ssign To field.

4. Modify the task description, as necessary, in the **D**escription field. By default, the broken URL displays in this field.

5. Click OK. A task is added to your To Do list.

TASK Fixing Page Errors

When a FrontPage component is configured incorrectly or a page that a FrontPage component refers to is moved or deleted from your Web, you'll notice a small red triangle next to the page in the FrontPage Explorer's Outline view. You can determine why the error appears on the page by using the following procedure:

TIP: If you notice the red triangles after you import several pages that you know are linked correctly, choose the **T**ools I **R**ecalculate Hyperlinks command. The error triangle might be there because of the order in which pages were imported to the Web. Refreshing the Web resolves many, if not all, of these error messages.

1. From the All Pages list in Hyperlinks view, select the page that has the error triangle.

2. Choose **E**dit I **P**roperties (Alt+Enter) or right-click and choose **P**roperties from the pop-up menu. The Properties dialog box appears.

3. Click the Errors tab to see a description of the page error. Usually, when a page has an error, the Properties dialog box opens with this tab selected for you.

4. Click OK to exit the dialog box and return to the FrontPage Explorer. Resolve the error as indicated by the dialog box.

The Final Pass

What if, as you develop your pages, you forget to perform a spell-check on some of them? What if you change your mind and decide to rename your Web site and you don't want to go back through dozens of pages to edit the names on the page? New to FrontPage 98 is the capability of performing across-the-web spell-checks, text searches, and text replaces.

Performing an Across-the-Web Spell-Check

Use the across-the-web spell-check to give your pages a final run-through. You can add pages that contain any misspelled words to your To Do list.

To perform an across-the-web spell-check, follow these steps:

1. Save any opened pages to your Web so that they can be included in the spell-check.

2. If you want to perform the spell-check on only some of the pages in the Web, select the pages from Folders or All Files view.

3. From the FrontPage Explorer, choose **T**ools I **S**pelling (F7). The Spelling dialog box shown in Figure 34.8 appears.

Figure 34.8.
The Spelling dialog box enables you to perform across-the-web spell-checks from the FrontPage Explorer.

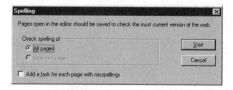

4. Choose **A**ll Pages to perform the spell-check on all pages in your Web or S**e**lected Pages to perform the spell-check on the pages you selected.

5. To add the misspelled pages to your To Do list, check the Add a **t**ask for each page with misspellings checkbox. If you leave this option unchecked, make note of the pages on which the spelling errors appear.

You learn about the task list in Chapter 6, "What To Do?"

Figure 34.9.
The Spelling dialog box displays a list of pages with misspelled words.

6. Click the **S**tart button. FrontPage performs a spell-check of all the pages in your Web. Pages with misspelled words will appear in the Spelling dialog box shown in Figure 34.9.

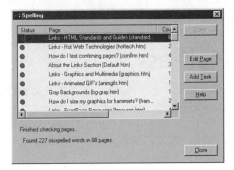

7. To edit a page that has misspelled words, click the Edit **P**age button. The page opens in the FrontPage Editor, and the Spelling dialog box displays the misspelled words. Step through all misspellings and correct them as necessary.

8. After you check or correct all spelling errors on one page, FrontPage asks whether you want to continue with the next document. Choose Next Document to continue or Cancel to stop the process.

9. To add a task from the Spelling dialog box shown in Figure 34.9, click the Add **T**ask button. Add the task in the New Task dialog box.

Performing an Across-the-Web Replace

Use the across-the-web replace feature of FrontPage 98 to search and replace any text or phrase on your pages. Note that this command searches and replaces text that appears on your Web page only while you view it in the WYSIWYG view of the FrontPage Editor. It does not edit any HTML code behind the scenes.

To perform an across-the-web replace, follow these steps:

1. Save any opened pages to your Web so that they can be included in the search.

2. If you want to perform the replace on only some of the pages in the Web, select the pages from Folders view.

3. From the FrontPage Explorer, choose **T**ools I **R**eplace. The Replace in FrontPage Web dialog box appears, as shown in Figure 34.10.

Figure 34.10.

FrontPage enables you to find a word or phrase on any or all pages in your Web with the Replace in FrontPage Web dialog box.

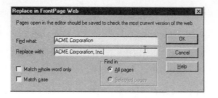

4. In the Find What field, enter the text you want to find in your Web.

5. In the Replace With field, enter the replacement text.

6. Choose Match **w**hole word only if the word or phrase you enter is likely to also appear at the beginning of a word. For example, if you want to find all instances of `can` but not `candle` or `canopy`, check this option.

7. Choose Match **C**ase if you want the replace command to locate all instances that appear in uppercase and lowercase exactly as you enter it.

8. Choose **A**ll Pages to perform the replace on all pages in your Web or S**e**lected Pages to perform the replace on the pages you selected from Folders view.

9. Click the **S**tart button. FrontPage finds and replaces the text as specified.

10. Click Close to exit the Replace in FrontPage Web dialog box.

 # Performing an Across-the-Web Find

Use the across-the-web find feature of FrontPage 98 to search for any page that contains a specific word or phrase. If, for example, you can't remember which of dozens of pages on your Web contains the phrase `going south to Florida`, you can enter the phrase and make FrontPage do the work for you.

To perform an across-the-web find, follow these steps:

1. Save any opened pages to your Web so that they can be included in the search.

2. If you want to perform the find on only some of the pages in the Web, select the pages from Folders view.

3. From the FrontPage Explorer, choose **T**ools | **F**ind (Ctrl+F). The Find in FrontPage Web dialog box appears. It is similar to the Replace in FrontPage Web dialog box shown in Figure 34.10.

4. In the Fi**n**d What field, enter the text you want to find in your Web.

5. Choose Match **W**hole Word only if the word or phrase you enter is likely to also appear at the beginning of a word. For example, if you want to find all instances of `can` but not `candle` or `canopy`, check this option.

6. Choose Match **C**ase if you want the find command to locate all instances that appear in uppercase or lowercase exactly as you enter it.

7. Choose **A**ll Pages to perform the find on all pages in your Web or S**e**lected Pages to perform the find on the pages you selected from Folders view.

8. Click the **S**tart button. The Find occurrences of "*phrase*" dialog box shown in Figure 34.11 appears. As instances of your search are found, the pages that include the phrase are added to the list in the dialog box.

Figure 34.11.

FrontPage enables you to find a word or phrase on any or all pages in your Web with the Find dialog box.

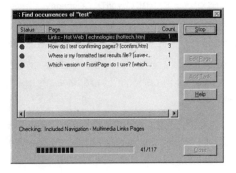

9. To edit the page on which the term appears, click the Edit **P**age button. To add a task to your To Do list, click the Add **T**ask button.

10. Click Close to exit the Find Occurrences dialog box.

 TASK

Getting Your Web Online

Your pages are hyperlinked, your spelling is checked, and your images are all nice, neat, and trim. You're ready to go to the Web now.

Use the Publish FrontPage Web command to transfer your Web to a service provider that has the FrontPage Server Extensions installed. When you use this command, you can copy changed pages, add pages to an existing FrontPage Web, and copy the root Web with or without child Webs.

NOTE: When you use the Publish FrontPage Web command to copy your Web pages from your local computer to a remote server, you are prompted to enter a name and password. Enter the name and password you use to transfer content to your remote Web directory in the Name and Password Required dialog box.

To publish your Web to the remote server, follow these steps:

1. Establish a connection with your Internet provider using normal login procedures.

2. Open the Web you want to publish in the FrontPage Explorer:

   ❏ Open the root Web to publish just it or to publish it and all child Webs.

   ❏ Open any child Web to publish only the child Web to your remote server.

TIP: You can also use the Publish FrontPage Web command to copy FrontPage Webs from the Personal Web Server to a file location on your hard drive (great for backup purposes) or to copy FrontPage Webs from your hard drive into the Personal Web Server (great for practicing new techniques before you put them on your server).

3. From the FrontPage Explorer, choose File | Publish FrontPage Web (Ctrl+B). The Publish dialog box, shown in Figure 34.12, appears.

Figure 34.12.
Use the Publish FrontPage Web command to publish Webs to a remote server that has the FrontPage Server Extensions installed.

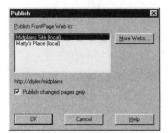

4. If the site to which you want to publish does not appear in the Publish FrontPage Web to list, click the **M**ore Webs button. The Publish FrontPage Web dialog box shown in Figure 34.13 appears.

Figure 34.13.
Enter the URL of the Web to which you want to publish your site in the Publish FrontPage Web dialog box.

5. Enter the URL of the server to which you want to publish your Web. If you have a domain name on a remote server, enter something like **http://www.*yourserver*.com**. If you have a subweb on a remote server, your URL might be something like **http://www.*ispserver*.com/~*yourweb***.

6. Choose OK. You return to the Publish dialog box.

7. To copy the entire Web, uncheck the Publish changed pages **o**nly option. Leave this checked if you are adding new or updated pages to an existing Web.

8. Click OK to publish your Web. FrontPage lists the pages in your current site and copies your Web pages to your remote server.

The Final Test

After you transfer your files to your remote site, browse through the site to make sure all hyperlinks work the way they should. If your server has the FrontPage Server Extensions installed, you can use the **T**ools | **V**erify Hyperlinks command while logged in to your remote site to verify the hyperlinks quickly. Check your pages once again, using various browsers, to see whether things look the way they should.

Publicizing Your Web

You can publicize your Web site in several ways. One way is to post messages in newsgroups that relate to your topic of interest. If your site has information of interest to those who frequent the newsgroups, post your URL so they can find your site.

I know you're excited about your new Web site and want to tell the world—but distribute your Web announcements sparingly, posting to only a handful of newsgroups at a time. Most who frequent newsgroups don't take too kindly to *spamming*— posting messages to dozens of newsgroups at the same time.

Another good way to publicize your Web site is to register your home page URLs with some of the many Web searches and robots, such as Yahoo!, Alta Vista, Excite, Open Text, and others. Some of these search engines also provide hyperlinks to sites from which you can send your URL to many other search engines at once.

Workshop Wrap-Up

Your Web is complete and resides on your remote server. Now you can begin the task of getting the word out. You've come a long way since the day you first opened the FrontPage box. Congratulate yourself for a great accomplishment! *You're on the Internet!*

In this chapter, you learned how to give your Web site the final once-over and publish it to a remote site. You have also learned three ways you can get your pages out to the world and which files you shouldn't transfer when your service provider doesn't use the FrontPage Server Extensions.

Next Steps

Where should you go next? The sky's the limit! Keep tabs of the new features being developed for the Web. Learn how to use custom scripting languages to enhance your site even further. Continue to develop your Web design skills to keep up with the latest and greatest features.

Q&A

Q: Can I perform an across-the-web replace on the HTML code?

A: The across-the-web replace works only on the text that appears on the WYSIWYG side of the page. You won't be able to change the "behind the scenes" code across the Web with this command.

Q: Are there any other areas where I can get technical information?

A: The Microsoft Knowledge Base, located on its Web site, has articles that address technical questions. There is a hyperlink to the Knowledge Base on MSN (go to MSSUPPORT if you're a member of the Microsoft Network). You can also find the Microsoft Knowledge Base at the following URL:

http://www.microsoft.com/KB/

Q: Once I post my pages on the Internet, can I remove them from my local computer?

A: Some people do this, but you may feel more comfortable knowing that you have another backup of your Web pages. If you decide to remove your FrontPage Webs from your computer, you can use the FrontPage Explorer's **F**ile I **P**ublish FrontPage Web command to create a backup copy of your Web. This copies the Web's configuration information in addition to its content. The Web can be restored very easily using the FrontPage Explorer's Import Web Wizard.

Q: After I connect online, I sometimes receive an `Unable to connect to Web server` message when I return to my Web in the FrontPage Explorer. How come?

A: This is a security measure. When you connect to a remote server, you disconnect from the server on your local computer. This prevents others from browsing files on your local computer. If you exit FrontPage and restart, you will be able to connect to the server on your local computer again.

Q: If I delete pages from my local FrontPage Web and then publish the updated site to my remote server, do I have to do anything special to delete the same pages on the remote server?

A: If you deleted pages on your local server and then publish your Web to a remote server, FrontPage detects the differences between the two sites. FrontPage will ask whether you also want to delete the same pages on the remote server. Choose **Y**es to delete one page at a time or Yes to **A**ll of you want to delete more than one page.

Q: Sometimes when I use the Verify Links command, the process seems to hang and a link is reported as broken. When I verify the broken link later in my browser, it takes a while to connect to the site but the link is OK. What happened?

A: On occasion, a server can be down for repair or experiencing a lot of traffic. The Verify Links command tests each link, but if a response is not received from a server within a short period of time, the link is marked as broken and FrontPage continues the test with the next link. You can add broken links to your To Do List and check them later to see whether the link is valid.

PART

VII

Appendixes

A
FrontPage Shortcuts

This appendix provides information on keyboard shortcuts used in FrontPage 98.

Keyboard Shortcuts

The Keyboard Shortcut or Toolbar Button columns in Tables A.1 and A.2 list any keyboard shortcuts or toolbar buttons that you can use to implement the menu command.

Table A.1. FrontPage Explorer hotkeys, shortcuts, and toolbar buttons.

Command	Keyboard Shortcut or Toolbar Button
File	New	Page	Ctrl+N; Standard toolbar: Create New Page
File	New	Task	Ctrl+T
File	Open FrontPage Web	Standard toolbar: Open FrontPage Web
File	Publish FrontPage Web	Ctrl+B; Standard toolbar: Publish FrontPage Web
File	Print Navigation View	Ctrl+P; Standard toolbar: Print Navigation View
Edit	Undo	Ctrl+Z
Edit	Redo	Ctrl+Y
Edit	Cut	Ctrl+X; Standard toolbar: Cut
Edit	Copy	Ctrl+C; Standard toolbar: Copy
Edit	Paste	Ctrl+V; Standard toolbar: Paste
Edit	Select All	Ctrl+A
Edit	Open	Ctrl+O
Edit	Delete	Del; Standard toolbar: Delete
Edit	Rename	F2
Edit	Properties	Alt+Enter or mouse right-click
View	Refresh	F5
Tools	Spelling	F7; Standard toolbar: Cross File Spelling
Tools	Find	Ctrl+F; Standard toolbar: Cross File Find
Tools	Replace	Ctrl+H
Tools	Show FrontPage Editor	Standard toolbar: Show FrontPage Editor
Tools	Show Image Editor	Standard toolbar: Show Image Editor
Help	F1; Standard toolbar: Help

Table A.2. FrontPage Editor shortcuts.

Command	Keyboard Shortcut
File	New	Ctrl+N; Standard toolbar: New
File	Open	Ctrl+O; Standard toolbar: Open
File	Save	Ctrl+S; Standard toolbar: Save
File	Preview in Browser	Standard toolbar: Preview in Browser

Command	*Keyboard Shortcut*
File I **P**rint	Ctrl+P; Standard toolbar: Print
Edit I **U**ndo	Ctrl+Z; Standard toolbar: Undo
Edit I **R**edo	Ctrl+Y; Standard toolbar: Redo
Edit I Cu**t**	Ctrl+X or Shift+Del; Standard toolbar: Cut
Edit I **C**opy	Ctrl+C or Ctrl+Ins; Standard toolbar: Copy
Edit I **P**aste	Ctrl+V or Shift+Ins; Standard toolbar: Paste
Edit I Cle**a**r	Delete
Edit I Select All	Ctrl+A
Edit I **F**ind	Ctrl+F
Edit I R**e**place	Ctrl+H
Edit I Hyperlin**k**	Ctrl+K
Edit I Proper**t**ies	Alt+Enter or mouse right-click
View I **R**efresh	F5; Standard toolbar: Refresh
Go I **B**ack	Standard toolbar: Back
Go I **F**orward	Standard toolbar: Forward
Go I Follow **H**yperlink	Ctrl+Click
Insert I Line **B**reak	Shift+Enter
Insert I **I**mage	Standard toolbar: Insert Image
Insert I Front**P**age Component	Standard toolbar: Insert FrontPage Component

Insert I FrontPage Component I

Insert HTML	Advanced toolbar: Insert HTML

Insert I Form Field I

One-Line **T**ext Box	Form Fields toolbar: One-Line Text Box
Scrolling Text Box	Form Fields toolbar: Scrolling Text Box
Check Box	Form Fields toolbar: Check Box
Radio Button	Form Fields toolbar: Radio Button
Drop-Down Menu	Form Fields toolbar: Drop-Down Menu
Push Button	Form Fields toolbar: Push Button

continues

Table A.2. continued

Command	Keyboard Shortcut
*Insert	Advanced |*	
Java Applet	Advanced toolbar: Insert Java Applet
Plug-In	Advanced toolbar: Insert Plug-In
ActiveX Control	Advanced toolbar: Insert ActiveX Control
Script	Advanced toolbar: Insert Script
Insert	Hyperlink	Ctrl+K; Standard toolbar: Create or Edit Hyperlink
Format	Font	Several buttons in the Format toolbar (Change Font drop-down menu, Increase Text Size, Decrease Text Size, Bold, Italic, Underline, Text Color)
Format	Paragraph	Use Change Style drop-down menu in Format toolbar to select paragraph or heading style; use Align Left, Center, or Right buttons in Format toolbar to align text
Format	Bullets and Numbering	Use Change Style drop-down menu in Format toolbar or Bulleted List or Numbered List buttons in the Format toolbar to select the list type; use Increase Indent and Decrease Indent buttons in the Format toolbar to create nested lists
Tools	Spelling	F7; Standard toolbar: Check Spelling
Tools	Thesaurus	Shift+F7
Tools	Auto Thumbnail	Ctrl+T
Tools	Show FrontPage Explorer	Standard toolbar: Show FrontPage Explorer
Table	Insert Table	Standard toolbar: Insert Table
Table	Draw Table	Tables toolbar: Draw Table
Table	Insert Rows or Columns	Tables toolbar: Insert Rows or Tables toolbar: Insert Columns
Table	Delete Cells	Tables toolbar: Delete Cells
Table	Merge Cells	Tables toolbar: Merge Cells

Command	Keyboard Shortcut
Table I Split Cells	Tables toolbar: Split Cells
Table I Distribute Rows Evenly	Tables toolbar: Distribute Rows Evenly
Table I Distribute Columns Evenly	Tables toolbar: Distribute Columns Evenly
Help	F1; Standard toolbar: Help
Help cursor	Shift+F1
Bold text	Ctrl+B
Italic text	Ctrl+I
Underline text	Ctrl+U
Cancel dialog box	Esc
Previous window	Shift+Ctrl+F6
Next window	Ctrl+F6

B FrontPage Reference

This appendix provides a directory of resources that will provide additional online reference material for Microsoft FrontPage and additional Web-related topics. All links have been verified as current at the time of publication.

This directory of resources will help you find additional information on topics or FrontPage tools discussed in this book. Topics include FrontPage resources, general Web information, Web developer information, CGI and Perl scripts, graphics and multimedia, and sources for ideas.

An online version of this directory of resources will be kept current on the Internet support site for this book at the following URL:

```
http://www.fpworkshop.com/
```

FrontPage Resources

You can find more information and support for FrontPage at the URLs discussed in the following sections.

Support Site for *Laura Lemay's Web Workshop: Microsoft FrontPage 98*

The support site for this book contains several sections that can assist you in developing and maintaining your Web pages using FrontPage. Among them are a user-to-user discussion group, a tips and tricks section, links to other helpful sites, graphics, and more:

http://www.fpworkshop.com/

Microsoft's Home Page

Go to Microsoft's home page for up-to-date information and links to product information, support, downloads, Internet workshop, and more:

http://www.microsoft.com

The FrontPage Home Page

The Microsoft FrontPage home page contains links to an overview of FrontPage, recent news, getting started, hosting and posting Web sites, Internet service provider information, and customizing FrontPage. Product information and support links are also provided:

http://www.microsoft.com/frontpage/defaultb.htm

FrontPage Server Extensions

You can visit a download area for UNIX and Windows NT versions of the FrontPage Server Extensions for the following servers: Microsoft Internet Information Server, NCSA, CERN, Apache, Netscape Communications Server, Open Market Web Server, and O'Reilly Web Site. Here is the URL:

http://www.microsoft.com/frontpage/softlib/fs_fp_extensions.htm

Microsoft Site Builder Workshop

The Microsoft Site Builder Workshop site contains information on creating and developing Internet pages. It also includes information on authoring, editing, designing and creating, programming, site administration, planning and production, demos, and how-to sites:

```
http://www.microsoft.com/workshop/
```

Microsoft SiteBuilder Network

The Microsoft SiteBuilder Network contains many resources, tools, tips, and tricks for Web developers with three levels of membership, from basic to advanced:

```
http://www.microsoft.com/sitebuilder/
```

Microsoft's Web Presence Provider Information

At the following address, you can obtain information for Internet service providers, including a Web hosting primer, frequently asked questions, and information about the FrontPage Server Extensions:

```
http://www.microsoft.com/frontpage/wpp.htm
```

WPPs (Web Presence Providers) That Use FrontPage Server Extensions

You can visit an up-to-date list of Internet service providers that host FrontPage Web sites at the following address:

```
http://microsoft.saltmine.com/frontpage/wpp/list
```

Free FrontPage Web Publishing Wizard

If your Internet service provider does not have the FrontPage Server Extensions installed, use the FrontPage Web Publishing Wizard to upload pages to your site. The wizard enables you to upload an entire Web or the pages that have changed since the past post. The wizard also warns you if any of your pages contain features that require the FrontPage Server Extensions. To obtain a free FrontPage Web Publishing Wizard for Windows 95 or Windows NT, go to

```
http://www.microsoft.com/frontpage/softlib/fs_fp_pbwiz.htm
```

FrontPage Developer's Kit

If you're a programmer, you can use the FrontPage Developer's Kit in conjunction with Visual C++ or Visual Basic to develop your own FrontPage Web and page wizards, Web templates, and bots. To obtain version 1.1 of the FrontPage Developer's Kit, go to

```
http://www.microsoft.com/frontpage/softlib/fs_fp_sdk.htm
```

General Web Information

The next sections provide a few sites that offer general resources for the World Wide Web.

Boutell.com World Wide Web FAQ

Boutell.com contains an introduction to the World Wide Web, information on how to obtain and use browsers, and pages about Web servers, authoring pages, and other resources:

http://www.boutell.com/faq/

Yahoo!: Computers and Internet: Internet: World Wide Web

The Yahoo! site contains many links to sites that have information about the World Wide Web. It offers links to WWW authoring, the best of the Web, books, browsers, caching, CGI, HTML, Java, JavaScript, page design, security, VRML, and more:

http://www.yahoo.com/Computers/World_Wide_Web/

Web Developer Information

Numerous sites provide information for developers. Many of them are described here. Categories include access counters, browsers, HTML standards and guides, and publishing and publicizing your Web.

Access Counters

If you want to track the number of times your pages are visited, you can include an access counter on the page. The following sites provide resources on how to accomplish this.

Adding Access Counters to Your Documents

How do you keep track of how many times your pages are accessed? The following site is a tutorial that tells you what to do:

http://members.aol.com/htmlguru/access_counts.html

Yahoo!: Computers and Internet: Internet: World Wide Web: Programming: Access Counts

This Yahoo! site provides links to all the counters you will ever need and more:

`http://www.yahoo.com/Computers/World_Wide_Web/Programming/Access_Counts/`

Browsers

The following sites will help you keep track of the latest available browsers and the features they include.

Browser Watch Browser List

The Browser Watch Browser List is a list of World Wide Web browsers and the operating systems (Windows, Mac, or UNIX) for which they are available:

`http://browserwatch.iworld.com/browsers.html`

Browser Watch Browser Stats

The Browser Watch Browser Stats is an extensive and thorough collection of browser statistics available for all browser types:

`http://browserwatch.iworld.com/report-table-browsers.html`

Browser Watch Plug-In Plaza

The Browser Watch Plug-In Plaza contains links to all the browser plug-ins that are currently available or in development:

`http://browserwatch.iworld.com/plug-in.html`

Yahoo!: Computers and Internet: Internet: World Wide Web: Browsers

This Yahoo! site contains links to browser usage statistics, capabilities, comparisons, helper applications, public access Web browsers, VRML browsers, and Usenet browsers:

`http://www.yahoo.com/Computers_and_Internet/Internet/World_Wide_Web/Browsers/`

HTML Standards and Guides

The following sites will assist you in learning HTML standards and keep you informed of the latest features that can be incorporated into your Web pages.

Beginner's Guide to HTML

The Beginner's Guide to HTML contains an introduction to producing HTML documents, with information on getting started, publishing, HTML tags, and more:

```
http://www.ncsa.uiuc.edu/General/Internet/WWW/HTMLPrimer.html
```

HTML Reference Manual

Michael J. Hannah of Sandia National Laboratories wrote an HTML reference manual that is very thorough and contains links to many other sources:

```
http://www.sandia.gov/sci_compute/html_ref.html
```

HTML Writer's Guild Home Page

Visit the home page for the HTML Writer's Guild, the premier organization of WWW page authors and Internet publishing professionals:

```
http://www.hwg.org/
```

Introducing HTML 3.2

Read W3C's new specification for HTML, developed in conjunction with IBM, Microsoft, Netscape Communications Corporation, Novell, SoftQuad, Spyglass, and Sun Microsystems:

```
http://www.w3.org/pub/WWW/MarkUp/Wilbur/
```

Author's Guide and HTML Reference for Internet Explorer 3.0

The Author's Guide and HTML Reference for Internet Explorer 3.0 is a thorough tab list that also contains many code examples:

```
http://www.microsoft.com/workshop/author/newhtml/default.htm
```

The Structure of HTML 3.2 Documents

The following site contains a summary of the features of HTML 3.2 tags:

```
http://www.w3.org/pub/WWW/MarkUp/Wilbur/features.html
```

The Web Developer's Virtual Library

You can visit an award-winning Webmaster's encyclopedia of Web development and Web software technology, which has a gallery, graphics, index, library, map, search, seminars, and top 30 sites, with thousands of links and tutorials:

```
http://www.stars.com/
```

The Web Developer's Virtual Library: HTML

The HTML section of the Web Developer's Virtual Library contains several links about creating and using Web pages:

```
http://www.stars.com/Vlib/Providers/HTML.html
```

Webmaster's Resource Center: Note and Links for Webmasters

The Webmaster's Resource Center is an excellent site that contains tools and references. Topics include HTML information, frames, books, Internet service providers, graphics, image maps, plug-ins, Java, JavaScript, browsers, CGI, Perl, publicizing, Web counters, and much more:

```
http://www.cio.com/webmaster/wm_notes.html
```

Yahoo!: Computers and Internet: Software: Data Formats: HTML

This Yahoo! site contains information on browser capabilities, extensions, forms, guides, tutorials, HTML 2.0, HTML 3.0, converters, editors, and much more:

```
http://www.yahoo.com/Computers_and_Internet/Software/Data_Formats/HTML/
```

The World Wide Web Consortium (W3C)

The World Wide Web Consortium is a group of individuals and organizations that support and develop the languages and protocols used on the World Wide Web. The Consortium's Web site contains information on HTML, graphics, 3D Web technology, fonts, style, SGML, and more:

```
http://www.w3.org/pub/WWW/
```

Publishing and Publicizing Your Web

Submit It! enables you to publicize a new Web site easily to several Web searches and cataloging services at once. The site submits to Yahoo!, Open Text, InfoSeek, Web

Crawler, Apollo, Starting Point, ComFind, BizWiz, Galaxy, What's New Too!, METRO-SCOPE, Lycos, InfoSpace, LinkStar, New Riders WWW Yellow Pages, Nerd World Media, Alta Vista, and Mallpark:

```
http://www.submit-it.com/
```

CGI and Perl Scripts

If you want to learn more about using CGI and Perl scripts with your FrontPage forms, the following links give you a good start. The links are arranged in two categories: sites that can help you learn how to develop scripts yourself and sites that have scripts you can use with your pages.

CGI Development

The following sites provide resources on CGI development.

The `cgi-lib.pl` Home Page

The `cgi-lib.pl` home page contains a standard library for creating Common Gateway Interface (CGI) scripts in the Perl language. The most up-to-date release of the library is found here:

```
http://www.bio.cam.ac.uk/cgi-lib/
```

Decoding Forms with CGI

This site provides a technical discussion of how to use forms with CGI scripts:

```
http://hoohoo.ncsa.uiuc.edu/cgi/forms.html
```

Index of Perl and HTML Archives

The following index contains links to several sites that contain information on Perl and HTML and on using CGI and Perl scripts with Web pages:

```
http://www.seas.upenn.edu/~mengwong/perlhtml.html
```

The Common Gateway Interface

This site is a primer on the Common Gateway Interface (CGI) and contains links to other pages about using CGI with forms:

```
http://hoohoo.ncsa.uiuc.edu/cgi/
```

Yahoo!: Computers and Internet: Languages: Perl

This Yahoo! site contains links and references about the Perl scripting language:

`http://www.yahoo.com/Computers_and_Internet/Programming_Languages/Perl/`

CGI Scripts That You Can Use

Check out the many CGI scripts that are available for you to use.

CGI Scripts for Windows NT and Windows 95 (Geocities Web Server)

CGI scripts by Ryan Sammartino include a hit counter, digital clock, simple guest book, and random image picker:

`http://www.geocities.com/SiliconValley/6742/`

Matt's Script Archive

Matt's Script Archive offers many public-domain CGI scripts, including a guest book, free-for-all link page, WWW board, counter, text counter, simple search, form mail, random image displayer, animation, countdown, and more:

`http://worldwidemart.com/scripts/`

Nuthin' but Links

The following contains links to several sites that provide public domain CGI scripts:

`http://pages.prodigy.net/bombadil/cgi.htm`

Selena Sol's Public Domain CGI Script Archive

Selena Sol's site has several CGI scripts and instructions, such as scripts for electronic outlets, a music catalog, forms processor, guest book, image maps, animation, Web chat, bulletin board, and more:

`http://www2.eff.org/~erict/Scripts/`

The Inter.Net Form/CGI Creator

If you aren't sure how to write your own CGI scripts, the Inter.Net Form/CGI Creator site can give you a good start. It features an online script generator. The forms require uncgi to work, and a link is provided for you to download it:

`http://the-inter.net/www/future21/formpro.html`

Graphics and Multimedia

Graphics and multimedia are gaining popularity on the Web. The sites that follow provide sources from which you can learn to develop graphics and multimedia for your Web pages. Categories include animated GIFs, clip art and image sources, retail and shareware graphics software support sites, Java and JavaScript, Microsoft ActiveX, Microsoft VBScript, and VRML/3D Web technology.

Animated GIFs

One way to provide animation on your pages is to develop animated GIF files. The site listed here provides a good start in learning to develop this type of graphic.

The Toolbox—GIF Animation on the WWW

For information on animated GIFs, check out the Toolbox. It is a resource for GIF animation on the Web and contains many pages and links that discuss creation and use of animated GIFs:

```
http://member.aol.com/royalef/toolbox.htm
```

Clip Art and Image Sources

Several sites provide clip art and images that you can use in your Web pages. The following sites contain a good collection of images or links.

Barry's Clip Art Server

Barry's Clip Art Server contains links to several sources of clip art for your Web pages. The clip art is available in a wide variety of categories:

```
http://www.barrysclipart.com
```

Microsoft's Multimedia Gallery

Microsoft's Multimedia Gallery offers free multimedia themes for your Web pages, including backgrounds, banners, navigation controls, images, sounds, and video clips:

```
http://www.microsoft.com/workshop/design/mmgallry/
```

Yahoo!: Computers and Internet: Multimedia: Pictures: Clip Art

Yahoo! maintains links to several clip art collections available for use in your Web pages:

```
http://www.yahoo.com/Computers/Multimedia/Pictures/Clip_art/
```

Yahoo!: Computers and Internet: Software: Data Formats: GIF

This Yahoo! site offers technical information about the GIF file format and the Unisys GIF/LZW controversy:

```
http://www.yahoo.com/Computers/Software/Data_formats/GIF/
```

Graphics Software—Retail

The following sections describe some links for product information and support for some of the most popular retail graphics programs. The links include information on products by Adobe, Corel Corporation, Fractal Design Corporation, and MetaTools.

Adobe Systems Incorporated

Adobe Systems Incorporated, makers of a wide variety of graphics programs, have several pages that provide product information and support.

Adobe Systems Incorporated Home Page

The Adobe Systems home page provides links to product support and information. Products include Adobe Acrobat, Adobe After Effects, Adobe Type Manager, Adobe Dimensions, Adobe Illustrator, Adobe Photoshop, Adobe PageMaker, and more:

```
http://www.adobe.com/
```

Adobe Acrobat

The following page is a download area for Adobe Acrobat and related items:

```
http://www.adobe.com/acrobat/
```

Adobe Acrobat Amber (Netscape Plug-In)

The Adobe Acrobat Amber is a download area for Adobe Acrobat Reader and related items, available in several software platforms:

```
http://www.adobe.com/acrobat/main.html
```

Adobe Photoshop

Adobe Photoshop is the graphics program of choice for many Web developers. You can find a product overview, details, help, and add-ons for Adobe Photoshop at this page:

```
http://www.adobe.com/prodindex/photoshop/main.html
```

Adobe-Compatible Plug-In Filters

For information on some of the most popular plug-ins available for Adobe Photoshop or Adobe-compatible programs, refer to the following sites.

Alien Skin Software

Alien Skin Software is the creator of the Black Box, version 2.0, a very popular set of plug-in filters for Adobe Photoshop or compatible applications. This site can sometimes be slow to connect:

```
http://www.eskimo.com/~bpentium/skin.html
```

Andromeda Software

Andromeda Software is the creator of the Andromeda Series of plug-in filters for Adobe Photoshop or compatible applications:

```
http://www.andromeda.com/info/AndromedaSeries.html
```

Corel Corporation—CorelNet

Corel Corporation's presence on the Internet is located at the following URL. This site contains product information and support for Corel's wide variety of graphics and desktop publishing software programs:

```
http://www.corelnet.com/products/graphicsandpublishing
```

Fractal Design Corporation

Fractal Design Corporation, creators of Fractal Design Painter and other ingenious graphics programs, has several useful pages that describe its products. Software updates and examples of artwork created with its software are also located here.

Fractal Design Corporation's home page contains links to product information, art galleries, download areas, and product support. Product information, support, downloads, and galleries are provided for Fractal Design's ingenious line of products. These include Fractal Design Painter, Ray Dream Studio, Ray Dream Designer, Fractal Design Expression, Fractal Design Detailer, Fractal Design Poser 2, and Dabbler 2. See also the section on MetaCreations, which follows. Here is the address for Fractal Design Corporation's home page:

```
http://www.fractal.com/
```

MetaCreations

The MetaCreations Web site features product information, support, and downloads for software produced by MetaCreations, which was formed when Fractal Design Corporation and MetaTools merged in 1997. You can find information on several 3D and 2D graphics software packages, including Real Time Geometry, Ray Dream Studio 5, Bryce 2, Bryce 2 Accessory Kit, Poser 2, Detailer, Painter 5, Kai's Power Tools 3, KPT Actions, Vector Effects, Expression, KPT Convolver, Kai's Photo Soap, Kai's Power Goo, Dabbler2, MetaPhotos, Infini-D 4, Final Effects 3, and more. Here is the URL:

```
http://www.metacreations.com/
```

Shareware Graphics Programs

Some of the most popular shareware graphics programs for the Windows operating system are covered in this section. These sites enable you to download the most current version of the software described.

Alchemy Mindworks

Alchemy Mindworks is the maker of several shareware graphics programs that can be of assistance in Web development. Most notable is the GIF Construction Set, which enables you to create animated GIFs. Graphic Workshop for Windows is also a very popular application.

Alchemy Mindworks Home Page

The Alchemy Mindworks home page provides links to software, books, and other resources about graphics development. Alchemy Mindworks is the creator of GIF Construction Set for Windows, GrafCat for Windows, Graphic Workshop for Windows, and many other shareware graphics utilities. The site can sometimes take a while to connect:

```
http://www.mindworkshop.com/alchemy/alchemy.html
```

GIF Construction Set for Windows

GIF Construction Set for Windows helps you create transparent and animated GIF files. The software is available for 16-bit and 32-bit Windows platforms:

```
http://www.mindworkshop.com/alchemy/gifcon.html
```

GrafCat for Windows

GrafCat for Windows prints a catalog of high-resolution thumbnails of your graphics. The program can print from 6 to 48 thumbnails per page:

`http://www.mindworkshop.com/alchemy/gctw.html`

Graphic Workshop for Windows

Graphic Workshop for Windows is a shareware graphics program that enables you to view, manipulate, and manage your graphics. The Web site includes support for TWAIN, PNG, MPEG, QuickTime, and multiple and interlaced GIF files:

`http://www.mindworkshop.com/alchemy/gww.html`

Lview Pro

Lview Pro is another popular graphics program for creating Web graphics. It is a 32-bit application for Windows 3.1 (requires Win32 application extensions), Windows 95, and Windows NT 3.51. You can download the most current version of the software from this site:

`http://world.std.com/~mmedia/lviewp.html`

Macmillan Computer Publishing—Windows Graphics Shareware Library

The Macmillan Computer Publishing site contains a collection of Windows graphics shareware programs, screen capture programs, and icon editors. You can find this library at the following URL:

`http://www.mcp.com/65528152318075/softlib/windows-utilities/wgraph.html`

Java and JavaScript

You can learn about using and developing applets and scripts with Java or JavaScript from several resources on the Internet. The following sites provide a good start.

Sun Microsystems JavaSoft Page

What are people doing with Java? The Sun site shows you what you can do and also offers information about the Java platform, JavaSoft news, products and services, and a developer's corner:

`http://java.sun.com/`

JavaScript Authoring Guide

The Netscape site contains information about authoring with JavaScript:

```
http://www.netscape.com/eng/mozilla/3.0/handbook/javascript/index.html
```

Yahoo!: Computers and Internet: Programming Languages: JavaScript

This Yahoo! site contains a collection of several different pages and sites that provide information about JavaScript development, including scripts you can use:

```
http://www.yahoo.com/Computers_and_Internet/Programming_Languages/JavaScript/
```

Microsoft ActiveX

Microsoft ActiveX, the Web technology platform used for Internet Explorer 3.0, provides the opportunity to make your Web pages come alive with interactivity and multimedia. You can find information on the following pages.

Browser Watch ActiveX Arena

The Browser Watch ActiveX Arena offers links to many ActiveX components that are currently available or in development:

```
http://browserwatch.iworld.com/activex.html
```

Microsoft ActiveX Controls

Download and try ActiveX controls for yourself; Internet Explorer 3.0 is required:

```
http://www.microsoft.com/intdev/controls/ctrlref-f.htm
```

Microsoft ActiveX Control Pad

The ActiveX Control Pad application enables you to quickly and easily develop Web pages that incorporate ActiveX features. The control pad is furnished as a part of Visual InterDev, but you can also download it from the following URL:

```
http://www.microsoft.com/workshop/author/cpad/
```

The Microsoft ActiveX Control Pad Getting Started Tutorial

The Getting Started tutorial gets you up and running in using the ActiveX Control Pad; Internet Explorer 3.0 is required:

```
http://www.microsoft.com/workshop/author/cpad/tutorial-f.htm
```

Microsoft ActiveX Component Gallery

Check out the Microsoft gallery of ActiveX controls; Internet Explorer 3.0 is required:

```
http://www.microsoft.com/activex/controls/
```

Microsoft HTML Layout Control

The HTML Layout Control application provides a means of laying out advanced Web pages that incorporate features used in Microsoft Internet Explorer 3.0. You do not need to download this application if you already have the Microsoft ActiveX Control Pad mentioned previously:

```
http://www.microsoft.com/workshop/author/layout/layout.htm
```

Microsoft VBScript

Microsoft VBScript, a subset of Visual Basic, provides a means of adding interactivity to your Web pages. It is a cross-platform language with great extensibility.

Microsoft VBScript Home Page

Visit the home page for Microsoft VBScript, with links to download areas, product support, and more:

```
http://www.microsoft.com/VBScript/
```

Online VBScript Language Reference

The following site provides an interactive online command reference for the VBScript language:

```
http://www.microsoft.com/vbscript/us/vbslang/vbstoc.htm
```

Hosting Visual Basic Scripting Edition

Consult the following guide, which outlines which version of VBScript is best for you:

```
http://www.microsoft.com/vbscript/us/techinfo/hosting.htm
```

Sound and Video

The following sections present some resources on sound and video.

Yahoo!: Computers and Internet: Multimedia: Sound

This Yahoo! site contains archives, MIDI sounds, MOD music format, movies, films and television, music software, speech generation, and Usenet links:

```
http://www.yahoo.com/Computers_and_Internet/Multimedia/Sound/
```

Yahoo!: Computers and Internet: Multimedia: Video

Another Yahoo! site contains animations, collections, festivals, institutes, morphs, MPEG, QuickTime, software, and technical information:

```
http://www.yahoo.com/Computers_and_Internet/Multimedia/Video/
```

Sources for Ideas

You can find sources for ideas in several areas. One way is to keep track of the "best of the Web" pages. Another way is to keep track of the types of sites that are getting the best ratings. The following are some links that can give you some ideas.

Cool Site of the Day

InfiNet's Cool Site of the Day includes its list of favorite Web sites. Links are arranged in today's cool site, iso-topically cool, and still cool (past cool winners):

```
http://cool.infi.net/
```

What's Hot and Cool on the Web

The What's Hot and Cool site provides links to several small, medium, and large sites. The sites are described as those with "strange, different, avant-garde, and just plain weird" contents:

```
http://kzsu.stanford.edu/uwi/reviews.html
```

Other Books in the *Laura Lemay* Series

The *Laura Lemay's Web Workshop* series offers more books in the area of Web development:

- ❏ *Laura Lemay's Web Workshop: 3D Graphics and VRML 2*. Sams.net Publishing. ISBN 1-57521-143-2.
- ❏ *Laura Lemay's Web Workshop: ActiveX and VBScript*. Sams.net Publishing. ISBN 1-57521-207-2.

❑ *Laura Lemay's Web Workshop: Creating Commercial Web Pages.* Sams.net Publishing. ISBN 1-57521-126-2.

❑ *Laura Lemay's Web Workshop: Designing with Style Sheets, Tables, and Frames.* Sams.net Publishing. ISBN 1-57521-249-8.

❑ *Laura Lemay's Web Workshop: JavaScript.* Sams.net Publishing. ISBN 1-57521-141-6.

❑ *Laura Lemay's Web Workshop: Microsoft FrontPage.* Sams.net Publishing. ISBN 1-57521-149-1.

❑ *Laura Lemay's Web Workshop: Microsoft FrontPage 97.* Sams.net Publishing. ISBN 1-57521-223-4.

❑ *Laura Lemay's Web Workshop: Net Objects Fusion 2.* Sams.net Publishing. ISBN 1-57521-278-1.

❑ *Laura Lemay's Web Workshop: Netscape Navigator Gold 3 Deluxe Edition.* Sams.net Publishing. ISBN 1-57521-292-7.

Other books by Laura Lemay include the following:

❑ *Laura Lemay's Java 1.1 Interactive Course.* Waite Group Press. ISBN 1-57169-083-2.

❑ *Official Marimba Guide to Castanet.* Sams.net Publishing. ISBN 1-57521-255-2.

❑ *Teach Yourself Java in 21 Days.* Sams.net Publishing. ISBN 1-57521-030-4.

❑ *Teach Yourself Java in 21 Days, Professional Reference Edition.* Sams.net Publishing. ISBN 1-57521-183-1.

❑ *Teach Yourself Java 1.1 in 21 Days, Second Edition.* Sams.net Publishing. ISBN 1-57521-142-4.

❑ *Teach Yourself Web Publishing with HTML 4 in a Week*, Fourth Edition. Sams.net Publishing. ISBN 1-57521-336-2.

❑ *Teach Yourself Web Publishing with HTML 4 in 14 Days,* Second Professional Reference Edition. Sams.net Publishing. ISBN 1-57521-305-2.

C

HTML Quick Reference

This HTML quick reference is different from those found in most other HTML books. Because FrontPage features many built-in HTML tagging functions, you do not have to touch your HTML Code very often. If you are familiar with HTML tags, you can use this quick reference as a guide to the commands and procedures that implement them. FrontPage supports HTML 3.2, with additional tags supported by Internet Explorer 4.0.

Consult the appropriate table for the information that you need. The tables are

Table C.1   ActiveX control tags
Table C.2   Cascading style sheet tags
Table C.3   Character styles and formatting
Table C.4   Font tags
Table C.5   Font and paragraph tags—Other
Table C.6   Form-related tags
Table C.7   Form field tags
Table C.8   Frame-related tags
Table C.9   Floating frame-related tags
Table C.10 Heading tags
Table C.11 Horizontal rule tags
Table C.12 Hotspot (image map) tags
Table C.13 Image tags
Table C.14 Line break tags

All the tables refer to HTML tags and the attribute names and values that can be applied to them. Italic type indicates an attribute value that you must specify, such as a URL, a numerical value, or a filename. There is also a reference to the chapter that discusses the tag in more detail.

The final column in each table shows the name of the field or the choice you make in the appropriate dialog box. In most cases, the dialog box associated with the tag is indicated in the figure caption. When this is not the case, the appropriate dialog box is listed for the tag.

The notation Use HTML Markup Bot indicates that you should use the HTML Markup Bot—discussed in Chapter 26, "Using Your Own HTML"—to enter your code. As an alternative, you can use HTML view in the FrontPage Editor and edit the code from there.

ActiveX Control Tags

To set ActiveX control properties, choose Insert | Advanced | ActiveX Control. The tags listed in Table C.1 can be set in the ActiveX Control Properties dialog box, unless noted otherwise. For additional information, refer to Chapter 25, "Using Java Applets and Netscape Plug-Ins."

Table C.1. ActiveX control tags.

Tag	Name	Value	Procedure or Option
object	align	absbottom	ActiveX Control Properties dialog box: Layout, Alignment, absbottom
object	align	absmiddle	ActiveX Control Properties dialog box: Layout, Alignment, absmiddle
object	align	baseline	ActiveX Control Properties dialog box: Layout, Alignment, baseline

Tag	Name	Value	Procedure or Option
object	align	bottom	ActiveX Control Properties dialog box: Layout, Alignment, bottom
object	align	center	ActiveX Control Properties dialog box: Layout, Alignment, center
object	align	left	ActiveX Control Properties dialog box: Layout, Alignment, left
object	align	middle	ActiveX Control Properties dialog box: Layout, Alignment, middle
object	align	right	ActiveX Control Properties dialog box: Layout, Alignment, right
object	align	texttop	ActiveX Control Properties dialog box: Layout, Alignment, texttop
object	align	top	ActiveX Control Properties dialog box: Layout, Alignment, top
object	border	*n*	ActiveX Control Properties dialog box: Layout, Border thickness
object	classid	*string*	ActiveX Control Properties dialog box: select a control or enter the class ID in the Pick a Control field
object	codebase	*string*	ActiveX Control Properties dialog box: Network Location, Code Source
object	height	*n*	ActiveX Control Properties dialog box: Layout: Height
object	hspace	*n*	ActiveX Control Properties dialog box: Layout: Horizontal spacing
object	id	*string*	ActiveX Control Properties dialog box: Pick a Control
object	name	*string*	ActiveX Control Properties dialog box: Name
object	src	*string*	ActiveX Control Properties dialog box: Network Location, Data Source
object	vspace	*n*	ActiveX Control Properties dialog box: Layout: Vertical Spacing
object	width	*n*	ActiveX Control Properties dialog box: Layout: Width

Cascading Style Sheet Tags

To assign a cascading style sheet style to a page element, click the Style button in the relevant Properties dialog box. The Style dialog box appears, after which you can set the properties shown in Table C.2.

Table C.2. Cascading style sheet tags.

Tag	Property	Value	Dialog Box Selection
span	class		Class tab: Class
span	ID		Class tab: ID
style	background-attachment	fixed	Colors tab: Attachment
style	background-attachment	scroll	Colors tab: Attachment
style	background-color	colorname	Colors tab: Background Color
style	background-color	rgb(n,n,n)	Colors tab: Background Color
style	background-image	url	Colors tab: Background Image
style	background-position	bottom	Colors tab: Vertical Position
style	background-position	center	Colors tab: Horizontal Position
style	background-position	center	Colors tab: Vertical Position
style	background-position	left	Colors tab: Horizontal Position
style	background-position	right	Colors tab: Horizontal Position
style	background-position	top	Colors tab: Vertical Position
style	background-repeat	no-repeat	Colors tab: Repeat
style	background-repeat	repeat	Colors tab: Repeat
style	background-repeat	repeat-x	Colors tab: Repeat
style	background-repeat	repeat-y	Colors tab: Repeat
style	border	colorname	Border tab: Color: Left, Right, Top, or Bottom; choose one of 16 default

Tag	Property	Value	Dialog Box Selection
			colors from the Color drop-down menu
style	border	*n*px	Border tab: Width: Left, Right, Top, or Bottom
style	border	dotted	Border tab: Style: Left, Right, Top, or Bottom
style	border	double	Border tab: Style: Left, Right, Top, or Bottom
style	border	groove	Border tab: Style: Left, Right, Top, or Bottom
style	border	inset	Border tab: Style: Left, Right, Top, or Bottom
style	border	medium	Border tab: Width: Left, Right, Top, or Bottom
style	border	none	Border tab: Style: Left, Right, Top, or Bottom
style	border	outset	Border tab: Style: Left, Right, Top, or Bottom
style	border	rgb(*n*,*n*,*n*)	Border tab: Color: Left, Right, Top, or Bottom; choose Custom from the Color drop-down menu and create a custom color in the Color dialog box
style	border	ridge	Border tab: Style: Left, Right, Top, or Bottom
style	border	solid	Border tab: Style: Left, Right, Top, or Bottom
style	border	thick	Border tab: Width: Left, Right, Top, or Bottom
style	border	thin	Border tab: Width: Left, Right, Top, or Bottom
style	border-bottom	*n*px	Border tab: Width: Bottom
style	border-bottom	*colorname*	Border tab: Color: Bottom; choose one of 16

continues

Table C.2. continued

Tag	Property	Value	Dialog Box Selection
			default colors from the Color drop-down menu
style	border-bottom	dotted	Border tab: Style: Bottom
style	border-bottom	double	Border tab: Style: Bottom
style	border-bottom	groove	Border tab: Style: Bottom
style	border-bottom	inset	Border tab: Style: Bottom
style	border-bottom	medium	Border tab: Width: Bottom
style	border-bottom	none	Border tab: Style: Bottom
style	border-bottom	outset	Border tab: Style: Bottom
style	border-bottom	rgb(n,n,n)	Border tab: Color: Bottom; choose Custom from the Color drop-down menu and create a custom color in the Color dialog box
style	border-bottom	ridge	Border tab: Style: Bottom
style	border-bottom	solid	Border tab: Style: Bottom
style	border-bottom	thick	Border tab: Width: Bottom
style	border-bottom	thin	Border tab: Width: Bottom
style	border-left	$n$px	Border tab: Width: Left
style	border-left	colorname	Border tab: Color: Left; choose one of 16 default colors from the Color drop-down menu
style	border-left	dotted	Border tab: Style: Left
style	border-left	double	Border tab: Style: Left
style	border-left	groove	Border tab: Style: Left
style	border-left	inset	Border tab: Style: Left
style	border-left	medium	Border tab: Width: Left
style	border-left	none	Border tab: Style: Left
style	border-left	outset	Border tab: Style: Left
style	border-left	rgb(n,n,n)	Border tab: Color: Left; choose Custom from the

Tag	Property	Value	Dialog Box Selection
			Color drop-down menu and create a custom color in the Color dialog box
style	border-left	ridge	Border tab: Style: Left
style	border-left	solid	Border tab: Style: Left
style	border-left	thick	Border tab: Width: Left
style	border-left	thin	Border tab: Width: Left
style	border-right	$n$px	Border tab: Width: Right
style	border-right	colorname	Border tab: Color: Right; choose one of 16 default colors from the Color drop-down menu
style	border-right	dotted	Border tab: Style: Right
style	border-right	double	Border tab: Style: Right
style	border-right	groove	Border tab: Style: Right
style	border-right	inset	Border tab: Style: Right
style	border-right	medium	Border tab: Width: Right
style	border-right	none	Border tab: Style: Right
style	border-right	outset	Border tab: Style: Right
style	border-right	rgb(n,n,n)	Border tab: Color: Right; choose Custom from the Color drop-down menu and create a custom color in the Color dialog box
style	border-right	ridge	Border tab: Style: Right
style	border-right	solid	Border tab: Style: Right
style	border-right	thick	Border tab: Width: Right
style	border-right	thin	Border tab: Width: Right
style	border-top	$n$px	Border tab: Width: Top
style	border-top	colorname	Border tab: Color: Top; choose one of 16 default colors from the Color drop-down menu
style	border-top	dotted	Border tab: Style: Top
style	border-top	double	Border tab: Style: Top

continues

Table C.2. continued

Tag	Property	Value	Dialog Box Selection
style	border-top	groove	Border tab: Style: Top
style	border-top	inset	Border tab: Style: Top
style	border-top	medium	Border tab: Width: Top
style	border-top	none	Border tab: Style: Top
style	border-top	outset	Border tab: Style: Top
style	border-top	rgb(*n,n,n*)	Border tab: Color: Top; choose Custom from the Color drop-down menu and create a custom color in the Color dialog box
style	border-top	ridge	Border tab: Style: Top
style	border-top	solid	Border tab: Style: Top
style	border-top	thick	Border tab: Width: Top
style	border-top	thin	Border tab: Width: Top
style	color	*colorname*	Colors tab: Foreground Color
style	color	rgb(*n,n,n*)	Colors tab: Foreground Color
style	float	left	Alignment tab: **F**loat
style	float	none	Alignment tab: **F**loat
style	float	right	Alignment tab: **F**loat
style	font-family	*fontname*	Font tab: Primary font
style	font-family	cursive	Font tab: Primary font
style	font-family	fantasy	Font tab: Primary font
style	font-family	monospace	Font tab: Primary font
style	font-family	sans-serif	Font tab: Primary font
style	font-family	serif	Font tab: Primary font
style	font-family	cursive	Font tab: Secondary font
style	font-family	fantasy	Font tab: Secondary font
style	font-family	monospace	Font tab: Secondary font
style	font-family	sans-serif	Font tab: Secondary font
style	font-family	serif	Font tab: Secondary font
style	font-family	*fontname*	Font tab: Secondary font

Tag	Property	Value	Dialog Box Selection
style	font-style	normal	Text tab: Style
style	font-style	italic	Text tab: Style
style	font-style	oblique	Text tab: Style
style	font-variant	normal	Text tab: Variant
style	font-variant	small-caps	Text tab: Variant
style	font-weight	100	Text tab: Weight
style	font-weight	200	Text tab: Weight
style	font-weight	300	Text tab: Weight
style	font-weight	400	Text tab: Weight
style	font-weight	500	Text tab: Weight
style	font-weight	600	Text tab: Weight
style	font-weight	700	Text tab: Weight
style	font-weight	800	Text tab: Weight
style	font-weight	900	Text tab: Weight
style	font-weight	bold	Text tab: Weight
style	font-weight	bolder	Text tab: Weight
style	font-weight	lighter	Text tab: Weight
style	font-weight	normal	Text tab: Weight
style	line-height	n	Text tab: Line Height
style	margin-bottom	$n$px	Alignment tab Margins: **B**ottom
style	margin-left	$n$px	Alignment tab Margins: **L**eft
style	margin-right	$n$px	Alignment tab Margins: **R**ight
style	margin-top	$n$px	Alignment tab Margins: **T**op
style	padding-bottom	$n$px	Alignment tab Padding: **B**ottom
style	padding-left	$n$px	Alignment tab Padding: **L**eft
style	padding-right	$n$px	Alignment tab Padding: **R**ight

continues

Table C.2. continued

Tag	Property	Value	Dialog Box Selection
style	padding-top		Alignment tab Padding: **T**op
style	text-align	center	Text tab: Text Alignment
style	text-align	justify	Text tab: Text Alignment
style	text-align	left	Text tab: Text Alignment
style	text-align	right	Text tab: Text Alignment
style	text-decoration	none	Text tab: Decoration
style	text-decoration	underline	Text tab: Decoration
style	text-decoration	overline	Text tab: Decoration
style	text-decoration	line-through	Text tab: Decoration
style	text-decoration	blink	Text tab: Decoration
style	text-indent	n	Text tab: Indent
style	text-transform	capitalize	Text tab: Transform
style	text-transform	lowercase	Text tab: Transform
style	text-transform	none	Text tab: Transform
style	text-transform	uppercase	Text tab: Transform
style	letter-spacing	n	Text tab: Letter Spacing
style	vertical-align	baseline	Text tab: Vertical Alignment
style	vertical-align	bottom	Text tab: Vertical Alignment
style	vertical-align	middle	Text tab: Vertical Alignment
style	vertical-align	sub	Text tab: Vertical Alignment
style	vertical-align	super	Text tab: Vertical Alignment
style	vertical-align	text-bottom	Text tab: Vertical Alignment
style	vertical-align	text-top	Text tab: Vertical Alignment
style	vertical-align	top	Text tab: Vertical Alignment

Character Styles and Formatting Tags

The procedures and options listed in Table C.3 appear in the Font dialog box, which is accessed with the Format | Font command. Refer to Chapter 10, "Composing and Editing Pages."

Character style tags can be assigned in the Font Properties dialog box. Font color can be set by using the Color drop-down menu in the Font tab or by clicking the Font Color button on the Format toolbar.

Table C.3. Character styles and formatting (Format | Font command).

Tag	Value	Procedure or Option
b	string	Special Styles tab: **B**old
blink	string	Special Styles tab: **Bl**ink
cite	string	Special Styles tab: Ci**t**ation
code	string	Special Styles tab: C**o**de
dfn	string	Special Styles tab: **D**efinition
em	string	Font tab: F**o**nt Style: Italic; Format Toolbar: Italic button
i	string	Special Styles tab: **I**talic
kbd	string	Special Styles tab: **K**eyboard
s	string	Font tab: Effects: Stri**k**ethrough
samp	string	Special Styles tab: **S**ample
strike	string	Font tab: Effects: Stri**k**ethrough
strong	string	Font tab: Font Style: Bold; Format toolbar: Bold button
sub	string	Special Styles tab: Vertical **P**osition: Subscript
sup	string	Special Styles tab: Vertical **P**osition: Superscript
tt	string	Font tab: Effects: **T**ypewriter
u	string	Font tab: Effects: **U**nderline; Format toolbar: Underline button
var	string	Special Styles tab: **V**ariable

Font Tags

The procedures and options referenced in Table C.4 appear in the Font dialog box, which is accessed with the Format | Font command. Refer to Chapter 10.

Table C.4. Fonts (Format | Font command).

Tag	Name	Value	Procedure or Option
font	color	#rrggbb	Font tab: **C**olor (drop-down menu); Format toolbar: Text Color button
font	color	colorname	Font tab: **C**olor (drop-down menu), select one of 16 predefined colors
font	face	facename	Font tab: **Fo**nt Style, choose from list; Format toolbar: Change Font drop-down menu
font	size	1	Font tab: **S**ize 1 (8 pt)
font	size	2	Font tab: **S**ize 2 (10 pt)
font	size	3	Font tab: **S**ize 3 (12 pt) or Size Normal
font	size	4	Font tab: **S**ize 4 (14 pt)
font	size	5	Font tab: **S**ize 5 (18 pt)
font	size	6	Font tab: **S**ize 6 (24 pt)
font	size	7	Font tab: **S**ize 7 (32 pt)

Font and Paragraph Tags—Other

The HTML tags shown in Table C.5 perform various font and paragraph formatting functions. You can implement them by inserting your own HTML code, except where noted. For additional information on inserting your own HTML code, refer to Chapter 26.

Table C.5. Font and paragraph tags (other).

Tag	Name	Value	Procedure or Option
basefont			Edit in HTML view
basefont	color	#rrggbb	Edit in HTML view
basefont	color	colorname	Edit in HTML view
basefont	face	face	Edit in HTML view
basefont	size	1	Edit in HTML view
basefont	size	2	Edit in HTML view
basefont	size	3	Edit in HTML view
basefont	size	4	Edit in HTML view

Tag	Name	Value	Procedure or Option
basefont	size	5	Edit in HTML view
basefont	size	6	Edit in HTML view
basefont	size	7	Edit in HTML view
big			HTML Markup Bot/Edit in HTML view
blockquote			Format toolbar: Increase Indent button
center			Format Toolbar: Center
div	align	left	HTML Markup Bot/Edit in HTML view
div	align	center	HTML Markup Bot/Edit in HTML view
div	align	right	HTML Markup Bot/Edit in HTML view
listing			HTML Markup Bot/Edit in HTML view
nobr			HTML Markup Bot/Edit in HTML view
plaintext			HTML Markup Bot/Edit in HTML view
small			HTML Markup Bot/Edit in HTML view
wbr			HTML Markup Bot/Edit in HTML view
xmp			HTML Markup Bot/Edit in HTML view

Form-Related Tags

The procedures and options shown in Table C.6 appear in the dialog boxes noted in the Procedure or Option column. Refer to Chapter 25.

Table C.6. Form-related tags.

Tag	Name	Value	Procedure or Option
form			Automatic when inserting form field on page
form	action	url	Options for Custom Form Handler: Action
form	enctype	mimetype	Options for Custom Form Handler: Encoding type
form	method	get	Options for Custom Form Handler: Method
form	method	post	Options for Custom Form Handler: Method
form	target		Form Properties: Target Frame

Form Field Tags

The procedures and options shown in Table C.7 appear in several different form field properties dialog boxes. Refer to Chapter 22, "Adding and Editing Form Fields."

Table C.7. Form field tags.

Tag	Name	Value	Procedure or Option
input	align	bottom	Edit in HTML view
input	align	middle	Edit in HTML view
input	align	top	Edit in HTML view
input	checked		Check Box Properties dialog box: Initial State, **C**hecked
			Radio Button Properties dialog box: **S**elected
input	class		Click **S**tyle button (refer to Table C.2)
input	id		Click **S**tyle button (refer to Table C.2)
input	name	*name*	Text Box Properties dialog box: **N**ame
			Radio Button Properties dialog box: Group **N**ame
			Push Button Properties dialog box: **N**ame
			Image Form Field Properties dialog box: **N**ame
			Check Box Properties dialog box: **N**ame
			Form Properties dialog box: Hidden Fields, **A**dd, **N**ame
input	size	*n*	Text Box Properties dialog box: **W**idth in Characters
input	src	*url*	Edit in HTML view
input	style	*string*	Click **S**tyle button (refer to Table C.2)
input	type	button	Push Button Properties dialog box: Button Type, N**o**rmal
input	type	checkbox	**I**nsert I Form Fiel**d** I **C**heck Box; Forms toolbar: Check Box button
input	type	file	Edit in HTML view
input	type	hidden	Form Properties dialog box: Hidden Fields, **A**dd
input	type	image	**I**nsert I Form Fiel**d** I **I**mage
input	type	password	Text Box Properties dialog box: Password field, **Y**es

Tag	Name	Value	Procedure or Option
input	type	radio	**I**nsert I Form Fiel**d** I **R**adio Button; Forms toolbar: Radio Button button
input	type	reset	Push Button Properties dialog box: Button Type, **R**eset
input	type	submit	**I**nsert I Form Fiel**d** I **P**ush Button (default selection); Push Button Properties dialog box: Button Type, **S**ubmit
input	type	text	**I**nsert I Form Fiel**d** I One-Line **T**ext Box; Forms toolbar: Text Box button
input	value	*value*	Text Box Properties dialog box: Initial **v**alue; Push Button Properties dialog box: **V**alue/Label; Check Box Properties dialog box: **V**alue; Radio Button Properties dialog box: **V**alue; Form Properties dialog box: Hidden Fields, **A**dd, **V**alue
option	choice		Drop Down Menu Properties dialog box: Choice, **A**dd, **C**hoice
option	selected		Drop Down Menu Properties dialog box: Choice, **A**dd, **S**elected
option	value		Drop Down Menu Properties dialog box: Choice, **A**dd, Specify **V**alue
select			**I**nsert I Form Fiel**d** I **D**rop-Down Menu; Forms toolbar: Drop Down Menu button
select	multiple		Drop Down Menu Properties dialog box: Allow multiple selections, **Y**es
select	name		Drop Down Menu Properties dialog box: **N**ame
select	size		Drop Down Menu Properties dialog box: **H**eight
textarea			**I**nsert I Form Fiel**d** I **S**crolling Text Box; Forms toolbar: Scrolling Text Box Button

continues

Table C.7. continued

Tag	Name	Value	Procedure or Option
textarea	cols		Scrolling Text Box Properties dialog box: **W**idth in characters
textarea	name		Scrolling Text Box Properties dialog box: **N**ame
textarea	rows		Scrolling Text Box Properties dialog box: Number of lines
textarea	wrap	off	Edit in HTML view
textarea	wrap	physical	Edit in HTML view
textarea	wrap	virtual	Edit in HTML view

Frame-Related Tags

The procedures and options referenced in Table C.8 are discussed in Chapter 18, "Frames: Pages with Split Personalities." The majority of the tags listed in Table C.8 are assigned in the Frame Properties dialog box, unless otherwise noted.

Table C.8. Frame-related tags.

Tag	Name	Value	Procedure or Option
frame	align	bottom	Edit in HTML view
frame	align	left	Edit in HTML view
frame	align	middle	Edit in HTML view
frame	align	right	Edit in HTML view
frame	align	top	Edit in HTML view
frame	border	false	Page Properties dialog box: Frames tab: uncheck Show **B**orders
frame	frameborder	n	Page Properties dialog box: Frames tab: check Show **B**orders
frame	framespacing	n	Page Properties dialog box: Frames tab: **F**rame Spacing
frame	marginheight	n	Frame Properties dialog box: Margins: Hei**g**ht
frame	marginwidth	n	Frame Properties dialog box: Margins: **W**idth
frame	name	framename	Frame Properties dialog box: **N**ame

Tag	Name	Value	Procedure or Option
frame	noresize		Frame Properties dialog box: uncheck **R**esizeable in Browser
frame	scrolling	auto	Frame Properties dialog box: Show **S**crollbars: If Needed
frame	scrolling	no	Frame Properties dialog box: Show **S**crollbars: Never
frame	scrolling	yes	Frame Properties dialog box: Show **S**crollbars: Always
frame	src	*url*	Frame Properties dialog box: Initial **P**age
frameset	cols	*n%*	Frame Properties dialog box: Frame Size: **W**idth, Percent
frameset	cols	*n*	Frame Properties dialog box: Frame Size: **W**idth, Pixels
frameset	cols	**n*	Frame Properties dialog box: Frame Size: **W**idth, Relative
frameset	border	false	Page Properties dialog box: Frames tab: uncheck Show **B**orders
frameset	frameborder	*n*	Page Properties dialog box: check Show **B**orders
frameset	framespacing	*n*	Page Properties dialog box: Frames tab: **F**rame Spacing
frameset	rows	*n%*	Frame Properties dialog box: Frame Size: Row Heigh**t**, Percent
frameset	rows	*n*	Frame Properties dialog box: Frame Size: Row Heigh**t**, Pixels
frameset	rows	**n*	Frame Properties dialog box: Frame Size: Row Heigh**t**, Relative
noframes			Add alternate content in No Frames view of FrontPage Editor

Floating Frame Tags

Floating frames, which you can browse in Internet Explorer 3.0 and later, can be inserted into your page using the HTML Markup component or by editing the HTML code directly. For more information, refer to Chapter 26.

Table C.9. Floating frame–related tags.

Tag	Name	Value	Procedure or Option
iframe	align		Edit in HTML view or use HTML Markup Bot
iframe	frameborder		Edit in HTML view or use HTML Markup Bot
iframe	height		Edit in HTML view or use HTML Markup Bot
iframe	marginheight		Edit in HTML view or use HTML Markup Bot
iframe	marginwidth		Edit in HTML view or use HTML Markup Bot
iframe	name		Edit in HTML view or use HTML Markup Bot
iframe	scrolling		Edit in HTML view or use HTML Markup Bot
iframe	src		Edit in HTML view or use HTML Markup Bot
iframe	noresize		Edit in HTML view or use HTML Markup Bot
iframe	width		Edit in HTML view or use HTML Markup Bot

Heading Tags

The heading tags listed in Table C.10 can be inserted from the Format toolbar, using the Change Style drop-down menu, or edited from the Format I Paragraph command, using the Paragraph Properties dialog box. Refer to Chapter 10.

Table C.10. Heading tags.

Tag	Name	Value	Procedure or Option
h1			Format toolbar, Change Style drop-down menu; Heading 1; Paragraph Properties dialog box: Heading 1
h2			Format toolbar, Change Style drop-down menu; Heading 2; Paragraph Properties dialog box: Heading 2
h3			Format toolbar, Change Style drop-down menu; Heading 3; Paragraph Properties dialog box: Heading 3
h4			Format toolbar, Change Style drop-down menu; Heading 4; Paragraph Properties dialog box: Heading 4
h5			Format toolbar, Change Style drop-down menu; Heading 5; Paragraph Properties dialog box: Heading 5

Tag	Name	Value	Procedure or Option
h6			Format toolbar, Change Style drop-down menu; Heading 6; Paragraph Properties dialog box: Heading 6
h1 thru h6	align	center	Paragraph Properties dialog box: Paragraph **A**lignment: center
h1 thru h6	align	left	Paragraph Properties dialog box: Paragraph **A**lignment: left
h1 thru h6	align	right	Paragraph Properties dialog box: Paragraph **A**lignment: right

Horizontal Rule Tags

For Table C.11, horizontal rules are placed on a page by using the **I**nsert I Horizontal **L**ine command. Properties are edited in the Horizontal Line Properties dialog box. Refer to Chapter 10.

Table C.11. Horizontal rule tags.

Tag	Name	Value	Procedure or Option
hr			**I**nsert I Horizontal **L**ine
hr	align	center	Horizontal Line Properties dialog box: Alignment: C**e**nter
hr	align	left	Horizontal Line Properties dialog box: Alignment: **L**eft
hr	align	right	Horizontal Line Properties dialog box: Alignment: **R**ight
hr	class		Style button (refer to Table C.2)
hr	color	#rrggbb	Horizontal Line Properties dialog box: Color: Custom (in drop-down menu)
hr	color	colorname	Horizontal Line Properties dialog box: Color: Choose one of 16 named colors from drop-down menu
hr	id		Style button (refer to Table C.2)
hr	noshade		Horizontal Line Properties dialog box: check **S**olid line (no shading)
hr	size	n	Horizontal Line Properties dialog box: Height: Pixels

continues

Table C.11. continued

Tag	Name	Value	Procedure or Option
hr	style		Style button (refer to Table C.2)
hr	width	n%	Horizontal Line Properties dialog box: Width: **P**ercent of Window
hr	width	n	Horizontal Line Properties dialog box: Width: Pi**x**els

Hotspot (Image Map) Tags

To enable the Image Properties toolbar, click on a page image. Then choose one of the buttons referenced in Table C.12 to create a specific hotspot in that image. By default, FrontPage generates image maps that are compatible with the FrontPage Server Extensions. To designate another method, choose **T**ools I **W**eb Settings. In the FrontPage Web Settings dialog box, choose the Advanced tab. Under Image Maps, **S**tyle, select NCSA, CERN, Netscape, or <none> from the drop-down menu. Refer to Chapter 9, "Getting from Here to There."

Table C.12. Hotspot (image map) tags.

Tag	Name	Value	Procedure or Option
area	coords	x1,y1,x2,y2[el]	Coordinates generated automatically when you draw a hotspot
area	shape	circ	Image toolbar, Circle button
area	shape	poly	Image toolbar, Polygon button
area	shape	rect	Image toolbar, Rectangle button

Image Tags

The tags shown in Table C.13 appear in the Image Properties dialog box. Refer to Chapter 15, "Working with Images and Sound."

Table C.13. Image tags.

Tag	Name	Value	Procedure or Option
img			Insert I **I**mage or Insert Image button on Standard toolbar
img	align	absbottom	Appearance tab, Layout, **A**lignment, absbottom

Tag	Name	Value	Procedure or Option
img	align	absmiddle	Appearance tab, Layout, **A**lignment, absmiddle
img	align	baseline	Appearance tab, Layout, **A**lignment, baseline
img	align	bottom	Appearance tab, Layout, **A**lignment, bottom
img	align	center	Appearance tab, Layout, **A**lignment, center
img	align	left	Appearance tab, Layout, **A**lignment, left
img	align	middle	Appearance tab, Layout, **A**lignment, middle
img	align	right	Appearance tab, Layout, **A**lignment, right
img	align	texttop	Appearance tab, Layout, **A**lignment, texttop
img	align	top	Appearance tab, Layout, **A**lignment, top
img	alt	*text*	General tab, Alternative Representations, Te**x**t
img	border	*n*	Appearance tab, **B**order Thickness
img	class		General tab, click **S**tyle button (refer to Table C.2)
img	controls		Video tab, **S**how Controls in Browser
img	dynsrc	*URL*	Video tab, **V**ideo source
img	height	*n*	Appearance tab, **S**pecify Size, **H**eight, in Pixels
img	height	*n%*	Appearance tab, **S**pecify Size, **H**eight, in Percent
img	hspace	*n*	Appearance tab, Hori**z**ontal Spacing
img	id		General tab, click **S**tyle button (refer to Table C.2)
img	ismap		Use Image toolbar to create hotspots (also refer to Table C.7)
img	loop	*n*	Video tab: **L**oop
img	loop	infinite	Video tab: **F**orever
img	loopdelay	*n*	Video tab: Loop **D**elay

continues

Table C.13. continued

Tag	Name	Value	Procedure or Option
img	lowsrc	*url*	General tab: Alternative Representations: Lo**w**-Res
img	src	*url*	General tab: Image **S**ource
img	start	fileopen	Video tab: Start, **O**n File Open
img	start	mouseover	Video tab: Start, On **M**ouse Over
img	style		General tab, click **S**tyle button (refer to Table C.2)
img	vspace	*n*	Appearance tab, **V**ertical Spacing
img	width	*n*	Appearance tab, Specify Size, **W**idth, in Pixels
img	width	*n%*	Appearance tab, Specify Size, **W**idth, in Percent

Line Break Tags

The line breaks tags listed in Table C.14 are inserted with the **I**nsert I **B**reak command and edited in the Break Properties dialog box. Refer to Chapter 10.

Table C.14. Line break tags.

Tag	Name	Value	Procedure or Option
br			Normal Line Break
br	class		Click **S**tyle button (refer to Table C.2)
br	clear	all	Clear Both Margins
br	clear	left	Clear Left Margin
br	clear	right	Clear Right Margin

Link Tags

The links identified in Table C.15 are created with the Create Link button in the Standard toolbar or with the **E**dit I Hyperlin**k** command. The Create Hyperlink dialog box (or the Edit Hyperlink dialog box) contains four tabs—Open Pages tab, Current FrontPage Web tab, World Wide Web tab, and New Page tab. Refer to Chapter 9.

Table C.15. Link (anchor) tags.

Tag	Name	Value	Procedure or Option
a	href	*filename*	Create Hyperlink or Edit Hyperlink dialog box: **U**RL
a	href	*url*	Create Hyperlink or Edit Hyperlink dialog box: **U**RL
a	methods	meth1,meth2[el]	Edit in HTML view
a	name	*name*	Edit I **B**ookmark command, **B**ookmark Name
a	rel	*relationship*	Edit in HTML view
a	rev	*revision*	Edit in HTML view
a	target	*window*	Create Hyperlink or Edit Hyperlink dialog box: **T**arget Frame; Page Properties dialog box: Default **T**arget Frame
a	target	_blank	Create Hyperlink or Edit Hyperlink dialog box: **T**arget Frame; Page Properties dialog box: Default **T**arget Frame
a	target	_parent	Create Hyperlink or Edit Hyperlink dialog box: **T**arget Frame; Page Properties dialog box: Default **T**arget Frame
a	target	_self	Create Hyperlink or Edit Hyperlink dialog box: **T**arget Frame; Page Properties dialog box: Default **T**arget Frame
a	target	_top	Create Hyperlink or Edit Hyperlink dialog box: **T**arget Frame; Page Properties dialog box: Default **T**arget Frame
a	title	*name*	Edit in HTML view
a	urn	*name*	Edit in HTML view

List Tags

The list tags referenced in Table C.16 are formatted using the Change Style drop-down menu in the Format toolbar, formatted with the Format I Bullets and **N**umbering command, and edited with the List Properties dialog box. Refer to Chapter 11, "Organizing Information into Lists."

Table C.16. List tags.

Tag	Name	Value	Procedure or Option
dd			Format toolbar, Change Style drop-down menu: Definition
dir			Format toolbar, Change Style drop-down menu: Directory List; List Properties dialog box: Other tab, Directory List
dl			Format toolbar, Change Style drop-down menu: Definition List; List Properties dialog box: Other tab, Definition List
dl	compact		List Properties dialog box: Other tab, check Compact Layout
dt			Format toolbar, Change Style drop-down menu: Defined Term
li			Automatic when adding list items
menu			Format toolbar, Change Style drop-down menu: Menu List; List Properties dialog box: Other tab, Menu List
ol			Format toolbar, Change Style drop-down menu: Numbered List; Format toolbar: Numbered List button; List Properties dialog box: Numbers tab
ol	start	number	List Properties dialog box: Numbers tab; Start At
ol	type	A	List Properties dialog box: Numbers tab; Choose A.B.C. style
ol	type	a	List Properties dialog box: Numbers tab; Choose a.b.c. style
ol	type	I	List Properties dialog box: Numbers tab; Choose I.II.III. style
ol	type	i (small I)	List Properties dialog box: Numbers tab; Choose i.ii.iii. style
ol	type	1	List Properties dialog box: Numbers tab; Choose 1.2.3. style
ul			Format toolbar, Change Style drop-down menu: Bulleted List; Format toolbar: Bulleted List button; List Properties dialog box: Plain Bullets tab

Tag	Name	Value	Procedure or Option
ul	type	circle	List Properties dialog box: Plain Bullets tab; choose unfilled circle bullets
ul	type	disc	List Properties dialog box: Plain Bullets tab; choose Solid circle bullets
ul	type	square	List Properties dialog box: Plain Bullets tab; choose square bullets

Marquee Tags

The marquee tags listed in Table C.17 are inserted with the Insert I Active Elements I Marquee command and formatted or edited in the Marquee Properties dialog box. Refer to Chapter 16, "Working with Animation and Active Content."

Table C.17. Marquee tags.

Tag	Name	Value	Procedure or Option
marquee	align	bottom	Align with Text: **B**ottom
marquee	align	middle	Align with Text: **M**iddle
marquee	align	top	Align with Text: To**p**
marquee	behavior	alternate	Behavior: Alter**n**ate
marquee	behavior	scroll	Behavior: Scr**o**ll
marquee	behavior	slide	Behavior: **S**lide
marquee	bgcolor	#rrggbb	Background **C**olor, choose Custom from drop-down menu
marquee	bgcolor	colorname	Background **C**olor, choose one of 16 predefined colors.
marquee	direction	left	Direction: **L**eft
marquee	direction	right	Direction: **R**ight
marquee	height	n	Size: Specify Hei**g**ht, in Pi**x**els
marquee	height	n%	Size: Specify Hei**g**ht, in **P**ercent
marquee	loop	n	Repeat: **C**ontinuously (unchecked) and enter number in times field
marquee	loop	infinite	Repeat: **C**ontinuously (checked)
marquee	scrollamount	n	Movement Speed: **A**mount
marquee	scrolldelay	n	Movement Speed: **D**elay
marquee	width	n	Size: Specify **W**idth, in Pi**x**els
marquee	width	n%	Size: Specify **W**idth, in **P**ercent

Java Applet Tags

For the tags discussed in Table C.18, refer to the following dialog boxes and chapters:

❏ Applet tags are added with the Insert I Advanced I Java Applet command and edited with the Java Applet Properties dialog box. Refer to Chapter 25.

❏ EMBED tags are added with the Insert I Advanced I Plug-In command and edited with the Plug-In Properties dialog box. Refer to Chapter 25.

Table C.18. Java applet tags.

Tag	Name	Value	Procedure or Option
applet	align	absbottom	Layout, Alignment, absbottom
applet	align	absmiddle	Layout, Alignment, absmiddle
applet	align	baseline	Layout, Alignment, baseline
applet	align	bottom	Layout, Alignment, bottom
applet	align	center	Layout, Alignment, center
applet	align	left	Layout, Alignment, left
applet	align	middle	Layout, Alignment, middle
applet	align	right	Layout, Alignment, center
applet	align	top	Layout, Alignment, top
applet	align	texttop	Layout, Alignment, texttop
applet	alt	text	Message for Browsers without Java Support
applet	code	appletFile	Applet Source
applet	codebase	codebaseURL	Applet Base URL
applet	height	n	Size, Height
applet	hspace	n	Layout, Horizontal Spacing
applet	paramname	paramName	Applet Parameters, Add, Name
applet	paramvalue	paramValue	Applet Parameters, Add, Value
applet	vspace	n	Layout, Vertical Spacing
applet	width	n%	Applet, Size, Width
embed	align	absbottom	Layout, Alignment, absbottom
embed	align	absmiddle	Layout, Alignment, absmiddle
embed	align	baseline	Layout, Alignment, baseline
embed	align	bottom	Layout, Alignment, bottom

Tag	Name	Value	Procedure or Option
embed	align	center	Layout, Alignment, center
embed	align	left	Layout, Alignment, left
embed	align	middle	Layout, Alignment, middle
embed	align	right	Layout, Alignment, center
embed	align	texttop	Layout, Alignment, texttop
embed	align	top	Layout, Alignment, top
embed	border	n	Layout: Border thickness
embed	height	n	Size: Height
embed	hidden	true	Hide Plug-In
embed	hspace	n	Layout, Horizontal Spacing
embed	src	data	Data Source
embed	vspace	n	Layout, Vertical Spacing
embed	width	n	Size: Width

Page-Related Tags

The page-related tags listed in Table C.19 are edited in the Page Properties dialog box, except where noted by another command name. Refer to Chapter 10.

Table C.19. Page-related tags.

Tag	Name	Value	Procedure or Option
! (comment)			Insert I FrontPage Component I Comment command, Comment dialog box (or enter in HTML view)
!doctype			Generated automatically by FrontPage Editor
base	href	url	General tab: Base Location
base	target	name	General tab: Default Target Frame
body			Generated automatically by FrontPage Editor
body	alink	#rrggbb	Background tab: Active Hyperlink, Custom color
body	alink	colorname	Background tab: Active Hyperlink, choose one of 16 colors

continues

Table C.19. Page-related tags.

Tag	Name	Value	Procedure or Option
body	background	url	Background tab: Background Image
body	bgcolor	#rrggbb	Background tab: Background, Choose Custom color
body	bgcolor	colorname	Background tab: Background, choose one of 16 colors
body	bgproperties	fixed	Background tab: Watermark
body	leftmargin	n	Margins tab: Specify Left Margin
body	link	#rrggbb	Background tab, Hyperlink, choose Custom color
body	link	colorname	Background tab, Hyperlink, choose one of 16 colors
body	topmargin	n	Margins tab: Specify Top Margin
body	text	#rrggbb	Background tab, Text, choose Custom color
body	text	colorname	Background tab, Text, choose one of 16 colors
body	vlink	#rrggbb	Background tab, Visited Hyperlink, choose Custom color
body	vlink	colorname	Background tab, Visited Hyperlink, choose one of 16 colors
head			Generated automatically by FrontPage Editor
html			Generated automatically by FrontPage Editor
isindex			Edit in HTML view
isindex	action	action	Edit in HTML view
isindex	prompt	prompt	Edit in HTML view
meta	content	url	Custom tab, System Variables
meta	http-equiv	refresh	Custom tab, System Variables
meta	name	name	Custom tab, User Variables
nextid			Edit in HTML view
style			General tab, Style button (refer to Table C.2)
title			General tab, Title

Paragraph Tags

The default paragraph style for the tags listed in Table C.20 is Normal. Styles can be changed with the Change Style drop-down menu in the Format toolbar or with the Format I **P**aragraph command, using the Paragraph Properties dialog box. Refer to Chapter 10.

Table C.20. Paragraph tags.

Tag	Name	Value	Procedure or Option
address			Format toolbar, Change Style drop-down menu: Address; Paragraph Format dialog box: Address
blockquote			Format toolbar: Increase Indent button
p			Default paragraph style when entering text; Format toolbar: Change Style drop-down menu: Normal
p	align	center	Format toolbar: Center button; Paragraph Format dialog box: Paragraph **A**lignment: Center
p	align	left	Format toolbar: Align Left button; Paragraph Format dialog box: Paragraph **A**lignment: Left
p	align	right	Format toolbar: Align Right button; Paragraph Format dialog box: Paragraph **A**lignment: Right
pre			Format toolbar, Change Style drop-down menu: Formatted; Paragraph Format dialog box: Formatted

Sound Tags

The sound capabilities listed in Table C.21 can be added to a page by using the **I**nsert I Backgrou**n**d Sound command. The Background Sound properties can be edited using the Page Properties dialog box. Refer to Chapter 16.

Table C.21. Sound tags.

Tag	Name	Value	Procedure or Option
bgsound	loop	*n*	Page Properties dialog box: General tab, Background Sound: Loop
bgsound	loop	infinite	Page Properties dialog box: General tab, Background Sound: Forever
bgsound	src	*url*	Page Properties dialog box: General tab, Background Sound: Location

Table Caption Tags

The table captions shown in Table C.22 are inserted with the Table I Insert Caption command and edited with the Caption Properties dialog box. Refer to Chapter 12, "Your Tables Are Ready."

Table C.22. Table caption tags.

Tag	Name	Value	Procedure or Option
caption	align	center	Edit in HTML view
caption	align	left	Edit in HTML view
caption	align	right	Edit in HTML view
caption	valign	bottom	Edit in HTML view
caption	valign	top	Edit in HTML view

Table Tags

The table tags referenced in Table C.23 are created with the Insert I Table command and edited in the Table Properties dialog box. Cells (TH, TR, TD tags) are edited in the Cell Properties dialog box. Refer to Chapter 12.

Table C.23. Table tags.

Tag	Name	Value	Procedure or Option
col	align	center	Edit in HTML view
col	align	justify	Edit in HTML view
col	align	left	Edit in HTML view
col	align	right	Edit in HTML view
col	span	*n*	Edit in HTML view

Tag	Name	Value	Procedure or Option
colgroup			Edit in HTML view
colgroup	align	center	Edit in HTML view
colgroup	align	justify	Edit in HTML view
colgroup	align	left	Edit in HTML view
colgroup	align	right	Edit in HTML view
colgroup	span	*n*	Edit in HTML view
colgroup	valign	baseline	Edit in HTML view
colgroup	valign	bottom	Edit in HTML view
colgroup	valign	middle	Edit in HTML view
colgroup	valign	top	Edit in HTML view
table	align	center	Insert Table dialog box or Table Properties dialog box: Layout, Alignment, Center
table	align	left	Insert Table dialog box or Table Properties dialog box: Layout, Alignment, Left
table	align	right	Insert Table dialog box or Table Properties dialog box: Layout, Alignment, Right
table	background	*url*	Table Properties dialog box: Custom Background, Use Background Image
table	bgcolor	*#rrggbb*	Table Properties dialog box: Cus-tom Background, Background Color (choose Custom color)
table	bgcolor	*colorname*	Table Properties dialog box: Custom Background, Background Color (choose one of 16 colors)
table	border	*n*	Table Properties dialog box: Border Size
table	bordercolor	*#rrggbb*	Insert Table dialog box or Table Properties dialog box: Custom Colors, Border (choose Custom color)

continues

Table C.23. continued

Tag	Name	Value	Procedure or Option
table	bordercolor	colorname	Table Properties dialog box: Custom Colors, Border (choose one of 16 colors)
table	bordercolordark	#rrggbb	Table Properties dialog box: Custom Colors, Dark Border (choose one of 16 colors)
table	bordercolordark	colorname	Table Properties dialog box: Custom Colors, Dark Border (choose one of 16 colors)
table	bordercolorlight	#rrggbb	Table Properties dialog box: Custom Colors, Light Border (choose one of 16 colors)
table	bordercolorlight	colorname	Table Properties dialog box: Custom Colors, Light Border, (choose one of 16 colors)
table	cellpadding	n	Insert Table dialog box or Table Properties dialog box: Layout, Cell Padding
table	cellspacing	n	Insert Table dialog box or Table Properties dialog box: Layout, Cell Spacing
table	frame	above	Edit in HTML view
table	frame	below	Edit in HTML view
table	frame	box	Edit in HTML view
table	frame	hsides	Edit in HTML view
table	frame	lhs	Edit in HTML view
table	frame	rhs	Edit in HTML view
table	frame	void	Edit in HTML view
table	frame	vsides	Edit in HTML view
table	frame	n	Edit in HTML view
table	frame	n%	Edit in HTML view
table	rules		Edit in HTML view
table	rules	all	Edit in HTML view
table	rules	basic	Edit in HTML view

Tag	Name	Value	Procedure or Option
table	rules	cols	Edit in HTML view
table	rules	none	Edit in HTML view
table	rules	rows	Edit in HTML view
table	valign	bottom	Edit in HTML view
table	valign	top	Edit in HTML view
table	width	n	Insert Table dialog box or Table Properties dialog box: Width, Specify **W**idth (in Pixels)
table	width	$n\%$	Insert Table dialog box or Table Properties dialog box: Width, Specify **W**idth (in Percent)
tbody			Edit in HTML view
tfoot			Edit in HTML view
th,tr,td	align	center	Cell Properties dialog box: Horizontal Alignment, Center
th,tr,td	align	left	Cell Properties dialog box: Horizontal Alignment, Left
th,tr,td	align	right	Cell Properties dialog box: Horizontal Alignment, Right
th,tr,td	background	*url*	Cell Properties dialog box: Use Background **I**mage
th,tr,td	bgcolor	*#rrggbb*	Cell Properties dialog box: Custom Colors, Background Color (choose Custom Color)
th,tr,td	bgcolor	*colorname*	Cell Properties dialog box: Custom Colors, Background Color (choose one of 16 predefined colors)
th,tr,td	bordercolor	*#rrggbb*	Cell Properties dialog box: Custom Colors, Border (choose Custom color)
th,tr,td	bordercolor	*colorname*	Cell Properties dialog box: Custom Colors, Border (choose one of 16 predefined colors)

continues

Table C.23. continued

Tag	Name	Value	Procedure or Option
th,tr,td	bordercolordark	#rrggbb	Cell Properties dialog box: Custom Colors, Dark Border (choose Custom Color)
th,tr,td	bordercolordark	colorname	Cell Properties dialog box: Custom Colors, Dark Border (choose one of 16 predefined colors)
th,tr,td	bordercolorlight	#rrggbb	Cell Properties dialog box: Custom Colors, Light Border (choose Custom Color)
th,tr,td	bordercolorlight	colorname	Cell Properties dialog box: Custom Colors, Light Border (choose one of 16 predefined colors)
th,tr,td	colspan	n	Cell Properties dialog box: Cell Span, Number of Columns Spanned
th,tr,td	height	n	Minimum Size, Specify Height, in Pixels
th,tr,td	height	n%	Minimum Size, Specify Height, in Percent
th,tr,td	nowrap		Cell Properties dialog box: Layout, No Wrap
th,tr,td	rowspan	n	Cell Properties dialog box: Cell Span, Number of Rows Spanned
th,tr,td	valign	baseline	Cell Properties dialog box: Vertical Alignment, Baseline
th,tr,td	valign	bottom	Cell Properties dialog box: Vertical Alignment, Bottom
th,tr,td	valign	middle	Cell Properties dialog box: Vertical Alignment, Middle
th,tr,td	valign	top	Cell Properties dialog box: Vertical Alignment, Top
th,tr,td	width	n	Cell Properties dialog box: Minimum Width, Specify Width, in Pixels

Tag	Name	Value	Procedure or Option
th,tr,td	width	*n*%	Cell Properties dialog box: Minimum Width, Specify **W**idth, in **P**ercent
thead			Edit in HTML view

About Theme-Related Cascading Style Sheets

When you apply themes to your FrontPage Webs and pages, a hidden folder named themes is created in your Web. Beneath this folder are subfolders that hold the cascading style sheets that define the images and fonts used in your Web pages.

If you are familiar with cascading style sheet properties, you can edit the cascading style sheets in your theme folders. The tables in this appendix serve as a reference to the theme elements that are configured in several different cascading style sheets.

Displaying Theme Web Folders

The folders that are associated with your Web themes are initially hidden. You'll need to set an option to display files in hidden directories in your Web if you want to view or edit the associated files.

To display the theme folders in your Web, follow these steps:

1. From the FrontPage Explorer, choose **T**ools I **W**eb Settings. The FrontPage Web Settings dialog box appears.
2. Click the Advanced tab.

3. In the Options section, check the Show documents in **h**idden directories checkbox.

4. Click OK. FrontPage asks whether you want to refresh your Web. Choose **Y**es. You will now see a folder named _themes and a subfolder that holds the cascading style sheet pages and images associated with each theme you use in your Web.

Files Associated with Themes

The themes folder, and subfolders, in your Web contain the graphics, settings, and cascading style sheet configuration files for the themes you use in your Web. In addition to several graphics images, there are several information and cascading style sheet files. If you want to change the graphics in your themes, you need to edit some of the cascading style sheet files (those with a .css extension). In this chapter, you'll learn which files contain information about the graphics you use in your theme. For further information about changing the fonts, text colors, and margins in your themes, refer to Chapter 27, "Using Styles."

Let's say, for example, that you have selected the Arc theme to use on your pages. Your Web contains a hidden folder named _themes/arcs, which contains all the images and configuration files for the theme. Of particular note are seven ASCII files, named as shown in Table D.1.

Table D.1. Configuration files associated with themes.

Filename	Function
color0.css	Defines the hyperlink, background, table, and heading colors used for your theme if you do not use Vivid Colors.
color1.css	Defines the hyperlink, background, table, and heading colors used for your theme if you use Vivid Colors.
graph0.css	Defines the images, font faces, font colors, and text alignment used in your Web if your Web does not use hover buttons.
graph1.css	Defines the images, font faces, font colors, and text alignment used in your Web if your Web uses hover buttons.
theme.css	Defines the navigation button, background color, and fonts used in your Web if default colors (no textured backgrounds) are selected.

Filename	Function
`arcs.inf`	An information file used to place the theme in Themes view. The file prefix is unique to the theme you select for your Web. Must use the same prefix as the `.utf8` file, described next.
`arcs.utf8`	An information file used to place the theme in Themes view. The file prefix is unique to the theme you select for your Web. Must use the same prefix as the `.inf` file, described previously.

Customizing Your Graphics

You'll notice quite a few graphics in your themes subfolders, and if you want to customize or replace them, you need to know which graphics serve which purpose. The `graph0.css`, `graph1.css`, and `theme.css` files, described in Table D.1, give you this information.

To open, view, and edit these files, follow these steps:

1. From the FrontPage Explorer, choose **V**iew | **F**olders, or select the Folders icon in the Views pane.

2. From the Contents pane in Folders view, right-click on the filename you want to open and choose Open **W**ith. The Open with Editor dialog box appears.

3. Choose Text Editor (`notepad.exe`) and click OK. The file opens in Notepad.

Graphics Cascading Style Sheet Files

The `graph0.css` cascading style sheet file identifies the graphics used in your Web when you choose normal (not hover) buttons. Table D.2 lists the cascading style sheet properties that define each of the graphics. The name of the associated graphic is defined by code that typically reads as follows:

`propertyname: url(imagename.gif);`

You can modify the files in the `themes` folders in your Web. You can also import your own images into your FrontPage Web and modify the filenames to use your own graphics instead.

Table D.2. CSS properties used with normal buttons.

CSS Property	Function
separator-image	Defines the image used for horizontal rules.
list-image-1	Defines the image used in the top level of a bulleted list.
list-image-2	Defines the image used in the second level of a bulleted list.
list-image-3	Defines the image used in the third level of a bulleted list.
nav-banner-image	Defines the image used for your navigation banner.
navbutton-horiz-normal	Defines the image used for buttons in horizontal navigation bars when the button is in its normal state.
navbutton-horiz-pushed	Defines the image used for buttons in horizontal navigation bars when the button is in its pushed state.
navbutton-vert-normal	Defines the image used for buttons in vertical navigation bars when the button is in its normal state.
navbutton-vert-pushed	Defines the image used for buttons in vertical navigation bars when the button is in its pushed state.
navbutton-home-normal	Defines the image used for the Home navigation button.
navbutton-next-normal	Defines the image used for the Next navigation button.
navbutton-prev-normal	Defines the image used for the Previous navigation button.
navbutton-up-normal	Defines the image used for the Up navigation button.

The graph1.css cascading style sheet file identifies the graphics used in your Web when you choose hover buttons. All the properties shown in Table D.2 appear in this file as well, but in many cases the graphics used in the theme are different. In addition to the properties shown in Table D.2, you'll see the properties shown in Table D.3.

Table D.3. Additional properties used with hover buttons.

CSS Property	Function
navbutton-horiz-hovered	Defines the image used for buttons in horizontal navigation bars when the mouse is hovering over the navigation button
navbutton-vert-hovered	Defines the image used for buttons in vertical navigation bars when the mouse is hovering over the navigation button
navbutton-home-hovered	Defines the image used for the Home navigation button when the mouse is hovering over the navigation button
navbutton-home-pushed	Defines the image used for the Home navigation button when the button is in its pushed state
navbutton-next-hovered	Defines the image used for the Next navigation button when the mouse is hovering over the navigation button
navbutton-next-pushed	Defines the image used for the Next navigation button when the button is in its pushed state
navbutton-prev-hovered	Defines the image used for the Previous navigation button when the mouse is hovering over the navigation button
navbutton-prev-pushed	Defines the image used for the Previous navigation button when the button is in its pushed state
navbutton-up-hovered	Defines the image used for the Up navigation button when the mouse is hovering over the navigation button
navbutton-up-pushed	Defines the image used for the Up navigation button when the button is in its pushed state

The `theme.css` cascading style sheet file defines a couple of other images used with your selected theme. The `top-bar-button` property is listed in the `.mstheme` section of the file, and the background image you use in your theme is listed in the `body` section of the file.

Table D.4. CSS properties used for banner and background images.

CSS Property	Function
top-bar-button	Defines the image used for the top navigation bar
background-image	Defines the background image used for your theme

Table D.5. CSS font properties assigned in `theme.css`.

CSS Property	Function
`.mstheme-topbar-font`	Defines the font family and color for the text used in the top navigation bar
`.body`	Defines the font family used for the normal text in your page
`h1 through h6`	Defines the font family for Headings 1 through 6

Table D.6. CSS font properties assigned in `color0.css` and `color1.css`.

CSS Property	Function
`a:link`	Defines link color
`a:visited`	Defines visited link color
`a:active`	Defines active link color
`body`	Defines background color and normal text color
`table`	Defines light table border color and dark table border color
`h1 through h6`	Defines colors for headings 1 through 6
`background-image`	Defines the background image used for your theme

Table D.7. CSS font properties assigned in `graph0.css` and `graph1.css`.

Style Sheet Section	Function
`.mstheme-bannertxt`	Defines the font and font properties used in the banner text. Properties set are font-family, color, text-align, and vertical-align.
`.mstheme-horiz-navtxt`	Defines the font and font properties used for the horizontal navigation bars. Properties set are font-family, font-weight, color, text-align, and vertical-align.
`.mstheme-vert-navtxt`	Defines the font and font properties used for the vertical navigation bars. Properties set are font-family, font-weight, color, text-align, and vertical-align.

Style Sheet Section	Function
`.mstheme-navtxthome`	Defines the font and font properties used for the "home" navigation button. Properties set are font-family, color, text-align, and vertical-align.
`.mstheme-navtxtprev`	Defines the font and font properties used for the "previous" navigation button. Properties set are font-family, color, text-align, and vertical-align.
`.mstheme-navtxtup`	Defines the font and font properties used for the "up" navigation button. Properties set are font-family, color, text-align, and vertical-align.

What's on the CD-ROM

Microsoft-Related Products and Utilities

- ❏ Internet Explorer 3.0
- ❏ Microsoft Internet Information Server
- ❏ Microsoft Visual Basic 5.0 Control Creation Edition
- ❏ Internet Assistant for Microsoft Word for Windows 95
- ❏ Internet Assistant for Microsoft Excel for Windows
- ❏ Internet Assistant for Microsoft PowerPoint for Windows 95
- ❏ Internet Assistant for Microsoft Access for Windows 95
- ❏ Internet Assistant for Microsoft Schedule+ for Windows 95
- ❏ Microsoft Word Viewer for Windows 95
- ❏ Microsoft Excel Viewer for Windows 95
- ❏ Microsoft PowerPoint Viewer for Windows 95
- ❏ Microsoft PowerPoint Animation Player for Windows 95

Internet and HTML Utilities

- ❏ Cute FTP
- ❏ Hot Dog Pro Web Editor from Sausage Software
- ❏ HTML Assistant from Brooklyn North Software Works

Graphics and Editing Programs

- ❏ Paint Shop Pro from JASC, Inc.
- ❏ Thumbs Plus from Cerius Software
- ❏ Snagit32 from TechSmith Corp.
- ❏ Map This
- ❏ UltraEdit-32

Web Servers

- ❏ WebSite from O'Reilly and Associates

Perl 5

- ❏ Perl 5 for Win32 from Hip Communications

Java and JavaScript

- ❏ Sample Java Applets from the Web
- ❏ Sample JavaScripts from the Web

Compression Utilities

- ❏ WinZip from NicoMak Computing

INDEX

J-K

A VIACOM SERVICE

The Information SuperLibrary™

Bookstore

Search

What's New

Reference

Software

Newsletter

Company Overviews

Yellow Pages

Internet Starter Kit

HTML Workshop

Win a Free T-Shirt!

Macmillan Computer Publishing

Site Map

Talk to Us

CHECK OUT THE BOOKS IN THIS LIBRARY.

You'll find thousands of shareware files and over 1600 computer books designed for both technowizards and technophobes. You can browse through 700 sample chapters, get the latest news on the Net, and find just about anything using our

We're open 24-hours a day, 365 days a year.

You don't need a card.

We don't charge fines.

And you can be as **LOUD** as you want.

MACMILLAN COMPUTER PUBLISHING USA

A VIACOM COMPANY

Technical ----- Support:

If you need assistance with the information in this book or with a CD/Disk accompanying the book, please access the Knowledge Base on our Web site at **http://www.superlibrary.com/general/support**. Our most Frequently Asked Questions are answered there. If you do not find the answer to your questions on our Web site, you may contact Macmillan Technical Support **(317) 581-3833** or e-mail us at **support@mcp.com**.

Laura Lemay's Guide to Sizzling Web Site Design

Laura Lemay & Molly Holzschlag   *Casual-Accomplished*

This book is more than just a guide to the hottest Web sites; it's a behind-the-scenes look at how those sites were created. Web surfers and publishers alike will find this book an insightful guide to some of the most detailed pages. The latest Web technologies are discussed in detail, showing readers how these technologies have been applied and how they can implement those features on their own Web pages.

CD-ROM includes source code from the book, images, scripts, and more.

$45.00 USA/$63.95 CDN 1-57521-221-8   400 pp.

Creating Killer Interactive Web Sites

Adjacency with Ibanez   *Intermediate-Advanced*

Creating Killer Interactive Web Sites is a one-of-a kind look into the secrets of one of the world's preeminent Web design firms: Adjacency. Providing the most in-depth analysis of Web design ever published, this guide brings a new standard to the integration of design and interactivity in creating successful sites. Explains the art of integrating interactivity into a well-designed Web site. Offers proven techniques to entice site visitors.

Gives detailed case studies of sites that successfully integrate design and interactivity.

$49.99 US/$70.95 CDN   1-56830-373-4   256 pp.

Teach Yourself Web Publishing with HTML 4 in a Week, Fourth Edition

Laura LeMay   *New-Casual*

Teach Yourself Web Publishing with HTML in a Week, Fourth Edition is a thoroughly revised version of the shorter, beginner's soft-cover edition of the best-selling book that started the whole HTML/Web publishing craze.

Covers the new HTML Cougar specifications, plus the Netscape Communicator and Microsoft Internet Explorer 4 environments, as well as style sheets, Dynamic HTML, and XML.

Teaches Web publishing in a clear, step-by-step manner, with lots of practical examples of Web pages. Still the best HTML tutorial on the market.

$29.99 US/$42.95 CDN   1-57521-336-2   600 pp.

Paul McFedries' Microsoft Office 97 Unleashed, Professional Reference Edition

Paul McFedries' et al.   *Accomplished-Expert*

Microsoft Office 97 Unleashed, Professional Reference Edition teaches the user advanced topics, such as the VBA language common to Excel, Access, and now Word; how to use binders; a crash course in the Active Document technology; new Internet and intranet tools; and the integration of scheduling and communications in Outlook.

Shows the reader how to turn the Office suite into a fully integrated business powerhouse and Internet and intranet publishing tool.

Focuses on information-sharing across applications and networks, not just using the applications. Microsoft is the largest suite producer in the market today, with more than 22 million users.

$49.99 US/$70.95 CDN   0-672-31144-5   1,600 pp.

Add to Your Sams.net Library Today
with the Best Books for Internet Technologies

ISBN	Quantity	Description of Item	Unit Cost	Total Cost
1-57521-221-8		Laura Lemay's Guide to Sizzling Web Site Design	$45.00	
1-56830-373-4		Creating Killer Interactive Web Sites	$49.99	
1-57521-336-2		Teach Yourself Web Publishing with HTML 4 in a Week, 4E	$29.99	
0-672-31144-5		Paul McFedries' Microsoft Office 97 Unleashed, Professional Reference Edition	$49.99	
		Shipping and Handling: See information below.		
		TOTAL		

Shipping and Handling: $4.00 for the first book, and $1.75 for each additional book. If you need to have it NOW, we can ship product to you in 24 hours for an additional charge of approximately $18.00, and you will receive your item overnight or in two days. Overseas shipping and handling adds $2.00. Prices subject to change. Call between 9:00 a.m. and 5:00 p.m. EST for availability and pricing information on latest editions.

201 W. 103rd Street, Indianapolis, Indiana 46290

1-800-428-5331 — Orders   1-800-835-3202 — FAX   1-800-858-7674 — Customer Service

Book ISBN 1-57521-372-9

END-USER LICENSE AGREEMENT FOR MICROSOFT SOFTWARE

Microsoft Visual Basic, Control Creation Edition

IMPORTANT—READ CAREFULLY: This Microsoft End-User License Agreement ("EULA") is a legal agreement between you (either an individual or a single entity) and Microsoft Corporation for the Microsoft software product identified above, which includes computer software and may include associated media, printed materials, and "online" or electronic documentation ("SOFTWARE PRODUCT"). By installing, copying, or otherwise using the SOFTWARE PRODUCT, you agree to be bound by the terms of this EULA. If you do not agree to the terms of this EULA, do not install or use the SOFTWARE PRODUCT; you may, however, return it to your place of purchase for a full refund.

Software PRODUCT LICENSE

The SOFTWARE PRODUCT is protected by copyright laws and international copyright treaties, as well as other intellectual property laws and treaties. The SOFTWARE PRODUCT is licensed, not sold.

1. GRANT OF LICENSE. This EULA grants you the following rights:

a. Software Product.

Microsoft grants to you as an individual, a personal, nonexclusive license to make and use copies of the SOFTWARE for the sole purposes of designing, developing, and testing your software product(s) that are designed to operate in conjunction with any Microsoft operating system product. You may install copies of the SOFTWARE on an unlimited number of computers, provided that you are the only individual using the SOFTWARE. If you are an entity, Microsoft grants you the right to designate one individual within your organization to have the right to use the SOFTWARE in the manner provided above.

b. Electronic Documents.

Solely with respect to electronic documents included with the SOFTWARE, you may make an unlimited number of copies (either in hardcopy or electronic form), provided that such copies shall be used only for internal purposes and are not republished or distributed to any third party.

Redistributable Components.

(i) Sample Code. In addition to the rights granted in Section 1, Microsoft grants you the right to use and modify the source code version of those portions of the SOFTWARE designated as "Sample Code" ("SAMPLE CODE") for the sole purposes of designing, developing, and testing your software product(s), and to reproduce and distribute the SAMPLE CODE, along with any modifications thereof, only in object code form provided that you comply with Section d(iii), below.

(ii) Redistributable Components. In addition to the rights granted in Section 1, Microsoft grants you a nonexclusive royalty-free right to reproduce and distribute the object code version of any portion of the SOFTWARE listed in the SOFTWARE file REDIST.TXT ("REDISTRIBUTABLE SOFTWARE"), provided you comply with Section d(iii), below.

(iii) Redistribution Requirements. If you redistribute the SAMPLE CODE or REDISTRIBUTABLE SOFTWARE (collectively, "REDISTRIBUTABLES"), you agree to: (A) distribute the REDISTRIBUTABLES in object code only in conjunction with and as a part of a software application product developed by you that adds significant and primary functionality to the SOFTWARE and that is developed to operate on the Windows or Windows NT environment {"Application"); (B) not use Microsoft's name, logo, or trademarks to market your software application product; (C) include a valid copyright notice on your software product; (D) indemnify, hold harmless, and defend Microsoft from and against any claims or lawsuits, including attorney's fees, that arise or result from the use or distribution of your software application product; (E) not permit further distribution of the REDISTRIBUTABLES by your end user. The following **exceptions** apply to subsection (iii)(E), above: (1) you may permit further redistribution of the REDISTRIBUTABLES by your distributors to your end-user customers if your distributors only distribute the REDISTRIBUTABLES in conjunction with, and as part of, your Application and you and your distributors comply with all other terms of this EULA; and (2) you may permit your end users to reproduce and distribute the object code version of the files designated by ".ocx" file extensions ("Controls") only in conjunction with and as a part of an Application and/or Web page that adds significant and primary functionality to the Controls, and such end user complies with all other terms of this EULA.

2. DESCRIPTION OF OTHER RIGHTS AND LIMITATIONS.

a. Not for Resale Software. If the SOFTWARE PRODUCT is labeled "Not for Resale" or "NFR," then, notwithstanding other sections of this EULA, you may not resell, or otherwise transfer for value, the SOFTWARE PRODUCT.

b. Limitations on Reverse Engineering, Decompilation, and Disassembly. You may not reverse engineer, decompile, or disassemble the SOFTWARE PROD-UCT, except and only to the extent that such activity is expressly permitted by applicable law notwithstanding this limitation.

c. Separation of Components. The SOFTWARE PRODUCT is licensed as a single product. Its component parts may not be separated for use by more than one user.

d. Rental. You may not rent, lease, or lend the SOFTWARE PRODUCT.

e. Support Services. Microsoft may provide you with support services related to the SOFTWARE PRODUCT ("Support Services"). Use of Support Services is governed by the Microsoft policies and programs described in the user manual, in "online" documentation, and/or in other Microsoft-provided materials. Any supplemental software code provided to you as part of the Support Services shall be considered part of the SOFTWARE PRODUCT and subject to the terms and conditions of this EULA. With respect to technical information you provide to Microsoft as part of the Support Services, Microsoft may use such information for its business purposes, including for product support and development. Microsoft will not utilize such technical information in a form that personally identifies you.

f. Software Transfer. You may permanently transfer all of your rights under this EULA, provided you retain no copies, you transfer all of the SOFTWARE PRODUCT (including all component parts, the media and printed materials, any upgrades, this EULA, and, if applicable, the Certificate of Authenticity), **and** the recipient agrees to the terms of this EULA. If the SOFTWARE PRODUCT is an upgrade, any transfer must include all prior versions of the SOFTWARE PRODUCT.

g. Termination. Without prejudice to any other rights, Microsoft may terminate this EULA if you fail to comply with the terms and conditions of this EULA. In such event, you must destroy all copies of the SOFTWARE PRODUCT and all of its component parts.

3. UPGRADES. If the SOFTWARE PRODUCT is labeled as an upgrade, you must be properly licensed to use a product identified by Microsoft as being eligible for the upgrade in order to use the SOFTWARE PRODUCT. A SOFTWARE PRODUCT labeled as an upgrade replaces and/or supplements the product that formed the basis for your eligibility for the upgrade. You may use the resulting upgraded product only in accordance with the terms of this EULA. If the SOFTWARE PRODUCT is an upgrade of a component of a package of software programs that you licensed as a single product, the SOFTWARE PRODUCT may be used and transferred only as part of that single product package and may not be separated for use on more than one computer.

4. COPYRIGHT. All title and copyrights in and to the SOFTWARE PRODUCT (including but not limited to any images, photographs, animations, video, audio, music, text, and "applets" incorporated into the SOFTWARE PRODUCT), the accompanying printed materials, and any copies of the SOFTWARE PRODUCT are owned by Microsoft or its suppliers. The SOFTWARE

PRODUCT is protected by copyright laws and international treaty provisions. Therefore, you must treat the SOFTWARE PRODUCT like any other copyrighted material except that you may install the SOFTWARE PRODUCT on a single computer provided you keep the original solely for backup or archival purposes. You may not copy the printed materials accompanying the SOFTWARE PRODUCT.

5. DUAL-MEDIA SOFTWARE. You may receive the SOFTWARE PRODUCT in more than one medium. Regardless of the type or size of medium you receive, you may use only one medium that is appropriate for your single computer. You may not use or install the other medium on another computer. You may not loan, rent, lease, or otherwise transfer the other medium to another user, except as part of the permanent transfer (as provided above) of the SOFTWARE PRODUCT.

6. U.S. GOVERNMENT RESTRICTED RIGHTS. The SOFTWARE PRODUCT and documentation are provided with RESTRICTED RIGHTS. Use, duplication, or disclosure by the Government is subject to restrictions as set forth in subparagraph (c)(1)(ii) of the Rights in Technical Data and Computer Software clause at DFARS 252.227-7013 or subparagraphs (c)(1) and (2) of the Commercial Computer Software—Restricted Rights at 48 CFR 52.227-19, as applicable. Manufacturer is Microsoft Corporation/One Microsoft Way/Redmond, WA 98052-6399.

7. EXPORT RESTRICTIONS. You agree that neither you nor your customers intend to or will, directly or indirectly, export or transmit (i) the SOFTWARE or related documentation and technical data or (ii) your software product as described in Section 1(b) of this License (or any part thereof), or process, or service that is the direct product of the SOFTWARE, to any country to which such export or transmission is restricted by any applicable U.S. regulation or statute, without the prior written consent, if required, of the Bureau of Export Administration of the U.S. Department of Commerce, or such other governmental entity as may have jurisdiction over such export or transmission.

MISCELLANEOUS

If you acquired this product in the United States, this EULA is governed by the laws of the State of Washington.

If you acquired this product in Canada, this EULA is governed by the laws of the Province of Ontario, Canada. Each of the parties hereto irrevocably attorns to the jurisdiction of the courts of the Province of Ontario and further agrees to commence any litigation which may arise hereunder in the courts located in the Judicial District of York, Province of Ontario.

If this product was acquired outside the United States, then local law may apply.

Should you have any questions concerning this EULA, or if you desire to contact Microsoft for any reason, please contact the Microsoft subsidiary serving your country, or write: Microsoft Sales Information Center/One Microsoft Way/Redmond, WA 98052-6399.

LIMITED WARRANTY

NO WARRANTIES. Microsoft expressly disclaims any warranty for the SOFTWARE PRODUCT. The SOFTWARE PRODUCT and any related documentation is provided "as is" without warranty of any kind, either express or implied, including, without limitation, the implied warranties or merchantability, fitness for a particular purpose, or noninfringement. The entire risk arising out of use or performance of the SOFTWARE PRODUCT remains with you.

NO LIABILITY FOR DAMAGES. In no event shall Microsoft or its suppliers be liable for any damages whatsoever (including, without limitation, damages for loss of business profits, business interruption, loss of business information, or any other pecuniary loss) arising out of the use of or inability to use this Microsoft product, even if Microsoft has been advised of the possibility of such damages. Because some states/jurisdictions do not allow the exclusion or limitation of liability for consequential or incidental damages, the above limitation may not apply to you.

CD-ROM
Installing the Disc

The companion CD-ROM contains an assortment of third-party tools and product demos. The disc creates a new program group for this book and utilizes Windows Explorer. Using the icons in the program group and Windows Explorer, you can view information concerning products and companies and install programs with just a few clicks of the mouse.

Some of the utilities and programs mentioned in this book are included on this CD-ROM. If they are not, a reference to a Web site or FTP location is usually provided in the body of the reference. If a reference is missing, up-to-date information can almost always be obtained from a comprehensive shareware site, such as Beverly Hills Software (www.bhs.com), TUCOWS (www.tucows.com) or CINet (www.shareware.com) for third-party Windows 95/NT products.

System Requirements for This Sams.net CD-ROM

The following system configuration is recommended in order to obtain the maximum amount of benefit from the CD-ROM accompanying this book:

Processor:	486DX or higher processor
Operating System:	Microsoft Windows® NT 4.0 Workstation or Windows 95
Memory:	24MB
Hard disk space:	9.5MB minimum
Monitor:	VGA-or-higher resolution video adapter (SVGA 256-color recommended)
Other:	Mouse or compatible pointing device CD-ROM drive Web browser such as Netscape or Internet Explorer
Optional:	An active Internet connection

To create the program group for this book, follow these steps:

Windows 95/NT 4.0 Installation Instructions

1. Insert the CD-ROM disc in your CD-ROM drive.

2. With Windows 95 or Windows NT installed on your computer and the Auto-Play feature enabled, a Program Group for this book is automatically created whenever you insert the disc in your CD-ROM drive. Follow the directions provided in the installation program.

If Autoplay is not enabled, using Windows Explorer, choose Setup.exe from the root level of the CD-ROM to create the Program Group for this book.

3. Double-click on the Browse the CD-ROM icon in the newly created Program Group to access the installation programs of the software or reference material included on this CD-ROM.

To review the latest information about this CD-ROM, double-click on the About this CD-ROM icon.

NOTE: For best results, set your monitor to display between 256 and 64,000 colors. A screen resolution of 640×480 pixels is also recommended. If necessary, adjust your monitor settings before using the CD-ROM.

Technical Support

If you need assistance with the information in this book or with the CD-ROM accompanying this book, please access the Knowledge Base on our Web site at

```
http://www.superlibrary.com/general/support
```

Our most Frequently Asked Questions are answered there. If you do not find the answer to your questions on our Web site, you may contact Macmillan Technical Support at (317) 581-3833 or e-mail us at support@mcp.com.

NOTE: If you are having difficulties reading from our CD-ROM, try to clean the data side of the CD-ROM with a clean, soft cloth. One cause of this problem is dirt disrupting the access of the data on the disc. If the problem still exists, whenever possible, insert this CD-ROM in another computer to determine whether the problem is with the disc or your CD-ROM drive.

Another common cause of this problem may be that you have outdated CD-ROM drivers. In order to update your drivers, first verify the manufacturer of your CD-ROM drive from your system's documentation. Or, under Windows 95/NT 4.0, you may also check your CD-ROM manufacturer by going to \Settings\Control Panel\System and selecting the Device Manager. Click on the plus sign next to the CD-ROM option and you will see the information on the manufacturer of your drive.

You may download the latest drivers from your manufacturer's Web site or from:

```
http://www.windows95.com
```